Succeeding with Objects

Decision Frameworks for Project Management

Succeeding with Objects

Decision Frameworks for Project Management

Adele Goldberg
and
Kenneth S. Rubin
ParcPlace Systems, Inc.

ADDISON-WESLEY PUBLISHING COMPANY, INC.

Reading, Massachusetts · Menlo Park, California · New York
Don Mills, Ontario · Wokingham, England · Amsterdam · Bonn
Sydney · Singapore · Tokyo · Madrid · San Juan · Milan · Paris

Sponsoring Editor: Peter S. Gordon
Associate Editor: Helen M. Goldstein
Senior Production Supervisor: Helen M. Wythe
Production Coordinator: Marybeth Mooney
Manufacturing Coordinator: Evelyn M. Beaton
Cover Illustrator: Rebecca Cannara
Composition: Jacqueline Davies
Text Design: Wilson Graphics & Design (Kenneth J. Wilson)
Cartoon Illustrator: Rebecca Cannara
Line Art Illustrator: Scientific Illustrators

Text printed on recycled, neutral pH paper.

Library of Congress Cataloging-in-Publication Data

Goldberg, Adele.
    Succeeding with objects: decision frameworks for project
management / Adele Goldberg and Kenneth S. Rubin.
        p. cm.
    Includes bibliographical references and index.
    ISBN 0-201-62878-3
    1. Object-oriented programming (Computer science) 2. Industrial
project management.   I. Rubin, Kenneth S.   II. Title.
    QA76.64.G63 1995
    005.1'1—dc20   94-34913
                                                                         CIP

1 2 3 4 5 6 7 8 9 10-MA-98979695

For their love and support, we dedicate this book to our families.
From Adele to Dennis, Rachel, and Rebecca.
From Kenny to my parents Manny and Joyce, and my wife Jenine.

I wake up each morning determined to change the World and also to have one hell of a good time. Sometimes that makes planning the day a little difficult.

E. B. White

This book is written for technical managers who wish to be successful in the use of object-oriented technology. It contains our advice, distilled from 20 years of direct experience in the creation and use of the technology—programming languages, development tools, and methods for analysis and design.

What This Book Is About

Our original intent was to present a prescription that details, step by step, what an organization—its managers, developers, support teams, and customers—should do to be successful in the use of object-oriented technology. The prescription was going to be something like: Plan so that incremental results will be delivered every three months; use "some language" as the programming language; limit team size to no more than eight developers, including a tester, documentor, and code librarian; and assign a corporate-funded reuse engineer to each team. However, no single prescription for managing object-oriented technology was appropriate. Differences in culture and long- and short-term goals create remarkably large variations in a potential prescription. A company might have only C programmers who believe C++ is easier to learn. A company that is accustomed to project staffs with 40 or 50 developers might not appreciate how to do the work with only eight. And some companies have no structure with which to support and finance a corporate-level competency center staffed with reuse engineers.

What we have written instead is an explanation of how to construct your own prescription. We examine the decisions you need to make, and the issues that enter into the decision-making process. Each related decision has to be made in a coordinated fashion, one leading to the other so as to provide a coherent project-management plan. Although you are the one who needs to make these decisions for your organization, we do make recommendations, and we tie these recommendations to the conditions under which we have seen success and failure. Specifically, we provide examples of decisions derived from 39 project case studies we conducted over a four-year period.

Object-oriented technology involves organizational change. Objects suggest new ways to develop software that alter the relationship between customers and developers, and between developers and business experts. Objects influence how development teams acquire the skills needed for effective use of new analysis, design, implementation, testing, and integration techniques. A commitment to objects is a commitment to change your organization's structure, processes, and resources. This book helps you manage the changes that attend object-oriented technology.

Our emphasis in this book is on project-management practices for professional software development teams. Although we are object advocates, we do not try to sell you on objects alone. Rather, we are interested in showing you the benefits that come from applying object-oriented technology in the context of good project management.

Who Should Read This Book

We expect the reader to be an information systems project manager or a manager of technical managers, someone with a desire to find better processes and techniques for building software systems. This person may not have caught the object wave yet, but is trying to learn what is involved in committing his or her organization to the use of the technology. Most likely, this person will be a project leader when the organization initiates its first object-based project, and will be involved in making many of the management decisions we propose.

Although this book is written for a project manager, everyone involved with the project team should read it to understand their roles within an organization that is using object-oriented technology. We do not assume that the reader has experience in the use of object-oriented technology, so we provide a managerial introduction to the basic concepts. We also provide an overview of the important issues related to managing software projects: planning, organizing, staffing, directing, and controlling. As such, this book can serve as the blueprint for a basic software engineering course. To support this objective, we include additional readings about each topic. This book is not intended to be a substitute for the literature on object-oriented languages, databases, tools, or other technical aspects that you might wish to study.

Book Organization

Broadly, the book is organized around a set of frameworks for helping you make management decisions affecting software projects. Chapter 1 defines the essential characteristics of a decision framework—its principles, goals, maxims, and decisions. In Chapter 2, we introduce the first decision framework: Defining project goals and objectives. We define what we mean by a project, setting the stage to explain the kinds of process-improvement and resource-improvement projects that are needed to base software development effectively on the use of object-oriented technology.

A brief managerial overview of object-oriented technology—defining the concepts and terminology—is provided in Chapter 3. The primary focus of the chapter is to point out the benefits of using the technology in the context of the second decision framework, which asks you to examine what you value in products, processes, and resources, and to decide what about objects can help you obtain what you value. Constructing this value proposition for objects is the first step in creating the organization's rationale for a long-term commitment to the technology.

The next chapter, Chapter 4, discusses how to get started with object-oriented technology to fulfill your value proposition. We suggest that you initiate a first software development project in advance of having the details about how to transition your organization to one in which objects are effectively employed. The details make more sense if you have some experience and if you are ready to make a commitment to the strategic use of the technology. Indeed, many companies will not make a commitment to new technology until they can assess the outcome of a first project. You may also decide to initiate a special technology center to provide a focal point for gathering and assessing information about object-oriented technology.

Chapter 4 tells you what you have to do to get started. Having a real task—planning a first project—as you read the subsequent chapters can help you understand the importance of the details we provide. The details describe software development practices directly altered by a commitment to objects. These are:

- Selecting a product process model

- Setting up a project schedule and controlling to meet the schedule

- Selecting a reuse process model

- Selecting a project team structure

- Selecting a software development environment

- Setting up a training plan

- Selecting measures for assessing, controlling, and predicting process, resource, and product attributes

These seven topics are covered in the following 16 chapters. Process models plus planning and control take up the first four of these chapters. Reuse, covered in the next three chapters, focuses on the process needed to make systematic reuse a reality. We do not provide a technical explanation of how to design for reuse, as that level of detail is outside the scope of management concerns. The discussion of team structures and how they relate to the goals of a project is presented in the next two chapters. (We have relegated the important but detailed job descriptions for team roles to an appendix.) Software development environments—what they are and how to select them—take up the next four chapters. These chapters include definitions and criteria for selecting analysis-and-design method tools, programming languages, libraries, tools, and databases. Chapters 18 and 19 review subject areas and proficiency levels required by members of a team using object-oriented technology, and describe the kinds of training that can be used effectively with the different team members. And then Chapter 20 encourages you to set up a software measurement program, with the goal of measuring progress on individual projects and on transitioning your organization into one that is a mature user of objects. The last chapter recapitulates our main recommendations, restated as the pitfalls of poor decision making.

We conducted case studies of 39 projects that used object-oriented technology. These case studies, along with our own experiences, are used to illustrate the decision frameworks and our recommendations. The demographics of the case studies are relegated to an appendix, best read only by those curious about the source of this information.

When and How to Read This Book

We offer ten project-management decision frameworks, each of which is defined by a principle, a goal, several steps, and several maxims. To help you identify these framework elements, look for the following symbols in the margins. They mark where each element is introduced, and look like this:

Project Goals and Objective

Framework Principle. You should know where you are going, so you will know whether you have arrived.

Benefits of Objects

Framework Goal. Set realistic expectations for how object-oriented technology can help you to achieve your software development goals and objectives.

Framework steps:

Make an Initial Commitment to Objects

- Make the decision to use objects
- Obtain an initial management commitment to the use of objects
- Select an initial process model and software development environment
- Select and set up an initial pilot project
- Assess the outcome of the initial pilot project

A maxim:

Planning

Confidence comes from the planning process, not from the plan.

There are three possible pathways through the book, depending on your primary interests and level of involvement with object-oriented technology: a fast track, to review the decision frameworks; a foundation track, to explore fundamental concepts and acquire a basis for making choices; and an adoption track, to find information as you need it.

Fast track. This book contains a lot of detail, not all of which is necessary or appropriate to cover on your first reading. The detail will be important when you actually have to do the work—when you have to set up a project, decide on the team members, plan a training program, set up a corporate reuse program, determine which measures give you the information you need, and so on.

To help you circumvent the details, we provide a list in Table P.1 of the chapter sections (including their subsections) that offer a quick path through the guidelines. The fast track includes only those sections that describe the principles, goals, maxims, and steps of the project-management decision frameworks. In addition to the listed sections and tables or figures, you should read the chapter opening and the summary provided at the end of each chapter. The fast-track material assumes a knowledge of terminology and of background material provided in other chapters, which you can read opportunistically.

Foundation track. Any reader who is uncertain about the terminology we use, or about the fundamental concepts underlying the proposals we make, should read the chapters in the foundation track. This track consists of Chapters 1 through 3 plus the chapters listed in Table P.2 that have a check mark in the column titled "Definitions and Choices." The material in this part of the book presents our opinions about how to make the various project-management decisions.

Table P.2 provides additional pathway information. Case studies contain the experiences of other practitioners and illustrate many of the decisions in the project-management decision frameworks. In Table P.2, we placed a check mark next to the chapters that include case-study illustrations. The table also identifies which chapters contain the descriptions of the frameworks themselves.

Adoption track. You can also read this book in an opportunistic fashion. First read Chapters 1 through 3. You are then ready for your first project. Chapter 4 can help you select this project. The decisions you make to formulate and carry out a product development project are typically ordered as follows: set goals and objectives, select the project process model, create a plan including how to measure progress and results, select the team, select the tools, train the team, carry out the project, revisit the process and planning decisions with the team, and intermittently assess progress and results. As you come to each of these steps, you can read the relevant chapters on each framework, as cited in groups in Table P.2, independently. If you are setting up a reuse program, you will also want to pay special attention to the three chapters on a reuse process model.

Acknowledgments

This book has taken a long time to complete. At times our confidence that we could distill our experiences rationally would falter—these were the times when we would encounter a new client with an even newer kind of problem. It took some time to realize

Table P.1 A Recommended Fast Track through the Book

Chapter	Chapter Title	Sections to Read	Tables/ Figures
1	Introduction	§ Basic Principles and Maxims	
2	Establish Project Goals and Objectives	§ Projects—Transitioning from Current to Desired Situation	
		§ Framework for Defining Project Goals and Objectives	
3	Determining Benefits of Object-Oriented Technology	§ Framework for Determining How Projects Benefit from Using Object-Oriented Technology	
4	Make an Initial Commitment to Use Object-Oriented Technology	§ Framework for Making an Initial Commitment to Objects	
		§ Select and Set Up an Initial Pilot Project	
		§ Set Up a Special Object Technology Center	
5	What Is a Process Model?	§ Summary only	
6	Select a Product Process Model	§ Framework for Selecting a Product Process Model	
7	Plan and Control a Project	§ Summary only	
8	Case Studies of Process Models	§ Summary only	
9	What Is Reuse?	§ The Value of Reuse	
10	Reuse Process Models	§ Framework for Selecting a Reuse Process Model	
		§ Set Up a Process for Maintaining Reusable Assets	
11	Organizational Models for Reuse	§ Organizational Model Maxims	Table 11.1
		§ Corporate Reuse Issues—Large and Small (first four sections only)	
12	Select a Team Structure	§ Summary only	Fig. 12.1
13	Case Studies of Teams	§ Summary only	
14	Expectations for a Software Development Environment	§ Summary only	

continued

Table P.1 *continued*

Chapter	Chapter Title	Sections to Read	Tables/ Figures
15	Analysis and Design Methods and Tools	§ Summary only	Table 15.1
16	Languages, Libraries, Tools, and Databases	§ Summary only	Tables 16.1 and 16.2
17	Select a Software Development Environment	§ Framework for Selecting a Software Development Environment	
18	What Is in a Training Plan?	§ Subject Area Proficiency Levels § Training Plan	Table 18.2
19	Set Up a Training Plan	§ Framework for Setting Up a Training Plan	
20	What Is Measurement?	§ Framework for Setting Up a Software Measurement Program	
21	Failing with Objects	Entire chapter	

that the ever-changing problem situations were, in fact, the key to writing a book of value. We then stopped looking for answers and started formulating the questions. We thank our clients and the people who attended our courses and talks, spread over five continents and as many years, for sharing their time and experience.

We thank the 26 organizations willing to open their project doors to us, allowing us to participate in their projects and project postmortems. We hope they will understand that our nondisclosure agreements with their companies prevent us from naming them here. We also appreciate the assistance of our colleagues at ParcPlace Systems for being willing sounding boards: Tw Cook, Marek Jeziorek, David Leibs, K. Ross Looney, Patrick McClaughry, Paul McCullough, David Pellegrini, Mike Robicheaux, and David Smith.

A special debt of appreciation goes to our reviewers, who patiently explained where our explanations could be greatly improved. Thank you to: Brian Alexander, Dennis Allison, Mike Crooks, John Davis, James Falek, Steve Fraser, Martin Griss, Marie Lenzi, William Lively, and Efrem Mallach. We hope we did justice to John and Martin's extensive suggestions. And we are especially indebted to Dennis, whose forcefulness in getting us to rewrite the original draft undoubtedly led to a more readable and acceptable manuscript.

Our special and fondest thanks to our personal artist, Rebecca Cannara, who provided the cartoon artwork that resulted in the cover characters, the team role characters, and the many chapter cartoon illustrations.

Table P.2 Chapters Containing Information About Software Development Practices Altered by the Use of Object-Oriented Technology

Framework	Chapters	Definitions and Choices	Framework Principles, Goals, Maxims, and Steps	Case Study Illustrations
Process Model	5	√		√
	6		√	
	8			√
Plan and Control	7	√	√	
	8			√
Reuse Process Model	9	√		
	10		√	
	11			√
Team Structure	12	√	√	
	13			√
Software Development Environment	14	√		√
	15	√		√
	16	√		√
	17		√	√
Training	18	√		
	19		√	√
Measurement	20	√	√	
Team Job Descriptions	Appendix	√		

Finally, we would like to thank the folks at Addison-Wesley whose careful eyes and ears allowed us to produce a quality edition—to Peter Gordon, who has been our book mentor for many years, and to the editorial and production staff, including Robert Chamberlain, Helen Goldstein, Eileen Hoff, Margo Shearman, and Helen Wythe.

Adele and *Kenny*
February, 1995
Palo Alto, California

Contents

Preface   v

Chapter 1   **Introduction to Principles, Maxims, and Decision Frameworks**   1

Some Software Engineering History   2

Background on Object-Oriented Technology   6

Today's Object-Oriented Perspective   8

Basic Principles and Maxims   9

   The Principle of System Architecture   10

   The Principle of Decision Making   10

   Management Communication   11

Project Management Decision Frameworks   11

   Establish the Goals for the Use of Object-Oriented Technology   11

   Use Object-Oriented Technology in Software Development   12

Background on Case Studies   13

Summary   15

Additional Reading About the History of Software Engineering   16

Chapter 2   **Establish Project Goals and Objectives**   19

Goals and Objectives   19

Projects—Transitioning from Current to Desired Situation   20

Framework for Defining Project Goals and Objectives   21

   Understand the Business Mission and Business Processes   23

   Understand Business and Team Values for Software Development   26

   State the Desired Situation in Terms of Goals and Objectives for Products, Processes, and Resources   27

   Assess the Current Situation   29

Assessment of the KandA Widget Company—An Example   31

Case Study Results   33

Summary   36

Additional Reading About Project Goals and Objectives   37

Chapter 3   **Determining Benefits of Object-Oriented Technology**   39

What Is an Object?   39

A Class Describes a Set of Objects   42

Objects Form Applications, Frameworks, and Components   43

What Does It Mean to Be Object-Oriented?   45

What About Objects Helps Build Systems?   49

Objects Separate Interface from Implementation   50

Object Models Closely Map the Real World   50

Objects Come in Different Sizes   51

Objects Live All the Way Down   51

Additional Benefits of Objects   52

Objects Are a Means of Attacking Complexity   52

Objects Build Systems Resilient to Change   53

Objects Allow Partial Systems to Work   54

Objects Represent Natural Units for Reuse   55

Framework for Determining How Projects Benefit from Using Object-Oriented Technology   56

Determine Whether and How Object-Oriented Technology Contributes to Obtaining What You Value in Software Development   56

Determine Projects Needed to Achieve Valued Objectives Through the Use of Object-Oriented Technology   58

Case Study Results   58

Summary   60

Additional Reading About Objects   61

Chapter 4   **Make an Initial Commitment to Use Object-Oriented Technology**   63

Framework for Making an Initial Commitment to Objects   64

Receive an Initial Introduction to Objects   64

Obtain an Initial Management Commitment to the Use of Objects   66

Make the Business Case   66

Manage the Expectations of Management   68

Select an Initial Process Model and Software Development Environment   70

Select and Set Up an Initial Pilot Project   71

Guidelines for Choosing a Pilot Project to Develop a Software System   71

Mechanics for Setting Up the Initial Pilot Project   73

Decide Who Will Staff the First Project   74

Decide on the Training Plan   75

Assess the Outcome of the Initial Pilot Project   76

   Assessment Methodology   76

   Assessment Report   78

Set Up a Special Object Technology Center   80

Summary   82

Additional Reading About Making a Commitment to New Technology   83

Chapter 5   **What Is a Process Model?**   85

Process Model Definitions   85

Example Process Models   87

   Waterfall Model   87

   Spiral Model   89

   Recursive/Parallel Model   90

There Is Not One Process Model for Objects   91

Strategies for Developing with Objects   94

   Iterative Development   94

   Incremental Development   95

   Prototyping   96

   Consuming Reusable Assets   102

   Producing Reusable Assets   104

Case Study Results   105

   Product Process Models   105

   Reusing   106

   Prototyping   108

   Illustration 1: Time-Driven Process Model   110

   Illustration 2: Customer Information System   111

   Illustration 3: CASE Tools   112

Summary   114

Additional Reading About Process Models and Prototyping   115

Chapter 6   **Select a Product Process Model**   117

Additional Strategies for Developing with Objects   117

   Partitioning   117

   Integrating and Managing Changes   121

   Documenting   122

Quality Assurance Strategies When Developing with Objects 124

How Quality Relates to Other Development Strategies 124

Uncovering Defects During Development 125

Testing Object Implementations 127

Recording Defects 132

Framework for Selecting a Product Process Model 134

Agree on Maxims 135

Verify Software Development Goals and Objectives 136

Select Project Strategies, Activities, and Their Ordering 136

Select Methods for Each Activity 137

Case Study Results 137

Product Process Models 137

Example Partitions 138

Summary 141

Additional Reading About Product Process Models That Use Object-Oriented Technology 142

Chapter 7 **Plan and Control a Project** 143

What Is a Project Schedule? 144

Planning Under Uncertainty 147

State Clearly What You Know and What You Do Not Know 148

State Clearly What You Will Do to Eliminate Unknowns 149

Make Sure That All Early Milestones Can Be Met 149

Plan to Replan 150

Planning Resources 150

Framework for Planning and Controlling 151

Identify Required Milestones 152

Identify System Capabilities 153

Identify Tasks 154

Estimate the Cost of Each Task 157

Account for Costs 160

Monitor and Control Project Execution 161

Summary 166

Additional Reading About Planning and Controlling Projects 168

Chapter 8   **Case Studies of Process Models**   169

   Milestone-Driven Process Model   169

      Illustration 1: Measuring Progress   170

      Illustration 2: Documenting Progress   174

   Security-Driven Process Model   180

      Illustration 3: Control Based on Need to Know   180

   Just-Do-It Process Model   182

      Illustration 4: No Formal Design   182

   Creating a Reusable Asset Process Model   185

      Illustration 5: Create a Reusable Framework   185

   Concept Development Process Model   190

      Illustration 6: Available Prototypes   190

      Illustration 7: Prototyping Partnership   196

   Summary   200

   Additional Reading About Case Study Experiences   201

Chapter 9   **What Is Reuse?**   203

   Why the Hype About Reuse?   203

   Reuse in Software Development   207

      Cloning Is Not Strategic Reuse   209

      Reuse with Objects   210

   The Value of Reuse   212

      The Reuse Producer/Consumer Equation   212

      Reuse Claims   214

   Case Study Results   216

      Illustration 1: Reusable Assets Need Support   217

      Illustration 2: Reusing a Binary Asset   218

   Summary   219

   Additional Reading About Reuse Definitions and Expectations   220

Chapter 10   **Reuse Process Models**   221

   Framework for Selecting a Reuse Process Model   221

   Define Reuse   224

Set Up a Process for Populating a Library of Reusable Assets 225

    Identify and Prioritize Categories of Reusable Assets 225

    Acquire Reusable Assets 230

    Certify Reusable Assets 234

    Classify and Represent Reusable Assets 237

    Store Reusable Assets 240

Set Up a Process for Sharing Reusable Assets 241

    Communicate the Availability of Reusable Assets 241

    Locate and Retrieve Reusable Assets 242

    Understand and Use Reusable Assets 244

Set Up a Process for Maintaining Reusable Assets 245

Case Study Results 246

Summary 248

Additional Reading About Reuse Process Models 249

Chapter 11 **Organizational Models for Reuse** 251

Organizational Model Maxims 251

    Reuse in the Virtual Hallway 252

    Reuse as a Form of Technology Transfer 252

    Reuse Is a Maintenance Responsibility 253

Reuse Organizational Models 253

    Ad Hoc Model 254

    Supply and Demand Model 255

    Expert Services Model 256

    Product Center Model 259

    COTS Model 261

Corporate Reuse Issues—Large and Small 262

    Multilevel Reuse Efforts 262

    Motivating Reuse 264

    Initiating a Corporate Reuse Program 266

    Reuse Maturity 268

    A Small-Company Question 268

Illustrations of Reuse 269

    The Reuse Process of a Software Vendor 269

    Reuse in Japan 271

Case Study Results 274

Summary 275

Additional Reading About Reuse Organizational Models 275

Chapter 12   **Select a Team Structure**   277
What Is a Team?   277
A Team Has Structure   280
Kinds of Teams   282
Application Productization Team   282
Application Prototyping Team   285
Framework Team   285
Cross-Project Team   287
Reuse Team   289
Maintenance Team   291
Retaining Team Members   292
Framework for Selecting a Team Structure   292
Decide Which Teams Are Needed   293
Identify the Roles Needed for Each Team   294
Decide on the Style for Managing Each Team   295
Determine How Communication Will Take Place   296
Find Team Members   296
Summary   298
Additional Reading About Team Structure   299

Chapter 13   **Case Studies of Teams**   301
Illustration 1: Subteams Based on Enterprise-wide Analysis   302
Illustration 2: Geographically Distributed Teams   305
Illustration 3: Framework Team Support Obligations   308
Illustration 4: Enterprise-wide Framework Team   309
Illustration 5: Two Pollinator Team Examples   310
Illustration 6: The Star Trek Team Model   311
Summary   314

Chapter 14.   **Expectations for a Software Development Environment**   315
Users as Developers   316
There Are Different Kinds of Developers   316
Development Is Done at Different Levels   317
Coordination of People, Processes, and Resources   319
Portability and Interoperability   321
Cross-Platform Portability   321
Distributed Open Systems   322
Client/Server Architectures   324

Retaining an Investment in Prior Technology   327

   Keep As-Is and Coexist   327

   Keep Temporarily Until Complete Transition   328

Illustration: Reengineering a Mainframe World to a Client/Server Open Systems Architecture   330

Summary   332

Additional Reading About Expectations for a Software Development Environment   332

Chapter 15   **Analysis and Design Methods and Tools**   335

Process Models, Methods, and Notations   335

What Is Analysis?   337

What Is Design?   339

Analysis and Design Techniques in Support of Object-Oriented Concepts   340

Choosing Analysis and Design Methods   344

Summary   350

Additional Reading About Analysis and Design Methods   350

Chapter 16   **Languages, Libraries, Tools, and Databases**   353

Choosing a Programming Language   353

   Multiple Levels of Encapsulation   356

   Bounded and Unbounded Polymorphism   356

   Single and Multiple Inheritance   357

   Static and Dynamic Type Checking and Method Binding   357

   Runtime Support for Object Lifetimes   358

   Hybrid versus Pure Languages   358

Libraries   359

Programming Tools   359

   Implementation Strategy   360

   Interaction Strategy   364

Object-Oriented Databases   368

   How to Choose a Database   370

Summary   372

Additional Reading About Software Development Environment Choices   372

Chapter 17   **Select a Software Development Environment**   375

    Framework for Selecting a Software Development Environment   375

        Assess the Current Resource Situation   376

        Understand the Software to Be Developed   379

        Determine the Characteristics of the User Environment   379

        Establish a Program for Evaluating Options   380

    Case Study Results   382

        Software Development Environment Camps   382

        Choice of Programming Languages   386

        Choice of Databases   387

        Illustration 1: Languages Face-off Using Multiple Comparisons   388

        Illustration 2: Languages Face-Off Using a Single Large Comparison   389

        Illustration 3: Methods Face-off Using a Survey Approach   390

        Illustration 4: Champions Face-off Face to Face   392

    Summary   393

    Additional Reading About Evaluating Software Development Environments   394

Chapter 18   **What Is in a Training Plan?**   395

    Subject Areas   396

        Concepts About Object-Oriented Technology   396

        Object-Oriented Analysis   397

        Object-Oriented Design   398

        Framework Design   399

        Implementation Environment   400

        Project Management   401

        Other Subject Areas   401

    Subject Area Proficiency Levels   405

        Proficiency Levels   405

        Time to Attain a Proficiency Level   406

    Training Formats   408

        Prepared, Face-to-Face Presentations   409

        Mentoring   411

        Self-Study   412

    Training Plan   413

Case Study Results   416

Summary   418

Additional Reading About Training   419

Chapter 19   **Set Up a Training Plan**   421

Framework for Setting Up a Training Plan   421

Determine Skills of Team Members   422

Define Desired Skills of Team Members   423

Define Training Resources and Activities   423

Case Study Results   424

Illustration 1: The Reading Club   424

Illustration 2: Continuing Education Programs   426

Illustration 3: Mentoring Success Story   428

Illustration 4: A Popular Idea—Quick Start Training Projects   430

Illustration 5: A Bad Situation That Got Better   432

Summary   435

Chapter 20   **What Is Measurement?**   437

What Is a Measure?   437

The Goal-Question-Metric Approach   440

Measuring Size, Productivity, and Effort   443

Length Measure: Lines of Code   445

Length Measure: Number of Object Abstractions   446

Functionality Measure: Function Points   447

Measuring Quality   452

Reporting Quality in Terms of Defects   454

Measuring Complexity   455

Inherent and Added Complexities   456

Object-Oriented Design and Code Complexity Measures   456

Measuring Reuse   458

Measuring Potential Reuse   459

Influence of Reuse on Size Measures   459

Influence of Reuse on Effort Measures   460

Framework for Setting Up a Software Measurement Program   462

    Define Project Goals and Objectives   463

    Determine Measures Based on Goals and Objectives   464

    Use Measurement Data to Assess, Predict, and Control   464

    Update the Measurement Plan   465

Summary   466

Additional Reading About Measurement   467

Chapter 21   **Failing with Objects**   469

Good Project Management Leads to Success   470

Poor Project Management Leads to Failure   470

The Last Word   474

Appendices

    Appendix A Primary Case Study Data   475

    Appendix B Suggested Survey Questions for Project Managers   481

    Appendix C Team Member Job Descriptions   493

Glossary of Terms   503

References   519

Index   529

CHAPTER 1

Introduction to Principles, Maxims, and Decision Frameworks

S ucceeding with objects means that you make the best use of object-oriented technology to achieve your organization's goals and objectives. In this context, we use the term *technology* to encompass all aspects of software engineering, from programming languages to analysis-and-design methods to measures of progress, productivity, and quality. By *object-oriented technology*, we mean technology that uses objects fundamentally.

We cast our understanding of how to use object-oriented technology in the form of decision frameworks. A *decision framework* is an organized sequence of decisions that you must make. For each decision, you define technical terms, weigh organizational and technical issues, and make choices about products, processes, and resources. The term *framework* is used in this book in two ways: to describe a set of management decisions, and to describe a set of objects that interact to form the architecture for an application. In each case, framework refers to a coordination of parts that form a basic structure for processing within some domain. In the first case, the domain is project management, while in the second case, the domain is software architecture. We avoid ambiguity by always identifying the project-management usage as a "decision framework."

This book presents ten decision frameworks to help you structure your thinking and enhance your ability to succeed with object-oriented technology. Given all the possible decisions you could make in setting up and managing a software development project, these ten decision frameworks represent the key decisions that you have to make. We encourage you to refine these decision frameworks to match any special needs of your organization.

Some Software Engineering History

Before we explore strategies for successful use of object-oriented technology, let's take a look at the history that forms our basic understanding of good software engineering practices. This history is important because the basics seem to have been ignored in many 1990s commercial organizations seeking to build large and complex software systems.

We start our review of history in 1968 because it was around this time that people with considerable software experience first reflected on the problem of engineering large systems.

Fred Brooks was living the mythical man month.

Apollo software was being readied for the next year's landing on the moon.

ESS1—AT&T's electronic switch—had been shipped.

J. Licklider's paper "Man-Computer Symbiosis" had been published in the IRE (now IEEE) *Transactions on Human Factors in Electronics* in March 1960, and broadly read in the software community.

The C. Bohm and G. Jacopini paper on programming without GOTOs, leading to further development of structured analysis and design, had been published in the *CACM* two years earlier ("Flow diagrams, Turing machines, and languages with only two formation rules," *Communications of the ACM*, 9:5, May 1966).

It was after the Summer of Love and the ascendancy of San Francisco's acid rock culture.

OS/360 was released.

Sketchpad, JOSS, and Grail were in use.

There was no DEC VAX, Xerox PARC, or Intel 4004.

The B5000, CDC 66000, and PDP-8 vied for attention.

Christopher Alexander had published his *Notes on the Synthesis of Form*, admonishing designers to look for repeatable patterns in architecture design.

Earlier, in 1956, Doug Ross presented his first paper on Gestalt programming at the Western Joint Computer Conference, in which he talked about a behavioral perspective on programming:

> Standard programming practice is to be replaced by simple and unambiguous expression of the desired characteristics of behavior, the expression itself in effect tying together integrated units of computer behavior.

Other still-timely ideas about programming followed:

> Mel Conway, in his paper "How do committees invent?" in the April 1968 issue of *Datamation*, argued that the system being produced will tend to have a structure that mirrors the structure of the group producing it, whether or not this replication of structure was intended.

> Doug Engelbart presented his Online System (NLS) at the 1968 Fall Joint Computer Conference, demonstrating in the course of a few hours the way multimedia video communications and interactive information management can augment human intellectual skills.

> Edsger W. Dijkstra circulated his work on the THE operating system, and published in the *CACM* the now-notorious correspondence on GOTOs being considered harmful, arguing for ways to structure code closer to the statement of the solution than was possible with the spaghetti code prevalent at the time.

> Ole Johan-Dahl, Bjorn Myhrhaug, and Kristen Nygaard published the definition of Simula-67, the first programming language based on creating object descriptions and object interactions.

A NATO conference on software engineering was held in October 1968 in Garmisch, Germany [Nauer and Randell 1969]. The conference organizers coined the phrase *software engineering* as a provocative term to "imply the need for software manufacture to be based on theoretical foundations and practical disciplines traditional to engineering." The highlights of the conference were discussions related to process: how to produce quality software efficiently, how to provide customer-oriented service, and how to protect a business investment in software. Good software engineering was equated with good project management.

Conference attendees agreed that systems should be built in layers and modules. They introduced notions of top-down and bottom-up design. They also emphasized that developers should produce systems gradually, in stages. At each stage, the developers should attempt "to define what a given component should do, before getting involved in decisions as to how the component should provide this function." Attendees identified the need for special notations to aid communication during the design process. Large development groups are inevitable. To manage these groups, the attendees discussed the need for structure in communication and decision making. Among the other conference results: Maintenance was defined to include adapting to a changing problem, not just correcting blunders. Metrics were acknowledged as necessary to measure development progress—adequacy and stability of interface details being a better measure than lines of code. Feedback devices must be built into all systems and processes to support continuous improvement.

Bob Bemer, of the General Electric Information Systems group, was at the Garmisch meeting to introduce the software factory, an environment for program construction and use. Doug McIlroy, from Bell Telephone Laboratories, argued the case for mass-produced software components. And Edsger W. Dijkstra, of the Technische Hogeschool Eindhoven, conceived a design process for constructing a complex system—layering virtual machines in such a way that a variable at one layer is a constant at another. Alan Perlis, chair of the Computer Science Department at Carnegie Mellon University, summarizing the discussion on design, made these points:

1. A software system is best designed if test is interleaved with design.

2. A simulation which matches the requirements contains the control which organizes the design of the system.

3. Through successive repetitions of this process of interlaced testing and design, the model ultimately becomes the software system itself.

The conference attendees agreed that the design concepts essential to building maintainable software systems are modularity (to isolate functional elements of the system), specification of the interface (to supply documentation needed to train users, to understand requirements, and to provide maintenance support), and generality (required for extensibility). Software must be thought of as open ended—that is, it must be extensible.

The NATO conference was held when computers were large and programming was a part of a large and complex endeavor. Personal computers represented a stark contrast to these large systems of 1968. In the 1970s and 1980s, we witnessed a dramatic change in the computer industry, with the evolution of hobby computers into personal, home, and business computers. Traditional mainframe systems-development organizations were forced to contend with the use of hobby computers as desktop work environments. The nature of the professional's programming tasks changed considerably. Creating code to fit into machines with only 32K, 64K, or 128K of memory was not a systems problem so much as it was a tour de force in practical programming.[1] When making changes or mov-

---

[1] Think of 32K as about 10K–15K lines of code in assembly, or 8K of BASIC interpreter plus about 2500 lines of code in BASIC.

ing to another platform involved rewriting more than 20 percent of the code, common wisdom said it was cheaper and faster to start over again. But modern personal computer programs have 32, 64, even 128 megabytes of code—and growing—enough to be called a system. This is enough code for managers not to want to throw it all away when the company changes platforms—enough code to need more than a few programmers to understand and modify it. Still, these systems are a far cry from fully functional COBOL MVS environments, weighing in at multimillions of lines of code.

When PC-centric vendors started to produce bigger systems and to sell tools to developers of large systems, they adopted and marketed object-oriented technology as though it were a recent innovation aimed at solving all their systems-building needs. Perhaps the reason these developers treated objects as new is that they had just discovered that the principles underlying object modeling make an important difference—they had just discovered the need to design before coding, to think in terms of systems, not programs. Perhaps all the fuss about objects and the supposedly new way to program occurred because this was the first time these developers had to build large systems.

What is actually new—the striking difference between now and the time before computers were personally affordable—is the immediacy of both computers and computing in everyone's lives. There has been a dramatic change in who uses and who has to understand computers and computer software. In the past—even the recent past—production systems had to be understood only by computing professionals. Now, in the 1990s, managers and users expect to understand systems to ensure that they accurately represent business models. End users expect to refine system capability easily—to specialize systems to meet their requirements. The desire to make systems customizable means that the system model has to be visible and understandable to the user. The visible system model must mimic the manager's or user's world view. This requirement forces us to emphasize clear architecture. This change is one of emphasis, not of kind.

The issues raised at the NATO conference—leading to proposed organizations and management structures—were the same then as they are now, despite several critical differences in both accessibility of computing power and diversity of access. The technical solution from the past—even some of the terminology—is the same as the object-oriented solution proposed today. Objects are not new. They were tested, were found to work, and are still around. But they continue to be used successfully only where appropriate organizational and management contexts are created.

Today, we are faced with two cultures—large systems and personal computers. In businesses today, these cultures are commingling. The large-system culture depended for its success on modular architectures, clear interfaces, and generality. The decades since 1968 were spent refining processes and coding style, creating new documentation and testing techniques, and generally figuring out how to take advantage of the significant advances in hardware technology. Inevitably, costs decreased and computing power and multimedia opportunities increased. Personal computers were transformed into full-featured business workstations. Faced with this transformation, the home-brew personal-computer culture, with its just-do-it mentality, has had to rediscover the importance of good architecture and supported processes. Object-oriented technology is needed by both cultures. And it will continue to be used by both cultures—but only if we adopt the recommendations that follow from the large-system culture's advice on good project management.

The recommendations made in 1968 echo throughout this book.

Background on Object-Oriented Technology

It was fortuitous that research into object-oriented technology in the early 1970s, carried out by the Smalltalk group at the Xerox Palo Alto Research Center (PARC), dealt with programming-language design as a question of pedagogy: When we create a language that allows people to access and manipulate information, how will we teach these people how to use the language? Learnability strongly influenced both the design of programming languages and how people would interact—both physically and logically—with computer systems. Thus, programming-language research in the seventies was intimately tied to the design of interactive development environments, graphical user interfaces, and programming by reusing pre-existing capability.

Early forms of object-oriented technology were created primarily for the benefit of one person—the individual programmer. The goal was to empower the individual to direct the computer to do very complex and interesting things—things that in the past required hundreds of programmer months to accomplish. The individual should be able to create entertaining, graphical applications, such as a simulation of household finances, complete with scheduling and economic models, an interactive game, or solutions to school physics problems. Every user was expected to learn how to program. Programming was viewed as the preferred way to command the computer to retrieve and analyze information.

Network computing, with its potential for sharing information in a dynamic, geographically dispersed fashion, was anticipated but was not emphasized. Programming was considered a personal and somewhat isolated activity. Hence, most of the issues that would eventually be considered when teams began to use object-oriented technology—including organizational and coordination issues—were ignored during the early development years at PARC. To a lesser extent, the notion of distributing shareable computing resources across the network was also ignored.

Early development of object-oriented technology anticipated and actively supported three individual programmer activities:

- Managing the specification of complex information models

- Customizing existing applications to meet personal preferences

- Composing innovative graphical user interfaces

The individual programmer was not expected to be a computer scientist or a software engineer. Researchers paid a lot of attention to whiz-bang computer-based painting, animation, music, document processing, and video. They also paid attention to graphical ways of representing and accessing information. And they made a special effort to implement these features on personally affordable—and transportable—computing systems.

To realize the goal of empowering the individual, researchers focused on creating programming language systems, primarily Smalltalk and LISP derivatives. These language systems supported the description of events found in the real world (simulations), and provided a set of techniques for graphical presentation and interaction. Programming tools combined conventional techniques for source-code editing and debugging with navigational aids for locating and incorporating existing software components. The languages and tools were augmented by rich libraries of software components—new software could be created through composition and refinement of existing components, thereby letting programmers build from the work of others. This system structure was directly derived from the pedagogical premise that it is easier to learn how to do something by modifying what already exists than it is to create abstract concepts and all of the concrete realizations of those concepts.

The resulting software development environment, made up of source code, source-code editors and debuggers, code browsers and inspectors, enabled a new programming style: programming by refinement and exploratory programming [Barstow, Shrobe, and Sandewall 1984]. *Programming by refinement* is the ability to create new software by specifying differences from existing software. *Exploratory programming* is the incremental development of a program, or set of programs, based on incomplete specifications. The developer, uncertain of the complete functional and architectural details of the desired system, creates as much as possible, and lets the interim result dictate the direction of further development. Interim results contribute to development by enabling early design review and feasibility analysis, as well as early testing by target users.

The fundamental technology used to create this new form of development environment is called object-oriented technology. It manifested itself in the form of new languages composed of *objects* as encapsulated representations of behavior and the information needed to carry out the behavior, *classes* as descriptions of sets of objects, and *message-passing* as the way to coordinate and communicate among objects. Simula [Dahl, Myhrhaug, and Nygaard 1968] was the first such language. Simula extended ALGOL 60 with objects and message-passing. Smalltalk-80 [Goldberg and Robson 1983] was the first language and system to consist entirely of objects, classes describing sets of similar objects, and message-passing as the only way to invoke actions and to share information. Existing languages, such as LISP, Pascal, C, and COBOL, continue to add object-oriented constructs. Direct-manipulation graphical interfaces and icon-oriented presentations were used to create visual representations of objects on bit-mapped display screens. Dynamic cross-referencing and navigational tools (browsers), and dynamic analysis tools (inspectors and debuggers) were easily implemented, because objects lend themselves to uniform query about their structures and interrelationships, about the messages to which they respond, and about the messages they send to other objects.

Today's Object-Oriented Perspective

By the late 1980s, the market was familiar with the concepts of object-oriented software. The benefits of exploratory programming and programming by refinement, and the advantages of the new tools, had accrued to individual application developers. These developers typically used object-oriented languages and tools to create simulations of physical or conceptual processes (for example, financial or economic dynamic models) with novel graphical interfaces to improve the users' understanding of, and involvement with, the underlying physical or mathematical models. Three potential benefits attracted these programmers:

- Rapid application development, despite the lack of well-specified requirements

- One-to-one mapping of descriptions from real-world entities to interacting computer-representable objects

- Maintainable software systems

The sponsoring organizations made their decisions to use object-oriented technology without understanding how the new form of development might influence overall group project management. These decisions did not present a serious problem when the resultant software was delivered to a small population of local users, when the problems being solved were intimately understood by the programmers themselves, or when the solutions were used by these same programmers.

However, the use of object-oriented technology in the absence of formal project management represented a risk for mainstream development projects. These were projects that had used large teams of programmers, often geographically dispersed, programming in COBOL/4GL languages on mainframe computers. They now wished to share in the development and reuse of objects. These projects have to meet corporate development guidelines. They involve business experts, analyzers, designers, and documentors, as well as programmers. The project results have to be used for a long time, and have to be maintained by programmers who were not involved in the original development.

For years, we have given talks to large audiences of these mainframe programming teams to introduce them to object-oriented technology. We had to convince our listeners that the technology was not something to fear just because it appeared to be new. In the beginning, the audiences consisted mostly of programmers. We would say: "Who here is a programmer? Raise your hand. Now keep your hand up if you are a *good* programmer."

We would then ask what made these self-proclaimed good programmers good. Our intention was to show that the good programmers would continue to be evaluated as good, despite a transition to object-oriented technology. The response to our question was not uniform. In California's Silicon Valley or on Route 128 outside Boston, Massachusetts, most developers consider themselves the best. Between three and four percent of the programmers elsewhere kept their hands in the air to declare that they were good. And they said they were good because they know technology and meet their schedules within predefined performance and space constraints.

By 1992, the answers changed. The programmers said they were good because they understood the business. The makeup of our audiences changed as well. More technical and business managers started to attend the seminars. Now when we give talks, we have to convince these managers that just because software claims to be object-oriented does not mean that the software is necessarily good. We ask our audiences why they are so interested in the technology. They indicate that it is an item on the purchase check-off list. They often do not know why.

To obtain the benefits of a new technology, you must understand the technology. You must understand who should care about object-oriented technology, and why. You must know why objects are on the check-off list, which means you must know the basics of good project management.

Basic Principles and Maxims

Good project management is based on principles, maxims, and coordinated decisions translated to practice. A *principle* is a rule or a fundamental truth that guides you in making decisions, regardless of organizational situation. Each decision framework for the use of object-oriented technology is based on a principle. It is not acceptable to make a decision that violates the principles. A number of maxims are also associated with the frameworks. Like a principle, a *maxim* is a guideline that is helpful in making decisions. Unlike a principle, a maxim's applicability is situation dependent. Maxims are rules of thumb derived from personal experience, your current collection of "battle scars." For example, Benjamin Franklin, espousing the maxims of life, reported:

> A penny saved is a penny earned.
> Early to bed and early to rise, makes a man healthy, wealthy, and wise.

While Shakespeare's Polonius proffered:

> Never a borrower nor a lender be.

One of the case study projects we examined suggested a maxim of sorts:

> Time misused is a software developer's four-letter word.

Tom Gilb is a master at identifying basic truths about software project management. As examples of what we mean by a maxim for software development, we quote these from Gilb's *Principles of Sotware Engineering Management* [Gilb 1988].

> *Disasters.* Disasters don't happen by accident; they are entirely creditable to your own management.

> *Fail-safe minimization.* If you don't know what you are doing, don't do it on a large scale.

> *The third wave.* You may forget some critical factors, but they won't forget you.

> *The promise.* Never make promises you cannot keep, no matter what the pressure.

The Principle of System Architecture

Principle of System Architecture

The system structure reflects the culture and organization of the group that creates it.

The principle of system architecture is the principle recommended by the participants at the 1968 NATO conference on software engineering. This principle defines a relationship between the kind of system you build and the kind of organization you manage. As a software system grows in size, it inevitably grows in complexity. Management tasks become proportionately more complex. The principle predicts that the result of a software development project will be a direct consequence of the way the development team is structured. Well-organized, modular organizations produce well-organized, modular system results; poorly organized, monolithic organizations beget haphazard, spaghetti-coded systems without clear architectural boundaries.

Consider the desired properties of a system you wish to build, and see what these properties imply about the group culture and structure that should exist to create the system.

The Principle of Decision Making

Principle of Decision Making

All project-management decisions should relate to the project's stated goals and objectives.

A second principle—the decision-making principle—governs all of the decision frameworks we propose. The most important action that can be carried out to assure a project's success is to state clearly the project's goals and objectives at the outset of the project. Every task within the project should have a purpose that is aligned with the project's stated goals and objectives. And all team members should understand the relationship between any decision and the goals or objectives.

Management Communication

Everyone makes decisions in a project, so everyone should know what is going on. Everyone should understand how each action helps to meet the goals and objectives. All team members should know the technical and organizational information that affects their ability to do their jobs.

> All project information should be shared with team members.

Shared Vision

Each decision framework implicitly includes a communication step: communicate decisions, communicate values, communicate expectations, and communicate plans. Communication is needed to make sure that every team member is aware of and understands the organization's work culture. This step is needed to make sure that team members make their own on-the-job decisions within the context set by the project goals and objectives.

Project Management Decision Frameworks

A developer, who at the time had four years of experience working on a team building an object-oriented system, told us:

> There is a large cultural component to a successfully functioning development process. It embodies organizational values and commitments. These must be internalized and evolved into a system and practices that make sense within the context of the organization. A process of this kind cannot realistically be developed off in the corner or bought off the shelf. It must be grown, practiced, and refined within the organization. Not to say that outside "experts" cannot impart much valuable knowledge. However, to a large degree, this information must be digested and massaged into a suitable process from within the organization.

This advice from an early adopter of object-oriented technology introduces the long-term and learned nature of successful project management. It is why we cannot give you specific, organization-independent answers. But we can ask the questions, and direct your own efforts to reach conclusions in the context of your organization's activities. We organize our questions and advice as decision frameworks in two basic categories:

- Establish the goals for the use of object-oriented technology

- Use object-oriented technology in software development projects

Establish the Goals for the Use of Object-Oriented Technology

The first category consists of three decision frameworks. These frameworks ask you to:

- Define project goals and objectives

- Determine how projects can benefit from using object-oriented technology
- Make an initial commitment to the use of object-oriented technology

Chapter 2 introduces the project goals and objectives framework, which asks you to plan a series of process- and resource-improvement projects. You first expose your business and team values by defining the attributes of the products you wish to create, and the processes and resources you will use to create these products. These preferred product, process, and resource attributes describe your desired work context for developing software. You can then assess your current approaches to software development. The assessment will determine which improvement projects you should carry out.

The object-oriented technology framework in Chapter 3 asks you to combine your ideas about what you value in products, processes, and resources with your expectations for object-oriented technology. Specifically, it asks you to determine the role that objects play in meeting your goals and objectives for software systems. To meet the obligations of the framework, you will need to define what it means to be object-oriented, and the benefits you expect from the use of object-oriented technology.

The third decision framework—making an initial commitment to use objects— addresses the issues that appear when you introduce the new technology into your organization for the first time. Many organizations will not make a commitment until they can assess the outcome of a first project. They cannot agree on models for software development processes and resources until they can demonstrate some initial capability. Hence this framework, presented in Chapter 4, focuses on carrying out and assessing a first demonstration project.

Each decision framework has an underlying principle and goal. All decisions should be consistent with the principles and lead to the goals. The principles and goals for the first three decision frameworks are listed in Table 1.1.

Use Object-Oriented Technology in Software Development

There are seven decision frameworks in the second category that ask you to:

- Select a product process model
- Set up a project plan and control
- Select a reuse process model
- Select a team structure
- Select a software development environment
- Set up a training plan
- Set up a software measurement program

Table 1.1 Establish the Goals for the Use of Object-Oriented Technology—Decision Frameworks, Principles, and Goals

Decision Framework	◈ *Principle*	◨ *Goal*
Project goals and objectives	You should know where you are going, so you will know whether you have arrived.	Determine goals and objectives, and set up a structure for decision making in which all decisions are traceable back to these goals and objectives.
Benefits of object-oriented technology	Object-oriented technology is not the goal of a project, but a means to attain the goal.	Set realistic expectations for how object-oriented technology can help you to achieve your software development goals and objectives.
Make an initial commitment to objects	Commitment in the form of a well-resourced demonstration project is needed to introduce new technology successfully.	Choose and be successful with a first project that demonstrates the contributions that object-oriented technology can make to your organization, and that lays the foundation for making strategic decisions.

The frameworks ask you to plan, organize your work effort, staff your teams, direct and control the work flow—all of this to make effective use of object-oriented technology in meeting overall project goals and objectives. These decision frameworks embody principles consistent with good software engineering. The goals for each framework are designed to create effectively managed software development in your organization. The principles and goals are listed in Table 1.2.

Background on Case Studies

Over the last several years, we have been involved either as participants or observers in a large number of projects for building software systems and applications based on the use of object-oriented technology. These development projects used either Smalltalk-80 or C++. Increasingly, our involvement turned to organizational and methodological issues, as these issues became important to the successful development and deployment of the applications built using these language systems. Underlying all the prescriptions we provide, then, is the knowledge that comes from participating in a variety of projects: analyzing enterprise-wide requirements, designing reusable frameworks, and building specific systems. In addition to experience with clients, we have personally managed numerous development projects over our 35 cumulative years of work. Like all project managers, we now know how much better we would have done, if only . . .

Table 1.2 Use Object-Oriented Technology in Software Development—Decision Frameworks, Principles, and Goals

Decision Framework	◈ *Principle*	◍ *Goal*
Product process model	Incremental decision making, development, testing, and integration produce effective project results.	Select project activities, their ordering and methods, according to project goals and objectives and the guidelines of the organization.
Project plan and control	Planning and execution are interleaved activities, whereby partial plans are set, carried out, and the results used to do further planning.	Develop a project schedule, and a way to control execution to schedule, that builds management trust and meets management development expectations.
Reuse process model	Reusable assets are strategic products of the organization.	Set up a structure in which to plan and manage the process of acquiring, distributing, and maintaining reusable assets throughout the organization.
Team structure	The team structure mirrors the needs of the process model and, where appropriate, the structure of the desired outcomes.	Identify the purposes, roles, managerial styles, and communication channels that build the teams needed to meet the organization's goals and objectives.
Software development environment	Team members work together most effectively when there is a strategy for coordinating methods, tools, libraries, languages, databases, and delivery.	Set up a development environment for all team members that enables the team to create, maintain, and deliver applications.
Team training plan	Success with a new technology depends on proper education of all team members in the use of the technology.	Develop a training plan to give your team members the additional skills they need to use new processes and resources to achieve desired results.
Software measurement program	Effective software measurement is an essential engineering activity.	Set up a measurement program to identify the data you require, a means of collecting this data, and a way to use the results to meet goals and objectives.

The success or failure of software development projects is best understood from empirical data. Our primary source of data in the use of object-oriented technology, in addition to our personal experience, is a set of case studies of 39 projects at 26 companies. By prior agreement with these companies, we will not disclose their names, but we will use data about the projects to substantiate and clarify our recommendations.

We initiated our studies in 1990. That year, there was an observable increase in the interest managers showed in the technology. Repeatedly we were hearing from these managers that everything was new—too new—and that it was simply too hard to take advantage of the technology. We knew that this should not be so. As vendors of the technology, we knew it must not be so. We set out to understand what was really going on, to percolate the experiences of the projects we studied in a way that would help new projects to avoid mistakes, to leverage successes, and, most important, to understand the cost of introducing object-oriented technology.

We carried out our studies in two phases, which we refer to as Phases 1 and 2 in describing case study results throughout this book. The demographics are presented in Appendix A, with the survey used in Phase 2 provided as Appendix B. The reuse questions in the Phase 1 questionnaire were incorporated into a survey prepared by another organization—Technology Transfer International—for a similar study it conducted in Japan.[2] The data from the Japan study were provided for our use and are reported in this book.

Much of the data we collected are from projects that date back to the late 1980s or early 1990s, although we have augmented the examples in this book with more recent projects. The early nature of projects in the case studies raises the question whether the data are still valid, in particular whether the maturation of the technology affects any of our conclusions. The case studies raised our awareness of issues, but our everyday experience as consultants and managers directed our recommendations for resolving these issues. We base our consultations with our clients on the material in this book. We ask our clients to make the decisions identified in each framework, and help our clients coordinate their plans based on these decisions. The primary data that would change should we do the case studies today are the demographics: More projects, with more use of the growing offerings in analysis-and-design methods, are available to us for study.

Summary

The important ideas of object-oriented technology are mature ideas, based on experience and practices developed over almost 30 years. But the basics seem to have been ignored in many nineties commercial organizations seeking to build large and complex software systems. We briefly reviewed the history of software engineering, and observed that the

---

[2] The report, *Software Reuse in Japan,* is available directly from Technology Transfer International, Inc., Colorado Springs, Colorado, USA.

ideas recognized as early as 1968 remain relevant today. We also provided an even briefer history of the invention of object-oriented programming languages and development environments, and touched on three potential benefits that attract developers to the use of objects: rapid application development, one-to-one mapping of descriptions from real-world entities to objects, and maintainable software systems.

We then defined what we mean by a decision framework, a principle, and a maxim. And we introduced the foundation principles and a maxim that govern our recommendations for creating a management plan for effective introduction and use of object-oriented technology. These were the principles of system architecture and decision making, and the maxim for management communication.

A decision framework is an organized sequence of decisions that you must address to be successful with object-oriented technology. Decisions have to be coordinated. Decisions cannot violate basic principles that we set out. We introduced two categories with which we organize our discussions about ten project-management decision frameworks: establish the goals for the use of object-oriented technology (Chapters 2–4), and use object-oriented technology in software development (Chapters 5–20). A summary of the principles and goals of these decision frameworks was also provided. These principles form the basis of our recommendations for selecting methods, techniques, and supporting tools for different kinds of project process models.

The chapter concluded with a brief introduction describing the sources of information we used to formulate our recommendations. In addition to our personal management, consulting, and training experiences, we studied 39 software development projects at 26 companies, and participated in interviews with six companies in Japan. The projects we studied demonstrate that use of object-oriented technology can improve software development productivity—it can help companies meet their system goals in less time and with fewer developers. These projects lend evidence that organizing projects to take advantage of reusable assets can encourage companies to develop systems based on consistent definitions of business processes and elements. These projects and our own direct experience convinced us that the benefits of object-oriented technology are best met in the context of well-managed projects.

Additional Reading About the History of Software Engineering

ACM Turing Award Lectures: The First Twenty Years, 1966–1985, ACM Press: Reading, Mass., 1987.

> Each year, the ACM—a professional society for computer scientists, teachers, and developers—selects a member of the computing sciences community to receive the prestigious Turing Award. The honor is conveyed during the ACM Annual Meeting, at which the recipient delivers a lecture reporting on his or her history of research and teaching. This book is a compendium of the first 25 years of lectures, and provides a clear perspective on critical issues in past computer research and development programs.

Byte Magazine, August 1981.

This issue of *Byte Magazine* was dedicated to the introduction of the Smalltalk-80 language and its associated object-oriented approach to program development environments. The feature articles, written by members of the Xerox PARC Smalltalk research team, represent the first major publication about the language and its environment. The issue is considered a collector's item and may require some effort to find.

Goldberg, A., ed., *History of Personal Workstations*, ACM Press: Reading, Mass., 1988.

This book contains papers by the many people who created the hardware and software of the personal workstations of the fifties, sixties, and seventies. It includes material on Doug Engelbart's NLS project, Alan Kay's Dynabook, the Xerox Alto workstation hardware and software, and many others. The papers were originally presented at a conference of the same name. Excerpts from the conference, including all video shown by the presenters, are available on videotape from the ACM.

Wexelblat, R., ed., *History of Programming Languages I*, Academic Press: New York, 1981.
Bergin, T., and Gibson, R., eds., *History of Programming Languages II*, forthcoming. Preprints appear in *ACM SIGPLAN Notices*, March 1993.

Twice now, separated by 15 years, the ACM has sponsored an event to celebrate the invention and use of programming languages. The languages discussed in these books are survivors. They all were introduced at least ten years prior to the conference, and all were still in widespread use at the time of the conference. Each language is presented by its creators, highlighting why the language was invented, the process of invention, and some thoughts on the language's influence. The first edition includes Simula; the more recent edition covers popular object-oriented languages—CLOS, C++, and Smalltalk.

Yourdon, E., ed., *Classics in Software Engineering*, Yourdon Press: New York, 1979.

Ed Yourdon has compiled a collection of seminal research articles and reports dating from 1965 to 1978. The collection includes the Bohm and Jacopini paper we reference in this chapter, as well as Dijkstra's original harangue against the GOTO statement. There are several papers debating programming styles with and without GOTO statements, discussions on structured programming and on the concept of chief programmer teams. The earliest paper in the volume is Dijkstra's "Programming Considered as a Human Activity," generally cited as representing the start of the structured programming revolution. This book will save you the time of hunting the library shelves. Every student of software engineering practices should read most of the papers reprinted here. Their age in no way diminishes their value.

CHAPTER 2

Establish Project Goals and Objectives

First a story, as told to the congregation by a rabbi on the eve of a new year.

> A rabbi boarded a train, one on which he often rode and one whose conductor, therefore, recognized him. The rabbi reached into his coat pocket for his ticket. Not finding it, he began a search of his belongings. The conductor stopped him: "Rabbi, I know you must have the ticket somewhere. Don't bother searching now. You can send it later, when you do find it." But the rabbi kept searching. When approached by the conductor yet again, the rabbi replied: "You do not understand. I know you trust me for the ticket. But—where am I going?"

Like the rabbi in the story, many organizations have no idea where they are going. Each course of action seems as promising as the next. In some organizations, people go off in different directions. Not only do these people not know where they are going, they are not all going there together. You might argue that this chaos is good, since someone might end up in an interesting place—the old monkey-at-the-keyboard approach to book writing—but the risk of not getting anywhere is much too high.

Goals and Objectives

The story of the rabbi illustrates the theme of the first project-management decision framework, summarized by the following principle:

Framework Principle. You should know where you are going, so you will know whether you have arrived.

This decision framework—for defining project goals and objectives—is the initial stage of the effort to establish goals for the use of object-oriented technology. The framework goal is:

Project Goals and Objectives

Framework Goal. Determine goals and objectives, and set up a structure for decision making in which all decisions are traceable back to these goals and objectives.

Goals and *objectives* are statements of desired outcomes. An objective is time-targeted and measurable, while a goal is not. In this sense, goals and objectives differ in the amount of detail or precision we use to define them. For example, an organization might have a goal to be the best producer of graphical software widgets. An objective corresponding to this goal is to have a 50 percent share of the market for graphical widgets within two years. The objective is used to evaluate the extent to which the desired outcomes have been achieved.

There are business goals and system goals. Business goals refer to financial, market positioning, or operational properties of the organization. System goals address the specific attributes of three different entities: products, processes, and resources.

Product   Any artifact available as a consequence of a process, such as a software system

Process   Activities and methods used to build products

Resource   Person, tool, environment, or other asset that is an input to a process that yields a product

System goals and objectives should be defined in terms of these three entities.

Projects—Transitioning from Current to Desired Situation

The purpose of a project is to change a current situation into a desired one. We use the term *situation* to refer to the available products, processes, and resources. The general form of a project is shown in Fig. 2.1. The *current situation* is the way the organization uses processes and resources to develop and maintain software products. The *desired situation* embodies the kinds of products that the organization wishes to develop, and the preferred development processes and resources. Within this context, a *project* is a set of activities that uses the current processes and resources to create or maintain a product, or that modifies these processes or resources to be more like those defined by the desired situation. An *assessment* is a project that examines the current situation and provides information to set goals for the desired situation.

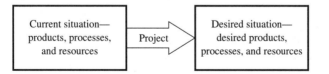

Figure 2.1   General Form of a Project

Longer-term goals are not defined in terms of object-oriented technology, but rather in terms of the results that the technology can help achieve. When you introduce object-oriented technology into an organization, you need a variety of shorter-term projects—in particular, resource- and process-improvement projects—whose goals and objectives are defined in terms of the successful adoption of object-oriented technology. In this and future chapters, we use the diagram shown in Fig. 2.1 to describe the different types of improvement projects that are needed to change a software development situation to use object-oriented technology successfully. We define the following projects:

Chapter 6	Process-improvement project to change the product development process model
Chapter 7	Process-improvement project to change the planning and controlling process, and create a project schedule
Chapter 10	Process-improvement project to establish a reuse process model
Chapter 12	Resource-improvement project to create the appropriate teams
Chapter 17	Resource-improvement project to select a software development environment
Chapter 19	Resource-improvement project to develop a plan to train team members
Chapter 20	Process-improvement project to establish a software measurement program

Framework for Defining Project Goals and Objectives

The first decision framework asks you to determine your goals for improving products, processes, and resources. This framework consists of the following steps:

***Project
Goals and
Objectives***

- Understand the business mission and business processes

- Understand business and team values for software development
  - Determine what you value in the products you produce
  - Determine what you value in the processes you use to create products
  - Determine what you value in the kinds of resources that should be available

- State the desired situation in terms of goals and objectives for products, processes, and resources

- Assess the current situation

Figure 2.2 illustrates the elements in defining projects. There are five inputs to a statement of the desired situation. All project goals should be aligned with the business mission and processes, and with the organization's and each team member's values for software development. Expectations for the use of object-oriented technology and assessment of the current situation must also be considered.

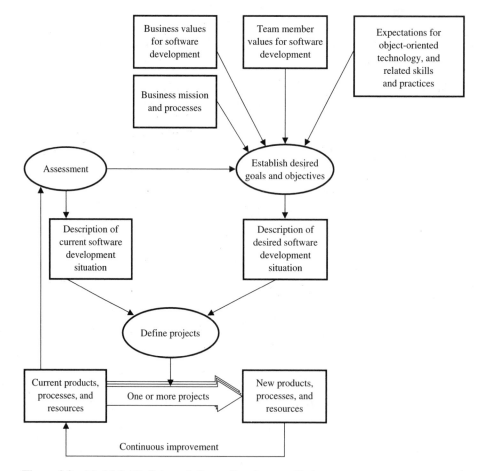

Figure 2.2   Model for Defining a Software Development Project

Assessing the current situation helps the manager to understand the abilities and limitations of the organization's current development processes and resources, and the nature of existing products. With knowledge gained from the assessment, the manager can determine not only what should change, but also what is feasible to change in a reasonable time frame. The assessment can uncover information that is used to define the desired situation.

The arrow from new products, processes, and resources to that of the current ones indicates continuous improvement, whereby the situation resulting from a project becomes the new current situation, and the project-definition activity repeats.

Understand the Business Mission and Business Processes

The business mission statement of an organization describes management's principal goals. In effect, it directly or indirectly prescribes the behavior of everyone in the organization. An organization will have difficulty making effective business decisions, including decisions about how to develop its computer systems, unless it has a good understanding of its mission. Thus, it is critical that the mission statement be well articulated, effectively communicated, and easily understood by everyone in the organization. Many companies publish their business mission statements in their shareholder reports or corporate brochures. A brochure for Matsushita Electric states its mission as the basic management objective written by the company's founder in 1929:

> Recognizing our responsibilities as industrialists, we will devote ourselves to the progress and development of society and the well-being of people through our business activities, thereby enhancing the quality of life throughout the world.

The brochure reviews the company's current business activities—the manufacture and sales of electric and electronic products—in terms of this statement.

Business process reengineering. A business's mission must be supported by its business processes. In Fig. 2.2, we show that the business mission and processes are input to establishing the desired software development goals and objectives. This figure assumes that the statements of business mission and processes are understood and appropriate. Suppose they are not. Then how are the mission and processes established? *Business process reengineering* (BPR) is one approach.

According to the advocates of business process reengineering, a radical redesign of business processes is needed if a business is to achieve dramatic improvements in critical, contemporary measures of performance, such as cost, quality, service, and speed [Hammer and Champy 1993]. BPR assumes that task-oriented jobs are obsolete, and that companies must reorganize work around business processes. This reorganization is accomplished by examining the many distinct tasks being carried out in the organization's current business situation, and then reorganizing work in terms of new processes.

Figure 2.3 shows a model for how BPR influences the desired software development situation. In this model, the organization carries out a special BPR project that constructs

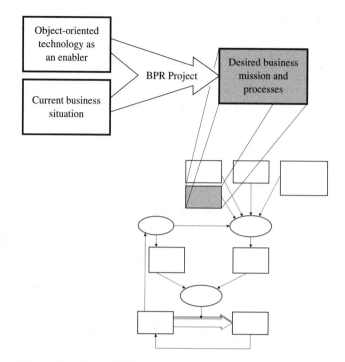

Figure 2.3   How BPR Influences Getting to the Desired Software
Development Situation by Establishing the Processes
That Support the Business Mission

a business vocabulary shareable across the enterprise, identifies the information important to running the business, and develops the new business processes. The results of the BPR project define the desired business situation of the organization, corresponding to the business mission and process box shown in Fig. 2.2.

BPR deemphasizes the use of new technologies to enhance, streamline, or improve the current approach to doing business. Instead, technology is treated as an enabler that allows the business to do things that it is not already doing. In Fig. 2.3, object-oriented technology is shown as an enabler of the BPR process (that is, as input to the BPR project). The desired software development situation must include product, process, and resource goals and objectives that support the use of object-oriented technology commensurate with its role as a BPR enabler.[1]

---

[1] Object-oriented technology also provides a special solution for carrying out a BPR project. Some object-oriented analysis methods provide concepts and techniques that can be used to model not only the current business processes, but also the desired ones. The same methods can also be used to model the requirements of specific systems. The synergy between these two models—business and systems—can reduce the possibility that system analysts will misinterpret the statement of desired business processes. There can also be a greater degree of traceability from the analysis and the design of systems, back to the business process goals and objectives.

Mottoes. Many organizations develop mottoes as a means of summarizing their mission statements. For example, the following are mottoes of some major U.S. companies:

Burger King	Have it your way
DHL	Faster to more of the world
FedEx	When it absolutely, positively, has to be there overnight
Ford Motor Company	Quality is job 1
Lucky Supermarkets	The low price leader
New York Times	All the news that's fit to print
Novell	Customers first, employees second, shareholders third
Paul Masson Wines	We will sell no wine before its time

A good mission statement and motto pervades an organization. With a commitment to training and effective leadership, every employee knows and understands them. More important, every employee uses the mission statement and motto as the basis for decision making. Tom Peters [Peters 1987] tells the story of a junior telecommunications expert at FedEx who took the initiative to rent a helicopter, fly to a snowbound mountaintop location, and fix a cable broken in a snowstorm—all to get the company back on-line, delivering packages overnight. The company financially rewarded this personal initiative because the employee appropriately interpreted the company's motto. Another example of how a worker took initiative at FedEx was told to us by a consultant in business process reengineering:

On a normal daily pickup run, a FedEx employee shows up at a sidewalk FedEx drop-off box. When he goes to remove the deliverables from the box, he realizes that he does not have the proper key to open the box. What should he do? Leave the packages in the box and take the other packages to the airport? Go to the dispatch center for the key, and take a chance that he can still get back to the airport on time? The driver chooses a third alternative. He takes a monkey wrench out of his truck, unbolts the drop-off box from the sidewalk, tosses it in the back of the truck and heads straight to the airport. The box is promptly opened and the packages sent to their destination—arriving, as the motto states, overnight. The employee is subsequently praised and rewarded by his supervisors for exercising good judgment.

Why discuss these examples in the context of a book on object-oriented technology? Simply stated, new technology must be aligned with the business mission. Technology that derails or displaces organizational goals is detrimental to the health of the organization.

Understand Business and Team Values for Software Development

You should understand what your organization and your team members value in how they develop software and in the kinds of software they develop. What each team member values is a personal opinion, but one that has to be appreciated at a team or organizational level.

Figure 2.4, entitled "What Do You Value in Software Development?," displays a set of questions. These questions ask you to consider what you value in software development, as stated in terms of products, processes, and resources. Answer these questions to describe your desired work situation. Ask each member of the team to answer these questions. Users are team members, so solicit their input as well.

In exploring questions of value, make a list of the characteristics or attributes that make you feel good about a product, process, or resource. For example, in describing a successful product, you might state that the product architecture is well designed in the sense that it is highly modular. Similar statements can be made about processes and resources. A process might be successful because it reduces the number of defects introduced; it might be considered effective and therefore good because it leads quickly to a stable design. You might simply say that a process is good if it is fun to use. Many strongly held opinions are about resources; for example, software engineers value having the fastest computers with the highest-resolution color displays, and having access to the fastest worldwide communications networks.

What do you value in a software development effort? Answer in terms of the following:

Product	Make a list of the attributes of a software product that make the product successful.
Process	Make a list of the attributes of a software development process that support your ability to create the kinds of products you value.
Resource	Make a list of the attributes of the resources for software development that contribute to a successful process.

Figure 2.4   What Do You Value in Software Development?

State the Desired Situation in Terms of Goals and Objectives for Products, Processes, and Resources

The next step of the decision framework is to translate the business mission and processes, and the business and team values into statements of software development goals and objectives.

The statement of goals and objectives, in some absolute sense, describes your ideal. This ideal is a baseline against which you can assess your current situation to determine departures from the ideal. You then formulate projects to transform the current situation into something closer to the ideal. If you choose a series of projects, you may revise your vision of the ideal based on the results from each project. You might prefer to assess your current situation before you state desired goals and objectives, as the assessment may identify practices you wish to continue. Any assessment procedure, however, implies assumptions as to what your desired situation should be. It will identify where your situation does not match the baseline set by the assessment, and will suggest goals you can incorporate into your statement of a desired situation.

Example of a desired situation. The following is a list of responses, categorized by product, process, and resource values, given by participants in our seminars to the questions in Fig. 2.4.

Product values	A well-designed system, which means:
	The system meets end user requirements
	The system is complete
	The system is testable
	The system is easy to extend
	The system execution meets performance criteria
	The system contains zero defects
	The system can be maintained at a reasonable cost
Process values	A well-managed project, which means:
	Schedules are predictable
	Results are delivered on time
	Results are delivered within budget
	Processes can be reused
	Change requests are handled in a timely way
Resource values	Appropriate and sufficient resources, which is known if:
	Team members understand their tasks
	Staff feels satisfied
	Reusable assets are available
	Staff is adequately trained to use the selected technology
	Appropriate tools are available

Next, goals and objectives for a desired software development situation are defined, representing the business and team values in terms of measurable attributes of products, processes, and resources.

Product goals and objectives

These product goals and objectives express the desire for a complete and understandable system, one that meets customer needs and is easily extended.

- The services of the delivered system fulfill the needs of the client/user (no less, and preferably no more), according to an assessment of 100 current customers.
- The system consists of a set of subsystems, each with a well-defined interface.
- Documentation describes all of the desired system capabilities.
- Existing subsystem implementations can be added or modified without having to change the implementation or specification of any other subsystem.

Process goals and objectives

These process goals and objectives involve end users to obtain their agreement on system functionality. The process model emphasizes reusing, not reinventing, as a way to meet deadlines and budget constraints.

- End users preview and approve all functionality prior to final system implementation.
- Reuse consideration precedes any development.
- Project schedule always shows detailed tasks for the coming month.

Resource goals and objectives

These resource goals and objectives focus on developing team members who can use the desired processes and tools to create the desired products.

- Team members are trained and disciplined in creating modular architectures, ones that are easy to extend.

- Team members understand the value of appropriate reuse.
- Team members know how to document their work in an understandable way.
- Team members know how to work with (non-technical) end users to solicit and respond to feedback on subsystem design.
- Tools are available for creating, documenting, and testing modular specifications and implementations.
- Tools are available for monitoring the interactions among subsystems and the potential overlap of functionality.

After using this value-driven approach to define goals and objectives, communicate the results to all team members.

Assess the Current Situation

The final step of the framework is to assess the current software development situation. We try to understand the current situation so we can decide what should be changed. In an assessment, we ask three questions: What is the perspective to be used? What are the attributes that are of interest from this perspective? And what is the scale along which the attributes can be measured? For example, a software project manager might be interested in the time needed to complete subprojects, which is measurable in terms of the number of staff hours per project activity. Or the quality assurance manager might be interested in the perceived quality of a delivered product, measurable in terms of the number of defects reported per week.[2]

We assess products, processes, and resources. We assess the products that the organization currently delivers and supports, and the processes that were used to develop these products. We examine, for example, the product-development process, analysis-and-design methods, test and documentation techniques, and change-control policies. Each organization has existing resources consisting of software development environments, teams, computer hardware, and software tools. We assess the attributes of these resources as well.[3] When possible, we do so in terms of the desired situation we have set as a baseline.

---

[2] We offer more detail on issues of measurement in Chapter 20.

[3] See Chapter 15 and Chapter 16 for ways to assess analysis-and-design methods and programming environment tools.

In addition to providing information about the current situation, we can use the assessment to guide us in describing a desired situation. The techniques offered by the Software Engineering Institute (SEI) at Carnegie Mellon University are examples of such assessment procedures.[4] SEI developed a Capability Maturity Model (CMM) that can be used to perform software process assessments and software capability evaluations [Humphrey 1989, Paulk *et al.* 1995]. The CMM is a model that proposes a vocabulary, a set of priorities for attacking software problems, and a measurement to provide reliable and consistent appraisals. Software process assessments help software organizations prioritize their process improvement needs; software capability evaluations help acquisition agencies identify risks in awarding business to contractors. A software process assessment measures the maturity level of an organization's processes along an ordinal scale ranging from one to five. Each maturity level is defined by a set of process goals, and is the basis for predicting the most likely outcome of subsequent software projects.

The CMM states that organizations assessed at higher maturity levels are capable of developing software in a well-defined, organized fashion, and are more likely to complete a software project successfully than are less mature organizations. In addition, more mature organizations are in a better position to introduce new technologies, in that they are better able to measure resource productivity and product quality. SEI defined the desired process situation; its assessment determines the extent to which an organization meets SEI's ideal.

Specifically, the CMM describes five levels, with Level 3 the first level at which the organization is considered sufficiently mature to handle the introduction of new technology. At Level 3, an organization has a well-documented, supported process with which software quality is tracked; the process is used by both management and engineering staffs, and changed as required. Capability at Level 1 is characterized by instability in planning and execution, and reaction-driven commitment systems. Most organizations worldwide assess at this level.

Does this mean you have to achieve Level 3 before considering object-oriented technology? Our answer is no. The interest in objects rekindles interest in project-management practices, creating an opportunity to get your organization working toward Level 3 and better, coincident with your use of object-oriented technology. Moreover, the technology has immediate benefits that make it a risk to wait because your competitors probably are not waiting.

But there is a downside. Unless you are at Level 2, you do not have a good measurement program in place and have not collected data on which to base a comparison. Consequently, you will not easily quantify any improvement due to the use of object-oriented technology. According to the SEI findings, there is also a risk that you will not suc-

---

[4] The SEI maturity model is one of several recommended approaches to assessment. See also the Reuse Maturity Model from the Harris Corporation [Koltun and Hudson 1992] and the Six Sigma from Motorola [Harry and Lawson 1992].

ceed because your processes are nonexistent or broken. Our recommendation is to put a simple first process model in place that leverages strategies encouraged by the use of object-oriented technology, and to document what you plan to do. You have to start somewhere. Postproject reflection on your documented experience is a good start to working toward higher CMM levels.

Assessment of the KandA Widget Company—An Example

Suppose we are the KandA Widget Company.[5] The mission of the business is to be the dominant widget provider in the world. The company makes all kinds of widgets, big and small. Indeed, the motto is:

> A widget for every occasion; a widget for all.

Specific objectives for the coming year include: owning 70 percent of the world widget market, and developing five new markets in countries where the company currently has no presence. The KandA Widget Company has the long-term goal of making KandA Widgets a household name.

Goal setting in the KandA MIS department is based on the company's mission statement and motto. The MIS goal is to provide the information-technology infrastructure for a company that dominates the world widget market, selling any kind of widget anywhere. The MIS department services all other departments of the company, such as accounting, sales, widget inventors, and so on. Members of all departments are aligned for the purpose of obtaining 70 percent market share and penetration of five new territories. MIS developers are currently working on four projects to develop a new customer-service response system, an opinion poll for the public relations department, a new inventory control system for local distributors, and a new order processing system. There are three applications waiting to be developed, and two others that must be maintained. Each of these projects has its own product goals and objectives.

Another project exists at the KandA Widget Company. The goal of this project is to modify the company's current software development situation, where necessary, so that the company can improve the speed with which it can develop new graphical, interactive applications. To formulate this project, the managers assessed the company's current development situation to determine objectives for change. Let's suppose that the KandA Widget Company was assessed as the worst case—SEI Level 1: the engineers operate in an ad hoc or chaotic manner, with an insufficient sense of teamwork. They are unwilling or unable to create clear specifications of the content of the next product release. Source

---

[5] We intend the KandA Widget Company to be a representative company, describing the melting pot of information obtained from the case studies. This approach allows us to mask any less favorable descriptions about any one case study.

code is not under formal version and configuration management, little QA is performed, and, according to customer surveys, inadequate documentation is supplied with the products.

How did this situation occur? Fast growth at the company contributed somewhat, matched by insufficient management interest in, or understanding of, the software development process. Marketing contributed as well—insisting on large individual results, rather than smaller attainable results delivered incrementally. The KandA Widget Company's desired-situation objectives are: Understandable and easily extended software systems, built with end user involvement and reuse of artifacts from prior development projects, and built by developers who understand the technology they must use. An assessment shows that the company's widgets and system software products meet technical objectives, and have better than industry-average reliability. Future product plans do aim to meet market needs. The problem is that the processes and resources available to projects are not sufficient to produce these products in a timely way, nor with the new product features identified by marketing. The assessment states:

1. Documentation of subsystem interface specifications is inadequate. Users of subsystems require better documentation, including examples for effective use, so they can incorporate the subsystems without additional assistance.

2. Better requirements specifications and design documentation are required, so that software can be modified by developers who did not write the original code.

3. Developers do not agree with the development plans created by management. Plans need team sign up.

4. Existing tools are insufficient for source-code change control.

5. There is no way for management to track progress short of simply believing the reports from engineering managers.

6. Responsiveness to customer incident reports needs to be improved so that customers have direct and immediate feedback as to how issues are being addressed.

7. Teams are not protected from interruptions or diversions. As a result, they are not focused on well-defined tasks, but rather react on a daily basis to the problem of the day.[6]

What plans for improving the situation should the KandA Widget Company make? Improvement might involve setting up several situation-improvement projects.

---

[6] DeMarco and Lister succinctly document that engineering schedules are most likely met when team members create them. They also document that dates set by managers without team support are rarely met, and that interrupted work is unproductive time [DeMarco and Lister 1987].

Process improvement goals

- Define better techniques for involving team members in setting product objectives and schedules.

- Define clear corporate guidelines for requirements specifications and product documentation, and then communicate the guidelines to all team members.

- Adopt a new product process model that incorporates the new corporate guidelines and the new software development tools.

- Create a better way to capture and track defect reports, and to report the status of product changes to customers.

Resource improvement goals

- Install tools for reaching closure on product features, assigning subsystem ownership, tracking subsystem development, and controlling and releasing versions and configurations.

- Train team members so they know how to provide adequate requirements specifications and design documents.

- Obtain better tools for source-code change control.

The desired situation often differs from the current situation in many ways. Removing each difference may involve multiple projects. For example, if new technology is ultimately to be used, a project to retrain the team may be needed. If special tools will be used, there may be a project to evaluate commercial alternatives.

For the KandA Widget Company, there are seven areas of improvement. Each involves a separate project. Some can be done in parallel, and some might be combined. For example, the introduction of new tools may involve a change in the product process model. Each of these kinds of projects may be managed differently, in a way appropriate to meeting the goals for different application products, obtaining reusable product assets, or improving resources (tools, team skills). KandA's management must decide which of these projects will benefit from the use of object-oriented technology. We discuss how to make these decisions in the next chapters.

Case Study Results

We categorized the goals and objectives from the case studies according to different kinds of projects: projects to create specific product results, projects to create reusable product results, projects to improve resources, and projects to improve processes. It was more difficult to obtain statements of measurable quality objectives for the projects we studied than to obtain the goal statements, indicative of a lack of emphasis on collecting data at the studied sites. A sampling of statements follows.

Projects to Create Specific Product Results

Business

Create a family of network-manager products—defining a common look and feel—to manage effectively all of our company's products that reside on communications networks.

System

Create a core system module containing the common parts and functionality required to manage all networks. Then create specific personality modules that can plug into the core.

Business

Support the business with a customer information system that manages the complete revenue cycle of the business ($20 million in fees).

System

Create software systems that will have long life, and be quickly changeable in response to changing business conditions and regulations. Use new technology in the near future, especially cooperative processing.

Quality Objectives

Handle 1.3 million customer records and 12 transactions per second.
Interoperate with existing CICS, DB2, PL/1 programs.
Support 400 concurrent users.

Business

Create a product that is a software development environment for creating real-time call processing systems.

System

Provide ability for customers to program the product.
Support customizable configuration of functionality.

Quality Objectives

Get factor of five increase in development productivity (as measured by lines of code per developer per day).
Cut amount of code to 1/5 or 1/10 of the 16 million lines of an existing, comparable product.

Business	Consolidate and replace existing information management systems.
System	Build a system that can be flexibly changed.
Quality Objectives	Process more than 5 million loans overnight. Handle 100 simultaneous users. Provide two-minute response time. Deliver system on time within limited budget.

Business	Create a call management system that supports all of the activities of the company's services organization.
System	Must be evolvable as customer needs change. Must be configurable to support policies governing variety of technical support personnel and customer communication channels (telephone, FAX, e-mail, electronic bulletin board). There must be many levels of secure access. All user times must be logged, and automatic logout must be supported.
Quality Objectives	System must be available 24 hours a day, 7 days a week, 365 days a year. System must support 150–300 simultaneous users and approximately 10,000 calls per week. Information must be available on-line and real-time to all service sites with a one-year call history. Database transactions must be completed within 5 seconds (worst case).

Projects to Create Reusable Product Results

Business	Reduce time to create the compilers for each new oscilloscope (from several years to several months or weeks).
System	Create a reusable compiler-compiler that would take as input the instruction set for a new instrument, and generate a compiler as output.

Business	Give customers access to shipment information and the ability to initiate shipments, to improve customer service.
System	Create an on-line source information capture, eliminating manual data entry. Create an application infrastructure of reusable parts.

Projects to Improve the Resource Situation

Business	Prove or disprove the claims that developers using object-oriented technology are more productive.
Systems	Objectively measure the productivity of the developers when using object-oriented technology to develop a mainstream corporate application. Draw conclusions by comparing the productivity of the same developers when creating the same application using traditional technology.

Summary

Our concern is not only with the nature of a product that is built using object-oriented technology, but also with the processes and resources an organization needs to build such products. The framework for defining goals and objectives asks you to determine your goals for improving products, processes, and resources. When you introduce object-oriented technology, you will change your current software development situation into a situation that can make best use of processes and resources based on objects, and you will do so in the context of your organizational needs. These new processes and resources must be useful in developing the kinds of products you wish to produce. Your plans should take into account the business mission, business processes, business and team values for software development, and the assessment of the current products, processes, and resources.

We invented a story about the KandA Widget Company to illustrate our ideas about assessing the current software development situation, and about initiating projects that lead to the desired use of object-oriented technology. We also provided several example statements of business and system goals and objectives, drawn from case study projects. These examples should help you understand the kind of statements you should prepare for each project you set out to do.

Additional Reading About Project Goals and Objectives

Gilb, T., *Principles of Software Engineering Management*, Addison-Wesley: Wokingham, England, 1988.

Tom Gilb is a master of communicating timeless and classic knowledge of the software development process. This book discusses the importance of clear project objectives, in the context of an evolutionary development process in which knowledge of specific quality objectives is key to ensuring proper project management. Gilb's use of quality templates, discussed in our Chapter 20, is a particularly good way of defining the objectives associated with a software development project.

Humphrey, W., *Managing the Software Process*, SEI Series in Software Engineering, Addison-Wesley: Reading, Mass., 1989.

This book is a result of Humphrey's personal experiences and research conducted at the Software Engineering Institute at Carnegie Mellon University. It presents a framework and techniques for evaluating and improving the process of software development based on five levels of software process maturity. Humphrey's stated intention is to help you assess the quality of your current software process, what you should do to improve your process, and how you can get started.

Paulk, M. C., Weber, C. V., Curtis, B., and Chrissis, M. B., *The Capability Maturity Model: Guidelines for Improving the Software Process*, Addison-Wesley: Reading, Mass., 1995.

This book is the authoritative description of the Capability Maturity Model (CMM) and how to interpret its practices. It includes a case study of IBM Houston's Space Shuttle project—an SEI Level 5 rated project—and, in an appendix, a comparison of CMM with ISO 9001. The book is intended as a companion to [Humphrey 1989].

CHAPTER 3

Determining Benefits of Object-Oriented Technology

Organizations can benefit from the use of object-oriented technology, but only if they understand the technical nature of the technology, and how to interpret these technical details in the context of how to develop better software systems. We address both the concepts and a business interpretation that inform you of what you can reasonably expect from object-oriented technology.

What Is an Object?

To understand a software system, we examine the behaviors the system carries out, and the parts of the system responsible for these behaviors. We can also examine how the system carries out its behaviors, defined in terms of code and data. In the context of software, *behavior* is something that the software can do, and *implementation* is how the behavior is defined in computer executable code.

An *object* is a description of a set of behaviors that occur in the real world. Of course, we can create an imaginary world. Then, an object can be the description of a set of behaviors in this imaginary world.

Figure 3.1   A World of Traffic

Sometimes an object represents the behavior of a tangible thing in the real world, such as the car or the person or the road or the traffic light exhibited in Fig. 3.1. An object can represent the intangible things in the world as well, such as timing and synchronization. Given the behaviors associated with cars, people, roads, traffic lights, all timed and synchronized, we have a set of related behaviors that interact to model a real world of street traffic. A car has behavior. It starts. It stops. Its engine idles. Its acceleration increases. A person has behavior. A person runs, walks, waits, pushes buttons, plans a route through the streets. A road has behavior. It holds cars or people. It cracks from winter frost. It steams from summer heat. Cars and people and roads and timers and synchronization can all be represented in a computer as software descriptions.

An object is defined in terms of the behaviors that it demonstrates. For example, a car object is an entity that defines the behavior of a car—to accelerate, slow down, turn right, to transport a passenger, and so on. As a consequence of its behavior, the car could be in motion or stationary. The car object can also describe physical properties of color, style, size of fuel tank, or the legal properties of having a registered owner or liability insurance.

Every object has a well-defined interface that specifies the behavior of the object in a manner that is independent of its implementation. This interface defines the collection of *services* that can be invoked by other objects. The implementation of an object describes how to carry out its services. This includes information private to the object, accessible to other objects only if services exist to provide such access. Similarly, the algorithms that implement services are private to the object. No other object can rely on how another object implements its services. This ability of objects to hide internal structure, thereby defining services independent of implementation, is called *encapsulation*.

Message sending. A fundamental notion of software systems described in terms of objects is that all processing and transfer of information is carried out as a consequence of messages that are sent among the objects. We invoke the services that an object can carry out by sending messages to the object. To get a car to move forward, we send it a message asking it to move some distance. To assign an owner to a car, we send the car a message that it has been purchased by a particular person or other entity that can serve as a car owner. To find out how much fuel the car currently holds, we ask the car to tell us its current fuel level.[1]

A computer program involving objects is a sequence of message-sends. Example message-sends are shown in Fig. 3.2.[2]

traffic light turn green
car move forward
motorcycle wait
pedestrian check signal
bicyclist check signal

Figure 3.2 Some Possible Messages in the World of Traffic

When an object receives a message that it understands, it invokes some behavior. This behavior is part of the definition of the object. Various kinds of objects can understand the same message, yet respond differently. In creating a simulation of traffic flow, we might specify that objects approaching an intersection will respond to a message indicating that the traffic light has turned to yellow. Some cars might speed up and race through the intersection, while slower cars or a bus or a person might come to a stop. This ability for different kinds of objects to respond differently to the same message is called *polymorphism*.

Object composition. Objects can be defined in terms of other objects. The parts-whole relationship among objects decomposes an object into behaviors that are best grouped as independent object descriptions. A car consists of its registration, repair history, and warranty. And, should we be interested in the behavior of the car's constituent components, we would model the car's doors and lights and wheels and windows, and so on. A door, a light, a warranty, an owner—these are all objects. A door might consist of a handle, a

---

[1] It is common practice in the object world to anthropomorphize objects, and to refer to objects as though they are real and can receive and send messages. Although we do not really "talk to" cars or car parts, or "ask" car parts for information or action, we describe the object model as though such conversations actually take place. In our examples, we will provide only partial descriptions of the example objects.

[2] We do not use the syntax of any particular programming language other than to express the message-sends in an English-like command format.

lock, a window—again all described as objects. When an object is described in terms of other objects, it can *delegate responsibility* for fulfilling services to these component objects.

Here is an example that demonstrates the advantage of delegating responsibility to a component object. A car door lock is typically mechanical, requiring that a physical key be inserted and turned for the lock to be released or engaged. Responsibility for securing the car is delegated by the car to its door, and in turn is delegated to the door lock. Suppose that we create a new kind of lock—an electronic one. A remote-control device releases and engages the lock. Now suppose that when we create a new car, we give it doors with these new locks. The behavior of the car does not change. It still responds to messages to lock and unlock its doors. The behavior of the doors does not change either. But the actual kind of key needed does change, and the impact of this change is confined to the lock object.

The ability to characterize an individual object as a set of behaviors enables us to capture our understanding of how responsibility for information and information processing is grouped in a real or imaginary world. The ability to compose new objects from existing objects enables us to reuse the behaviors supplied by other objects. Such reuse enhances our understanding of the world that we are trying to model. We divide our world into parts that represent the smallest levels of ownership of information and services that we wish to study or control. We then combine these parts to create new parts.

A Class Describes a Set of Objects

A *class* defines a set of objects that provide a particular set of services and have a particular set of properties. An *instance* is a member of the set.[3] Classes offer an approach to sharing—all instances of a class reuse its services and properties. Conceptually, classes are themselves objects because they are software descriptions with well-defined interfaces. They provide services, like any other object, such as creating instances and sometimes answering questions about all instances of the class.

In our model of the world of cars and traffic, it becomes apparent that while there are many different cars, they all behave in the same way, perhaps differing only in the time to accelerate to a fixed speed or to stop when the brake is applied. Likewise, there are many drivers. They behave in basically the same way, but they differ in reaction times and some might therefore fail to brake fast enough when the traffic light changes. For our purposes, the fact that some cars have four-wheel drive, or that some have two doors and others have four, is not relevant, so these distinctions need not be described. We might then define a single class that we name Car, with services to accelerate, stop, brake, turn on, turn off, move forward, and back up.

---

[3] More formally, the basic concept of object-oriented technology is data abstraction. We define objects in terms of data types, where each type defines a set of methods. There may be many instances of a data type, each of which has the same behavior. The data needed to carry out the behavior is private to each instance. A class is a data type that defines a set of instances.

Classes can be described in terms of other classes. We say that a class can be described as a *subclass* of another class—called its *superclass*. The subclass inherits all of the services already defined for the superclass. Figure 3.3 provides an example hierarchy of vehicles, distinguished by their mode of operation. All vehicles share the ability to start, stop, and move. Some kinds of vehicles have behavior that is specific to the domain of operation. For example, an Air Vehicle is able to take off and land.

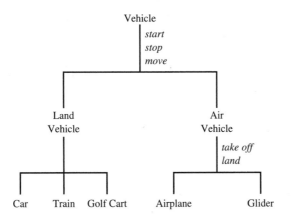

Figure 3.3 Sample Class Hierarchy for Modeling Vehicles

When representing traffic, we need not concern ourselves with the differences in land vehicles—that there are cars and trucks and motorcycles and bicycles, all intermingled on the road. But suppose that our purpose in capturing aspects of the real world is to model passenger capacity. Or suppose that we wish to analyze the different road configurations that distinguish roadways for commercial vehicles, such as trucks and buses, from those for non-commercial cars and motorcycles. Then distinguishing these differences in land vehicles becomes a critical aspect of describing the objects.

Capturing similarities and differences among objects—by placing the shared behaviors in a superclass and the unique ones in subclasses—accomplishes two objectives. First, it gives us a clear behavioral model of the relationships among aspects of the world. Second, it allows us to express how changes in behavior should be propagated. Any change in a superclass immediately propagates to the subclasses. New behaviors can be attributed to a subclass without affecting the behavior in its superclass. Describing a subclass is known as refining the superclass's behavior.

Objects Form Applications, Frameworks, and Components

An *application* is a set of interacting objects. The functionality of an application is defined in terms of the behavior provided by the objects that participate in the application. For example, an application for coordinating the transportation of cargo consists of objects representing trucks with cargo capacity, truck drivers, schedules, destinations, and roadways.

We can define an application in sufficiently general or abstract terms, so that we can change the objects that provide the expected behavior without changing the implementation of the basic application itself. This extends the usefulness of the application. Applications written in this style are referred to as application frameworks. An *application framework* is a set of objects that interact to form the basic structure and processing of applications within a given domain. The objects that provide the general behaviors required by the application framework are called *components* of the framework.

An application framework for coordinating the transportation of cargo provides the structure for combining individual carrier cargo capacity, routes, and prices. A specific trucking company creates its transportation system by specifying the trucks it has available, the routes it can take, and its pricing structure. The computation of cargo loading and route optimization is included in the framework. The framework is general when it does not assume that the cargo is carried by trucks on roads, but rather by cargo carriers on routes. Then a specific shipping company creates its transportation system by specifying ships as the cargo carriers and identifying the ships it has available, the routes it can take, and its pricing structure.

Suppose we create a software system that provides travel agency services for planning family car vacation trips. The software system produces a travel itinerary that identifies routes, gas stations, hotels, restaurants, and sights to see, and computes trip expenses. These system behaviors depend on information such as the car to be used, the budget for hotels, the number and ages of the travelers, their eating habits, and sight-seeing preferences. The behaviors support two applications: a trip planner, and a trip simulator that lets customers preview a proposed trip.

Objects in the travel agency planner and simulator send messages to car objects to simulate a trip based on the description of the car, the family, and sightseeing preferences. The applications are not implemented with specific details about cars, people, or preferences.

Any kind of vehicle—bus, truck, or motorcycle—can support the behavior of a vacation trip. The head of the travel agency recognizes that the ability to plan trips for any kind of vehicle represents an opportunity to expand the business to plan trips for commercial transportation vehicles, such as tour buses or trucks, or to plan motorcycle trips. To extend the software systems, the developers create new components representing buses and motorcycles that carry out the behavior that is provided by cars—the behavior on which the travel applications depend.

One day a bicyclist sees the poster for the travel-planning service, and asks for help in planning a cross-country tour. Does the travel agency turn the bicyclist away? Of course not—not when a new revenue opportunity presents itself. The basic travel-planning and simulation frameworks are applicable to bicycles that support the expected behaviors.

Now, let's suppose that to attract new customers, the agency decides to offer discount packages by making special arrangements with hotels, restaurants, and tourist sights. The framework that supports the travel planner and simulator has to be changed to account for the change in the business involving discount packages. The change in the framework does not change how the individual components are defined. Applications and application frameworks are systems with well-defined interfaces. In the case of frameworks, the interface specifies expectations for components that can participate in the finished application, or expectations for specializing the framework to produce an application. A change in business assumptions typically requires changes in frameworks and components, to the extent that the framework is not sufficiently general.

What Does It Mean to Be Object-Oriented?

Many people tell the story of the CEO of a software company who claimed that his product would be object-oriented because it was being written in C++. Some tell the story without knowing that it is a joke. The use of a language that provides object-oriented constructs does not render the result object-oriented.

What does it mean to be *object-oriented*? The answer depends on whether the question refers to a programming language, a user interface, an application, a database, or an analysis or design method. The question takes on a different appearance if we attach the adjective to something other than software. Consider, for example, an object-oriented curriculum or an object-oriented government. We want a definition that makes sense for the many kinds of artifacts we wish to label as object-oriented.

Table 3.1 lists some of the ways people define the term object-oriented. The various approaches fall into several categories, depending on whether object-oriented technology is viewed as construction tools and materials (what it is built with), execution behavior (how it operates), abstract models (what it deals with), modular architecture (how it is structured), or the basis for future systems (what more you can do with it). All of the categories, with the exception of the construction tools and materials, matter in determining whether a system is object-oriented. The last category emphasizes the contribution the technology makes to maintenance—the ability to change the system in such a way that the changes propagate immediately to all desired parts of the system.

Table 3.1 Typical Definitions Asserted for "Object-Oriented"

Definition Categories	How People Define "Object-Oriented"
What it is built with	Written in C++ or Smalltalk. Written using a GUI builder. Code generator. Built from reusable assets.
How it operates	Processing involves asking, not telling. Processing involves identifying a tangible entity and sending it a message.
What it deals with	The system describes abstractions that model a problem.
How it is structured	The basic units that make it up are well-defined separate modules. The basic units are easy to integrate. The basic units are general descriptions of classes of things. The system is built out of generalizations that are specialized, and described in terms of encapsulation, polymorphism, and inheritance.
What more you can do with it	You can extend the system, with changes propagating throughout the system as desired, and without duplicating effort or breaking unrelated parts of the system.

Our rule of thumb for determining whether something is object-oriented is this:

> Something is object-oriented if it can be extended by composition of existing parts or by refinement of behaviors. Changes in the original parts propagate, so that compositions and refinements that reuse these parts change appropriately.

Let's see how the various categories are defined in the context of this rule of thumb.

What does it mean to be an object-oriented language? A language is object-oriented when its representational capabilities are object-oriented—that is, when it exhibits the following three properties:

Encapsulation	The language supports the representation of information and information processing as a single unit that combines behavior with the information needed to carry out the behavior
Polymorphism	The language makes it possible to send the same message to different objects and elicit a distinct but semantically similar response from each
Inheritance	The language supports the definition of a new entity as an extension of one or more existing entities, such that the new entity inherits existing behavior and information

Object-oriented languages make it possible to define system parts in terms of their interfaces, to define new parts as compositions of existing ones, and to create new parts that inherit and then refine the behavior of existing ones. Both C++ and Smalltalk are object-oriented languages. Most 4GL scripting languages are not object-oriented, because they use traditional procedural language constructs to specify information structures. Although these constructs permit structures to be built as combinations of other structures, they do not provide ways in which to describe behaviors abstractly. An object-oriented language has to provide ways in which the developer can describe a system in abstract terms that can be specialized either through delegated responsibility or through refinement of inherited behaviors. Both delegation and inheritance make it possible to extend the system in such a way that the change immediately propagates to all other system parts that are dependent on the changed part.

What does it mean for a user interface to be object-oriented? We think about a user interface from various perspectives: how it operates, what it deals with, how it is structured, and what more you can do with it. Our considerations about a user interface focus on the user interface itself, not the consequences of having used it.

With a modern user interface, the user makes a selection from a menu, double clicks on a picture or drags a picture onto another one to invoke a command. For example, a bus can start or stop; a bus can move or reverse itself. A picture on the screen represents the bus. A menu displays a list of bus behaviors. Think of a selected picture as an object, a selected menu item as a message, and—you have a user interface that supports the ideas of object-oriented processing. Regarded this way, an object-oriented user interface is a visual object-oriented programming language [Burnett, Goldberg, and Lewis 1995].

Another interpretation of what it means for a user interface to be object-oriented depends on whether the user interface provides an interaction model that presents the elements of the work environment in an organized way that encourages meaningful use of applications. The interpretation is based on what the user interface deals with.

Another way in which a user interface can be object-oriented involves the structure of the user interface, specifically what kinds of components and operations are made available. Does it have general descriptions of visual widgets like lists, radio buttons, and slide bars, or visual forms like dialog boxes or property sheets? Does the user interface support composition and refinement of visual components, and is it possible to create new application user interfaces by combining or inheriting from existing ones?

What makes an application or tool object-oriented? The fourth way to consider whether a user interface is object-oriented overlaps the question of whether an application is object-oriented. You determine the application or the user interface's end-user customizability. Suppose your application has several screen views, each of which has a textual label. You want all of the labels to be pictures instead. Can you make this change? If not, it is not extensible. When you make the change, do you make it once so it applies to all of the screens? If not, you do not have the benefit of change propagation, which we expect from a well-structured object-oriented application.

A development environment, such as a user-interface construction kit, is a special kind of application. A way to consider whether it is object-oriented is to examine its implementation architecture. What are the parts that make up the construction kit, and can the kit and its parts be extended?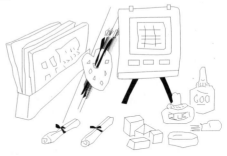

An application is object-oriented when the functionality of the application is composable and refinable, or when the kinds of objects managed by the application can be extended. Few applications are object-oriented in this sense. A development environment is object-oriented when new kinds of development tools can be composed out of the existing ones through composition or refinement. An operating system may be object-oriented for the same reason. Simply having the ability to dispatch messages to some module (object) does not make an operating system object-oriented. The litmus test is whether the operating system provides support for creating objects using composition and refinement, for maintaining references to objects, and for managing message flow among the objects.

Databases can be object-oriented. Databases are object-oriented when they store object models. Object-oriented databases provide mechanisms for representing, storing, and retrieving objects. Object-oriented databases store the information or data associated with objects, and the object behaviors that make use of this data. Some object-oriented databases allow you to invoke and execute these behaviors within the database management system. Responsibility for updating or analyzing information stored in the database can reside with objects also stored in the database. It should be possible to extend the object model, adding new kinds of objects.

When is an analysis-and-design method object-oriented? A *method* is a specific way of carrying out an activity, a step-by-step procedure that takes you from a set of inputs to an end result.[4] Object-oriented analysis-and-design methods provide techniques for find-

---

[4] This definition for *method* applies whether the method is for analysis, design, or implementation. To avoid confusion, however, we use the word method only when referring to an analysis or design method. We do not use the Smalltalk terminology in which a method is the code implementation for an object's behavior.

ing objects (an analysis method), or for structuring object relationships in the context of a system architecture (a design method), or for managing the process of creating objects (a project-management method). Generally, the goal of an object-oriented analysis-and-design method is to model a problem domain in terms of a collection of interacting entities, each of which provides a well-defined set of behaviors (services).

So far, we have focused on using a method to create something that is object-oriented. We have given you a description of what you do with a method, not of the method itself. Methods prescribe what to do. Changing what to do changes the method. Hence it makes little sense to describe a method as extensible. According to our extensibility criterion, it is not correct to call a method object-oriented.

It may be correct to say that the outcome of a method is object-oriented. That is, if you use a method to construct an object model, it does not mean that the method itself is object-oriented, but rather that it produces an object-oriented artifact. This is the converse of the notion that using an object-oriented language does not in itself guarantee an object-oriented result. We bow to the language common in the object community, and will use the term "object-oriented method" in this book, but to mean that the outcome of the method is an object-oriented model—not that the method itself is object oriented.

What about curricula and governments? How are curricula and governments to be called object-oriented? Take the notion of having sets of modules that can be combined dynamically, depending on dynamically determined results (such as tests). Modules can be structured to give students study assignments and learning exercises, all of which can be modified to suit the personalities and interests of individual students. A curriculum designed in this modular format is an object-oriented curriculum. This same notion of modular parts, tailored to changing circumstances, applies to organizational structures. Consider the framework of interacting parts, regulated by law, that composes a government. Delegation of responsibility to operating units, loosely coupled dependencies among these operating units, and reuse of policies and procedures—these are the hallmarks of an object-oriented government.

What About Objects Helps Build Systems?

The powerful features of objects support the ability to create systems made up of independent parts and systems that can be extended without duplicating effort or breaking unrelated parts. Independence and extensibility naturally lead to reusability, maintainability, and portability of software systems. Four characteristics of objects facilitate software systems development: objects separate interface from implementation; objects closely map the real world; objects come in different sizes; and objects live all the way down—from analysis to design to implementation.

Objects Separate Interface from Implementation

An object depends only on the services of other objects, stated in terms of the messages it sends to those objects. Any change in the way an object fulfills its service obligations does not change the behavior of the clients of those services. Moreover, an application can add new behavior, either by adding new objects or by extending the definitions of existing ones, without changing already tested services.

Object Models Closely Map the Real World

Object models can represent the real world as you understand it. Specifically, the real world can be represented as a collection of interacting entities, each of which exhibits well-defined behaviors. It is not necessarily true that the world is a collection of interacting entities, but the object-oriented approach assumes that the aspects of the world in which you are interested can be modeled in this way.[5]

What is it about objects that helps us closely map the real world to the software world?

- Objects are descriptions of behaviors and the properties found in real-world entities, concepts, and relations.

- Objects interact by sending messages, mirroring the way their counterparts in the real world work together to get information, give information, and invoke actions.

- Object behavior names are derived from the real-world domain, and these names are shareable across objects that support semantically similar behaviors.

- Objects are composed of other objects, reflecting the real world's part-whole relations.

- Object groups can be defined generally in terms of classes that collect the common characteristics of a set of real-world objects into a single description. Or object groups can be defined in terms of instances that serve as examples for other instances.

- Objects are described in terms of hierarchies of behavior, capturing the real world's notion of type classification.

Changes in a real-world domain can be reflected as comparable changes in the objects that describe the analysis model, and as consequential changes in design and implementation. The amount of change should be proportional: A small change in the problem

---

[5] This statement says that objects are not *in* the world but *of* the world.

domain should beget a small change in the analysis, design, and implementation, while a major revision should be just that—a major systems rewrite. Meyer calls this idea Modular Continuity [Meyer 1988].

Objects Come in Different Sizes

We use the word "objects" to refer to the variety of different descriptions that occur during system development. All the parts of a system are similar in that each has a well-defined interface. New parts are made by combining existing ones, and the new parts themselves have well-defined interfaces. Parts become wholes; wholes become parts.

We have not defined or constrained the granularity of an object. In fact, there is no single standard definition of an object size. Large systems are commonly divided into subsystems, each of which provides well-defined services, such as storage and retrieval of information, or printing and graphical display of information. A subsystem can be viewed as an object that provides these or other services. Development environments treat an application as a large object—a collection of objects that work together to provide a well-defined set of services (that is, the application's interface). Objects, subsystems, and applications are all defined in terms of interfaces that describe what they do, not how they do it. Anything specified by its interfaces can be treated the same with respect to composition and refinement. In this sense, they are all objects.

Objects Live All the Way Down

Objects can represent the analysis model. Objects can represent the design model. And objects can express the constructs of the programming model. Moreover, the same objects discovered in earlier stages of development can live on in later stages. There is little controversy on the point that objects appear everywhere.

There is some disagreement as to whether the analysis objects will be retained in the design model, or whether the design objects will exist in the code. Why should analysis objects show up at design time? Because doing so provides the maintenance advantages that come from retaining a close match between the design architecture and the problem description. The analysis model forms the basis for constructing the design model. Design adds to the analysis model by taking into account technology requirements. The analysis model objects might not be retained precisely as they were specified during analysis. When examined in the context of architectural decisions, an analysis object may be altered. For example, the model-view-controller architecture used in the Smalltalk-80 system factors system capability among the domain model, graphical presentation of aspects of the model, and user-interaction support. Use of this architecture encourages developers to factor an analysis object, which provides behavior for both information semantics and user-interface support, into the three kinds of design objects: a model, one or more views, and a controller for each view. If we retain sufficient information to trace what changes were made, we can map the single analysis object to the (in this case) three design objects.

Why should design objects show up in code? The rationale is the same. The design objects, and by extension analysis objects, show up in the code to retain the maintenance advantages of linking the implementation directly to the problem description. Programming languages add the syntax and semantics of coding constructs to the design objects. The consequence is that the implementation might contain objects that are somewhat different from the objects found in the design. But if we retain a trace as to why this difference was necessary, we will be able to determine which implementation objects change if the system requirements change.

The notion that objects live all the way down offers the opportunity to reduce the number of transformations between analysis, design, and implementation. This reduction in transformations translates to a reduction in errors, which in turn should translate to less maintenance work. The primary reason for maintenance is to make changes that reflect changes in the business. The changes in code should be safer to make because we know why we are making them. We know why an object exists in the code, and can be better informed when we need to remove or modify it.

Additional Benefits of Objects

Objects Are a Means of Attacking Complexity

Certain problems are intrinsically more complex than others. What does object-oriented technology provide that helps to model this complexity, without adding to it? When we encounter complexity, our first instinct is to eliminate it. But our premise is that it is not possible to eliminate the complexity—we have selected a problem to solve at a particular level of detail.

If we cannot eliminate complexity, we should at least try not to make things worse by adding more complexity. Our solution is to create an understandable object model of the real-world situation by defining objects that map directly to the real-world entities, and by retaining this model throughout the product life cycle.

We can do better still. We can organize complexity so that it is manageable. Each object can be simple, and linked to the specification of the desired system capabilities it supports. The collection of interacting objects displays the complex behavior, organized as a series of message-sends that model real-world processes. The static and dynamic relationships among objects describe and organize the way a complex system behaves.

Objects Build Systems Resilient to Change

To be resilient means to be flexible. The term resilience also connotes being cheerful, tying flexibility to joy. Many developers are quick to report that creating software with application development environments based on objects is more fun. You don't have to be afraid to try things out. The development life cycle is fast enough that you can experiment and learn, while retaining high levels of productivity. You may be prototyping, fixing defects, or incorporating changes in specification. You can incrementally add new objects, provide new implementations for existing objects, remove part or all of an existing object. The system keeps running. It keeps running even if the latest change is wrong. Errors do not propagate to unexpected places.

Let's review an example of resiliency, where even fundamental changes in systems-level components, such as the memory manager, do not break the system.

As early as 1973, Smalltalk played a central role in the research at Xerox PARC. In 1977-78, research management at PARC proposed a special workshop to convey to top Xerox management the essence of the software opportunity: Many office products could be created quickly using a general-purpose workstation and specializations of software system components. The Smalltalk-76 system was selected as the basis for creating a hands-on software learning laboratory with which the president of Xerox and his top directors could each compose different simulations of Xerox copier-duplicator centers, factory production lines, document work flow, and so on. Smalltalk-76 was the first of the Smalltalk systems to support inheritance, and the simulation framework was designed so that new simulations created subclasses of workers, stations, and customers. Close to show time, we discovered that the memory manager, a critical systems-level object, could not handle the high degree of subclassing used by the simulation framework. A change in the implementation of the memory manager was proposed, without a change in its interface. The proposal was reviewed, implemented, and tested within a few days. The revised software learning laboratory was used without a glitch.

Why can objects create systems that are resilient to such fundamental change? Objects are self-contained units that encapsulate the information and algorithms needed to fulfill their contractual obligations. Emphasis on well-defined interfaces that separate the "what" from the "how" means that the "how" can be changed without affecting objects—the clients—that rely on the "what." Consistently applied, this eliminates side effects that occur when shared information or algorithms are altered. New functionality can be added as independent objects, subclasses of existing classes of objects, or new objects that extend an existing interface. This ability to add objects facilitates safer maintenance and encourages exploratory development.

Objects Allow Partial Systems to Work

Systems structured with objects can be partial, yet functioning. By a partial system, we mean that the architecture of the system is defined, specifically in terms of the contracts (interface) between all required parts. But the implementation or elaboration of each part is not as yet completed. We liken this to the idea of launching a boat that is still under construction (Fig. 3.4).

Figure 3.4   Objects Support Launching Incomplete Systems

Objects are self-contained. They describe behaviors and information in one place. The separation of "what" from "how," of interface specification from implementation, means that the system can be built in stages. First, the system can be laid out at a high level in terms of the interfaces between subsystems or applications. Each of these can then be independently analyzed, designed, and implemented, because they rely only on contracted behavior, and on the eventual existence of objects that implement these behaviors.

Object interactions are defined in terms of messages sent between objects. Most object systems delay identifying the object that will receive a message until the latest possible time. This deferred identification makes it possible to introduce a new object that conforms to the interface specification, and to do so even at runtime. In this way, exploratory development can take place, by incrementally creating new objects or refinements of existing objects, and experimenting with modifications of the system.

It is not necessary to have all of the objects available to run a part of a system. Some capabilities, such as printing or graphical display, may not be needed. Object-oriented development environments do not force you to have everything specified and included to try out partial functionality.

The ability to experiment—by building executable partial systems—encourages an exploratory or incremental style of development. A critical aspect of this style is that individual objects are made available as they are completed; all of the objects do not have to be fully implemented before system integration can take place. Prototyping, as an activity for obtaining information, relies on the idea that you can build a partial system to get the desired information in a cost-effective way. Moreover, the ability to create functioning partial systems makes it natural for developers to create extensible application frameworks—partial systems that are completed by adding components or subclasses that implement the incomplete aspects of the framework.

Objects Represent Natural Units for Reuse

Reuse reduces effort. We reuse a design so that we do not have to expend the effort to create a new design. Reuse is easy to see in the world of concrete objects. We build houses out of bricks, slats of wood, window frames, doors, stairs. These different kinds of objects have a design that is copied over and over again, and used to construct different house forms. This same idea of reuse of hardware components to construct similar results, yet different forms, also exists in the automotive and electronics industries, and elsewhere. The basic notion is that we describe a component, and then copy that component for reuse. If the design for the component changes, presumably to improve the component in some way, then future consumers benefit from the change. Prior consumers do not benefit, unless the constructions are taken apart and the old component is replaced with the improved version. Car owners experience this phenomenon when their cars are recalled by the manufacturer to replace a faulty part, or when they need to replace a component in the normal course of car aging.

From everything we have said, it follows that objects—as self-contained units with well-defined interfaces—form the basis for composing subsystems. The basic concepts of object-oriented technology suggest ways in which software designs and implementations can be reused:

Encapsulation	Reuse the functionality of an object through its external interface
Polymorphism	Reuse a common vocabulary for services
Inheritance	Reuse common behaviors and properties

Each of these reuse mechanisms is a way objects share their descriptions. For each approach to sharing, change in the reused object propagates differently to the reusers. The choice of which form of sharing to employ affects how long-term maintenance will be carried out. Of course, reuse with objects is not inherent in the use of object-oriented technology, but rather is a consequence of explicit reuse design goals.

Framework for Determining How Projects Benefit from Using Object-Oriented Technology

The object-oriented technology framework is the second stage of the effort to establish the goals for the use of object-oriented technology, following the first stage of setting project goals and objectives. This decision framework asks you to determine how your projects can benefit from using object-oriented technology. Specifically, you want to align your organization's values for products, processes, and resources, with the benefits you can expect from using object-oriented technology.

Historically, people confuse the goal—the end of a process—with the means to reaching the goal. The confusion has been especially noticeable with object-oriented technology. Hence the choice of principle.

> *Framework Principle.* Object-oriented technology is not the goal of a project, but a means to attain the goal.

The foundation of this principle is that longer-term goals are not defined in terms of object-oriented technology, but rather in terms of the results that the technology can help achieve. The goal for this decision framework is a plea for common-sense planning.

> *Framework Goal.* Set realistic expectations for how object-oriented technology can help you to achieve your software development goals and objectives.

The goal is reached by following two steps that direct you to construct a statement of your value expectations for objects.

Benefits of Object- Oriented Technology

- Determine whether and how object-oriented technology contributes to obtaining what you value in software development

- Determine projects needed to achieve valued objectives through the use of object-oriented technology

Determine Whether and How Object-Oriented Technology Contributes to Obtaining What You Value in Software Development

The purpose of this first decision-framework step is to match your expectations for object-oriented technology with your goals and objectives for successful software development. Earlier, we stated eight benefits of using object-oriented technology to build and maintain software systems. You need to decide whether these potential benefits meet your software development needs.

In Chapter 2, we ask you to answer a set of questions to help you identify what you value in the products you produce, and in the processes and resources you use. Most

likely, you value a great deal that technology cannot bring to you, things for which you, as a manager or developer, strive—such as a sense of importance in your organization. Being an agent of change—bringing object-oriented technology into your organization—may in fact bring you a sense of importance. But this personal and social goal is not specific to the use of objects. Consider what you now know about object-oriented technology. What do you know or what have you heard about objects that might help you to bring about change in your organization—change that can better position you to get what you value?

Object-oriented technology can help you get what you value, for example, if you need to create complex systems that have to be maintained by developers other than the ones who originally designed and coded the systems. Do you know your customers' requirements, and are these requirements stable over time? If not, the ability to develop the systems incrementally and to get your customers' early involvement in using partial results can help you create the right systems. Perhaps your customers can participate more in your development when the analysis-and-design models more closely map the customers' real-world model. If you value meeting deadlines, and perhaps getting to market faster than the competition, the ability to reuse past results can speed the development process. Perhaps you value letting your customers specialize the system themselves. The extensibility features of object-oriented systems could be of interest to you.

One major user of object-oriented technology stated the organization's expectations for the use of object-oriented technology in the form of the following value proposition:

- Introduction of object-oriented development tools should immediately create two to three times improvement in development productivity (defined as function points per month; see Chapter 20).

- After one year, the use of advanced tools and common development practices based on object-oriented technology should create five times improvement in development productivity.

- Within three years, the availability of utility objects for general reuse should create ten times improvement.

- Additional availability of reusable application frameworks should create 200 times improvement after three to five years.

These are dramatic expectations. We do not claim that these numbers should represent your objectives for the use of objects. Our point here is not to make your value-expectation decisions for you, but to suggest some ways in which objects might help meet your development goals and objectives, and to request that you explicitly state your expectations. The important idea is that you start by determining what you value in products, processes, and resources. Then you look to object-oriented technology, determine whether the technology can help you get what you value, and write clear statements of value expectations. Before moving to the next step, you have to do a reality check—you have to examine your organization and its ability to make the changes necessary to meet your expectations.

Determine Projects Needed to Achieve Valued Objectives Through the Use of Object-Oriented Technology

Having now set your objectives for the use of object-oriented technology and decided that your organization is prepared to consider change, you have to decide which aspects of your current situation you should change to meet these objectives. You need to plan the (possibly parallel) projects that will take you from your current situation to your desired one. These will be process- and resource-improvement projects that:

- Change your product process models and how you plan and control your projects

- Set up a program for creating and maintaining reusable assets

- Build new team structures and team member skills

- Bring in new software development methods and tools

- Set up a program for appropriate measures of progress and results

The projects you choose have to be aligned with your value expectations. We recommend that you choose the projects that minimize the risks associated with meeting these expectations, notably projects that make sure that your organization has the long-term skills and other resources necessary for leveraging your technology choice. Using the example of the prior section, the strong emphasis on productivity and reuse implies that this example organization's first projects have to evaluate new tools, determine how developers will be trained in the use of the technology and supportive tools, and initiate efforts to obtain reusable assets.

Process- and resource-improvement projects are the topics of the remaining chapters of this book.

Case Study Results

We asked interviewees in Phases 1 and 2 why they chose object-oriented technology. In Table 3.2, we list the top 14 reasons.

Most case study project managers expected to complete their projects faster. Some expected maintenance to be easier and perhaps cheaper; only one project had enough maintenance experience to report success in this area. Interviewees from all of the com-

Table 3.2 Why Objects were Chosen By Case Study Projects

Reason	No. of Projects Selecting the Reason
Reduce development time; reduce amount of software to create	13
Participate in state-of-the-art technology, apparent market momentum	9
Improve long-term maintenance	8
Follow dictum of prior work—that is, use whatever a prior project decided to use	5
Create desired GUI, especially for accessing a database	5
Improve system structure to help organize applications (better representation of architectural concepts), manage complexity	4
Obtain design consistency	3
Obtain better user involvement; enable customers to configure systems	3
Improve ability to evolve the product, handling the rapid pace of business change	3
Follow standard; since standard is expressed in object terms, use object-oriented technology	2
Solve reusability problem	2
Obtain flexibility	1
Obtain better consistency in analysis, design, and code models	1
Improve ability to test with independent modules	1

pleted projects indicated that they had met their initial expectations for object-oriented technology.

In one case, in which there was an expectation to have better user involvement, the managers told us that they are doing better, but they still do not understand how to get user involvement to the level of their expectations. One project manager, in stating that the original reason for choosing object-oriented technology was to be able to reuse results of one project in other projects, said that the result the team experienced was "stunning"—all of their new applications are now customized from existing subsystems. The key exceptions to realizing expectations were tied to development time and maintenance. The projects took longer than expected because of the effort required to learn object-oriented technology and the lack of reusable assets for initial projects. There is simply insufficient evidence to draw conclusions about maintenance.

The managers were correct in their belief that they would have to change their development product process model to meet their expectations for object-oriented technology. In one of the unsuccessful projects, the manager stated that the team did not get the productivity boost that was expected for two reasons. First, reuse is not possible until the libraries of reusable artifacts exist. Yet, the organization did not plan for the development and introduction of reusable artifacts when setting time-to-market expectations. Second, the organization selected object-oriented technology too early; the particular products (language, tools) selected were simply not ready for production use. The team was diverted from its primary task by trying to help fix the problems with the purchased products.

Summary

We defined objects to be descriptions of sets of behaviors that occur in real or imaginary worlds. Objects interact by sending messages to one another to give information, to get information, and to invoke actions. We can describe objects in terms of other objects, either as compositions or refinements. A class describes a set of objects that carry out the same behaviors the same way. In many object-oriented languages, objects are instances of classes, and classes can inherit their descriptions from other classes. Classes can thereby form a hierarchy, in which a subclass inherits or shares the description of its superclass. An application is a set of interacting objects. A special kind of reusable object is an application framework, a set of objects that interact to form the basic structure and processing of applications within a given domain.

By our definition, something is object-oriented if its architecture is modular; its parts are described in terms of encapsulation, polymorphism, and inheritance; it describes abstractions that model a problem; processing is based on message-sending; and it can be extended through composition and refinement. This definition applies to system analysis-and-design methods, development tools and environments, languages, databases, applications, and user interfaces.

The potential benefits of object-oriented technology were explained, focusing on how the technology can be used to create well-defined architectures and analysis models that correspond to the problem domain model. Both architectures and models support rapid application development, and the creation of understandable and maintainable systems. These benefits include: separation of interface from implementation, closely mapping the real world, uniform definition regardless of object size, and applicability throughout the development process. Objects are a means of minimizing added complexity and organizing inherent complexity. They allow you to build systems resilient to change; even partial systems work.

The framework for determining the benefits of using object-oriented technology asks you to tie the decision to use objects to your statement of what you value in products, processes, and resources. To gain management support for and commitment to the use of object-oriented technology, you will have to convince management that your value expectations for objects are critical to the organization's success.

Additional Reading About Objects

There is more than enough material now to fill your bookshelves with object folklore and object lessons. We list here only four books, two for nontechnical managers (by Cox and Taylor), one for developers (by Meyer), and one for technical managers and developers (by Booch). Read these books to get additional perspective on the definition of objects, the benefit of choosing object-oriented technology, and how the technology can be effectively used. The Taylor book is by far the easiest one to read and is the best starting point for nontechnical managers.

Booch, G., *Object-Oriented Analysis and Design with Applications*, Benjamin Cummings: Redwood City, Calif., 1994.

This book is really three books in one. The first section provides a good overview of the basic concepts associated with object orientation. This material should be accessible to people with limited knowledge of object-oriented technology. Object-oriented novices should read Taylor's book first, then read the first section of Booch's book. The second section provides an introduction to the Booch notation, a high-level description of a development process and several project-management topics. This material is essential for learning the Booch notation. The final section provides five example applications that illustrate development using the Booch notation and C++.

Cox, B., *Object-Oriented Programming: An Evolutionary Approach*, Addison-Wesley: Reading, Mass., 1986.

This book is primarily about how object-oriented technology and reuse play a role in building software systems. Specifically, Cox discusses the concept of how reusable components— Software-ICs—can be plugged together to form quality software systems. Cox uses the Software-IC point of view to introduce the Objective-C programming language. The book describes how features such as inheritance, encapsulation, and message-passing are supported by Objective-C. It also provides a hands-on tutorial for creating several software systems to illustrate the concepts and the language.

Meyer, B., *Object-oriented Software Construction*, Prentice Hall International Series in Computer Science, Prentice Hall: New York, 1988.

This book discusses many of the software engineering principles and object-oriented concepts that underlie the development of production-quality software systems. It is particularly well known for its treatment of the issues surrounding assertions and programming by contract. The book uses the programming language Eiffel to illustrate the various concepts. Developers will find it particularly useful, though all but the most technical of managers may be overwhelmed.

Taylor, D., *Object-Oriented Technology for the Manager*, Addison-Wesley: Reading, Mass., 1991.

This book is intended to give managers a quick, high-level introduction to object-oriented technology. The book's margins provide a summary of the main text, one sentence per paragraph. It is possible to read just the margins in about one hour, yet learn many of the important points about the technology. Although Taylor oversimplifies many technical issues, the book can serve as a good, first introduction to developers with no experience using object-oriented technology. It is especially well suited for upper management.

CHAPTER 4

Make an Initial Commitment to Use Object-Oriented Technology

It's what you do now, when you don't have to do anything, that makes you what you want to be, when it's too late to do anything about it.

R. J. Gary

By the time the rules of the game are clear, the windows of opportunity will have closed.

Santhanam C. Shecker

We argue in other chapters that the fundamental concepts of object-oriented technology are not new. We use this argument to eliminate any fear that you are being asked to experiment, to take a risk on unproven ideas. At the same time, we ask you to look forward to what you want to be—at how you want to develop your software systems aligned with your business needs. You should experience some fear that unless you start to act now, by the time the future arrives, it will be too late. You can start now with an initial project that teaches you some of the theory and practices of object-oriented technology, and that keeps the windows of opportunity open to you.

Framework for Making an Initial Commitment to Objects

And so we turn our attention now to the framework for making an initial commitment to objects. The principle and goal for this framework were chosen to emphasize the basis for selecting a pilot project.

Framework Principle. Commitment in the form of a well-resourced demonstration project is needed to introduce new technology successfully.

Framework Goal. Choose and be successful with a first project that demonstrates the contributions that object-oriented technology can make to your organization, and that lays the foundation for making strategic decisions.

The principle emphasizes the need for a long-term vision, while the goal states that the first project should be a proof-of-concept—demonstrating that you can obtain the benefits you expect from object-oriented technology, and proving that your organization has (or can learn) the skills needed to obtain these benefits.

The framework consists of five steps that define a process for introducing object-oriented technology into an organization.

Make an
Initial
Commitment
to Objects

- Receive an initial introduction to objects

- Obtain an initial management commitment to the use of objects

- Select an initial process model and software development environment

- Select and set up an initial pilot project

- Assess the outcome of the initial pilot project

You will likely select several pilot projects, projects that will serve as prototypes or experimental undertakings prior to full-scale operation. Each pilot project will focus on one or more aspects of introducing object-oriented technology into your organization. Each will serve as guides through some unknown process or use of a resource. Pilot projects are learning experiences, and consequently we expect the team to take the time and effort to instrument each project so as to monitor and assess the experience. Each pilot project should expand the organization's commitment to the use of object-oriented technology.

Receive an Initial Introduction to Objects

The process of introducing object-oriented technology into an organization starts when the first serious discussions about the technology begin to take place, before management makes the strategic decision to try it. We have seen organizations receive their initial exposure to objects in one of four ways: through advanced technology studies, consulting assistance, grass-roots movement, or enlightenment from above. Exactly which way is best, or even possible, is a function of the organization's culture.

Advanced technology model. Many organizations have an advanced technology group whose charter is to investigate the state of the art of methods, languages, tools, and databases. These groups are often the first to experiment with object-oriented technology to determine how well it matches the requirements of the organization. Individuals in these groups attend tutorials at professional conferences, read articles in newsletters, magazines, and journals, and use various commercial and academic tools to carry out experiments. Normally they choose simple problems to solve—indicative of the types of problems to be solved within the organization—to evaluate the effectiveness of the method, language, database, or tool. An initial exposure through the advanced technology group typically has a strong technical focus, which risks ignoring the organizational issues that attend the use of object-oriented technology.

Consulting assistance. Some organizations receive their initial exposure to object-oriented technology through external consulting groups, possibly from a system integrator who has extensive experience with object-oriented technology. Contract consultants and vendors also introduce organizations to object-oriented technology. Successful adoption, however, depends on the existence of internal champions working on the day-to-day details, at least one of whom is a senior manager.

Grass-roots movement. Technical developers can be attracted to object-oriented technology by reading trade magazines or attending tutorials and conferences. These developers talk with other developers, and the word starts to spread. The ideas of object-oriented technology then appear informally in technical work within the organization. Invariably, first-level technical management begins to hear the rumblings. The seeds have been planted and the roots start to take hold. At this point, the organization has to be careful because there is a risk that the developers will overwhelm the managers with their desire to use object-oriented technology. Management can catch the enthusiasm, wanting to encourage the developers, and can forget to make sure that the proper infrastructure is in place. Grass-roots support is necessary but not sufficient.

Enlightenment from above. In some organizations, management dictates the use of object-oriented technology in carrying out strategic plans. Typically this comes about when managers attend seminars or trade shows, or read about object-oriented technology successes. Suitably inspired by these articles, upper management excitedly dictates new game rules. The risk in this approach is that no one—no developer—is willing or able to play by the new rules. Management has to elicit grass-roots support.

Case study experience. Eleven companies in the case studies learned about object-oriented technology through their advanced technology groups. The first experience with the technology for another 11 companies came through a grass-roots movement. The management of seven companies demanded that object-oriented technology be used, while four other companies learned about the opportunities from consultants.

Obtain an Initial Management Commitment to the Use of Objects

You now know about objects and have decided to bring them into the organization for well-defined reasons. To a large extent, it does not matter who "you" are—we assume you had the responsibility to explore new technology opportunities, and the credibility within the organization to initiate the first efforts to take advantage of these opportunities. Regardless of organizational structure and lines of authority, we encourage you to make sure that you have a commitment from the highest-level managers. Bringing in object-oriented technology is a strategic decision because it influences all aspects of software systems development, and because its benefits depend on corporate-wide collaborations.

Make the Business Case

You want management committed, not just involved. We have a framed cartoon in our office that shows a plate of ham and eggs beside a pig and a chicken. The caption states: "In a bacon-and-eggs breakfast, the chicken is involved and the pig is committed."

To get management committed, you must develop a business case that clearly indicates the expected costs, benefits, and return-on-investment that you expect as a result of using object-oriented technology. Much of this information can be derived from the value proposition that you construct in following the steps of the second decision framework: Benefits of Object-Oriented Technology (Chapter 3). Your business case must include compelling arguments that support your value proposition. These arguments are founded on greed, fear, or logical reasoning based on the characteristics of the technology.

The greed approach relies on your ability to convince management that they will lose money if they do not adopt object-oriented technology. The fear approach, related to greed, relies on your ability to show management that competitors are using object-oriented technology and therefore already have a competitive advantage. If, however, you find yourself in the most unfortunate situation, where you cannot convince management based on a greed or fear argument, you will be forced to use logic, a much less powerful means of persuasion. You will need to provide plausible arguments—other than those based on greed or fear—for adopting object-oriented technology.

Motivation by greed. Greed is a most powerful means of persuasion and is often effective in convincing management that object-oriented technology is appropriate. The basic argument goes like this.

> Well, boss, did you know that Company M started using object-oriented technology last year and is saving a ton of money during their maintenance and update releases? In addition, Company R has been using object-oriented technology for more than two years, and with their reuse library they are making it to market *X* times faster than their competitors.

To motivate management convincingly that they are losing money by not using object-oriented technology, you will have to show them examples of companies that have earned a more-than-reasonable return on their investment in the technology. In the past it has been particularly difficult to use this argument because there were insufficient examples upon which to draw. As more companies have had the time to develop their object strategies and have been forthcoming with their success stories, this argument is becoming easier to use.

Motivation by fear. The fear argument relies on your ability to show how direct competitors have already started to use object-oriented technology. A good case of fear can be instilled in management if you can show that direct competitors are being successful at capturing market share because they are spending less time fixing old products and more time building newer, more interesting products.

Motivation by logic. Motivation by logic involves using well-articulated, interrelated arguments to convince management that the organization can benefit from object-oriented technology. With each argument, you ask the manager to examine the inherent logic, as opposed to the emotion aroused by the argument. A purely logical argument takes the technical characteristics of object-oriented technology and discusses how each characteristic, alone or in conjunction with others, can help address a business problem. For example, you might point out how object encapsulation helps hide implementation details from the user of a component. This separation decouples the user of a software component from seeing any changes in implementation, and should lead to more predictable maintenance results.

Our initial approach for acquiring management commitment is to develop a business case based on logical reasoning about the benefits of object-oriented technology, supplemented with examples that incite greed and fear. Often, commitment to the business case will depend on a demonstration of the technology's viability within the organization. You pick a pilot project. You carry it out. You report on the pilot experience as part of the ongoing development and maintenance of the business case.[1] The purpose of this pilot is threefold. First, seeing is believing—proving to management that the technology makes sense in the context of the kinds of software you need to create. Second, it shows that your organization can indeed bring in the new technology and successfully carry out a demonstration. And third, it grounds the concepts in terms of a real result that management can relate to because the example is about the organization's business. These three reasons for the proof-of-concept assume that you pick an example that is useful to, or related to, your organization's business.

Case study experience. During the case study interviews, we asked the interviewees how they ultimately sold management on the idea of object-oriented technology, regardless of their initial exposure. Seven organizations demonstrated a proof-of-concept example. Five had experienced dissatisfaction with prior approaches to software development, and four were afraid of losing market share. Another four organizations expressed a desire to have a timely response to market, and believed object-oriented technology could be useful in meeting this objective. Three organizations said that a graphical user interface (GUI) was needed, and therefore they picked object-oriented technology. Choosing objects because GUI = objects is a manifestation of the confusion surrounding object-oriented technology. Another three organizations chose objects because they were convinced that it would be the best technology for creating portable solutions.

The fact that there are only a few examples of selling by means of greed and fear is not surprising since half of all the projects we studied started before 1990. There simply were not many examples at that time from which to form a greed- or fear-based argument.

Manage the Expectations of Management

You have just completed a great sales job, so now you are potentially in trouble. Management is committed and waiting. The question is, do you really know what management expects from you? And are you confident that you can deliver?

---

[1] The organization should periodically re-examine its business case for objects to verify that the assumptions and value expectations remain consistent with the organization's overall strategy.

The technology magazines abound with experience papers discussing the introduction of object-oriented technology. They are consistent on one theme—management and developers must have shared expectations. Here is an example from an article published in early 1993. It starts with the expectations of the proponent of object-oriented technology, expectations that were not met.

> When I proposed to take an object-oriented approach to the database component of a state-of-the-art automotive diagnostic tool, I expected debate. I expected to discuss the merits of the proposal, so I prepared carefully reasoned, diplomatic rebuttals for all of the objections I expected the customer to raise. I was even prepared to hear them veto my ideas altogether.
>
> Instead I received (and naively accepted) a signal to go ahead, without discussion. In a contracting relationship, structured around short-term projects, this made the situation very dangerous. I knew the methodology would provide numerous benefits in the medium to long term, including lowered cost and higher quality, both of which were very explicit and sincere goals of the customer. However, there was no up front discussion of the costs and risks of the approach, nor of the time it would take to achieve any given level of results. This led to unrealistic expectations and unnecessary disappointments.

Notice that the author realized his naiveté. He never engaged management in a conversation to set realistic expectations. He quickly acknowledges what he should have done.

> A better approach would have been to insist on a discussion of the benefits in productivity and quality, along with a detailed and realistic projection of the costs and risks involved. More time spent up front on keeping expectations realistic would have made life easier for me, my workers and my company's and customer's project managers.
>
> Dale Hunscher
"Stories from the frontlines"
Object Magazine
Jan./Feb. 1993

It is not just management that has expectations. The development team members are trying something new. They expect you to train them and support them, to help them be successful. Depressed software developers do not do good work. Software developers become depressed when they feel that their managers expect something that the developers simply cannot do, because there is not enough time, resources, or training. Sometimes managers want something that no one knows how to do. Management has to listen to the developers and cooperate with them in setting goals and objectives.

Select an Initial Process Model and Software Development Environment

In Chapter 6, in combination with Chapter 5, we define the various strategies and activities that enter into successful product-development processes. And in Chapter 17, we discuss how to evaluate analysis-and-design methods, programming languages, tools, and databases. When you plan your first project that employs object-oriented technology, you have to select initial development processes and resources in advance of making all the strategic decisions we emphasize in these later chapters. In many organizations, evaluation of software development tools is done in combination with carrying out the first project. This means that the first project not only serves as a proof-of-concept, but it also assists in evaluating technology options. In addition, it can serve as the basis for training a core team of developers who will provide internal mentoring on later projects.

In planning the first project, you have to decide how many of the new processes and resources you will introduce. There is a trade-off as to whether you introduce, in one fell swoop, object-oriented technology in all aspects of development, or whether you approach the task incrementally. The choice depends on the extent to which you and your staff are prepared to assimilate change in the organization, and which processes and resources are important to upper management when making a strategic commitment.

If your culture demands an incremental approach, we can offer some hints. First, make sure you have a long-term vision of where you want to be. Then you can change incrementally by choosing one full technology dimension and leaving the others as they are. For example, most software development environments interoperate with applications or databases created in a non-object-oriented way. You can bring in a new programming language, but keep the old database. You can bring in a new analysis method, but keep a prior programming language.

We do not recommend picking hybrid solutions for a single dimension, unless your developers are very sophisticated adapters or your cultural biases dictate the choice. Changing only partially with hybrid solutions—such as languages that mix traditional (non-object-oriented) with object constructs, or analysis-and-design methods that mix object modeling with data-flow modeling—makes it too easy to revert to the old ways. Just at the point where the learning becomes the most difficult, and it is important to focus on trying out the new ideas, people have a tendency to fall back on what is familiar to get the job done. And it is possible they will not get the job done the way you want them to do it. So the full benefits of the new technology will not be assessable.

Choose a technology that will apply across multiple projects. It would be unfortunate to have to do a new evaluation for every project.

Select and Set Up an Initial Pilot Project

Your initial pilot project can serve different purposes. You can use this first effort with object-oriented technology to evaluate software development options (analysis-and-design methods, process models, languages, databases, tools, or styles for training). Or you can use the pilot to establish new process models or build team skills. Most often, however, the pilot is a software development project carried out to demonstrate the organization's ability to make effective use of object-oriented technology.

Guidelines for Choosing a Pilot Project to Develop a Software System

The following are project characteristics on which we base our choice of a first pilot project whose purpose is to demonstrate that the organization can produce a software system that makes use of object-oriented technology:

Criticality	The importance of the project results to business needs. Criticality measures the extent to which the organization views the project as being on one or more critical paths.
Duration	The estimated elapsed time from start to completion of the project.
Future leverage	The extent to which this project will leverage future projects—that is, whether the artifacts or the acquired skills will be useful in future projects.
Inherent complexity	The extent to which the problem is complicated, regardless of how it is solved. Some problems are inherently more complex than others.
Perceived triviality	The extent to which a problem is perceived to require little time, sophistication, or effort to solve. This does not necessarily reflect the actual time, sophistication, or effort needed to solve the problem.
Problem domain	The domain associated with the problem—for example, an accounting, transportation, or process control domain.
Visibility	The extent to which the project is known about or discussed, or to which it exerts influence within an organization. Management visibility refers to the level of management that is familiar with the project. Peer visibility refers to the extent that technical developers on other projects are familiar with the project.

Given these definitions, our advice on picking an initial pilot project consists of the following guidelines.

Avoid trivial projects, or projects perceived to be trivial. If you choose a trivial project, then you lose no matter what the outcome. If you satisfactorily complete the project, skeptics will dismiss your success as meaningless because you chose a problem that could have been solved with any technology. If you fail, critics will most certainly have a field day with the fact that you couldn't even solve the trivial problem, let alone some real one. Don't get caught in a no-win situation. Keep in mind that triviality is subjective. Something is trivial if no one cares whether the result is obtained. The someone of importance, of course, is management or customers.

Avoid overly critical projects. If a project is too important—if it is on the critical path of other activities—there is a natural tendency to be overly conservative about a technology transition. Such conservatism may prevent an organization from trying out many of the ideas associated with objects. The most critical project often has the most constraints and is therefore a poor first choice.

Don't replace the most optimized legacy system. Mature organizations are likely to have a substantial inventory of existing systems that have been used and maintained over a long time. These systems are very well tuned to the needs of the organization. You might choose to reimplement a legacy system as your first project because you are familiar with its functionality and because it was scheduled for eventual replacement. But it is not likely that the performance of the first object-oriented implementation will compare well to that of a legacy system that has been tuned over many years. Much of the work on the legacy system has gone into specialized memory, time, or storage-based tuning. The initial object-based result will not have the benefit of this long-time performance enhancement. You will end up with a system whose immediate comparison with the past shows poor performance and no additional functionality. An important reason for replacing a legacy system is to obtain a more maintainable result, which is harder to demonstrate to management in the short term.

Choose a project with sufficient visibility to ensure desired resources and influence. It is important that the initial project have sufficient management visibility to ensure that adequate resources, including good people, are allocated. Also, you want to make sure that the project has sufficient visibility to influence the development of future projects. Resources are applied to the more critical projects. So there is clearly a balancing act you have to perform to make sure that the project is important, yet not so important as to create fear of trying out new ideas.

Choose a problem that objects are good at handling, something with inherent complexity. Object-oriented technology excels at problems that are inherently complex in terms of the numbers of behaviors and interactions. Pick such a problem, stacking the deck in favor of objects.

Choose a project that takes long enough to build team skills. The project has to take enough time to allow the team members to acquire real project experience. The first project should take between 6 and 18 months. This is the time it takes to acquire functional skills in most subject areas, as we define in Chapter 18.

Get something tangible accomplished early and often. On the first project, in fact, you should set milestones that you can meet about every month. Choose milestones that demonstrate progress to both the team members and to those watching the project.

Make sure that the project schedule fits into the organization's overall schedules. In larger companies, there is usually an overall plan for developing multiple projects. The duration of the initial project must not delay the transition to other projects scheduled to begin at some future time.

Don't expect to obtain reusable results. It should not be the goal of the first project to create reusable assets. You simply do not have enough experience. You do not know enough to make the strategic choices for reusable assets, you most likely do not have a robust reuse process in place, and, most important, your first software artifacts are likely to be of lower quality than you need for long-term and general use throughout the organization. This idea complements the general management dictum that first-time learners are not the ones you rely on to create a long-lived product result.

Mechanics for Setting Up the Initial Pilot Project

Now that you have selected the first project, you have to select the process model (see Chapters 5 and 6), set up the measurable objectives (Chapters 2 and 20), and choose the team structure (Chapter 12).

On this first attempt, it is very important that you understand what you did and how well you did it. Make sure that you state your goals and objectives clearly, especially making sure that you collect the information you need to perform the desired measures. Ensure the team structure matches the kind of project you are doing. Should you choose to do multiple pilot projects, consider the ideas we present on cross-project team support (Chapter 12).

Decide Who Will Staff the First Project

Choosing the members of the initial project team can be problematic. Where do you get the people and how will they be trained? We provide some relevant insight in Chapters 12 and 18. It is simply easier to attain your goals if someone who is knowledgeable is available to help you. So the big issue in staffing the first project is finding the proper mix of learners and mentors. Sometimes the learners are your internal developers, whereas the mentors are consultants you hire or qualified internal developers.

If you decide to use mentors, there are four different ways they may interact with your people, analogous to the use of mentors in training (Chapter 18). Figure 4.1 illustrates these different approaches and implies their relative merit based on a hypothetical pricing structure in which price is proportional to value.

Consultants do the work. Your people contract the work outside. This contract is equivalent to outsourcing. Your people learn nothing. Without proper legal safeguards, you may not even own the result. On the upside, if you find the proper people, you are likely to obtain a successful first result. Unfortunately, you have done very little to convince upper management that their own people can do the job. At best, you have shown them your good judgment in choosing expert consultants. Since this approach does not build in-house competence, it should be avoided.

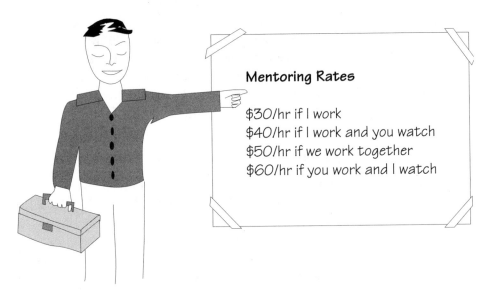

Figure 4.1   Working with Consultants

Consultants do the work, your people watch. Your people can look over the shoulders of the people doing the work. Presumably they absorb some of what they are seeing by osmosis. However, your people are still not doing the work themselves. In the end, you still have the same management issue as in the first approach—it isn't clear that your people can do the work. This approach makes sense if you are under heavy schedule pressure. Or you might use this approach if you wish only to have a maintenance organization, not a full development team.

Consultants and your people work together. Your people finally get to be hands-on, arguably the best way to learn. You can divide the work between your people and the consultants. Typically the consultants get the difficult architectural assignments and the requirement to explain decisions to the rest of the team. Your people tackle the more straightforward elements of the project. At project completion, your people have gained the experience of working with a good object-oriented design, and are likely to have more of a sense of ownership than in either of the previous approaches. Upper management is likely to feel that their own people can attack future problems.

Your people work and the consultants watch. Your people do the work and the consultants oversee the construction of the project in the role of mentors. As such, the consultants have the primary responsibility to provide guidance and insight into the development effort. They are involved in all significant activities, especially reviews. In the end, your people have done most of the interesting work, and have gained experience and confidence that makes them valuable, reusable resources for your next projects. Upper management has good reason to believe that future projects will be successful, preferably without further assistance from the consultants.

Case study experience. Of the 39 projects in the case studies, 25 let the people in the company do the work, without any consultation by experts. Consultants did all of the work on two projects, did the work with the project team members watching on three projects, and worked with the team members on five projects. On the remaining four projects, the team members did the work while the consultants watched. The current industry trend is to use mentors who mostly watch and direct internal developers.

Decide on the Training Plan

Based on the style of development you have selected, the kind of project, and the people, you can select a training plan. You might, of course, staff the first project entirely with already trained personnel. But our experience is that the first project serves as a training ground for at least some of the team members. We cover this idea in Chapter 19.

Assess the Outcome of the Initial Pilot Project

The project is over. How did you do? What did you learn? First and foremost, did you reach your goals and objectives? The ability to answer these questions, needless to say, depends on your having set the goals and objectives in the first place. When we did the case studies, we discovered two things. First, some projects had difficulty convincing themselves—let alone us—that they were successful because their goals and objectives were not clear. They had to reverse engineer their accomplishments to figure out whether they had met the needs of the organization. Second, we found that our interviews served as a good basis for assessing a project. The interviews were especially successful when the entire team was present. The discussion allowed team members to share their disappointments as well as what excited them. Often we found that team members and managers said different things. So the group session served to clarify what worked and what did not, allowing all team members to learn from one another and to build a stronger foundation for future projects.

You should assess your people after the first project. How well have the team members of the first project learned object-oriented skills? Your next step is likely to be a series of pilot projects, carried out concurrently, or the first production development. See whether these veterans of the first project can serve for any of the follow-on efforts. What did you learn about the tools you selected, and the techniques for analysis, design, and implementation? Part of your assessment procedure should be to discuss these questions and make the answers part of the organization's newly evolving culture.

Figure 4.2 illustrates a midcourse assessment process. The current situation represents today's products, processes, and resources. The desired situation is defined by the organization's long-term strategic goals for its use of object-oriented technology. Optionally, the midcourse assessment may compare or benchmark the organization's current situation in terms of other companies that are using or adopting object-oriented technology. A benchmark allows management to compare their progress with that of other companies. It also allows them to review the efficacy of their goals in terms of the goals of other companies.

Assessment Methodology

To carry out the midcourse assessment, you decide who will conduct the assessment, what will be assessed, and what information sources will be available to provide assessment details.

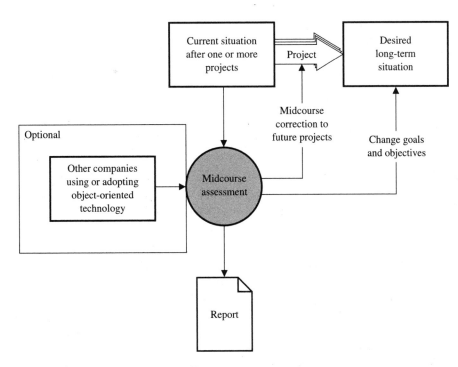

Figure 4.2   Midcourse Assessment Process

Who will conduct the assessment. The assessment should be carried out by unbiased personnel. Participants who are directly involved with the object program are biased and should not conduct the assessment. You should use qualified personnel from another group or outside consultants. Outside consultants with benchmarking experience are a good choice if you also wish to benchmark your organization against other organizations that are adopting object-oriented technology.

What will be assessed. The goal of a midcourse assessment is to determine the extent to which you are meeting the long-term object-oriented technology program goals and objectives. In theory, you should assess the degree to which all of the goals and objectives are being met. In practice, it may only make sense to focus on a subset of the goals because not all goals may be addressed by the object program at a particular time (especially early on).

Assessment information sources. A comprehensive assessment should involve personnel who are responsible for setting up the object program, including: sponsors, management, and technical staff members. It should also involve customers of the program, including: developers, management, the quality assurance team, and so on. In addition, external object-technology consultants who are working on the program should be included. If software products have been developed as part of the program, they should be available to the assessors as well.

Assessment Report

An assessment report should indicate the degree to which each desired objective is being met. Since objectives are measurable, the principal way to conduct an assessment is to measure each objective and report its results using the scale associated with the measure. Quality Templates can be used to define the relevant information for each objective (see Chapter 20).

It is important to provide a series of planned values for each objective. Each value represents the expected measure of the objective at some target date. For example, if you set a four-year objective to achieve a 20-fold decrease in the time needed to develop software, an assessment after the first year is likely to show that you are still far from meeting this objective. However, you can much more accurately assess your overall progress toward the final objective if your interim objectives are to have a twofold decrease after the first year, a fivefold decrease after the second year, and a tenfold decrease after the third year.

As consultants, we have provided assessment and benchmarking services to our clients. Many of them do not have numerically defined and measurable objectives. To assess and benchmark these organizations, we have adopted a less formal but practical approach based on a scorecard as shown in Table 4.1. Each column of the scorecard corresponds to a particular dimension of the object program. A dimension typically corresponds to several related process, product, or resource objectives. Similar dimensions are grouped together on the same scorecard. For example, there might be a Product Process Model scorecard that contains dimensions such as: testing (how good is your object-oriented testing capability), coding (how good are you with your selected programming language), interproject reuse (how well you support effective interproject reuse), configuration management (how good is your configuration management process), and so on. Of course, the specific scorecards and dimensions are designed for each organization.

The first column of a scorecard lists the set of activities that have been carried out by the organization. An activity is either an entire project or major work within a project such as: Provide Smalltalk Introductory Training, Pilot Project 1, and Develop Testing Guidelines. Each row of a scorecard assesses the extent to which the activity supports each dimension. Each cell in the table is divided in half.

Figure 4.3 provides a legend for interpreting the contents of these cells. The top half of a cell is either empty or contains a bullet. A bullet indicates that the activity was planned to address the dimension; an empty cell indicates that the activity was not

Table 4.1 Assessment Scorecard

| | Dimensions | | | |
Activities	Dimension 1	Dimension 2	Dimension 3	Dimension 4
Activity 1	●/√		●/√	
Activity 2		●/X	●/?	●/√
Activity 3	●/√		●/X	●/?
Activity 4		●/√	●/X	●/√
Activity 5	●/?	●/?	●/√	
Comparison	●	○	◐	◖
Theory/Practice	Theory	Practice	Practice	Theory
Overall Assessment	◖	○	◉	●

planned to address the dimension. The lower half of each cell contains either a √, an X, or a ?. A √ indicates that the activity did address the dimension at some level. An X means that the activity did not address the dimension at all. A ? means that the assessors did not have sufficient information to reach a conclusion. This approach makes the resulting measurement of each dimension a ternary outcome. If we had an appropriate measure for each dimension, we would have numeric assessments for each dimension, instead of the symbols.

The last three rows of a scorecard contain aggregate assessment information for each of the dimensions. The first of these rows represents a comparison or benchmark against other companies with which the assessors have had experience. Figure 4.4 describes the comparison assessment scale, ranging from far behind to well ahead of the pack.

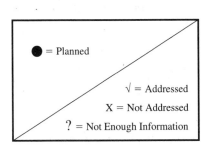

Figure 4.3 Legend for the Scorecard Activity Cells

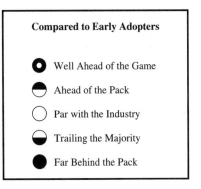

Figure 4.4 Comparison Assessment Scale for the Scorecard

The second of the last three rows is the theory/practice scale. In this row, you assess whether an organization's support for a particular dimension is based on theory, practice, or best practice. Theory means that you have thought about the topic, perhaps even written a document, but you have no practical experience. Practice means that you have direct experience, and best practice means that you have enough direct experience to choose the best approach for your organization.

The last row of the scorecard is the overall aggregate assessment of the dimension relative to the overall goals. Figure 4.5 describes the overall assessment scale. The assessment of a specific dimension is based on the aggregate coverage of all of the activities, plus an adjustment for how important the assessors feel the dimension is in your overall plan.

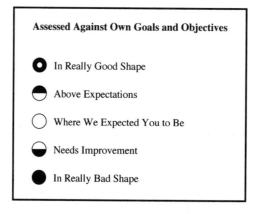

Figure 4.5   Overall Assessment Scale for the Scorecard

An assessment of a particular project is likely to have four to ten different scorecards. Upper managers to whom we have presented these cards find them intuitive and easy to understand. In addition, when subsequent assessments of the object program use this same reporting approach, management can observe the progress of the project by comparing the Overall Assessment row of each card with the same row and card of the previous assessment.

Set Up a Special Object Technology Center

From the outset, an information center is important to the success of a program to introduce new technology into an organization. It gives a home to the knowledge accumulating in the organization, and a place where interested parties can get information, regardless of the organization's state of the art in the use of objects. You can consider setting up a special object-oriented technology center at any time in the process of bringing objects into your organization.

As Steve Fraser, a software engineering researcher from BNR, said, a staff member of an object-oriented technology center should greet people with this analogy:

"Hi, I am from the U.S. Peace Corps. I am here to help you help yourself."

The idea behind a special center is to provide a nucleus of expertise, a well-known place to which interested managers and developers can turn when they want to share the benefits of object-oriented technology. Many organizations make use of this idea, often with different centers for different kinds of technologies or skills, each providing assistance to multiple projects. There are usability centers, statistical analysis centers, and even documentation design centers. The staffers act as mentors on projects across the organization.

The purpose of these centers is to help the organization to:

- Communicate experiences with other interested parties in the organization. Successful companies seem to have self-motivated people who make sure that others know what works and what does not work, whether in administrative processes or software development processes.

- Scale up using a controlled process to make sure that the organization does not unnecessarily repeat technology evaluations and initial experiences.

The list that follows contains some ideas about the roles and responsibilities of an object-oriented technology center, taking a very broad view of the possible activities.

Knowledge discovery	Bring resources into the organization from external sources. This responsibility includes providing a library of books, journals, reports, and videotapes, as well as arranging for experts to speak on object-oriented technology topics.
Technology transfer	Transfer capabilities from the center to line organizations. This responsibility includes providing mentors, setting up training opportunities, setting up pilot projects, and perhaps devising projects in which people from other organizations can participate. This last service provides a form of apprenticeship program.
Setting standards or guidelines for products, processes, and resources	Set guidelines for the use of object-oriented technology in the organization, including customizing any acquired resources. An example is to set guidelines for process models, testing, or reuse. Center activities could include monitoring guidelines and defining preferred implementation approaches, such as choice of hardware or recommended software products.

Technology support	Provide a help desk or other technical support services, and perhaps carry out project reviews.
Managing external relationships	Carry out and report on evaluations of external products and resources, acting as a single point of contact for outside vendors. This responsibility could include helping a project evaluate the appropriateness of various choices.
Center management	Coordinate efforts, making sure that information gets from projects into the center, between projects both inside and outside the center, and generally making sure that other centers of expertise understand and can apply object-oriented concepts.
Marketing	Proactively make members of the organization aware of the services available in the center, and update management on the center's accomplishments. This responsibility includes lobbying for appropriate support, promoting activities to outside organizations where such credibility or awareness is important (perhaps to the organization's customers), and creating newsletters and seminars whose content is provided by members of the center.

Many of the services might actually be carried out by an outside contractor and managed by someone in the object-oriented technology center. Many of the roles identified correspond to roles in the reuse process model (Chapter 10). It is possible that the object-oriented technology center includes the roles we identify in Appendix C to administer the reuse process, carrying out the organization's reuse plan.

Practically speaking, small organizations are not going to have a formal structure that provides all of the services we have identified. Nonetheless, these organizations should provide those services that are critical to early success—notably setting standards and providing technology support. They can always add more services over time.

Summary

The third decision framework gives advice on how to make an initial commitment to the use of object-oriented technology. We reviewed the five steps of the framework, examining the need to get the organization to treat the decision to use objects as a strategic one use of object-oriented technology. We reviewed the five steps of the framework, examining the need to get the organization to treat the decision to use objects as a strategic one and making sure that team members are prepared to learn and use new technology. It is important to get management buy-in to a business case for the use of object-oriented technology. We emphasized that the first project you choose to do is an important learning experience. You can use this first project to demonstrate your ability to create systems based on objects. You can test a new process model or analysis-and-design method. You can also use this first project to learn about and evaluate software development environments, and to train a small group of developers who will form the core of object-oriented technology expertise in your organization.

We reviewed the characteristics of software development projects and summarized which characteristics to look for when selecting your first development project. We gave advice on the mechanics of setting up the first project, notably making sure you state measurable objectives and select an appropriate process model and team structure. We also gave advice on how to staff the project, describing ways in which you might use outside consultants to help you get started. Our recommendations are that you staff a project with at least one expert, and that you let consultants act as mentors rather than have them do the project for you.

The final step of the decision framework asks you to assess whether you are making progress towards meeting your goals and objectives. To assist you in carrying out this step, we suggested a midcourse assessment process leading to an assessment report—a scorecard that indicates the degree to which each desired objective is being met.

At any time in the process of introducing objects into your organization, you should consider setting up a special technology center that houses the information you gather and provides consultation to interested groups. We provided a list of the roles and responsibilities for staffing such an object-oriented technology center.

Additional Reading About Making a Commitment to New Technology

Bouldin, B. M., *Agents of Change: Managing the Introduction of Automated Tools*, Yourdon Press: Englewood Cliffs, New Jersey, 1989.

This book provides practical information regarding how to introduce new technology (specifically CASE tools) into MIS organizations. Bouldin focuses on people-related issues that must be addressed to transfer new technology successfully. She provides specific advice on how to obtain management and developer commitment to introduce new technology in the face of resistance, fear, and resource constraints, echoing much of our own advice.

CHAPTER 5

What Is a Process Model?

M any process models come into play when managing an organization. Different process models are used in managing software development—for example, process models are needed for:

Developing products

Maintaining products

Managing reusable assets

Building development teams

Training team members

Measuring products, processes, and resources

In this chapter, we focus on product process models. The other process models are covered in subsequent chapters.

Process Model Definitions

A *process model* states an order for carrying out activities. It includes rules for inputs and outputs for each activity, whether it is appropriate to redo an activity and, if so, when or why. Some models state the purpose of team reviews. And some answer questions about the use of prototyping, the role of reuse, and how to direct incremental integration. The choice of process model affects the way a team is structured, when and how team members interact, who has responsibility and authority for each aspect of the project, and even the format of reviews and reports.

Process models are important because they provide the basis by which we answer five critical questions:

Planning	What is it that we are going to do to meet goals and objectives?
Authority	How can we influence what is happening to get where we want to be?
Prediction	Where will we get to—that is, where are we going?
Assessment	Where are we in the process, and why?
Traceability	How was a particular result achieved—for example, how is a particular piece of code linked back, through design and analysis, to goals and objectives?

More formally stated, a process model is a collection of maxims, strategies, activities, methods, and tasks, which are organized to achieve a set of goals and objectives.

Maxims. *Maxims* embody opinions or beliefs that act as a foundation for choosing activities, strategies, methods, and tasks. Example maxims for software development are:

- Assessing and managing risk is important to success.

- It is better to understand the problem before developing a solution.

- Intermediate deliverables increase developer and customer confidence.

Strategies. A *strategy* for software development describes and directs the larger vision of how activities in a process will be carried out, without worrying about the details of the techniques or tasks involved. Two strategies of interest in setting up process models for the use of object-oriented technology are prototyping and reusing.

Activities. An *activity* is a step you take to accomplish some purpose. Possible process model activities are: analysis, design, implementation, documentation, integration, implementation testing, and maintenance. Our use of these terms follows common practice.

Analysis	Understand the problem to be solved in terms of requirements to be fulfilled
Design	Develop an architecture and details for a solution that fulfills the analysis requirements
Implementation	Express the design in computer executable form

Documentation	Describe the salient aspects of the analysis, design, and implementation
Integration	Combine independently created parts so as to form a coherent whole
Testing	Uncover any detectable implementation defects
Maintenance	Improve or modify the system

Methods. A *method* is a specific way of carrying out an activity. For example, structured analysis is a method for doing analysis. Object Behavior Analysis is a method for doing object-oriented analysis [Rubin and Goldberg 1992]. There are methods for quality assurance, tracking project progress, testing software, and so on.

Tasks. A *task* is a specific use of a method within a given process model. Each task is defined by a statement of the desired outcome, when the task takes place relative to other tasks, and may include other pertinent information such as the resources needed prior to beginning the task and the process model activity supported by the task.

Example Process Models

There is the Waterfall Model. The Spiral Model. The Recursive/Parallel Model. Each offers different strategies for ordering activities, and each chooses different mechanisms by which management can control the process.

Waterfall Model

Each of the popular product process models was devised for a specific purpose. For example, a sequential process model is a strategy for defining and tracking progress toward well-defined milestones or checkpoints. As a result, it is well received in the community of government contractors because the contractors can align payments with deliverables. A schedule is a sequence of tasks. Tracking consists of verifying that a task has been completed. Execution is very linear. Indeed, it is the linear nature of the process that is so appealing. Just lay out the tasks and do them, start to finish.

The most popular sequential model is the Waterfall Model [Royce 1970, Boehm 1981], which expects a sequence of activities to be followed in order:

- Understand the new system requirements (analysis)

- Determine an appropriate mapping of requirements to system architecture (design)

- Implement each component of the system (code and test)

- Combine all components to form the desired system (integration)

These are appropriate activities in creating a software system. Every project manager expects to carry out each of these activities, somehow, and to produce the necessary outcomes:

- Requirements specification

- Design document

- Code verified that it meets requirements

- Parts integrated and verified that they interact appropriately

Underlying the Waterfall Model are the following maxims:

- Goals are best achieved by targeting well-defined and documented milestones, dividing development into well-defined sequential stages.

- Technical documents are understandable by nontechnical users and managers, and these nontechnical participants can communicate effectively with analysts.

- Every detail about requirements and functions can be known in advance before the software is developed, and these details remain stable throughout development.

- Testing and evaluation can be efficiently carried out at the end of development.

The Waterfall Model fell into disfavor because users could not state clearly, in advance of seeing a running version, how a dynamic and complex system should function. Moreover, the model appears to be inflexible—once an activity has been completed, it is not to be changed unless an error is detected (although the actual model was less restrictive, its application typically was more so). Ed Yourdon, in his book *Decline and Fall of the American Programmer* [Yourdon 1992], points out more problems with the Waterfall Model:

- Is based on paper

- Takes too long to see results

- Depends on stable, correct requirements

- Makes it difficult to trace requirements to code

- Delays detection of errors until the end

- Does not promote software reuse

- Does not promote prototyping

- Is not practiced in a formal fashion

The Waterfall Model was originally well received because it identified a reasonable and logical staging of activities. Unfortunately, the model did not explain how to modify a result—it provided no guidance for why and when to review a prior result for possible change. This rigidity raised questions about the continued usefulness of the model. The irony of most development projects that use the Waterfall Model is that the managers do not agree with the underlying maxims, yet they select process models based on them. Often, the requirement to produce deliverables (mostly documents) to get follow-on funding dictates the sequential, partitioned approach to development activities, even when the managers believe another approach would be a better fit.

Spiral Model

Boehm later modified the Waterfall process model, producing a series of spirals that explicitly includes prototyping. The Spiral Model is a strategy for reducing risk [Boehm 1988]. Boehm described it as risk-driven, as opposed to document-driven or code-driven, because of its emphasis on cycles of work, each of which leads to a risk analysis before proceeding to the next cycle. Each cycle begins with the identification of objectives for a part of the product, alternative ways to accomplish the objectives, constraints associated with each alternative, and then an evaluation of the alternatives. Where uncertainty is identified, various techniques are used to reduce any risk in choosing among the alternatives. Techniques include simulations, user focus groups, and analytic modeling. Each cycle of the Spiral Model ends with a review that discusses the current outcomes and the plans for the next cycle, with the purpose of getting sign-up by all team members for the next cycle. The review can determine that further development will not meet the stated goals and objectives of the project, and so the spiral ends.

Maxims underlying the Spiral Model state:

- An activity starts with an understanding of the objectives and risks involved.

- Based on evaluating alternative solutions, use the tool(s) that best reduce(s) risks.

- All related personnel should be involved in a review that terminates each activity, and plans for and commits to the next activities.

- Development can proceed in increments at each stage.

To use this model, you have to be particularly good at identifying and managing risks.

Boehm [Boehm 1988] introduced another model, which he called the Transform Model. This model has been studied under the research topic of automatic programming. The goal is to describe the result you want in terms of formal specifications, which can then be translated into executable implementation at the latest possible time. All modifications to requirements are reflected in changes to the specification, not to the code. The executable code is regenerated from the modified specifications. In this way, code does not evolve over time into unrecognizable structures (or rather, into structures only recognizable as "spaghetti"). The use of 4GL languages to generate applications is an example of carrying out this kind of process model strategy.

Recursive/Parallel Model

The Recursive/Parallel Model recognizes that during any software development effort, the analysts and designers work on some requirements and defer working on others. According to a key proponent of the model [Berard 1993], the basic approach is to decompose a problem systematically into independent components, then reapply the decomposition process to each of these components to decompose them further (the recursive part). This process can be applied to each component simultaneously (the parallel part). Reapplication continues until some completion criteria are met. Composition has a role as well. Larger components are decomposed; new components are created as compositions of existing components. The process that will be applied—in whole or in part—to each of the components is analysis, followed by design, followed by implementation, followed by testing. This model has often been described as "analyze a little, design a little, implement a little, test a little."

For the Recursive/Parallel Model to be effective, the components must be as independent of one another as possible—which presumably is why advocates of this process model often choose object-oriented technology. In contrast, functional decomposition— by definition—leads to descriptions of functions that are closely coupled to one another. Subfunctions exist only to support the parent function.

Maxims for the Recursive/Parallel Model include:

- Development should focus on working in parallel on independent components.

- Systems should be designed as compositions of independently created components.

In addition to the proposals for Waterfall, Spiral, and Recursive/Parallel models, there is a Fountain proposal [Henderson-Sellers and Edwards 1994], a Cluster emphasis [Meyer 1990], and Round-Trip Gestalt Engineering [Booch 1991]. The maxims underlying each of these more recent proposals follow from an admonition of Heinlein: "When faced with a problem you do not understand, do any part of it you do understand, then look at it again."[1]

---

[1] Quoted in [Booch 1991], from R. Heinlein, *The Moon Is a Harsh Mistress*, Berkeley Publishing Group: New York, 1966, p. 290.

There Is Not One Process Model for Objects

A common fallacy in the software industry is that there is one process model that will work for projects that use object-oriented technology. The search for a single, universal process model has generated a lot of discussion, papers, books, and consulting fees. But one process model does not fit all software development situations. Large organizations have more than one product process model because they build several types of software products. In the case studies and projects with which we have been involved, every product process model has been specially tuned to fit the situation. As we argue here, there is not just one process model, and there are several strategies you should consider when you construct your own process model for your particular type of project.

Several companies we studied use a variety of product process models to build their systems. During an evaluation study at one company, we identified and classified five types of projects labeled as: First-of-Its-Kind, Variation-on-a-Theme, Legacy Rewrite, Creating Reusable Assets, and System Enhancement or Maintenance. These project types illustrate why different process models are required.

First-of-Its-Kind Project. The goal of a First-of-Its-Kind project is to build the initial version of a system. In this case, there are no domain-specific components available at the start of the project, which can be refined to create the desired result. There may be some general purpose reusable assets, such as utilities, that can leverage the effort. Because there is often no experience in creating software of this type, more time is needed to analyze the problem domain. Sometimes the domain model is familiar. You might understand what it means to report personal income taxes to the government, having done so on paper, but this might be the first software version of the process.

On a First-of-Its-Kind project, uncertainty creates risks and demands special planning. The process model followed in a First-of-Its-Kind project has to take into account the uncertainty of the requirements for the first version of an application. Consequently, it is important to have a general view of the software requirements. It is often harder to partition these projects into tasks that can be done in parallel than it is to divide better-understood efforts.

In Chapter 8, we illustrate the process of building a system without a complete understanding of the domain model, using our own experience in developing the tools that support the Object Behavior Analysis method prior to distilling all the details of the method.

Variation-on-a-Theme Project. The goal of a Variation-on-a-Theme project is to build a derivative work by refining an existing result. This might involve taking an existing reusable software asset and modifying it according to its rules of usage. The derivative might be built from an existing framework and the components that specialize the framework. New components might be created as well. Or the derivative might be built from an existing application that is modified to add new business functions.

On a Variation-on-a-Theme project, the structure of the software framework or application to be refined dictates the process model. The critical difference in projects of this category is that the risk is much lower than in First-of-Its-Kind projects. What has to be done is already defined by the nature of the software asset—framework or application—that will be reused. An initial task, then, is to understand the reusable asset and its rules for modification. Each Variation-on-a-Theme project may differ according to these rules. It is not likely that some generic process model documented in the literature will have a lot to say to the team doing this kind of project.

In the case study project that created a framework for visualizing financial data, the framework was used to create three applications during the course of a year. These were banking applications that dealt with bonds, currency, and interest rates. At the time of our interview, a fourth application dealing with equities had just begun. Also, based on the experience of developing three applications, the framework itself was being revised.

Legacy Rewrite Project. An organization may choose to create a system using object-oriented technology that is a rewrite of a legacy system. Because the organization has already built the system at least once before, the Legacy Rewrite project will have some of the characteristics of a Variation-on-a-Theme project. For example, the process model will include activities for examining the existing system model to extract requirements and to understand the legacy implementation architecture. The Legacy Rewrite project may also have many characteristics of a First-of-Its-Kind project, such as having to create a new architecture and not having available appropriate reusable assets based on object-oriented technology. In addition, there are all of the risks that attend any first-time project using a new technology. The project process model will need activities to address these risks.

Several case study projects described in Chapter 8 used existing systems as an initial source for requirements. These were rewrite projects, not efforts to create new applications that could interoperate with legacy systems.

Creating Reusable Assets Project. A particular project might have as its goal creating one or more reusable assets.[2] This kind of project is much like other software development projects in that it is necessary to understand requirements, create a maintainable design, and implement, document, and test the solution. It is different in that the require-

---

[2] If a project is expected to create a reusable asset, then this expectation should be made an explicit goal. Not all projects should be expected to create artifacts that can be successfully reused in other projects. We discuss this assertion in the chapters about reuse (Chapters 9, 10, and 11).

ments have to take into account the needs of multiple projects, the documentation has to indicate how the software interfaces to other software and how this software can be specialized, and testing must include reuse evaluation—making sure that the design of the artifact is general enough to be useful in as yet unknown situations.

Projects that create reusable assets often require additional time to rework the software so that it is general enough to be useful for a variety of applications. The process model typically defines activities for creating concrete examples that are then generalized, and activities for making sure that the concrete examples can be recreated by specializing the more general version. Often the concrete examples already exist in the organization, and this project team retrieves them for generalization. Or the effort to create reusable assets is embedded in a larger project that initiates the concrete examples.

Projects to create reusable assets found in our case studies include: a bank's framework for visualizing financial data; an instruments company's framework for creating user interfaces to test equipment; and, in several companies, frameworks for network configuration management.

System Enhancement or Maintenance Project. In a System Enhancement or Maintenance project, core utilities or system frameworks are modified. Projects such as these are often relatively small in scope. The purpose is to make a set of modifications to some existing utility or framework to support new functionality. This category of project does not include rewriting a framework or application in its entirety.

Developers assigned to these kinds of projects must have a good understanding of the utility or framework to be enhanced, or an ability to learn about the utility or framework at a much deeper level than is necessary when simply reusing it to build Variation-on-a-Theme applications. A person may be capable of modifying a utility or framework without being able to create one. Also, as with the original developers, these people have to be concerned with low-level system or business issues. In other words, they have to be willing to sweat the details so that the First-of-Its-Kind and Variation-on-a-Theme programming tasks concentrate only on the novel business aspects of each new problem.

In an instruments company we studied, the system framework used to manage the user interface and network access was modified several times in response to new ideas for graphical widgetry and to connect to additional sources of information.

The choice of product process model depends on the goals and objectives of the project, the scope of the project, the skills of available team members, organizational constraints placed on selection of technologies and methods, and the set of values you wish to realize. Differences in process models also come from other development details, such as: the extent to which the target system model is well understood, the extent to which documents exist that describe requirements and designs, whether 4GL code generators can be used to create the required functionality, and the desire to incorporate reuse.

Strategies for Developing with Objects

Iterative Development

If the Waterfall Model is inadequate, spiraling through planning and review cycles is too cumbersome, the transform approach is still futuristic for building systems generally, and the Recursive/Parallel Model too trite, is there any model that does work? Ask any objectologist, and you will likely hear that the correct model is iterative development.[3]

The act of reviewing a prior result for possible change is referred to as iteration. What people seem to mean is: We do not have to get it all done the first time around—we can come back later. Just get done what we know, and we'll add more later, or we'll fix the coding of it later, or we'll replace this function later, and so on. Later we will figure out what we needed. So the iterative process model seems to be a strategy for doing things later!

Project managers are rightfully concerned that the iterative process may never reach closure. They wonder how to specify a project plan when they are uncertain as to the number of iterations. They do not believe that artificially declaring the number of iterations to be three or five or eight is the best solution to this problem. These project managers are also wary of using the opportunity for iteration to justify shoddy or incomplete work, of not doing the job correctly or well the first time around—after all, the developers can always come back later!

The real intent of *iterative development* is to allow for the controlled reworking of part of a system to remove mistakes or to make improvements based on user feedback. This approach is based on two maxims described in [Cockburn 1993]:

- We get things wrong before we get them right.

- We make things badly before we make them well.

By adopting these maxims, we agree to approach the development life cycle as a learning experience. After each iteration, we evaluate the result and plan, in the next iteration, to improve the correctness of the system and the quality of its design.

There are times when a problem is new enough or difficult enough to justify iteration. Developing a reusable framework often requires that the framework be used and reworked several times before we have enough confidence in its quality and potential for reuse. For this kind of development, it is very difficult to know whether a framework is indeed reusable without the benefit of having actually used it. In such circumstances, a wise manager plans for rework based on feedback.

---

[3] An *objectologist* is one who practices and preaches the benefits of object-oriented technology. The first temple of objectology was in Oslo, Norway, but the cult was fruitful and multiplied in the sunshine of California.

Using the word "iterative" more often comes from the desire to justify a nonsequential activity. Perhaps the process requires five steps to be completed, but the developers feel more comfortable doing the third before the second, and some of the fifth before the third. To justify their chaotic working style, these developers claim that they do a little bit of each step linearly, with the right to back up when new information is discovered. Work is applied opportunistically. Perhaps the right process model name, then, should be the *Opportunistic Model*. That is, you do not have to carry out the steps sequentially, but rather in the order that is most opportune based on the situation at hand. This is much the way a person might solve a jigsaw puzzle (Fig. 5.1)—rarely left to right, but rather as pieces are discovered.

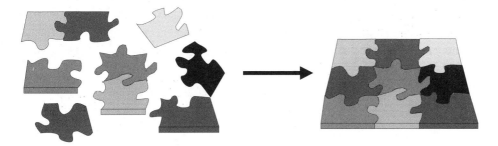

Figure 5.1   Opportunistically Solving a Jigsaw Puzzle

Incremental Development

An increment is something added or gained. To increment is to make progress toward completing whatever next task is at hand.

Incremental development is a strategy for making progress in small steps to get early tangible results. Our suggested maxim comes from Benjamin Franklin: Small strokes fell great oaks. Incremental development is an explicit avoidance of the "Big Bang" theory of software development.[4] The incremental approach requires that a problem be partitioned into several subproblems so that each can be developed in turn. As each partition is completed, it is tested and integrated with the other completed partitions of the system. At each stage, the partially completed system can be evaluated to influence the development of future partitions. If resources are available, and partitions are sufficiently independent, partitions can be developed in parallel.

---

[4] The Big Bang theory of software development is analogous to the Big Bang theory of the creation of the universe. The basic idea is that the universe came into existence in one large explosion. The corresponding software idea is that you do years of analysis, then years of design, followed by much coding, and then, finally, miraculously, the entire software system is delivered at once.

The terms "iterative" and "incremental" are often used interchangeably when describing process models. However, they are distinct and independent development strategies. Iterative development supports the reworking of portions of the system. Incremental development allows systems to be partitioned and developed at different times or rates. Iterative and incremental development can be used separately or together.

For example, a small-scale but technically challenging project may not be partitionable. Several iterations will be needed to make sure the resultant system meets expectations. On the other hand, the manager of a large-scale project, when creating a familiar kind of system, can partition the work effort to develop and deliver capability in an incremental fashion without reworking any particular partition. Many contemporary projects use some combination of incremental and iterative development. These projects are large enough to require partitioning, and the capability of an individual partition may be unfamiliar enough to require planning for rework based on user feedback.

Prototyping

Prototyping is a strategy applied to most process activities. The purpose of *prototyping* is to seek the information needed to make decisions. Prototyping can help reduce the risk of making mistakes in setting requirements or in designing the system architecture.

A *prototype* is a preliminary, or intentionally incomplete or scaled-down, version of a system. It may not be sufficiently engineered for robust product delivery, yet the existence of the demonstration supports the belief that the full product can be developed. The term *rapid prototyping* refers to the process of quickly building and evaluating one or more prototypes.

Figure 5.2 Prototype for the Outside Inn, Col. Falls, MT. Richard Smith, architect.

Many disciplines employ prototyping as a standard strategy. For example, an architect constructs a physically scaled-down prototype of a house (such as the one shown in Fig. 5.2), skyscraper, or landscape, placing the prototype in a context resembling the actual environment (a street, a set of other houses or skyscrapers, and so on) to provide a visualization of the proposed result for the potential purchaser.

In the past, an automobile designer would hand-tool the first working version of a new car. The working model could be driven by engineers, test drivers, and potential customers, to give feedback on the car design and performance. The difference between the model and the one at the car dealer is that the one for sale incorporates feedback from the use of the model, and has been constructed using a large-scale manufacturing process. Today's car designers often use computer-aided design systems to model cars. With these models, the designers explore the design space, and look to reduce the costs associated with building the physical model. Tomorrow's car designers may use virtual reality technology to let drivers take the prototype out for a drive.

Connell and Shafer [Connell and Shafer 1989] describe a software prototype as a dynamic visual model that serves as a communication link between end user and designer. Their ideas were framed in a fourth-generation-language (4GL) context of display-screen painting and report writing, where users can create mock-ups of screens and pages for retrieving data from a relational database. Much of what they say is appropriate to object-oriented technology as well.[5] They say that a prototype is

- A requirements definition medium

- A means for providing users with a physical representation of key parts of the system before full implementation

- Functional after a modest amount of effort

- Flexible so that modifications can be done with minimal effort

- Not necessarily complete or intended to be the final system

Why prototype? Despite requirements statements, surveys, and other instruments for soliciting end user input, users are rarely able to express clearly what they want, and often prefer something other than what they get. Unfortunately, this is the most costly type of development problem because it often happens very early in the project (during specification), and is detected very late in the project (at delivery). This situation occurs because decision makers lack key information.

Several research studies support the need to improve the early stages of development. One study [Ramamoorthy *et al.* 1984] reported that 34 percent of errors discovered in the course of conventional software development (basically projects using the Waterfall Model) were due to the functional specification being incorrect or misinterpreted. As shown in Chart 5.1, another 22 percent were attributable to errors in design or implementation of a single component, and 12 percent occurred because the requirements were incorrect or misinterpreted.

---

[5] Indeed, the authors have recently recast their thinking to serve the object community [Connell and Shafer 1995].

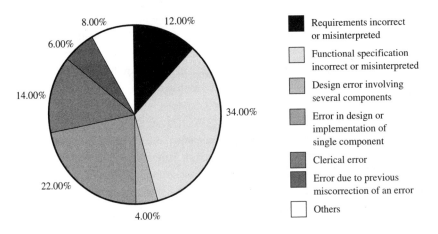

8.00%   12.00%

6.00%

14.00%

34.00%

22.00%

4.00%

Requirements incorrect
or misinterpreted

Functional specification
incorrect or misinterpreted

Design error involving
several components

Error in design or
implementation of
single component

Clerical error

Error due to previous
miscorrection of an error

Others

Chart 5.1   Sources of Errors in Software Development

Fitting prototyping into a product process model. There are different kinds of prototyping activities, depending on the motivation: analysis prototyping, design prototyping,
vertical prototyping, and feasibility prototyping.

Analysis prototyping	An analysis prototype enables target users to interact with an executable but partial mock-up of the product. The purpose is to help clarify requirements and solicit new ideas. Because complex interfaces are hard to document, the analysis prototype can be included in the requirements documentation.
Design prototyping	A design prototype is developed to explore and understand the system's implementation architecture. This prototype can form the basis for performance and space evaluation, and for checks on redundancies or inconsistencies in the design. Performance analysis of a design prototype can identify bottlenecks, places where engineering effort is needed before a product version can be created.
Vertical prototyping	A vertical prototype is used to understand a slice or partition of a problem and its solution, where underlying concepts are not well understood and where a complete functional result for the slice is needed for explanatory purposes.

Feasibility prototyping

A feasibility prototype is used to demonstrate whether something is possible. Can a particular architecture be employed? Does a particular way of connecting to a database give adequate performance? Is it possible for this team to learn to program in that language? Can this system design handle 1000 transactions on this platform in less than a millisecond using this language and that database? It can also be used to determine whether technology is suitable for an organization—for example, whether it can be learned by existing team members. Other kinds of prototypes may serve as feasibility prototypes.

To evolve the prototype or not. When project managers express concern about object-oriented technology, it is often because they sense a loss of control—they cannot figure out whether the project team is making progress. The programmer rolls around in the system as if in a sandbox—building sandcastles, knocking them down, building anew. The purpose is to explore, to understand, to show off to playmates the latest castle turret design. Exploration is fun. The ease of use of tools and languages based on object-oriented technology helps make programming fun—which is useful, because the programmer learns what is feasible, what kinds of foundations are needed to hold up different structures, and what it is like to have a three-turret castle surrounded by a deep moat. Prototyping is a way of learning.

Prototyping is a fast and productive way to answer questions about requirements and design. But prototyping promotes the misconception that the only process model when using object-oriented technology is a strategy for iteratively evolving a prototype. The presumption is that you do not have to know much detail about the requirements. You simply start coding and let the product unfold, letting castles appear out of the wet sand. Build something, add to it, knock it down, build something else. It is hard to throw things away. Don't. Build something new by changing what you already have.

Object-oriented technology changes the role of prototyping. In the past, development models such as the Spiral Model incorporated prototyping as a way to reduce the risk of getting the user interface wrong. These prototypes were sequences of screen views that depicted what the product would look like to the user. They gave an illusion of the functioning system. But the typical object-oriented development environment invites prototyping of full functionality—actual working functionality that can be used and commented upon by the target customers. It is appropriate to prototype at this deep level to make sure that the feedback from the target customers informs the analyzers and designers about work flow, function details, and performance. But the implementation of a prototype is not necessarily product quality, designed for long-term maintainability. Rather it is often quickly glued together, to be tried and then rewritten. As such, the implementation should be thrown away.

But prototypes are not simply kept or thrown away. These are two extremes. Rather, parts of a prototype are retained when the next prototype or the product version is created. For example, to study some aspect of a system, a prototype might have to include considerable infrastructure. When the study is completed and the next prototype begins, the infrastructure can be discarded and the rest retained.

The design prototype has a higher probability of evolving into product software than other types of prototypes. The environment in which the design is studied is more likely to be the same as the one to be used in product development. The design prototype studies how the product will be implemented. After a series of studies, the design prototype is likely to represent a satisfactory approach that can be retained and expanded.

An analysis prototype might evolve into the product as well. Suppose that you have a library of software components, including sets of interacting objects that represent core business processes, and a consistent approach to creating a business application user interface. Prototypes can make use of these reusable assets. Assuming that the reused assets were of product quality, it is likely that a completed product can evolve from this initial prototype by modifying the implementation in response to user feedback and space/performance objectives. Of course, asking a developer to create a prototype rapidly, and also expecting to evaluate the quality of the implementation, establishes conflicting goals. Consequently, analysis prototypes are typically thrown away.

Prototyping successes and failures. What distinguishes the successful uses of prototyping from the failures? We have observed in many examples of prototyping (many of which we reported in [Goldberg and Rubin 1990]) that on successful projects, the prototypers:

- Understand the purpose of the prototype and use it only for that purpose.

- Take the time to understand the technology to be used and the prototyping process.

- Assemble an appropriate team to do the prototype: project leader/documentor, analysis prototyper, and design prototyper.

- Evaluate team and deliverables.

- Involve target users early in the process.

- Are willing to repeat the prototyping process to understand better the underlying architecture.

- Set proper evaluation criteria at the beginning of each stage of prototyping, and firmly base completion on these criteria.

- Build prototypes based on an existing approved company library of reusable code, controlled by an assigned librarian.

Where the project fails, the prototypers:

- Do not understand what a prototype is and how it should be used.

- Do not understand the process well enough to set up the team correctly.

- Do not know when to stop evolving a prototype and start anew—that is, they overextend the process.

- Do not know when to continue to try to meet the desired evaluation criteria— that is, they prematurely terminate the process.

- Do not use supportive object-oriented development environments or tools, but only an object-oriented language.

- Believe that a reasonable prototype is an acceptable product.

Prototyping gets mixed reviews for two reasons. First, there is a tendency to be excited when the anticipated application first works, even though the application is in fact a first prototype. Hoping to beat competitors to the marketplace, a manager might be tempted to deliver the prototype. Development systems based on object-oriented technology have been criticized for their ability to make it fast and easy to create good demos—fooling nontechnical observers. So the good news is the bad news when proper management controls are not in place.

Second, the processes never seem to converge. Rather than one analysis prototype, there are two, three, or more; rather than one design prototype, there are several. In smaller organizations, the product is often developed by the same people who did the prototyping, adding to confusion as to which stage of development the project is at and whether the final product will ever be delivered.

Even more important is to adopt a work model that requires clear statements of goals and objectives for each activity within the project, so that it is possible to monitor progress toward completion. The pitfalls of prototyping can be avoided by having a clear agreement—before you start work—on how the prototype will be evaluated. Then you will know when to end. It is useful to assign clear authority to a single person for evaluating and declaring the prototype finished. It is also useful to create a clear role for differentiating the development of prototypes from products, essentially to assign some developers to be "professional prototypers." In addition, it is useful to budget time and set milestones to acknowledge that a prototype will likely be thrown away after the information-gathering phase.

Consuming Reusable Assets

Consumption of already completed artifacts is a strategy for completing a task with as little effort as possible. This strategy has to be complemented by efforts to produce these reusable assets. A *reuse producer* creates reusable development artifacts. A *reuse consumer* attempts to reduce work effort by reusing these artifacts. Whenever a solution to a problem is needed—whether the problem is related to analysis, design, or implementation—the first question the consumer asks is, does the solution already exist? If so, reuse it. A partial solution may exist. Reuse it, adding the remaining functionality.

The *producer/consumer process model* for software, a process model that intermingles projects that produce reusable assets with those that consume reusable assets, is a popular analogy for understanding the economics of software development. The decision to reuse is based on an assessment that understanding and incorporating the existing solution takes less effort than the work that is needed to develop a new solution. An organization must be willing and able to incur the upstream costs of reuse production in order to reduce the downstream development costs through reuse consumption. An organization can manage costs and make reusing an effective part of its product process model by setting up an internal group that plans and manages the process of acquisition, distribution, and maintenance of reusable assets. The structure and function of this group is a topic in Chapters 10 and 11.

Reusing promotes consistency and quality. Reusing artifacts across multiple projects yields two benefits: users of applications that solve the same problem have a consistent solution across all applications, and improvements to the solution propagate to all of these applications. Moreover, reusing a tested solution, one that has proved to be reliable through repeated use, can directly improve the quality of the applications that incorporate it.

Reusing should be appropriate. Reusing has to be appropriate. By *appropriate reuse*, we mean that the reusable solution is germane to meeting the goals and objectives of the task in which reuse is considered. Reusing may not be appropriate if the reusable solution adds functionality or implementation details that make the result inappropriate for the target market, unable to meet quality objectives, harder to maintain, or harder for users to learn.

Reusing requires trust. Developers will only reuse existing solutions that they trust will behave as prescribed, with the required level of quality. Developers trust themselves, and they trust other developers whom they know. If a developer thinks highly of another developer's skills, he or she projects this trust onto the solutions provided by this developer. Our proposed solution, given in Chapter 10, is to have the organization set up a process that developers can trust to populate the shared library with quality reusable assets.

Reusing should fit into the process model. There are two ways in which reusing takes place in a product process model. The first way focuses on reuse within a project: *intraproject reuse*. The basic idea is to create unique solutions for the parts of a system, and ensure that these solutions are reused throughout the project.

The second way in which reusing takes place focuses on reuse across projects: *inter-project reuse*. For each identified task, developers first look to see if an appropriate (reusable) solution already exists.

Figure 5.3 points to where reuse could take place in a project's process model. The opportunities occur throughout the life cycle. First you set the project goals and objectives. Have you solved this problem before? If so, reuse the solution.

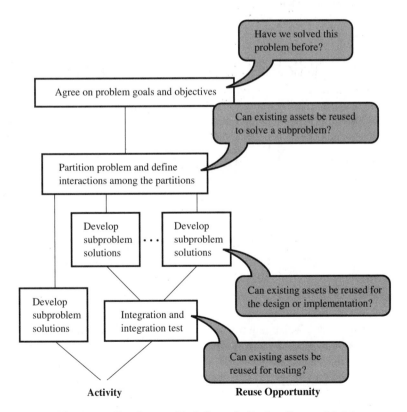

Figure 5.3   Reuse Can Occur at Each Step of a Product Process Model

Partitioning the problem represents an opportunity for reuse. Have you done systems like this before? Are the prior partitionings applicable? If you can start from an existing way of partitioning, then it is possible that one or more of the existing partition solutions can be reused.

For a partition, are there existing analyses or designs that can be reused? Are there reusable test suites or existing implementations? To deliver a partition, you need documentation for the end users. You may also need training. Existing documentation formats and training courses and examples might be reusable.

As an example, the problem of creating a customer-help application may be similar to that of the accounting department's complaint-handling application. In searching for potential reuse, you notice that the analysis for the complaint application divided the problem into two partitions: problem management and call processing. The specific requirements for the problem-management partition do not look at all like the ones you need for the help application. But the call-processing partition seems quite similar. The capabilities embodied in complaint call processing and that needed for the help application are the same. So you can reuse the requirements. On further examination, you notice that the design and implementation of complaint call processing is precisely what you need. Reuse it all. You can then focus your resources to create the problem-management partition for the help application.

Suppose the call-processing partition does not serve your needs in the help application. You proceed to do the analysis and design, leading to the specification of a set of subsystems that includes printing reports. You go back to the organization's reusable assets and discover that an appropriate printing subsystem already exists. In fact, it was used successfully by the complaint application, lending confidence that it is a tested solution. Reuse it.

Reuse consumers seek out appropriate reuse opportunities throughout the entire product process model.

Producing Reusable Assets

The emphasis on reusing throughout development raises the question, where do the reusable assets come from? The producer effort to create reusable artifacts is a separate but not independent effort from the projects staffed by consumers. Creating reusable artifacts is an important goal that changes the view of software as a liability to that of an asset. Producing useful assets that can be trusted by potential consumers requires focus and special design skills. It also requires a special software development process model.

First, reuse producers create results that are valued not as independent and completed end-user functionality, but rather as resources that will contribute to other projects. The producers must have a multiproject perspective. They use activities such as domain analysis to determine the requirements that are shared across similar systems in the organization. Second, the reuse producers carry out special tasks to increase the potential reusability of the artifacts, tasks that replace the as yet unattainable crystal ball. One such task is variant analysis, which helps producers to identify and prioritize likely variations of an artifact [Barnes and Bollinger 1991]. Information from variant analysis is used to design artifacts that can be adapted—extended or refined—for anticipated consumer use.

Other reuse producer tasks include creating reuse-oriented documentation and applying special reuse evaluation. The documentation must state assumptions and limitations of the artifact, and point out expected ways to compose from, extend, or refine the artifact. Reuse evaluation benefits from variant analysis to identify the test cases. For a framework, we ask for a description of the category of applications that can be derived from the framework, and test to see whether applications of this type can in fact be derived. For components, we ask whether the descriptions are sufficiently general that they can participate in diverse applications of interest to the organization. A more detailed discussion of testing is in Chapter 6.

In practice, reuse producers and consumers work in an interleaved fashion. The production of the reusable frameworks and components, and the production of products are linked processes. The reuse producers need to see what consumers have done to decide what is generally useful. And the reuse consumers need to try out software from the producers to provide the feedback needed to decide whether the results are indeed general purpose and valuable enough to be called assets. In Chapter 12, we delegate responsibility for producing reusable assets to Framework Teams and Reuse Teams that work closely with Application Teams to improve the organization's ability to develop quality software.

Case Study Results

Product Process Models

A surprising outcome of our case studies was that the successful commercial projects claimed to use the Waterfall Model. They used it because it was familiar, because measures for evaluating progress were easier to implement, or because it was dictated by some standards committee. But they modified the model in three key respects:

- Added prototyping to clarify the requirements and design

- Emphasized reuse of software artifacts to speed development

- Integrated partitions as they were completed, to obtain early usage

Each of these modifications heightened the manager's feeling that he or she was losing control of the project. Here are some of the issues these managers raised:

Prototyping never seemed to end.

Some engineers wanted to distribute a subsystem for use by other engineers as soon as it passed testing. This added management complexity—a configuration then includes both code that is under test and code that continues under development. Who owns the subsystem being tested? Who can modify it? What version is being used by which developers? How are versions maintained consistently across reusers?

Reusable artifacts often include a broad set of capabilities to be more general than any single reuse situation requires. Thus reuse often meant that the system included functionality that was not required, increasing the system size and development effort.

Reuse did not decrease the amount of code to be tested. Isn't it a benefit of reuse that large portions of a system can be acquired with only integration testing? But the testers we talked with did not trust the quality of the reused code.

One of the teams referred to their process model as a "protocycle" rather than a life cycle. They needed a new approach—that is, new compared with textbook Waterfall, because both data and process models were being developed in parallel. This parallel development resulted in two analysis models that differed considerably from the desired situation. So each of the modeling processes was complemented by a series of prototypes written in Smalltalk, the selected programming language. The company used prototypes to figure out the functionality of the system, give tangible evidence that they were accomplishing something (anything), and get early feedback from customers. However, the project leader complained that they did not really do proper prototypes because they "completed too much before giving the demo to the customer." This team member thought that their life cycle was unbalanced, with its heavy focus on evolving prototypes.

Similarly, another team referred to their prototype as their "software breadboard." The manager of this project had some interesting uses for the prototypes they developed: Use the prototype as a training environment before the final system is complete. We take a similar approach at our own company. The prototype—if it looks just like the final system—permits early development of the user documentation, and can be used to pretrain the sales force and presell the product.

Reusing

Table 5.1 and Table 5.2 summarize the answers we received from the case study managers when we asked them to describe their reasons for reusing. Most reuse concerns were linked to issues of time and quality. Will the team have enough time to understand the reusable assets? Will the assets support standards requirements? And will the assets demonstrate the performance required in this project? Reuse is considered valuable because it promotes standards and communications through a shared vocabulary. It speeds up getting started and getting finished. Reuse should improve the quality of the resulting system if the reuse parts have a strong quality track record. The managers indi-

Table 5.1 Quoted Case Study Responses to the Questions: Why Is Reuse a Valuable Objective? Why Not?

Reuse is valuable because:	*Reuse is not valuable because:*
Commonalty is easier to support.	Generalized components may not fit performance requirements.
External consistency is promoted by incorporating standards.	Time to learn new components may not fit project timetable.
Reuse increases the ability of otherwise diverse groups to discuss problems.	Standards can be limiting.
Reuse reduces costs.	
Reuse makes it easier to get started, even when the reusable component is not a perfect fit.	
Reusing speeds up delivery time.	
Reusing already tested results improves quality.	

Table 5.2 Quoted Case Study Responses to the Questions: When Do You Believe That You Should Reuse? Should Not Reuse?

You should reuse when:	*You should not reuse when:*
You need to conserve resources.	Design objectives cannot be met by doing so.
It increases the pool of functionality.	You have to force a fit by making too many changes.
Doing so provides guidance for design.	Reusable components provide features that make the result inappropriate to the target market.
The reusable components improve the quality of the product.	Reusable components provide excess functionality.
Knowing parts of the system lets you predict development time.	The reusable component interface is not well understood by the project team.
Reusing is faster.	The reusable components are proprietary to a specific project.
Current assumptions match component assumptions.	
Components have proved to operate correctly in other situations.	

cated that reusing is not a good idea when there is not a good fit, either because performance expectations cannot be met or the time to learn about the reusable components causes development to take too long.

Prototyping

Ten of the case study projects did no prototyping. Of these projects, three were successful and five were ongoing at the time of the interviews (one is known to have finished successfully later). In most of these cases, the project involved re-creating a product that already existed in another form or for which there were comparable products already in the market.

Of the 16 projects that reported one prototype, one was unsuccessful and four were ongoing. Most of these projects reported that they continually evolved a single prototype until they obtained user acceptance. The primary risk of this process is that there is no architecture, resulting in the delivery of products that are not designed for a long-term life in the marketplace. Another risk is the inability to carry out orderly testing and to develop stable documentation, so that shipped products demonstrate low quality.

Six projects created two prototypes, five reported three prototypes each, and two reported five prototypes each. Successful teams that decided to create prototypes did so for various reasons. The list that follows contains the reasons they reported, categorized by different goals.

Make sure the system does the right things:

- Test concepts

- Obtain product definition

- Determine full functionality

- Design user interface

- Design subsystems

- Get customer sign-off to minimize changes and confusion after delivery

- Provide a context for discussion when parties have different backgrounds or speak different languages

Make sure the system does things right:

- Determine system behavior model

- Test alternative algorithms

Improve the implementation of the current or future system:

- Help identify classes for reuse

- Design framework for applications

- Help estimate construction time

Improve processes and resources:

- Create proof of concept to get a contract

- Test new tools (languages, development environments)

- Determine whether a technology works in a particular environment

- Learn a technology—a language, a set of tools, a set of techniques

- Gain business advantage before final system delivery by enticing customers and the press with an early demonstration of a product

- Train technical support and sales force early

Object-oriented technology retires many of the truisms associated with traditional software development prototyping. From our experience, we have learned that:

- It is NOT bad to throw away an implementation. (Even an implementation that took a lot of time and energy to build can and should be thrown away, when it was not planned to be the production version, its design is incomplete, and especially if it is poorly written.)

- It is NOT the case that only display screens are easy to prototype. (Use of object-oriented techniques for composition and specialization make it possible to prototype rapidly at all levels of a system.)

- It is NOT the case that the language for prototyping is necessarily different from the production programming language (that is, an object-oriented 3GL language can serve both purposes).

- It is NOT the case that the performance of the prototype is irrelevant (performance certainly does matter if the prototype is to be used in target-user studies).

- It is NOT the case that it is acceptable for prototypes to break easily (again, if the prototype is to be used in target-user studies, it is critical to handle errors gracefully).

Illustration 1: Time-Driven Process Model

Although an organization might use several process models, each model should be well defined in the sense that the team knows what it did and, if asked to do so, can repeat its actions. The term "well defined" is not a qualitative statement about how well the process leads you to a successful product. You must be aware of what you are doing so you can evaluate how your actions affect your ability to meet your goals and objectives. And then you can make improvements by changing these actions.

The following case study illustrates our point. The company had an identifiable process model. They introduced object-oriented technology, but felt unsuccessful. Their process wasn't working for them.

The team members of one project we studied told us that they were able to become more productive solely because they changed their development strategies and maxims, with no change in analysis-and-design methods, programming language, or development tools. The project was a large-scale telecommunications network management system. It used a combination of C and C++, running on Unix workstations under the X window manager, and accessing an Informix database. The first two releases of the system were developed in an ad hoc manner. Release 1 was created by doing a prototype to expose the requirements, and then the resulting system was coded. The effort involved up to 30 people for 18 months. Release 2 involved 30 people over a 16-month period. This second system was 140,000 lines of C++ code; the largest change was to replace the database with a file manager.

The process model used in the first two releases was a simple form of the Waterfall Model. That is, activities progressed logically from a complete analysis to a complete design to a complete implementation to system integration and test, never looking back once an activity was presumed complete. Moreover, Release 1 had to continue to work until Release 2 was introduced. The single development team was left to do the sustaining engineering and the new development simultaneously. Insufficient resources meant that defects in the first release were not fixed fast enough to maintain a quality operation, and the new release could not be completed fast enough to satisfy customer expectations.

For the third release, the project manager decided to experiment with a new approach to the product process model, one the team members had devised. Their goal was to create software subsystems that were less dependent on one another, and easier to maintain than the prior, monolithic system. This goal was directly reflected in the structure of the project. Simply stated, their idea was to create small, self-empowered teams, each owning the problem of developing a particular subsystem. The teams competed with one another in a race to "beat the clock." This approach directly addresses the perceived problem of slow response to customer requests. Each team was to resolve all issues surrounding the completion of a given subsystem. Each had full responsibility to create the required features of its subsystem, to obtain and respond to customer feedback, and to get done fast. Each team knew how to design using objects and was responsible for quality assurance.

Twenty people (including ten developers originally on the Release 2 project) were assigned to Release 3. The result was a faster cycle time than experienced with earlier releases. Release 3 subsystems took from 6 to 12 weeks for integration and system test, and used five testers, in comparison with the 6 months and 15 testers needed for Release 2. Release 3 met all of its functionality requirements, satisfied customers, and created a system that is more modular than prior systems. In comparison, earlier releases were considered failures because customers were dissatisfied and the software was hard to change.

The company had been using object-oriented technology for some time. In the case of the third release, the only thing that changed was the process model and the decision to train the team members on appropriate use of the process model. The manager set up a process model and team structure designed to elicit and reward the desired behavior: fast cycle time. And the project succeeded. We are neither criticizing nor praising past or current approaches. What this company's experience demonstrates is that restructuring the process model alone, and training the team to use the new model, can significantly improve software development.

Illustration 2: Customer Information System

It is interesting to see the specific series of prototypes created by successful projects that did a lot of prototyping. Let's start with the project with the most prototypes. This was the first time that an object-oriented approach was going to be used by this group of developers, and by the company. No one in the same industry had reported any experience with objects, and none of the developers had any experience. The technical team chose object-oriented technology because it focused on the model or simulation aspects of system building, allowing the system architecture to be based on the structure of the underlying problem domain. They had learned from prior experience that there would be a long-term maintenance reward if they could design the new system so that the business logic was kept separate from the user interface aspects of individual applications. In particular, the team wanted to design both technical and organizational artifacts of the new system as replaceable components. Technically, their goals were to:

- Reduce application bulk

- Speed development

- Lengthen the lives of applications

- Preserve application descriptions

- Reduce design transformations

- Promote component reuse

Several analysis prototypes were created, and the decision was made to use object-oriented technology. A pilot project was carried out to test an idea for a front-end control program, primarily to see what object-oriented programming was like. This was done on a personal computer in Smalltalk. A paper-based model of message dispatching was devised, and then a prototype was built to check out the model. Although we count this as one prototype, in reality four models were devised and implemented. The last was retained for use in the product.

Another pilot project was carried out to make sure that the team understood the methods they would follow. Specifically, they designed and built a small piece of the system to understand their design techniques and to determine whether they lacked any tools for creating the complete system. They also wanted to understand performance issues. They wrote the prototype code in a language that resembled Smalltalk, but whose output was a standard 3GL.

At this point, the team and its management were comfortable that they could do the actual system using an object-oriented approach. Two more prototypes were built. The first was a prototype design for a task-driven user interface. It tested whether users would be able to learn and interact with the new system in their interrupt-driven offices. The second was a design prototype of the business logic to explore different ways of packaging this logic for reuse.

This project is an example of how to apply prototyping successfully. The team knew it was inexperienced, and specifically used prototypes to learn about the technology. The team knew that its success would be measured on the acceptance of the system by users, and so prototypes served to get early user feedback and commitment.

In fact, the team eventually divided itself into two teams to continue benefiting from pilot projects. One team worked ahead of the other with the intention of discovering potential problems. They could look for method shortcomings or the lack of necessary tools, and they could explore alternative designs, without slowing down work on parts about which the team had already reached agreement.

Illustration 3: CASE Tools

The next case study involves a large telecommunications company, with a variety of software development projects, geographically distributed throughout the world. The company needed to coordinate development and distribution to the dispersed sites. One of two projects we examined developed real-time software. Its goal was to create a new software environment for programming and customizing call-processing services. Ultimately, a CASE tool kit was created for design and simulation of real-time systems. It is now a delivered product, which provides the ability to capture and reuse design components, and graphically to monitor and debug designs. Its selling point is that it makes it possible rapidly to prototype distributed, event-driven systems that use synchronous or asynchronous communication.

This project revealed how a team that had the goal of creating a prototyping environment itself used prototypes. We were disappointed that there was no controlled management approach to the use of prototypes. We counted three prototypes, one to check out routing algorithms, one to determine whether the visualization of the telephony concepts would be adequate, and one to test the application of the tool set. This third prototype could have counted as four prototypes since it involved creating and testing two editors, the state machine, and the user interface look of the desktop.

Unfortunately, the team was never given the time to design an architecture that would support all the functionality of the various prototypes, once this functionality was understood. The team consisted of a few mature designers, who knew the real-time domain, and a lot of younger programmers without real-time design experience. The team was very loosely structured, with everyone doing prototyping and evolving the prototypes. Problems in evolving the prototypes showed up when the team evaluated their success in reducing code redundancy—that is, in getting intraproject reuse. At the time of this evaluation, there were 47 team members, few of whom showed an interest in reuse. After five years of development effort, the product still did not have sufficient functionality to be minimally useful. Adding more functionality was difficult because the system contained redundant ways of carrying out most tasks. The developers were worried that they had paid insufficient attention to reuse—that the system and the development process had not benefited from the decision to use object-oriented technology. Here is a quote from one of the team members which highlights this point:

> Fifty percent increase in code bulk between [versions] 3.2 and 3.3 indicates to me that new functionality is being added but little reuse is occurring. It also means that the design of new functionality is less than optimal. This should come as no surprise since it is accepted in the OO community that "useful abstractions are usually. . . discovered, not invented," to quote Ralph Johnson. To achieve reuse, a period of little code growth (i.e., limiting new functionality) would be required, with time devoted to cleaning up existing functionality. This should result in a sharp decrease in code size along with much improvement in the design. . . .

> In my mind this issue raises an important question: How can the imperatives of successful object-oriented design be accommodated within the philosophy and practice of project management in this organization?

How indeed?!!

Summary

A process model is a collection of maxims, strategies, activities, methods, and tasks that is organized to achieve a set of goals and objectives. There are many process models that come into play when managing an organization. In this chapter, we focused on the product process model or life cycle for producing a software result. To illustrate why there may be multiple process models within a single organization, we distinguished among different kinds of projects: First-of-Its-Kind, Variation-on-a-Theme, Legacy Rewrite, Creating Reusable Assets, and System Enhancements or Maintenance. Having a well-defined product process model means that you know what you did, and, if asked to do so, you could repeat your actions. The example case study of a time-driven process model emphasized the value of being aware of what you are doing so you can improve the processes you are using.

After reviewing the maxims that underlay various process models—Waterfall, Spiral, and Recursive/Parallel—we drew a distinction between the iterative and incremental development strategies. The intent of iterative development is to allow for the controlled reworking of part of a system to remove mistakes or to make improvements based on user feedback. The word "increment," on the other hand, means to add or to increase. While iterative development supports the reworking of portions of the system, incremental development allows systems to be partitioned and developed at different times or rates, and tested and integrated as they are completed.

Two additional software development strategies alter the form of a product process model: prototyping and reusing. A prototype is a preliminary version or model of all or part of a system. We create a prototype to obtain the kind of information that helps us reduce errors that come from uncertainty. Creating prototypes during the early stages of development is a way to increase user involvement and confidence that the right system will be built. To reuse means to make use of something that already exists when creating something new. Reusing occurs throughout a development process. Its purpose is to reduce work effort, remove redundant effort, improve the quality of initial development, and create solutions that are consistent across multiple applications.

We are strong advocates of systematic reuse. Reusable artifacts should be treated as assets that are critical resources for the organization's software development projects. Reuse occurs as a planned engineering activity. You have to plan to create reusable assets, and you have to plan to reuse them. Given the different activities that reuse producers and consumers have to carry out, we advocate that a reuse producer group be structured as separate but interrelated with the consumer groups.

Effective use of object-oriented technology involves a judicious mixture of strategies for iterative development, incremental development, reusing, and prototyping, selected according to the type of product project. Case study illustrations described how different projects combined these strategies.

Additional Reading About Process Models and Prototyping

Connell, J. and Shafer, L., *Structured Rapid Prototyping*, Yourdon Press: Englewood Cliffs, New Jersey, 1989.

Connell and Shafer discuss a full software development process for rapid prototyping. They provide compelling arguments that a process model that incorporates prototyping is effective for developing many types of solutions. Although the book is written from a 4GL perspective, the fundamental prototyping concepts apply equally well to object-oriented technology.

DeGrace, P. and Stahl, L. H., *Wicked Problems, Righteous Solutions: A Catalogue of Modern Software Engineering Paradigms*, Yourdon Press: Englewood Cliffs, New Jersey, 1990.

DeGrace and Stahl are particularly interested in process models that can be used to solve wicked problems. By definition, these problems are not well formulated. They can be fully understood only after they are solved. The authors point out how wicked problems may be addressed by several process models: Waterfall, Whirlpool, Incremental and Spiral, Prototyping, All-at-Once, Video, and Cleanroom Models.

Smith, M. F., *Software Prototyping: Adoption, Practice and Management*, McGraw-Hill: London, 1991.

The Smith book also discusses a prototyping approach to software development. Whereas Connell and Shafer provide a detailed development process, Smith provides more background motivation and addresses a wider range of topics nourished by prototyping. Many parts of this book are little more than bulleted lists of ideas. However, these lists can be mined for a wealth of insight.

CHAPTER 6

Select a Product Process Model

Yᴏu have to do a project, and you need to choose a process for carrying out that project which takes into account your decision to use object-oriented technology. In Chapter 5, we recommend general strategies for organizing your work effort—iterative and incremental development, prototyping, and consuming reusable assets. There are a number of other strategies you should consider that focus on particular kinds of activities. Specifically, you should select a strategy for decomposing work to be developed incrementally or in parallel (partitioning), a strategy for combining or managing changes to work whether carried out incrementally or in parallel (integration), a strategy for documenting, and a strategy for quality assurance. You organize your decisions for selecting a product process model using the next project management decision framework.

Additional Strategies for Developing with Objects

Partitioning

If you are going to see the benefits of object-oriented technology, then you have to create a work style that promotes identifying and working on well-defined and manageable system components—components that you can develop and release incrementally, components that suggest subteam structures that encourage parallel work, and components that are easier to associate with reuse opportunities. Thus a critical development strategy is how you partition your work effort, where your rationale for partitioning can focus on any one of these three objectives.

A *partition* is a set of capabilities that identifies the boundaries of a subproblem. The choice of partitions naturally influences the way the project will be managed. Managers coordinate the development of a set of partitions, planning resources for individual partitions, setting milestone dates, facilitating re-partitioning efforts, and assuring the quality of each partition. The partitions might be selected to match project resources. Where resources are limited, the partitions can be selected to match a reasonable division of effort to produce acceptable incremental releases.

To base development on partitioning, a project manager must:

- Make sure that the team members understand the objectives in working on a partition—that they understand the business goals and objectives supported by the partition, and how the development of a partition leads to meeting the objectives of the project as a whole.

- Obtain agreement on the capabilities and the external interfaces of partitions.

- Set up a communication channel for (re)negotiating capabilities and external interface specifications.

- Set up regular reviews.

Reviews are important because work is going on in parallel, and subteams that depend on one another have to keep abreast of individual partition results and issues. Communication can take the form of regular meetings in which progress and any proposed changes are reviewed. Frequency of the meetings depends on the overall project schedule. In addition, electronic forms of communication can keep the groups up to date on change proposals, to avoid surprises.

The choice of partition also influences how the system is developed. For purposes of analysis, partitioning subdivides the problem description into related sets of user requirements. For purposes of design, partitioning defines the subsystems of the system architecture. Analysis partitions are not necessarily subsystems. A subsystem is a design artifact used to describe a coordinated set of objects that work together to provide a set of services.[1] The collection of subsystems and how they relate defines the architecture of the system. Analysis partitions are analysis artifacts whose realization at design time may span one or more subsystems. To understand the difference better, imagine that the system must support transactions that query a database and print results. Transactions that perform related queries are classified into the same analysis partition, whereas each transaction at design time may require the services of one or more subsystems (e.g., database and printing subsystems).

During analysis, you define partitions in terms of desired system capabilities. A goal of analysis is to elaborate on these capabilities, and possibly decide to move capa-

---

[1] That is, from the object point of view, a subsystem is an embeddable application.

bilities from one partition to another. Design partitions are more formally defined in terms of the specifications of their external interfaces. One design partition relies on another by assuming that the external interface will be supported. These interfaces represent contracts, which the teams working on the partitions must either fulfill or negotiate to have changed. Any team making use of another team's results can assume that the contract will be fulfilled. A team can create stubs, code that doesn't do anything except represent the interface of the yet-to-be-delivered solutions of other teams. In this way, one team can proceed with its work, relying on future deliveries from the other teams to replace the stubs.

You can take either a breadth-first or depth-first approach to partitioning. The breadth-first approach, as illustrated in Fig. 6.1, starts with a high-level analysis. It is most often associated with an enterprise-wide or domain analysis. You do an overall analysis of the whole problem, and then create partitions for development purposes. The partitions are fully developed (designed, implemented, and tested) in parallel, depending on available resources.

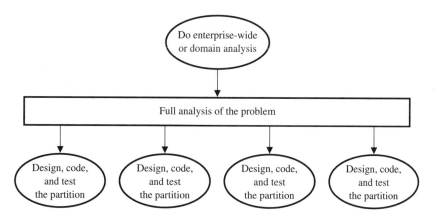

Figure 6.1   Breadth-First Partitioning

The enterprise-wide or domain-analysis partitioning is often associated with efforts to identify reusable assets before one or more systems are developed.

A variant of the breadth-first approach lets you partition the problem, and do an analysis of each partition in parallel. The first partitioning will be an approximation because, as you proceed with your work, carrying out the detailed requirements analyses, the boundaries may need to be realigned. When all analyses are completed, they are combined into a single set of analysis artifacts. Then the problem is repartitioned for development based on this unified analysis. This approach is illustrated in Fig. 6.2.

A depth-first approach (Fig. 6.3) partitions the problem and takes each partition all the way from analysis to implementation and testing. You can arrive at the partitioning in a number of ways:

■ Understand the pristine life cycle of the proposed system. Most business situations have a natural time-ordered sequence of activities (life cycle). In manufacturing, this might be the sequence for building a physical product, such as a car or a motor. In retail, this might be the sequence for acquiring an item of inventory, making it available for sale, and selling it. Pristine means pure; the life cycle

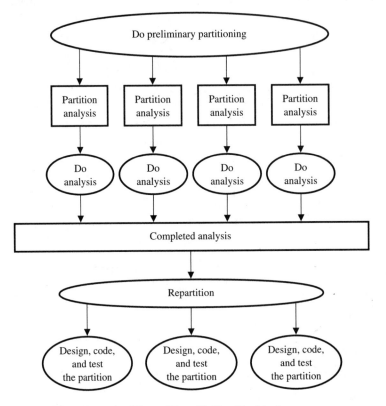

Figure 6.2   Alternative View of Breadth-First Partitioning

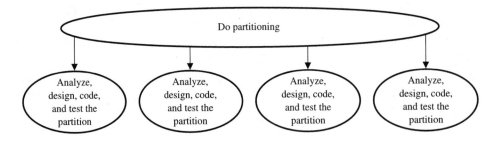

Figure 6.3   Depth-First Partitioning

is not adulterated by the details of scaling up to handling more than one business element (physical product, inventory item, and so on) at a time.

- Use an existing system model (analysis pattern) to determine the major clusters of behavior.

- Use past experience. You have built such a system before, so you know the basic partitions.

- Guess the high-level tasks. If you have no other idea, make something up that will help you better understand the problem. Prototyping might be a useful technique to explore possible divisions.

In setting your analysis strategy, keep in mind the following maxims:

> **Think before you act.** When in doubt, don't code, analyze.
>
> **Prototype for clarity.** Look for analysis prototyping opportunities to help clarify requirements.
>
> **Just get started.** Be willing to be wrong in early partitioning.

Process Model

The third maxim encourages you to use an iterative development style, because detailed analysis of the partitions will suggest ways in which you should rework the higher-level partitioning.

Integrating and Managing Changes

You need not wait until the work on all partitions has been completed to begin integration (as illustrated in Fig. 6.4). Independent of how you partition, as soon as a partition has been completed, it should be integrated with other completed partitions, and released for use by teams still developing other partitions. Projects successful with object-oriented technology never leave completed work sitting on a shelf waiting for a monolithic integration.

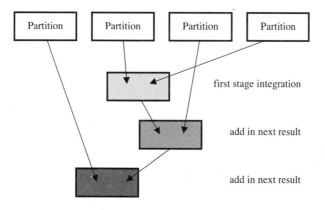

Figure 6.4   Incremental Integration of Partition Results

As each partition is completed, it is delivered to the customers. Most likely a "customer" is some other partition that is still under development, one that created stubs for the expected partition capabilities. Integration requires a test to make sure that the solution for a partition fulfills its contract with its target customers and does not create unexpected conflicts in the way partitions interact when brought together (in particular, performance degradation or space usage). Introduce capabilities gradually; the less you understand, the more important it is to do so.

Most projects using object-oriented technology try to partition their effort so that tangible results can be released every two or three months. These partitions are integrated with the work of other subteams or customers who have agreed to receive and give feedback on preliminary results. Incremental integration within the project team should take place frequently. Indeed, a goal of most mature developers is to remain synchronized with other developers, able to integrate changes continuously. Incremental integration is possible where an object or collection of objects forms a clear boundary for work assignment, and the subteams fulfill the contracted relationships among the partitions. Both a process and support tools are needed to manage rapid change, but the good news is that objects provide enabling technology.

Documenting

Decide early in the development process on the kind of documentation you want to produce. This decision will affect your choice of work environment, tools, and criteria for transitioning between development activities. Can you say that an activity is complete if the documentation is not? Here are some of the documentation-related decisions you might make:

- When you will create documents

- How you will communicate requirements to designers

- How you will capture consistent user interaction guidelines

- The form in which you will express designs

- Whether and how you will document the interface agreements when you partition

- Whether and how there will be on-line user documentation

- How you will review documents for accuracy

- Whether and how the product process model will be documented

- How you will document decisions

The introduction of object-oriented technology does not change the need for documentation. However, because of the extensibility afforded by the technology, a new level of documentation is required to guide customization. Moreover, the fact that objects can closely map the real-world situation (with vocabulary common to the real world) leads us to a new goal for documentation, indeed for implementation—that a business manager can look at the specification of the external interfaces and relationships among the objects in the system, and understand the model these objects represent.

Document the external interfaces and relationships of the objects in the system. The choice of granularity for presenting the various objects depends on the target reader. Interfaces to applications belong in the user manual. Interfaces to frameworks and other reusable components provided in a development environment belong in the developer's (or specializer's) manual. And interfaces for all objects belong in the maintainer's and reuser's manual. Developers, maintainers, and reusers also need details about the ways one system component relies on or delegates effort to another component, including components that may not otherwise be exposed. Plauger, in [Plauger 1993], implies an interesting way to measure the quality of documentation. In a discussion of software copyright and patent law, he notes that it is legal to reengineer a system to figure out what the system does when this information cannot be understood in any other way. He suggests that a measure of a well-designed system, and consequently its documentation, is that reengineering is not required to borrow the system's ideas.

Object-oriented technology has inspired some new ideas relating to documentation. First, new notations have been invented for capturing and communicating the salient elements of an analysis and design involving objects (for example, Booch Notation [Booch 1994] and OMT [Rumbaugh *et al.* 1991]). Second, emergence of domain frameworks encouraged researchers to revisit Christopher Alexander's foundational work on the architecture of buildings [Alexander, Ishikawa, and Silverstein 1977]. Alexander's notion of design patterns is being adopted by researchers such as Johnson [Johnson 1992] as a way to document object models that can be reused across projects. Johnson recommends that patterns be used to document many of the design details embodied in a framework, and thus assist the programmer in reusing the framework without a detailed understanding of the implementation.

Third, increased expectations about on-line documentation have led to some ideas for applying Donald Knuth's concept of "literate programming" [Knuth 1992]. Trygve Reenskaug and his colleagues [Reenskaug and Skaar 1989] have been working on a multimedia document production system, which incorporates object relationships as documentation elements and is capable of generating executable Smalltalk code. In other words, their approach centers the process model on the development of documentation for analysis and design, with executable code as the side effect rather than the central focus. The approach has incorporated formal ideas about analysis and design, embodied in an analysis-and-design method called ORASS (Object-Oriented Role Analysis,

Synthesis, and Structuring) [Reenskaug *et al.* 1992]. A similar use of literate programming for C++ has been explored by M. S. Hyman [Hyman 1990].

Quality Assurance Strategies When Developing with Objects

Quality is a catchall term that refers to external product attributes, such as reliability, maintainability, understandability, usability, correctness, system safety assurance, and so on. It also refers to the attributes of the processes and resources used to create and support the product.

Some development managers link product quality to the quality of the development process. This leads to an interpretation of quality as conformance to standard processes. These standards may simply be code-style guidelines, or they may be detailed procedures for the development process. Managers often claim that the way they will obtain quality is by following some standard, as though consistent use of a documented process or method alone will produce a quality product. Standards can provide a framework for producing quality software; they do not guarantee results. A quality process combined with quality individuals produces quality results.

There are a number of questions to consider in determining your approach to quality assurance, such as:

- When will you assess the quality of your products, processes, and resources?

- How will you uncover defects?

- How will you test object implementations?

- How will you record quality assurance results?

How Quality Relates to Other Development Strategies

The choice of process model strategies associated with object-oriented technology—iterative and incremental development, prototyping, and consuming reusable objects—influences the quality assurance strategy.

The iterative development strategy is a plan to rework a system partition, improving the partition's quality with each iteration. You expect all but the last iteration to have quality issues. When you agree on a quality plan for a partition, you can set your sights on the final outcome and examine the current iteration for any deviations from plan, or you can establish quality objectives specific to each iteration. Because you expect significant changes from iteration to iteration, you do not want to lock in the test suites too early.

The incremental development strategy partitions a system into parts that are developed and released separately, over time. You need to assure the quality of the artifacts that make up a release. Incremental development suggests that you check quality more often, and possibly at a more detailed level. With each release you have an opportunity to check both the part of the product that was created, and how these parts were created, giving you the possibility of improving the process and resources as you enter into developing the next increment. Incremental integration gives you the chance for more frequent checks on how the parts fit together. With incremental development, the goal is to complete a part of the product, anticipating additional capability in the next increment. This development strategy makes it worthwhile to develop regression test suites for each part as the part is developed. For additional information on fitting testing in with incremental development see [McGregor 1994].

Prototyping is both a development strategy to reduce risk, and a quality assurance technique to uncover misunderstandings and to get answers to development questions. You always evaluate the prototype to determine whether you obtained the information you were seeking from it. As always, when following a process—here, prototyping—you are interested in how well you are carrying out the process, and some process evaluation is appropriate. Whether you test the quality of the implementation of the prototype, however, depends on the purpose of the prototype. For example, the goal of an analysis prototype is to understand better the customer's problem. It should not be necessary to provide complete code testing of such a prototype. The goal of a design prototype is to explore architectural ideas; its code may not survive the transition to product.

Where a series of prototypes is developed, partial results may survive from one prototype to the next. In the interest of early quality assurance, it may be preferable to test these results prior to continued reuse. Often you reach a point where you need to have customers use the prototype over a long period of time, even to do production work. The prototype stops being an unsupported sample and starts to be a supported experiment. More formal implementation testing of the prototype may make sense. The decision to test is based on a determination of the risk of not testing, following the recommendations of [Hetzel 1988].

Two questions about quality assurance must be answered when the process model includes a strategy for reusing: What do you have to examine when you reuse an artifact, and what do you have to examine when you change a reused artifact? Assuming that the artifact has passed independent quality assurance, and you use the artifact as it is delivered, you should expect only to look at your use of the artifact, not at the artifact itself. If you have to change the artifact, then there are a number of possible scenarios for quality assurance, which we discuss in a subsequent section.

Uncovering Defects During Development

The number of defects in a product, process, or resource is a measure of quality. A *defect* is any deviation from desired outcome—an imperfection, a difference between desired and observed results. It can be something in a software development artifact that would not exist if the development process were perfect—if no developer errors were committed and no requirements omitted.

Defects can be introduced during any software development activity. Analysis defects occur when requirements are either not captured, or are captured improperly. Design defects occur when quality objectives (performance, reliability, and so on) of the project are not met. Typical causes are poor architecture or algorithm design. Code defects include syntactic and semantic errors. Documentation defects include failing to document at all, or inaccurately documenting a capability or spelling errors.

There are a number of techniques that can be used to uncover defects. Table 6.1 shows our view of how to rate the detection potential of several techniques in uncovering defects in analysis, design, code, and documents. Prototyping, as discussed in Chapter 5, is an excellent way of uncovering defects during analysis and design. However, it is a poor way of detecting code defects. *Inspections* apply statistical process control techniques to evaluate documents resulting from all development activities. These techniques not only identify defects, but also identify software process improvements to prevent the occurrence of defects in future artifacts. When rigorously applied, inspections have proved to be an excellent way of uncovering analysis, design, and documentation defects, and are a good way to uncover code defects [Gilb and Graham 1993]. Reviews and walkthroughs are far less structured than inspections and have proved to be only a fair way of uncovering defects.

Testing is a fair way to identify defects in the analysis, design, and documentation results. It is an excellent way to detect defects in the code. Only testing and prototyping can identify defects that occur when a system is executing.

Correctness proofs use mathematical formalisms to establish the correctness (lack of defects) in software artifacts. Formal methods are a good way to uncover defects during analysis and design. However, they are currently difficult to apply and are limited to semantic defects. A correctness proof of code is an excellent way to know that the code will solve the proper problem. However, proving the correctness of large amounts of code is itself a difficult problem.

Table 6.1 Defect Detection Potential of Several Techniques

	Analysis Defects	Design Defects	Code Defects	Documentation Defects
Prototyping	Excellent	Excellent	Poor	Not Applicable
Inspections	Excellent	Excellent	Good	Excellent
Reviews and Walkthroughs	Fair	Fair	Fair	Good
Testing	Fair	Fair	Excellent	Not Applicable
Correctness Proofs	Good	Good	Good	Not Applicable

Testing Object Implementations

Inspections, reviews, and walkthroughs are not much different when your work is based on object-oriented technology. The goals and procedures remain the same, although the details of what you look for may change. In the following discussion, we use the term "member function" when referring to the code implementation for a message. For example, you can look to see whether:

- All public messages are commented correctly

- Messages received but not sent are documented as to intended use

- Any reimplementation of an inherited member function does not simply duplicate the implementation in the superclass

- All subclasses conform to the expectations of the superclasses for providing deferred functionality

- Subclasses do not implement inherited messages for the purpose of blocking functionality

- No superfluous redundancies exist

- All redundancies are documented as to why they are required

- All public functions are documented with an example of use

Many traditional forms of testing apply to systems built with object-oriented technology, such as:

- System test cases, implemented in the form of software uses of the system (usually referred to as ad hoc tests)

- Coverage analysis, to determine which parts of the system have been exercised sufficiently (branch analysis, state condition analysis)

- Capture and playback, replaying recordings of scripts of human use of a user interface

- Code reading and other forms of walkthrough

Applying these four approaches provides the kind of confidence you want before shipping a software product. Tom Love documents a testing case study in his book on lessons learned from using object-oriented technology [Love 1993]. Using these four approaches in combination, a team that developed a class library for Objective C reported the following:

- Eighty percent of the product code was proclaimed to be error-free based on finding and fixing errors with ad hoc test cases and user interface scripts, and using coverage analysis to determine which parts of the system had been sufficiently exercised.

- Thirteen percent of the software went through a code reading by team members.

- Seven percent was given special attention, either additional test cases or team reviews.

The team found 40 percent of the errors using ad hoc test cases, 40 percent by replaying scripts of the human user interface, and 20 percent by using code reading and sheer chance. In the first year of shipping the product, customers found only five errors in 30,000 lines of source code, in contrast to an industry average of ten errors per 1,000 lines.

We have chosen to organize the discussion of testing in a way that is consistent with our description of the structure of systems built using object-oriented technology as discussed in Chapter 3.

Member functions. Traditional black-box testing should be used to assure that the member function behaves as specified. Traditional white-box code testing is also appropriate, with the caveat that, although useful, test coverage analysis is not as significant. Most member functions tend to be very small. Moreover, the complexity of traditional case statements is relegated to message dispatching in object-oriented systems. Consequently, there are far fewer branches to white-box test. For those systems in which pre- and postconditions can be specified, you have to ensure that, when the preconditions are valid, the member function guarantees the expected postconditions.

Classes. Member functions are the natural smallest unit for testing. In practice, however, they are not comparable to the functions of traditional unit testing, where it is expected that functions can be individually tested. Being in the same class means that the member functions have a solidarity—they belong together and should therefore be tested together, as a unit.

Except for simple accessing member functions that just store or return an attribute's stored or computed value (where the computation does not depend on information from other objects), implementations require the services of other member functions. Testing a member function requires that these other member functions be present. The usual way to create a test harness is to replicate existing implementations, many of which are found in the same class as the member function to be tested. But if the class as a whole is part of the test context, most of the replication is not necessary. Hence the class turns out to be a better choice for unit testing.

Following a structure-based approach to class testing, you isolate and test those member functions that do not rely on any other member functions. You then test those that rely only on other member functions found in the same class. And then you branch out to test member functions that rely on those in other classes. Of course, you must have tested the member functions of those classes first. Then you can treat them as black boxes, testing only that a member function uses the already tested services correctly. It will help if you create a member-function dependency graph to define the order for testing.

State-based testing is also used for classes. This approach assumes that each object can be defined with a finite number of states, that there are a finite number of transitions between states, and that each state is uniquely identifiable through a set of member functions. Assuming all states can be reached from a given set of initial states, it should be possible to construct test cases that exercise an object into and out of all states. A particular state-based approach can be found in [McGregor 1994].

Behaviors defined for a class specify the behaviors of an instance of the class, and in some languages, the behavior of the class itself. You have to test both. You create one or more instances of the class and test the instance behaviors; you use the class itself to test the class behaviors (somewhat circular but obvious, a critical test of class behavior is the ability to create instances).

Class hierarchies. A class's complete specification is distributed in a hierarchy (defined with single or multiple inheritance). The two principal testing challenges when testing class hierarchies are polymorphism and inheritance.

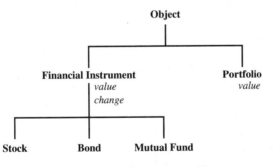

Figure 6.5   Example Business Domain Classes

Polymorphism removes case-statements from the code, making coverage analysis more complicated. For example, Fig. 6.5 shows simple business domain classes. There is a hierarchy of financial investment classes, each of which can respond to the messages *value* to determine the market value of the investment, and *change* to determine the gain or loss in the investment. There is also a Portfolio class, whose instances hold on to a collection of different types of Financial Investments. The Portfolio has a behavior for computing its value that adds up the market values of each financial instrument in the portfolio. In an object-oriented implementation, this computation is done by sending the message *value* to each financial instrument. In a traditional implementation, this is done with a case statement that tests for each type of financial instrument and calls a uniquely named function (such as *bondValue*) to compute the type's market value. In this case, traditional coverage analysis will ensure that all specialized market value functions are executed. However, in the object-oriented case, test cases have to ensure that all possible receivers (here, different financial instruments) are covered when testing a message statement. Languages that support type checking at compile time, of course, make this problem easier.

With inheritance, testing questions are: What has to be tested when a new class (subclass) shares the description of a prior class (superclass)? What aspects of a subclass have to be tested when the superclass is changed? In the following, we provide a summary of the kinds of testing to consider.

> *Scenario: Add a subclass that augments the superclass.* If the subclass only adds new capability, and in no way touches the implementation of the superclass, then you only have to test the subclass.

> *Scenario: Add a subclass that reimplements (overrides) superclass behavior.* You are obligated to retest all client code that sends the corresponding message to an object that might be an instance of the new subclass. (We say "might" because, in systems that support dynamic binding, you cannot be certain of the class of the receiver.)

> *Scenario: Create a concrete subclass that specializes an abstract superclass.* In some systems, a superclass represents an abstract object that specifies which member functions a concrete subclass must implement. Test to make sure that all responsibilities assigned to the subclass are implemented. Retest all client code that sends the corresponding messages to an object that might be an instance of the new subclass. Retest any superclass methods whose implementation depends on a concrete subclass implementation.

> *Scenario: Change the implementation of a member function in the superclass.* If every use of the member function relies solely on its public interface, then you only have to test that the new member function fulfills its interface requirements. If any member function within the superclass itself has knowledge of the prior implementation, then it must be tested. In some systems, it is possible that subclasses have access to the implementation details of a superclass as well. These would have to be tested. Alternatively, you could design systems—superclasses and subclasses—without such knowledge of implementation details. In effect, you make subclasses access implementation through public interfaces.

> *Scenario: Add a variable to a superclass.* As long as all you have done is add a variable, and you trust the compiler to recompile the necessary class descriptions correctly, then you just have to test the use of the new variable within the class. Otherwise, one of the other scenarios applies.

Scenario: Remove a member function from a superclass. The test must assure that no system part relies on the deleted member function. In languages where you must have a declaration in the superclass to provide a redefinition in a sub-class, simple deletion may be disallowed. A subclass implementation (or other client) might defer part of its implementation to a member function provided in the superclass. Deleting the member function breaks the subclass.

Abstract versus concrete classes pose an additional testing challenge. Abstract classes capture common specifications for a set of related classes. Typically we cannot create instances of abstract classes because one or more behaviors must be implemented by a subclass. For example, Fig. 6.5 illustrates a financial-instruments hierarchy whose root is the class Financial Instrument, with subclasses Stock, Bond, and Mutual Fund. Financial Instrument is an abstract class in that it does not specify how to compute *value* and *change*. An appropriate way to test the implementation defined for class Financial Instrument is to create and test an instance of one of its concrete subclasses. Another possible testing approach is to create a default implementation for each unimplemented behavior in the superclass. For example, you might define class Financial Instrument's *value* and *change* behaviors to return random numbers within an acceptable range. If you are able to define default testing behaviors for all such unimplemented behaviors in an abstract class, you will then be able to instantiate the "abstract" class and test its instance.

Applications or subsystems. An application or subsystem is a collection of interacting objects. You test the specifications for the objects independently, and then you test how the objects work together. When the objects are brought together, you may uncover errors due to the absence of a message-send (such as one needed to set up a precondition), or the absence of a receiver for a message that is sent. Essentially, you have to test the pathways of message-sends that implement all the application's behaviors [Jorgensen and Erickson 1994]. In addition to testing the sequences of member function executions linked by messages, you have to test all sequences invoked by any legal event. These tests are essentially those associated with integration testing. You have to test from the point of view of behavioral interactions, rather than structural relationships. These behavior-oriented test cases should come from the use scenarios constructed during analysis (for more detail on use scenarios, see Chapter 15). In addition, traditional testing of the graphical user interface, if any, is needed and applies to object-oriented systems.

Frameworks and components. Testing frameworks starts with testing classes and class hierarchies. The added challenge in testing a framework is evaluating whether it can be specialized to create the kinds of applications for which it was designed. The framework itself is testable only if one or more specializations are created, which are then tested as you would test completed applications. Preferably, any specializations would be created using the components provided with the framework. If there is a default version for the framework, then it can be tested instead.

Recording Defects

Grady and Caswell [Grady and Caswell 1987] studied defect measures across projects at Hewlett-Packard and discovered that defect counts reported by different projects varied by a factor of 45 because of differences in the way defects were defined and recorded. To avoid this problem, we provide definitions and templates to record incident, defect, and change information in a standard way. We recommend that you use these templates, which work just as well for projects that use object-oriented technology as for those that do not. Note that Humphrey also offers suggestions on logging forms [Humphrey 1995].

Incidents. An *incident* is an undesirable or unexpected result that is detected during product development or in the field. You can capture information about an incident using the template shown in Table 6.2. Scales for Severity, Priority, and Status have to be defined by the organization.

Table 6.2   Template for Recording an Incident

Aspect	Description
Identification	A unique number or other unique identifier
Description	Description of what happened, when and how it happened
Originator	Name of person or organization reporting the incident
Product Descriptor	Specific aspect of the product referenced by the incident
Configuration	Hardware and software configuration in which incident took place
Attachments	Additional information that may help reproduce the incident, including software that recreates the problem
Record Date	Date that the incident was recorded
Severity	Severity from the originator's perspective
Priority	Urgency from the originator's perspective
Responder	Persons assigned to handle the incident
Status	Current status of the incident
Cause	Why the incident occurred (known after the incident is closed)
Resolution	How the incident was handled if incident is closed
Resolution Date	Date that the incident was resolved and communicated to Originator
Comments	General comments that capture the discussion of possible causes and solutions
Incident References	References to other incidents that are similar to this incident

Table 6.3 Template for Recording a Defect

Aspect	Description
Identification	A unique number or other unique identifier
Reference	Reference to the incident report(s) that uncovered the defect
Originator	Developer who created the defect report
Product Descriptor	Which part of the product is affected
Development Activity	Development activity during which the defect was introduced into the product
Cause	Why the defect occurred
Priority	Urgency for fixing the defect from the perspective of the development organization
Responder	Persons assigned to handle the defect
Status	Current status of the defect
Changes	References to change reports that describe how the defect was repaired
Attachments	Additional information provided by the Originator that may help describe the defect (may be useful for regression testing)
Comment	General comments reporting the handling of the defect

Defects. A defect is recorded when there is an incident report whose resolution requires engineering effort. We recommend the use of the template shown in Table 6.3 to capture information related to a defect.

Changes. Whenever you create a defect report, one or more changes may be made to remove the defect. Each organization must define the guidelines for establishing when a modification to a product, process, or resource constitutes a change. For each change, we recommend the use of the change template shown in Table 6.4. It is necessary to record the affected artifact or artifacts and determine whether changes have a Reuse Implication. In addition to keeping track of the percentage of reused assets that are faulty, you may also need to notify the reuse team when you change a reused asset.

Here is an example classification for the Type of Change entry in the Change Template, tailored to object-oriented technology:

Change in Interface

Change in Implementation

Change to Base class (superclass)

Change to Derived class (subclass)

Table 6.4 Template for Recording a Change in a Deliverable

Aspect	Description
Identification	A unique number or other unique identifier
Description	Description of the required change
Product Descriptor	Which aspect of software development product has been changed
Reuse Implication	Comment on whether and how a reused asset was modified
Type of Change	Classification of the change that was applied to a system artifact
Change Date	Date when the change was introduced into the product
Responder	Persons responsible for making the change
Cost	Cost to implement the change (in staff hours)
Status	Status of the change, such as tested, reviewed, done, rejected
Reference to Fix	Reference to system components, versions, or files that create the changes
Dependencies	Reference to other needed changes, or installation requirements when integrating the change
Comment	General comments reporting the handling of the change
References	Reference to the defects repaired by the change
Disposition	What was done and why

Making a change to the system implies that an activity is scheduled to create, test, and review the change. The Cost entry is the number of staff hours necessary to complete the change. A change may involve code, a change to a model, a change to a document, and so on. Reference to Fix tells where these new artifacts can be found. Making one change might be contingent upon making other changes or executing various installation procedures. Dependencies refers to these requirements.

Recording the defects, linking them to incidents and product changes, gives you data that will be important in assessing your current ability to produce products, using existing processes and resources. This data is useful both for producing a quality product and for planning future improvement projects.

Framework for Selecting a Product Process Model

Selecting a new product process model is a process-improvement project, as illustrated in Fig. 6.6.

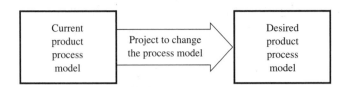

Figure 6.6   Process-Improvement Project to Change the Product
Development Process Model

The principle underlying the decision framework for selecting a product process model describes the fundamental form that your process model should take when object-oriented technology is employed. This principle is based on the idea of incremental work effort.

Framework Principle. Incremental decision making, development, testing, and integration produce effective project results.

Incremental work effort should produce incremental results so that you can show progress constantly. Incremental integration and delivery let you obtain continual feedback from users on both functionality and quality. Incremental delivery means you spend less time getting next-step products to the market. The framework goal focuses on selecting the process model, and the steps remind you of what to do.

Framework Goal. Select project activities, their ordering and methods, according to project goals and objectives and the guidelines of the organization.

- Agree on maxims

- Verify software development goals and objectives

- Select project strategies, activities, and their ordering

- Select methods for each project activity

*Product
Process
Model*

Agree on Maxims

Maxims are personal. They come from the battle scars carried by experienced team members. Agreeing on the maxims is the team's opportunity to draw on the wealth of knowledge they have as to what works and what does not work. The choice of maxims helps direct the choice of product process model. We recommend that you consider the following maxims:

Understand the (sub)problem to be solved and the risks involved before you act.

All activities should be selected so as to meet agreed-upon problem goals and objectives.

*KandA
Battle Scars*

You have better control of the development process if you maintain traceability—that is, if you are always in a position to answer these questions: Why have we obtained this result? If I make this change, what is affected?

You can obtain more feedback if you develop incremental results by dividing the problem into smaller problems (partitions) that can be solved by smaller teams.

You can get done faster if you work on as many partitions as possible in parallel.

You can enhance quality if you integrate partition solutions as early as possible.

You can reduce the risks in a development process by judicious use of prototyping in all activities.

You can lower development time and costs, and improve quality, if you reuse prior work whenever appropriate.

Verify Software Development Goals and Objectives

Your choice of process model relies heavily on your goals and objectives. Make sure you know what kind of project you are carrying out. Are you building an application or a reusable asset? Are you expecting to change your processes or resources as a result of this project?

All of the team members should know and understand the goals and objectives. Have these goals and objectives been stated as simply as possible? Does everyone agree that the problem statement is the right one to attack, or should the problem be restated or divided into simpler problems?

Once the goals and objectives have been stated, ask the team members whether they think that a solution is already implied. Make sure that the solutions they have in mind are in fact solutions to the problem. The answers lend insight into the team's understanding of the problem. Perhaps discussion alone is insufficient—some actual results may be needed to help the team members understand what needs to be done. An initial, high-level analysis might be appropriate. In complex situations, an initial analysis is generally productive. It clarifies the scope of the work, brings up many misunderstandings early, helps identify an initial partitioning, and lends confidence that the team is properly focused.

Select Project Strategies, Activities, and Their Ordering

The purpose of this step is to choose the activities of your process model. Depending on the kind of project, you are going to do one or more of the following activities: planning, analysis, design, implementation, integration, testing, documentation, delivering results, and managing changes. You have to figure out how these activities fit together—the order in which they will be carried out and the criteria you will use to decide when to transition from one activity to another. Select your process model activities and ordering based on the general strategies of iterative and incremental development, prototyping, and consuming reusable assets, and the specific strategies we describe in this chapter for partitioning, integration, documentation, and quality assurance.

Selecting the process model activities is easiest when you have done a project like this before, and you were successful. You reuse the process model. You might also be able to skip some activities because you can reuse results from prior projects. Many developers say that they never do analysis, just design. The design-only approach is often used in very technical domains where understanding of the problem comes from many years of working on similar projects. The problem is understood; the new situation just introduces different constraints demanding a new design. Perhaps the requirements are known because it is a Variation-on-a-Theme project—analysis and initial design are known, and you just need to add a new visual widget, improve the performance, or connect to a new database.

Select Methods for Each Activity

Let's suppose, however, that the project is the first project of its kind in your organization. It is big. It is complex. What do you do? You have chosen your strategies. Now you have to choose the tactics with which you will do analysis and design, how you will integrate results, what roles prototyping and reusing will play, how you will maintain quality, and the kind of documentation you will produce.

Although we provide some examples of tactics, notably in the case study illustrations, for the most part this book maintains a higher level of discourse. There are a number of books available that focus on how to carry out specific activities that are referenced in the chapter sections on additional reading.

Case Study Results
Product Process Models

The case study project leaders were all asked what process model they used. Table 6.5 contains a summary of their responses. The character *s* indicates a successful project, *u* unsuccessful, and *o* ongoing. There is no particular indication in this summary that one process model works better or worse than another. There is one reference to a model we have not discussed, the Fountain Model [Henderson-Sellers and Edwards 1990]. This model presents the notion of clusters of classes that progress through different parts of the life cycle at different times. Among the people we interviewed, this model made it hard to get an aggregate measure of progress. Another reference in the table is to a special model devised by a consultant.

Table 6.5 Process Models Used by the Case Studies

Projects	Status	Product Process Model
4	s	close to Spiral Model, one time called "Tornado" as a variation on iterative and another time called a Spiral, which had a Fountain within Spiral phases
1	s	incremental product releases
2	o	incremental product releases
4	s	Waterfall Model
1	o	Waterfall Model
7	s	incremental prototyping until result was declared a product, sometimes called "rapid interactive prototyping" and one time called "protocycling"
6	o	incremental prototyping
2	u	incremental prototyping
5	s	none
4	o	none
2	s	in-house, one called time-based competition and reported on in Chapter 5, another close to Spiral
1	s	special invention

Example Partitions

The case studies provide examples of a number of interesting high-level partitions. One case study company was developing a new systems infrastructure that supported its objectives in collecting data on land lease management. This new system was written in the Smalltalk-80 language, executing on multiple workstations (PCs and Unix), and making use of both relational and object-oriented databases. The full system included an image-processing system for scanning, storing, and retrieving lease documents. At the outset of the project, based on the pristine life cycle of acquiring and managing rights to land from which raw materials are obtained, the following partitions were identified:

Prospect for rights acquisition

Acquire rights and obligations

Manage rights and obligations

Manage gas and gas products

Dispose of rights and obligations

Support and comply with regulations

Another approach to partitioning is illustrated by projects that build a user framework and a set of tools that work within the framework. The first example is from a CASE vendor. The user framework consists of an interface to a relational database, visual widgetry, and common user services. Within the framework, there are a number of editors. The team, in developing the editors, identified a set of services shared by all editors, as well as the need for a screen painter. The partitions identified were:

User framework

Screen or window painter

Services common to all editors

Document editor

Data model editor

Data flow diagram editor

A similar project targeted a set of tools for modeling information to be stored in relational databases. The partitions were:

Database framework (interface to storage)

Mainframe-to-client-workstation conversion service

Data modeler tool

Data dictionary designer tool

Metadata query tool

The interest in client/server architectures motivates a fairly common partitioning between user interface tasks, business logic, and communications with service providers, the most common being a database management system. We conducted a small survey in one of our seminars to understand whether, when offered these partitions, project managers would be able to map their efforts into these client/server boundaries. Our survey indicated that all but three out of 26 responders could easily use the provided partitions to describe their systems. The three distinguished responders were implementing systems with pixel processing, scientific algorithms, or special legacy system access. All the projects had elected to use object-oriented technology, and all emphasized graphical user interfaces and access to databases. We concluded from this introductory survey that the four basic parts—user interface, business logic, communications, and database management—represent a reasonable initial partitioning for systems requiring a client/server architecture.

A different approach to determining partitions involves paying attention to the flow of information. In one case study, the information that flows through the system is about customers who request assistance with products bought from the company (the technical support help desk). As shown in Fig. 6.7, the system consists of two layers: the Services Information Model and the Applications. The Services Information Model represents a number of different data sources. Applications use these data sources to navigate through information about customers, customer contacts, service providers, and products. They are built with User Interface Construction Tools. Partitions within the Services Information Model filter facts and activities: information management, problem management, and process management.

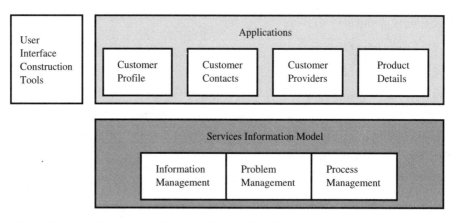

Figure 6.7   Architecture for a Technical Support Help Desk

The next partition example was also derived from an analysis of the flow of information, in this case the flow from the design of a computer chip to its manufacture. Figure 6.8 represents the architecture for this system. Each of the nine boxes indicates a separate software partition on which work proceeded independently. A chip design is given to a process engineer who creates the production specification (Spec Services). This specification goes to a planner, who figures out a manufacturing plan driven by customer demand. The outcome of planning is a build plan that goes to scheduling, where the specification is used to derive resource requirements. The scheduler dynamically determines resources and starts to pull in materials. The schedule then goes to physical manufacturing, which is carried out by robots taking materials to gas chambers and etching the actual chips.

The team members of this project told us that a critical factor for success with large projects (notably ones that form teams to work on independent partitions) is the use of regular reviews throughout the development. At the review, the subteams present their current understanding of the interface contracts that they must fulfill. In this way, any proposed changes can be communicated and negotiated. Where changes are not handled in this controlled manner, the integration is more likely to fail.

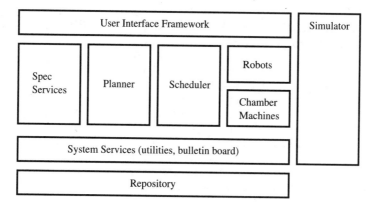

Figure 6.8   Architecture for a Manufacturing System

Summary

The nature of object-oriented technology implies the use of a product process model that emphasizes partitioning the problem to make it possible to work on incremental releases, incremental integration, documentation, and quality assurance. Careful up-front partitioning offers several benefits. It helps you focus effort on appropriate work increments. And it provides a way to divide the project staff into subteams able to coordinate effort based on defining partition boundaries (agreeing on the interface specifications), and testing and integrating completed partitions. According to the Principle of System Architecture—the system structure reflects the culture and organization of the group that creates it—the choice of partitions, and the decisions to prototype and reuse prior results, have to be reflected in the way the team is staffed and organized.

Quality has to be planned and tracked. The choice of process model strategies associated with object-oriented technology influences the quality assurance strategy, defining when to check for defects, what kinds of artifacts and processes must be checked, and how prototyping can help uncover misunderstandings early in the process. We discussed how to uncover defects using prototyping, inspections, reviews, and walkthroughs, and testing object implementations. These techniques not only identify defects, but also identify software process improvements to prevent the occurrence of defects in future artifacts. We also outlined techniques you should follow for recording incidents, defects, and changes made to remove the defects.

This chapter discussed how you select a product process model, following the four steps of a decision framework: agree on maxims, verify goals and objectives, select project activities and their ordering, and select methods for each activity. The discussion about selecting methods emphasized taking advantage of the incremental work effort that is appropriate when using object-oriented technology.

Additional Reading About Product Process Models That Use Object-Oriented Technology

Coleman, D., Arnold, P., Bodoff, S., Dollin, C., Gilchrist, H., Hayes, F., and Jeremaes, P., *Object-Oriented Development: The Fusion Method*, Prentice Hall: Englewood, New Jersey, 1994.

> The authors present the Fusion method, an amalgamation of analysis-and-design methods selected so as to unify the thinking of Rumbaugh, Booch, Shaler-Mellor, and Wirfs-Brock. This book is important in its attention to process—to the sequencing and applicability of the Fusion techniques. The purpose of the recommended process model is to illustrate the dependencies and relationships among different development phases. The authors fully recognize that real developers will not follow this ideal process approach, but do expect developers to produce the full set of Fusion analysis-and-design artifacts.

Jacobson, I., Christerson, M., Jonsson, P., and Övergaard, G., *Object-Oriented Software Engineering: A Use Case–Driven Approach*, ACM Press: Reading, Mass., 1992.

> Jacobson recommends use cases, a way to represent software requirements that can be understood by users, and yet can be applied by technologists to build and test the system that implements these requirements. This book is a comprehensive description of Objectory, a way of applying use cases to gather requirements, create an architecture, test and maintain systems—generally for making software development a "rational industrial (engineering) process."

Special Issue of the *Communications of the ACM* on Object-Oriented Software Testing, September 1994.

> Each September issue of the *Communications of the ACM* contains a collection of papers on a special topic. For the last three years, the topic has been related to issues in object-oriented technology. In the September 1994 issue, six papers deal with integration testing, class testing, ways to automate testing, and how testing fits into the product process model.

CHAPTER 7

Plan and Control a Project

We will be better and braver if we engage and inquire than if we indulge in the idle fancy that we already know—or that it is of no use seeking to know what we do not know.

Plato

P*lanning* is the set of activities needed to describe how a project will be conducted. The description or *plan* includes a breakdown of work to be done, the time dependencies of tasks, and the allocation of personnel and materials. One aspect of a plan is a schedule. *Controlling* is the set of activities that ensures that the project executes according to its plan. Special planning and controlling are required for software projects that use incremental and iterative development and prototyping because of the uncertainty inherent in these forms of development. You have to create a project plan in spite of unavailable information, and still maintain a sense of control over the project. You have to schedule and report progress on project milestones and the tasks leading to these milestones, without micromanaging the opportunistic tactics developers use to complete tasks. Moreover, tasks have to be aligned with the activities of the selected product process model.

What Is a Project Schedule?

A *project schedule* is a time-ordered sequence of deliverables and how these deliverables are to be obtained. Preparing a schedule is often the best way to organize work effort, to communicate how work will get done toward meeting project goals and objectives, and to select the basis for tracking progress. The units of work in a schedule are tasks. Tasks must be completed to produce the deliverables. *Milestones* mark progress in the schedule, and are chosen to identify major project accomplishments, such as delivering a first version of the system or passing a design review. The schedule specifies the resources needed to carry out each task. We base the formation of a schedule on system capabilities, tasks, and milestones.

System capabilities. A *system capability* is a statement of what the system is supposed to do. *External system capabilities* are the user-visible features, or system requirements. The development team adds design requirements, or *internal system capabilities*, to assist in implementing the system requirements. So a system capability is something that describes a set of system behaviors, of measurable value either to the user or to the developer.

Tasks. A *task* is the smallest unit of work on a project schedule which contributes to a milestone. Each task occurs only once in a schedule. Its status is either "completed" or "not completed." Tasks must be specified at a level of detail that makes it possible to identify a well-defined output and an objective criteria for determining whether the output has been obtained.

Tasks are often different because you are using objects, simply because tasks must be aligned with the activities of the product process model. We explain in Chapters 5 and 6 how activities differ when you choose to use object-oriented technology, assuming iterative and incremental development, prototyping, and consuming reusable assets are new to you. There are special tasks for how quality assurance, documentation, and integration take place.

Table 7.1 displays the detail appropriate to describing a task. The first six items in the table name and describe the task in terms of its purpose, related subtasks, and importance to the project. Often you will schedule a task at a level of abstraction that can be defined in more detail. This more general task is a *supertask*. The deliverables of subtasks combine to form the larger supertask deliverable. Although the project manager needs to identify subtasks in order to schedule resources, upper management is usually interested only in supertasks.

A *figure-of-merit* is an indicator of importance that computes the partial completeness of a milestone. A value between 0 and 1 is assigned to each task by the project manager. This number indicates the importance of the task in meeting the milestone. The sum of all figures-of-merit of tasks leading to a single milestone should be 1.

Table 7.1 Information Associated with a Task

Aspect	Definition
Name	Unique identifier for the task, often intended to be informative
Description	High-level description of the task's goal
Purpose	Why the task deliverable is required
Subtasks	List of subtasks, if applicable
Deliverable(s)	Description of the deliverable(s)
Figure-of-merit	A number between 0 and 1 that indicates the importance of the task in meeting its associated milestone
Capabilities	System capabilities (external or internal) created by the task
Process model activity	Process model activity supported by the task
Risks	Description of risks associated with a task that contribute to determining the likelihood factor
Likelihood factor	A number between 0 and 1, where 1 indicates that the task can definitely be done, and 0 that it cannot be done
Planned start date	Specific date the task should start, which defines the start date for any subtask
Expected duration	The amount of time required to complete the task, which reflects the time by which all subtasks will have completed
Required resources	People and material assigned to do this task and all of the subtasks
Actual start and finish dates	Actual dates on which work on the task started and finished
Actual resources	Actual resources that were required to carry out the task
Deviations	Description of any deviations from the planned task

A task is classified according to the capability it creates, and the process model activity it supports—analysis, testing, integration, and so on.[1] This information is used for cost accounting and reporting purposes. Risks and a likelihood factor are associated with the task to identify technical or financial uncertainty. Likelihood is expressed as a number between 0 and 1, where 1 indicates the belief that the task will definitely be completed as scheduled. The likelihood for a supertask is the minimum of the likelihoods of all its sub-

---

[1] Our use of capabilities in the table corresponds to an aspect of planning that Boehm and others refer to as work breakdown structure [Boehm 1981].

tasks. Task likelihood factors should be kept up to date as the project progresses, as uncertainties are removed and dependent tasks completed.

Each task has a planned start date, expected duration, and required resources. Resources are people and materials, such as computer equipment and development tools. Dates, durations, and resources of supertasks have to account for subtasks, as noted in the table. You should track the project history by recording actual task results: dates, resources, and any deviations from plan. The deviations are used to improve the scheduling process when you plan future projects or replan the current project.

Milestones. A milestone is a convenient point in the schedule at which the organization wishes to mark progress. A sequence of tasks is carried out to reach the milestone. Figure 7.1 shows an example plan to reach the following milestone: Script Editor is tested. This plan assumes that the Script Editor is already implemented. The figure illustrates a sequence of three tasks (shown in rectangles) needed to achieve the milestone (shown in a rounded-corner rectangle).

The legend in the figure helps in interpreting the task- and milestone-related information. We show each task's planned start date, expected number of workdays to completion (duration), system capability to be created, and supported process model activity.

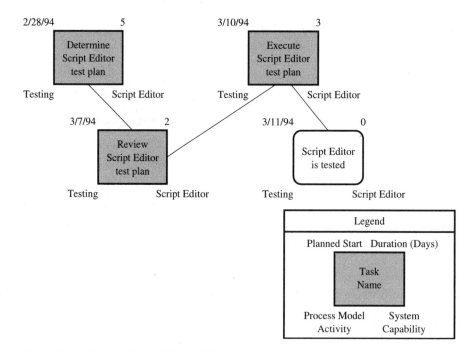

Figure 7.1   Example Plan to Meet a Milestone

In a degenerate case, a supertask and a milestone might be the same—when there is only one supertask and no other tasks leading to a milestone— but conceptually these are two different ideas. Generally, a milestone is selected because the organization recognizes or has guidelines for when to check project progress, regardless of the tasks that have to be done. Milestones are also selected to identify project-specific accomplishments. A supertask is intimately tied to tasks needed to accomplish the specific project, and provides a convenient placeholder for describing a related decomposition of tasks.

Planning Under Uncertainty

Several years ago, we were having a business dinner in New York City with a representative from a large client firm. The representative claimed his organization is able to schedule a four-year project, involving approximately 100 team members, and be confident of the start and stop dates for every task within plus or minus two days. He wanted to know whether he would be able to do the same when using object-oriented technology on the project.

We were, to say the least, amazed, and asked how their planning capabilities could be so accurate.

"Easy," said the client representative. "We have developed the same project many times over the past 30 years. We always use the same hardware, software, and development approach. We really know how to solve this problem!"

"Ah ha!" we responded. "There is no direct equivalent that we have to offer. Modern object-oriented technology has not been in existence for 30 years, and we certainly do not have 30 years of experience solving the same problem. Surely you must know this?"

"Well, yes," said the client representative with a grin. "But don't worry, I am still interested in object-oriented technology. Just because I can tell you with great accuracy that it is going to take me four years doesn't mean that I want it to take me four years. I prefer to do it in one year!"

Our client knew that experience with a particular problem and experience with the technologies used to solve the problem help the project manager create precise plans with confidence. The only projects you can plan that have no risks are ones that are fully determined in advance. Our client also realized that new technologies bring new opportunities. Short-term inaccuracies in project plans trade off against the long-term benefits of object-oriented technology.

Object-oriented technology allows you to manage the risk of a project with unknowns because it supports the use of prototyping, and of incremental and iterative development strategies. Although these strategies allow you to carry out development in the presence of uncertainty, the uncertainty complicates planning and control. You create a prototype to explore unknown parts of the problem (analysis prototyping) or the solution (design prototyping). If you are doing prototyping, by definition the project has uncertainty in it, and you cannot expect to know the full plan in advance. Incremental development as used with object-oriented technology requires that a problem be partitioned into subproblems. As you complete each partition, you test it and integrate it with the other partitions. At each stage, you evaluate the partially completed system to determine what replanning, if any, is needed to develop future partitions. You do not know in advance, for purposes of planning, how the evaluation of completed partitions will affect the other, yet-to-be-completed partitions. Also, there are times when a problem is new enough or difficult enough to require iteration. If you do not know how many iterations will be necessary to complete a part of the system, you cannot specify the actual linear sequence of tasks that the project must carry out.

To contend with this uncertainty, we recommend a planning strategy in which you:

- State clearly what you know and what you do not know

- State clearly what you will do to eliminate unknowns

- Make sure that all early milestones can be met

- Plan to replan

State Clearly What You Know and What You Do Not Know

Plan smart. You have to know what you know.

Create as detailed a plan as possible using the information of which you are certain. Avoid creating detailed plans for those aspects of the system for which you are lacking important information. In other words,

Plan truthfully. Avoid planning beyond the limits of your understanding.

Plan and Control

The risk in creating plans in the presence of uncertainty is that management and customers will view the plans as absolute commitments. You can mitigate this risk in two ways. First, make sure that you know what you know, and state this information clearly (as the Risk entry in the Task description). Second, state your level of confidence that you can complete each task, based on clear statements of what you do not yet know (as the Likelihood factor). If management accepts your risk analysis, there is less chance they will be surprised. For example, when new information becomes available, management will expect you to change any tasks related to this information, especially tasks with low likelihood factors.

Suppose you find that tasks with very high likelihood factors are not executing according to plan. Why not? Perhaps you thought you knew something that you really did not know. At least now you are in a position to figure out why you are off plan—what it is that you erroneously thought you knew. The benefit of early and frequent deliverables is that you can quickly discover many of these situations. Also, by involving team members in the planning process, you not only enable them to take ownership of the plan, but you increase the overall information base for planning and reduce the risk of overlooking important information.

State Clearly What You Will Do to Eliminate Unknowns

Plan and Control

Plan to be smart. Ignorance can be tolerated if there is a plan to learn.

If you tell your managers you cannot plan because you do not know something, then these managers have the right to ask you how you will figure it out, and when you will have the necessary information.

Tell them. Put into your plan, as a task, a description of the work to obtain the information you still need. Of course, you do not know how the deliverables from these information-gathering tasks will translate into the next steps—you have to do the tasks first. But it is possible that you can predict likely outcomes and show these as alternative tasks, with appropriate risks and likelihood factors. Obviously, if not much information is known, the effort to obtain information may involve a major research program. Management may naturally decide the risk is too high, and change its goals.

Make Sure That All Early Milestones Can Be Met

Plan and Control

Plan to prove yourself. Earn the right to make changes.

Plan frequent deliveries. Schedule milestone deliveries every three to six months.

Show that you are making progress. Build a plan that will give the team a good track record—a good history of providing incremental results. It is essential that a project plan be constructed so that all early deliverables can be met. Doing so builds confidence among the developers, managers, and customers.

One particular case study project was required to provide a complete schedule and final delivery date for the project. The manager knew that many of the project details were unknown, and could not be known for some time. However, he still provided a complete project plan that charted a path to the final goal. The manager made sure that all of the early milestones were extremely well understood and could be confidently achieved. The team subsequently met all of the planned early milestones, on schedule. These early successes earned the trust of management. So, when the manager needed to replan the schedule to reflect what was learned during the early part of the project, his management was receptive.

Plan to Replan

Plan and Control

Plan to replan. Confidence comes from the planning process, not from the plan.

The most important strategy for planning under uncertainty is to plan to replan. Treat the plan as a living document. It should explicitly include tasks to revise itself. By making the replanning task a scheduled part of the project, the project manager declares it will be necessary to replan the schedule based on experience gained during earlier parts of the project. Uncertainty is treated as a normal, expected part of the development process.

At a workshop on object-oriented design held in a western U.S. skiing resort in 1994, Ward Cunningham (an experienced objectologist and inventor of the class-responsibility-collaborator design technique) offered the comment that "everything I needed to learn about object-oriented programming, I could have learned on a black-diamond run." A skier starting an "experts only" (black diamond) downhill run has a clear end goal in mind: safe arrival at the bottom, with speed and style. The entire trip down the mountain is not preplanned, although the general process is understood and the first few tasks are scheduled. The skier proceeds downhill, looks two to three turns and bumps ahead, and expects to replan as conditions change during the journey. Managing projects that rely on incremental and iterative development, that use prototyping and take advantage of exploratory development environments, is a lot like skiing black-diamond runs—best done a few turns and bumps at a time.

Planning Resources

A benefit of the Waterfall Model is that resources assigned to a completed activity can be released and reassigned to other projects. Iterative and incremental development imply that the use of resources is not allocated to single time slots, but is spread throughout the project. For example, the business analyst in the Waterfall Model works during the analysis activity only, which occurs up front in its entirety. This same analyst in a project using an incremental development strategy has to be available to do the analysis activities as they occur—and they are distributed throughout each increment for the duration of the project. As a result, projects using object-oriented technology have to retain resources for longer durations, or the organization has to plan the tasks of multiple projects as though they were in a single project, or the organization has to provide a cross-project team that coordinates allocation of special resources.

Resource planning can be more complex when object-oriented technology is used because of the project uncertainties. The desire to coordinate resources across multiple projects adds to the complexity. Resource requirements must be tied to scheduled tasks, yet not all tasks can be scheduled when the initial resource plan is created. This dilemma is resolved depending on whether you have fixed or dynamically allocated resources.

Fixed resources. Many successful case study projects simplified their resource planning by assigning a fixed set of resources for the duration of the project. Where the project was the company's first use of object-oriented technology, it was simply easier to assign a stable team to take the project from inception to delivery. Resources were often allocated by determining the amount of work planned to be done in parallel. In other cases, management simply dictated resources. Available resources influenced the task breakdown and the order in which tasks were carried out. Where the project's size required fewer than 12 developers, the developers fulfilled multiple roles. The issue of resource planning was reduced to deciding on the proper team members to play these roles for the duration of the project.

Dynamically allocated resources. On large projects, and in organizations with multiple projects and limited resources, it is typically not possible to assign a fixed number of resources for the duration of a project. Rather, resources are moved between projects on an as-required basis. Consequently, the managers must generate detailed resource utilization plans. The most practical approach is to create short-term resource plans and replan your resources when you replan your schedule, assuming that the resources will be made available. The problem is that personnel availability has to be fluid, which is difficult to do but easiest when the role is that of a specialist. Example specialty roles are those of the usability expert, design reviewers, or data schema designer. People who perform these specialized jobs can be added and removed from projects on shorter-term assignments.

Framework for Planning and Controlling

Planning under uncertainty must be interleaved with task execution: plan what you know, plan how to get what you do not know, and plan to replan based on the information you gather. The decision framework goal for planning and controlling is to change the process by which planning and controlling projects is carried out. The process improvement project is depicted in Fig. 7.2.

Figure 7.2 Process-Improvement Project to Change the Planning and Controlling Process, and Create a Project Schedule

The decision framework for planning and controlling a software project is therefore based on the following principle and goal:

Framework Principle. Planning and execution are interleaved activities, whereby partial plans are set, carried out, and the results used to do further planning.

Framework Goal. Develop a project schedule, and a way to control execution to schedule, that builds management trust and meets management development expectations.

The six steps of the decision framework follow from the goal. These steps are specific to planning and controlling software development projects.

Project Plan and Control

- Identify required milestones

- Identify system capabilities

- Identify tasks

- Estimate the cost of each task

- Account for costs

- Monitor and control project execution

Identify Required Milestones

A project schedule is expressed in terms of milestones. Progress is reported in terms of these milestones. An important first step in establishing a project schedule is to understand required milestones. Many organizations have one or more preferred patterns for developing products. These patterns will often provide suggested milestones for the organization's software development projects.

For example, one of the case study organizations required that each software development project include the following milestones in its project schedule:

- Feasibility prototype completed

- Market viability report based on the feasibility prototype available

- First technical prototype completed

- Prototype usability study completed

- Engineered product released for test

- Alpha (internal) release of product available

- Updated product, based on alpha feedback, released for test

- Beta (external) release of product shipped to customers for test

- Updated product, based on beta feedback, released for test

- Master copy of product released for manufacturing test

- First customer release of product shipped

Individual project managers in this organization set up their project plans based on this general, reusable pattern for project milestones.

In addition to identifying required milestones, the project manager should also identify the overall project constraints for meeting these milestones. There are several kinds of constraints that apply to most projects. Principal among these are resource constraints, such as people, time, and money. On a given project, one of these constraints typically dominates the project-planning process. For example, many of the projects in the case studies were time driven. The primary factor influencing the planning of these projects was to meet the goals and objectives—the final milestone—by a specific date. Tasks to meet project milestones were arranged so that the final milestone was achieved by the desired date. When this is not possible, either the final date is extended, or the scope of the deliverables is reduced, or the project is canceled because the desired goals and objectives cannot be achieved in the time allotted. Many of the case studies failed to meet time-driven milestones when management refused to change system requirements to match the available time.

A winning strategy is to deliver results frequently to build management trust in the development team and to obtain good customer feedback. Our experience indicates that it is useful to schedule intermediate milestones at three- to six-month intervals.

Identify System Capabilities

The goal of a software development project is to deliver a particular set of system capabilities. As we stated earlier, there are two types of capabilities: those that are defined by the users of the systems (external, analysis capabilities), and those that are required or defined by the designers (internal, design capabilities). A partial set of external system capabilities is often specified in a requirements document provided by the company's marketing department, or in a client proposal. The complete requirements are not known until after analysis is completed. Internal system capabilities are specified by the designers as necessary for achieving the external system capabilities.

The specific set of external and internal system capabilities must be known in order to establish milestones and tasks in the project plan. The degree to which the capabilities are known at the beginning of a project will differ from project to project. For Variation-on-a-Theme, Legacy Rewrite, or System Maintenance projects, it is likely that most if not all of the capabilities will be known at the start. For First-of-Its-Kind or Creating Reusable Assets projects, capabilities may only be known as the project unfolds. The partitioning strategies we discuss in Chapter 6 can be used to uncover system capabilities.

Identify Tasks

A project's schedule is a reflection of the selected product process model. Since process models differ among types of projects, the structure of a schedule will differ as well. As described earlier, we expect each task in the schedule to identify the process model activity it supports. The order in which tasks are carried out should reflect the ordering of process model activities.

Project plans are inherently sequential—one task follows the completion of another. There are no cycles or loops because, after all, there is no time machine available to the project manager. Tasks can be done in parallel, contingent upon task interdependencies and available resources.

Plan at a strategic level, not at a tactical level. If the method you choose to carry out an activity (for example, for analysis or design) specifies detailed steps—develop the object model, determine the system interface, develop an interface model, and so on—you could choose to have a task for each of these steps. But be careful because this choice fabricates some beautiful rational ordering where in fact you will operate in a more opportunistic fashion. The tactics for developing software using object-oriented technology are too small-grained and vary too much from analysis to design to implementation. Planning at a tactical level requires that you show a level of detail that is incomprehensible in a sequential project plan based on incremental and iterative development strategies.

Incremental development. Incremental development is used when all or some of the partitions are known at the beginning of the project. The initial project schedule accounts for the development of each known partition. You may not know precisely how each partition will be created. But even with such unknowns, you can create a skeletal task list for each, based on your selected product process model.

Figure 7.3 illustrates the structure of a plan that displays the expectations for incremental development. It shows that you start by scheduling the supertasks for creating each increment. In subsequent planning, you will decompose these supertasks into subtasks. For example, your product process model may require testing and integration after each partition is implemented. If so, you can place these subtasks on the schedule.

An initial project schedule may have islands of unconnected tasks because when you devise your initial plan you may find it easier to place the partitions in the plan without

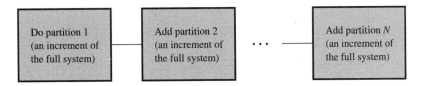

Figure 7.3   Planning Incremental Development

clear connections to one another or to general milestones. You next create tasks for obtaining the information needed to complete the schedule. As you carry out these tasks and more information becomes available, you should be able to connect the islands.

Iterative development. The iterative development strategy asks you to plan to obtain a result, and then to plan to rework the result because you know in advance that the process of getting the result will provide information that will affect the statement of requirements or the solution approach. Iterative development requires an open-ended schedule. But what do you do in an organization that demands more precision?

Figure 7.4 is the schedule diagram typically drawn by developers who wish to illustrate opportunistic development. It shows a plan for achieving the milestone called Delivery of Order Entry. The diagram is derived from iteration in the process model—the arrows that loop back denote endless opportunity to rework each result.

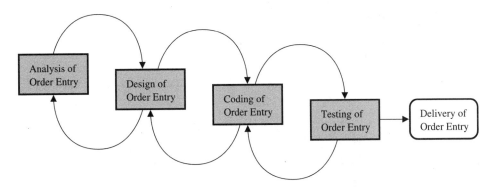

Figure 7.4   Tasks Are Scheduled According to an Opportunistic Development Strategy

But this is a nonsense project plan. Time does not go backward, and schedules cannot go on forever. A project schedule is sequential and finite, with tasks ordered by time. So how can you schedule this milestone and still indicate the desire to use iteration? The answer is that you show the tasks needed to create the deliverable, not the iterating activities. On the schedule, you identify the sequence of tasks leading to the initial result, and also the reconsideration task that occurs after the result is obtained so that it is clear that a change in the plan can occur. Figure 7.5 illustrates the structure of a plan that incorporated replanning based on an iterative development strategy. The initial plan showed only the first two tasks in the figure; the plan was revised four times to incorporate four revisions of the initial result.

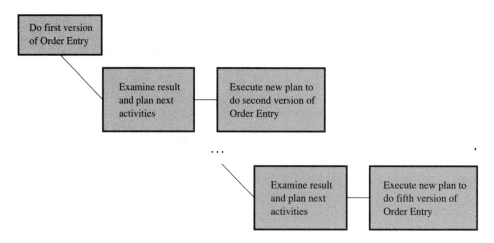

Figure 7.5 Planning Iterative Development

Size of tasks. It is likely that a task, like Do first version of Order Entry, is too large for planning purposes. Iteration offers no help in resizing, but incremental development does: Treat the large task as a supertask and divide it into subtasks. For example, add tasks to create order, update order, and print order. The new plan is shown in Fig. 7.6. These are the subtasks for each iteration of the supertask shown in Fig. 7.5 to create a version of Order Entry.[2]

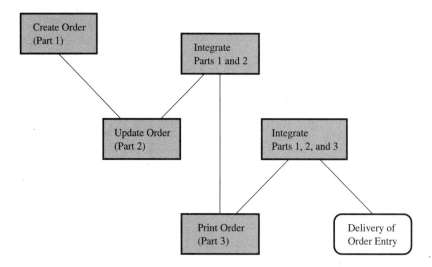

Figure 7.6 A Supertask Is Decomposed into Subtasks

---

[2] It is of course not a requirement that all the increments of Fig. 7.5 be carried out using the same pattern of subtasks.

The tactics for carrying out each task in Fig. 7.6 can differ depending on the size and the kind of task. You want to schedule tasks at a level at which you are comfortable that the developers can be fully responsible to describe how to accomplish the tasks. You do not want to microplan. Show only the details you need for reporting purposes; show only those tasks for which you can reasonably assign figures-of-merit, risks, and likelihood factors. Do not try to show the opportunistic details of how you will apply an analysis, design, or implementation method.

Duration of tasks. By scheduling at a strategic level, leaving tactics to the developers, you let developers decide how to do their work. Sounds good, but as a manager you have the responsibility to control the use of your resources. No problem. You can retain control, but give developers the authority to carry out the tasks, by scheduling well-defined tasks that require no more than one or two weeks to carry out. Scheduling short task durations is risk containment. Perhaps the developers won't do the right things. But you will find out quickly, before it is too late to fix the problem. If you assign a task that lasts six months, you stand the chance of losing five- or six-months' effort—even jeopardizing the success of the project. If you are comfortable with this risk, then it is of course your choice to schedule tasks with longer durations.

Estimate the Cost of Each Task

The next step of the decision framework is to estimate the cost involved in carrying out the project. Cost estimates are needed at the granularity of tasks, milestones, system capabilities, and the project as a whole. By costs, we refer to the resources needed to accomplish the work, including time and people.

There is little historical data on the cost of developing projects using object-oriented technology. What little data does exist is spread over many different kinds of projects. Yet all cost-estimating techniques, other than guessing, require historical data. Consequently, at this time, it is difficult to apply any rigorous form of cost estimation for projects using objects.

Because you have to do something, and because you must understand why collecting data now will prove useful in the future, we discuss four techniques for estimating costs: historical models, decomposition, expert opinion, and analogy. Using a historical model involves comparing the current project to past projects along some dimension, such as lines of code. Decomposition refines the estimate into a collection of estimates for individual tasks. Expert opinion and analogy appeal to luck and experience in estimating a project or individual tasks.

Historical models. Historical models use parameterized formulas to estimate development effort. These formulas are based on data collected for a significant number of completed projects. A formula, parameterized by factors believed to influence development, is fitted to the available historical data.

The Constructive Costing Model (COCOMO) proposed by Boehm is an example of a historical model [Boehm 1981]. The basic formula is simple:

$$\text{effort} = a\,(\text{size})^b$$

The person using COCOMO for estimation must determine which of three types of systems is to be built: organic, embedded, or semidetached. Values for a and b are defined for each system type. The variable *size* is the number of thousands of delivered source instructions that are anticipated to be in the resultant system. The three values are combined in the formula to compute the effort to complete the system, as measured in person-months.

To account for the many factors (other than lines of code and system type) that influence the duration of a project, Boehm proposed 15 cost drivers that can be used to adjust the estimate of work effort. Cost-driver attributes fall into four categories: product (an example attribute is database size), computer (execution time), personnel (analyst's ability), and project (use of software tools). Each attribute is assessed a ranking along a continuum (from very low to extra high). Based on the ranking, the estimator finds a value for the attribute from a table. All attribute values are multiplied together to compute an adjustment factor, which is itself multiplied by the original formula result to yield an adjusted estimate.

$$\text{adjusted effort} = (\text{product of all cost factors}) * \text{effort}$$

The quality of COCOMO estimates depends on the ability of the estimator accurately to determine system type and cost factors, and predict lines of code. Boehm has admitted that the accuracy of the detailed version of COCOMO on data from his projects is only 80 percent, between 68 and 70 percent of the time. Boehm estimates a 20 percent error in data collection, so he cannot claim better than 80 percent accuracy. COCOMO was developed to prepare TRW proposals for defense projects. Thus the published table of project type coefficients and cost-driver factors is specific to TRW defense projects. Any organization adopting COCOMO is expected to recalibrate the values in the tables to reflect its specific organizational history and conventions. Any organization adopting COCOMO for use on a project using object-oriented technology should replace lines-of-code measures by those for object abstractions. To parallel properly the ideas behind COCOMO, these object abstractions should be the ones found in the implementation, not the analysis or design object models. (Chapter 20 revisits this point.)

Jenson and Bartley describe an estimation model for predicting the software development effort when object-oriented technology is used [Jenson and Bartley 1991, Stamelos 1993]. Based on the data available from 16 projects (all developed by the same programmers at a single company), they claim that the best predictions were produced by a non-linear, exponential model, using the number of objects as the only significant independent variable (the number of operations and interfaces had no statistical influence on the actual software development effort). Their formula is derived from a least squares fit of the number of analysis objects in a small sample set. The size of the sample set creates doubt as to whether we can safely eliminate other parameters, such as the number of operations or interfaces.

The advantages of a historical model such as the one proposed by Jenson and Bartley is that it attempts to predict the cost of the project very early in the development life cycle using information that is actually available at the time, such as the number of objects that exist in the analysis object model. This approach is in contrast to COCOMO, which uses lines of code as the independent variable for predicting effort, even though an accurate count of lines of code is not available until the implementation is completed. The accuracy of the Jenson and Bartley approach is of course dependent on the extent to which the analysis method leads to accurate requirements.

Decomposition. Decomposition breaks the project into smaller and smaller tasks until the tasks are small enough and familiar enough to be accurately estimated. For each task, a different estimation technique may be used. For example, the way you estimate the effort to create a graphical user interface may be substantially different from the way you estimate effort to create an application domain model. The project estimate is the sum of the estimates for individual tasks.

Estimates, in practice, are based on a standard "average" effort, adjusted for any unusual difficulty of a task. This approach is repeatable and learnable to the extent that there are clear guidelines on how to decompose a project into smaller tasks. The techniques and standard averages are applicable to all systems that can be decomposed in a similar manner. Systems with radically different structures may require their own special decomposition techniques. Decomposition at a scheduling level is invariably at a task or system-capability level, not equated to developing individual objects. And so this technique is not undermined just because object-oriented technology is chosen.

Expert opinion. Relying on expert opinion is like saying, make a best guess. This technique, of course, is not repeatable or learnable by others, since a guess is based on individual wisdom. Expert opinion is the most common estimation technique for new users of object-oriented technology—typically an object consultant provides the estimate. Delphi studies have shown that experts are best at estimating short-term projects. This leads one to conclude that, where managers are not technical experts, they should defer cost estimates to a consensus formed between the manager and the technical team members.

Analogy. Estimating by analogy is another technique that relies on history and wisdom. The estimator notices that the project is similar to something done before. The effort for a similar previous project is taken as the initial estimate for the new project. The initial estimate is then adjusted according to the differences between the two projects. Estimation by analogy is only repeatable and learnable if there is a concise way to express how projects can be compared—that is, how to identify differences and know, with any accuracy, the importance of the differences. It is useful only when the organization has collected work effort data from multiple prior similar projects.

This technique is often applied when estimating projects that use object-oriented technology. Consultants can provide valuable input if they have comparable data on one or more similar projects from other organizations. The consultants' estimates, a combination of expert opinion and analogy, can be improved if they are involved in training and/or mentoring the development team, and appreciate the productivity characteristics of the individuals and the team.

We recommend that if you have some experience estimating client/server projects, you use these estimates adjusted by 10 to 25 percent to account for unknowns (err on the side of a larger adjustment based on how much experience you have with object-oriented technology). We picked client/server because many of the concepts of building systems based on a client/server architecture apply to the use of objects. Moreover, your client/server experience will be relatively new and will take into account newer hardware and software technologies.

Account for Costs

Cost accounting is collecting and assigning project cost data to appropriate accounting categories. You collect cost data so that you can tell where resources—time, money, people—are expended on a project. You can use this information to report on execution of the current project and to estimate the costs of future projects based on some historical model.

Earlier we provided you with a template that describes the information you should associate with each task (Table 7.1). The template specifies cost-accounting categories for each task: time (actual duration), people and materials (actual resources), process model activity, and system capabilities. You might want to augment the template with other cost categories. You have to decide what information you will put in each category. For example, you have to select your process model activities and use the names of the activities for this category. Similarly, the system capabilities should be named and used consistently across all tasks in a project. Under resources, you should account for team members and the roles they played, machines, special software, and so on, with some reference to costs such as salary and depreciation.

Time must be the actual *uninterrupted staff hours* spent to accomplish the task. The choice of this measure follows the recommendations of [DeMarco 1982]. Staff-hours is a normalized measure of effort to which other measures can be related, such as the number of people and the total time spent on tasks. DeMarco and others have provided convincing data that indicates productivity declines rapidly when developers are not given uninterrupted time to concentrate on their work.

The record of costs should also state who provided the data so that any potential biases will be recognized. Most development organizations have accounting systems that gather much of this data, often through personal timecards with project/task charge numbers reported daily or weekly.

Monitor and Control Project Execution

Now you have a plan and you have some estimate of the effort involved to execute the plan, and you know what information you have to collect. You must now decide on how you will ensure that the actual project work goes according to plan. You have to measure performance against plan to reveal where you are in reaching milestones and completing tasks, how you are progressing with respect to cost expectations, when and where deviation exists, and to institute corrective action when necessary. That is, you have to monitor and control your project.

How you should *not* track project progress. At the OOPSLA'93 Workshop on Processes and Metrics for Object-Oriented Software Development, one participant told the story of his first major object-oriented effort. The following paraphrases his report:

> The project schedule was set by analogy to similar work using FORTRAN. The team was accustomed to considerable freedom—reporting progress on completion of subroutines and number of lines of code. But the customer of the project, aware that the team was inexperienced with object-oriented methods and languages, wanted more detailed progress reports, and assurance that the project remained in control.
>
> The team chose to report system size and development progress using the number of classes produced. A class in this project was a C++ class or main routine. Problem domain analysis produced about 75 classes. Architectural design added another 425 classes. The number 500 thus became the basis for reporting progress.
>
> Monthly review meetings with the customer focused on the total number of classes—designed, implemented, unit tested, and integrated. As the number of classes exceeded the estimated 500—because new classes were added to support detailed design and implementation—the customer began to question the project manager's effectiveness.
>
> Good design practice suggested ways to factor classes for better reuse. Abstract class hierarchies were constructed to capture shared behavior. The number of classes increased—appropriately, but nonetheless unacceptably to the customer. The customer neither understood the cause for the increase, nor permitted a change in the way progress was measured. The project technical managers, all first-time users of object-oriented technology, panicked. The project manager, to pacify the customer, ordered, "No more classes!"

The implementation reverted to case statements, classes that handled too much behavior, and so on. The progress-tracking approach now inappropriately drove the design decisions.

This story demonstrates that the basis for tracking and reporting project progress can be critical to a project's real and perceived success. A project manager needs to make sure that work proceeds on schedule and within budget. Upper management is interested in the same data, although usually with less detail. The question is, what data provides the best indicator of project progress?

The story indicates that the implementation completed so far, whether lines of code or numbers of class definitions, is a poor indicator of progress. For example, if you expect to create 100,000 lines of code, and you have completed 65,000 lines of code, you might presume that the project is 65 percent completed. This fails to recognize the possibility that the remaining 35,000 lines of code will require relatively more effort to create, or that a significant portion of the existing 65,000 lines may be rewritten during subsequent development. Moreover, resource consumption—people, time, money—cannot be used as a measure of project completeness. Fifty percent time used or dollars spent does not mean 50 percent of the targeted system is completed. It might be necessary, for example, to spend the majority of the project capital budget the first day of the project. Or the first half of the project time might be spent by a few people doing analysis. We are interested, however, in tracking actual resource consumption to planned consumption.

How you should track project progress. When we discussed how to set up the project plan, we focused on: milestones, supertasks, and tasks to which individuals can be assigned without being micromanaged. When we discuss how to track and report project progress, we ask questions about these milestones and tasks, as well as system capabilities and quality assurance.

Specific questions about progress depend on your organization's expectations for reports and what specific people want to know.[3] The CEO, in asking how a project is going, expects to be told if the product will ship on time. The chief architect asks the same question but expects to know if the design is working to support the desired system capabilities.

Milestones. Milestones are often the most important elements for reporting progress, since they were placed on the schedule specifically for that purpose. You can report which milestones have been achieved and, for the others, how much work remains to be done. You compute the relative completion of a milestone by summing the figures-of-

---

[3] We recommend you follow a Goal-Question-Metric (GQM) approach to define the questions you expect to be able to answer, and the actual information you will need to formulate the reports. We describe GQM in Chapter 20.

merit of all tasks leading to the milestone. The sum of the figures-of-merit of all completed tasks denotes progress on the milestone.

Tasks. Tasks are the most abundant source of progress-related information. There are numerous measures that you might apply to tasks in order to generate reporting information. The most obvious is a simple count of the number of tasks completed, perhaps reported as a ratio to the number of total tasks (for example, 100 out of 200 tasks are completed). Although this ratio is easy to compute, by itself the ratio does not provide deep insight into overall project progress. Alternatively, you may choose to count tasks with specific characteristics. For example, you might ask, how many of the critical tasks have better than a 50 percent chance for completion? Up-to-date likelihood information is available in the task templates.

System capabilities. System capabilities are the end-user visible and design behaviors that the system must support. An informative way to report project progress is in terms of which system capabilities are completed. Often, delivery of a system capability is represented as a milestone. In this case, you report the progress of delivering a particular capability in the same manner as reporting the progress of a milestone. If the completion of a capability is not directly associated with a milestone, then you can determine which tasks support a capability and report those tasks that must be completed before a capability can be completed. You can also report the likelihood factors for the incomplete tasks. The minimum of the likelihood factors for the tasks indicates the likelihood that the system capability will be completed according to plan.

Quality. Quality relates to the characteristics of the system being developed. Many project managers equate project progress to the introduction of higher levels of product quality. This may range from the quality of the design to the rate of introduction and removal of defects. Oftentimes there are specific quality-related tasks on the project schedule. Describing which of these tasks are complete is another way to report progress.

Report on whether a project is under control. A project is considered under control if it is progressing at an acceptable rate, if schedule deviations are minimal, and resource consumption is within established parameters. As we saw in the earlier example for tracking progress by number of implementation classes, a poor choice for a measure of progress can give the appearance that a project is out of control, even when the project is quite stable and well managed.

Another way to determine whether a project is under control is to examine the extent to which there are deviations from scheduled tasks. Good planning under uncertainty should substantially improve your overall schedule, and specifically reduce the expected task-level deviations. However, given the level of uncertainty that accompanies incremental development, iterative development, and prototyping, some deviation is expected. When such deviations occur, you should record them in the deviations field of the affected task. This information can then be examined to determine why deviation occurred and whether there is a control problem. Additionally, you should also examine the rate of new tasks that are introduced into the project schedule. The rate should be proportional to the level of uncertainty. A large number of new tasks to meet a milestone that was thought to be well understood is an indicator that the project might be out of control.

Examining the level of actual resource consumption is another way to determine whether a project is under control. The project schedule indicates the planned level of resource consumption per task. As the project progresses, actual resource consumption for each task is recorded. Large deviations of actual consumption from plan are indicative of poor cost estimating or poor control. Analysis of the derivations should help improve cost estimating or determine where the project needs better control. Also, tracking consumed resources allows you to determine whether you have sufficient resources to complete the project given current resource estimates for the remaining tasks.

Maintain project control. You maintain control by assigning tasks with short durations so that you have frequent checkpoints. Each task has a well defined deliverable that you evaluate at each checkpoint. You also maintain project control by agreeing on a work model for authorizing and completing activities. Much of the prior discussion assumed that you are able to decide whether you have completed work. The work could be a full partition, or an activity within a partition. The purpose of a work model is to give the project manager who is planning under uncertainty a way to control activities and a way to maintain team focus.

Why is a work model needed? Suppose you choose to build a prototype of a user interface for querying a database. The desired outcome is a user interface that can be used without instruction by people who know how to handle the hardware devices, but who have never used computer-based database query tools. Your developers build an initial prototype that includes all of the visual widgetry but only some of the underlying functionality. They show it to potential customers, each of whom offers some new ideas. The developers create a second prototype. The customers have more ideas—they ask for a way to generate report forms. The developers see this as a good enhancement to the original product idea, so they stop working on testing the user interface and start producing a prototype report writer. Eventually, the customers are satisfied, but the developers have a new idea—color can be added, or icons can be animated. Another prototype is started. There always seems to be a good reason to do another prototype. STOP!!

The project manager asked for a prototype of the user interface, as specified, to do usability studies. The studies were incomplete before the developers started adding features. The project is indeed unfocused. How do you take control of the situation? Our solution is a work model that represents a fundamental set of activities a manager should do in planning, executing, and evaluating each task in the development process. We suggest that before you make a decision to create a prototype or initiate any planned activity where there is some uncertainty, you follow the steps shown in Fig. 7.7. The steps of Fig. 7.7 are also shown in Fig. 7.8, but in the format that we recommend for a schedule.

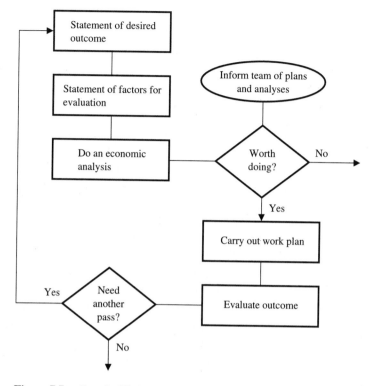

Figure 7.7   Generic Work Model

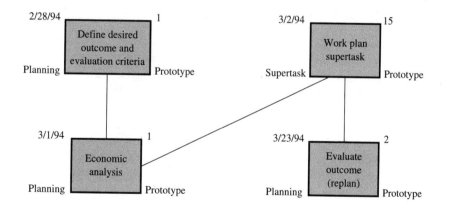

Figure 7.8   Task Structure for a Prototyping Activity

The first step is to write a clear statement of why you are doing the activity and what is to be done. The statement identifies a desired outcome—for example, the design for a user interface for a database query tool. Next, write a clear statement of how you will evaluate the work to determine whether the task is completed—that is, whether the outcome has been obtained. In other words, restate the desired outcome in terms of measurable objectives. Continuing the example, you might write down five queries that you would expect ten people to be able to carry out successfully during a half-hour session with the prototype. You also characterize the ten people with respect to their backgrounds.

The third step is to state, from an economic point of view, why it is worthwhile to do the work. How much effort is acceptable to find out the answer to the question you ask as your statement of desired outcome? You do your work at some cost, with the expectation of achieving some benefit—you are spending something to get something (people, money, time, lost opportunity). You state up front what you want to get, and determine whether it is worth paying to get it—before you do the work. You need to do a resource analysis. You want to be clear that you are spending resources to obtain information that is valuable to you. You want to be able to stop spending the resources once the effort crosses the financial threshold you have set.

Share the statements of desired outcome and evaluation factors, and the economic analysis with the team members. Make sure everyone understands why a work plan is being carried out. Consensus is not required—lest no work begin—but team members participating in the task should be able to contribute to the work plan. Someone, of course, has to be in charge and make the go/no-go decision. But clear statements about what is being done—and why—help create a culture of open communications. If the activity is worth doing, then do it. Monitor what is going on.

Evaluate the outcome using the identified evaluation criteria. Evaluate the outcome even if the plan is not completed but the time allotted has passed. Perhaps, as project manager, you want to reconsider the decision that it was worth doing. Only continue working on the task if, not having obtained the original outcome within the boundaries of the economic analysis, you write down a new statement of desired outcome, and so on.

In this way, when you are working on a task, you know why you are doing it, and how to determine when to stop working on it. You also have recorded information that will be useful as you gather metrics about your development processes so that, in the future, you can improve your statements of outcome, evaluation factors, and analyses. Following this work model requires a project manager who is able to say no—no to new ideas that do not lead to the stated outcome, and no to spending resources in unplanned ways.

Summary

This chapter discussed how to plan and how to control a software development project that uses the incremental, iterative, and prototyping strategies for a product process model. We defined a project schedule as a sequence of deliverables that identifies the way these deliverables will be obtained. The purpose of preparing the schedule is to organize work effort, to communicate how work will proceed toward meeting project goals and objectives, and to form a basis on which to track progress. In the context of using object-oriented technology, we defined schedules in terms of system capabilities, tasks, and milestones.

We emphasized that the ability to plan software projects depends on how much information you have available. One advantage of using object-oriented technology is the ability to get started on a project despite the presence of unknowns. Incremental and iterative development and prototyping are used in situations where uncertainty about system requirements exists. This complicates planning and controlling activities. Because you have to plan despite the uncertainties, and you have to have a sense of management control over your project, we offered several planning strategies: state what you know, state how you will eliminate unknowns, and plan to replan based on the information you gather.

We introduced the decision framework for planning and controlling, with the requirement to interleave planning with execution, given the desire to plan projects despite uncertainty about what to do and how to do it. The goal of the framework is to develop a project schedule, and a way to control execution to schedule, that builds management trust and meets management development expectations. The goal is obtained by following six steps. In the first three steps, you identify required milestones, system capabilities, and tasks. A winning strategy is to deliver results frequently to build management trust in the development team and to obtain good customer feedback. Our experience indicates that it is useful to schedule intermediate milestones at three to six month intervals.

Tasks should be aligned with the project purpose and process model activities. Every task must have a measurable outcome. We provided a template for how to describe tasks in terms of a figure-of-merit (its importance in meeting its milestone), likelihood factor (an indicator of whether the task can be completed), and estimates for time and other resources. A task is also described in terms of the system capabilities created by the task. You schedule tasks at a level at which you are comfortable the developers can be fully responsible, and a level at which you can reasonably assign figures-of-merit, risks, and likelihoods, showing only the details needed for reporting purposes.

In the final three steps of the framework, you estimate costs, account for costs, and monitor and control project execution. You estimate the cost of each task to understand the cost of milestones and of the project itself, and account for costs in terms of the uninterrupted staff hours and other resources needed to complete the task. This information contributes to future project cost estimating. We described current ideas about techniques for cost estimating: historical models, decomposition, expert opinion, and analogy.

Once you have a plan, you should not track progress on the amount of the implementation completed so far, nor on the amount of resources consumed, although you should keep track of resource consumption relative to what you estimated was required. We provided examples of how to report milestones based on the figures-of-merit of the tasks contributing to meeting each milestone, tasks based on completion likelihood factors, completed system capabilities, and effort to assure system quality. Finally, we introduced a generic work model that you can use to maintain project control in the face of planning under uncertainty.

Additional Reading About Planning and Controlling Projects

Boehm, B., *Software Engineering Economics*, Prentice Hall: Englewood Cliffs, New Jersey, 1981.

This book is the classic text on software cost estimation. Boehm not only discusses the basic economic framework of cost estimation, he introduces the now well-known COCOMO estimation model. Boehm derived COCOMO by examining the development attributes of 63 software projects created at TRW. The book provides a comprehensive description of the three levels of COCOMO (basic, intermediate, and detailed), each of which uses increasingly more detailed project information to obtain more accurate estimates. Many of the characteristics of COCOMO are found in derivative estimating models. Some of the COCOMO characteristics are still useful for estimating object-oriented software development projects.

DeMarco, T., *Controlling Software Projects: Management, Measurement and Estimation*, Yourdon Press: Englewood Cliffs, New Jersey, 1982.

Although DeMarco published this book in 1982, it contains timeless wisdom on how to plan, control, and measure the progress of software projects. Two of the prominent thoughts he seeds are: The project estimating role should be separated from product development by establishing an estimating group, and a single process model cannot be used for all projects.

Thayer, R., ed., *Software Engineering Project Management, IEEE Computer Society Tutorial Series*, Order Number 751, IEEE Catalog Number EH0263-4, 1988.

The IEEE Computer Society does a lot of your research homework for you by creating tutorial books that are compendiums of significant papers on various topics. Thayer's assemblage of papers on software project management lives up to the goals of the IEEE tutorial series. It reprints papers dating from 1969 (including Brooks's first description of the mythical man month) to 1987, and includes original offerings from Boehm, Yourdon, and others. Papers on planning introduce ideas about how to apply corporate software development policies, evaluations, and estimation techniques, and how to schedule. The section on controlling a software engineering project emphasizes controlling to plan, using walkthroughs, inspections, and audits, and applying software configuration management.

CHAPTER 8

Case Studies of Process Models

Illustrations from the case studies highlight different partitioning techniques, and provide examples of how plan-and-control, testing, and documentation are incorporated into various process models.

Milestone-Driven Process Model

The Milestone-Driven Process Model is one in which fixed milestones are defined and all activities are selected for the purpose of meeting these milestones. The principal maxim of the model, as in the Waterfall Process Model, states that goals are best achieved by targeting well-defined and documented milestones. Process models are often devised to satisfy upper management's need to be kept informed of progress toward completion in terms of tracking previously agreed upon milestones. This need is the driving force behind the Milestone-Driven Process Model.

Another name we could give to the Milestone-Driven approach is Contract-Driven Process Model. Instead of satisfying upper management of the same company through an informal or indirect contract, we satisfy some outside person or organization with whom we have a formal contract. The formality of a contractual relationship dictates formal specification of milestones, reviews, and reporting. For example, U.S. DoD 2167A is a set of guidelines for meeting a contractual relationship to develop software for the U.S. government. One of our case studies was bound by U.S. DoD 2167A requirements. The process model of this project illustrates how such contracts dictate the product process model, regardless of internal culture or choice of technology.

Illustration 1: Measuring Progress

A division of a large computer hardware and software systems company develops measurement and testing instruments. A project to build a front-end graphical display and control of signal measurement instruments was started in 1984 and was completed two years later. Specifically, the project goal was to transfer the primary interface from the front panel of an instrument to the screen of a general-purpose computer, to make it easier to interface with a group of instruments. A secondary project goal was to create a system that could easily be extended by customers using their own software and hardware. At project inception, the company had begun a company-wide internal effort to improve its processes. This motivated the project leader to set as an additional project objective creating a better way of measuring and reporting progress.

The project met its functionality goals, and in this sense was considered successful by the team and its direct management. However, the project missed management's schedule by one year, a 100 percent slippage.

Maxims. Five maxims underlie the process model for this project. (Derived from the interviews, these maxims were later confirmed by the project manager.)

Management is needed only for a team that is larger than six members.

Code should be quickly prototyped to gain operational understanding and experience, and then thrown out.

Prototypes help us learn, and the learning can be used to redo our work.

Measure progress in terms of meeting life cycle milestones, not individual performance.

Everyone is responsible for testing and documenting.

The first maxim came from experience and company management style. At the point at which seven or more people join together, the communication barriers are high enough to warrant making it someone's responsibility—that is, the manager's—to facilitate communication.

Process model. The manager of this project adheres to an iterative style of development and prototyping, advocating the Fountain Model approach to process control. The manager defined this model as allowing parts of a system to be developed in parallel and to be simultaneously at different stages of development. He was interested in this process model because it accounts for reusing artifacts in some but not all parts of a system. When you reuse, you get done faster. So reusing components to develop some parts of a system and not others can create a situation in which various parts of a system are at different stages of development.

Despite his preference for the Fountain Model, the manager was required to act as though he were following the Waterfall Model. As he said to us, Waterfall was "imposed on the project to tie software development to the more conservative management orientation of the hardware managers." The project's process model consisted of five phases:

Definition phase	Define external functional specifications
Design phase	Partition design into objects and define internal design and functionality of each object
Coding phase	Create, test, debug objects
System testing phase	Test entire product
Production release phase	Release with no remaining known defects and an acceptably low defect detection rate

Marketing specified requirements for the project: Reconstruct an existing product using modern technology, and add new functionality to support some new measurement techniques invented by a university professor who was a consultant to the project. In the definition phase, a requirements specification was produced consisting of object definitions written in terms of Smalltalk-like class descriptions. Marketing could not understand this notation, and relied on verbal explanation during face-to-face meetings to confirm that the correct requirements had been captured.

Design partitions were based on an architecture idea from the Smalltalk-80 system called Model-View-Controller [Krasner and Pope 1988]. This architecture factors the system into objects for presentation, objects for interaction, and objects for computation based on a business or domain model. In this project, the Model objects contain data about the hardware, or data collected from measurements or computations. Figure 8.1 contains a diagram of the partitions.

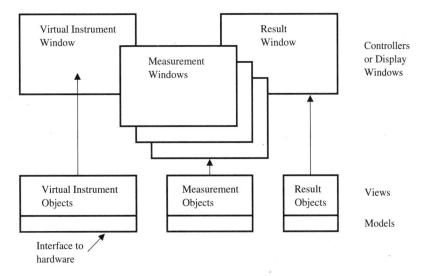

Figure 8.1   MVC Partitioning of Instrument Control System

During the design phase, the team invited Ed Yourdon to teach a course on structured analysis and design, but decided later that this method was incompatible with their ideas about development with object-oriented technology. They then created some of their own techniques for proposing class definitions. These techniques were remarkably similar to those later found in CRC Cards [Beck and Cunningham 1989] and Responsibility-Driven Design [Wirfs-Brock, Wilkerson, and Wiener 1990]. These techniques helped move the team from thinking in terms of structured analysis and design toward thinking in terms of objects.

Despite the claim that the hardware-oriented management of the company imposed a Waterfall Model, the team maxims led to a strong reliance on prototyping. Prototyping was used primarily to learn how to create a user interface that met the dual goals of user configurability and ease of use. Three designs for the user interface were prototyped and tested.

In the Coding Phase, the team started out using C. They had evaluated C++, but felt that it was not mature enough to meet their project goals. (Another team in the same company which had chosen C++ for a similar project was delayed due to problems with the language compiler and its libraries.) As the project progressed, they found themselves modifying C to add object-oriented constructs—essentially reinventing Objective C. Also, another group in the company was using Objective C to create similar systems, so the team switched to Objective C. They could now share code and ideas with the other group.

Project schedule. When the project time schedule was first put together, the team assumed that they would create 25 classes. This assumption came from prior experience in creating a 15-year-old system written in a non–object-oriented language. The schedule for this project—one year—was set by management based on their perception of the market window. It was a time-driven schedule, which did not consider the effort involved in creating 25 object descriptions. At first, the development team thought they could meet management's schedule. However, consultation with the corporate measurement group yielded a more pessimistic estimate of two years. The longer time frame included time to learn about object-oriented technology. They expected the team to grow to as many as 20 people at its peak staffing.

In the end, the project did take two years. The original six members of the team grew to 24, augmented by consultants who were delegated some of the work. Except for mentoring by the consultants, no special training was provided for team members. However, the team did work together to locate, read, and learn from the code of other systems that they thought represented good designs using object-oriented technology.

The project produced 100,000 lines of source code, organized in about 300 class definitions! The team also reused libraries purchased from a vendor of Objective C products. The project leader believed that the growth to 300 classes was the result of the designers' and engineers' constant focus on creating generalizations to meet the goal of flexibility. The engineers (in the manager's words) "got hooked on objects."

Measuring progress. The team's fourth maxim requires progress to be measured. Management wanted measures that indicated the status of the project through its different phases. In particular, the measurement program devised by a special corporate group dictated the following goals:

- Show progress of a project throughout the phases in its life cycle

- Indicate when a project has passed from one phase of the life cycle to the next

- Monitor changes to product definition, internal design, and code

- Improve resource and schedule planning to help coordinate project staffing, determine development cost, and forecast future schedules

- Flag any new process problems that a project might have

These goals imply that clear boundaries exist between phases (a Waterfall Model assumption). In hardware development—which dominates the company's culture—it is possible to organize phases with such precise boundaries. But in software, the phases were not this clearly delineated, and so the goals frustrated the team members.

Management wanted a regular monthly report of progress, tied to milestones. Using a Waterfall Model, this requirement translates to reporting the percentage completeness of the current life cycle phase, assuming all previous phases are 100 percent complete and all subsequent phases have yet to start. The project leader admitted to us that he did not know how to report numbers in this fashion while using the Fountain Model, although he did find a way to devise acceptable reports. He chose to report the completion percentages for each of the parts being worked on simultaneously—one subsystem is 80 percent defined, another subsystem is 10 percent designed, and so on. This satisfied his manager's desire to monitor progress.

To measure progress in a project involving objects, the team counted how many classes were completed relative to plan. Completion was determined by phase: percentage of the design completed, percentage of the code completed and tested, percentage of the class definitions documented and ready for production release. For each class, completion was measured in terms of how many methods were complete (relative to the behaviors determined during requirements analysis), and the stability of the definition.

Use of the CRC concepts also provided a mechanism for tracking progress: monitor the number of cards created and the number of variations in cards. When existing cards remained unchanged, although new cards might be added, the design was considered stable.

This project is interesting because of the explosion of classes. The original plan called for 25 classes, but the actual system had 300 classes. The project manager used the phrase "Zen of objects" to explain that as work proceeded, they began to understand more about the power of objects in modeling the design. So they added abstract classes, and classes that defined more functionality than originally planned. Because they were in a hybrid world, they had not anticipated that they would use objects to represent the small-grained units in the system (data structures, utilities, and so on). The number 25 represented large-grained objects—subsystems or stand-alone editors or applications; the final count of 300 included all objects. Nonetheless, management had heard 25 and, as the number increased, expressed concern that the project was out of control. Given that the team missed shipment deadline by a year, the manager indicated that, in this sense, perhaps the project was indeed out of control! We would guess that the missed deadline really indicates poor estimation capability.

The team's error was in reporting all objects in the same way. They should have set and reported progress on the milestones to complete the large-grained objects (as we discuss in Chapter 7).

Illustration 2: Documenting Progress

We interviewed a manufacturing software group that is part of a large hardware and software systems company that sells a variety of software systems. The business goals of the project we studied were defined by the terms of a government contract:

- Create a computer integrated manufacturing (CIM) system that runs on workstations and on the fabrication-line equipment, creating a paperless operation to coordinate all aspects of semiconductor wafer fabrication, from planning and scheduling to real-time embedded machine and process control

- Support the capability to produce integrated circuits rapidly in small volumes at low cost

System goals and objectives defined the characteristics of the CIM system:

- Produce a modular, low-cost facility for producing wafers

- Reduce the cycle time for production of a single wafer from several weeks to a few days

- Produce a wafer fabrication line for less than $30 million

- Demonstrate significant improvement in product quality and yield

The project had to create both hardware and software to meet the business and system goals and objectives. For the software part of the project, the architecture team had additional goals:

- Develop a distributed object-oriented system architecture for a next-generation microelectronics fabrication facility

- Specify the conventions, rules, and standards that define the development environment and that guide the development process

The software requirements were not well understood. They had to be derived by constructing a vision of what a CIM system should do, and what CIM software needs to do to support this vision. The funders then had to approve the vision and the associated software concepts.

The project managers we interviewed felt that all team members were well versed in the project goals, their functional role, and how they were being measured. There was no focus on reuse during analysis, but the team expected a big reuse payoff during design. This expectation led them to spend time searching for leverageable abstractions during high-level design. A major extension of the analysis prototype resulted from the decision to reuse the Smalltalk-based office automation package called the Analyst. This extended the capabilities of the system to back-office accounting and reporting, as well as the required manufacturing planning and scheduling.

Maxims. The process model maxims for this project were the same as those for the Waterfall Model, both because it was a government contract and because the primary experiences of all team members were in using the Waterfall approach. However, early experience with object-oriented technology changed the team maxims. By the end of the project, the now experienced object users offered the following maxims:

> Start small. Don't ramp up too fast.

> When starting a program, get senior people who understand the technology, or get people trained so that they have direct experience using the technology. Have the small number of initial people be the mentors or leaders for developing independent partitions.

> System engineers (technology experts) are critical members of the development team. For every ten designers (essentially for every two partitions), a system engineer is needed to review work done independently, and make sure that the system-level objectives for performance and reuse are being met.

> Pick a development and delivery environment that lets you easily isolate problems and fix them quickly, especially in the field.

> Reuse before you build.

These are operational maxims. They emphasize training, leveraging experience, and focusing on creating reusable results. The role of the system engineer was described to us as someone who could see the big picture and create frameworks that could be specialized to carry out multiple tasks. This system engineer was also responsible for monitoring the team's progress toward quality objectives. In this sense, the system engineer served as the team's object-oriented technology expert.

Process model. We interviewed the software managers and some team members. It wasn't clear from the conversations whether the project was research or an attempt to create a sellable product. The two government funders themselves were of mixed opinion: one wanted a product and the other a research result. Fortunately, the funders were paying the team to realize a vision, without a specific set of requirements for the software. In this sense, the project was research-oriented, and so the team saw no possibility of a failure. They would not be penalized for new ideas. They could try out new approaches and enabling technologies, and spend more money on training related to these technologies than the company usually allocates. The team did a lot of prototyping. The goal of the design prototype was to create a general framework that could be used to develop manufacturing applications. The team hoped this framework would be turned into a sellable product.

Ultimately, the software requirements were specified by translating the team's vision of what it thought would be worthwhile and feasible to do into U.S. DoD 2167A documentation format. The document in this format was reviewed and accepted by the government. In the end, the project created a working CIM system that has since been put into production use in several companies.

The process model was initially a Waterfall Model because the team needed to specify and meet milestones acceptable to the government funders. After initial training in the use of objects, the team felt that this process model was inappropriate because it did not easily support the development of a system based on objects. Specifically, they would not be able to meet the milestones and the dates associated with them. (This turned out to be quite true. The initial milestones were not met, although the project objectives and final dates were met—both on time and under budget.)

The process model that evolved was closer to a Spiral Model, but used evolutionary prototyping. Several prototypes were developed, to verify the domain analysis and to help make technical decisions, such as the choice of implementation language and design architecture. Key components—a resource specification editor and a screen layout editor—were also prototyped.

Figure 8.2 charts the system's development by quarterly date and delivery milestone. The documentation plans are indicated in the figure by abbreviations:

SRS—Software Requirements Specification

STP—System Test Plan

SDD—Software Design Document

STD—System Test Document

STR—Software Test Report

The need to produce these documents forced a top-down approach on much of the work.

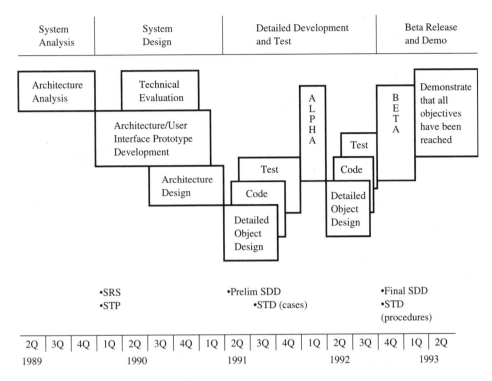

Figure 8.2 Product Development Process

This figure was produced in June 1989 for an internal presentation. In reality, analysis took a little longer and the user interface prototyping happened later. With hindsight, this actual timing made sense as there was no pressing need to have the user presentation model until the underlying information model was better understood as an outcome of the analysis period.

Timeline.

The following timeline identifies the team buildup and training program:

Aug 87	Proposal for project submitted
Aug 88	Proposal funded
Oct 88	Start of five-year project
Jan 89	Staffing effort, three people by April
May 89	Developed required specification documents and testing plans; agreement to explore object-oriented technology

Jan 90	Start of hiring ramp up to 30 people, mostly developers
Aug–Dec 90	More training in object-oriented design and system technologies
1Q91	Detailed development and test; preliminary design document completion by 4Q92
1Q93	First deployment, start productization program

For analysis, the Shlaer-Mellor approach was chosen [Shlaer and Mellor 1988]. In the development phase, they chose an object-oriented database to store CIM resource information. The production database had to be a multiuser system that could handle up to 10 gigabytes a month of information exchange. The language chosen for developing the initial prototype was Smalltalk. It was chosen after a lengthy evaluation process, with various LISP systems as the primary competitors. Smalltalk was later selected as the production language as a consequence of successes with the prototypes.

No graphical user interface builder was available at the time, so the team created an in-house tool. This in-house tool was used by the language vendor as an exemplar to create a commercial user interface builder. When the commercial version became available, the team retrofitted their system to use it. Tools for version and configuration control to support up to 30 developers on the engineering team were obtained from another outside vendor.

The first six months of the project felt somewhat unproductive to team members because many were untrained in large-scale software development and many were switching careers. Team members had an average of seven to ten years' experience in developing software using C and/or using structured analysis and design. Some of them had experience in manufacturing, but some did not. There was a training bottleneck as they were being asked to learn object-oriented analysis, design, and programming techniques, a new programming language, and a new analysis method (Shlaer-Mellor). An intense training sequence attempted to rectify this problem. The team agreed up front that most of the analysis prototypes could be thrown away, although parts would likely survive into design. They identified the manufacturing-process engineers as users and experts to be interviewed during analysis. As they produced models, they talked the models through with the domain experts, including representatives from other manufacturing companies. An SA/SD CASE tool was used to capture, store, and share analysis information, even though it was mismatched to the Shlaer-Mellor analysis models and notation.

Documentation. As an outcome of analysis, the team produced an SRS—Software Requirements Specification. The structure of the SRS, as defined by U.S. DoD 2167A, includes separate sections for the presentation of data, function, and control flow. Even though the project developed object models that combine the descriptions of function and data, and cast control flow in terms of contracts between objects, this information was disguised by mapping it into the required SRS format for delivery to the government. The large effort to map object requirements into a functional/data/control flow decomposition format was error prone and did not add anything of value beyond meeting the formal documentation requirement. Due to the mismatch, the team leaders proposed to the government alternative formats that retained the object descriptions. Probably because of the visionary nature of this project, the government supervisors were willing to entertain alternatives to the standard reporting structure.

Monthly status reports had to be filed with the heads of research, factory system management, internal technology, and others. There were many potential customers for the results of this project—inside the company, inside the government, and in other companies in the industry. Ongoing communication with all of these customers was important to ensure continued funding. Prototypes were used as a form of documentation, as a way to solicit new ideas from potential customers.

Testing. In their self-evaluation, the team remarked that testing needed the most improvement. They decided on the class as the unit for testing. The developers themselves created test cases and carried out the unit tests. A test harness was built and shared among team members, but only 20 percent of the developers used it.

The final system executes on and interfaces to wafer fabrication machinery. An appropriate system test would be to connect the proposed software to the actual machinery and run it for a while, but the actual host machines were not available until very late in the development life cycle. Instead, the system test consisted of exercising a simulation of these machines against the software. The simulator, built by one of the team members, had access to a database of actual production runs. Once the actual machines became available, integration testing involved putting the system into pilot use on the factory floor.

At the time of delivery, January 6, 1993, the system consisted of more than half a million lines of code. During the first four months of use, and despite the inability to do integration testing on real hardware, all reported problems were quickly isolated and fixed, often on the spot, without "putting a hiccup in the process." More integration testing was needed to isolate performance problems. When a performance problem was uncovered during the pilot production use, the team was able to redesign, reimplement, and reinstall entire mechanisms within one to two weeks. The project leader attributed these maintenance capabilities to the choice of object-oriented technology and to the particular delivery environment selected.

The outcome of this project was a successful pilot product delivered on time and under budget. It set a new world record for the fabrication cycle time of a silicon wafer.

Security-Driven Process Model

The next case study illustrates a partitioning based on the requirement to maintain maximum security during the development process. No one team member, other than the project manager, ever sees or understands the system as a whole. The purpose is to make sure that no team member can take complete knowledge of the system to a competitor. This process model is appropriate when the team is populated primarily by individuals who might collaborate with competitors, such as potential spies or, as in this project, outside consultants.

Illustration 3: Control Based on Need to Know

This project was done by a team within an advanced technology group of a financial services company. This company uses strategic new information systems technology to maintain a competitive edge in its core business functions. The primary goal of the project was to create a financial framework that could be specialized for each financial services agent. A secondary goal was to test the company's ability to use object-oriented technology to create an extensible framework supporting the sales of new products.

At the time of our interview, the result of the project had been in use for three months. But, from the point of view of the project leader, the result was never delivered, and never would be delivered.

Maxims. There was a critical maxim that defined the process model for this project, and thereby the team structure: No single contractor or nonmanagerial employee can know the whole system.

This maxim is based on the reality that people are critical assets of any business, but people move on, to find other jobs with competitors. In this particular situation, the team was highly leveraged by consulting experts in object-oriented technology, consultants who would move on and so could not be allowed to acquire the proprietary knowledge that gave the company its competitive edge.

An upper management dilemma: The project leader views software as organic—never done and always evolving. Organic software isn't delivered, it is just used and evolved. This leader recognizes that software is like clay and can be forever molded to meet changing needs. But he adds that documenting organic software is a waste of time, because it will keep on changing. Documentation implies completion. And so he makes it difficult for the organization to know its own assets.

Process model. The project lasted 18 months, with 17 team members. The project maxims dictated the team structure, which was what the interviewee called Guru-Oriented. The team was divided into subteams, with one to five members. Each subteam worked on an independent layer of the system. The guru—here, the project leader serving as the master architect—determines what is needed and states the requirements to the appropriate sub-team. Team members working on one layer do not have to know anything about the other layers, other than the part of the public interface that they need to use. Each subteam was autonomous in the sense that it had been delegated authority to figure out how to meet its assigned requirements. Upon receiving its assignment, each subteam independently brain-stormed, prototyped, designed, prototyped, and so on until a solution was completed. This solution was then presented to the project leader as a recommendation.

The partitioning shown in Fig. 8.3 was selected to define the independent system lay-ers. The architecture supports the need to store data in a relational database while execut-ing applications that use a distributed object model.

Application Layer (support for creating customized applications)
Business Model Layer (general business objects shared by all applications)
Semantic Layer (extensions to the base technology, including adding features to the language of choice—Smalltalk—and extending the user interface capabilities)
Distribution Layer (managing distributed objects)
Persistence Layer (object storage)
Database Layer (linking objects to a relational database)

Figure 8.3   System Partitioning

This process of exploring design options continued for several months. The guru-leader had a secret wish list of everything he wanted, but chose not to share it. Rather, he incrementally doled out assignments, waited to see what the team members were able to build, and then chose the next problem to tackle after seeing the latest results. Integration was done by the project leader.

Where else do we see process models and teams structured in this way? This approach has a flavor of Mills's chief programmer [Mills 1971], who does all assign-ments and acts as the center for all communications. But secrecy is not usually associated with a chief programmer, who usually tries to convey the big picture—in both words and architecture—so that team members can provide the needed support. The more likely analogy is to projects that control information on a "need to know" basis—many govern-ment contracts involving classified information have to operate this way.

The Security-Driven Process Model is not inherently flawed, but it is risky for an organization. Because only one person is familiar with the system as a whole, the organization's future use of the system is in jeopardy if this person is hit by a bus (our usual euphemism for no longer available to the organization).

Reuse. Several cultural factors in this organization limit its ability to reuse. The development organization does not have a tradition of cross-organizational sharing. There is no centralized technology organization. Also, there was a fundamental conflict on the project. An important goal was to create a reusable framework, one that could be specialized to meet the various needs of the company's financial services agents on different projects. The approach to developing that result required special intraproject security measures. But once the result was developed, intraproject security issues no longer applied, and cross-project issues had to be addressed. People who are supposed to reuse the result have to have some knowledge about what they are being asked to reuse. What kind of knowledge do they have to have, and how much of that knowledge will be available? For example, names of some objects and their methods may be secrets, the existence of some functionality might be a secret, architectural specifics might be a secret, or implementation details might be a secret. Inter-project security might still be required, but the secrecy limits potential reuse.

Just-Do-It Process Model

Just do it and it is done. This approach is sometimes referred to as the Code-and-Fix Process Model: Write some code, use it, and fix the defects discovered as a result of use. Analysis is not considered to be one of the activities of the process model. This approach is most often found in groups of fewer than six team members, all of whom are technically adept and find it easier (and probably more fun) to get started writing code as soon as possible. It has the advantage of less formality, and works best when the problem is well understood and the resultant system is not very big. The disadvantage is that the result is often difficult to maintain.

Illustration 4: No Formal Design

An instruments manufacturing company had a large number of network manager products, each with its own look, feel, and functionality. Some of these products had aged significantly and could no longer be effectively maintained. New networks were being developed by the company. And so it was time to create new network managers. Indeed, it was time to create an approach by which network managers could be built more quickly.

The goals of the project were:

Business   Create a family of network manager products with a common look and feel that allow a network administrator to manage resources, performance, faults, and security on one or more networks.

System	Create a core system module containing the common parts and functionality required to manage all networks. Then create specific "personality modules" that can plug into the core.
Business	Expect the customers to buy the core module and at least one personality module.

This project was carried out by a team of eight people doing their first project using object-oriented technology. They used Smalltalk to create a PC-based software system to configure the company's hardware product components. The resulting software has a kernel framework that handles the functions specific to managing all networks, but does not have network-specific knowledge. Network-specific information is defined in a personality module, which is a subsystem that can be combined with the kernel framework to form a product. At the time of the interview, the team had developed a kernel framework that they believed was reusable for creating future products, and had successfully completed and shipped two personality modules.

Maxim. The team used the following maxims:

You cannot do it right the first time.

You need to be able to change without starting over.

Process models. Team members reported that they used a traditional structured approach to system development. The team was organized in a traditional way, with a chief technologist who created the specification and the design. No analysis was carried out; no design documents were produced.

After the project was completed, two team members wrote a document that described the several different process models that the team used. These models map well to the different project types that we suggest in Chapter 5.[1]

Create Reusable Asset	Build the kernel framework using a Just-Do-It Process Model approach
Variation-on-a-Theme	Build a personality module
System Enhancement	Add a subsystem to the kernel framework or to a personality module

The kernel framework sets the user interface guidelines for any product to be created by customizing the framework. When creating a personality module, a prototype was created

---

[1] The company referenced in Chapter 5, for which we did consulting, is not the same as the one described in this case study.

first to obtain a mock-up of the graphical user interface. This prototype did not have to be functional, and was regarded as throwaway code.

Timeline.

The project timeline was as follows:

Late 88	Conceived the product concept
Mar 89	Started exploring the Smalltalk language and tools
June 89	Started prototyping the framework
Oct 89	Demonstrated completed prototype to management
Nov 89	Decided to create the product version. Consultant brought in to advise on how to manage the product development process
Jan 90	Implemented most of the old product functions, then overhauled the design to handle remote access from a dumb terminal
Apr 91	Completed customer evaluation
May 91	Shipped product to first customer

The timeline indicates that the process model focused on prototyping to support the desire to have quick results. The team covered a lot of ground using tools to support object-oriented technology. What the team found out was that, despite fast results, this approach does not lead to a good architecture.

The engineering team consisted of a project manager with 13 years of experience in developing software communication products, a lead engineer with experience on IBM PC computers, and three senior software engineers, each with ten years of experience. Only one of the five knew Smalltalk. In addition, the team included a development quality engineer, and a project engineer working in the company but not directly reporting to the project manager. This project was not the first one to use object-oriented technology in the company. A representative from a prior project that had used Smalltalk acted as a mentor/consultant. The team had little formal training in methods, and blindly followed the advice of a consultant just to start coding, managing the sources with a source code version control system. This process seemed both fun and productive. At first, the team was pleased with the resulting products.

When the team members were probed during the interview, however, the darker side of the Just-Do-It Process Model emerged: The team was not happy with the system's current maintainability.

They believed that system test should have been easier than it was. They said that they often do not understand the consequences that a change might create. As a result, they do not feel that they can predict how long it will take to remove all of the system defects.

The source of their problems? According to them, the source was the lack of a formal design architecture—the failing of the Just-Do-It Process Model.

The team commented that object-oriented languages and tools seem to encourage the Just-Do-It Model. Start coding. Evolve the code as you explore the design space. Eventually you code in all the functionality, then do some testing to convince yourself that the system is not easy to break, and you are done. Predictable and safe maintenance is lost, not because of objects, but because of the choice of process model for using objects that leads to poor design.

Creating a Reusable Asset Process Model

The process model for creating a reusable asset is distinguished by two characteristics: the up-front acknowledgment that considerable rework will be required, and the need to evaluate the generality of the asset. Evaluating the generality of a component is difficult. Although some clever people can devise good evaluation cases, the best way to evaluate an asset is to have it reused by developers who have serious product deadlines. The benefit of use in a real project is that the evaluation situation is not contrived.

Two of our case studies had a primary goal of creating reusable frameworks and components. At the time of the interviews, both had deployed to reusers. The first case study project was unsuccessful in the sense of finishing very late; the second was successful in creating its follow-on releases, but at the time of the interviews was experiencing support problems.

Illustration 5: Create a Reusable Framework

The goal of this case study project was to produce a new set of CASE tools competitive with those that already existed in the marketplace. The new version was to make the user interface of an existing product more like those of market competitors (that is, graphical). Business and system goals can be summarized as:

Business	Create an integrated set of CASE tools that support the full life cycle. The tools are to be used within the company and sold as products.
Business	Design and implement a more modern user interface for both the new set of tools and an existing product, which had similar functionality.
System	Maintain functionality of the existing product. Use a desktop paradigm for a new user interface. Create an application window painter and other tools that work with the existing product architecture. Use a client/server architecture. Create a development repository for the new architecture.

This project was primarily a re-architecting of an existing product, maintaining the functionality of this product and adding a limited set of new features (graphical interface, window painter, and some additional presentation views). Perhaps because this product was not entirely new, the development team was highly optimistic about their ability to finish in a short amount of time—despite the decision to use technology that was new to the team and to the company. Although the deadline was missed by a year, they did successfully ship a product that met the business and system goals.

Maxim. This company uses the following maxim to structure teams:

> A productive team can be built by bringing in less-experienced people to work under experienced coaches.

This maxim works best on Variation-on-a-Theme projects. The experienced leaders understand how to proceed, quickly learn what inexperienced people can be asked to do successfully, and can dynamically balance learning/teaching and doing. This model does not work well when developing new systems or First-of-Its-Kind architectures, as this particular team found out when it set out to create a new architecture to reimplement an existing product. With hindsight, one manager told us that the company needed to move toward a Maven Model[2]—small teams of highly skilled developers, who follow the project to completion and take personal pride in the result.

Process model. The team chose to create a reusable framework that supported the general services of a window-based user interface. The framework included editors that manage user interaction events, and facilities for sharing information among multiple editors (such as a clipboard). The team referred to the editors as applications.

The timeline for product development is shown here. It indicates that time was built in for rework; in fact, it shows that the scope of the framework was not finalized until much of the code that uses the framework was completed. Rework was driven by experience that was acquired while trying to create specializations using intermediate versions.

Timeline.

Oct 87	Began work on the functional specification.
Jan 88	Completed functional specification. Began evaluating development environments and designing the high-level architecture.
June 88	Finalized high-level architecture design.

---

[2] Maven is a Yiddish word for an expert, one who knows all the answers to everything in his field. It is meant in a positive way.

July 88	Selected Smalltalk as the development environment. Fifteen developers began coding the subsystems representing the basic architecture. Application prototypes were developed in parallel.
	Team consisted of one to three programmers per editor, and a technical manager who also programmed the object editor.
Sept 88	Completed coding of main windowing services.
Jan 89	Began coding of applications and additional subsystems for the architecture. Architecture coding completed in July, while application coding proceeded until Dec 90.
Mar 89	Finalized scope of project.
Nov 89	Beta tested the software.
Oct 90	Shipped product to first customer.

The original time schedule planned first customer shipments after two years; the actual development took three years. The slip included a longer time to get to beta. The instability of the software demanded a year's refinement and rework until the result was acceptable.

Six people formed the initial team. Prototypes for the new CASE editors were built during the period when the development environment was being chosen, and were presented to the project advisory committee as proof of concept. Early prototyping was used to identify the classes that would be needed, especially those that could be reused across applications. At the same time, the prototypers stress-tested the proposed new development environment. Prototyping was also used as a training exercise in the use of the language and development tools.

At the same time as application prototyping was being done, the overall architecture of the system was designed. The preliminary plan was to divide the system into a technical layer and an application layer. After considerable rework, the architecture was refined to that shown in Fig. 8.4. The three partitions in the technical layer were: services to manage a windowing interface, services to interface with a database or repository, and services common to all editors. This last set of services consisted of: Object Editor, which was a general editing framework used in most of the process-oriented applications; and Tree Editor, which was a framework for applications that represented information as tree structures. (This technical layer can be purchased today from a vendor of operating systems or application development environments, but was not as widely available in 1988.)[3]

---

[3] Actually these were available on the computers of choice—IBM PCs—but from Hewlett-Packard, who was under a copyright infringement lawsuit (which HP eventually won). The case study company did not want to rely on the vendor at the time.

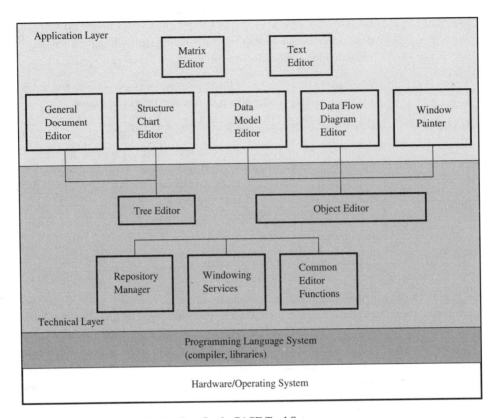

Figure 8.4   Architecture for the Case Study CASE Tool Set

Team. The team structure was modeled on the two layers of the system architecture, with the more senior people assigned to work on the technical layer, and the junior members on the application layer. Each of the application teams developed its own classes to support its particular editor. The programmers were given a great deal of freedom in design, reading manuals and books like those from Shlaer-Mellor and Booch [Booch 1991] to direct their efforts. Classes were not shared among the application teams during the initial prototyping period. This led to some redundancies, but the teams felt it simplified coordination. Later they found that this separation also meant that changes in one editor had no impact on the other editors. They liked this except when the changes needed to be shared (for consistency purposes, for example).

During the process of developing the various editors, a skilled designer joined the team. This designer reviewed all prototypes to find redundancies and common functions. He discovered that two frameworks were possible: the Object Editor and the Tree Editor. Only the Object Editor was built during this project because only one special use of the

Tree Editor was expected. There was not sufficient time in the development schedule to specify a more general version of the Tree Editor. Later, this decision was revisited and the more general tree-editing framework was developed.

By December 1988 the team consisted of 23 people. Five were managers, one of whom had three years of Smalltalk experience and who led the framework development for the editors. Seven were senior developers with an average of less than five years of experience. Only half the team members were fluent in Smalltalk. Outside consultants were employed to review the project for architectural design and appropriateness of the development environment. The consultants recommended that the team size be reduced by approximately one-third, retaining the more experienced system designers and programmers who knew Smalltalk. The time schedule for the project simply did not support the training time needed to bring inexperienced personnel up to speed on Smalltalk. More significantly, it appeared that the senior people were less productive than they could be, because they were spending a considerable portion of their time assisting junior people.

The team took the approach that unit testing should be done at the method level, which was quite time consuming. Application programmers tested at the user interface level as well. Testing involved eight to ten people for three months. These were not the same people as the coders.

The project experienced considerable delay because the team had little experience with the design of this kind of system and with the programming language. The software development environment was also unstable, with the vendor delivering six months later than promised. Technical problems with the language system's OS/2 version and its support for Presentation Manager persisted throughout the project.

Upper management expectations. Upper management really did expect object-oriented technology to be a silver bullet, which can be attributed at least partly to the optimism of a high-level consultant to the management team. They criticized the development team for being too slow. The project suffered from the inexperience of the team members, who did not know how to create a system software product and had to learn on the job. Management should not have been surprised by the lack of such system features as robust error handling—but they were. Our own view of this project is that some pretty remarkable people managed to deliver a product—despite buggy system software, despite a lack of experience in creating and testing frameworks, despite a decision to use all new technology—only one year later than management's too-short time schedule.

The framework was built to meet the stated goals of the project—creating a reusable framework was not itself a goal. The framework-and-applications approach turned out to be successful in that several follow-on products were created, building on the code that resulted from the first development project. Unlike the large-team approach of the first project, the second project needed only two designers, and three or four coders. As reported to us, a third product reused 50 percent of the code that was developed for the second one, basically selecting from existing editors. This reused code equaled 90 percent of the code of the third product—that is, the third product was mostly a repackaging with a few additional features.

Concept Development Process Model

The next two projects share a common characteristic: incomplete or poorly defined requirements. The goal of each project was to create a set of tools that support analysts in applying a business or technical method, but the method itself was not well articulated.

This form of process model tends to use exploratory prototyping, which we earlier defined as the ability to entertain radical changes in the system architecture as requirements change. Prototyping was used to discover what the tools should do, and to understand better the method to be supported by the tools.

Both projects started out with exploratory prototyping, but eventually settled on a more evolutionary approach. These two projects were not among our formal case studies, but were carried out by teams within our company, ParcPlace Systems.

Illustration 6: Available Prototypes

The ParcPlace Systems Object Behavior Analysis (OBA) method provides concepts, techniques, and steps for conducting object-oriented analysis [Rubin and Goldberg 1992, Rubin and Goldberg 1993]. Between 1989 and 1991, the method was carried out using paper and pencil, which involved an excessive amount of bookkeeping for customers with large and complex problems. OBA supports full traceability of analysis results: all artifacts, such as objects and the services of objects, are traceable back through the decision process to original goals and objectives. The ability to trace decisions requires a lot of bookkeeping, which is best done with computer assistance. Because the paper-based implementation did not scale up to large projects, the OBA team was denied valuable feedback on the effectiveness of the method. It was necessary to develop an OBA tool set to facilitate the analysis of large projects to test the scaleability of OBA techniques.

Over time, the OBA tool set project changed. In retrospect, it evolved in four phases. It started as an exploratory effort to see what, if anything, could be accomplished in the way of an OBA tool set. The result was a proof-of-concept tool, which demonstrated that OBA-like tools can help people analyze large projects. (It also demonstrated the usefulness of the concepts underlying OBA.) The second phase was based on a contract with another company. The purpose of the contract was to define the architecture of an OBA tool set that handles much of the requirements of any CASE tool, such as multiuser support and connection to a commercially available database. This second project resulted in a better understanding of what was missing in the OBA method, as well as a prototype architecture for a robust CASE tool, and the prototype tools themselves.

The goals of the third phase were to revise the method, create complete method documentation, and create a fully functional prototype of the first deliverable product. At the time of writing this description, the OBA effort is in its fourth phase, to create a product version of the OBA tool set.

Was OBA one project or four? Chapter 2 defines a project to be a set of activities to take you from a current situation to a desired situation. Projects differ according to their goals and are structured differently because their goals are different. In this sense, each phase is rightly a different project. So we will treat the OBA work as four different projects. Here we discuss only the first two projects, individually examining their goals, maxims, process models, and team structures.

Project 1—Exploratory Prototype

The goal of the first tool development effort was to provide on-line support for capturing some of the artifacts that result from the application of the OBA method. There was no formal requirements specification; there were no stated quality objectives. The resultant software was an exploratory prototype to see what was involved in creating OBA tools in the Objectworks\Smalltalk environment.

Maxim. The maxim that guided development during this project was:

> When the end functionality is unknown, it is better to prototype the partial functionality that is known than to attempt to develop a full requirements specification. The prototype can then be used as a testbed for developing new functionality.

Process model. This project was structured as a series of prototypes. Each prototype was an incremental extension of the previous prototype, and was made available to users of the OBA method. As a result, based on user experience, a subsequent prototype might rework parts of the previous prototype to make it more effective.

Table 8.1 describes each prototype by resources, goals, and activities. The original OBA tool set prototypes were based on tables of information—for example, scripts and glossaries. Hence, the goal was to develop a framework for tables. Resources to carry out the project were supplied by both ParcPlace and SEMATECH, a U.S. consortium of semiconductor companies.

Available prototypes. The first three prototypes were used by ParcPlace, SEMATECH, and its member companies. The initial project goal was to support many ParcPlace customers in conducting OBA on large and complex projects, and to obtain additional user feedback on the usefulness of the method. To meet these goals, it was decided that the

Table 8.1   OBA Project 1 Prototypes

Prototype Resources	Goals	Activities
Table Framework 2 people part-time for one month	Develop a table viewing and editing framework in Objectworks\Smalltalk 4.0.	▪ Identify existing table framework for possible reuse ▪ Examine and define strengths and weaknesses ▪ Define and carry out modification plan
Version 1.0 6 people from SEMATECH for 3 months	Develop preliminary requirements for an OBA tool set (based on Pen and Paper Approach) and develop the first prototype to support these requirements.	▪ OBA-based analysis of requirements ▪ Design, code, and test tools ▪ Evaluate and rework
Version 1.1 1 person, part-time for 2 months	Add additional tool support to Version 1.0.	▪ Evaluate Version 1.0 prototype ▪ Improve table framework ▪ Develop loader/unloader framework
Version 1.2 1 person, part-time for 2 months	Evolve Version 1.1 by enhancing support for OBA artifact traceability. Improve loader and table frameworks.	▪ Develop a Rich Text Format (RTF) writer ▪ Improve table framework ▪ Develop trace framework
Version 1.3 and Version 1.4 2 people (one from each company), part-time for 2.5 months	Develop new architecture based on the transactions that would support multiple users accessing a database. Improve the interoperability of the tools.	▪ Develop an architecture document ▪ Design and implement the transaction-specific portions of the architecture ▪ Redevelop all tools to use this architecture

OBA tool set would be an available prototype. *Available prototype* is a term that we have coined to describe a prototype that is distributed in a limited way, for purposes of gathering information from a larger user base, but which is not a product (and therefore is not officially documented, supported, or sold in a product sense).

There are several risks when prototypes are made available for use outside of the development organization. The kind and level of support and the availability of future updates must be addressed. It is a prototype, but the users might become dependent on its availability. In addition, because a prototype does not necessarily have the same quality as a product, an organization must realize that a poor prototype can create prejudices against the organization's products. ParcPlace used a well-defined process to distribute and support the prototype. The prototype was available only to students of the ParcPlace object-oriented methodology course who signed a licensing agreement that acknowledged the prototype status of the software. Prototype recipients were encouraged to use the prototype and to provide feedback directly to the OBA development team, who released changes to remove defects, and created the follow-on prototypes.

Analysis and design. During the development of each prototype, analysis and design activities were carried out in an opportunistic fashion. A small set of requirements was derived from the existing paper-based model of OBA for each of the prototypes. These requirements were captured in either a text document or simple OBA format. Most of the time was spent in design—whiteboard discussions using OBA techniques. As early prototypes became available, the OBA tool set itself was used to derive parts of the design. In fact, the first use of the OBA tool set was to remove several particularly nasty design defects in a table framework.

Reuse opportunities. Reuse opportunities come in two complementary forms: utilization of existing assets, and creation of new reusable components. All of the prototypes were developed in the ParcPlace Objectworks\Smalltalk Release 4.0 environment, and thus benefited from more than 300 classes and 8000 methods that are available for code reuse. In addition, prior to the start of this project, ParcPlace had developed a preliminary table framework for internal use. The activities of the Table Framework prototype adapted this existing framework to meet specific OBA requirements.

While building the prototypes in this project, we created two reusable frameworks: table and loader/unloader. These frameworks were reworked as prototypes evolved. Experience over the years has convinced us that good frameworks evolve only by being used in many diverse situations. It is premature to declare a framework reusable until you have at least three independent examples of successful reuse. Versions 1.1 and 1.2 created four new situations for using the table framework. Each use identified missed opportunities for generalization, or uncovered a poorly designed object protocol.

Project 2—Contracted Exploratory Prototype

The Version 1.4 prototype provided tools that supported approximately half of the OBA method as it was defined in late 1992. Many ParcPlace customers were using the prototype tool set to conduct OBA within their organizations. It was now time to investigate tools to support the remaining half of the OBA method, and to begin planning for productization. As part of the planning process, ParcPlace had discussions with many of its OBA users. One organization in particular liked the concepts embodied in the first project prototype. But their specific project needs required a more functionally complete tool set. ParcPlace viewed the extension of the prototype to include this additional functionality as a prerequisite to eventual productization. Recognizing a mutually beneficial opportunity, ParcPlace agreed to construct the next generation prototype under contract, which allowed the in-house team to grow from one to three people.

The first activity of this new project was to develop a high-level requirements document to describe the behavioral requirements of the OBA tool set. These requirements were organized by OBA method steps and by topic (e.g., graphical, team support). In addition, a set of quality objectives were defined. These included:

Resilience to change	Adding new OBA artifacts and tools, developed as the method evolves, must not interfere with existing system function.
Operating environment	Tools must operate with a variety of persistent storage mechanisms (e.g., RDBMS, OODBMS, file system).
Performance	There can be no more than a several-second interaction response delay, despite the need to deal with many thousands of artifacts. Browsing performance must be optimized.
Multiuser	Tools must support 20 simultaneous users, provide transaction-based editing, and be able to merge artifacts created by multiple users.

The partitions for the tool set shown in Fig. 8.5 were selected to meet the system objectives. A separate partition was created to understand the ways in which the OBA tools interact with the rest of the development environment. There was also a separate partition for handling the connection to a database, and another for an artifact manager to handle reading, writing, creating, and deleting artifacts. Two partitions focused on the ways in which the tools would interact with information stored in different formats. The i/o manager handles connections to external storage media, while wrappers transform representations of information stored in non-OBA formats. Tools manipulate artifacts, and each artifact can have one or more relationships with other artifacts. A separate partition solves the problem of maintaining consistency among all of these relationships.

The first three prototypes focused on adding OBA tools to support all of the OBA steps. The process of building these prototypes was much the same as for Versions 1.2–1.4. The next major result of this effort was a prototype of a new artifact-management architecture. The early versions assumed that the analysis models resided in memory. In this activity, the tool set was modified to store artifacts externally—in a relational or object-oriented database—to handle larger projects and to facilitate multiuser interaction.

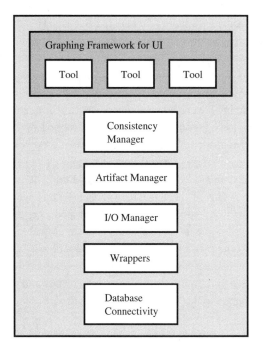

Figure 8.5   OBA Tool Set Architecture

The first generation of the new architecture was developed as a two-week rapid prototyping activity. The analysis and design techniques were derived from the OBA approach, although considerable time was spent in group sessions that brainstormed different architectures. The prototype code was further partitioned so several people could work simultaneously. Integration cycles were on the order of every couple of hours, rather than days or weeks.

Documentation. During this process, most of the major design choices were documented, along with some of the choices that were discarded as dead ends. The completed document contains the architecture requirements, the associated design choices, and the resulting prototype. This document was the basis for the first formal design review. The contract required only a usage review, but the developers required a design review because it was a project goal to use this architecture and its prototype as the basis for a product.

With a new architecture in place, the next activity was to port the current prototype to the ParcPlace VisualWorks environment. The resulting prototype, containing all of the ported tools, became OBA Tool Set Version 2.0.

Reusing. The team next constructed a multiuser database version of the tool set. The goal was to connect the OBA tool set to a relational database system, based on reusing the ParcPlace Database Connectivity package, which immediately enabled access to a variety of different databases, including Oracle and Sybase. To support access to multiple data-storage products, a layer was introduced between the application and the specific database connection layer (Fig. 8.5 Wrappers). This design choice later proved to be correct when the team was able to add support for in-memory and object data management system representations with a minimum of fuss. With the addition of the external data storage, performance tuning was required to get a usable prototype.

One important prototype activity remained—construction of a Graph Viewing framework. ParcPlace had developed a prototype graphical framework for another project, which was reused. Reuse reduced a multimonth framework development effort to three weeks of effort to understand the framework and to customize it.

The team developed two of the three required artifact viewers. The third viewer (a Harel State Chart Viewer) proved much more difficult than expected, and was abandoned because the current version of the OBA method did not collect sufficient information to generate the dynamic object model diagrams. This feedback was exactly the kind of method-related feedback expected from developing a prototype. A goal of the next project was thus established: Find out why the necessary information was not captured, and determine whether a change to the OBA method is required.

Testing. It was important to test the prototypes because they were made available to users who depended on them for real work. Because of the development strategy, limited resources, and "as-is" distribution policy, no regression test suites were created. Hindsight indicates that because the prototype was evolving incrementally, parts of the system that were developed during an earlier increment continued to exist during later increments, although many were slightly (and some significantly) modified in the process. Use of regression tests would have saved development time. This experience introduced a new maxim for future projects:

> When the development strategy is to create a series of available prototypes, use of regression tests for the stable parts of the evolving prototype will save development effort.

Illustration 7: Prototyping Partnership

A second ParcPlace project that created a series of available prototypes was done in partnership with a customer, a management consulting firm interested in supporting its business-modeling method with a set of computer-based tools. The method had been in use for some years, but was not supported by tools. The team that was building the tools was not well versed in the method, unlike the OBA tool set project. They used the development process to learn about the method.

Maxim. The project leader emphasizes the role of documentation in stating the development team's primary maxim (one also advocated by Gerry Weinberg [Weinberg 1971]):

> If it is not written down, dated, and distributed, it is not real.

"It" refers to anything—any part of the software development process including requirements, functional specifications, and decisions. Writing clarifies thinking. Careful and precise documentation of plans, decisions, and requirements builds confidence and understanding between the customer and the development team. The defining documents lead to agreement on what each prototype should attempt to explore.

Another strong motivation for this maxim is that teams of mostly senior people (true for this project) can keep a lot of information in their heads. They forget to communicate critical decisions to other team members. These senior people often work alone, and are inclined to institute rather sweeping changes with possibly negative effects on other developers. Documentation is a way to force communication, and to help mold a team approach.

Process model. The documentation was not about milestones. If so, the process model used on this project would have been dictated by contracted milestones, and we would have seen a Milestone-Driven Process Model. Rather, the documentation was about requirements for a prototype.

This project, like that of the OBA tool set, used a very generic process model, as shown in Fig. 8.6. In spite of the existence of a contract, a fixed sequence of tasks leading to a final result could not be predetermined. The agreement between contractee and developers required a series of prototypes to be built. Each prototype would make progress toward understanding the product system. Each prototype would seek information—information that the contractee agrees, in advance of doing the prototype, is important to obtain.

Resources for the project were stable throughout all prototyping efforts. At the outset of the project, a 12-person team was hired, including a project manager, a documentor, and a quality assurance manager (who built testing tools as well as the test cases). They were all highly skilled software systems developers, with several years of experience using object-oriented technology. Those team members who were not already fluent in Smalltalk either learned on their own, or took the ParcPlace Smalltalk and methodology courses.

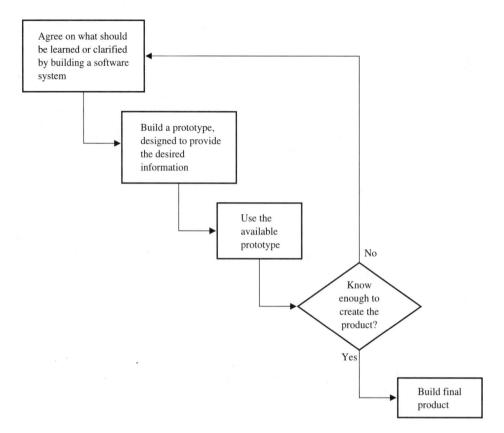

Figure 8.6   Getting to a Product Plan Using Available Prototypes

The goals for each prototype were:

Prototype 1   Demonstrate to the chief methodologist (the client) what
                     aspects of the method are currently understood by the team,
                     by building tools that reflect this understanding.

Prototype 2   Develop an architecture for the tools, based on an improved
                     understanding of the method.

Prototype 3   Create the architecture and implementation as the basis for
                     the first product. Add use of a relational database.

The first prototype was an analysis prototype that was thrown away after demonstration and discussion with the customer. This prototype exposed differences in understanding. Moreover, the prototype highlighted some additional opportunities. As a result, the customer changed requirements, which of course affected the next design effort. From building the team to completing the first prototype, three months passed.

The second prototype was a design prototype that reused some of the code from the first prototype. Implementation was quick—three months. The third prototype was a design prototype, with all new code. The project manager insisted on throwing away all of the code from the second prototype because he felt that trying to evolve to a new architecture would take longer than starting over again.

The team is currently evolving this prototype into a first product release. In anticipation of this use of the third prototype, documentation was created, consisting of a requirements specification, a detailed functional specification, and a detailed description of the user interaction model and graphical screens. The documentation includes goals and objectives, guidelines, and requirements and usage scenarios. The requirements consisted of the following topics:

Business modeling environment

Programming environment

Support expectations

Testing requirements

System utility requirements

These topics indicate that the goal was to create both a business modeling environment and an application generator. The business modeling environment uses outlining tools for gathering data, business structures, and glossaries. Support means on-line help; testing refers to debugging aids, use of undo in the editors, and so on; and system utilities include connections to relational databases. These categories became the basic partitions.

The customer did a formal inspection of the documentation, with all team members participating. The purpose of this inspection was to make sure that everyone understood the structure and details of the whole effort (in sharp contrast to the Security-Driven Process Model). Given that there were 120 distinct requirements, the inspection was time consuming. But because a number of significant misunderstandings were uncovered, the time was considered worthwhile.

At the time of writing this description, the third prototype has just been completed and reviewed. Work is proceeding to create the actual product based on the third prototype. The product process model will create four product releases, each one incrementally adding features. The purpose of doing the product incrementally is to get to market sooner and get earlier real-world experience. The architecture from the prototype defined the partitioning for the product.

Clearing up some evolving confusions. During the course of interviewing the project manager, we questioned whether he really threw away code. We ultimately agreed that there are several ways in which people use the phrase "evolving a prototype."

First, you can identify problems and try to fix those problems in place, much the way you might patch an arm or a nose on an existing statue. We use the term "iterative development" to identify this way of reworking a result.

Second, you can evolve by adding functionality, not by changing existing code. Sort of like adding a clay dog to stand next to a clay man, or a new wing to a house. We use the term "incremental development" for this process.

Finally, you can start over again and rethink the architecture for the next prototype. Once you have a plan for what to do, you might look around to see if code exists that you can salvage and reuse. This code could come from a prior prototype. Keeping with the analogy, you might redesign a new statue consisting of several figures and decide to reuse an existing man's head but create a new body, or take the fireplace from the old house to use in the new house. Does this mean that the prior prototype evolved? We use the term "evolutionary prototyping" for this process. Evolutionary prototyping ultimately looks like incremental development, but each new increment extends some but not all the parts of the prior increment.

All three uses of the phrase "evolving a prototype" are popular in the vocabulary of developers. When this project manager spoke of "throwing away a prototype," he agreed that the third situation might occur. But he would not agree that the new prototype had evolved from the prior one.

Summary

We provided examples drawn from seven case study projects to highlight some of the issues involved in setting up an effective product process model. These projects illustrate five different approaches to a process model, which we labeled milestone-driven, security-driven, just-do-it, creating a reusable asset, and concept development. Although we are not fond of all these models—notably, the security-driven dependence on gurus and the just-do-it approach both concern us—the experiences of these various projects should help you understand the kinds of decisions you have to make, the role that partitioning plays in planning the project, and the way in which a work model based on making prototypes available can help you to better understand a problem situation.

Specifically, these case studies reinforced our belief that it is a bad idea to track project progress by monitoring the number of objects created (illustration 1). They indicated that architecture dictates or heavily influences the process model of a project (illustrations 2 and 3), and that the lack of design, in this case associated with lack of training, creates testing and maintenance problems (illustration 4). Illustration 5, which documented the usefulness of a prototyping strategy when building frameworks and tools, has some important team structure messages—suggesting the importance of creating right-sized subteams to work in parallel. Similarly, illustrations 6 and 7 based their process model strategies on incremental development of prototypes. In addition, illustration 7 emphasized the overall importance of documentation in focusing team members.

Additional Reading About Case Study Experiences

Brooks, F. P., *The Mythical Man Month*, Addison-Wesley: Reading, Mass., 1975.

This book of essays is intended for professional software development managers. The essays examine the technical and managerial lessons that Brooks learned while managing the IBM OS/360 team from 1964 to 1965. Brooks's advice is rich in maxims such as: "How does a project get to be a year late? One day at a time." The insight that Brooks communicates is timeless.

Davis, J. and Morgan, T., Object-Oriented Development at Brooklyn Union Gas, *IEEE Software*, 10(1), 67–75, January 1993.

This paper documents the authors' experience in creating a new customer information system at the Brooklyn Union Gas Company to handle data from gas meters (downloading data from hand-held terminals), billing, cash processing, credit and collection, and field service orders. It points out different projects-within-a-project that led to the released system, as well as the successful maintenance experienced to date. The system was built using a modified version of PL/1 on an IBM mainframe.

Harmon, P. and Taylor, D., *Objects in Action: Commercial Applications of Object-Oriented Technologies*, Addison-Wesley: Reading, Mass., 1993.

The Object Management Group (OMG) is a consortium of companies that provides a forum for sharing experience and setting guidelines on the use of object-oriented technology. In 1993, the OMG held a contest to find successful applications of the technology in different industries and for different purposes. This book presents the winning contest entries.

Murphy, G., Townsend, P., Laberge, P., and Juzenas, M., Engineering Software With Objects, Chapter 3 in Meyer, B., and Nerson, J. M., eds., *Object-Oriented Applications*, Prentice Hall: Englewood Cliffs, New Jersey, 1993.

The Meyer and Nerson book is a collection of papers that document designs of several technical projects, all carried out using the Eiffel language. The Murphy *et al.* paper is the only chapter that provides detailed information about the project process model. The project was carried out in a Canadian telecommunications company for the purpose of creating a network trouble-reporting system. The advice is consistent with our recommendations, cleverly written with "voices" of management, development, and technology transfer commenting on theory versus practice.

CHAPTER 9

What Is Reuse?

The essence of reuse is using what already exists to achieve what is desired. We create reusable artifacts, and we reuse these artifacts. The term *artifact* refers to any result of a process model activity, including code, data, analyses, and plans. An *asset* is any artifact that has been certified (by someone or some process in the organization) for reuse. Our goal is purposely to create reusable assets, and to make these assets generally available throughout the organization.

Why the Hype About Reuse?

Look at the reported reuse success stories that credit object-oriented technology with good reuse results. *Computer World* tells how EDS used two languages to develop the same application.[1] The article attributes much of the project's success to the reuse of artifacts or components in the Smalltalk programming environment. The results were:

PL/1	19 calendar months	152 person months	265,000 LOC
Smalltalk	3.5 calendar months	10.4 person months	22,000 LOC

Forbes publicized another corporate success story about American President Company,

---

[1] White Paper on Object Technology: A Key Software Technology for the 90s, *Computer World*, May 11, 1992.

Ltd. (a shipping company).[2] By reusing objects,

> the data processing department was able to concoct custom software in a fraction of the time that it would have taken with traditional programming techniques. . . . Programming time for one market share report was cut from seven months to seven weeks. . . . The company was able to more than double international volume, from 215,000 containers in 1984 to 491,700 in 1989.

Communications Week says that Smalltalk and its reusable libraries offers an "eight to 15-fold performance gain over procedural approaches."[3]

And *Computer World* tells how AMS (a large systems integrator) has

> constructed a library of reusable software objects for generic programming tasks such as database interaction, user interfaces and error correction. . . . Their experience shows that more than half of all applications can be constructed from previously developed blocks of code, and when that happens, programmer productivity jumps by 35 to 100 percent.[4]

Impressive numbers. Hard to ignore. Unforgettable!

We do not know whether the advertised numbers are accurate or not. The fact is, we see the numbers, our customers see the numbers, decision makers see the numbers. They are unforgettable. It would be negligent for a CIO, an IT manager, or us not to investigate. Something is leading everyone to believe that there is at least an order of magnitude productivity improvement to be gained from reuse with objects. Why?

Objects are pluggable components. First, productivity gains should come because objects make you think about creating components that can be plugged together. With objects, reuse is a natural part of development. A useful analogy involves Lego® blocks.[5] These toy blocks are popular because they give children of all ages an endless ability to build different structures. As explained by an executive of the toy firm, the importance of the Lego idea is that it de-emphasizes how to do things in favor of what to do. The blocks focus the child on what is to be built, rather than how to build, because all of the parts fit together accurately—with just the right amount of friction—to make building easy.[6] Lego

---

[2] Pitta, J., Oops: why dirty your hands with programming code when you can just wave your hands and get the computer to do what you want?, *Forbes*, 145(6), 162–63, March 19, 1990.

[3] Cox, J., Psst! Smalltalk Gains C/S Favor, *Communications Week*, Nov. 1, 1993.

[4] Betts, M., AMS has suite deal: Reusable Software, *Computer World*, 14(42), Oct. 18, 1993.

[5] Richard Pawson of CSC Index provided us with his version of the Lego and restaurant analogies at the Index Summit meeting in March 1993. We have taken some liberty in extending the restaurant idea.

[6] The good interface makes Lego blocks easy to take apart, which is an important property of a toy designed for exploratory construction.

blocks are easy to reuse, and very hard to create because it is hard to design the edges that fit together so well. The dream is that end users will have the software equivalent of Lego blocks: a set of software parts with well-defined interfaces (edges), with which they can rapidly compose and recompose a variety of applications. Just as Lego users expect expert toy makers to create the blocks, end users expect expert developers to create the right software objects.

Objects are customizable components. The second reason why objects should improve productivity is that objects make it easier to design and implement applications that can be customized by the end user. Customizing objects is a special form of reuse that we explain by analogy to restaurants and cafeterias. Picture yourself in a restaurant. You sit down at the table. The waiter hands you a menu. It has a list of dinners, including the daily specials. None is perfect, but at least one is appealing. You order it. The waiter goes to the kitchen, places the order, and eventually brings it to you. As in the old school of software development, the chefs determine the choices, there is a limited number of choices, and the customers vote with their pocketbooks. Figure 9.1 labels this approach "supply-side information management."

A cafeteria represents an alternative kind of restaurant. The chefs prepare the dishes—condiments, salads, relishes, pastas, potatoes, meat, and so on. There is a clear set of options, laid out on a buffet table, and replenished regularly. The customers create their own meals by selecting any of the options in any quantity. Figure 9.2 labels this approach "demand-side information management." It is the goal of the new school of software development, where customers create their own applications by combining components (objects) made available by the experts.

Figure 9.1 Supply-Side Information Management— Software development by asking the experts to do it all

Figure 9.2 Demand-Side Information Management—Software development by components composition

The kitchen and software development staffs have a shared goal: reduce or eliminate the number of customer requests to substitute one component for another. These special requests in the supply-side system disrupt an otherwise well-managed process. They create a food preparation (a software development) backlog. The cafeteria approach—the demand-side system—handles the many customer differences in meal combinations by letting the customers create the combinations themselves. The chefs are left to prepare the core food offerings. The teams that produce reusable assets can do the same, by providing the reusable components that can be used by business programmers or end users to compose an application.

In the cafeteria, customers do not go into the kitchen to create the dishes, and the customers do not change the options. But perhaps a chef notices that a large number of customers create the same basic meal, by combining the same dishes. By making this combination a new option at the buffet, the chef can get more customers through the line faster. The software chef can do the same, by noticing the kinds of subsystems that business programmers often compose from existing components, and providing prefabricated, high-quality versions of these subsystems. Parts become a whole and the whole can become a part—a feature of objects.

Often a chef stands at the cafeteria line to slice the turkey or cut the beef, as shown in Fig. 9.3. The customers could serve themselves, but not all customers use a knife as well as the chef. The chef makes sure that the customers get their preferred parts of the fowl or roast, just as they need it. A software chef has to provide similar specialty work. Regardless of the size and variety of components that are available, some preparation is best handled by an expert.

Too many choices (large buffets) can overwhelm the hungry customer. Shopping malls have food courts consisting of several small food shops (Fig. 9.4). Organizing the choices into these shops—related collections of food choices—makes it easier to choose a

Figure 9.3   Chef-Assisted Cafeteria Line—Expert developers are still required

meal: first pick the general kind of food, and then choose the specific items. Libraries of reusable software assets can be organized in a similar manner. The library is the software shopping mall, and application frameworks with related components are the software food shops. The customer picks the appropriate framework and then creates a meal by specializing the framework using the associated components.

Figure 9.4   A Food Mall—Choices of libraries of reusable components

Cafeterias are not always preferred. The food choices are sometimes dried out, over-cooked, not quite what the customer wants. Ordering from the waiter, the customer can make special requests, demand freshly cooked food. To make sure that the cafeteria presents hot, fresh food—all the time—requires attentive management. Likewise, reuse in software development can become stale, not meeting developers' current requirements. A well-managed reuse process is required to ensure that the reuse opportunities remain fresh.

Reuse in Software Development

One way to understand reuse is to think of a reusable artifact as a box, and then to describe whether and how you can see inside the box and use what is inside the box. There are black boxes, glass boxes, and white boxes. They differ by how much information you are given when you reuse, and whether you can make modifications. Boxes get used as-is or by-adaptation. To use *as-is* means to reuse an artifact without making any modifications to it. *By-adaptation* means to reuse only after modifying the artifact in some way.

Black box reuse. *Black box reuse* lets you see only the outside of an artifact. When the box refers to a software artifact, then black box reuse lets you see only the interface—what the software artifact does, not how it does it. Black boxes can be combined with other boxes because you can plug them together via the visible interface. If boxes form a hierarchy, then a sub-kind of black box can be created because the visible interface is inherited. Black boxes can be reused in two ways: by reference or by replication. Referencing a black box means using some unique identification to access the box's services. Replicating means copying the box, without the ability to modify it. The essential idea of black box reuse is to make use of the artifact's services without being able to adapt what the box can do or how it does it. To the extent that no change is desired, black box reuse offers a protected way to share information or services.

A black box is reused as-is. If it is well constructed, then its quality is acquired by the reusers. Reusers have to test their use of the black box interface, but do not have to retest the black box itself. If the black box is changed in any way by its owners, reuse by reference guarantees that the change is shared. Changes do not propagate when the black box is incorporated by replication (copying).

Glass box reuse. *Glass box reuse* lets you see the inside as well as the outside of an artifact, but you can only see, you cannot touch. You can use only its external interface, although you can see its internal structure as well. In this sense, glass boxes are the same as black boxes, except that the reuser can understand what the box does by understanding how it carries out its responsibilities. Sometimes it is critical to know how a box works to be able to use it. Also, seeing inside existing boxes helps reusers learn how to build their own boxes.

There is a negative aspect of the ability to look inside the glass box. You can see private information, such as the information representation of an object, or the algorithm used in an implementation. You might rely on the representation or the algorithm. Box implementors—both the black and glass variety—have the right to make changes to the insides (changes that don't affect the interface specification), without worrying about how the changes affect reusers. Any reuser dependencies on inside information could create errors when the box is modified.

White box reuse. *White box reuse* lets you see and change the inside as well as the outside of an artifact. A white box can always be treated as a black or glass box. But in addition, it supports several other forms of reuse. A white box can share its internal structure or implementation with another box via inheritance or delegation, effectively creating a new and separate box by sharing the implementation details. The new box might retain the old implementation as-is or by-adaptation. It is not necessary in some systems actually to copy the implementation—it is referenced by forming an implementation hierarchy. A box in the hierarchy has the same behavior as a box higher in its hierarchy, but can add new behaviors or refine existing ones. An example was provided in Chapter 3. A vehicle hierarchy was presented in which all vehicles inherit the ability to start, stop, and move. Each kind of vehicle might use the same implementation of move, but implement start and stop differently.

A white box is typically used by-adaptation. It can offer more to reuse, but it can also create more opportunities for the reuser to be affected negatively by a change. Reusers are obligated to test anything new that is created, and to retest any of the white box's as-is use of other things (see the testing discussion in Chapter 6). Changing the white box can have direct and dire consequences on any reusers, so maintenance can be more costly than with black box reuse.

Because of the potential impact of changes, some systems do not treat the world as black and white. They add tones of gray—different ways of controlling which parts of a box can be seen (such as levels of encapsulation), and by which reusers.

A special kind of black box reuse: transformational reuse. *Transformational reuse* is an approach to reuse in which you provide a description or specification of what you want, and let a black box program generate the implementation details. This program is usually called an application generator.

The use of application generators indicates a trend in software development toward higher-level specification languages. Developers specify what they want to do at a level that closely matches the problem on which they are working, and rely on generators to produce the implementation. In this way, productivity can be greatly increased because developers create and maintain only a single specification that can run on multiple hardware/software platforms. For example, many commercial visual construction editors are used to specify a user interface design: screen layout, properties of the visual components, and the manner in which the components exchange information. The executable code is generated from the specification and adapted to specific platforms when needed and, for performance purposes, cached for repeated execution.

Cloning Is Not Strategic Reuse

Cloning is copying. Initially the copy is an exact replica. The problem is that there is no obligation over the long term for the copy to be the same as the original. The original can change without changing the copy; the copy can change without reflecting the change back to the original.

Cloning is a way of gaining autonomy. Reusers take responsibility for the systems that they are creating. Insofar as they do not want to burden their own projects with adapting to changes in the asset, these reusers take a copy and never look back. They view the copy as a way to get started faster. It is also a useful way to make use of the expertise of other people—for example, by cloning a framework that has a useful architecture.

Cloning is an attitude. Initially, you do the same thing when you clone as when you reuse. The difference lies in your intention: Will you maintain the integrity between original and copy? Cloning takes two forms: The reused part can be changed by the reuser independent of what anyone else does; or, if the original part is changed by someone else, the reuser can ignore the changes. With cloning, multiple versions propagate through different systems. Systems with old versions of reusable parts will break differently than systems with newer versions, which compounds the maintenance problem.

Reuse presents an opportunity to reduce maintenance effort. Cloning does not.

Reuse with Objects

At various stages of development, there are special groupings of objects that participate in the development process and that might be reused. We can reuse, for example, applications, class specifications, class implementations, instances, algorithms, analysis-and-design models, and the more advanced forms of reuse—frameworks and patterns.

Applications. An application is a set of interacting objects that provides well-defined services. An application can therefore be thought of as an object. The strategic direction of operating system design today involves the notion of resource managers that support the ability of applications to interoperate. Each application is viewed as an object that can reference other applications, either by sending messages to invoke services, or by embedding an instance of another application. Application reuse is effectively black box reuse.

Class specification. All instances of a class reuse the behavior that is defined by the class's interface specification. One class may be a subclass of another class (its superclass), thereby inheriting the interface specification of the superclass. The subclass might provide its own implementation of some aspect of the inherited interface. Classes that are not related by inheritance might carry out similar behaviors, providing their own implementations—that is, they reuse an interface specification by cloning.

Class implementation. The class implementation provides a definition of the behavior and properties of a group of objects. A subclass can be created from a class to reuse the class's implementation. Subclassing is an example of white box reuse, supported via delegation or inheritance.

It is rare that you would consider using a single class in isolation. You are more likely to consider the class in the context of a framework or application, or as part of a hierarchy of specifications.

Instances. Objects can be used to compose larger objects—that is, objects are described in terms of several parts, each of which is itself an object. Such composition is black box reuse. The larger object reuses the services of its parts without knowing how the services are implemented.

Algorithms. An algorithm is a way of carrying out some desired behavior—a step-by-step specification of what should be done. Algorithms can be independent of data structure. In Smalltalk systems, common search algorithms (select:, detect:, reject:) are implemented in an abstract class called Collection, which is a common superclass of classes such as Set, Array, and Dictionary. Some mathematical notions such as absolute value are implemented in the abstract class Number and are available automatically to subclasses Integer and Float.

An algorithm can be fully specified but partially implemented. The remaining partial implementation will be provided by subclasses of the class containing the specification, or by components delegated responsibility for the expected behavior. For example, a control algorithm for a generic window might first test to see whether the screen cursor is inside its boundaries, see if it wants control, and, if so, take some action. Subclasses of this generic window class would then specify what it means to want control and to take some action.

Analysis-and-design models. Analyses and designs are abstract reusable assets that have little reliance on implementation decisions. This enables their reuse during the early stages of a project when they are most likely to have the most widespread influence. It is generally believed that the only way to get an order-of-magnitude improvement in productivity and quality is to reuse analyses and designs. Reusing earlier stage results gives the potential for also reusing later-stage results—implementation, tests, and documentation.

Software frameworks. A software framework is a set of interacting objects that provides a well-defined set of services, and a well-defined way in which control is transferred among the objects. A framework can define a default application by providing a minimal implementation. Most frameworks are incomplete or abstract. They are completed by incorporating components that fulfill expected roles, or by adding subclasses that provide the anticipated implementations. By supporting a variety of specializations, the framework can be reused to create many similar applications.

Patterns. As we mentioned in Chapter 6, object-oriented technology researchers are trying to codify a kind of reusable asset called design patterns. A *design pattern* is a recurring design structure or solution. The goal of the research effort is to identify design patterns found in object-oriented systems, and to catalog them in a systematic way. A designer who encounters a familiar design problem should be able to apply a design pattern as the design solution, without having to rediscover it. Each pattern solves only one design problem or deals with only one design issue. Each design pattern identifies the participating classes, instances, roles and collaborations, and distribution of responsibilities.

A framework might consist of several patterns, but a pattern is not a framework. A pattern is intended to be something less than a complete application or framework. Whereas MVC is a framework, within the MVC design there are several patterns. One pattern is decoupling data representation (model) from graphical screen presentation (view), yet assuring that if the data is changed by actions within one view, all views will maintain a consistent presentation. This consistency is made to work by the dependency relationship between views and models. Whenever the model changes, it broadcasts an update message to all dependent views, which then can update their screen presentations.

Gamma *et al.* [Gamma *et al.* 1995] identify this pattern, called an Observer, in their catalog of design patterns. Their catalog is an attempt to suggest useful software design patterns. An Adaptor makes the interface specification of one object conform with that of another; an Iterator knows how to traverse object structures; and a Flyweight defines how objects can be shared.

The word "pattern" is thus quite general. A pattern is an exemplar, a model from which something can be made and one that deserves to be imitated. Unfortunately, "pattern" is sometimes used interchangeably with the word "idiom," which at best confuses the intention. An idiom is a form of expression—a grammatical construction—peculiar to a language. It often signifies something other than its grammatical or logical meaning, and, as such, an idiom is not likely to translate literally into another language. (For example, the English "you are driving me up a wall" means "you are irritating me," not that you are forcing me to travel up a wall of a room or building.) This contradicts the purpose of a design pattern, which is to provide a design structure or template that can be implemented in any number of programming languages, and would be recognized across languages.

The effort to codify design patterns, and to create design pattern catalogs, provides a common design vocabulary that should improve communication among developers and make design experience more generally accessible. Ultimately, the reason that we focus on reuse is that reinvention is more costly and more likely to recreate errors. If we have done something before, and it worked, then we want to know about it and build from it, not start over again. A design pattern, then, is one of many ways we can try to capture and share the history of software development.

The Value of Reuse

The Reuse Producer/Consumer Equation

How can you get value from reuse? Barnes and Bollinger draw a picture that summarizes the answer. You can get value from reuse if the cost of producing reusable assets is (significantly) less than the savings you experience from consuming the assets. Figure 9.5 is adapted from [Barnes and Bollinger 1991] to illustrate the idea. Design with reuse is not free. There is a cost to consumption associated with determining that a reusable asset is appropriate, and understanding how to integrate the asset into the system. In Chapter 11, we outline the full reuse process, which emphasizes the nature of producer and consumer costs.

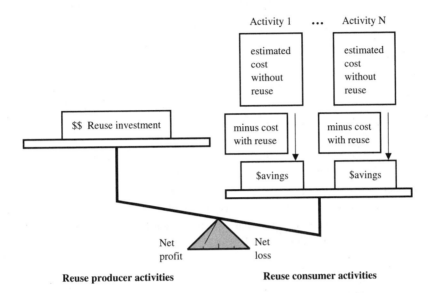

Figure 9.5   Reuse-Investment Relation. Adapted from [Barnes and Bollinger 1991].

The reuse-investment relation or cost equation depends on what you create. Some software components are more valuable to reuse than others. The judgment about relative value is yours to make, but there are several obvious dimensions to what constitutes value. First, components that solve more difficult and complex problems—which require significant expertise to create and maintain—are generally more valuable than components representing simple algorithms or data structures.

Second, components that are well designed for adaptation in your organization's situations are more valuable than ones whose adaptation requires major change to the assets. Domain-specific application frameworks that represent your business domain and can be customized to create your many applications are often more valuable than a generic system utility. Many organizations tie their value expectations for object-oriented technology to the availability of reusable application frameworks. This expectation is reasonable because all or most applications in a corporate MIS setting refer to a fairly small but critical set of behaviors that model the backbone of the corporate environment.

Third, black box components are often considered less costly to reuse than white box, simply because there is less to know and less to do in order to embed the component. In the long run, maintenance of black box reuse should be less costly if there is a commitment that the specification interface will not change significantly. Black box reuse assumes that hiding implementation is always the better solution. It assumes that the same implementation fulfills the desired system quality objectives for all potential reusers of the component. In practice this is not often true; it is often critical to be able to select among alternative implementations or write a new one. Black box reuse is not less costly when you do not get what you need. There are times when white or glass box reuse is important, in particular when adapting a domain application framework to specific delivery requirements.

Reuse Claims

We are constantly bombarded with reuse claims or management demands that make us uncomfortable. We review some of these claims to show why they are not reasonable, and to introduce several reuse definitions that will be useful in future discussions.

Potential reuse. One claim often made is that, at the outset of a project, it is possible to stipulate the actual percentage of newly developed artifacts that will be reusable on future projects. Such a claim is valid only if there is some way to measure the likelihood that an artifact will be reusable. We call such a measure *potential reuse*.

We do not know a way to prove that an artifact will be reusable on future projects. Indeed, we offer the following maxim claiming that reusability can only be demonstrated, not proved.

Potential Reuse

> **Reuse is demonstrated.** Reuse cannot be *proved* prospectively; it can only be *demonstrated* retrospectively.

We can only demonstrate, after the fact of another project's reuse, which artifacts were reused. However, it may be possible to establish some measure of the likelihood that an artifact will be reused. This measure could be used to select good candidate artifacts for a reuse library. Three factors influence potential reusability and might contribute to such a measure: inherent reusability, domain reusability, and organizational reusability. Some weighted measure based on these three factors could quantify potential reuse.

Inherent reusability

Inherent reusability is the likelihood that an artifact is reusable based on its internal properties. For example, if we take an arithmetic object and examine its interface, and find that it provides support only for multiply, divide, and add, we might conclude that this object lacks inherent reusability because it does not support subtraction. An account object that credits but doesn't debit might also lack inherent reusability. Also, we might conclude that an artifact is completely specified but poorly constructed, and therefore has low inherent reusability.

Domain reusability

> *Domain reusability* is the likelihood that an artifact is reusable based on whether the organization's future application domains are similar to the domain for which the artifact was first created. An airplane-engine object, which exhibits high inherent reusability, probably has no domain reusability inside a telecommunications company.

Organizational reusability

> *Organizational reusability* is the likelihood that the organization's reuse process model will support the reuse of this artifact. For example, even an artifact with high inherent and domain reusability can't be reused if it can't be found.

Effective reuse. Most reports based on the actual reuse achieved on a project are not sufficiently informative to be of real value. We have all heard claims such as: 90 percent of my product was built from reusable artifacts. But what was reused? In most claims of this ilk, it is implied that the percentage of reuse is the amount of code that the team did not have to write. What is not clear is whether the calculation of reused code takes into account the operating system, the database management system, or the windowing system, all of which contribute to the actual executing application. What about including artifacts other than code when calculating reuse? Suppose the code represents only 20 percent of the size of all artifacts created during the life cycle, and 90 percent of the code was reused. The number to report isn't necessarily 90 percent code reuse. Rather, we could report 18 percent artifact reuse for the entire project assuming nothing other than the code reuse.

The maxim we suggest is:

> **Label the numbers.** Reuse numbers have to be tied to a specific description of what is being measured for the numbers to be meaningful.

Effective
Reuse

Effective reuse is a measure of both the type and the quantity of reuse that occurs on a given project.

Expected reuse. A third claim we have heard is that it is possible to predict the type and the quantity of reuse a project will achieve. We call this *expected reuse*. Managers use expected reuse as a way to predict the cost of a project. For example, a manager might believe that a project will get done faster because 70 percent of the resulting system is going to be developed from reusable artifacts. How does the manager know, in advance of doing any of the work, the quantity of the artifacts that house the requirements or the design or the implementation or the testing? One way to know is when the project is the same as one done before. Or the project is a Variation-on-a-Theme project, and it is clear that the prior project with the similar theme left the organization with a fairly robust and substantive library of potentially reusable assets. It is sometimes easier to predict reuse in terms of system capabilities, such as database connection or visual widgets for a user interface. Be wary of accepting system objectives that set expected reuse for any First-of-Its-Kind or Legacy Rewrite projects.

Case Study Results

In our case study interviews, we asked what should be reusable. The most frequent answers were:

- Analyses

- Design ideas or patterns

- Design components

- Code artifacts

- Documentation

- Test cases and test suites

The least frequent answer was: People and their experiences with previous projects. Although it is true that software, documentation, and other artifacts are the result of applying experience, the easiest way to reuse experience is to make sure that experienced people are doing the work.

To the case study participants, reuse was mostly reuse of code—code obtained either from a vendor or from prior projects within the organization. Smalltalk class libraries and the AT&T C++ task library were popular examples. Various vendors supplied database interface code, 4GL-like forms creation or user interface layout code, and, in some cases, even complete applications. Some of the case studies reported reuse of style guidelines and of specifications based on protocols defined by standards organizations.

Most of the teams we studied said they were reusing when members of the same or different teams copied code from one another as a way to get started. They depended on the original developer to provide information about the code to be copied, and then accepted responsibility for all future maintenance within their own projects. Code gets passed on from reuser to reuser, without an apparent support obligation. We were often told that a project experienced about 60-80 percent reuse (in the sense that 60-80 percent of the code in the resulting product was not written by the current development team), mostly reusing vendor-supplied libraries (data structures, graphical widgets, and the like).

Illustration 1: Reusable Assets Need Support

We studied three projects at a test equipment manufacturing company. All of the projects had as a goal the creation of reusable assets. All were staffed by highly skilled developers with university computer science degrees. Two of the projects used C++, which is generally the language of choice for this company. The third project used Smalltalk. We also interviewed four user groups—developers who reused the assets—to find out consumer experience with the reusable assets.

The first project created a compiler-compiler that took as input the instruction-set grammar of a piece of equipment and produced a compiler. Producing a new compiler for an instrument was a lengthy effort because there was little compiler-writing expertise in the company. Reuse was viewed as a way to share specialized expertise. The compiler-compiler was created over a one-and-a-half year period, with lots of personnel changes. After 144 months of effort, the first release was completed by three software engineers working with one documentor. It was about 25,000 lines of C code, later rewritten in C++.

At the time of the interview, six different groups had successfully used the compiler-compiler in creating their products. These product teams had no formal compiler-writing expertise. Using the tool, they reduced the effort of creating a compiler for new machinery from the anticipated two years down to (at the most) two months. It took several years to learn enough to write the compilers, whereas it took only several months to translate expertise about a machine instruction set into the grammar for the compiler-compiler. The compiler-compiler was supplied as a tool in binary form. No changes were ever made by the reusers to the tool itself, both because the representation format was binary, and because the teams had no expertise in making such modifications. The tool, as-is, performed as needed.

The second project created a framework with which instrumentation software could be created, with emphasis on the user interface. It incorporated the compiler-compiler. The framework represented a significant investment in understanding and expressing the company's ideas about graphical presentation of, and interaction with, the information about a piece of test equipment and its use. The developers viewed themselves as experimenting with the ideas embodied in the asset. But the reusers were on product deadlines.

The business goal of this second project was to make it easier and faster to create instrument controls. The reason for using objects was to reduce the amount of code that had to be written to create new instruments. This goal was achieved. The reusable framework provides a common user interface and architecture for managing information. It is changed by deriving new classes and pluggable new components. Another system goal was to create a framework that users can customize by adding their own widgets. The framework designers chose to attain this goal by having the clients of the framework program new widgets in C++. Framework reusers complained to us about having to learn C++ and pointed out that management was mistaken in thinking that C++ was learnable simply through use of the framework.

The framework developers used an approach similar to what we called the Concepts-Driven Process Model. They created a series of prototypes, making each one available to the user community. They did not do code walkthroughs or special testing. After the first 18 months of effort, four to six software engineers (including a documentor and a quality assurance engineer) had created 30,000 lines of uncommented C++ code.

Potential reusers acquired the source code at the outset of their projects, and modified that code as they deemed necessary. We interviewed four reusers, who made use of a variety of reusable assets provided by the company, including operating systems, the compiler-compiler, measurement packages, and the user interface framework. Most of the reusers had similar reuse experiences, with 50–80 percent effective reuse of the framework code being loaded into the test equipment product. Projects lasted on the average 18 months. They differed depending on the specialty of the instrument and the ability to leverage prior algorithm work.

The framework software was cloned by all of the reusers. The software became a part of the product, losing its identity as a reusable asset because the reusers felt that they needed to have full control over all of the software delivered with their products.[7]

Other product programs in the company heard about the user interface framework—not from the original developers and extenders/maintainers, but from one or more reusers. Thus the asset they acquired often came from a reuser, in whatever form the reuser had transformed it.[8] At the time of our interview, a support crisis was brewing. The original developers had not set up an infrastructure for support. In fact, they had released a significant corporate contribution without certifying it as a "product." They did not keep track of their reusers, and the versions used in the product divisions were not likely to be replaceable with any upgrades to the framework.

Illustration 2: Reusing a Binary Asset

Here is a story of another company that obtained a binary asset from a third-party vendor—a compiler for a new language that supported object-oriented concepts. Unfortunately, the compiler did not perform as expected. The vendor was not responsive to the maintenance needs of the reusers. So, unfortunately, the company obtained the source code to fix the compiler themselves and gave knowledgeable feedback and code changes to the vendor. The compiler never worked correctly, never generated sufficiently optimized code, and suffered from a long compile-link cycle time.

---

[7] The need for a product team to take control of all software in its product is a corporate culture issue that has to be resolved by higher levels of management. A product team's insistence on cloning reusable assets in this manner runs counter to the opportunity to reduce corporate-wide costs by sharing maintenance of reusable assets.

[8] In fact, the original creators of the user interface framework found out about some of the indirect reusers as an outcome of the interviews with us.

The product written in the new language was not getting finished while the company and its management dealt with creating a better tool. After three years, $20 million, 100 software engineers, 2000 class definitions and 350,000 lines of code, no product existed. We surmise that had the source code not been available, management might have stopped the product program earlier, and saved millions of dollars on an effort that ultimately failed to deliver a timely product to the market. The company had no compiler expertise but went ahead and tried to modify sources anyway. And the vendor did not focus its business on creating an improved reusable asset. It takes knowledge and careful management to decide to modify a sophisticated asset; it takes considerable business acumen to know when not to adapt such an asset.

Summary

The essence of reuse is using what already exists to achieve a goal and benefiting from future improvements in the reusable artifacts. Object-oriented technology creates a renewed interest in reuse for two reasons. First, objects encourage you to think about creating independent components that can be plugged together to form new results. Second, the use of objects emphasizes the design and implementation of applications and application frameworks that can be customized.

In this chapter, we distinguished techniques for reuse: as-is or by-adaptation. Black box reuse is as-is only—reusing based on external specification. Glass box reuse lets you see how an artifact implements its specification, but you can still only reuse based on the externally visible capabilities. White box reuse permits reuse by-adaptation. You can change the way the artifact provides its services to make it better suited to your new purpose. Transformational reuse is a special case of black box reuse, whereby a program examines a specification and generates the appropriate implementation. Each form of reuse has its advantages and disadvantages. A critical concern is the propagation of changes so that when the original artifact changes, reusers benefit from this change.

Object-oriented technology provides a mixture of black, white, and glass box forms of reuse. Different kinds of objects participate in the development process and can be reused—objects that constitute an analysis object model, a design object model, or an application framework. These objects include applications, class specifications, class implementations, instances, algorithms, analyses, and designs. The current industry trend is to focus on black box reuse because it is presumed to be safer for less skilled programmers, and to provide more assurance that future objects, distributed on networked workstations, will be compatible.

You have to be careful with the general claims you and others make about potential, effective, or expected reuse of objects. Potential reuse is the likelihood that an artifact will be reusable, which cannot be proved prospectively and can only be demonstrated retrospectively. Effective reuse is a measure of the type and quantity of reuse that actually occurred on a given project, while expected reuse is the measure of reuse that we predict the project will experience. You have to tie any reuse counts to a specific description of what is being measured for these two measures to be meaningful. To understand fully the contribution that reuse can make in software development, you must measure reuse across all life cycle phases. And remember: Anything can be reused, especially the experience of the people in the organization.

Additional Reading About Reuse Definitions and Expectations

Biggerstaff, T. and Perlis, A., eds., *Software Reusability: Volume I, Concepts and Models*, ACM Press: Reading, Mass., 1989.

>The first of a two-volume set, this book is a collection of papers that discuss concepts and models of software reuse as seen by some of the top researchers in the field. The more theoretical papers establish a framework for thinking about reuse, and expose the issues that confront practitioners wishing to take advantage of reuse opportunities. Practical approaches to reuse are categorized as composition-based or generation-based systems. The papers on composition-based reuse deal with classification of modules, parameterized programming, templates, and schemas. Generation-based reuse is described in terms of application generators and program transformation techniques.

Freeman, P., ed., *Tutorial: Software Reusability*, IEEE Computer Society Press: Washington D.C., 1986.

>Of historical interest, this book is a collection of papers on software reusability: basic concepts, techniques, and research. The technique papers include contributions from noted researchers such as Jean Ichbiah on reusability in Ada, L. Peter Deutsch on reusability in Smalltalk-80, David Parnas on promoting reusability via information hiding, and Rubén Prieto-díaz on reusability classification schemes. Kernighan describes reusability within the Unix operating system, and Matsumoto introduces the requirements for a software factory with examples from the Toshiba Corporation.

Proceedings of the Workshops for Institutionalizing Software Reuse (WISR).

>The proceedings of these workshops contain the most recent knowledge and issue discussions about reuse. The 1992 workshop, held in Palo Alto, California, was attended by more than 65 people, including researchers from universities and industrial research laboratories, and practitioners from both large and small companies. They came together to share their experiences and identify key issues that stand in the way of making systematic software reuse a significant part of the software development process. Papers in the proceedings discuss a consensus reuse process, reuse maturity model and reuse terminology, management and technology transfer, domain analysis and engineering, designing for reuse, component certification, and tools and environment issues surrounding reuse. If you have Internet access, copies of the WISR'91, '92, and '93 proceedings and working reports are available via anonymous ftp at gandalf.umcs.maine.edu. Look in the /pub/WISR/wisrN directory, where N is the workshop number ('91=4, '92=5, '93=6).

CHAPTER 10

Reuse Process Models

euse requires trust, and trust requires an accepted process. When you cannot base your trust on knowing and respecting the developers, you have to be able to trust the process that acquires, distributes, and maintains the artifacts. Chapter 5 talks about developing with reusing as a strategy, whereas this chapter emphasizes how to manage the acquisition, distribution and maintenance of the reusable assets. The benefits of reuse are achieved through a carefully planned and managed process model.

Framework for Selecting a Reuse Process Model

The framework for selecting a process with which to manage reuse in your organization asks you to set up a reuse process that your developers will trust. The project described by the framework is a process-improvement project, as depicted in Fig. 10.1.

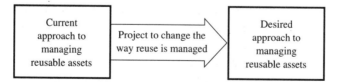

Figure 10.1   Process-Improvement Project to Establish a Reuse
Process Model

There are other projects related to reuse, all resource-improvement projects. One project sets up a team with the expertise to carry out the reuse process. We discuss this project in Chapter 12. Another project develops reusable assets using a product development process such as the ones we discuss in Chapters 5 and 6.

The principle for selecting a reuse process model reflects our attitude about reuse:

Framework Principle. Reusable assets are strategic products of the organization.

The statement of principle is loaded with special words:

asset	Something of value
strategic	Something vital, intended to last a long time
product	Something that meets the organization's quality objectives so it can be delivered to external customers

Reusable assets are products, not by-products. A product is tested, documented, trusted, something you are proud of, and something you encourage others to use. A product can be software or services, such as a software system or the technical support for the system, training materials, or the training itself.

Two maxims about reusable assets make it clear that we want reuse to focus on a small number of strategic products that represent the way the organization wishes to create software systems. These maxims are:

Give focus. Collecting everything is not useful.

Give direction. Collecting redundant assets is not useful.

Assets in the library can represent both specifications of what to do and implementations of how to fulfill the specifications. Multiple conflicting specifications for the same asset lead to inconsistencies and should be avoided. Multiple implementations for the same specification make sense when they offer clear alternatives for different delivery platforms, different performance profiles, or different language implementations.

The people we interviewed often did not agree with these maxims. The typical assumption underlying early efforts to provide libraries of reusable assets was: The more the merrier. The more there is, the more the developers have available to select from and the greater the likelihood that a developer's needs will be fulfilled by the library. We take a much more conservative point of view, because it takes considerable effort to create and maintain assets that the organization recommends and the developers can trust. The library should contain assets that have a high potential for reuse, especially those with good domain reusability. For example, if an organization is involved in the banking industry, Financial Instrument components are more likely to be of interest than Nuclear Reactor Control components. All banking applications will have a Customer component, but not all will include a Margin Account.

Strategic components are the ones that give the highest return on investment. As this chapter illustrates, the overhead cost of certifying, classifying, storing, locating, retrieving, understanding, using, and maintaining components can be high. To justify these costs, large-grained components such as editors and applications that offer greater effective reuse are a better strategic investment than finer-grained components such as data structures or utility objects. Finer-grained components that are reused extensively, or that require significant expertise to create, give a high return on investment and can be considered strategic as well.

The goal for reuse in an organization and for this decision framework is:

Framework Goal. Set up a structure in which to plan and manage the process of acquiring, distributing, and maintaining reusable assets throughout the organization.

The framework for setting up a reuse plan consists of four major steps.

- Define reuse

- Set up a process for populating a library of reusable assets

- Set up a process for sharing reusable assets

- Set up a process for maintaining reusable assets

Reuse Process Model

Following the steps to set up a reuse process model, the manager of the process-improvement project leads the effort to formulate a reuse process model that accounts for the following thirteen decision areas:

Define	Decide what should be reusable and how to reuse
Identify	Determine the specific artifacts that are to become reusable assets of the organization
Acquire	Build, buy, or contract to obtain reusable assets
Certify	Set and follow guidelines to determine acceptability of a reusable asset
Classify	Select and apply a method and notation for organizing and labeling the reusable assets
Store	Choose a method for storing assets so they can later be located and retrieved
Communicate	Select a method for making potential reusers aware of and interested in reuse opportunities (an alternative label for this step is "Proactive and Reactive Marketing")

Locate	Choose a method for finding stored assets
Retrieve	Choose a method for taking possession of an asset
Understand	Choose a method for determining the purpose of the asset, and its analytic, design, or operational characteristics
Use	Choose a method for integrating an asset into the new context
Update Assets	Choose methods for extending, updating, and repairing the assets in the library
Update Reusers	Choose a method for updating the systems that use modified assets

The decisions you make must help the development, maintenance, and reuse teams work together to create a positive reuse attitude. Selecting an organizational model that encourages and pays for the reuse process is covered in Chapter 11.

Define Reuse

The two substeps in defining reuse for your organization are:

- Decide what things you want to be able to reuse

- Decide how you want to reuse

These topics are discussed in detail in Chapter 9. It is not necessarily the case that you need or want to manage all possible kinds of reusable assets, nor that all techniques are applicable for you. Some of the organizations we studied preferred only black box reuse of business elements; others aimed for glass box reuse of frameworks and transformational reuse involving business-related application generators. Still others tried a mixture.

What business benefits do you require from reuse, and therefore what do you want to reuse? Is cloning acceptable, or do you prefer black box reuse only? Answering these questions defines reuse in your organization. Make sure that everyone in the organization accepts this definition and understands the benefits that the organization expects to obtain from the reuse program. One user of object-oriented technology must now deal with an early failure to answer these questions. This organization now has a library populated by all sorts of artifacts—Smalltalk class definitions in source code format, VBXs (Visual Basic components) in binary format, C code—many providing the same services and each requiring different tools and ways to reuse. The organization's developers are overwhelmed with every possibility for defining reuse.

Set Up a Process for Populating a Library of Reusable Assets

The next step of the framework is to make reusable assets available. This involves five substeps:

- Identify and prioritize categories of reusable assets

- Acquire reusable assets

- Certify reusable assets

- Classify and represent reusable assets

- Store reusable assets

Identify and Prioritize Categories of Reusable Assets

Decide which reusable artifacts you wish to manage as reusable assets. To do so, consider one or more of the following: the structure of your business, the needs of existing or planned projects, your organization's computer architecture, and the opinions of potential reusers.

Identify assets useful to a business unit. The goal is to acquire reusable assets that support the business. Look for these assets in the structure of the business. Organizational boundaries can identify independent business units, each with responsibility for creating, delivering, and supporting its own products. As a result, each business unit may have needs that are peculiar to its products and infrastructure. You can manage reusable assets for individual units. In addition, there are assets that transcend the business units. These are system-level domain-independent assets, such as general business objects, user interface frameworks and widgets, graphics and charts, network communication utilities, and database connection utilities. These kinds of assets are shareable across business units.

One investment bank divided itself into two sectors, each representing a distinct target market. One sector sells financial instruments only to large pensions, and the other sells publicly traded stock. Within the sectors, there are lines of business that further delineate the marketplace. This delineation fluctuates as the financial market opportunities change. Sectors are stable, lines of business are not. In using organizational boundaries to seek reusable assets, the sector offers a more stable context in which to identify business elements such as pensions, customers, financial instruments, and financial transactions.

Many organizations today are reconsidering how they run their businesses. These organizations are going back to first principles to discover processes that facilitate the development, delivery, and servicing of products. Reengineered business processes usually provide good definitions of both the underlying business information and the business processes that use it. Therefore, another approach to finding strategic reusable assets is to consider how each of these new processes might be represented by software assets. For example, a business process reengineering of an order entry system might identify objects that represent purchasing, invoicing, and exception signoff.

Often it is productive to identify reusable assets at different levels of generality. Take for example one of our case studies, which we recast here in terms of a soda pop produc-er. This company believed that their assets could be organized into three levels of gener-ality, as shown in Fig. 10.2. At the highest level, they placed assets that would exist in any business—such as Customers, Accounts, Contracts, and administrative applications like Payroll, Personnel Management, and Accounting. The next level focused on assets that are reusable across companies in the same industry. In the soda pop industry, this might mean recipe research results, recipe patents, processes for producing syrup, processes for bottling and packaging for shipment, and contracts with distributors.

| Assets of interest to any business |
| Assets of interest to any company within the industry |
| Assets specific to the company |

Figure 10.2   Possible Levels of Reusable Assets

The last level expresses the differences among companies within an industry. For soda pop, this would be the assets that distinguish, say, PepsiCo® from the Coca-Cola® Bottling Company—specific recipes, specific ways of managing contracts, specific nature of the distribution network. The case study organization believed that it could and should sell the assets at the highest level to any business. They expected to share some of the assets from the middle level with their competitors, to the extent that such sharing allowed for better industry growth. They believed that their ability to create specializa-tions for their company gave them a competitive edge. This three-level approach is com-mon in many industries. We have seen examples in the financial community, petroleum industry, manufacturing, and health services organizations.

The KandA Widget Company decided to take a similar approach to identifying reusable assets. KandA management negotiated a purchase of the soda pop producer's business-level reusable assets, and used these to create new adminstrative applications. The information systems department formed a special group to identify possible widget-specific assets. The result of the special study was a specification for widget catalogs and ordering systems which could be specialized to create seasonal catalogs and to account for holiday special-ordering policies. The management believes the designs for these new systems are a competitive advantage and is not likely to share them with other software widget companies, but perhaps the dress shop next store might be interested?

Identify the needs common to multiple projects.   There are a number of strategies that can be used to identify assets that are reusable across multiple projects. Here we discuss domain analysis, on-the-fly identification, and harvest-after-the-fact. These identification strategies can be done independently or in combination. The goal is to come up with potentially reusable assets. In the best of worlds, the assets you identify are the ones already reused on several projects. Both on-the-fly identification and harvest-after-the-fact assume examples exist. In the absence of an experiential basis for identification, domain analysis is required.

Domain analysis attempts to understand the basic abstractions in a discipline [Arango 1994]. The goal of domain analysis is to determine a general domain model from which it is possible to develop multiple applications. In the telecommunications industry, a common abstraction is a model for configuring networks. The model can be specialized to represent different specific networks. As we describe in Chapter 8, one case study model was created for managing nodes on a network. The model was specialized by adding personality modules that describe particular networks.

The U.S. Department of Defense (DoD) launched an aggressive program to create a library of reusable assets that can be shared across all software development carried out by branches of the armed services.[1] This program is the RAPID project, started in 1989 with the first phase completed in 1991. The effort started with a contract to SofTech, Inc., to carry out a domain analysis.[2] SofTech devised a domain-analysis method that was applied in 1992 to an analysis of the Army Supply Domain. (SofTech refers to their approach as Domain Engineering, which relies on analysis to identify reuse opportunities and implementation of the reusable components.) The notion of a domain, in SofTech terms, is a group of related systems that share a set of common capabilities and/or data: personnel, finance, command and control, logistics. A domain can contain subdomains—logistics contains maintenance, supply, and transportation.

Domain analysis can be used to identify common abstractions in business as well as technical domains. The result of a business domain analysis, for example, could be an abstraction of the collection of business applications that compose the soda pop company's order and billing system. The purpose of a technical domain analysis is to identify technical abstractions. For example, one of our case study projects did an analysis of what it means to create compilers, which led to the definition of a compiler-compiler.

The outcome of a domain analysis is the identification of reuse opportunities across applications in a domain. Across personnel, inventory, accounts receivable, and medical

---

[1] One of the authors was invited to provide a formal review of this project in April 1992 for the U.S. Defense Department's Director of Defense Information.

[2] Reports documenting the SofTech work are obtainable from the company in Waltham, Massachusetts. See for example, *Final RAPID Center Reusable Software Component Procedures*, 3451-4-326/4, June 1990, and *Reuse Opportunities Report* 1213-53-210/5 and *Domain Definition* Report 1213-53-210/3.1, March 1992.

systems, one might find data entry, data storage, data reporting, search algorithms, and sort algorithms. Domain analysis attempts to uncover system-level domain-independent items, and to show how they relate to one another. The benefit of this approach is that the potentially reusable assets are identified before any projects are carried out, and are available for all of the projects.

In domain analysis, you require the luxury of studying the problem domain before developing specific applications. Having identified reusable assets with domain analysis, you still do not know that the assets support reuse in your organization. Only demonstrated experience on several projects can give you such assurance. An effective reuse program takes time.

However, many organizations have neither the time nor the desire to identify reusable assets in this manner. Faced with short-term deadlines and an aggressive approach to exploiting new technology, these organizations immediately begin simultaneous development of several applications. Although they have forgone domain analyses, these organizations still wish to achieve high levels of effective reuse across their projects. Rather than relying on luck, they assign one person or a team of people to work with the ongoing projects. This person's or team's role is to identify cross-project reuse opportunities. If they identify potential reuse from one project, they attempt to cross-pollinate the other projects.

This approach to identifying reuse is called *on-the-fly identification*. Its benefit is that reuse is handled "just in time," with projects indirectly helping one another through a cross-project team that picks up assets from one project and deposits them in another. The term "pollination" is used to characterize the process. Pollination, of course, complicates communications and project management in that otherwise-independent projects are now connected by an independent team that attempts to keep in touch with team members of multiple projects and to get them to agree on common software.

In *harvesting-after-the-fact*, you identify and extract any artifacts that are sitting around waiting to be picked up. An organization that has not performed a domain analysis, and has not attempted to identify reusable assets during project development, can attempt to harvest reusable assets after several applications have been completed. It is easier to see that something is reusable when it has already been reused.

By examining existing applications, we can identify components that occur repeatedly in similar roles and responsibilities. Reusable assets are created by harvesting and unifying these components. The drawback to harvesting, compared with domain analysis or on-the-fly, is that already completed applications can benefit from the newly formed reusable assets only if they are retrofitted to include these assets.

Early adopters of object-oriented programming languages are likely to have a portfolio of code artifacts without the accompanying object-oriented design and analysis artifacts. This situation may exist either because the applications were developed during a time when object-oriented analysis-and-design methods were immature, or because the organization did not emphasize the creation and maintenance of these artifacts. Regardless of the cause, if only implementation artifacts exist, then it may make sense to reverse engineer them to reconstruct an object-oriented design and perhaps even a set of requirements, and provide more detailed documentation. The result will be more understandable reusable assets that can be used earlier in development.

Identify assets linked to the organization's computer architecture. Corporations today treat their computing architecture, physical as well as logical, as a strategic decision. The expectation is that new corporate architectures will be long-lasting. In most cases today, the natural choice is a distributed open-systems architecture that is multiplatform, extensible, and able to support interchangeable parts. Since the choice of architecture is so strategic to the organization, the reusable assets for developing systems based on this architecture are likewise strategic. Thus, a good way of identifying reusable assets is to examine the generic elements of the corporate computer architecture.

For example, a client/server architecture that retains legacy databases has at least four critical components, each of which suggests a set of reusable assets:

mainframe database	Reusing database, including middleware or accessors
desktop clients	Reusing application frameworks, application generators, and presentation formats
workstation servers	Sharing applications or computations
network	Reusing network communications utilities

Identify assets requested by potential reusers. Assets can be identified by interviewing members of the organization's development community to determine what assets they think will be useful in developing future systems. For example, in the DoD project referred to earlier, RAPID personnel interviewed project staff to learn the kinds of software they would expect to find in the library. Ten categories were named:

Forms, as front ends to the database

Communications/networking

Table generators

Report generators

Access security

Data dictionaries

Relational database management

Searching and sorting

Date/time conversion

Basic building blocks of any software system, such as data structures, input validation routines, string manipulation routines, and file management

Acquire Reusable Assets

Several options are available for acquiring reusable assets:

- Purchase existing product from commercial vendor

- Contract for development with vendor

- Share with another internal project

- Build your own

You cannot expect to rely on outside vendors to provide you with all of your reusable assets. The maxim that underscores this statement is:

It's your business. No one knows your business better than you.

You have to provide the strategic insight on your business abstractions. You have to turn to your own internal resources for domain expertise. You have to be prepared to build the assets yourself. Or you have to convince your competitors to cooperate in building those assets that are shareable in the industry, but that do not represent unique competitive advantage. Our construction rule-of-thumb is reflected in a maxim taken from [Barnes and Bollinger 1991]:

Shop for knowledge. Build reusable parts for local expertise; buy reusable parts for outside expertise.

Acquire Reusable Assets

You need to assess the resources you have available for acquiring reusable assets. Specifically, who in your organization has the requisite skills to create reusable assets, and who will understand the assets and be able to maintain them? Other issues to consider include:

Resource availability	Are the assets you want already available from someone else?
Asset ownership	Who will legally own the asset?
Price tag	What is the most cost-effective way to get the asset?

Timing	You are on a deadline. Someone else did something that is useful to you. Is what they did good enough, and worth the price, so that you can finish on time?
Asset format	Will the asset come in the form that you need?
Certification guidelines	Do the assets meet your certification guidelines, or do you have to do more work?

Who can do the acquisition work? One of the first considerations in determining how to acquire reusable assets is to decide who can do the work. Do your candidates know how to design and build reusable assets? Do they have the necessary domain knowledge? Often a partnership is needed between contractors who are experts in designing for reuse, and staff members who know the subject matter.

It is possible that a contractor has unique expertise and understands the domain. You may believe that the contractor can do the task better than the internal development team. But no one knows the specifics of your business better than you. You build to get what you want, to retain ownership of the intellectual property, and to develop your own expertise.

Building reusable assets requires a skill that is best learned through experience—by building assets. If your own teams never try, they never will have the skill to do it on their own, leaving you forever reliant on outside contractors. The process of building reusable assets is a way to understand something fundamental about your business. By building the assets yourself, you might discover some new business opportunities!

Who will be able to maintain the assets? After the assets have been acquired, you have to be able to use and maintain them. You need to determine who has the skills to do this. If you contracted the development, are you satisfied with the ability of your in-house team to maintain what it did not create? Your company now has a result that it may not understand. A long-term and strong relationship with the contractors may be needed because, as the iterative development strategy suggests, good reusable assets often evolve after intermingled use and modification.

Resource availability. When you set out to create a reusable asset, you may discover that your in-house teams can do the work. They have the requisite know-how. But they might be assigned to other, equally important tasks.

One of our clients lacks the resources to develop reusable assets. In fact, they do not have the resources to develop any new systems. They purposely do not staff for development, only for maintenance. This organization has decided to rely on outsourcing all development.

Asset ownership. Legal issues with respect to reuse deal with one principal question: Who owns the developed asset? Ownership means the right to resell the asset or to reuse it in other projects. Does the contractor have the right to worldwide company internal use, the right to resell as an independent product, or the right to embed the asset as part of other products? There is no legal issue if the company paying for the development is the same as the one doing the development work. If someone else does the work, then the questions having to do with the rights of the contractor and the rights of the developer should be resolved before the work is started.

Often a contractor must learn a company's strategic business as a prerequisite to building the software. So, there is a control issue when the contractor reapplies this know-how in working with competitors. The know-how comes in two forms: experience with solving a strategic problem, and the actual reusable assets. Ownership of the assets is, of course, controlled by writing a clear contract. Ownership of new knowledge in a contractor's head is not controllable.

In one of the case studies, we saw a variation of this problem. A large corporation contracted development of a prototype with a small consultancy—experts in the use of object-oriented technology. The prototype was part of a much larger effort, mostly being done with an in-house development team. The consultants determined that the fastest way to create the prototype was to reuse object models they had independently implemented. The consultancy did not create these models as supported products that could be licensed by their customers, but rather as leverage for any contract work.

The in-house team participated in the prototype development. When the prototype was completed, they had a problem in moving to product development. The product was to be built in a different software environment, and so a rewrite of the reused objects was necessary. The consultancy's reusable object models, which formed the foundation for the prototype, did not yet exist in the target software environment. The consultancy insisted on significant additional funds to port their reusable assets to the production environment, with continued full ownership. The larger corporation pointed out that all code in the prototype was already its property and therefore the in-house team or other contractors could and would do the port, presumably at a more acceptable price.

The written contract was very clear. All code used in the prototype was the exclusive property of the large corporation. The consultancy had carelessly included its assets in the prototype without regard to the letter of the contract. In the end, the corporation found an alternative source for this part of their product, licensing a product from another company that made no use of the consultancy's code.[3]

---

[3] In this case, the contract was well written from the point of view of both parties. The large corporation saw an opportunity to reduce its development and long-term maintenance costs by buying a product that was developed and supported by a third-party software vendor. The vendor's product was not complete at the time the contract was written, so the corporation decided to participate financially in the product development. This assured their early access and input into the productization process. Both parties in this contract benefited from the outcome.

Other contracting questions have been discussed in a paper by John Favaro of the European Space Agency [Favaro 1993]. He observes that if a contracting organization acquires all rights to the software, there is little motivation for the contractor to develop reusable software, assuming that the task of creating reusable software is outside the scope of the contract. Favaro points out that in the case of the agency he studied, the software actually remains with the contractor, and the agency acquires only a nonexclusive license for the software. Procurement rules differ across countries and companies. Copyright laws offer limited protection for the sale of reusable assets. These too differ across countries.

The best advice we can give you, of course, is to consult a legal professional, recognize that laws change over time, and take the cheapest route: ask before you act.

Price tag. What are the economics of creating a reusable asset? Other than the obvious initial development costs, how do you pay for maintenance? Is there a licensing or internal payback fee to incorporate the result in new applications? The best economics for a company would be to purchase reusable assets in an open marketplace, much the way hardware components are purchased today. The company's application development environment would be able to access and incorporate the assets into new applications. The problem is that, unlike hardware, there is no significant manufacturing cost to replicating software and no easy way to make sure that the use of the assets in all of the distributed application software is paid for. Unless a mechanism for reimbursement for the value of the components in distributed applications is adopted, a software components industry will be economically unsuccessful.

This particular topic is a favorite of Brad Cox [Cox 1992], who has proposed reimbursement on a royalty basis, much the way entertainers are paid royalty each time their music is played on the radio. Cox thinks his idea of "superdistribution" will be able to keep an accounting of components use in applications because computers live on networks and network monitors can log usage. This approach, however, carries the overtone of being taxed for usage, which is a runtime fee that most people do not like. They view the fees as a limit on their right to compile the results of their own development effort. They ignore the value of libraries of reusable assets, having used shared algorithm libraries without charge for many years and ignore the purchase fees for operating systems. Until the software consumer's mindset about paying for reuse of software is changed, a components industry cannot grow.

Timing. Companies often do not develop reusable assets because it is a lengthy and costly process when done well. Making the investment implies considerable foresight on the part of the company (or some very costly experience that provides critical hindsight). Having the reusable assets may pay off in future development—development is faster, and the results are more consistent with agreed-upon company guidelines. When reusable assets can be leveraged, there is less development work to do, and future products get to market faster.

Asset format. Will the asset come in the form you need? Do you need to have the source code for the reusable asset, or is a nonmodifiable form acceptable? Vendors see source code as exposing their critical investments, and want to be protected from cloners. They eloquently make the excuse that it is "safer" to take a components-based approach to reuse. They mean: Treat the reusable assets as black box capability to be reused as-is. They intend no customization other than that which they have already built into the components and exposed in the external interfaces.

For code reuse, access to source code gives reusers a sense of ownership in that they can choose to make changes—experiments or necessary patches that precede the vendor's release timeframe. However, such access requires that the vendor inform reusers as to which aspects of the reusable implementations are the basis for reuse, and which are just there to support the details of the implementation. Also, a vendor's reusable assets might not pass your certification guidelines. You may need source code to modify the assets to pass your internal requirements.

There is another reason for preferring source code. Many people are just learning about object-oriented technology. You learn to program by reading good programs, and you learn to design by reading good designs. Reading source code from skilled object-oriented vendors can be a useful way to learn.

Certification guidelines. Organizations often adopt standards for software formatting and documentation. Projects carried out within the corporation are expected to follow these guidelines, encouraging understandability through their consistent use. Outside vendors are less likely to know about or follow these guidelines. What influence do you have over an outside vendor to obtain assets that meet your guidelines?

Certify Reusable Assets

Certification assures that the assets meet some level of quality. It is necessary to certify in order to warranty the software, to assert the fitness of an asset for use in product development. It is not possible to certify some quality aspects of reusable assets, in particular it is not possible to warranty that a reusable asset is safe to use. Safety is an external product measure; safety can be measured only in the context in which the asset is used. For example, you can certify that a rifle works as described, but you cannot certify that it is safe for you to go hunting with it. Safety depends on the situation in which the asset is used.

To overcome the barriers to reuse arising out of unfamiliarity with the creator of an asset, the organization has to decouple the trust for an asset from the trust in a particular developer, and shift this trust onto the certification process that admits the asset into the shared library. To set up an effective certification process, you should

- Determine the overall certification goal

- Decide how to certify each kind of asset

- Consider the potential liability associated with certification

Determine the overall certification goal. The overall goal of certification must answer the question, what is it that we want developers to trust about the assets that we have in our reuse library? The U.S. Government STARS project (Software Technology for Adaptable, Reliable Systems) wants to guarantee—have people trust—that the software assets implement their requirements and that their execution will be error free in their intended environment [Davis 1991]. The CARDS project (Central Archive for Reusable Defense Software) wants to guarantee—have people trust—that reusable assets will be qualified on the basis of their form, fit, and function [Moore 1991].

Many organizations certify at different levels. You might certify one asset to be used in commercial applications of a non-life-threatening nature, but would not accept the same asset in a NASA project where human lives are at stake. You might certify some assets for creating prototypes, but not for products.

In the first step of the reuse decision framework, defining reuse, we asked you to decide what you want to reuse. Here we ask you to state which assets must go through a well-defined certification process, and at what level. Given the cost of certification, you might wish to limit which assets go through the process.

Decide how to certify each kind of asset. There are potentially many different kinds of assets that need certification, and it is likely that each will have to possess different attributes to meet the certification requirements. It is also likely that we can determine attributes for the same asset that discriminate levels of trust. The purpose of this step is to state these attributes, for each kind of asset, at each level of trust.

This choice of the appropriate set of attributes is dependent on the kind of asset involved, and the trust level desired. Sample dimensions along which attributes are chosen include collateral material, quality measures, and potential reuse. For example, the CARDS project needed to state the attributes of an asset that ensure form, fit, and function. The term "certified" was used to refer to an asset that possessed these attributes. Different kinds of assets may display form, fit, and function differently, and so different sets of attributes were needed.

Certification—associated collateral material. Certification might ensure the existence of the proper collateral materials for assets being added to the library. These materials accompany an asset into the library, and are used to explain the asset to potential reusers. For example, at a minimum, a class implementation should have documentation, test cases, and use cases. The documentation describes the overall purpose of the class as well as the specific interface to each service (text description and type of the formal input/output parameters). At the very least, the test cases must provide a minimal form of testing to be performed when the asset is reused. The use cases are provided to show the potential reuser how to incorporate the class in one or more situations.

As another example, the STARS reusability guidebook requires the following documentation to accompany each library submittal:

Part description

Submitter data (who submitted)

Component constituents

Component history

Component relationships

Component attributes

Restrictions

Disclaimers

Software support

Miscellaneous instructions

Releases

Deliverable media description

Media

Certification—quality measures. Certification properties have to be understood in terms of the number of defects, performance characteristics, readability of the code, and so on. Here we explain the idea of quality measures by example. In Chapter 20, we formally define quality measures.

Part of the recommended certification process devised by SofTech involves evaluating artifacts based on maintainability measures. The standards they recommend create four levels of certification, depending on whether the code was independently tested, whether all function is provided (completeness), and whether it is documented:

Level 1	No additional testing or documentation, and level of completeness is unknown
Level 2	Level of completeness is verified and reported
Level 3	Test suites were executed and provided
Level 4	Fully tested/documented, meets standards of CSRO (Center for Software Reuse Operations)

Table 10.1 Loral Certification Requirements

Test	Required Result
Passed inspection	meets standards
BAT cyclomatic complexity rating	result < 10
Number of error reports after delivery	result < 15
Number of years since delivery	result > 1
Number of projects that used code	result > 1
Supporting documents exist	test, design, requirements

Test suites are to be constructed as reusable assets, and deployed as part of regression testing as the assets change over time. Level 4 documentation is targeted at reusers, to help them integrate the asset into their systems.

An example of a test plan comes out of work at Loral Software Productivity Laboratory [Bourgeois 1992]. Table 10.1 lists the tests that must be passed at Loral to conclude that a code artifact is certified for reuse.

Certification—potential reuse. The likelihood that an asset is reusable is based on the similarity between the domains of future applications and those for which the asset was constructed. So the asset needs to be characterized by its intended domain, and any constraints placed on the way it is to be used.

Consider potential liability. Given that the reusable assets have been certified at some quality level, a project manager who makes use of the assets should expect to hold someone accountable for the certification claims. A project manager has the right to assume that any problems will be resolved in a timely way. Developers expect reusers to make sure that they are acquiring and maintaining the right assets, and to make sure that the assets meet the reuser's quality expectations. So reusers too have a responsibility—to provide feedback on their experiences in trying to reuse assets.

Classify and Represent Reusable Assets

Having a large quantity of potentially reusable assets is useless if the assets cannot be found. This problem is also faced in other disciplines such as library sciences, botany, and zoology: How do we organize a large body of information so that it supports the needs of information users? The classification problem is to identify common characteristics that can be used to organize information, as in the Dewey decimal system. Unfortunately, there is no equivalent system for classifying software.

All organizations must answer the following three questions:

- What classification structure should be used?
- How will assets be cataloged using this structure?
- What is the representation form of the assets that are to be stored?

Other decisions, such as storing, locating, and retrieving artifacts, all depend on the answers to these questions.

Classification schemes. A classification scheme provides a means by which assets can be cataloged, retrieved, and evaluated. There are three common approaches to developing classification schemes: enumerative, faceted, and keyword or attribute.

An *enumerative scheme* divides the universe into a collection of domains and subdomains. The Dewey decimal system used by many U.S. libraries, and the system used by professional societies for classifying papers in journals (e.g., the scheme used by the *ACM Computing Reviews*) are enumerative schemes. A new artifact is classified by choosing the predefined domain that best describes it. This approach works well if the universe of discourse lends itself to a predetermined hierarchy. Whereas this might work well for U.S. book libraries, it is not the best approach for a software library in which the structure grows as new modules are added. In addition, since an object-oriented model describes classes and their relationships, it would be surprising to know these classes prior to developing any models. If you are from the camp that believes in full enterprise analysis prior to developing any system, an enumerative scheme might work.

A *faceted scheme* relies on synthesizing a classification from a set of basic categories. You might think of this as the Chinese menu approach to ordering dinner: choose one item from the soup column, one item from the rice column, one item from the poultry column, and so on. In classifying software, each column in the menu corresponds to a facet that represents a distinguishing category.

A facet can be a dimension of a particular domain. The domain of interest for the European Esprit project REBOOT is code [Karlsson, Sørumgård, and Tryggeseth 1991]. To organize this code, the project uses a faceted classification scheme that employs four facets:

Abstraction	An artifact can be characterized with a noun, such as stack or flight manager
Operations	Artifacts have operations, such as arithmetic, enumeration, and stack manipulation
Operates On	Objects on which this artifact acts, such as integers, set, list, resource
Dependencies	These are nonfunctional dependencies and similar characteristics that make reuse of the artifact more difficult, such as C++ based, Unix based or HOOD based

To support the flexible retrieval systems associated with a faceted scheme, you will need to identify the terms within a given facet. You may choose to organize the terms into a graph assigning conceptual distance values to the edges. These distance values allow you to search for near, rather than exact, matches. You can change the terms in a facet as well as the distance values to reflect your evolving understanding of how to characterize the reusable assets.

The faceted approach is much more common for classifying software assets than is the enumerative approach. The U.S. DoD uses a faceted approach, classifying metrics, abstracts, problem reports, and user feedback, as well as the artifact and its associated documentation and use tests. Whereas none of the case study projects chose the enumerative scheme, three projects chose the faceted scheme. In addition, we have encountered several projects outside of the case study projects that have also adopted a faceted approach.

The *keyword/attribute scheme* is a simple approach to classifying. An asset is classified by assigning one or more keywords or characteristics to it, with no constraints on the choice and number of keywords. Typical keywords might be analysis artifact, design artifact, or code artifact. In effect, a facet is a categorization of keywords with distance values. An attribute-based scheme predefines the choice and number of characteristics, but not the set of all possible values for these characteristics. Typical attributes might be: author, creation date, and project name.

This approach to classification is by far the most common. Most adopters of this approach, including the majority of the case study projects, combine keyword and attribute-based classification.[4] It is not surprising that this is the most popular form of classification. It is easy to understand and is well defined, and there are plenty of existing systems that embody the approach. However, the keyword approach does not take advantage of the description of objects. Inheritance, for example, cannot be expressed well using keywords, and can only be expressed superficially using attributes.

Classification and representation. We draw a distinction between classification and representation. Imagine that you have analyzed a system using OBA and implemented it in Smalltalk. The development life cycle results in different types of artifacts such as behaviors, which OBA chooses to represent as scripts, and class descriptions, which the developers represent as Smalltalk code. That is, different types of artifacts have different representations.

In object-oriented systems, analysis and design supply the units to be classified: objects, classes, class hierarchies, subsystems, applications, and frameworks. Object

---

[4] The attribute-based approach is part of almost every classification system, including enumerative and faceted. For example, it may make sense to be able to search by author regardless of the primary classification scheme.

encapsulation reduces the scope of the classification problem to the object's external interface. Polymorphic protocols provide a ready-made classification scheme. Objects with similar protocols may be substitution-compatible if other semantic criteria are met.

To illustrate, let's look at Fig. 10.3. Inheritance is useful for classifying objects. In the diagram, Air Vehicle and Land Vehicle are both special types of Vehicles. The classification scheme can directly benefit from this information as one means for organizing artifacts—by inheritance. However, the definition of any class is incomplete unless you consider the behavior and information provided by all of its parent classes (transitively until the root class is reached). Inheritance effectively spreads the definition of a class over a set of classes in a hierarchy, thus increasing the difficulty of providing a noninheritance form of classification.

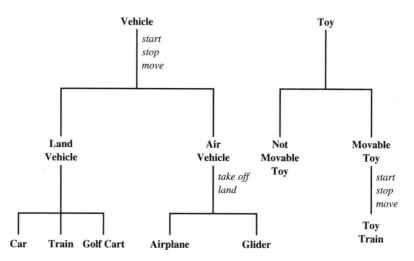

Figure 10.3   Sample Class Hierarchies for Modeling Vehicles

Suppose we search for objects that can start, stop, and move. We would retrieve any Vehicle, in particular any Land Vehicle or Air Vehicle, which inherits this protocol. Suppose our system also has objects representing Toys, and movable toys know how to start, stop, and move. Our search based on the polymorphic protocol (start, stop, and move) would retrieve these toys, such as the Toy Train, as well.

Sophisticated classification schemes for object artifacts should use the representation inherent in these objects.

Store Reusable Assets

Assets have to be stored in a way that makes it possible for developers to locate and retrieve the assets. We can store the classification information in a different way from the way we store the actual assets. For example, we can store the classification scheme in a relational database and the actual assets in a flat file system. Alternatively, the hierarchical structure of a file system and the corresponding names of the directories and files can be used to capture the classification scheme. If we use a relational database, we can store the assets in tabular format along with keyword and attribute fields for classification. Using this storage approach, structured queries can be used to locate and retrieve assets. Unfortunately, the relationships in object models are often complex and do not map well to the simple table structure of relational databases. Using a relational database requires software that projects object models onto table structures. Alternatively, object-oriented databases could be used.

Set Up a Process for Sharing Reusable Assets

Sharing involves three substeps for learning about the existence of, finding, and using the reusable assets:

- Communicate the availability of reusable assets

- Locate and retrieve reusable assets

- Understand and use reusable assets

Communicate the Availability of Reusable Assets

How do people know what reusable assets are available? Here is a story to consider:

> One of the authors used to work at the Xerox Palo Alto Research Center. The center provided a work environment for about 200 researchers plus various other administrative services, including a comprehensive library of books and periodicals in computer science, physics, optical science, and so on. The librarian maintained a daily presence in the research programs. She attended technical and business presentations, read all technical reports and group progress reports, and networked with her counterparts at Stanford, University of California at Berkeley, and other local high-technology companies. The result was that a researcher would often arrive in his or her office to find a book or periodical with a note from the librarian: "This item is probably of interest to you." She was usually on target.

Now that's a communication service!

Now consider situations you have been in when reuse was effective. Most programmers we know claim that they always reuse not just their own tools and software but ones created by colleagues in the company. They find out about these tools and software at meetings, in the cafeteria, in the hallway.

Both the librarian and the hallway represent communication in the form of *opportunistic marketing*. In the first case, the marketeer was proactive—the librarian understood the problem situation and, when she saw the opportunity to bring value to the research effort, proactively delivered information. In the second case, someone stated a problem and someone with a reusable solution reactively provided it.

Personal contacts work well on a small scale, but not in the larger context of an organization's reuse process. As in the public marketplace, marketing communication is needed to inform potential customers that the products exist—through advertisements, newsletters, and seminars. The purpose of marketing is aggressively to inform developers that reusable assets do exist, to make sure that the strategic assets are well known and that the mechanisms for finding less strategic assets are also understood.

The companies studied in Japan handled their marketing communications by providing hardcopy catalogs of the contents of their libraries—in fact there was no actual place or organization called the "library." The catalogs were indexed by keywords and referenced a contact from whom you could obtain the asset.

A second communication problem involves broadcasting the need for assistance. A developer might place a problem statement in an accessible location—a physical kiosk, an electronic bulletin board, on the Internet—or contact an agent, like the Xerox librarian, who does a search and produces a solution.

Most organizations in the case studies relied on hallway encounters or company-wide seminars to communicate reuse opportunities. In support of its effort to promote reuse in the development of Ada applications, IBM created an object-oriented technology reuse group in Poughkeepsie, New York. This group developed Ada programs that were shared throughout IBM. Various IBM divisions maintain a computer server that acts as a "kiosk" of information about assets that can be obtained from the reuse group.

Locate and Retrieve Reusable Assets

Locating assets depends on the decisions you make about classification, representation, storage, and communication. Most developers prefer to describe the assets they want and then leave it to tools to satisfy the request. The extent to which this automatic search is possible depends in part on the storage representation. Most storage representations cannot support sophisticated queries and reasoning. For example, the Unix grep (string search) command is one way of locating assets in a file-based scheme whose representation is textual. However, it is up to the user to interpret the file and line information that is returned, which is often cluttered with noise (mismatches) because of the limited semantic selection of the search.

More sophisticated storage facilities do leverage the native asset representation. For example, tools like the ParcPlace Smalltalk browsers help developers locate classes by exploiting the inheritance relationships that exist among classes. The same browsers allow the developer to cross-reference other relationships, such as senders of messages, and implementors of methods. In all, there are more than 10 different ways of locating Smalltalk components, all leveraging the underlying Smalltalk representation.

Even with sophisticated representation techniques, the developer may often want to supplement the official classifications with user-defined schemes. In the ParcPlace Smalltalk browser, there are two user-defined classification levels: categories and protocols. Categories are used to group classes that have something in common. The classes Character, Date, Magnitude, Time, and TimeZone are stored in the category Magnitude-General. The second level of classification is the protocol, which is used to group related methods within a particular class. For example, the class Date contains the following protocols: comparing (methods for determining whether one date is before, after, or equal to another date); accessing (methods for accessing day, month, and year); and arithmetic (methods for adding and subtracting days); as well as protocols for inquiries, converting, printing, and private.

The most common scheme for locating assets is based on keyword and attribute-based searching. The following techniques may be supported:

- Wild card search—introducing wild cards (denoting "anything") into the search string

- Thesaurus—locating synonyms of the requested asset

- Phrase search—multiword searching

- Boolean combination—forming a conjunction or disjunction of search parameters

- Automatic stemming—allowing stem words to match larger morphological units—for example, the word "switch" matches switches, switching, and so on

The majority of the case study projects used retrieval tools that support some form of keyword or attribute-based locating.

In place at the U.S. DoD Center for Software Reuse Operations is the Defense Software Repository System (DSRS), an on-line tool for user search and retrieval, and formulation of descriptions for storage of assets. DSRS implements a faceted classification scheme for assets. Assets are stored with measures, abstracts, problem reports, and suggestions. The storage medium is a commercial relational database.

Bell Northern Research experimented successfully with CD-ROMs to store its library of reusable code [Fraser 1991], and created a tool to help designers locate software using keyword searches. AT&T has a reuse "help desk" staffed with reuse experts who can help developers find and use reusable assets, notably frameworks and components, and assist the developers in understanding how to refine the frameworks.

The steps of locating and retrieving assets can be coupled when the circumstances permit. Circumstances might dictate a separation of the two activities:

- Security: just because you found something doesn't mean you are allowed to retrieve it.

- Perhaps the nature of the library requires that you create a purchase order after you locate the asset.

- The physical structure of your library might be such that you locate with one system and retrieve with another.

The task of locating is simplified if you focus on fewer larger-grained reusable assets, such as application frameworks. When you first set up your library, we recommend that you focus on classifying fewer and more powerful assets, rather than on finding better classification schemes.

Understand and Use Reusable Assets

As another maxim states: You cannot use what you do not understand. How you understand and how you use an asset are tied to the representation of the asset itself, in combination with the collateral material, tools, and methods for understanding and using the asset.

Suppose you are redeveloping a business application for the KandA Widget Company. The original version generated a character-based screen report of the number of widgets sold over the past year. The new application is supposed to present this same information using a bar chart. Fortunately, a previous project developed a set of charting widgets that were certified and stored in a shared library managed by the KandA IS department. You know they are in the library because you recently received an announcement in the form of an e-mail message. You use the locating and retrieval tools to fetch the bar-chart widget.

What exactly did you retrieve? Just the code for the bar chart? If so, will this be sufficient information for you to determine how the chart works, and whether it will satisfy your current charting needs? How about a user's document? What about scenarios for exercising the capabilities of the chart? What about test cases to assist you in verifying the correct operation of the bar chart once it is embedded in your application? In practice, although the asset itself may contain sufficient information for you to understand it, you always benefit from supportive collateral materials. You benefit even more from the assistance of an expert, who uses the retrieval tools, finds the asset for you, and shows you how to integrate it into your system!

Reuse-oriented documentation should suggest the best ways to use an asset, should provide examples of how to use it, and might suggest any integration pitfalls. Good documentation is often the lowest-cost additional work to help make assets more reusable.

Set Up a Process for Maintaining Reusable Assets

Maintaining reusable assets involves two substeps:

- Update reusable assets
- Update the reusers

Well-considered policies will help you deal with the long-term maintenance and evolution of reusable assets. The policies must address questions such as:

- Who is responsible for correcting defects in assets?
- When can evolutionary demands permit backward compatibility to be broken?
- How will you keep track of the reusers?
- How will delivered applications be affected by a new version of a reused asset? That is, when a delivered application has reused an asset in which a defect has been repaired, does the delivered application immediately take the new version of the asset and incorporate it, take the new asset at its next major release point, or perhaps never take the asset?

Suppose that you have created dozens of applications, made out of hundreds of reusable parts. And the person who wrote one of those parts finds a problem. The problem might be a missing feature, a change in business semantics, a poorly named function, an algorithm that runs slower than necessary. The problem is solved. The component is changed. And the revised part goes on the shelf, ready for future reuse.

New reusers benefit from the revision. But what about the earlier reusers? To benefit from a revision, they must first discover that a part used in their system has been revised, and then they must remove the original part and replace it with the revised one.

Somehow reusers have to be informed. They must know what is in their system and they must know a new version is available. Somehow the changes to the reused part have to propagate as desired. How this is done depends on the organization's policy for updating its systems. Are updates deferred until the reusers decide to make the change? Or must updating be immediate? The changes could be ignored. The reuser can choose to continue with the older version. The term "cloning" refers to this option.

You can avoid the issue of convincing reusers to update by taking advantage of network-based object servers through object request brokers. Reusers never copy an asset and link it into their own system code. Rather, they set up a call to their broker. The broker is responsible for passing messages to the latest implementation. This approach is best used with large-grained objects (applications).

Perhaps you don't agree that the reusers need to update. After all, their programs appear to work already. Whoever instigated the revision will know about the revised part and will be prepared to make the change. The rest of the reusers haven't figured out that there is an improvement necessary. If they don't know it's broken, why fix it?

Is this the way to run a business? If vendors kept their improvements a secret from their customers, would they still be in business? Especially when a business change is reflected in reusable parts, the organization should expect all reuses to change.

When a company purchases a code library from a software vendor, it does so with two expectations. The first is that there will be technical support, and the second is that the vendor will improve the code, to maintain the marketability of the product. It is our experience, in working for such a vendor, that our customers update their use of our offerings. Indeed, as a vendor, we maintain a record of all customers for the explicit purpose of getting them to update. We take both a reactive and a proactive approach to maintaining both our software and our customers as reusers. We maintain a support hotline—a reactive maintenance device. If we find a major problem, we proactively contact the affected customers. Moreover, based on customer feedback, we update our products and again proactively contact customers about these updates.

If you expect this from an outside vendor, why wouldn't you expect this from the internal provider of reusable assets? A list of reusers needs to be maintained so that updated information about the assets can be shared. Or the reusers have to have direct access to the creators of the reusable assets to ask questions. One company we know of supports an electronic kiosk at the different development sites worldwide. Lists of reusers are maintained per kiosk. When the assets change, a message about the change goes to the kiosk for affected reusers. It is up to the reusers to browse the kiosk regularly.

To fulfill the potential for reuse, some questions need to be answered. How do parts maintainers contact the reusers? How do maintainers of a system find out which parts are in the system, and track the sources of these parts?

There is a way. But much of what we have to say about maintenance hinges on how reuse is paid for in the company. Who is in charge of creating the reusable assets? Who takes responsibility for communicating the availability of assets? That is, whose job is it and who pays the salaries and expenses? The next chapter proposes several models, distinguished by the decisions they make in each of the steps of the reuse framework. We use these models to make recommendations about maintenance.

Case Study Results

Figure 10.4 summarizes three different reuse and reuse maintenance situations found in the case studies. The situations refer to maintenance of binary code and source code. Similar maintenance issues exist for assets other than code. The binary form of an analysis, for example, is read-only access to the analysis object model, or supporting scripts, glossaries, and diagrams.

The first scenario we label As-Is Reuse. As we explain in Chapter 9, the reusable asset is taken as-is by the reuser. Reuse depends only on the external aspects of the asset, so that an updated asset, which does not eliminate services or change the semantics of an existing service, can simply replace its prior version. This maintenance process is shown as Fig. 10.4 (a).

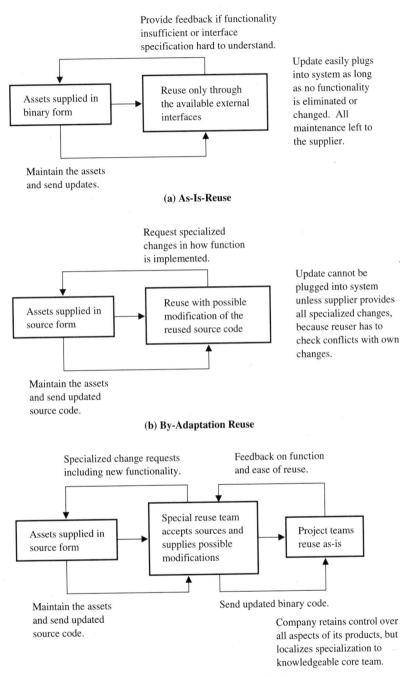

(a) As-Is-Reuse

(b) By-Adaptation Reuse

(c) Adaptation by Central Team Only

Figure 10.4   Ways to Maintain Reusable Assets

The second scenario we label By-Adaptation Reuse. White box reuse leads the reuser to make modifications to the reusable asset. Updated reusable assets cannot simply be plugged into the reuser because there may be change conflicts. This maintenance process, shown as Fig. 10.4 (b), is more costly than the as-is reuse, because it is necessary to handle the recoding, integration, and testing implied by the potential conflicts. Moreover, the supplier ought to provide details of the changes to help in the conflict checking. When the reusers are relatively unsophisticated software developers, or when they have limited resources, this approach is not appealing. The tendency is to clone the reusable assets and avoid the maintenance opportunity.

The third scenario, labeled Adaptation by Central Team Only, is shown in Fig. 10.4 (c). As in the second scenario, white box reuse leads the reuser to make modifications to the reusable asset. However, the only developers with white box access are members of a central expert reuse team. The organization-specific or project-specific changes are made by these experts, and then passed in black box or glass box form to the reusers for as-is reuse. This combines the first two approaches, giving a sense of ownership of the reusable assets to the organization, yet localizing the burden of maintenance on more expert developers.

Our point in reviewing the options here is to emphasize that it is important to treat the use of reusable assets as a business. The creator of the assets, or some responsible party, should have a commitment to maintenance. The reusers of the assets should have a commitment to upgrading. Reuse requires knowledge and good project controls to make sure that long-term maintenance is not jeopardized.

Summary

To change the process by which you manage reuse, you have to select a reuse process model that treats reusable assets as strategic products of your organization. In this chapter, we suggested the steps for selecting a reuse process model. First, you have to decide on what reuse means. Specifically, decide what you want to have available as reusable assets, and the way you want to reuse: as-is or by-adaptation. We recommend that you focus on strategic assets, frameworks that represent your industry and that can be customized to create applications specific to the way you want to run your business within that industry. We also recommend that you plan to create these frameworks yourselves but seek cooperation with other businesses in your industry to collaborate to create the business components that do not represent a competitive disadvantage if shared.

Next you decide how you will populate a library of reusable assets, distribute the assets, and maintain both assets and reusers. We identified specific decisions that lead to a process by which you treat reuse as a business within your organization. Reusers should be able to trust the assets because they trust the process. The discussions in this chapter were detailed, outlining the many options available to you today. It is essential that you decide on your long-term goals for reuse, at the outset of putting the reuse process in place, and that you construct initial policies for certification and classification. It will be very costly to have to carry out this work after you have already accumulated a significant library of reusable artifacts, especially if certification levels will affect the acceptability of existing applications. We also recommend that you focus your efforts on creating fewer, more powerful reusable assets. If there are fewer assets, they will be easier to locate. You need not expend initial efforts on creating retrieval schemes and tools.

Developers as reuse consumers have to be aware of which reusable assets are available; developers as reuse producers have to understand what their potential customers (reuse consumers) will find useful. The reuse process model encourages broad communication between consumers and producers, which we liken to a software vendor's proactive and reactive marketing programs and technical support operations.

Additional Reading About Reuse Process Models

Biggerstaff, T. and Perlis, A., eds., *Software Reusability: Volume II, Applications and Experience*, ACM Press: Reading, Mass., 1989.

>The second of a two-volume set, this book is a collection of papers that focus on the applications of reuse and the experience derived from such applications. The papers review the tools that foster reuse, focusing on the constructs of object-oriented programming languages such as Eiffel and Smalltalk-80. Case studies illustrate reuse in business applications, telephony, and process control software. Some quantitative studies in software reuse are reported which attempt to characterize the nature of reuse in several projects. How do programmers approach reuse? What knowledge do they need and what can we provide to encourage reuse? Papers by Soloway and Curtis attempt to answer these questions. Additional papers review the research on automatic programming and various ideas about encouraging reuse through tools in program development environments.

IEEE Software, Special Issue on Systematic Reuse, 11(45), September 1994.

>This issue of *IEEE Software* contains articles organized by William Frakes and Sadahiro Isoda which emphasize the importance of systematic reuse, with an appraisal of the risks in implementation as well as the risks in leaving such a program to your competitors. Papers in the issue discuss management, measurement, legal issues, economics, and how to design for reuse through iterative refinement.

Schäfer, W., Prieto-díaz, R., and Matsumoto, M., *Software Reusability*, Ellis Horwood: United Kingdom, 1994.

>This book grew out of the First International Workshop on Software Reusability held in Dortmund, Germany, in 1991; the workshop deliberations and contributed papers were molded into chapters that survey and analyze the key issues in software reusability. These issues include domain analysis, managerial and organizational structures for supporting reuse, formal methods, and tools and environments. The opening historical overview provides an interesting perspective on research goals and the status of government-funded research projects (worldwide). All of the chapters together provide a starting point for anyone entering this area of research and practice, and therefore interested in a full literature review. A wealth of tactical ideas is represented in the surveys, although many of the tactics presume large-scale organizational investment.

CHAPTER 11

Organizational Models for Reuse

Lunacy is to continue to do the same thing and expect a different result.

Unknown

A software organization, faced with the challenges to remain competitive, has no choice but to embrace a systematic reuse process. The question is, what should be the extent of the investment? The framework for selecting a reuse process model suggests you make decisions in 13 areas. Your decisions are driven by your organizational model for reuse.

Organizational Model Maxims

As practitioners, we have managed research programs. We have directed engineering projects. We have shipped numerous successful products. And we have taught and consulted with thousands of customers. The one element that reappears in all of our endeavors is that we rely on the skills and work ethics of the people in the groups we manage. This trust is the basis for two maxims for successful reuse.

People make reuse work. Reuse happens when people cooperate.

Reuse is a technology transfer opportunity. The best way to transfer technology is to have the people who created it help the people who want to use it.

Reuse Organization

A third, and likely more controversial maxim, directs your attention to the long-term nature of the systems you build, and the benefits of maintaining synchronicity between the reusable assets and their reuses.

***Reuse
Organization***

Reuse is a maintenance imperative. Systems that reuse assets should be updated when the assets are changed.

Reuse in the Virtual Hallway

Picture an engineer, pacing around his office, and up and down the hallways late at night—mumbling to himself—until a colleague bumps into him, maybe literally.

"What are you doing?" she asks.

"Thinking," he says.

"What about?" she asks. He explains his problem. She smiles. She has solved a similar problem.

"Come along," she urges. "I will show you my solution."

And together they go to her office to find the solution.

We all recognize this chance encounter. It sets the stage for an effective form of reuse—people helping one another. Someone knows something that someone else needs to know. The developers may not be working on the same project, but they work in the same company and are interested in sharing their expertise. Reuse is often initiated in the hallways, the cafeteria, the restroom, seminars, or other forums. A communication hallway is anywhere.

But we can't rely on chance physical encounters to make sure people get the help they need. We can't rely on the right people being in the same geographic location. Some kind of organizational structure has to create a hallway for communication, a guarantee of chance encounters.

We need a virtual hallway.

Reuse as a Form of Technology Transfer

Technology is rarely transferred successfully without an expert participating in the transfer process—someone who was an active participant in the creation of the technology. The reason is simple: The people who believe in the technology, who understand it, have the passion and the patience to make sure that potential users succeed.

Reusing someone else's result is rarely an easy task. The reuser quickly tires of the effort when no one is around to help. Written documentation is okay when all you need to do is look up a fact or a definition, but not as useful when you want to understand how to adapt something to your situation.

Historically, transfer of an innovation or engineered technology to other divisions of the same company succeeds only when the people who did the original work join the development team that is chartered to make use of the technology.

We need to make sure that reusable assets get transferred.

Reuse Is a Maintenance Responsibility

Reusable assets promote consistency among the reusing systems. It is just as important to remain consistent as it was to start out that way. As the business changes, reusable assets representing business elements and processes will change as well. To remain consistent, the applications that made use of the assets need to be updated. This does not happen by chance.

A critical part of your reuse plan is to make sure that the original goals of reuse are maintained throughout the life of the organization's software systems. When a reusable asset changes, the reusers have to be proactively informed. Replacing the reusable asset with its updated version can be just as tiring or cumbersome as it was to use the asset in the first place. Again, assistance by knowledgeable people is appropriate. You need an organizational model that helps the maintainers of the reusable assets participate with the reusers in making sure that the updates are done correctly and in a timely way.

We need up-to-date and consistent use of reusable assets.

Reuse Organizational Models

What structure should be supported to create a company-wide virtual hallway that encourages successful technology transfer and consistent use of the latest versions of reusable assets? Four possible structures were seen in the case studies. We call these:

- Ad Hoc Model
- Supply and Demand Model
- Expert Services Model
- Product Center Model

Another approach you might consider is the Commercial-Off-the-Shelf (COTS) Model, which assumes that all assets are acquired from commercial vendors. The COTS Model leans toward purchasing reusable assets rather than crafting them internally. Most organizations will support a mixture, depending on commercial availability and requirements for proprietary technology. Most organizations will ramp up their reuse effort by starting the library with purchased assets (usually system utilities, tools, and general-purpose application frameworks) and gradually adding assets developed by an internal reuse team.

Table 11.1 on page 260 characterizes the way each of the organizational models addresses the recommended reuse process.

Ad Hoc Model

The Ad Hoc Model for managing the reusable assets of a corporation is, as the name implies, a model of somewhat arbitrary behavior—everything is welcome. The more choices in the library, the happier the potential users will be because it is more likely that there will be something they can use. The model is illustrated by Fig. 11.1.

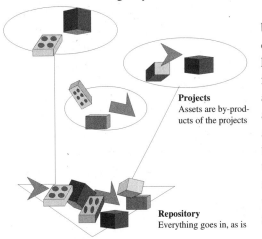

Projects
Assets are by-products of the projects

Repository
Everything goes in, as is

Figure 11.1   Ad Hoc Model

The appeal of this approach is based on quantity. There is no measure of success based on whether the library has assets that are useful to current and future projects. Trust in the developers and supporters of the process that adds artifacts to the library is not available. As a result, the reusers must assume that anything they retrieve is suspect with respect to usefulness, reliability, and robustness. Such libraries can be viewed as corporate-sanctioned flea markets.

We do not like this model. Except for the purchased assets, the model encourages developers to build systems out of salvaged designs and implementations, which were left around in an accessible storage location without having been certified for any purpose and without any commitment to support.

We assume that creating reusable assets was not one of the goals of the project from which the artifacts were salvaged. Making the project artifacts generally useful did not contribute materially to the project's goals. Yet the Ad Hoc Model says that the project can supply reusable assets. There are two possibilities: either nothing special was done to promote reusability, or effort was expended to transform the project artifacts into more generally useful assets. In the first case, the project artifacts were simply offered as assets—reuser beware! In the second case, we have a resource question. Since effort was expended to promote reusability, something else—some other project objective—probably suffered.

The argument in favor of the Ad Hoc approach is that product projects create well-tested analyses, designs, and implementations. These might have been purposely designed for reuse as a way of improving the quality of the product. The assets in the library come as a by-product of well-managed projects. Therefore, the assets are trustworthy.

We do not buy this argument. Just because an artifact can be trusted in the situation for which it was designed does not mean that it can be trusted for reuse in other situations.

Supply and Demand Model

The second model we call the Supply and Demand Model.[1] It is essentially the same as the Ad Hoc Model, as illustrated by Fig. 11.2, with the key distinction that there is a well-defined and accessible marketplace where assets are placed and potential reusers can shop. As with the Ad Hoc Model, the Supply and Demand Model encourages anything and everything to enter the market and to compete for attention. Redundancy gives the shoppers choices. No importance is placed on having a singular approach that can be shared across projects.

The idea of a marketplace is that demand creates supply—what is in the marketplace is determined by what buyers want. Buyers state what they want by shopping, taking some things and not other things, and perhaps complaining when something they want does not exist. Somehow the marketplace is managed, and the managers can pass on the complaints to potential suppliers. Assets that are never used are removed after some pre-determined length of time. Assets that are frequently used are given a positive review by buyers, and are advertised by these buyers as the preferred assets. The preferred assets are treated as the quality choice. Market acceptance is the only certification process.

See Table 11.1 for how the Supply and Demand approach handles the recommended reuse process.

On the surface, both the Ad Hoc and Supply and Demand Models look like cheap and easy ways to achieve reuse. Many of the reuse process steps are not addressed, yet a potentially large library of assets can be obtained. But these are not artifacts that can be trusted, since certification was not done. And these are not artifacts that necessarily represent strategic assets—no proactive identification and acquisition ties these artifacts to the needs of the corporation.

Where the artifacts are developed internally, there are hidden costs.

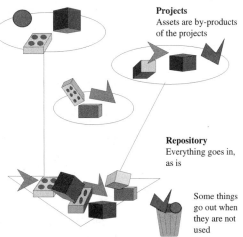

Projects
Assets are by-products of the projects

Repository
Everything goes in, as is

Some things go out when they are not used

Figure 11.2   Supply and Demand Model

Developers spend time creating artifacts, and submitting them to a communal pot, without assurance that these artifacts are useful to others, can be found within the large pot, or are even understandable if found.

---

[1] Howard Baetjer, an economist from George Mason University, first presented us with this modification of the Ad Hoc Model. He has documented his ideas about a components industry in [Lavoie *et al*. 1993].

And certainly the developers are not paid to maintain these assets—they are paid to meet the goals of their assigned projects. When the artifacts are developed externally, there is a possibility that this approach represents a process that can be trusted. Knowledgeable external developers form businesses to sell reusable assets. They are motivated by marketplace economics to create quality software and to provide customer support and maintenance. But as we note in Chapter 10, your strategic business assets are not likely to be available from external vendors.

Expert Services Model

In the Expert Services Model, the organization creates a reuse competence center, which is staffed by an independent Reuse Team responsible for identifying, acquiring, certifying, and storing the reusable assets in a shared library. The team's reuse process certifies that the assets can be trusted as parts of products to be sold or used internally. Included on this team are reuse technology engineers, skilled developers knowledgeable in reuse development, certification, classification, storage, and retrieval. These reuse engineers have at their disposal a complete set of tools for supporting their reuse activities.

The team's certification process stipulates that the assets must meet the product guidelines of the organization. This point is often lost in the excitement of creating as large a library as possible to give maximum opportunity for reuse. But the goal should be to create a library whose size is proportional to the set of assets considered to be strategic to the organization. By focusing reuse on strategic products, the library is likely to be small and can more likely serve as a recommendation to development groups. The Expert Services Model picture, Fig. 11.3, shows the product guidelines as a fence that keeps out uncertifiable contributions.

The Reuse Team can identify and acquire assets using any of the techniques outlined in Chapter 10. In doing so, an objective of this team should be to minimize, or even eliminate, redundancies in the library. These unique assets would then express the corporation's preferred (perhaps only) way to accomplish a particular set of capabilities.

What is unique about this model is that the Expert Services reuse engineers are available to work on specific projects. When a new project is started, the project leader interviews the engineers on the team and "hires" one or two engineers, depending on project requirements. These engineers provide the project with intimate knowledge of the corporate library and the tools for working with the library. In addition, they bring their knowledge of when and how to reuse appropriately in a given situation. This exchange of knowledge is what we mean by a Virtual Hallway. Assigning reuse engineers to projects turns the possibility of chance encounters into a defined working relation.

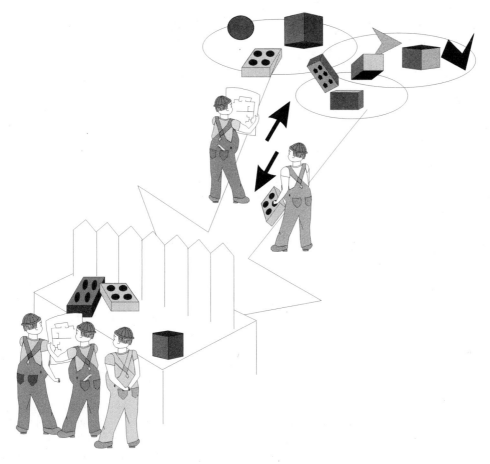

Figure 11.3   Expert Services Model

The reuse engineers are effective resources for leveraging the assets in the reuse library. They are obligated to make sure that appropriate reuse is realized. However, their overall evaluation is based on how well they apply their knowledge to help the project meet its stated goals and objectives.

When the project ends, the engineers return to the reuse competence center. They take back their experience in working on the project—experience that can be reused on future assignments. They also take back recommended improvements to existing assets, including defect fixes and extensions. Reuse team members are familiar with and keep records of the projects they work on and the assets they reuse. So all projects that are reusing an asset that has been fixed or extended can be notified of an update. (The organization must still decide what policy it will use for updating reusers.)

Another important service provided by the Reuse Team is to create reusable assets by harvesting project artifacts. When working on a project, a reuse engineer can recognize that a newly developed artifact has high potential reuse within the organization. The reuse engineer can harvest the artifact and take it back to the Reuse Team where it can be developed into a generally reusable asset. This saves the specific project the time and money needed to perform the work, and it ensures that knowledgeable people do the work.

The Expert Services approach can handle each aspect of the reuse process, as shown in Table 11.1.

When an organization adopts the Expert Services Model for organizing reuse, it states that reuse is an important, sanctioned activity. However, this activity costs money. Who's going to pay? One alternative is to have the organization pay for the assets created by the Reuse Team as a form of overhead, although we prefer to think of it as an investment. Another approach is to ask projects, especially those that will use the developed assets, to contribute financial resources. We recommend that such a charge-back approach be deferred for at least two years, during which time the Reuse Team can create the initial assets under corporate funding and build up a reputation for quality. Otherwise, the funding projects will be tempted to avoid charges by ignoring opportunities for reuse. That is, we recommend initial corporate funding as an investment to prime the reuse pump. This corporate-level support is an excellent way to create an appropriate culture of cross-project reuse: it shows that corporate-level management is serious about reuse.

It may appear that there is a substantial financial cost in setting up the Expert Services Center. However, for the value received, it is likely to be cheaper than other alternatives. This conclusion is based on an age-old maxim that if you don't know what you are doing, don't do it on a large scale. In this context, what we are doing is supporting a reuse process. This requires that people be trained in concepts and tools to identify, develop, certify, classify, store, locate, and retrieve assets. In large organizations, this can be a considerable and misplaced investment in training. Do we train everyone because one day they may need the skills, or only those who need it now? Do we buy supporting tools for everyone, or just some subset? Shouldn't we wait until the process is stable before unleashing it on the large number of corporate developers?

The Expert Services Model concentrates the new skills required to manage a reuse process in the hands of a small team of experts. The cost of developing this team is small relative to the effort involved in training all software developers. The reuse effort can get started faster because the smaller team can start out working with less formality, deferring decisions about some of the reuse steps. And the Reuse Team can more easily learn from experience. Time and real projects will teach the corporation about its certification and classification needs. These needs will influence the choice of tools for these two steps, as well as for storing, locating and retrieving. A smaller team can be more cost-effective in adapting to any needed changes in techniques and tools.

Thus, the Expert Services approach is likely to be a cost- effective way of getting a reuse effort under way. As reuse becomes more commonplace in the organization, the need for reuse engineers to be assigned to projects should diminish. The tools for accessing the reuse library should stabilize, as should the certification and classification schemes. These can then be included in the standard training programs, further decreasing reliance on a central team of experts. As reusing becomes a standard part of the development process, the cost of reuse will be translated into the savings in creating new systems and maintaining existing ones. The idea of charging expenses from projects back to a central Reuse Team can be dropped in favor of recognizing that the corporate investment in reuse is saving money throughout the organization.

Product Center Model

Figure 11.4 shows the Product Center Model, which is much the same as the Expert Services Model but with the people in the hallway omitted. As with the Expert Services Model, the main characteristic of the Product Center Model is that responsibility for the reuse process model is assigned to an independent Reuse Team. There are two differences between the models. First, the Product Center Model does not provide the reuse engineers who are loaned to projects. And second, this model expects individual project developers to view reuse as a standard part of the development process and to

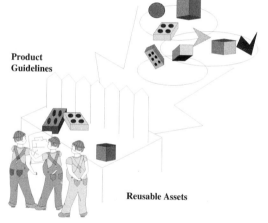

Figure 11.4   Product Center Model

know how to locate, retrieve, and use the reusable assets. The tools associated with accessing the library have to be given to these developers, along with appropriate training and documentation.

Table 11.1 describes the reuse process steps as they apply to the Product Center approach.

The Product Center assumes a certain amount of organizational maturity because it provides no reliable way to assure communication between the team that developed the reusable assets and the potential reusers. Potential reusers are expected to locate and

Table 11.1 Summary of the Reuse Process Model and Decisions Made by Each Reuse Organizational Model

	Ad Hoc	*Supply and Demand*	*Expert Services*	*Product Center*	*COTS*
Identify	—	—	All appropriate means	All appropriate means	Monitor market brochures and other collateral materials to identify opportunities; survey potential users
Acquire	Anyone submits anything	Anyone submits anything	All appropriate means	All appropriate means	Purchase reusable assets from outside vendors
Certify	—	—	Multilevel certification procedure	Multilevel certification procedure	Vendor reputation
Classify	—	Keyword as provided by the marketplace	Informal or formal classification scheme	Formal classification scheme	Done by vendor through market positioning, or redone internally
Store	File system	File system	File system, database, or special repository	File system, database, or special repository	From any other model
Communicate	Word of mouth	Word of mouth	Reuse engineers provide input to projects	Word of mouth, developers ask Reuse Team, or formal help desk	From any other model
Locate	Word of mouth or file system tools	Word of mouth or file system tools	Reuse engineers find the assets using reuse team's tools	Search tools based on mature classification scheme	From any other model
Retrieve	File finder	File finder	Reuse engineers retrieve the assets using the team's tools	Access tools based on search capabilities	From any other model

continued

Table 11.1 continued

	Ad Hoc	Supply and Demand	Expert Services	Product Center	COTS
Understand	—	—	Reuse engineers provide the understanding	Reuser's manual; possibly with help from member of Reuse Team, or formal help desk	From any other model
Use	Standard file system and programming tools	Standard file system and programming tools	Standard programming tools, with advice from the engineers	Standard programming tools, help on request	From any other model
Maintain	—	Prune supply based on long-term perceived demand	Reuse engineers update based on feedback from reusers	Reuse Team updates based on feedback from reusers	Handled by software vendor
Update Reusers	—	—	Projects to be redone as the assets are improved, assisted by reuse engineers	Communicate available updates, updating left to organization policy	Communicate available updates, left to reusers to adopt or not

retrieve assets on their own. They must have knowledge of the tools to perform these tasks, and they must understand how the assets are cataloged. These tools and the knowledge of the library are likely to be new to the reuser, requiring some training. A Reuse Team representative might provide help, as could a formal help desk or an informal electronic bulletin board.

COTS Model

The central assumption of this next model is that all of an organization's reusable assets will be acquired from outside vendors of such software—vendors of what are usually referred to as Commercial-off-the-Shelf (COTS) packages. No reusable assets are created or modified by the organization.

Most interest in this model comes from organizations that use what they purchase as-is, or that have an internal group that combines the assets into various configurations for internal users. Many people believe that this will be the dominant model for software construction in the future: Buy a large number of existing components from a commercial vendor, and then plug them together. The effect on the reuse process is shown in Table 11.1 under the column labeled COTS.

The COTS Model is really reuse by end users. It represents several decades of purchasing practice. The availability of COTS packages for developers really answers only the question of how the organization will handle acquisition. When components are acquired for use by a systems development organization, such an acquisition model still leaves open the questions of how certification, classification, and the other steps will be handled to assist the developers in meeting the organization's quality guidelines. One of the other four reuse organizational models will still have to be adopted.

Corporate Reuse Issues—Large and Small

Two more business issues are often raised in conversations about a reuse process model. First, at what level of the organization do you position the reuse effort, and should the effort be duplicated at multiple levels? Second, how will we get our recalcitrant developers to reuse the work of others?

Multilevel Reuse Efforts

A reuse effort can be created at more than one level of the organization. The number of libraries and the level at which they are managed depends on the structure of the organization. The idea of multiple reuse centers is consistent with our earlier discussion on the potential to use organizational boundaries as the basis for identifying assets. We have seen several possible organizational schemes that make sense. In Fig. 11.5, each box represents a library associated with an organizational entity.

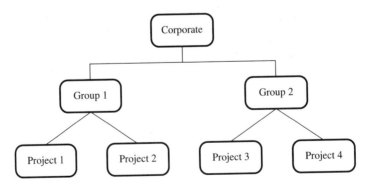

Figure 11.5   Libraries Can Exist Within Each Organizational Entity

Line of business. A business line may have several projects of the same type, and, therefore, we could argue for a reuse effort at this level. However, business lines are unstable because they are constantly realigned with market opportunities, so we do not recommend placing a reuse center at this level.

Corporate. There are reusable assets that are more general than the business-oriented ones that would be created at the division level. In particular, there are enterprise-wide analyses, frameworks for managing business processes, and tools and support utilities such as communication software, which can be managed at this level to encourage sharing among the divisions. Periodically, it might make sense for the corporate reuse organization to harvest some of the assets created at the group level for inclusion in a more widely available corporate library.

Group or division. A group or division represents the largest subunit of business functionality within an organization. It is often the case that this level contains multiple business functions, and therefore multiple projects, which share common business processes and information models. This level has the greatest potential for identifying strategic assets. Since there are multiple groups, it is likely that independent reuse efforts will exist.

Project. We recommend that every project have intraproject reuse as a development goal. This goal is to reduce the creation of redundant artifacts, and to ensure that unique solutions are reused throughout the development effort. A project can maintain its own library of reusable assets and can make use of assets maintained at higher levels of the organization. Projects should not reuse components found in the libraries of other projects because these components were not necessarily designed for general use. In Fig. 11.5, for example, Project 1 can reuse only from its own library and those from Group 1 and Corporate. Artifacts from projects need to be promoted to higher levels through a formal reuse process.

Given reuse efforts at multiple levels, a number of issues related to the reuse process model need to be addressed. First, certification requirements may differ at each level. There is an implicit expectation that the higher the business level, the greater the potential for widespread use, the less likely developers know one another, and therefore the greater the need for a trusted process. Moreover, potential reusers need to understand and trust the possibly different certification processes at each level. A question of liability has to be answered. Regardless of the level at which the asset is certified, it should be retested based on the guidelines given in Chapter 6.

Regardless of the organizational model selected, classification schemes are best shared at all levels, making it possible for projects to access reuse assets managed at every level. Communication is more complex when there are multilevel reuse efforts with possibly different classification schemes. Special effort may be needed to coordinate information from the multiple sources and to support communications among the reuse teams themselves. And finally, maintenance has to include updating the reusers.

Motivating Reuse

Even the best reuse process model—one that creates the most appropriate and best-designed reusable assets—will not in itself guarantee that the assets will be reused. Assets will be reused only if the people are motivated to use them. So the question we have to answer is how to motivate project managers and developers. How do you motivate people to overcome their inherent biases of: "Why work extra to benefit someone else?," "I can do it better," or "I won't use it because I didn't build it"? Suggestions we have heard are:

- Pay developers royalty when their contributions are reused

- Pay developers when they reuse an existing asset

- Penalize developers when they miss an opportunity to reuse an asset

Royalty payments. When reuse is not part of the culture, some unnatural acts take place in the name of promoting reuse. The most common aberration is paying developers a royalty every time their assets are reused. Let's imagine for a brief moment that this idea has merit. It seems practical, since the royalty-based model is one used extensively for non-software reusable assets such as books. However, how do we determine when one developer's work ends and another's begins, especially when inheritance is employed?

Let's say that Developer 1 creates Asset A, which provides three services. But no one wants to use Asset A until Developer 2 creates Asset B as a subclass of A, adding one new service. Along comes Developer 3 who decides to use Asset B, benefiting from the reuse of all four services. Who should get paid royalties, Developer 1 or 2, or both?

Perhaps it should be Developer 2 for creating the useful Asset B. However, Asset B is defined in terms of A. Shouldn't Developer 1 be compensated as well? Yes, you say? Well, then, what should be the division of royalty between Developers 1 and 2? Maybe this should be prorated based on the number of services each developer provided. Or maybe it should be prorated based on the number of services Developer 3 wants. What if Developer 3 would never have considered Asset A without the new service in Asset B? From the economics of value-based pricing, B provides more value than A. Developer 2 can argue for a greater share of the reward. And if Developer 1 dissents, Developer 2 will simply say, "Fine, I'll reimplement my services without you"—completely missing the point of reuse from a corporate perspective.

Now, imagine how complicated this could be in the presence of multiple inheritance with multiple developers.

There are other problems with the royalty model. Developers might choose to reuse their own artifacts or those of a friend to steer the royalties. Are we encouraging developers to create their own little software businesses within the company? This royalty model does not motivate the desired behavior of appropriate reuse, nor does it focus developers on the reason we really hired them—to meet the goals and objectives of their assigned projects.

Bribing to reuse. Paying developers to reuse existing assets is like paying developers to write lines of code. Once they understand the measure, they will do whatever they can to maximize it. In this case, developers will attempt to reuse whatever they can, even when it is not justified. We are more interested in *appropriate reuse* than in maximum reuse. Appropriate reuse is an economic choice—we realize an overall savings by reusing an asset versus not reusing an asset. Remember:

> **Reward drives behavior.** People demonstrate the behavior for which they are rewarded.

Reuse Rewards

So, the way to get developers to reuse is to set their goals and objectives so that reuse is the most logical strategy. Reward the developers for meeting their goals and objectives.

Many project managers understand this. When given the opportunity to pay developers to reuse—they call it bribing the engineers—they don't. Why not? Because project leaders know that if you provide extra payment for something, then engineers will redirect their efforts to that task, to the detriment of more valued project activities. Reuse should be a part of the job, and not perceived or rewarded as something extra.

Punish for not reusing. Can we penalize developers for not reusing? Although punishment can sometimes prevent undesired behavior, it does not promote the proper development atmosphere. Surely a reuse reward system cannot be designed around punishment (an oxymoron in the making). And again, punishing a developer for missed opportunities tends to promote inappropriate reuse.

Rewarding appropriate reuse. To help you think about rewarding for appropriate reuse, ask yourself: What do you expect a member of your development team to do, ignoring any expectations you may have for consuming reusable assets? Write it down. Then review your list as you read this section.

Based on what people in the case studies value in products, processes, and resources (Chapter 2), some developer expectations are to:

- Create a quality product

- Get done on time

- Understand user needs

- Get all the functionality into the system

- Write code

- Write documentation about the code

- Document the design of the system

- Document the use of the system

Now ask yourself, do you pay the members of the development team to do the things on this list, or to do something else? How do you measure the performance of these team members? And what is the basis for bonuses and salary increases? Write this down.

Why does getting them to reuse assets change things? Frame the answer in terms of your list of expectations. Perhaps reuse leads to a better quality product, one that is done on time, with all desired functionality and documentation. Consuming reusable assets has to create a result that the users need, that is complete, tested, and well documented. Reuse can contribute to meeting these developer expectations.

Reuse is not the goal, it is the means to a goal. Rewarding people for reuse itself is misguided. We are more likely to have developers reuse if we lend appropriate support to the reuse effort, and we set up the reward structure to motivate it. Provide help, such as the reuse engineers of the Expert Services Model, so that reuse doesn't add an extra burden to the developers. Make sure that the reusable assets contribute to the objectives of projects—for example, represent and implement strategic business processes that need to be consistent across applications. And if you know that reusable assets should be used— if you know what appropriate reuse is for the project—make it an objective of the project to employ these assets. You pay your developers to meet the goals and objectives of a project. You should set these goals and objectives so that the most reasonable way to meet them is to reuse.

Initiating a Corporate Reuse Program

Chapter 10 describes the steps of a reuse process model. Ultimately, you need to provide support for each of the steps. You can get started by establishing the basic policies of your reuse program, followed by initial identification and acquisition of reusable assets.

Your first step in setting up a corporate reuse program is to choose the reuse manager, someone responsible for making the many policy decisions. If it is possible to assign additional resources to the effort, then fill the reuse team roles in the following order: reuse administrator, reuse engineer(s), and reuse librarian.[2] The role of the reuse administrator is to identify and acquire assets. If the scope of the reuse program is small enough, the reuse manager can take responsibility for managing the program and acquiring the initial assets. At least one reuse engineer is required early to take responsibility for developing possible assets or consulting on projects, carrying out the policies set by the reuse manager.

The manager, alone or with the newly formed team, proposes a definition for reuse, what the organization should reuse, and how reuse should take place (with or without the possibility of modifying the reusable assets). The reuse manager and administrator can now identify which reusable assets are needed, and set the priorities for acquisitions based on how soon the organization will need each asset. Alternatively, the two-person team can form a cross-project team for the purpose of harvesting assets from existing projects to form the basis for the reuse library.

Success with reuse depends on making sure that developers are interested in reusing assets and are aware that the assets exist. The next important step is to develop a communications strategy for advertising the availability of assets, and giving potential reusers a way to ask questions and report ideas and problems.

The next activities put in place policies for certification and classification. It is best to develop at least minimal one-level certification criteria, defined by required collateral materials. Collateral material should include a reference manual and data on who created the asset, when it was acquired, and who is responsible for maintenance. Later you can add guidelines for quality measures and reuse evaluation.

It is important to create a classification scheme early on, unless you are confident that the library will be very small (fewer than 25 retrievable items). Since the library will likely evolve over time, we recommend a faceted classification scheme.

Only after these initial steps are taken should you worry about tools. And the first tools should be simple ones—a file system or database with associated tools for storage and retrieval. If you follow the Expert Services organizational model—which we recommend until reuse becomes standard practice—these tools will be used only by the reuse team members. Because you will not have to worry about training all developers on these specialized tools, your selection is simplified.

If you do not have the resources to establish the Expert Services model, then consider creating a short one- or two-day course about the company's reuse process to make

[2] Chapter 12 elaborates on the idea of a Reuse Team. Job descriptions for the specific team roles are provided in Appendix C.

sure that individual project developers are aware of the goals and benefits of the reuse program.

Reuse Maturity

Reuse maturity is a way to assess the organization's reuse effectiveness. The Harris Corporation prepared a five-level maturity model for reuse: Initial/Chaotic, Monitored, Coordinated, Planned, and Ingrained [Koltun and Hudson 1992]. Levels are distinguished by motivation, planning for reuse, breadth of reuse involvement, responsibility for making reuse happen, approach to reusing, reuse inventory, classification activity, technology support, and metrics gathering.

The Harris Reuse Maturity Levels are prescriptive, whereas the four models we offer are descriptive, based on the case studies. Our Ad Hoc and Supply and Demand Models correspond to the Harris Initial/Chaotic level 1. Expert Services is similar to Harris Planned level 4, and the Product Center corresponds to the Harris Ingrained level 5. We did not see models in the case studies that corresponded to the Harris levels 2 and 3, although we might have split our models into additional ones based on the organizational group within which reuse took place. This division would have given us a mapping to Harris levels 2 and 3, which depend on whether reuse takes place at the work group or department levels.

Your long-term goal is to have the reuse benefits provided by a Product Center. But this presumes that reuse is pervasive in your organization's culture. You cannot install culture; it is something that evolves over time. Thus we see the Expert Services Model as an excellent stepping stone to the Product Center. It puts all the elements of a well-managed reuse process in place, but relies on experts who can mentor the process and make it easier for projects to get started reusing. You can use the COTS Model to obtain some initial assets. We recommend that you start with the Expert Services Model, relying on the reuse engineers for at least two or three years, and then evolve toward the Product Center.

A Small-Company Question

We have presented the reuse organizational models in the context of reuse in large corporations. If you work in a small company, the overhead of the reuse process model may seem much more than is necessary or more than you can handle. Many of the problems with access to expertise and communication may not exist. After all, you are small and everyone knows each other, so the virtual hallway is an actual hallway. Perhaps you do only one project at a time, so coordinating multiple projects is not an issue. What you worry about is making sure that future projects benefit from the efforts of the current one. The same team members will do all of the projects, so you do not have to worry about the long-term storage and retrieval issues. They will simply know what is available and where to find the reusable assets.

All of this may be true. Nonetheless, the reuse process model contains decisions that you will still have to make. It is just that some decisions will be to do nothing. No action is still a decision.

In the next chapter, Chapter 12, we introduce a variety of ways in which you can achieve reuse at the project level when a formal reuse team does not exist. These ideas about team structure are useful to smaller organizations.

Illustrations of Reuse

The Reuse Process of a Software Vendor

In looking for an illustration of a reuse process, we sought one that involves most of the activities of the reuse process model. A vendor that sells object-oriented reusable assets, such as ParcPlace Systems, Inc., is a good choice. ParcPlace sells and supports application development environments that include tools, a class library consisting of frameworks and components to support development of applications written in Smalltalk, and special applications built using these other products. Products of the company are available to external as well as internal customers. The ParcPlace Systems approach internally is a Product Center Model; the availability of a consulting organization to help customers use the development tools and libraries creates a relationship characteristic of the Expert Services Model.

Identifying. The marketing team identifies what frameworks and components should be part of the product line, in accordance with the product strategy set by the chief technical strategist. Each product line has a product marketing person who talks with customers—external and internal—to determine new features.

Acquiring. From time to time, ParcPlace purchases both frameworks and components from other companies, but mostly builds its own software. The company's development team consists of experts in object-oriented technology, including framework designers, reuse evaluators, and prototypers.

Certifying. Certification means that a developed or purchased artifact has met the product guidelines of the company. Because ParcPlace distributes full sources for most of its reusable objects (allowing white box reuse), the developers have to be careful that products can be supported in the face of customer refinements. To this end, the company has four levels of certification:

1. Available only to the internal development team for review and discussion

2. Available to internal projects for use in their prototyping efforts

3. Available as a prototype to special customers who have acknowledged the non-product status

4. Available as a product sold by the sales team and supported via the technical hotline

A ParcPlace development team includes an integrator, much like the reuse librarian, who makes the decision to include a system change in an internal release of one of the products. Project leaders for different development teams report to the engineering manager. At staff meetings, the project leaders discuss and negotiate the exchange of artifacts that can be reused across internal projects for prototyping. The third level is handled as special cases, either by the manager in charge of corporate-level technology partners, by the manager of the consulting team, or by the sales manager. Certification as a product to be sold by the sales team is done by the product marketing manager in conjunction with the engineering manager.

Classifying. Classification is handled within the tool sets of the various application development environments, in terms of source code browsers and special framework editors. Classification is therefore considered a product feature. Initial classification is done by the developers, with input from the documentors.

Storing. Artifacts that are part of the development process are stored as files on shared file servers, although much of the information is now being moved to either relational or object-oriented databases.

Communicating. External communication—between the company and its paying customers—relies on the marketing literature and seminars handled by the product marketing manager, and face-to-face contact by the sales team. Internal communication relies on informal face-to-face meetings, electronic mail, and hallway conversations.

Locating, retrieving, understanding, and using. These reuse steps are handled by the team members using the tools that the company sells. External customers use the same facilities.

Maintaining. ParcPlace uses a formal process by which change requests—to remove defects, add features, or create new products—are discussed, prioritized, and scheduled. The engineering manager works with product marketing to determine changes, in the context of the plan prepared by the company technical strategist and any contractual obligations.

Updating reusers. There are three classes of reusers: development team members, internal projects, and customers. The development teams are obligated to update as part of the ongoing development process. Internal projects decide when to update according to their own delivery schedules, but ultimately have to update. External customers make the decision to update based on whether the new versions represent sufficient added value. Presumably the value was predetermined by marketing before the company made the decision to do the development. Nonetheless, it becomes the responsibility of the sales team, and notably the sales engineers and members of training and consulting, to help the customers understand the value of the new versions. Sales and marketing know who the reusers are because the company maintains a database of all customers who have bought products, and proactively contacts them when a new release is available.

The way ParcPlace runs its business is consistent with our view of a reuse process model that serves the needs of multiple projects carried out in a corporation.

Reuse in Japan

We participated in a study of reuse in Japan involving six very large and long-term projects. The interviews were conducted by Technology Transfer International, Inc. (TTI), of Colorado Springs, Colorado, under funding agreements with several U.S. based organizations. One of the authors participated as a contributing author and reviewer, and so we had access to the raw data as well as the analyses offered by TTI. The focus of attention in these studies was the phenomenon known as the *software factory*, which is fully detailed in a book by Michael Cusumano [Cusumano 1991], editor for the TTI report.

The primary targets of the research were outsourcing and reuse, and nominally the influence of these on the various phases of the software life cycle. Seven Japanese organizations participated. They were selected for their experience with reuse practices in creating production systems (ENICOM, Fujitsu, Hitachi, Oki, and Toshiba) or their commitment to incorporating software outsourcing on a large scale (SIGMA Systems Corporation, IPA Software Technology Center). All of the companies were in the business of software development and integration; six of them had external customers (customers who did not work for their company) for business, systems, process control, CASE, or planning software.

For the most part, these companies rely on hardcopy documentation and paper catalogs describing software assets. They do agree that reusable assets span all phases of the development life cycle to include analyses, designs, and test suites, as well as code. TTI applied techniques supported by Quantitative Software Management, Inc., a company that supplies comparison metrics for 2600+ projects, to determine whether the Japanese companies managed their projects well. The Japanese projects were assessed in terms of defect rates as a function of project size, duration, and manpower. All of the Japanese projects were found to be "as good as or better than" most other projects in the comparison database. And TTI concluded that these projects were good models for others to study.

The team members interviewed in Japan made impressive claims about the productivity improvements they derived from systematic reuse:

- Reduced development time by 10-50 percent

- Improved productivity by 15-50 percent

- Improved quality by 20-35 percent

Some of the reuse occurred during the requirements analysis phase. We hypothesize that the greater reduction in development time was due to reuse during analysis. During analysis, the goal is to identify the opportunities for reuse so that management can turn opportunity into reality. Most of the reused code consisted of small modules (less than 1000 lines of code, with fewer than ten inputs or outputs).

Much was said about reusing tools. One example given was that of a simulator (hardware and software), which was used to test distributed interactive systems via data paths and control paths. These companies have yet to take advantage of object-oriented technology, although most noted its future possibilities.

When asked their opinion about training developers to understand the goals and processes for systematic reuse, the managers all thought more training was needed, and worried that costs could increase by as much as 20 percent to pay for the increased training.

What is reused? The TTI study incorporated our questions about the definition of reuse and what is reusable. The answers from the Japanese companies were consistent with those from other companies we interviewed. They added that reuse involves adhering to a defined corporate reuse process. Reuse is critical as a way to propagate common processes, policies, and products across projects. The Japanese companies focused on reuse as a way to control costs rather than as a way to improve business practices. This focus can be attributed to the nature of the businesses interviewed. All were software development organizations, rather than information systems departments, which use technology to give their corporation competitive leverage.

Reuse libraries. For those companies that maintained libraries (five of the seven), the content focused on a narrow domain and were acquired through ad hoc extraction from existing projects. Librarians worked at the project level, leaving to others the responsibility for monitoring and promoting reuse. According to the study, reuse librarians:

- Collect standard patterns, modules, and other reusable assets

- Catalog and manage those common-use assets

- Help developers find what they need

These tasks are consistent with the use of the term "library" as a place to gather, catalog, and assist in retrieval of information. A typical Japanese reuse library supports multiple projects, contains source code modules, and uses multiple classification schemes. Storage in mainframe databases was common. Librarians assume much of the responsibility for testing and maintaining the assets. Few companies could say how libraries were pruned; those that did said it was left to the judgment of the department manager or an asset was simply deleted if not used after two years.

Questions of scaling up. The Japanese companies offered the following advice for managing large-scale reuse:

- Use tools to enforce management controls

- Keep libraries small and therefore strategic

- Keyword search on libraries of reusable components is unsatisfactory

- Incremental product improvements reduce risk and let you respond to requests faster

- Components should be organized so that most are derived from a few critical or common elements

Measures. To impose and monitor strict standards for outside contractors, measures are critical to the Japanese companies, all of which emphasize outsourcing. Management measures were used to estimate costs, monitor component usage, and create incentives for reuse. Most measures characterized components by size and function, and reported defects and usage data.

Requirements for reuse success. The participants in the study were asked what is needed in a successful reuse program. They concluded (as summarized in the TTI report) that the following features are necessary:

Critical mass	Availability of sufficient reusable assets
Intelligibility	Ability to understand code written by others
Incorporation	Ability to link reusable assets into new requirements
Cultural transfusion	A way to transfer corporate reuse culture to subcontractors
Attitude	A way to overcome the conservative views of older software engineers

The TTI study raises the issue of promoting reuse among outside contractors. The Japanese companies were very experienced with the problems of directing subcontractors—of providing explicit requirements and quality objectives, and of making sure a contractor is willing to build from the results created by the company and other subcontractors.

Case Study Results

Eighteen of the 19 companies in the first case study phase reported some effort to create a corporate-wide reuse program. Only seven of these companies attempted to formalize the way in which reusing was supported. In the 39 projects we studied, 38 expected to have corporate-wide reuse, although most fell into the style of the Ad Hoc or Supply and Demand Models (see Chart 11.1, which summarizes the reuse models of the projects that had some form of reuse program). Most believed that some form of separate reward structure would be needed to create a reuse culture.

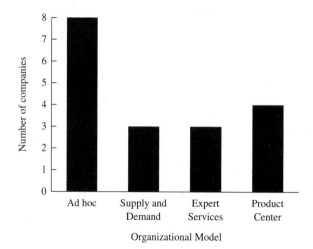

Chart 11.1   Case Study Use of the Reuse Organizational
Models

Of the three projects that were attempting to set up an Expert Services approach, two were created as research activities.

All of the Japanese companies in the TTI study claimed they follow a well-defined reuse process, manage a central reuse library, and have successful reuse across their projects. They use the Product Center Model. However, the typical arrangement in these companies is to place several outsourcing projects under the umbrella of a common manager. What otherwise looks like interproject sharing—across the outsourced projects—is in fact intraproject reuse. Indeed, an excellent way to make sure that reuse occurs is to take an interproject situation and convert it to an intraproject one. The single manager is motivated to remove redundancies and lower project costs. The six case studies in Japan all made sure that the multiple outside contractors were not paid to do the same work.

Summary

We likened the reuse process to communication in a virtual hallway and to an exchange of expertise typical of technology transfer. We also pointed out that reuse is a maintenance responsibility, to make sure that the organization retains, throughout the maintenance period, all the initial benefit of creating systems with consistently designed and implemented assets. We outlined five models for managing a reuse process: Ad Hoc, Supply and Demand, Expert Services, Product Center, and COTS. Only the Expert Services and Product Center Models fulfill the principle that reusable artifacts should be managed as strategic products of the organization.

We asked two critical questions about reuse programs. First, at what organizational level do we position the reuse effort? A reuse process model can be managed effectively at multiple levels of an organization: at the corporate level, or the group or divisional level. Additional consideration must be given to sharing assets among the multiple reuse libraries, and to coordinating differences in certification procedures. Second, how will we get recalcitrant developers to reuse the work of others? Appropriate reuse should be part of the organization's culture. An organization that provides explicit reuse support—training, experts, and useful libraries of strategic assets—will not have to bribe its development teams. The way to get developers to reuse is to set their goals and objectives so that reuse is the most logical strategy. Reward the developers for meeting their goals and objectives.

We also showed how reuse can be treated as a software business by summarizing the way a vendor of object-oriented technology manages its reuse process. This view of reuse management as akin to running a software business to sell reusable assets—in which you take into account both proactive marketing and reactive support—is a useful way to plan your long-term investment in reuse. We concluded with a description of case study reuse organizational models.

Additional Reading About Reuse Organizational Models

Fafchamps, D., Organizational Factors and Reuse, *IEEE Software*, 11(5), 31-41, September 1994.
   This paper is a report on studies carried out at Hewlett-Packard (HP) on why people sometimes resist reuse and which organizational models appear to encourage reuse more than others. The author cites four models observed at ten HP sites: the lone producer, nested producer, pool producer, and team producer. Here the word "producer" is used to mean the developer of reusable assets, in contrast to the consumer who is the reuser. The nested producer model assigns a member of each product team to the role of providing reuse services and expertise. In the team producer model, the reuse team corresponds to the same organizational structure as other development teams, and lets these consumers set the priorities. The nested producer model did not work well at HP, whereas the team producer role worked best. This team producer model is like our Product Center.

Poulin, J. S. , Caruso, J. M., and Hancock, D.R., The business case for software reuse, *IBM Systems Journal*, 32(4), 567–594, 1993.

    This paper contains a set of measures used by IBM to define the effort saved by reuse. These measures distinguish the savings and benefits of reuse from those obtained by applying accepted software engineering techniques. The return-on-investment model provided by the authors, populated with data based on the proposed measures, yields a business justification for reuse and the basis for assessing the outcome of a corporate reuse program.

CHAPTER 12

Select a Team Structure

A symphony orchestra best illustrates [the idea that each individual's contribution is uniquely important]. While the orchestra's overall performance is a careful blend of many instruments, each musician is a highly competent and disciplined contributor. Individual performers occasionally stand out, but the entire orchestra is far more than the sum of these parts, and a single sour note by any individual could damage the entire performance.

from [Humphrey1995]

You cannot manage people into battle.
You can manage things;
you lead people.

Admiral Grace Murray Hopper

I f you have a process for development, reusable assets, and good plans, you still don't have a project. You need the individual team members and the team structure in which they can effectively work.

What Is a Team?

A *team* is a group of people who work together in a coordinated way to meet a clear set of goals and objectives. There are three essential aspects about how teams function: roles, management, and communication.

The first aspect is that people play different roles. A *role* is a job type, a related set of activities. Roles are often labeled with common names, such as manager, analyst, or designer, to denote the set of activities. Some example roles are shown in Fig. 12.1. We describe a team in terms of roles rather than in terms of people because a person can play one or more roles on a team. For example, Ann plays the role of analyst when she is responsible for developing the requirements specification. She also plays the role of analysis prototyper when she constructs a prototype of some proposed system capabilities.

Figure 12.1   Software Development Roles

The second aspect about teams is that the people are lead by managers, who tell them what they need to do, organize them to carry out their tasks, and monitor them to determine whether they are making progress. There are three distinct managerial or leadership roles: technical, people, and administrative. The technical leader role is responsible for the project's technical solution. This role is sometimes called the chief architect. The people manager role is responsible for motivating team members and attending to their day-to-day needs. We discuss a specific instance of this role (called the Object Coach) in more detail later in this chapter. The administrative manager role is responsible for planning and controlling the execution of team tasks. This role has overall responsibility for meeting the project goals and objectives, for reporting upward, and for ensuring that resources are available.

On small projects a single person may play all three managerial roles. On larger projects, each of these roles may require full-time dedicated team members. The team may be structured so that a different person plays a role on a rotating basis. We have seen very productive teams managed in this way.

The final aspect of how a team will function is determined by how team members communicate with one another. Organizational reporting obligations dictate formal communication requirements; teams usually evolve their own unique informal communications style. Smaller teams, in which everyone has access to everyone else, communicate informally. The team is closely knit, working in the same office space and relying on folklore to reinforce decisions. Even in a small team, written documentation that captures reasons for the decisions is important, especially if team membership changes often.

Often, the layout of the team's physical environment—individual or shared offices, common areas, meeting rooms—is designed to encourage communication. One of the case study teams chose to create office cubicles surrounding an open space. They placed a large table and chairs in the open space, and brought their computers to this common table. These team members did the prototyping, and felt that they needed to talk to each other frequently, help each other, shout out the availability of new system components, and so on. The layout of the physical environment encouraged the desired immediate interaction.

Members of different teams have to share information, such as plans, tasks, and results. *Linking pins* are the roles that allow multiple teams to communicate [Thomsett 1993]. The idea is simple: If two or more teams are to communicate effectively, someone or something has to take on the task of making sure that communication takes place. A common way to do this is through liaisons—people from the different teams  attend one another's meetings and reviews. Or they work directly on one another's teams, as in the Expert Services Reuse Model from Chapter 11. Linking pins are also useful on large projects that have been divided into subprojects. Someone, usually the team manager or a technology specialist, keeps an eye on each subproject and communicates decisions and questions that cross subprojects.

A Team Has Structure

Purpose, managerial preference, and communication needs influence the team structure. By *structure*, we refer to the arrangement of team roles, which affects how team members communicate with one another, how assignments are allocated, how reporting is handled, and so on. In Chapter 5, we show that different process models apply to different kinds of projects. Likewise, different team structures exist to mirror the differences in process models. Larry Constantine [Constantine 1993] approaches this problem in a similar fashion, identifying models of team culture based on closed, random, open, and synchronous communication. Here we look at the models we observed in the case studies: hierarchical, egoless management styles, military, and battlefield commander.

Hierarchical Team Model. In hierarchical teams, there are layers of authority for delegating responsibility and carrying out action. The higher the roles are in the hierarchy, the more likely it is that they have authority for decision making, and the less likely it is that they are doing the hands-on work. Flat organizations prefer to mix decision making with day-to-day development responsibility. The former is considered more autocratic, although there is no reason a hierarchical structure has to ignore democratic consensus building. Harlan Mills proposed a structure based on a chief programmer [Mills 1971]. His proposal was to replace large project teams with smaller, tightly organized, and functionally specialized teams, each led by a guru, someone who basically does all of the critical work but assigns smaller utility tasks to a supporting staff. On large projects, the idea of the chief programmer may seem infeasible, but it might work well on smaller partitions—assuming the availability of gurus.

The more people on the team, the more likely a hierarchical organization is put in place to facilitate communication. The selected team structure often reflects the partitioning of the problem. This is the case in Illustration 2 of Chapter 8, whose system partitioning is shown in Fig. 6.8 in Chapter 6. The team structure, given here in Fig. 12.2, indicates several project managers, each with responsibility for two or more of the partitions.

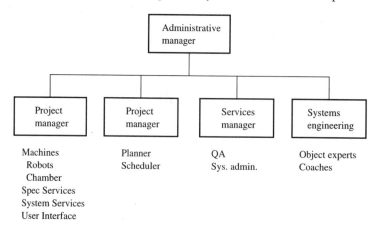

Figure 12.2   Hierarchical Team Structure

There is a box in this figure for systems engineering. Systems engineers were treated as the critical communication resource, the team linking pins. They were experts who provided advice and support to the partition teams. They were supposed to make sure that each team met its system-level and reuse objectives.

Egoless Team Model. Another team structure is popularly referred to as the Egoless Model, after the term "egoless programming" coined by Weinberg [Weinberg 1971]. The idea is to create a structure in which goals are set by consensus, and group leadership is a rotating function. People share their work openly. The same artifact may be owned by different people at different times. All egoless programming teams share a willingness to exchange their artifacts, have them reviewed in open meetings, and happily accept any criticisms. Egoless teams are typically small, with a considerable exchange of personnel between tasks.

Military Team Model. An alternative to the Hierarchical Model is the Military Model. We asked a manager at EDS, a large system integrator known for its military origins, how he felt about the company's reputation for having a military style of organization and management. He responded with pride that the military model is to train, train, train the personnel so they have the background and good judgment to be given full responsibility when on the job. When a soldier is on the battlefield, there is rarely time to ask for approval; the soldier has to be delegated authority to act. So the Military Model combines the notion of a hierarchy for planning and overall decision making, with full delegation of responsibility and authority when on the job.

Battlefield Commander Team Model. A derivative of the Military Model is the Battlefield Commander Model. The leader sets the strategy and identifies the critical problems. The staff is made up of experts who are assigned different tasks, and are asked to use their expertise to propose solutions to the questions and to report back. The leader makes the final decisions. No one on the staff is ever told the full strategy, in case of capture by the enemy. The Battlefield Commander style is that used in the case study we introduce in Chapter 8 as the Security-Driven Process Model (Illustration 3). The organization's maxim was that the company had to be protected from any single person knowing the whole system. The team on this project was highly leveraged by experts in object-oriented technology. Of the 17 team members, six were hired consultants, each with more than five years of experience in the use of the technology. The team was divided into subteams corresponding to the independent layers of the system design. Each subteam consisted of as few as one and as many as five team members.

The team was led by the master architect, an expert in the business area and an experienced technologist. His manager referred to him as the guru who understood the whole project, determined the architecture, and managed the subteams by giving them incremental tasks. All communication among subteams was channeled through this guru, who, in turn, never told any single team member everything about the project. As a result, none of the outside consultants could have information that might endanger the company's competitive position.

Kinds of Teams

We next explore four team structures that we have seen work effectively in both large and small organizations: Application (productization and prototyping), Framework, Cross-Project, and Reuse Teams. Application and Framework Teams are formed to produce application and reusable framework product results, whereas Cross-Project and Reuse Teams are formed primarily to support the reuse process model.

Application Productization Team

The most common structure is the Application Team. It is responsible for the analysis, design, implementation, delivery, and sometimes maintenance of a software product. This team specifically interacts with the client to determine requirements. And this team should be tasked to be reuse consumers whenever appropriate.

The image of most application teams is that the implementors on the team are following a design based on a requirements specification. The developers march in an orderly fashion to implement the designs, much the way band members are obliged to play a composition according to the sheet music.

Three important ideas about the Application Team are:

- The process model defines the activities that map to useful roles on the team.

- When the process model involves partitioning, the partitions define independent subprojects, each with its own team members, and each needing to coordinate with the other subprojects.

- Objects provide a common language by which all team members, regardless of their roles, can communicate.

A general view of process model activities is shown in Fig. 12.3, in which we itemize the activities for developing a partition; there may be more than one partition, and therefore more than one occurrence of these activities. The roles associated with these activities are named in Fig. 12.4. An expert in using object-oriented technology should participate on the team, especially for the first effort. We added two roles to the Application Team to provide this expertise: an object technology expert to provide hands-on assistance, and an object coach to provide ongoing reviews and consultation that serve to teach team members in the context of working on the project. These two roles can be played by the same person, depending on the team-to-coach ratio, and on the amount of actual development the expert is to do.

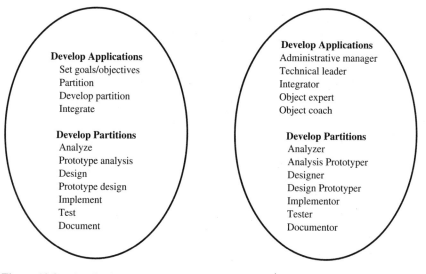

Figure 12.3   Application Team Activities   **Figure 12.4**   Application Team Roles

Object-oriented technology affects the team in other ways as well: object names, object interfaces, and object relationships become the lingua franca of the team. Regardless of roles, everyone on the team uses a common object vocabulary, based both on the terminology of the technology and on the terminology of the problem domain. Incremental development accentuates the communication requirements because all team members remain engaged throughout the development cycle, creating or revising partial results at any point in the development cycle. Parallel development of partitions encourages communication based on the well-defined interfaces to objects.

Figure 12.5 depicts roles in the Application Team and their critical communication pathways. Analyzers work with prototypers to create both the requirements specification and running examples that users can review. Prototypers work with users to test whether requirements have been correctly captured and to help users clarify requirements. Similarly, designers work with prototypers to explore the feasibility of different architectures, and these design prototypers may work with users to make sure that quality objectives will be met. Analyzers and designers work together to make sure that the requirements are understood and implementable. Designs are implemented by coders, so the designers and coders must constantly exchange information to make sure the code is consistent with the requirements. Testers work with analyzers to form the system level tests, and with designers to create subsystem tests. They also work with the implementors to create and execute unit level test cases. Documentors, coaches, technology experts, and team leaders clearly must work with all players on the team. Since the work is done incrementally, there is a constant flow of information back and forth.

Figure 12.5   Communications Among Application Team Members

Application Prototyping Team

Prototypers are explorers. They do not develop what is already understood, because their job is to help understand what is not known. We depict them as members of a jazz band, rather than a marching band. Jazz players are encouraged to improvise. Their musical output is evaluated on its contribution to the group effect, not on whether it corresponds to the sheet music. Similarly, prototypers are evaluated on the results they create, not on how the results are obtained.

If an analyzer or designer on an Application Productization Team does the prototyping as well, then a separate Prototype Team is not required. Having a separate Prototyping Team, however, allows its members to focus on creating prototypes, without concern that their work will mistakenly be evaluated as products. Creating separate teams emphasizes the difference between prototyping and productization.

Framework Team

When an organization decides to create a general framework that can be reused by a number of different Application Teams, it can form a special development group we call the Framework Team. Many of its activities are similar to those of an Application Productization Team, with the exception that the product is intended to be reusable—a template that is general or abstract. The Framework Team might also develop components that the other teams can use to complete a framework. Team members are reuse producers, and therefore must develop under the guidelines of the organization's criteria for reusable assets. This typically means that they have additional responsibilities for evaluating and documenting the reusability of the product.

A Framework Team can be an independent team, or it can be a subteam within a larger project. If a project is expected to have a high degree of internal reuse, and many of the reusable components have to be developed, it might make sense to have two subteams. The Framework Subteam develops a reusable framework and components, and the Application Subteam makes use of the components to create the application. In this case, the Application Subteam is the sole customer of the Framework Subteam.

A Framework Team is not the same as a Reuse Team. The distinction is that the Framework Team only creates a framework product, whereas the Reuse Team is responsible for carrying out the entire reuse process. A responsibility of the Reuse Team could be to create a framework as a subproject.

Figure 12.6 displays activities for developing frameworks, in which the project is partitioned by the framework and its various components, and each partition might be developed by independent subteams. The roles listed for these activities in Fig. 12.7 distinguish two kinds of evaluators: framework evaluators and component evaluators. Evaluation is not a testing job in the usual sense. Rather, the purpose of the evaluation is to determine whether the software can be used in situations for which it was not specifically designed. The evaluation information is input to the reuse certification process.

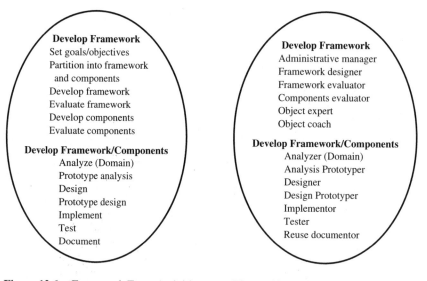

Figure 12.6   Framework Team Activities   **Figure 12.7**   Framework Team Roles

Evaluating a framework involves creating typical as well as atypical scenarios to see whether new applications can indeed be created by specializing the framework. This evaluation often means developing new components that can be plugged into the framework. Components are evaluated to see whether they interact correctly with an existing framework, and whether they are independently reusable with other frameworks or applications. The evaluator adds value by discerning new uses for the components, and thereby providing a measure of the software's potential reuse.

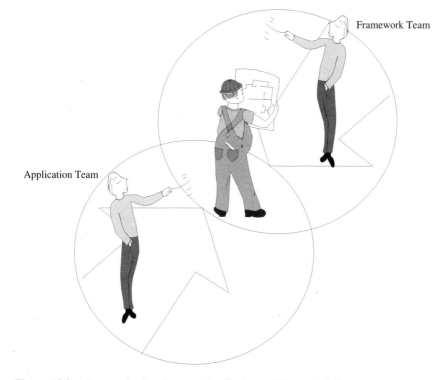

Figure 12.8   Communications between Application and Framework Teams

The Framework Team has a framework designer, who has the special skills needed to render the reusable abstractions of a problem domain as a collection of objects. The Framework Team also includes the roles that are typical of any application development team, including an analyzer. Depending on the breadth of the framework, analysis could be a domain analysis. Communication between the Framework and Application Teams is handled either by overlap in development team members, who implicitly carry requirements and design concepts back and forth, or by the addition of a special linking-pin role to provide the information exchange, as shown in Fig. 12.8.

Cross-Project Team

A company might have several projects going on at the same time. To facilitate sharing results across projects, a special team is formed that we call the Cross-Project Team. To encourage reuse, a team of pollinators constantly moves from application project to application project. Their goal is to pick up reusable artifacts from one project and deposit them in another. Using this model, an organization can achieve some of the benefits associated with having reusable components available before an application project is started.

The Cross-Project Team is part of an interteam communications mechanism. It is essential that reuse pollinators be able to communicate and work with members of each of the Application Teams. They have to be object technology experts who are capable of extracting reusable artifacts from one project, and helping team members in other projects reuse these artifacts. The Cross-Project Team is often self-managed, and is usually small relative to other teams in the organization.

What does this team do? Team members involve themselves in many projects, learning and reviewing the artifacts produced by the projects. Potentially reusable components are identified and acquired as-is. This team typically develops no software. As team members visit projects, they notice opportunities for reuse and communicate these to the project team members. These activities are listed in Fig. 12.9.

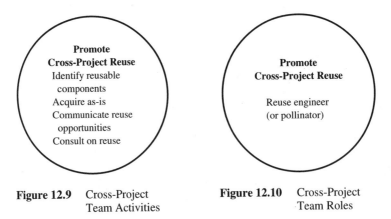

Figure 12.9   Cross-Project Team Activities

Figure 12.10   Cross-Project Team Roles

The principal role on the Cross-Project Team is a pollinator, whom we usually call a reuse engineer (Fig. 12.10). These reuse engineers are knowledgeable about object-oriented technology, and focus on identifying, acquiring, and communicating reuse opportunities.

The efforts of the Cross-Project Team will be a waste if their communications are ignored. They need some kind of authority to have teams adopt the suggested reuse opportunities. One way to assign authority is to staff a Cross-Project Team with a council of technical leaders or administrative managers who meet regularly in place of informal "visits."

The Cross-Project Team represents an attempt to create pathways by which otherwise independent projects can communicate. In this regard, they form a virtual hallway.

The team members, as shown in Fig. 12.11, involve themselves in the various projects, moving from one to another as the demand arises. Forming a Cross-Project Team is a useful strategy for organizations that are not prepared to pay for a formal Reuse Team, or cannot wait until the Reuse Team is functional. Indeed, the assets acquired by these reuse engineers could become the initial contributions to the organization's library of reusable assets.

Cross-Project Team

Application Teams

Figure 12.11   Communication Between the Cross-Project Team and Multiple Application Teams

Reuse Team

The charter of the Reuse Team is to manage the reuse process model. The activities of this process model are shown in Fig. 12.12, with the corresponding roles in Fig. 12.13. The latter figure identifies six roles for the Reuse Team: reuse manager, administrator, librarian, engineer, evaluator, and maintainer.

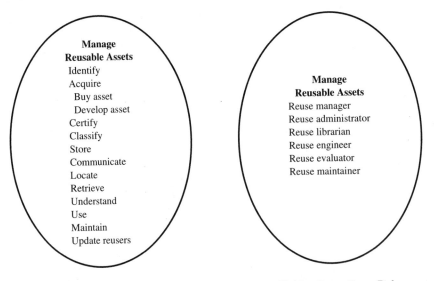

Figure 12.12   Reuse Team Activities   **Figure 12.13**   Reuse Team Roles

The special roles for the Reuse Team were designed to handle the steps of the reuse process model. The reuse manager is in charge of the overall organization of the Reuse Team, and is involved in making the policy decisions associated with the reuse process. All other roles directly or indirectly report to the manager. Moreover, the reuse manager is the chief reuse cheerleader for the company.

The reuse administrator identifies and acquires assets, and must communicate with the reuse librarian who is responsible for asset certification, classification, and storage. The administrator will work with the reuse engineers to identify the reusable assets that are missing from the library based on the engineers' project experiences. The reuse engineer knows what is in the library—knows how to locate, retrieve, understand, and use the assets. The engineer helps others use the assets, and can often fulfill the role of reuse maintainer as well as developer and consultant. Reuse engineers will interact with the librarian to learn about new assets in the library, to offer new contributions to the library, and to participate in maintaining existing assets. All reuse team members are responsible for communicating—proactively and reactively—about reuse opportunities.

The Reuse Team handles all the steps of the reuse process model, including acquisition of reusable assets. It is possible that the Reuse Team will choose to build the assets, in which case the team can form a Framework Team to do the work. In the Expert Services Organizational Model, the Reuse Team provides one or more reuse engineers to work on an Application Team or a Framework Team. The reuse engineers bring their knowledge of the reuse library. They make the contents of the library available to the team when appropriate. This scenario is depicted in Fig. 12.14. Alternatively, the reuse engineers can be organized into a team that acts more like a Cross-Project Team.

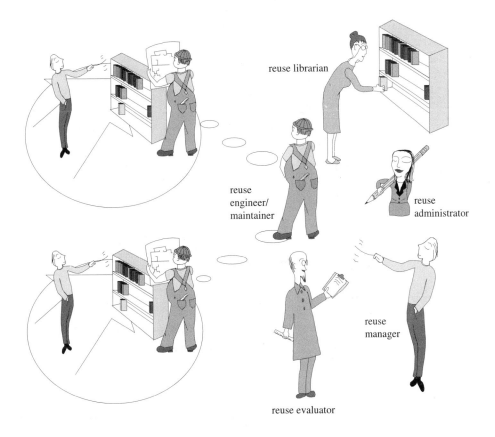

reuse librarian

reuse engineer/ maintainer

reuse administrator

reuse manager

reuse evaluator

Figure 12.14   Reuse Team Engineers Work on Application Teams

Maintenance Team

You may think of other teams that your organization needs. An obvious one to consider is a Maintenance Team (or Sustaining Engineering Team). The Maintenance Team can be responsible for all incremental enhancements to a released product. It can also be responsible for removing all defects uncovered during a product's lifetime. The team members of a Maintenance Team are similar to those on the Application Productization Team. Mature organizations separate the work involved in maintaining existing products from the work involved in creating new products. Where such separation is not arranged, new development often suffers while the more immediate needs of sustaining engineering are carried out.

In Chapter 11, we propose that reuse is a maintenance opportunity. The Maintenance Team could very well be the same as the Reuse Team, or minimally be tightly coordinated, because an anticipated benefit of reusing is that a change in a reusable asset will propagate to all systems that made use of the asset. If the majority of new development is based on reuse, then it follows that most of maintenance is linked to maintaining the reusable assets. The Reuse Team is responsible for maintaining the reusable assets; this same team could effectively make sure that the reusers are updated as well. Consider the (future) possibility that applications are described as compositions of reusable assets distributed over a network. Maintaining these assets on a network server centralizes the maintenance effort; application systems always access the latest version.

Retaining Team Members

The seemingly high investment needed to acquire and train team members on object-oriented technology raises a critical question: How do you retain them? This question is an issue because the market momentum behind object-oriented technology creates a big demand for your people's new skills. There are three answers: make them successful, let them have fun, and make sure they are compensated competitively.

Make them successful. Developers stay in organizations where they feel successful. They feel successful when they work on well-managed projects so that they can create results that contribute to the organization's success, and especially when what they create is used by the target customer. People leave poorly managed projects; they leave poorly managed companies. They also feel successful when they see that their involvement with new technology leads to career growth that is available within the organization.

Let them have fun. Developers enjoy learning new technology, but they expect to be able to apply their new skills on the job. If you train people on object-oriented technology, and then assign them to a COBOL maintenance project, they will undoubtedly look for another job.

Compensate competitively. Developers have to eat too. Sometimes people stay because they cannot, financially, afford to leave. If you pay unusually high salaries, or provide stock options or other financial rewards, then you might get away with not providing a success-driven or fun work environment. The reality is that currently a large demand exists for a short supply of experienced objectologists. You cannot rely on financial tactics alone to retain your people; you must make sure that your people feel successful and are having fun.

Framework for Selecting a Team Structure

Setting up a team structure is a resource-improvement project, as identified in Fig. 12.15. It involves assessing the current situation to understand the various planned projects that require teams, and assessing the team members currently available. The goals and objectives for the desired situation identify which teams and which roles on each team are needed, how the teams should be managed, and how communication should take place within a team and among collaborating teams.

Figure 12.15   Resource-Improvement Project to Create the Appropriate Teams

The purpose of the team-structure resourcing project is to make these decisions, and then to locate the team members who will work together within the identified structure. The principle for the framework follows directly from the Principle of System Architecture:

> *Framework Principle.* The team structure mirrors the needs of the process model and, where appropriate, the structure of the desired outcomes.

The goal for the team structure decision framework summarizes the purpose of the project:

> *Framework Goal.* Identify the purposes, roles, managerial styles, and communication channels that build the teams needed to meet the organization's goals and objectives.

The five steps of the team structure decision framework are:

- Decide which teams are needed

- Identify the roles needed on each team

- Decide on the style for managing each team

- Determine how communication will take place

- Find team members

***Team
Structure***

Decide Which Teams Are Needed

You need to select a team for each project you set up. If a project has been partitioned, you need a team to create each partition. In this chapter, we recommended teams for product development, producing reusable assets, managing the reuse process model, prototyping, and maintenance. In other chapters, we recommend teams for selecting process models, evaluating software development environments, curriculum development and training, and measurement. You need to build a team for any project you set up.

Identify the Roles Needed for Each Team

The second step is to identify the roles needed for each team, and the people who will play these roles. Here is a maxim to guide your decision making:

Team Roles

> **Activities define roles.** The number and kinds of roles on a project are tied to the kinds of activities that have to be carried out to meet the project's goals and objectives.

For example, the fact that there is a project implies that there is a role for someone to be responsible for the project. If the project is partitioned into subprojects, there is likely to be a similar leadership role for each partition, and a role to integrate the partition results. With the project and each of the partitions, there is a process model consisting of a set of activities. There is a role to carry out each activity.

There are a large number of roles on a software development team in addition to those shown in Fig. 12.1, for example change manager, packaging and production control manager, and quality assurance. Quality is every developer's job, but someone should be assigned responsibility to ensure that quality objectives are met. After the software is delivered to the customers, additional roles are needed for maintenance and technical support.

Which people fill which roles depends on how many people are available, what kinds of skills they have, and what it takes to get the job done within budget. There are usually more roles on a team than there are team members. Since many roles are identified for each project, and not always enough people, look for roles and activities that have an affinity for one another. Consider grouping these as a single role. For example, two roles that could be grouped are: collect all action requests (ARs) and decide which ones will be worked on for the next release, and integrate all the changes. At ParcPlace, these roles were called AR Czar and Integrator.

End users.   The target end user, sometimes referred to as the customer, is a special role on every project. He or she is part of the project through all of its activities. The end user works with the analyzers to establish the requirements definition and quality objectives, evaluates the analysis prototypes, participates in usability testing, specifies the acceptance test cases, reviews all documentation, and evaluates releases. The role can be played by an actual end user, or by someone who knows what the end user requires. Here is a maxim about end users which highlights the central nature of the role:

Team Roles

> **Make the end user an insider.** Successful teams enroll the end user as an insider, an active member of the product team.

As an insider, the end user is committed to the team's success and is more likely to provide the time and effort needed to fulfill the responsibilities of the role. With the end user on the team, other members are constantly reminded of the project's goals and objectives, that is, to satisfy the end user.

Decide on the Style for Managing Each Team

To decide on the style for managing each team, you first have to understand the managerial philosophy of your company and the best way to realize the potential of your team members.

Two maxims are essential to good management:

Managers serve their teams. The role of managing is to make sure that team members have the information and resources they need to accomplish their jobs.

Team Management

Responsibility demands authority. People cannot be successful if they are given responsibility without authority.

Good managers know when to delegate. Managers can delegate only when they are willing to assign both authority and responsibility—it is impossible to do a job without the authority to obtain and direct required resources. Excellent managers know what kinds of tasks can be assigned to which team members; these managers develop team members to take ever more responsibility and authority. Excellent managers know that delegating authority does not diminish the manager's role.

We have seen successful projects that are completely self-directed. We describe one such project in Chapter 5—the case study referred to as a Time-Driven Process Model. The idea was to create small self-empowered teams, each owning the problem of developing a particular subsystem. Each team had full decision-making authority for solving its problem, and was held accountable for meeting both the organization's quality objectives and its delivery deadlines.

Some managers cannot give up responsibility. Perhaps they do not trust their own people. In any case, they keep a significant portion of the workload on their own desk, either ignoring the managerial role or letting the functional tasks slip deadlines. This leads us to introduce additional maxims:

Managers manage. The manager cannot be on the critical path of (hands-on) development.

Team Management

Developers control deadlines. A manager cannot meet a deadline to which the developers have not agreed.

DeMarco and Lister provide data that back up this last maxim [DeMarco and Lister 1987]. Their data make it clear that the only dates obtainable are ones that the developers own. By "own," we mean that the developers have participated in establishing the tasks, defining the duration and resources for each task, and estimating the team's ability to carry out each task.

Determine How Communication Will Take Place

For a decision to be accepted, does it have to be written down and transmitted to people in certain roles? Who on the team relies on whom for information?

In this step of the team structure decision framework, you have to decide what team members need to know, which team members need to communicate with one another, and the form of the communication. Alan Perlis, a highly respected computer scientist, teacher, and researcher, offered the following maxim at the 1968 NATO conference on software engineering:

> **The Perlis eight.** Organize teams so that no one person has to talk to more than about eight people in total—at the person's level, and up and down.

This complements our own maxim about team size:

Team Size

> **Divide to conquer.** Teams should be partitioned according to the target system partitioning so that a subteam consists of six to eight people.

Partitioning creates subprojects that can be understood by a few people. There is evidence for the divide-to-conquer maxim in the case study data. Of the 23 successful projects we studied, seven had eight or fewer participants. Thirteen of the 23 projects had 11-50 team members, and ten of these divided into subteams of fewer than eight members.

When there are multiple interrelated projects or subprojects, you need to decide what kind of interteam coordination is needed, and how you will support the communication process. Chapter 11 identifies one proposal for interteam reuse communication—the Expert Services Organizational Model—whose ideal for communication is to set up a virtual hallway whereby reuse engineers participate in each project.

Find Team Members

Job descriptions for the new roles needed when using object-oriented technology are provided in Appendix C. The descriptions identify role responsibilities, hiring manager, expected educational background, and basis for performance evaluation.

When searching for team members, we look for three principal characteristics: talent, motivation, and interpersonal skills, defined in the context of the team structure. From the perspective of object-oriented technology, talent is a measure of an individual's ability to apply object-oriented concepts, while motivation is a measure of the individual's willingness to learn and use the technology. Interpersonal skills are independent of technology, but are essential in a team environment. Although we generally favor team players over loners, we make exceptions for outstanding talent.

Properly motivated team members are essential to the success of a project. How can an organization find motivated team members among its own personnel? Most organizations take whomever is available—a risky approach. Some organizations invite candidates to apply for a job opening that requires the use of object-oriented technology. This approach provides a good indicator that the applicants are motivated, but does not ensure that they have the skills. Highly motivated but unqualified people can cause a project to fail, albeit enthusiastically. We prefer to build a team by proactively selecting people who either have or can learn the skills needed to fulfill the team roles.

If you don't know a person, how do you assess whether he or she has the requisite skills? One technique for selecting team members from internal candidates is to teach an initial course on the relevant subject areas and see who "gets it." Another approach, useful with both internal and external candidates, is to have the candidate perform a job-related task. When we interview candidates for a teaching position in our training department, we ask them to train us on a topic of their choice. We stage a typical classroom with ourselves as inquiring and skeptical students. We ask potential documentors to write a technical description, and we ask potential developers to create a small application in our preferred development environment.

American Express used four tools in building their teams: Tuckman's Model, Life Styles Inventory, Myers-Briggs Type Indicator, and team-building classes.[1] The Tuckman Model sees teams as passing through four stages: form, storm, norm, and perform. Most teams are quickly formed and enter the storm stage, where the various personalities clash as they try to fit themselves to the available team roles. A team with a one-year mission cannot afford to spend much time storming before it starts performing. Most experience shows that the storm continues while the team tries to perform, a somewhat suboptimal arrangement. The approach that American Express took in order to leave the storming stage and enter a more normalized situation was to apply psychological testing and team-building techniques.

The Life Styles Inventory identifies team members' constructive personality styles,[2] while the Myers-Briggs identifies team members' communication capabilities and personal preferences.[3] Results were used to select team members, to match apprentices and

---

[1] Based on a presentation by Andrew Pan of American Express at the ParcPlace First International User's Conference, July 31 to August 2, 1994, Santa Clara, California.

[2] The Life Styles Inventory was a questionnaire administered by Human Synergistics, Inc. It was sent to five people who know the team member to ascertain the external perception of this person.

[3] Myers-Briggs is a test each team member took which identifies personal thinking and communications styles and preferences. According to Myers-Briggs, there are 16 different personality types, each of which has a different manner of interaction with the other types.

coaches so they complemented one another, to assign people to roles, and to select tools that suited the team (for example, electronic brainstorming). The psychological models could select team members who are comfortable juggling multiple roles, who excel at communications in complex (cross-project) situations, or who are suitable for guiding and helping beginners.

Finding team members does not necessarily mean hiring them as regular employees. You, and they, might prefer a consulting arrangement. What roles can such consultants play? They can be the object technology experts on your first projects, mentoring your own employees. Or they can help you set up your product process model, help you find people, train, write documentation, or do reviews or testing. Some organizations are structured to do maintenance only. They hire outsiders to do all of the initial development and documentation, leaving a maintainable system as the product of their work. In this way, skills for creating new software come from outside the company. These skills are different from those needed to maintain existing software.

It is sometimes difficult to test the knowledge of expert consultants. How do you assess their talent before you hire them? Audition them. Call references. You can also contract with a well-known expert to help you evaluate the others. Be cautious of consultants who are experts by association—experts because they are employed by an organization that has built a reputation for expertise. Evaluate them on their individual merit.

As difficult as it might be to find experts, their assistance is essential, as this maxim states:

Team Members

Experience first. Every object-oriented effort requires at least one team member who is an expert in the technology.

Getting help early avoids wasting time and learning bad habits. Do not neglect to find the domain experts, who may also be your customers. They are team members too.

Summary

A team has a purpose, and is made up of different roles that perform the activities needed to fulfill the purpose. Teams are lead by managers. The role of management is to make it possible for the team to do its job—to provide resources, work environment, processes, and information. Team members communicate, both formally and informally, with themselves and with other teams. And teams have a structure that should mirror the structure of the process model used by the team members.

In this chapter, we identified several special teams found in projects that have successfully applied object-oriented technology. These are: Application Productization Teams, Application Prototyping Teams, Framework Teams, Cross-Project Teams, Reuse Teams, and Maintenance Teams. The Application Productization Team creates a software application for production deployment, while the Application Prototyping Team creates prototypes of the desired application. The Framework Team also creates a software result, but one that is designed to be reusable. The Cross-Project Team exists to assist multiple application projects in sharing artifacts. The team does no development. The purpose of the Reuse Team is to manage the formal reuse process model, and to create and maintain the organization's strategic reusable assets. And finally, the Maintenance Team is responsible for all ongoing development and defect removal. Most likely, you will need to organize one or more of these teams, perhaps evolving from the Cross-Project Teams, serving to encourage reuse, to a fully staffed Reuse Team empowered to create and maintain reusable assets.

We also presented the decision framework for selecting a team structure. To select a team structure, you first decide which teams you require, and next identify the roles needed for each team. The third step of the framework is to identify the style for managing each team. We identified four team-management styles: hierarchical, military, battlefield commander, and egoless. Depending on the management style and preference of team members, different forms of communication take place. Choice of communication style is influenced by the team structure, which should mirror the choice of product process model. The last step of the framework is to find the team members.

Our own preferences for setting up team structures were stated by the maxims we presented. We determine the activities that have to be carried out and then match team members to these activities. We always consider the end user a member of the team, and expect the manager to focus on making sure that information and resources are provided as required by the team. Team members should have authority as well as responsibility, should be trusted to do their jobs, and should be aligned with business and schedule objectives. Managers should never be on the critical path of development, and should never set deadlines without the agreement of the other team members.

Additional Reading About Team Structure

DeMarco, T. and Lister, T., *PeopleWare: Productive projects and teams*, Dorset House: New York, 1987.

> These authors not only write in a humorous and flowing style, but they provide more common sense in fewer pages than any other authors we know in the field of software engineering. The data they cite encourage engineering and personnel managers to set up sensible work environments for all team members—sensible in terms of sufficient space, tools, and concentrated time to get tasks done. The authors also provide good advice on how to encourage team members to be more productive, to care about quality, and to be creative in the context of well-planned projects.

CHAPTER 13

Case Studies of Teams

The case study projects and projects on which we consulted provided us with illustrations of the teams we describe in Chapter 12: Applications (Productization and Prototyping), Framework, Cross-Project, Reuse, and Maintenance Teams. Table 13.1 summarizes the number of these teams found in the case study projects, cross-indexed on whether the projects were successful, ongoing, or unsuccessful.

Illustrations 1 and 2 discuss Applications Teams, while illustrations 3 and 4 discuss Framework Teams. Illustration 5—pollinators—comes from two companies that were not part of the case study interviews. Pollination efforts (Cross-Project Teams) showed up in the case studies only in the form of an object coach. We have seen a number of these teams in non-case study projects, two of which we describe in this chapter. Illustration 6 also describes an Application Team, one modeled after the officers and personnel found in the "Star Trek" television and movie series.

Table 13.1 Correlation of Kinds of Teams to Project Completion Status

Type of Team	Successful	Ongoing	Unsuccessful
Application Team	14	5	1
Framework Team	4		
Both Application and Framework Teams	6	5	1
Reuse Team		1	

Illustration 1: Subteams Based on Enterprise-wide Analysis

To illustrate the way the team structure mirrors the development partitions, we present this case study from the Phase 2 interviews. The project was still in progress at the time of the interview, although several partial results had already been delivered to the target users, who had become dependent on the system to do their daily work. During the three years of development, different developers had participated at different stages. Anywhere from two to six team members worked on the project at any one time, and the project transitioned from an internal development effort to one that was contracted to an outside software house. However, this separate business was formed by internal personnel for the purposes of attracting people with object-oriented technology expertise who, it seemed, were not interested in joining the larger organization.

The project was done by a television broadcasting company in Belgium. This company is only five years old, and has the distinction of being the first commercial television station worldwide to be profitable in its first year of operation. Its mission and motto are:

Mission: Be the preferred family broadcaster.
Motto: <Company Name> gives color to your day!

The project goal is to create a tool that supports the director in administering television programming. Specific system objectives are:

1. Build an integrated planning application for coordinating all of the planners, for both strategic planning and daily planning, as well as for administering video-tapes

2. Automate existing programming processes

3. Create a user interface that is easy for existing television planning personnel to learn

4. Create access to a database of the videotapes available for television programs

We asked the development team to list its maxims. They were quick to respond:

Maxim 1: Look at the whole picture first to be fully prepared and to be able to attain the desired quality.

Maxim 2: Pay critical attention to the usability of the application because users expect a lot.

Maxim 3: The only way to be successful is to deliver partial results every couple of months—to make sure you are building the right system and to gain user confidence.

To adhere to Maxim 3, the team recognized that it needed a small number of customers who were willing to take the time to test the partial results. The sponsor of the project, one of the company television programming directors, became an enthusiastic user, providing the critical usage feedback. The team believed strongly that, throughout the incremental development, the basic problem domain components were stable because they had taken the time (about five months) at the outset of the project to do a complete enterprise-wide analysis. The analysis was carried out using a traditional approach (that is, not object-oriented). Workers in all departments of the company were interviewed to obtain a complete description of the company's processes—from obtaining rights for rebroadcasting a program, to scheduling and delivering a day of television. Throughout the rest of the project, team members treated the domain components derived from the enterprise-wide analysis as immutable.

System partitions were derived from the company's department boundaries, although, where commonalities were discovered, the boundaries were ignored in favor of bringing consistency to the analysis result. This attempt to recognize consistency forced some changes in the customer's (nonautomated) work arrangements.

The business partitions are listed here, in an order that reflects the flow of activities needed to arrange a day of television programs. In this list, the word "Product" refers to a videotape of a television program.

P1   *Product Management.* Obtain rights to purchase the Products and store information about program opportunities in the database. Be able to browse the database.

P2   *Videotape Management.* Order the tapes of the Product, on an as-needed basis, and store information in the database as to the Product's availability. Be able to browse the database.

P3   *Strategic Planning by the program director.* Covers two or three months of television seasonal planning, for each of three seasons. Planning is done on a five-minute resolution.

P4   *Tactical Planning.* Next level of detail. Programs in the planning chart are linked to the Products (and therefore indirectly to the Videotape). (This means: Link to the database element referencing the Product, rights for which have been obtained but the actual tape has not necessarily been ordered; test whether the window for broadcasting is open; check that the duration of the Product fits the reserved space; and so on).

P5   *Vision.* Put technical details about the Product in the database.

P6   *Refinement.* Fill in the programming holes, doing the commercials, trailers, and billboards. Link into the Commercial Department's separate database to get this information. Give planning details with a one-minute resolution.

P7   *Continuity.* Alternative representation of a day's programming, with each program sequenced by presentation time. Make sure all approvals and materials have been obtained. Be able to recalculate timing in real time as broadcasting is taking place. Give planning details with a one-second resolution.

P8 ·   *Trailer Management.* Similar to Product Management.

P9   *Press.* Export plan to a desktop publishing system.

The team's process model was based on three ideas: partial deliveries, incremental addition of features, and developing subsystems in parallel. The team thought that the key reason for providing partial deliveries was to involve users in improving the functionality and quality of the system. However, the team believed that they needed to be better at communicating with the users to manage user expectations and to prevent creeping featurism.

Partition 1—Product Management—was understood before the enterprise-wide analysis was carried out. In fact, four developers and an analyst spent 18 months to create the data models for a relational database, implement a query tool in a dialect of Smalltalk, and connect Smalltalk to the database. This query tool was not delivered until almost 18 months after the enterprise-wide analysis was completed and additional partitions had been developed. The developers who did the work were hired from the outside. Prior to making the decision to hire outside contractors, the company had spent six months trying to hire employees to do the development work, but was disappointed in its ability to attract qualified candidates from the small pool of computer scientists available in Belgium.

Two employees of the television broadcasting company joined with three object experts to form an independent software company. A sixth person joined the new company shortly thereafter. The company received a long-term contract to deliver a system covering all seven business partitions, guided by a steering group consisting of target users, and a project sponsor (who later became the first user). It took 2.5 months to translate the requirements specification into a design object model, which consisted of about 60 business objects. The entire team participated in this exercise so that the business experts and the software engineers would understand each other's needs.

Based on the partitions and resources consisting of six developers, the project was divided into three subprojects, each with two team members, to work in parallel. Each subteam was assigned complete authority to develop one of the partitions. One team worked on product acquisition, another on strategic planning support, and the third focused on the database level. These partitions were selected because they would produce core implementation objects—both the database hookup and the problem domain objects—that would be reusable when creating the other partitions. The team made this determination based on the enterprise-wide analysis.

Over time, several team members left the project, new people were added, and the subteams were reconstituted and assigned different partitions to work on. But there were always three teams, and each always had authority for at least one partition. This helped create an egoless development situation.

Most of the deadlines were reached on time. Updates to the initial release were done three times during a seven-month period, mainly to add functionality. Although these updates were planned in advance, the overhead for releasing versions to the end users was not well understood. Eventually an additional person was added to the project specifically to manage the release process. The end user was the project sponsor, who took the first prototype immediately into production and has been a satisfied user ever since.

This illustration emphasizes two essential aspects of Application Team structures. First, this team was divided into subteams according to the problem partitions, with each subteam delegated full authority to design, implement, and test. Having conducted an enterprise-wide analysis, all team members shared a common vocabulary for the domain and therefore for the object model. This facilitated their ability to work independently and successfully deliver incremental results to the end user. Second, the team involved its key end user early in the development process. This end user served as a requirements provider, aggressive tester, and avid supporter.

Illustration 2: Geographically Distributed Teams

This next case study illustrates an application project to design and implement a physician's workstation. The project goals were to:

Automate medical records

Automate orders to laboratories and pharmacies

Integrate appointment scheduling and billing

Provide in-home terminal access to a medical expert system

The business goal was to support a new approach to medical practices whereby both doctors and patients would have more direct access to medical histories, taking into account patient security issues. The system objectives included minimizing training for physicians, and fulfilling all legal medical record requirements. The customer needed to support 550,000 subscribers to its health program, who interact with 850 physicians. Users had access to intelligent workstations and dumb ASCII terminals.

The project process model and the analysis-and-design techniques had been defined by a separate corporate-level group, and were extended by the team members of the physician's workstation project to account for the adoption of object-oriented technology. This product process model defines a set of required tasks, including inputs and outputs. Each project manager maps the tasks in the process model to specific roles needed to build a desired system. For the project we describe, the team was partitioned according to the structure of the organization's computer systems architecture (kinds of workstations and network services). This team was very large (120 team members), and the project was expected to last at least two years. The team was geographically distributed in three cities. Prototypes were created to understand the system behavior model (work flow for the user) and to get early agreement on the user interfaces. Extensive written documentation was distributed to keep everyone informed about the team members and their roles.

The project team consisted of:

1	account manager
40	account staff and domain experts
1	administrative manager
22	ASCII terminal software developers
10	librarians, assistants
1	object administrator
10	prototypers
18	server developers
3	technical leaders
20	workstation software developers

The organization did the project under contract to a customer. So the team included an account manager who was responsible for managing the relationship with the customer, and for making sure that the project was profitable. This person had final authority for all decisions.

The administrative manager was responsible for deadlines, budgets, and resources. Reporting to this administrative manager were three technical leaders, one for each of the following subactivity areas: front-end workstations and ASCII terminals, back-end, and database systems. The front-end team was further divided into three groups, one for the graphical workstation, one for the terminal, and one to manage all of the prototyping efforts. All three subgroups were under the same team leader.

An object administrator role was played by a senior person who was responsible for keeping abreast of everything going on and for supporting requests for reuse. If a new reusable object was needed, this person produced it. Team members were explicitly rewarded for reuse in the sense that their performance appraisals included comments on their willingness and ability to reuse components. Technical leaders were responsible for motivating reuse. They held weekly meetings during which the teams discussed the components that were available and how they could be reused.

Analysis took 14 months, and then an additional six months were required to go from prototypes to design to production code. The system itself consisted of about 1000 class descriptions, with at most 15 methods per class. Much of the work went into creating the data models and screen presentations. There were 220 data tables, presented in almost 600 screens.

The team followed a formal change-request process when making changes in prototypes. This was made more complex because the customer who reviewed the prototypes was in a different geographic location. Here is a brief outline of the change-request process:

1. Prototyper reviews prototype with manager to see whether it is ready for customer use.

2. Administrative manager coordinates reviews with account manager at remote site, by generating a design review request.

3. Account manager sets up time with the customer/user.

4. Customer reviews.

5. As part of the review, not attended by the prototyper, a change may be identified, recorded in the review report, and sent to the prototyper.

6. Start over.

This process seems inefficient. The benefits of an intimate relationship between customer and prototyper are unavailable. The geographic distribution requires written notification of even small changes, and requires following a detailed process to get permission to do something that might be easy and obvious. This overhead discourages frequent reviews with the customer, but encourages clear documentation of the resulting prototype or system and tracking change requests. To overcome these inefficiencies, the project allowed alternative reviews involving user groups, thereby eliminating several process steps—those in which a third party sets up customer reviews without the prototyper's participation.

This Applications Team organized into three subteams mirroring the architecture for the target delivery system: subteams for developing software for workstations, ASCII terminals, and servers. These subteams were supported by an expert in object-oriented technology (who was called an object administrator but whose role corresponds to our description of an object technology expert). Prototyping was a central part of the project process model, so that ten out of the 70 developers were designated as prototypers. Since prototyping was critical to the process, it was disappointing to see that the communication problems associated with geographically dispersed development were heightened by denying the prototypers direct access to the target end users. It appears that the process model was selected because the customer was not really a part of the team, but was paying for the team and requiring justification for all expenditures.

Illustration 3: Framework Team Support Obligations

We interviewed several groups in one Phase 1 case study company, including two Framework Teams and several Application Teams that made use of the frameworks. Here we discuss only one of the Framework Teams. This team evolved from an existing research group because the charter for the entire research laboratory had changed to emphasize technology transfer. The software architecture group within the laboratory set up a project with the goal of designing a reusable user interface framework for creating instrumentation applications. They believed the framework would be of interest to several divisions in the company, and planned to market their ideas once the first release was completed.

We describe this project as Illustration 1 in Chapter 9. It makes extensive use of a compiler-compiler created by another laboratory project. The six members of the Framework Team were knowledgeable about the problem domain as well as user interface issues, both of which were important in the design effort. All team members were software engineers, and took responsibility for testing their own implementations.

When the Framework Team was ready for its first release, it had a waiting audience. These were the users of the compiler-compiler, interested in having a better user interface and tool set for instrumentation functionality. Two of these users received the initial release of the framework, and included it in their product software by adding algorithms and drivers specific to their instrumentation products. These customers said that they had no expectations of receiving support from the Framework Team, and in fact had no need to keep up with new releases unless there was a major defect fix or proof that the changes would reduce the cost of their products.

There are no rules within the corporation about sharing software across projects. If there are personality barriers, teams can simply decide not to share. There is no formal channel for distributing information about available software. In fact, the customers we interviewed found out about the framework mostly by word of mouth. The Framework Team told us that they wanted to maintain control of the framework as they expected to provide several incremental releases. They were planning to do new releases and training in the context of the recently established user group for the compiler-compiler. In contrast, the customers felt that the Framework Team members were not inclined to do sustaining engineering work, or to set priorities based on the product requirements of the other divisions. The team was still focused on doing research.

This situation is a typical one: The developers think they can be responsive to a growing customer base while they continue their prior development practices. This behavior rarely works. Initial product development is, for the most part, protected from any outside interruptions. The developers are not answering customer questions or putting out fires. First product release is the point at which most engineering teams split into two teams: sustaining engineers and new release engineers. A Framework Team coordinating with multiple Application Teams has to balance support with new development work.

Illustration 4: Enterprise-wide Framework Team

One organization chose to transition from a traditional mainframe environment to workstations, windowing systems, graphical user interfaces, and object-oriented technology. It contracted with a management consulting firm to handle the transition and to direct the new development project. The project was expected to be a five-year effort. Based on an enterprise-wide analysis conducted by the management consultants, a development team was assembled to reengineer many of the organization's key business systems. This initial development team was divided into two subteams because the organization itself is divided into two kinds of businesses. Each team was assigned approximately ten people.

Because of the new development architecture, the organization expected to develop many new infrastructure components. A third team was established to develop these components, to avoid redundant effort. We refer to this team as the Framework Team, because it was also responsible for developing tools and the basic application framework.

All of the project's team members were new to object-oriented technology. After an aggressive training program, the top three students were chosen to staff the Framework Team. Two object-oriented technology experts were brought in to mentor the teams. One was assigned to the Framework Team, and the other was assigned to the two Application Teams.

At the start of the project, the Framework Team was the center of activity. Tools were developed and made available to the other teams. Framework Team members acted as consultants to the Application Teams to assist them in using the tools. One of the team members was assigned the triage role (to figure out priorities and dispatch requests), and handled all incoming support requests. For the first couple of releases, this was a full-time job. When the application framework was completed, Framework Team members consulted with application developers on how to use it. This direct interaction allowed them to improve the framework for future applications.

As the project progressed, more of the attention began to focus on the Application Teams. With their tools and framework in place, these teams began to create the end-user applications. Although these applications contained the necessary business functionality, they did not operate efficiently enough for the end users. This defect required that the Framework Team improve performance by rebuilding pieces of the underlying framework.

The Framework Team was established within a single enterprise-wide project for the purpose of providing expertise in reuse to two Application Teams building many applications. Given its success as a separate team, and given the long-term nature and size of the project, the Framework Team will likely remain as a separate development unit in the company.

The lifetime of a Framework Team depends on the needs of the organization. A Framework Team created to make a single project successful can be disbanded once the goal is attained. Alternatively, given its positive experience with the Framework Team, the organization could sponsor the team as an independent development group. The charter of the new group would be to provide support for the reusable assets it created, and assistance in developing assets for other projects—that is, the organization would transition the Framework Team into a Reuse Team.

Illustration 5: Two Pollinator Team Examples

We have worked with two organizations (not a part of the case studies) that used a Cross-Project Team to achieve effective reuse across a collection of ongoing projects. Both of these companies were first-time users of object-oriented technology. Indeed, they were aggressive adopters because they were willing to use the technology for the first time on several concurrent projects. There are many risks in being so aggressive, one of which is ineffective reuse across projects. The Cross-Project Teams were created to address this concern.

Management of the first organization believes that effective levels of reuse can be reached only when there is a well-developed reuse process model. As a consequence, they created a Reuse Team to manage the reusable assets. This team consisted of one person who was responsible for all of the reuse roles. Reuse requires a long-term vision. Management expects a formal reuse process model and library to take a year or so to develop. Project deadlines, however, cannot wait a full year. When object-oriented technology was evaluated and selected, it was decided that four projects would be started at once. Establishing a Cross-Project Team was management's short-term solution for improving effective reuse, while buying enough time and experience to establish the Reuse Team.

The Cross-Project Team initially consisted of two people. One was the manager of the newly formed Reuse Team, and the other was a well-known senior developer within the organization. Both were knowledgeable about the organization's business, but both were new to object-oriented technology. Their primary responsibility was to attend the review meetings of all of the projects, so they could understand what each project was doing and be able to offer suggestions for reusing artifacts developed by other projects. Neither of the pollinators was an expert in developing reusable artifacts. Rather, they were keen observers and had enough business knowledge to understand where overlap existed among the projects. They added value by identifying these overlaps—pointing out that a particular part of the business had already been analyzed by another project, and the first group's work could be reused in a second or third project. The technical issues surrounding the reuse of artifacts were left to the project teams.

This approach was designed to avoid duplicate work. It is successful if projects can reuse the work of other projects and, by doing so, reduce their overall effort to reach completion. It does not address the longer-term issues of reuse maintenance. The organization set no particular guidelines or requirements for how reuse should take place. Unless team members on different projects collaborate, one team is likely to copy the artifacts of another, and change them to its own needs. One of the reasons the Reuse Team manager was assigned to the Cross-Project Team was to address these issues.

The second organization established a pollination subteam primarily to improve effective reuse across the many subprojects of one particularly large project. The Cross-Project Team consists of two people, both experts in the business of the company. One of the team members is a sophisticated object-oriented developer, the other a sophisticated information modeler. Together they are expected to ensure that appropriate, effective reuse occurs across all subprojects. In general, this pollination team operates much like the first organization's team. The primary difference between this team and the team in our first example is that this team was given the responsibility and authority to make policy decisions about how reuse is to take place across projects. In this way, the team is operating much like a formal Reuse Team.

Illustration 6: The Star Trek Team Model

The San Joaquin Delta College, a community college in the 107-campus California public college system, built the initial version of a new student information system: System 2000.[1] The college has an enrollment of 18,000 students and an annual budget of $60 million, supporting 600 full-time employees. The effort was initiated by a total reengineering of the administrative processes and procedures. Students, staff, faculty, and administrators will use System 2000 to access all of the functions needed to support their roles in the school, including course selection and enrollment, preparing and distributing grades and transcripts, collecting fees, planning degree requirements fulfillment, matching courses with faculty and physical classrooms, and creating reports required by the (California) state educational offices.

System 2000 was designed by the same team that developed and managed the original Unisys Burroughs mainframe COBOL applications (consisting of 1 million lines of uncommented COBOL code). The concept of System 2000 is a client/server-based

---

[1] Lee Belarmino and Matt Rosen of the San Joaquin Delta College—dressed in full Star Trek uniforms as Starfleet officers—described their teams in a presentation at the ParcPlace First International Users Conference, July 31 to August 2, 1994, in Santa Clara, California.

model, with the majority of the computing being done on the user's (Macintosh) desktop. A VAX minicomputer provides data and voice processing so that students can access the system, "talking" by pressing keys on the public telephone and receiving synthetic voice messages. The system was developed using ParcPlace's VisualWorks so that it would be easy to port to the hardware available at other colleges. On completion, the system represented 120 new application classes, accessing a relational database described by 225 relational tables.

Both for humor and understandability, team roles were identified with characters from both the old and new versions of the popular movie and television series "Star Trek." The germ of this idea came from recognizing that, as a team, the college systems staff was isolated, much like a starship in space. Since they work at a public college, the team leaders were restricted from hiring additional staff, including any consultants, and from replacing any existing staff. The ten full-time staff members, with an average of ten years' programming experience in COBOL, had little knowledge of object-oriented technology. Fortunately, their isolation meant that no one could tell them that their mission was impossible.

The five-year project was started in 1989, with an initial exploration phase carried out using the Hierarchical Guru approach. The guru is a technically knowledgeable person who provides leadership by example, and serves as an internal mentor while the team is trained on object-oriented technology. This guru had responsibilities similar to those of the Object Coach role. Associating the team structure with "Star Trek" roles, the approach relied on a combination of Kirk and Picard as project manager, a Spock as the technical and hands-on guru, Dr. McCoy as the designer who provided a user-oriented reality check, Wesley Crusher as the design prototyper with no fear of the unknown, and miscellaneous security personnel.

The initial exploration phase provided a plan for a system to manage student courses and services. The actual development project consisted of three teams: Architecture, Framework, and Application. The architecture was modeled on the Apple Corporation VITAL guidelines—a series of generic services and service linkages. Chekov served as the designer on the Architecture Team, relying on Sulu (the ship's navigator) to steer the team to use the architecture correctly. On the Framework Team, Sulu continued as a linking pin for architecture dissemination, Wesley Crusher did the database interface drivers and handled interprocess communications, Spock enhanced the development environment, and Scotty handled systems, network, and database details. Scotty, along with several other crew members, worked below deck, apparently operating without awareness of the system's architecture. The application domain problem was divided by the project manager and guru (Kirk and Spock) into 14 partitions, with full responsibility to develop each partition given to one team member. Partitions took about six months to develop, were reviewed by peers once a week, and as frequently by the target users.

Project management adopted the Battlefield Commander model for the postexploration phases. The battle plan was to direct reuse of the architecture by the framework developers (or toolsmiths), and to have the application developers specialize the frame-work. The Architecture Team is a special kind of Framework Team, focused on creating the technical framework for the client/server model. This dependency among the teams is shown in Fig. 13.1.

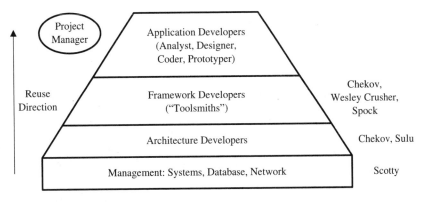

Figure 13.1   Support/Reuse Model for the Parts of San Joaquin Delta College's System 2000

System 2000 is currently managing registration for 14,000 San Joaquin Delta College students. The project was completed on time and within budget, ready for the start of the school year. A project that typically requires 30 staff years in a college information sys-tems department, in this case took ten staff years. The ten-person team will be reduced to five for maintaining the system, leaving the remaining staff available for new projects.

The San Joaquin Delta College experience illustrates a number of important points. First, COBOL programmers can build significant systems based on object-oriented tech-nology. To do so, the team effort had to be carefully factored to separate those activities requiring different skills levels: Architecture (or Technical Framework) Team, (Application) Framework Team, and Application Team. Assigned to the different teams according to their personal skills, individuals could learn without the frustration of being asked to do tasks that exceeded their current technical expertise. Second, the roles of Object Coach and Technology Expert were key to providing team leadership. And third, the team members' knowledge of how information systems support the college allowed the manager to delegate responsibility to them for the capabilities of each partition. Here we see that domain knowledge dominated technology expertise, the latter learnable with careful management and mentoring.

This project had two phases, each with its own style of management. The first phase used a Hierarchical Guru approach and the second the Battlefield Commander. Thus the pro-ject also demonstrated that team management structure should be flexible and should adapt to changing circumstances. And finally, the "Star Trek" theme gave the team an identity and a way to understand one another's roles. The theme added fun to the work environment.

Summary

We described a number of projects illustrating different application, framework, and cross-project teams. Additional examples of case study project team structures are presented in the context of process models in Chapter 8.

Perhaps the most surprising aspect of our case studies was the absence of formal reuse teams. Given the way in which objects are equated to reuse, we should have seen more effort to formalize the process of identification, acquisition, and maintenance. Framework Teams were quite common, showing up in 17 of the projects. Development organizations taking advantage of object-oriented technology recognize the benefits of creating domain-specific abstractions and of creating applications as specializations of these abstractions. But these same organizations do not manage these frameworks for corporate-wide distribution and maintenance. None of the case studies sought outside expertise to consult on setting up a reuse process, in direct contrast with the approaches taken by organizations focused on reuse but not on object-oriented technology. Lack of a well-managed reuse process model will inhibit otherwise well-intentioned organizations from realizing one of the key benefits of object-oriented technology.

The case studies illustrate that the application development team structures do mirror the structure of the process model. These projects partitioned the work effort, assigning partition development to subteams. Successful teams invariably had an object expert available, who brought to the project essential information that helped the teams avoid the mistakes experience teaches. No organization should do a first project without such assistance, either from an internal expert or an outside consultant.

The customer has become a true member of successful projects using object-oriented technology. Because the customer was a true member of the team, the projects were more likely to deliver results that the customer wanted and was able to use. The projects were better tested because incremental deliveries to the customer assured early feedback and ideas cultivated from actual use.

CHAPTER 14

Expectations for a Software Development Environment

A *software development environment* is the set of methods, languages, libraries, tools, and database services used to create software systems. We use this term in an all-inclusive manner to cover support for any part of a product process model—analysis, design, coding, testing, documentation, and so on.[1] Clearly the choice of software development environment is based on the environment's ability to improve the team's productivity. But your choice of software development environment for the use of object-oriented technology is also partially driven by a number of other expectations:

- Often users expect to be developers; the distinction between developers and users is becoming blurred.

- Team members within the same team, or across multiple teams, expect to coordinate their efforts.

- Users expect software systems to be portable across platforms, and to be able to interoperate with independently created systems.

---

[1] CASE, or computer-assisted software engineering, is an umbrella term for tools that support software development. It is often erroneously associated only with 4GLs and code generators, and so we do not rely on the term in this and subsequent chapters.

- Network-based systems present a client/server architecture in which developers expect to create and deliver software products.

- Organizations expect to retain prior software and database investments.

Users as Developers

A software development environment is created for a developer of a particular kind of software. You cannot evaluate an environment unless you know who should use it—what kind of developer creating what kind of software.

There Are Different Kinds of Developers

More and more, people who are neither trained nor paid to develop software are doing so. We expect the distinction between developer and user to become even more blurred over time, as reuse, visual construction builders, and other inventions for automating the coding process enable more people to give programmatic directions to a computer. Today, most large organizations have at least four kinds of developers: systems developers, business application framework developers, business application developers, and business people as developers.

Systems developers. Systems developers create software to be used by other developers. They create or enhance system-level components for managing the operating system, network communications, systems administration, and so on. They provide architectural frameworks for uses such as developing user interfaces and access to databases. They sometimes also provide special utility applications, such as text editors and drawing tools. The systems developers typically use 3GL programming languages, such as C, and they expect to be able to implement any component they desire.

Business application framework developers. Business application framework developers create software to be used by business application developers. This software is in the form of frameworks and components for specific business domains, such as banking and transportation. The business application framework developers most often use 3GL programming languages, such as C, C++, or Smalltalk.

Business application developers. Business application developers create software for end users. The applications are often created by refining domain-specific business or technical frameworks that they receive from framework developers. The business application developers use a 4GL programming language, a visual construction framework, or a framework that includes significant default functionality and an automatic code-generation capability. They are also turning to the various non-object-oriented languages whose newer tools support component composition, such as Visual Basic with its custom controls (OCXs).

Business people as developers. The business person as a developer is an information manager who uses a scripting system such as a spreadsheet, Hypercard-like editor, or a PC-based communications application. In this regard, the information manager writes programs, albeit in a custom scripting language. The results (spreadsheets, card stacks, or scripts) are primarily for personal use, but are often shared with colleagues. As new scripting languages become available that are targeted to specific uses, and are relatively easy to learn and to modify (spreadsheet macro languages are good examples), the information manager becomes a new kind of developer, creating software for carrying out business computations and what-if analyses. Unlike the other kinds of developers, business people are not professional developers in the sense of being paid to create software. Rather, they are paid to carry out business-related tasks. They develop software to help complete these tasks; they are tool users, not tool builders. In this sense, a business application that is extended by using a scripting language is a special tool for modeling business functions.

Development Is Done at Different Levels

Figure 14.1 shows the four layers of developers within an organization, with a fifth (lowest) layer that represents the system software provided by software vendors. The vendor

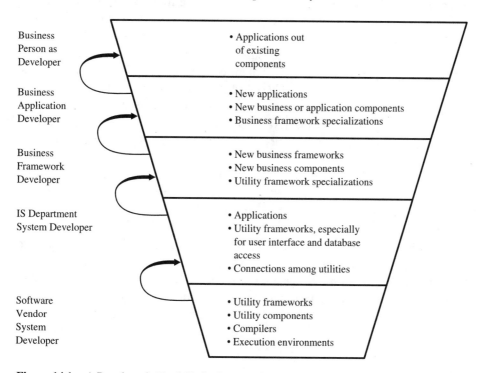

Figure 14.1 A Developer's Food Chain: Layers of Developers and What They Develop

provides the runtime capabilities of the development environment, which are then modified by the different kinds of corporate developers. Vendors often provide frameworks and tools that might otherwise be constructed by the IS department—for example, visual construction tools for building graphical user interfaces, and special database navigation tools.

The lowest three layers are built by Framework Teams, either technical frameworks such as operating system resource managers or database access frameworks, or business frameworks such as accounting or inventory management. The Application Teams appear at the Business Application Development layer, building on the technical and business frameworks provided by the layers below. The business person (traditional user) uses the products created by the Application Teams.

Users at each level are developers as well. The user at the IS department level uses the software created by vendors and develops software to be used by the business framework developer at the next layer. The business application developer in turn uses what the business framework developer creates, but may also develop software using a business-oriented scripting language. The relationships among the various layers create a software developer's food chain, wherein components produced by one layer of developers are consumed as components for the next layer.

In each layer, the knowledge and experience required to develop software differ. Users at the topmost layer have the least experience as software developers and the most knowledge as business professionals. Each class of developer works at a particular level of abstraction, using methods, languages, tools, and libraries to create components that are appropriate for that level. The development environment at any one level of abstraction should be sufficient for creating most of the components that are needed at that level. However, there are times when developers find it necessary to descend to the next lower level to add facilities that support components at their own level. If the developers are not permitted or equipped to extend the next lower level, they call upon the services of developers at that level to make the extensions for them. The backlog of requests for extensions can build up.

Object-oriented technology helps reduce the backlog by enabling developers to work faster, through reuse of components and refinement of frameworks. Potentially, the backlog never even occurs because the developer at one level can learn enough to develop at the level below. Why is this reasonable?

In a fully object-oriented environment, there are objects all the way down—at every layer. (Don't let the use of the word *layer* confuse you; think of a layer as a collection of objects that work together to provide a set of services.) The language of a layer consists of the names of objects in that layer and the messages that can be sent to invoke the services of those objects. The tools of a layer are objects that enable the developer to manipulate other objects. Libraries of objects are additional components with which the developer can customize the layer. If developers move to another layer, they find more of the same—just a different vocabulary and perhaps different sets of tools. It is feasible, therefore, to consider incremental learning, whereby a developer starts at a high level of a system, using objects that are familiar from the developer's real-world experience. At this system level, the developer learns about object concepts and how to develop software within a limited world, and then moves to the next level of detail. Developers who are willing to learn more, can.

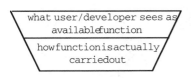 At each level, the developer makes use of what the objects provide, without worrying about how they are able to do so. These objects provide their services by calling on the services of other objects, often objects that reside in the layer below. The translation from what objects can do, to how they do it in the layer below, is transparent to the user. The user in the next (lower) layer, of course, sees these *hows* as lower-level *whats*.[2]

Coordination of People, Processes, and Resources

Coordination among developers is essential for the successful creation of software products. These developers might work within the same team, or they can be on multiple teams. When the software development environment encourages a layered approach, not only will team members at the same layer have to coordinate, but team members at adjacent layers will have to coordinate. At the very least, developers in one layer must provide the functionality needed by the developers in the next higher layer. For example, developers of a reusable framework must coordinate with those who use it, to make sure the framework is used properly, and to fix any defects that are exposed by such use.

Coordination among other project resources is also important. Software development projects create a variety of intermediate artifacts that need to be coordinated, which in turn requires process support for configuration management. *Configuration management* is a method for identifying the arrangement of system artifacts at discrete points in time. Individual artifacts may exist in multiple versions; these multiple versions are stored in repositories for general access by the developers. A configuration specifies which version of each artifact is being used. Tools for configuration management help to control changes in system parts, as well as to maintain the integrity and traceability of these changes throughout the development process. Just as developers are constrained to use the development capability at their appropriate system layer, so too must versioning be handled within the context of a development layer.

---

[2] The typical description of an object is that of a package of behavior and information whereby other objects know only what the object can do—that is, its behavior—not how the object implements its behavior. In Chapter 3, we discuss the separation of an object's external specification from its implementation.

Coordination policies. Each organization must select its preferred style of coordination based on its development processes, resources, and artifacts. This style takes the form of policies for coordinating artifacts. A *policy* is a system for administering permissions among a group of developers. Coordination policies come in two flavors: security and concurrency. A *security policy* is a coordination policy that allocates permissions to developers (such as read or write) based on user authentication and security clearance levels. Security policies define the rights of developers to access and change system artifacts. A *concurrency policy* is a coordination policy that allocates permissions to developers based on already allocated permissions and the rules for multiple-developer interaction. Concurrency policies settle conflicts between developers who are working on the same artifacts. There may be one policy that applies to all types of artifacts—analysis, design, code, test, and so on. Or, there can be a specific policy for each type of artifact. The organization selects a software development environment tool partly on its ability to enforce the selected policies.

Some security policy models are based on ownership, whereby changes are made only by assigned owners. Ownership-centric policies are popular because they make it easy to know who to contact when there is a problem. Consider the accountability of the Reuse Team. Anything taken from the library is owned by the Reuse Team, and they are solely responsible for any changes needed to update these assets. You can change something that you do not own for your personal use, but you cannot officially release these changes for use by others. The consequence is that developers who have ideas for changing an artifact have to negotiate with a perhaps more conservative owner.

Coordination as it relates to objects. Two coordination questions arise with respect to object-oriented technology: What are the artifacts to be coordinated, and what are the various configurations that you wish to be able to create?

Object-oriented methods are used to create and manage many different artifacts including analysis objects, design objects, implementation objects, test cases, and documentation. Most coordination issues are the same for object-oriented development as for traditional development, but there are a couple of special issues. First, assuming there is a clear separation of the object interface from its implementation, you should be able to track implementation versions independently of interface versions, and link specifications to the appropriate implementations. Second, you need to keep track of which version of any reusable asset is incorporated into a system.

Finally, system configurations are made up of modules or packages. When you are using object-oriented technology, *packages* are collections of classes and initialized instances of classes. Packages refer to other packages—the classes defined in one package might have instances in another package. Moreover, a package may extend a class that is defined in another package. When packaging is supported, software development tools for both individuals and teams must help developers maintain consistent references to versions of packages.

Portability and Interoperability

The choice of software development environment depends on the target user environment. But the user environment changes over time because technology opportunities change. For example, new hardware, operating systems, window managers, and graphical libraries become available. To protect the organization's investment in software, developers have to be able to make changes rapidly and with low risk of introducing defects. To meet these goals, developers expect a software development environment to support the development of systems that are portable across platforms, are open, and have a client/server architecture.

Cross-Platform Portability

Cross-platform portability is the ability to implement application software on one kind of machine and have it execute on a different kind of machine. There are two kinds of portability: one where you have to do something to get the application software to execute, such as recompile it; and another where a special layer of software, called middleware or a virtual machine, shelters the application from changes to the host system. The second kind of portability is often called *binary portability*. The developers do not require special knowledge about the target host systems or development tools for these systems. They simply move the binary representation of an application from one machine to another, and start up a runtime execution environment that can then execute the application.

Cross-platform portability allows developers to create applications on expensive machines, and deliver on machines that are more appropriate for everyday business use. The organization gets a high return on investment from its developers, while minimizing the cost of deploying applications to business sites that may have a variety of kinds of hardware. Maintenance costs decrease because only one platform-independent version of each application exists.

Binary portability works because the application relies entirely on a set of well-specified services provided by the underlying middleware, and not on how the services are implemented. The specifics of communicating with the host platform are transparent to the application. Full cross-platform portability might therefore require that applications use only services that are common to all of the platforms. Adherence to the lowest common denominator is limiting, and is eliminated when the middleware emulates functionality that is available on one host platform but not on others.

The most desirable middleware provides access to host platform capability where available and emulates only when the host is deficient. Developers write applications using the interface provided by the middleware. An example of a binary portability architecture for Smalltalk is shown in Fig. 14.2. The middleware, called an Object Engine, is different for each combination of processor, operating system, and windowing system. All Smalltalk objects execute using this Object Engine and are binary portable across platforms.

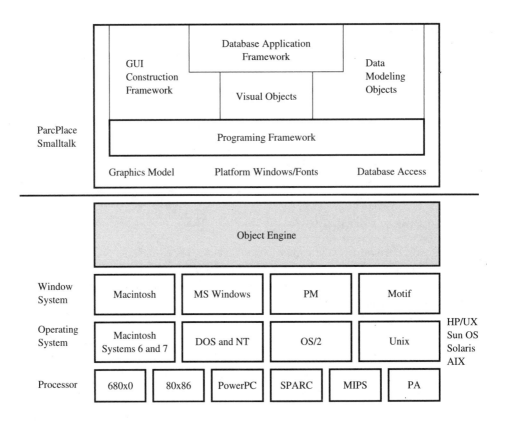

Figure 14.2   Portability Architecture for ParcPlace Smalltalk

Object-oriented technology offers a general solution to creating portable applications because object systems provide late binding of a specification to different implementations at runtime. For example, an application can specify a visual widget that is bound at runtime to the host platform's actual widget. Or a Smalltalk code method can be compiled at runtime to the instruction set of the host platform. This runtime capability is referred to as dynamic compilation [Deutsch and Schiffman 1984].

Distributed Open Systems

The idea behind open systems is simple. Software interoperates—even software from competing vendors—because it is delivered in the form of components that have well-defined interfaces. A text editor from one vendor, a spreadsheet from another, and a charting program from yet a third, can be plugged together and used with the appearance of being designed as a whole. An organization can buy best-of-breed solutions, and take full advantage of the cost competition and innovation of the open marketplace. Software bought today will work with software invented a year from now. And tomorrow's inventions can easily slip into today's niche. Open systems make today's purchases safe choices.

The open systems approach applies to any layer of the system. Interoperability is achieved by creating a well-defined interface, commonly referred to as the application programming interface (API). One application interoperates with another by calling on the services named in the API. Unfortunately, there is not just one API for each type of software component. Where multiple APIs exist, each with a different naming convention, a higher-level abstraction is used to provide a common interface for applications. The abstract interface automatically translates for whichever API is to be used. Objects are good for implementing this abstract layer. When used in this way, we refer to objects as the "glue" that binds an application to the many APIs.

When one object calls on another, it is possible that they reside on different computers, that is, that the application relies on objects that are distributed across a network of computers. Open systems and distributed architectures are complementary. Independent system parts can execute on the same or on different platforms. However, being distributed does not imply that a system is open.

The combination of distributed and open systems introduces an opportunity for object-oriented technology, which is uniquely suited to define objects that call upon one another's services, independently of the location of the objects, of which programming language was used to describe the objects, and of which network protocols are used for object-to-object communication. This capability is offered by a special system component called an *object broker*. All applications have access to the object broker to request services from other objects. The broker, in turn, knows how to access these other services because every application that wishes to provide services informs the broker when the application is first installed.

The ability to call on services from distributed objects makes it easy to update reusers. The reusable asset is maintained in one place known to the object broker. Reusers are automatically updated because the broker accesses the latest version of the object.

CORBA—Common Object Request Broker Architecture—is an example of an object broker for a distributed system [Object Management Group 1991]. Several vendors sell products that are either CORBA compliant—for example, the IBM DSOM (Distributed System Object Model)—or have their own object brokering mechanisms. Microsoft's Object Linking and Embedding (OLE) is an example of the latter. Over time, differences among approaches will likely be resolved.

Client/Server Architectures

A client/server architecture is one in which multiple processes interact, one calling on the services of the other. In application terms, one application has the role of client or master, and the other is the server or slave. The client requests information or an action from the server. Any process in a client/server architecture can fulfill both roles: a client can be a server for some other client. The use of a client/server architecture necessitates careful factoring so its functions can be distributed across multiple computers as needed.

Clients rely on what the servers provide, not on how the servers carry out their work. This basic idea—separating the *what* from the *how*—is central to object-oriented technology, so many people think that objects are the appropriate enabling technology for implementing a client/server architecture. The appropriateness of objects does not mean that client/server systems have to be developed using objects, merely that the similarity makes objects a good choice.

As shown in Fig. 14.3, any layer of a system, acting as a client, might call on the services of some other system, the server. Any client or client layer, and any server, can be made up of components provided by multiple vendors or by the organization itself. And the clients and servers might reside on different workstations. The ability to use low-cost

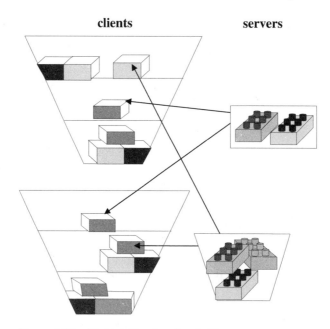

Figure 14.3   Multiple Vendors Supply Components
Accessible On Shared Servers

computers as the desktop clients, and to share services provided by high-performance workstations, represents a significant cost savings over the use of mainframe computers. Additional vendor software and workstations can be added to the organization's resources incrementally, and nearly transparently, as new services are required.

A typical application can be partitioned into four parts: user presentation and interaction, application logic (the software or "glue" that ties the user presentation to the business or technical model), the model itself, and management of business or technical data. These four parts of an application are shown in Fig. 14.4. The reason for factoring the application in this manner is to be able to use the right resources to support each aspect of the system.

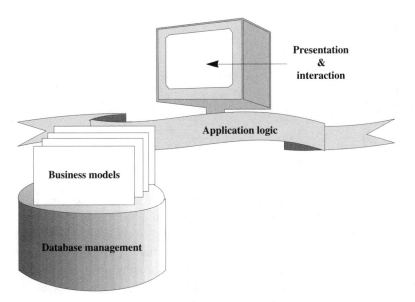

Figure 14.4   Typical Application Parts

Figure 14.5 shows several configurations of the client/server architecture. The configurations differ in the way the four parts of an application are distributed across client and server platforms. The sloped line in the figure draws the boundary between functionality and data that reside on clients (above the line) or servers (below the line). The vertical lines indicate the network that links the parts of the application. Objects that compose the application communicate by sending messages over this network. In the figure, we show clients and servers as singles or multiples, indicating that all combinations are possible, although not drawn. We use small blocks to denote objects, and show objects as being used throughout the system.

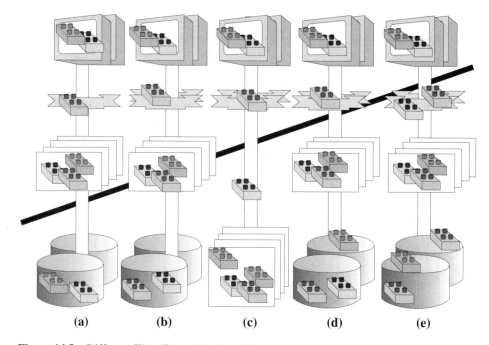

Figure 14.5   Different Client/Server Configurations

Configuration (a) depicts a common use of a client/server architecture, with the server being a database or file-based storage medium accessed by client applications. Configuration (b) indicates that the business processing can be done on both the client and the server. This decision is usually based on finding the appropriate processing capacity to carry out the computations, and ensuring security where required. In configuration (c), we eliminate the database. The database of static items is replaced by an executable business or technical model, waiting to be called upon for information or processing. When you take advantage of the idea that objects encapsulate the data they require, a separate static data store is not required. Configuration (d) indicates that the logic linking the user presentation and interaction to the business model could be factored and distributed across the client/server boundary. The last configuration represents remote presentation, where the client simply handles the operations for painting the screen. All other processing and information reside in one or more servers. This configuration essentially represents a computer mainframe with multiple terminals.

Does object-oriented technology require the use of a client/server architecture? No, there are plenty of object-oriented applications that do not have such an architecture. The choice of architecture is tied more to the goals and objectives of the organization, in particular to your desire for a distributed, scaleable, shared, open architecture. An organization that adopts both client/server and objects will create a powerful synergy.

Retaining an Investment in Prior Technology

An important software development consideration is the extent to which existing applications can be retained. This consideration is of especial interest when new applications are to be written using object-oriented technology, while existing applications are not object-oriented. This is referred to as the legacy problem—or opportunity, depending on your perspective.

Legacy systems cause a problem, not because they were written poorly, or because they have difficult interfaces, or because they were not written using today's preferred programming language. The basic problem with legacy systems is that they were designed for a set of assumptions that no longer holds. They were often written for mainframe computers without the benefit of independent database management systems. Or the database systems assumed that data and the use of the data should be separately managed. Few legacy systems provided users with graphical interfaces.

Another legacy issue involves the people who built the existing applications. You can retain these people with their current skills simply to maintain the legacy software. But these people are valuable assets—they know your business. It is usually easier to train people in the concepts and mechanisms of object-oriented technology than it is to build up the business expertise that existing people already have. We discuss how to reskill your people in Chapter 18. Here we discuss the use of legacy software: whether to keep the legacy systems as-is and find a way for them to coexist with new development, or to replace these systems.

Keep As-Is and Coexist

The conservative approach is to declare that what works should continue to be used, as-is. The legacy system becomes a single "object" in that its functionality is accessed via some existing or added interface. The idea is to create a layer of software that clearly specifies the legacy system's services in terms of the syntax of your selected object-oriented system, and translates any messages into calls to the existing software. Some people call such a software layer a "wrapper" because it encapsulates the legacy software, now treated as the hidden implementation of the counterfeit object. Figure 14.6 depicts a legacy system that is encapsulated within a wrapper object.

The wrapper solution enables the new software to interoperate with the old software. It requires you to maintain the legacy systems. Maintenance effort increases because changes in the legacy system may have to be reflected in the wrapper code. Some software development environments provide tools that automatically create wrappers. Several different approaches are available depending on whether the legacy software is to be included as part of the new software package, or treated as a server in a distributed system.

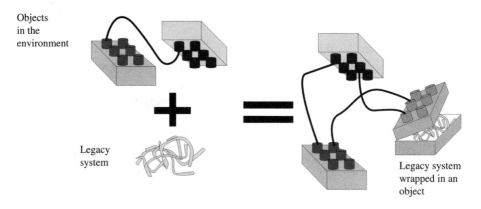

Objects in the environment

Legacy system

Legacy system wrapped in an object

Figure 14.6   Retaining a Legacy System by Adding an Object Wrapper

Keep Temporarily Until Complete Transition

If you intend eventually to replace the legacy system with an object-oriented one, then you can use an incremental development and integration strategy, replacing parts of the legacy system over time. It is possible to create a replacement system all at once, and then carry out a parallel test and deployment. But replacing all of a legacy system in one pass is often not practical and is generally risky, especially if you need to respecify the legacy system. By using a planned transition with incremental changes, you are more likely to maintain the users' trust.

The incremental approach works best when there are well-defined subsystems within the legacy software. These subsystems are the pieces that can be incrementally replaced—for example, database subsystems, or business logic subsystems, or user interface subsystems.

The first step is to understand the relationships among the various legacy subsystems. Specifying the functionality of a long-lived legacy system may be difficult. Reverse engineering tools may be helpful, as might design documents and organizational folklore. Once the architecture of the legacy system is understood, the evolution can begin.

Figure 14.7 illustrates one way to transition legacy software from a monolithic system containing a collection of embedded databases, to a set of applications made up of interacting objects and using a shared database. First you extract the embedded data and move the information into a shared database that can be accessed by both the legacy system and new applications, as shown in step (a). All new applications are built to access the shared database. You modify the legacy system (steps b and c) to access the databases in their new shared format. This modification often requires what we call software scaffolding.

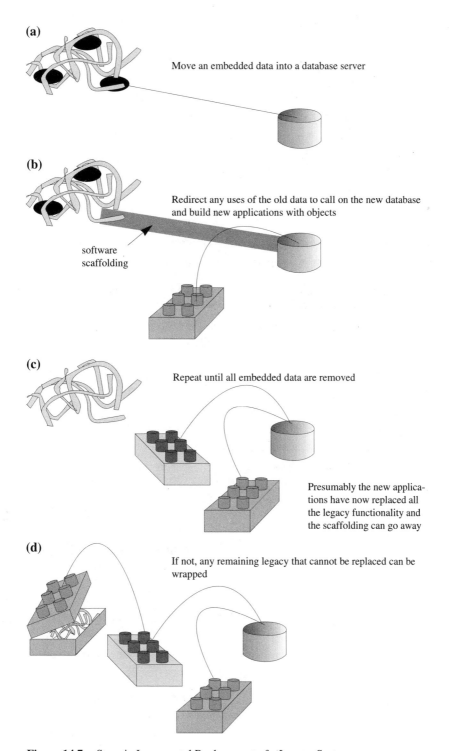

(a) Move an embedded data into a database server

(b) Redirect any uses of the old data to call on the new database and build new applications with objects

software scaffolding

(c) Repeat until all embedded data are removed

Presumably the new applications have now replaced all the legacy functionality and the scaffolding can go away

(d) If not, any remaining legacy that cannot be replaced can be wrapped

Figure 14.7   Steps in Incremental Replacement of a Legacy System

Software scaffolding is code that is used temporarily to bridge a gap between parts of a system, much as a painter constructs a scaffold that provides access to parts of a building. Scaffolds are torn down when the painter's task is completed. Since software scaffolds are temporary, it is best to plan the process carefully so that no one is surprised when the time comes actually to throw away the scaffolding code. Software scaffolding must be correct. Simplicity and safety are the critical design constraints for scaffold building.

Once the legacy system has been revised to remove all embedded databases and functionality that is linked to these databases, parts of the legacy system may still remain. You have to rewrite these to interoperate with the new software, or you have to create a wrapper object around them all.

Illustration: Reengineering a Mainframe World to a Client/Server Open Systems Architecture

American Management Systems (AMS), a management consulting and systems integration firm, moved a large mainframe legacy system onto a system with a distributed open systems architecture. The goals of AMS's Mobile2000 project were to create a graphical user interface to existing legacy code (reusing the legacy code without change), and to develop a process model for doing similar projects.

Mobile2000 is a customer service and billing system that supports large cellular carriers. It is a transaction-based system written in COBOL using IBM mainframe products: MVS/CSA, DB2, and CICS. It is a large system, measured by the approximately 200 on-line screens, 18,000 function points, and 800,000 lines of code written in the Intersolv APS Macro Customization Facility. The expanded version of the APS code totals more than 3 million lines of COBOL code.

Owen Walcher, in an experience report to the ACM OOPSLA'93 audience, stated that the key reason AMS was successful in revising Mobile2000 was because the original legacy system had an application architecture. System calls could be isolated from the actual application logic, so that the rewrite done on the client workstation and on the server mainframe did not require any application or top-tier code revision. All of the CICS commands, DB2 access, and systems-specific calls were embedded in a common software layer.

The revised Mobile2000 systems architecture consists of three primary components: client workstations (replacing 3270 terminals), servers (OS/2 server, Unix server, and the mainframe), and a communication channel that links clients and servers together.

AMS views objects as the glue that makes it possible to plug subsystems together. The subsystems or partitions of Mobile2000 are:

Common facilities	Security checking, error processing, printing, log-on and log-off, and so forth
Process manager	Tracking simultaneous use of multiple systems

Transaction manager	Protocol-independent network services providing datagram services
Business logic and data	Applying validation rules and maintaining customer service data
Presentation logic	Providing data and process access

All business logic and data access methods are in a single COBOL program that resides on the mainframe. To attach the workstation to a server, AMS developed a transparent communications level, whereby an object converts itself into a data stream. The data stream goes out on the network and the language interpreter on the server knows how to convert the data into either an object (for object-to-object coordination) or a query to a relational database. The first workstation subsystem was a reimplementation of the mainframe's Service Request Processing capability. Redesign of the data-input formats and use of a window construction tool made it possible to recreate quickly the mainframe customer information screens. This simplistic approach left AMS with software that frequently failed when they attempted to update the data on the server because no validation was performed in the workstation presentation software. Hence the next step was to migrate the business logic for validation from the mainframe to the client workstations.

The software on the mainframe server was a COBOL application. Using the APS Macro PreCompiler, AMS created a language that emulated the mechanisms of inheritance (similar to the way PL/1 was changed for the Brooklyn Union Gas project by Andersen Consulting). Owen describes the AMS approach:

> The crux behind the mainframe code is the first line in our source code is a $ program. It sets up your identification division. It sets up all of your working storage. It copies in common modules. It also does things like figuring out "am I being compiled as a 3270 program or as a GUI stored procedure?" By tweaking the macros just a little bit, we were able to completely recompile all those 200 on-line programs into callable stored procedures. Not bad for reuse. Each program has embedded business logic and data. So what we're doing is treating each of those COBOL programs as an object, and mapping from the GUI object, which is more domain-oriented, to the actual implementation. We're also migrating those COBOL programs off the mainframe onto the PC, and we're investigating running the COBOL programs themselves on the PC to perform all the validation prior to sending it to the mainframe, enabling us to ensure that the edits will be passed. Next, programs actually know whether they're a GUI program or a 3270 program so a user sitting at a 3270 console adding a customer and someone sitting right next to him on a GUI adding a customer, actually execute the same piece of code back on the server. It's just pointed to and entered in a different fashion. So we have no duplicated source. We just compile the same source down two different paths.

As their next transitioning step, AMS is throwing away the back-end program, and plugging their new applications directly into the database using SQL queries and updates. All new subsystems are designed using object-oriented analysis and design techniques. Their process model for using object-oriented technology is still evolving. In fact, they think that one of their failures was in not developing a large object model of the entire domain at the onset of the project. The lack of upfront domain analysis caused frequent reworking of the object model within their implementation language (Smalltalk) to take better advantage of inheritance, reworking that they believe would not have occurred if the object model had been based on a domain analysis.

Summary

You have to select a software development environment to meet the diverse requirements and expectations of developers and users. This chapter reviewed several requirements that can be met with special development tools, and expectations that influence the choice of the basic environment. Users expect to be developers, which complicates the question of who will use the software development environment and whether it is possible to select different environments for possibly diverse levels of analysis, design, implementation, and business knowledge. Despite the diversity of knowledge levels, it might still be necessary to coordinate work effort among developers and users. Coordination tools should help manage the efforts of multiple team members or of multiple teams.

The target user environment drives the choice of software development tools as well, because some development tools make it easier to maintain systems that will be changed by users, to port systems to multiple target platforms, or incrementally to add functionality provided by multiple vendors. We offered descriptions of cross-platform portability, distributed open systems, and client/server architectures as considerations in choosing a software development environment. Similarly, we discussed the need for special tools to assist in retaining access to legacy systems or to reimplement a legacy system using object-oriented technology.

Additional Reading About Expectations for a Software Development Environment

Magazines and Conference Proceedings: *Dr. Dobb's Journal* is typically a good source for up-to-date information about software development environments generally. *Object Magazine* focuses on development environments that claim to be object-oriented. You can also check the proceedings of popular software conferences, such as the ACM's OOPSLA (Object-Oriented Programming Systems, Languages, and Applications); ECOOP, the European Conference on Object-Oriented Programming; or the IEEE Computer Society International Conference on Computer Systems and Software Engineering.

Object Management Group, *The Common Object Request Broker: Architecture and Specification*, OMG Document Number 91-12-1, OMG Publications: Boulder, Colo., 1991.

Object Management Group, *Common Object Services Specification*, Vol. 1, OMG Document Number 94-1-1, Wiley and Sons: New York, March 1994.

The Object Management Group publishes a number of documents that provide guidelines, specifications, or comparisons of software development architectures, environments, and tools. The two listed here document CORBA and its associated naming, event, and life cycle services.

Shriver, B. and Wegner, P., eds., *Research Directions in Object-Oriented Programming*, MIT Press: Cambridge, Mass., 1987.

This book is a collection of papers that attempt to outline research issues of interest in the late 1980s. Much of the research continues today, so the papers remain timely reading. The papers cover language concepts, object-oriented environments, object-oriented databases, and theoretical concepts. The environments described include the multiparadigm system Garden by Steven Reiss and the special framework for user interface design called Impulse-88. The paper by Harold Ossher on how to specify large, layered systems is of special interest.

CHAPTER 15

Analysis and Design Methods and Tools

A perfect method should not only be an efficient one, as respects the accomplishment of the objects for which it is designed, but should in all its parts and processes manifest a unity and harmony.

George Boole

Second only to the choice of a programming language, the selection of an analysis-and-design method elicits considerable emotion. The energy is appropriately spent given the extent to which methods influence how you think about your problem domain, system architecture, and product process models. Until recently, analysis-and-design methods were equated to notation, and the software tools to support the methods were little more than computer-assisted drawing tools. In the last few years, software developers have become more sophisticated in their understanding of the benefits of complete and understandable methods, and are challenging the researchers and commercial vendors to make clear distinctions among the important ideas of process models, methods, and notations.

Process Models, Methods, and Notations

Three aspects of software development are often confused: process model, method, and notation. They are related but different. Chapter 5 defines a process model as a collection of maxims, strategies, activities, and methods that are organized to achieve a set of goals and objectives. We discuss several process models, those for developing products and those for establishing a reuse infrastructure.

A *method* consists of the concepts, techniques, and steps used to implement a process model activity.[1] A *notation* is used to communicate the artifacts that result from applying a method. The tokens of the notation may be graphical, textual, or some combination of the two.

Figure 15.1 illustrates the relationships among process models, methods, and notations. The left side of the figure illustrates possible activities of a process model, the middle enumerates example methods for carrying out these activities, and the right side shows example notations for capturing the results of methods.

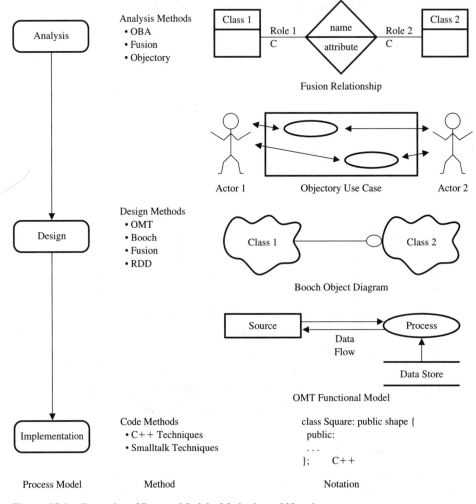

Figure 15.1   Examples of Process Models, Methods, and Notations

---

[1] We use the word "methodology" to mean the study of methods, and employ "method" when we wish to refer to a particular set of concepts and techniques.

What Is Analysis?

Analysis focuses on what a system is supposed to do, rather than on how it is supposed to do it. An *analysis method* is a set of concepts, techniques, and steps used to construct a model of the problem. Figure 15.2 illustrates a process for conducting analysis.

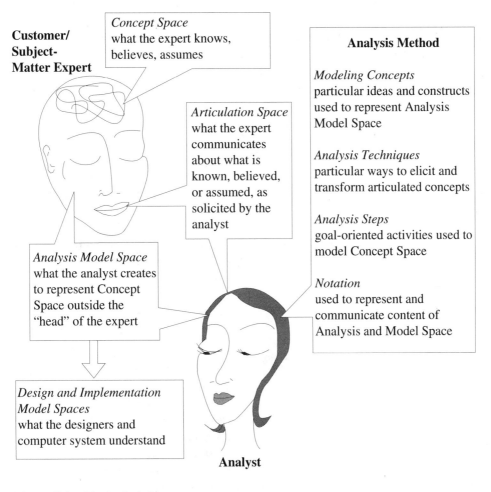

Customer/ Subject- Matter Expert

Concept Space what the expert knows, believes, assumes

Articulation Space what the expert communicates about what is known, believed, or assumed, as solicited by the analyst

Analysis Model Space what the analyst creates to represent Concept Space outside the "head" of the expert

Design and Implementation Model Spaces what the designers and computer system understand

Analyst

Analysis Method

Modeling Concepts particular ideas and constructs used to represent Analysis Model Space

Analysis Techniques particular ways to elicit and transform articulated concepts

Analysis Steps goal-oriented activities used to model Concept Space

Notation used to represent and communicate content of Analysis and Model Space

Figure 15.2   The Analysis Process

According to Fig. 15.2, analysis involves two individuals (actually two roles) working through three information spaces: Concept, Articulation, and Model.[2] The first person

---

[2] These ideas were developed based on our work with Gurdon Blackwell of Gemini Consulting, Morristown, New Jersey, and originally published in [Rubin and Goldberg 1993].

is a user or customer, a subject-matter expert who understands the problem to be solved. We assume the problem is quite complex, and is maintained in the expert's Concept Space—that is, in the head of the expert. The expert's understanding of the problem is multifaceted and highly associative. When the expert also develops the system, the principal manifestation of the concept outside of the expert's head is likely to be a direct solution—for example, a spreadsheet or interface to a database or specialization of an application framework.

The real challenge of analysis begins when the expert must communicate the concept to someone else—to an analyst, as depicted in the figure. Since the concept is often very rich and expansive, it is generally not possible for experts adequately to communicate their entire understanding in a single, holistic expression. As a result, they are forced to provide multiple explanations, verbal or written. The analyst prompts for and captures these explanations (we call this Articulation Space), and pieces them together into a coherent representation (Analysis Model Space).

Analysis is particularly difficult when the experts are unable to articulate what they know, or are uncertain or even incoherent as to their knowledge or beliefs. As Fig. 15.3 illustrates, the distance between the expert's brain and mouth can be large. What is clear-

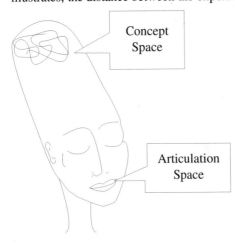

ly understood in the brain may be poorly expressed by the mouth.

The Modeling Concepts, Analysis Techniques, and Analysis Steps represented in Fig. 15.2 compose the analysis method that guides the way the analyst manipulates the Articulation and Analysis Model Spaces. The Modeling Concepts that come from object-oriented technology include objects, classes, class hierarchies, and other object relationships. There are also constructs for describing the dynamics of the system, such as scenarios, events, and object-level state models. A possible way to elicit what the expert knows is to request a walkthrough of the proposed system, which can be captured in a script.

Figure 15.3   Articulation of Knowledge May Be Difficult

Analysis Techniques and Analysis Steps direct and guide the analyst in transforming the information provided by the experts into the representations of the analysis model in Analysis Model Space. You can think of Articulation Space as a convenient place for the experts and analysts to meet. Here they agree on how they will talk with one another (possibly including the structure of sentences and definitions of words to be used). The precise nature of their exchanges depends on the Analysis Techniques. It is here that the various object-oriented analysis methods diverge. Although most methods agree on the concepts for modeling a problem, they disagree on the techniques for employing these concepts to create the analysis model. For example, Shlaer-Mellor [Shlaer and Mellor 1988] adapts entity-relationship modeling, equating objects to entities, while Object Behavior Analysis (OBA) [Rubin and Goldberg 1992] identifies system behaviors, using these behaviors to derive system roles and responsibilities.

Analysis Steps are goal-oriented activities that employ the Analysis Techniques to model the Concept Space in a form representable in Analysis Model Space. For example, OBA scripting is a technique, whereas OBA includes a step ("Create Script Model") that requires that scripts be created. Methods specify a preferred sequence for applying the steps, although in practice steps are applied opportunistically (as we discuss in Chapter 5). Figure 15.2 also shows the existence of Notation. Notation is used by the analyst to represent the analysis model in Analysis Model Space, in a manner understandable by the subject-matter expert.

A goal of analysis is to minimize the differences between Concept and Analysis Model Spaces.[3] In the best of all worlds, no transformation would be needed to move from Concept to Analysis Model Space—that is, each aspect in the expert's concept model would have a direct correspondent in the analysis model. One of the benefits of object-oriented technology is that the transformation from Concept to Analysis Model Space is considerably more natural and efficient than with other technologies. Indeed, some cognitive science research indicates that people think in terms of objects [Rosson and Alpert 1990].

The expert reviews the analysis model to determine whether it accurately depicts his or her understanding of the problem. If the distance between the analysis model and the expert's understanding is large, it will be quite difficult, if not impossible, for the expert to verify accuracy. Consequently, one of the principal requirements of any analysis model is that it be understandable to the expert. The extent to which this is possible is directly related to the nature of the Modeling Concepts and the notation used to represent the various aspects of the analysis model.

What Is Design?

Design is really two activities: architectural design and detailed design. Architectural design involves making strategic decisions about how system functionality is factored among independent system components, how components relate, and how control trans-

---

[3] Any transformation introduces the possibility of errors when moving from one space or representation to another. This is a failing of Structured Analysis and Structured Design—a significant number of large transformations is required when moving through the steps of the process.

fers from one component to another. It often includes a specification of how users give and receive information, and how the system communicates with other systems. Detailed design consists of tactical decisions, such as the choice of algorithms and data structures to meet performance and space objectives.

Figure 15.2 indicates that the development process continues from analysis to design and implementation. Developers change the analysis model by adding implementation constraints, such as the choice of user platform, the style of user presentation, or the database management system. To satisfy these constraints, the analysis model is transformed, for example, by the addition of objects to handle communication between the application and platform-specific components. The design may include a decision to use an existing domain or application framework, or other appropriate reusable assets. And so the analysis model can be transformed by mapping analysis objects onto corresponding reusable assets. The resulting design model can then be implemented using the development environment of choice.

Object-oriented analysis and design have much in common. The same object-oriented concepts, techniques, and notations used in analysis apply equally well in design. As a consequence, the same development tools can be used to support both activities. Often, these similarities make it hard to tell which activity is being carried out. As a litmus test, use the following: If the current task is specifying part of the problem, as the customer or expert deals with it, then the task is analysis. If the task is developing part of the solution, then it is design. In the presence of opportunistic development, it is not generally useful to force a distinction.

The lack of a clear distinction between analysis and design confuses critics of object-oriented technology, who complain that doing object-oriented analysis means solving rather than understanding the problem. These critics point out that there is often a one-to-one mapping between the objects in the analysis model and those in the design model. So they assume that the object-oriented analyst, by definition, creates a solution. What these critics see as a flaw is in fact one of the most important benefits of object-oriented technology—the representation of the solution is a direct consequence of the representation of the problem.

Analysis and Design Techniques in Support of Object-Oriented Concepts

Several analysis techniques have been proposed for finding objects in the problem domain:

- Highlighting requirements—Underline nouns and verbs in the requirements specification

- CRC cards—Brainstorm among a group of experts

- Scenario—Capture system behaviors in scripts or use cases

- Information engineering—Identify the information structure that is stored and maintained by applications, and map it to objects

Our own work on Object Behavior Analysis recommends scenarios.

Highlighting requirements. Highlighting refers to using a colored pen to mark significant passages of text in a document. Figuratively, if not literally, analysts who use this technique read a document and highlight the nouns and verbs. The assumption is that the nouns will be the objects of the system, the verbs will be the services of the objects, and the adjectives will be the attributes of the objects.

Both the Object Modeling Technique (OMT) [Rumbaugh *et al.* 1991] and Responsibility-Driven Design (RDD) [Wirfs-Brock, Wilkerson, and Wiener 1990] recommended the highlighting technique for finding the initial objects that represent the problem.

> Not all classes are explicit in the problem statement; some are implicit in the application domain or general knowledge . . . Don't be too selective; write down every class that comes to mind. Classes often correspond to nouns. [Rumbaugh *et al.* 1991, p. 153]

> Read through the requirements specification carefully . . . looking for noun phrases. Change all plurals to singulars, and make a preliminary list. It is likely, looking over that list, that you will mentally divide the items on it into three categories: obvious objects, obvious nonsense, and phrases you are not sure about. [Wirfs-Brock, Wilkerson, and Wiener 1990, pp. 37–38]

Two facts undermine the highlighting technique. First, it assumes that a complete, formal, and correct requirements specification exists. The existence of such a specification is almost certainly not true for large systems. Indeed, the absence of a requirements specification is often the reason object-oriented technology is chosen. Second, underlining nouns and the verbs in some document is not likely to yield satisfactory design results, because many of the key design objects are abstract and thus would not necessarily appear in any written description. This technique is biased toward accounting for the tangible aspects of a problem—those things that can be seen, heard, felt, smelled, tasted. It gives little advice on how to identify objects that represent the intangible policies, synchronizers, and coordinators that govern a business or technical situation.

CRC cards. CRC cards were invented by Ward Cunningham and Kent Beck [Beck 1993] as a way to help a group of people agree on objects that represent the problem (and the solution, since the CRC authors make no distinction between analysis and design). CRC stands for Class-Responsibility-Collaborators. The class represents the name of an object. Responsibilities describe what the object does in the system. And the collaborators are the other objects that are involved in carrying out the responsibilities. CRC focuses on which objects exist in the system, and how the objects divide the work to be done. Members of the group role-play the proposed uses of the system, taking turns pretending to be one of the objects on a card, and seeing whether the responsibilities and collaborators are sufficient for carrying out some scenario.

CRC does not provide a technique for finding objects, but a technique for reorganizing (and generalizing) already discovered objects.

> Rather than worrying about all possible issues that could be dealt with during design, CRC tells us that by focusing on classes, responsibilities, and collaborators early in the design, we will arrive at systems that make good use of objects . . . picking names and distributing responsibilities have the largest downstream effects, and therefore should be done first. [Beck 1993, p. 42]

The developers of CRC recommend capturing CRC results with a simple textual notation on ordinary index cards—these are often referred to as CRC cards. The "cards" are often self-sticking notes that are pasted all over conference room walls as a way to help the group manipulate the evolving object model. The developers' experiences show that cards can be used to represent a modest-sized system. RDD, and Booch in his revision to the Booch method [Booch 1994], both recommend the use of some form of CRC cards.

Scenario. A *scenario* is a sequence of actions that can take place in the problem domain. Constructing scenarios helps to determine the necessary behaviors of a system, and to assign responsibility for carrying out these behaviors to various roles, as played by objects. Both OBA and Objectory [Jacobson *et al.* 1992] recommend the use of scenarios.

In OBA, the technique of building scenarios is called *scripting*. The OBA scripting principles are adapted from those of cognitive psychology and artificial intelligence, which state that one way people store their understanding in Concept Space is by episodic memory. Episodic memory is a sequence of events that makes up a story or episode. By capturing the stories told by the expert, the analyst determines the roles and responsibilities required to represent the expert's understanding. OBA captures these stories in a format that uses the natural language expressions proposed by the expert, so the expert can determine whether the analyst correctly understands what is in the expert's Concept Space.

An OBA script consists of a series of contracts. Each contract is an agreement between two roles—the initiator and the participant. The initiator is responsible for performing an action, and the participant is responsible for providing a service. During design, objects are assigned system roles and their corresponding responsibilities. Initiators who are not participants are treated as objects that interact with the system unless the goal is to create a system simulation.

Objectory has similar goals: Sequences of actions are captured as *use cases* (a specific kind of scenario), and the objects that reside outside the system boundaries are called actors. Use cases identify three types of analysis objects: interface, entity, and control. Interface objects translate an actor's actions into events, and the system events into results an actor can understand. Entity objects model system information. And control objects are a catchall for behaviors not easily allocated to the other two types, essentially providing the glue that unites the other system objects.

Information engineering. Many object-oriented methods are evolutionary in the sense that they are extensions of traditional methods. One popular analysis technique that has been adapted for use with object-oriented technology is information engineering.

Information engineering builds conceptual models that describe the data required to operate an organization, activities that use this data, and the technologies for storing, maintaining, and manipulating the data. When applying the techniques of information engineering to object-oriented technology, the data orientation is recast in terms of object types, the ways these object types interrelate, and what events must occur to change the state of objects. Traditional information engineering relies on an enterprise-wide review of the organization to determine all of the information that might be needed and the events outside the system boundaries that invoke processing on this information. The information is packaged in data structures called entities. Entity types are related to one another, and usually entity-relationship diagrams describe the results of the analysis. An event model describes how an initial event triggers a series of system responses.

In object-oriented terms, entity models are cast as object models. Such techniques are generally useful if the problems to be analyzed are data-centric, and the system consists only of information-accessing behaviors. Otherwise, information engineering suffers from an inability to assist in modeling general behavior that is understood independent of data. Examples of methods that incorporate some form of information engineering include Fusion [Coleman *et al.* 1994], OMT, and Shlaer-Mellor. Fusion combines aspects of OMT and Booch. OMT combines data-flow modeling with entity-relationship and state-transition modeling. Shlaer-Mellor also combines information and state-transition modeling. Ptech [Martin and Odell 1992] is another hybrid approach that is founded on information engineering.

Choosing Analysis and Design Methods

Since you have chosen to use object-oriented technology, the only analysis-and-design methods you should choose from are those (1) whose Modeling Concepts (Fig. 15.2) are based on object-oriented concepts, and (2) whose end result is a model in Analysis Model Space which is close to what the expert understands, yet is expressed in the terminology of object concepts. The methods should provide Analysis Techniques that create both static and dynamic models of the system. The static model includes descriptions of the objects that exist in the system, their mutual relationships, and the operations that can be performed on the system. The dynamic model includes the legal sequence of operations on the system, as well as the sequence of messages among objects needed to perform system operations. Most of the conceptual differences among commercial methods have to do with which dynamic models are supported. (As an additional source on how to choose analysis-and-design methods, Hutt [Hutt 1994b] documents an approach to evaluating methods on a concept-by-concept basis.)

In addition, consider the following seven method characteristics.

Kind of information gathered. Good analysis-and-design methods provide a set of techniques for gathering information. These techniques are used to create a complete statement of the problem with which the domain experts concur, and the means for creating a solution that meets system quality objectives. If the goal of the project is to create reusable assets, then a consideration in selecting the analysis-and-design method is whether the method has techniques for developing reusable results.

Consistency requirements. Consistency is an attribute of a model in which all of the components are accurately and sufficiently related. Hence one of the earliest evaluation questions you should ask is, are the elements of the model properly related? In asking this question, you are probing the integrity of the model that the method can produce. Better methods prevent you from making mistakes that violate the basic concepts of the method, while acceptable methods at least have techniques that check to see whether violations exist.

Checks and balances must be part of the method, and should be enforced by method tools. Questions of accuracy belong to the method, but poor tools can confuse the question by allowing users to do things that the method actually does not recommend or allow. Make sure that the tools you choose either keep you from making mistakes or detect any method violations. This requirement means that simple notation drawing tools are of no interest as they are devoid of consistency management.

Another question that you might ask is, how do you know when you have modeled a complete problem or solution? Or perhaps a question more pertinent when using incremental development is, how do you know that you have done enough analysis work so that you can proceed to do some design and then some implementation? The second question refers to sufficiency, while the first to completeness. Both answers are tied to system partitioning techniques. The method must allow you to work on partitions independently, and clearly indicate where information is missing but not critical to continuing to next activities. And the tools associated with the method must support you in merging otherwise independently derived models. It should be clear from the notion of partitioning and independent work that, for large systems staffed by multiple analyzers and designers, consistency management will be the single most important issue.

Domain of applicability. Another basis for selecting an analysis-and-design method is its domain of applicability. Some methods apply only to applications based on sequential behavior, other methods handle concurrency, and still others are devised especially for real-time applications [Selic, Gullekson, and Ward 1994]. You should choose methods that support the characteristics of your domain.

Product process model. The methods you choose should also fit into your preferred process model. They should provide the expected inputs to activities of the product process model, especially documentation, and should not contradict the desired ordering of process model activities. Where the product process model has provisions for regular reviews, the methods should provide guidelines for reviewing the analysis and design models.

Is there something about object-oriented analysis-and-design methods that is especially useful or harmful to the ability to reuse? Reusing assumes that you can compose or refine something that already exists. Surprisingly, most object-oriented analysis-and-design methods proposed to date do not provide steps that focus on reusing. It is insufficient to make statements such as: "Now you are ready to pick a design—see if one already exists. Or if you have discovered a system event, see if a use case or script already exists to handle the event." Rather, a method must provide techniques and guidelines for how to fit these designs, use cases, or scripts into the evolving models. One useful example is a method that builds a common vocabulary for object names and messages, and makes a provision for incorporating existing vocabularies. As another example, OBA has a step that explicitly searches for existing architecture design objects, and reuses these designs by folding their roles and responsibilities into the models obtained using earlier OBA steps. These roles and responsibilities can then be factored or generalized as part of the overall OBA design process.

Maintenance considerations may also influence your choice of analysis-and-design method. We recommend that you select methods that retain sufficient information to explain why a particular object exists in the analysis, design, or implementation model. The explanation should trace back to assumptions, supporting facts, and the goals and objectives that led to the result. The objects that appear in the implementation should be consistent with those specified by the design model. Sometimes it is useful to be able to reverse engineer a system—that is, to derive the design model from the implementation. You may wish to evaluate the extent to which a method supports such reverse engineering.

Models created by analysis and design. One way to qualify a method is to determine whether the models you wish to produce can be derived from the information that is gathered and represented by the method. Let's suppose as an example that the model you wish to produce includes business rules that describe particular constraints the system must enforce. Alternatively, suppose you are required to generate a safety model for the system. Or perhaps you are required to deliver a performance model before you will be allowed to implement a solution.

Then the analysis-and-design methods you should consider are ones that either directly handle the requirement to elicit and represent these business rules or safety models or performance models, or can be augmented in order to derive the desired information. You evaluate the support provided by the method and its tools, and how much effort you have to expend to extract your required results.

Notations. Most methods can be compared by examining how the static and dynamic models are communicated—that is, what kind of textual representation or graphical diagram is recommended. A notation isn't right or wrong, only more or less effective at communicating results among team members. The goal is to choose the notation that is most effective for your teams. A good notation should have sufficient expressive power to model object concepts to the level of detail that you desire. Some notations have a larger vocabulary than others so they can represent greater levels of detail. You will also want a notation that allows you to represent analysis and design models at varying levels of abstraction.

A good notation is also one that can be learned and relearned quickly. Its symbols are meaningful and evocative. Can you guess how to interpret the notation? An expert in object-oriented technology certainly should be able to do so. Poorer notations express large semantic differences with small changes in tokens—the placement or orientation or scale of a token has deep semantic meaning that often only the notation designer can appreciate. This is in violation of the maxim of least astonishment:

Notations

Least astonishment. Notations should communicate information in a manner that minimizes surprise to the reader.

Since you may not always have tool support for drawing a notation, you will want a notation that can easily be drawn by hand.

Tools. It is not practical to consider methods independent of tools. Much of the effort involved in analysis and design involves handling information with complex interdependencies that have to be created and maintained over long time periods. Tools must be available to handle the information management aspects of a method. They also might generate complex diagrams and even some of the executable code.

All tools handle a single developer working on a single project. Some tools handle multiple developers working together on a single project, providing a shared repository, and a way to coordinate effort and to resolve any conflicts created by overlapping results. Multiple projects, often carried out at multiple sites, also require special tool support. Such tools are important in organizations that wish to provide a coordinated reuse program in which analysis and design models are treated as reusable assets.

Select tools based on the following criteria:

- The tool should provide explicit support for each step of the method.

- The tool should manage all of the information that the method requires you to collect or to specify.

- The tool should be able to handle the quantity of information you require (that is, it should scale to the size of your problem).

- The tool should include a mechanism by which you can check that the information you have collected is consistent.

- The tool should take on as much of the burden of layout and pretty-printing as possible for drawing the various diagrams.

- The tool should handle the number of simultaneous users on single or multiple projects that you require for your organization.

- Optionally, and depending on the kind of system you are building, the tool should be able to generate an initial executable implementation and hardcopy documentation. If any generated implementation is to be modified by the users, then the tool should provide a reverse engineering mechanism to make sure that implementation changes are consistent with the analysis-and-design models.

Table 15.1 summarizes some of the questions that you might ask as you review the different method offerings.

Why don't traditional methods suffice? Most organizations today use analysis-and-design methods that are not based on object-oriented concepts. They use traditional methods based on data modeling, functional decomposition, or data-flow diagramming. When such organizations wish to use an object-oriented language and libraries of reusable objects, do they have to change their approach to analysis and design? The argument in favor of change is a strong one. It is based on the disparity between traditional methods and the process models that are best suited to object-oriented technology, and between the analysis and design models created with traditional methods and the need for consistent object modeling throughout the life cycle.

Table 15.1 Summary of Method Selection Criteria

Selection Criteria	Description
Concepts addressed by the method	The method should support basic concepts that you believe are significant in solving your problem.
Is the choice a method or not?	Choose a method with concepts, techniques, and well-defined process steps, not merely a set of recommendations for a process model or a notation.
Notational appropriateness	The notation should be immediately understandable, and there should be a minimal subset for beginners. It should be drawable by hand.
Process model coverage	Choose a method that addresses well-identified activities of the process model.
Types of applications	Choose a method geared toward the kinds of applications your organization builds.
Customizability	If you expect to refine any method you choose, then select one that identifies appropriate aspects for customization. Alternatively, if you expect to compose several methods, make sure the inputs and outputs (or points of overlap) are complementary.
Evolutionary vs. revolutionary approach	Choose a method that is consistent with your organization's ability to bring in new technology (see Chapter 17).
Learnability	Make sure your people can learn the proposed method.
Traceability	Choose a method that maintains a clear and consistent mapping among artifacts.
Scalability	Choose a method (and related tools) that address the size problem you must solve. A method needs to scale up and scale down to the needs of a project.
Collateral material	Choose a method that produces the collateral documents required by your organization.
Tool environment	Choose tools that are well integrated, with an open access to the information collected using the different tools.
Marketplace momentum	Choose a method and tools that you are confident will have sustaining life in the marketplace, ones for which there is ample training and consultants available.

Traditional methods, especially functional decomposition, assume that all of the primary requirements are representable as functions that are related in a fixed hierarchical structure and can be implemented in the same fashion. This approach fails to take into account the incremental and iterative development strategies for building systems with object-oriented technology; it fails to recognize that people solve problems in an unstructured manner. Moreover, functions that are locked in a hierarchy tend to support only one specific superfunction. This makes reuse difficult, if not impossible.

Traditional methods are founded on the thesis that data and function should be separated so that new functions can be added that make use of a common source of data. Most of the techniques of traditional methods deal with how to model data. Any consideration of the desired functionality—which justifies the existence of the data—is thrown out by the time the data dictionaries are specified. The idea that data is independent of function contradicts the conceptual basis of object-oriented technology.

We have seen case study projects that successfully used traditional methods with object-oriented technology. There are two reasons they succeeded. First, they extracted a subset of the traditional methods for gathering requirements, and then they reverted to prototyping. Second, they used the traditional methods to define the data dictionary, and then relied on tools provided by the vendors of object technology products to help them map from this schema to the objects in the executing applications. They had to do the work twice to figure out the system behaviors and the associated data.

Is it reasonable to combine multiple methods? People combine methods when they do not find a single method that provides the techniques and steps leading, in their eyes, to a sufficiently complete result. Combining methods is risky, unless each method is focused on different activities—for example, one on requirements gathering and the other on constructing a design, and the artifacts from one method provide information useful to the other method. Otherwise, the effort to combine methods can become a research project to create a new method, starting with several existing ones. Be careful not to collect information required by a single method that has no value when the method is combined with other methods.

Is it reasonable to combine multiple notations? There are multimethod, multinotation products on the market today. The idea is appealing if you think of these tools as repository managers, whereby information gathered by one or more methods can be stored in a common representation and then shown in your preferred notation. One tools fits all projects, while still administering a single common repository. The idea is appealing, but its practical execution may not be. First, you risk creating a large data store of unrelated information, not well attuned to any one method. Second, you risk creating a situation in which the artifacts used in the organization are not consistent. If you choose this route, you will have to create your own consistency manager that crosses methods. You might want to choose one method but allow multiple notations, which makes sense only if the multiple notations can represent the artifacts generated by the method. The success of current tools providing multiple notations is clearly associated with the fact that the competing methods are all fundamentally similar with regard to the modeling concepts they support.

Summary

In this chapter, we clarified the distinction between process models, methods, and notations, and defined what we mean by analysis and design. We then reviewed the various techniques that have been proposed for finding objects in the problem domain, namely requirements highlighting, CRC cards, scenarios, and information engineering. We also provided a brief summary of the kinds of models that are often created to capture both the static and dynamic information about a system.

Choosing an analysis-and-design method is a complex endeavor that takes into account the kinds of information gathered, support for product or reuse process models, ability to check models for completeness and consistency, learnability, availability of tools for single or multiple developers on a project, and so forth. In keeping with the nature of this book, which explains the decisions you must make when adopting object-oriented technology, we do not advocate any one analysis-and-design method, but we do ask you to consider your choice carefully based on the criteria we outline in Table 15.1, placing considerable importance on support for consistency and traceability.

Additional Reading About Analysis and Design Methods

Arnold, P., Bodoff, S., Coleman, D., Gilchrist, H., and Hayes, F., *An Evaluation of Five Object-Oriented Development Methods*, Hewlett Packard Laboratories, Bristol, United Kingdom, Report No. HPL-91-52, June 1991.

  This study, conducted by Hewlett Packard, evaluates the methods of Booch, Buhr, OMT, RDD, and HOOD (Hierarchical Object-Oriented Design). Call 415-857-4573 for pricing and availability.

Hutt, A., ed., *Object Analysis and Design: Description of Methods*, Wiley and Sons: New York, 1994(a).

Hutt, A., ed., *Object Analysis and Design: Comparison of Methods*, Wiley and Sons: New York, 1994(b).

  In 1993, the OMG Object Analysis and Design Special Interest Group set out to create a technical framework for object-oriented concepts that would form the basis for comparing methods. The group created a survey that was filled out by developers of 21 methods. The responses were published as submitted in the first cited document. The second document describes how the committee processed the survey to compare the different methods.

Monarchi, D. E. and Puhr, G. I., A Research Typology for Object-Oriented Analysis and Design, *Communications of the ACM*, 35(9), 35-47, September 1992.

This article compares 23 object-oriented analysis-and-design methods to identify common themes, and strengths and weaknesses of such methods in general.

Definitive books on the object-oriented analysis-and-design methods:

Booch

Booch, G., *Object-Oriented Analysis and Design with Applications*, 2d Ed., Benjamin Cummings: Redwood City, Calif., 1994.

Fusion

Coleman, D., Arnold, P., Bodoff, S., Dollin, C., Gilchrist, H., Hayes, F., and Jeremaes, P., *Object-Oriented Development: The Fusion Method*, Prentice Hall: Englewood Cliffs, New Jersey, 1994.

HOOD

Robinson, P., *Hierarchical Object-Oriented Design*, Prentice Hall International: United Kingdom, 1992.

Object Behavior Analysis

Rubin, K. S. and Goldberg, A., Object Behavior Analysis, *Communications of the ACM*, 35(9), 48-62, September 1992.

Objectory

Jacobson, I., Christerson, M., Jonsson, P., and Övergaard, G., *Object-Oriented Software Engineering: A Use Case–Driven Approach*, ACM Press: Reading, Mass., 1992.

OMT

Rumbaugh, J., Blaha, M., Premerlani, W., Eddy, F., and Lorensen, W., *Object-Oriented Modeling and Design*, Prentice Hall: Englewood Cliffs, New Jersey, 1991.

Ptech

Martin, J. and Odell, J. J., *Object-Oriented Analysis and Design*, Prentice Hall: Englewood Cliffs, New Jersey, 1992.

RDD

Wirfs-Brock, R., Wilkerson, B., and Wiener, L., *Designing Object-Oriented Software*, Prentice Hall: Englewood Cliffs, New Jersey, 1990.

Shlaer-Mellor

Shlaer, S. and Mellor, S. J., *Object-Oriented Systems Analysis: Modeling the World in Data*, Yourdon Press: Englewood Cliffs, New Jersey, 1988.

SOMA

Graham, I., *Object-Oriented Methods*, Addison-Wesley: Wokingham, England, 1994.

CHAPTER **16**

Languages, Libraries, Tools, and Databases

An object-oriented programming language is a language for describing system behavior and information representation that includes the syntax and semantics of objects, relationships among objects, and object control based on message-passing. A library is a collection of services that the developer can call upon. The services for an object-oriented library will be packaged in the form of individual objects, object hierarchies, and collections of objects representing a framework, subsystem, or application. Tools associated with languages and libraries support the specification and execution of systems described in terms of object interactions, including interactions with objects in the library. A database holds the information that persists between uses of the system, such as application data and objects in the library.

This chapter continues our discussion of the basis for selecting a software development environment, with criteria for choosing a programming language, database, and related tools and libraries.

Choosing a Programming Language

The several object-oriented languages that are available commercially or as research results from universities differ in how they support basic object concepts, such as: encapsulation, polymorphism, and inheritance. These languages also differ in the support they provide for type declaration, runtime execution, and late binding of variable names to objects and message names to implementations. Table 16.1 summarizes the benefits and

Table 16.1   Benefits and Drawbacks of Language Mechanisms

Concept/ Mechanism	Benefits	Drawbacks	Languages
Object Abstraction			
Classes or templates	Capture similarity among like objects	Overhead for applications that have many one-of-a-kind objects	C++, CLOS, Eiffel, Objective C, Smalltalk
Encapsulation			
Multiple levels	Flexibility in controlling visibility	Reduces potential for reuse	C++, CLOS
Circumvention	Potential performance boost by avoiding message-passing as a way of accessing data	Violates an object's encapsulation and introduces tight coupling between objects	C++, CLOS, Objective C
Polymorphism			
Unbounded polymorphism	Flexibility in prototyping and maintenance to replace an object with another object that supports the required interface	Inhibits static type checking	CLOS, Objective C, Smalltalk
Bounded polymorphism	Provides additional information for type checking and optimization	Reduces the flexibility of object references	C++, Eiffel
Inheritance			
Of interface specification without implementation	Promotes behavior reuse and object substitution	In isolation no drawback, but if there is no implementation inheritance, then forces redundant coding	C++, Eiffel
Of implementation	Promotes code reuse	Inheritance hierarchies may not reflect object type specializations	C++, CLOS, Eiffel, Objective C, Smalltalk
Multiple	Useful when a class is viewed as a combination of two or more different superclasses	Can lead to exceedingly complex inheritance patterns, difficult to understand and maintain	C++, CLOS, Eiffel[1]

---

[1] A number of add-on packages provide multiple inheritance for Smalltalk programmers, although these are not widely used.

continued

Table 16.1 continued

Concept/ Mechanism	Benefits	Drawbacks	Languages
Typing			
No declarations	Less work for the developer	Omits important information that could improve implementation understandability	CLOS, Smalltalk
Formal declarations	Makes implementations easier to understand and provides necessary information for static type checking	More work for the developer	C++, Eiffel
Static type checking	Detects type errors before execution	May impede prototyping by rejecting implementations that could run	C++, Eiffel, Objective C
Dynamic type checking	Allows flexible construction and testing of implementations	Detects type errors only at runtime	CLOS, Objective C, Smalltalk
Binding			
Static	Avoids runtime lookup, or use of large amounts of memory to store compiled code for alternative execution pathways	Requires unique names for all system operations, and may require multiple code changes when requirements change	(C and Pascal)
Dynamic	Creates very flexible code that is resilient to the addition and removal of types	Incurs the overhead of binding at execution time, or the creation of extra code for alternative execution pathways	CLOS, Smalltalk
Both	Can choose the appropriate form of binding for the situation	Requires the developer to know the difference and to specify the information needed to support both	C++, Eiffel, Objective C
Object Lifetime			
Classes are objects available at runtime	Additional abstraction capability and runtime flexibility to modify and add classes	Overhead for maintaining the class information in the runtime environment	CLOS, Objective C, Smalltalk
Manual runtime storage reclamation	Allows the developer to control reclamation in special situations	Is error prone and forces the developer to deal with a low-level systems issue	C++, Objective C
Automatic runtime storage reclamation	Frees the developer from determining when space is to be reclaimed	Imposes an overhead on the runtime system to do the reclamation	CLOS, Eiffel, Smalltalk

drawbacks of these mechanisms. To understand the table fully, you may need to know more about some of the terminology, which we will explore in this section. The table indicates which of the commercially available languages support the listed mechanisms.

Ultimately, you choose an object-oriented language just as you would any traditional language. You see how well it fits your applications, execution requirements, machine availability, development culture, and so on. C++ and Smalltalk are the main contenders as the object-oriented programming language of choice. C++ was designed specifically to extend the capabilities of C, and is well suited to the systems programming community served by C. Smalltalk was designed as a simulation language, with careful consideration of support for graphical user interfaces, and is well suited to information systems applications.

Multiple Levels of Encapsulation

Object-oriented systems combine data and the behavior that operates on this data into a single unit called the object. Users of an object should know only the interface to the object—the names of the messages that can be sent to the object to invoke its behavior. The term "encapsulation" is the name for the ability of objects to hide information, thereby maintaining the interface independent of implementation.

Some object-oriented languages provide multiple levels of encapsulation. C++ provides three levels: public, private, and protected. Public methods, called member functions in C++, can be accessed by all client objects. Private member functions and data are fully encapsulated and unavailable to any but the defining class. Protected member functions and data are visible only to the defining class and its subclasses. In Smalltalk, all implementation information is accessible to the defining class and its subclasses, although some Smalltalk developers label a group of methods as "private" or "protected" to document the intention of confining visibility to the defining class or its class hierarchy. Information in CLOS goes into slots, each of which specifies its visibility. A slot can be read, written, or both. Encapsulation can be circumvented in some languages. For example, C++ allows a nonmember function, a member function, or an entire class to be declared a "friend," and friends of a class can access the class's otherwise private information.

Bounded and Unbounded Polymorphism

Support for polymorphism in an object-oriented language means that different objects can reuse the same behavior name for different implementations. There are two primary kinds of polymorphism, distinguished by restrictions on the relationship among classes reusing the same behavior name. Bounded or inclusion polymorphism limits reuse to classes defined within the same class hierarchy. For example, two subclasses of the same class can define the same behavior name. Unbounded or parametric polymorphism allows classes that do not share a common superclass to reuse a name. Bounded polymorphism is provided in languages with a formal type system, in which the compiler has more information about the set of objects to be used in a particular situation. Unbounded polymorphism gives more flexibility to the developer to add new types of objects that fulfill the responsibilities expected of components in a framework.

Single and Multiple Inheritance

Object-oriented languages support single or multiple inheritance. In single inheritance, a class can have at most one superclass; in multiple inheritance, a class inherits from two or more superclasses. In either case, the interface specification and implementation can be inherited. Multiple inheritance is a powerful tool for conceptual modeling, notably when class behavior is best defined as a refinement of several sets of (abstract) behaviors. Each superclass defines a cohesive set of behaviors that are implemented by the subclass.

For example, an object representing Seaplanes must be able to fly through the air and to glide on water. The Seaplane could be defined to inherit multiply from both a class that describes vehicles that fly (Plane) and one that describes a vehicle's behavior on water (Boat). With only single inheritance, the Seaplane has to be defined in terms of either the Plane or the Boat, and then extended through composition and delegation with the additional behavior it did not inherit.[2]

Languages that support multiple inheritance must address the issues of name collision and of repeated inheritance. Name collisions occur when a class inherits a variable or behavior with the same name from two different superclasses. A class that inherits from the same superclass more than once is an example of repeated inheritance. The question is whether there are one or several copies of the inherited variables and behaviors. Each language has rules that resolve these issues. However, the result of applying these rules is often an implementation of complex hierarchies that are hard to understand and maintain.

Static and Dynamic Type Checking and Method Binding

The type of an object indicates the role it can play in a system; an object is the type of its class and of any of its superclasses. Not all object-oriented languages require explicit type declaration, but all object-oriented languages do type checking at some point. Static type

---

[2] As another example, an object representing a data structure that is both sequenceable (able to respond to ordered add, delete, and enumeration messages) and indexable (able to respond to messages of the form at: index and at: index put: anObject) could be defined as the subclass of both a class that specifies sequenceable behavior and one that specifies indexable behavior. Another data structure could be sequenceable, not indexable, but streamable (able to respond to messages to retrieve the next item or store an item—next and nextPut: anObject). And yet another data structure could respond to all three. Using only single inheritance, the designer must choose how the three protocols—sequencing, indexing, and streaming—relate hierarchically, if at all, and reuse the protocol that does not fit the single inheritance model through composition and delegation. For example, indexable objects can be defined as subclasses of sequenceable objects. But streamable objects are not necessarily sequenceable or indexable, and so have to be independently defined with reading and writing behavior that references any kind of collection data structure, whether sequenceable or indexable.

checking takes place before the system executes to ensure that every message sent to an object will be handled by at least one method (that is, that the object is the type of a class that takes responsibility for the messages). With dynamic type checking, the type of a variable, argument, or return value is determined at runtime, when each is bound to a specific object.

Just as there is a choice when to determine the type of an object—at compile time (static type checking) or runtime (dynamic type checking), there is a choice when to determine which method (implementation) is associated with a named behavior (message). Static binding presumes that the compiler has all the information to determine that exactly one implementation will execute every time a particular message is sent to an object. It implies that every method is uniquely identifiable, and that no new method implementations can be created and executed at runtime. Dynamic binding provides more flexibility— no explicit message dispatching is required in the code (for example, no case statements are needed), and new method implementations can be created programmatically and executed at runtime. This flexibility is in exchange for some compile-time optimizations.

Runtime Support for Object Lifetimes

Objects are created as an application executes. At some point, a particular object will have fulfilled its responsibilities and will no longer be needed. Each object-oriented language provides some mechanism for creating objects and for allocating memory for an object's transient existence. When the space for the object is no longer needed, it must be recovered. Either the programmer is responsible for allocating and deallocating memory (as in C++) or the language system itself automatically allocates and reclaims storage (as in Smalltalk). Having the runtime language system perform the memory-management tasks eliminates errors of omission and commission: errors in not reclaiming storage which then slowly leak away available memory, and errors in reclaiming too early, which creates total chaos [Ungar and Jackson 1988].

Transient objects exist only during a single execution of an application. If the object outlives an execution of its creating application, it will need to be stored persistently so that it can be retrieved at a later time. Most language systems provide ad hoc mechanisms for moving binary or textual descriptions of objects to and from disk storage; the current industry trend is to make object persistence an intrinsic part of the system. Language bindings to object-oriented databases provide an additional mechanism for managing persistent objects.

Hybrid versus Pure Languages

Another consideration in choosing a programming language is its acceptability and learnability by the target developers. Hybrid languages combine mechanisms that provide support for object-oriented concepts with mechanisms that support procedural or functional programming concepts, grafting together two or more programming styles. Hybrid languages include: C++, which combines C with objects; Objective C, which is essentially a

Smalltalk preprocessor for C; CLOS, which combines LISP with objects; and OO-COBOL (or Object COBOL, depending on the vendor), which combines COBOL with objects. Smalltalk and Eiffel are examples of pure object-oriented languages, pure in the sense that they provide a single style of programming based on the description of interacting objects.

A hybrid language is a reasonable choice when all new development must be fully compatible with code written in an existing base language. Most pure object-oriented language systems, such as the several commercial Smalltalk offerings, provide interoperability support for accessing code written in procedural languages such as C or COBOL. A hybrid language is also helpful in managing the concerns of developers who have been asked to change languages. With a hybrid language, these developers can continue to use familiar tools and development processes, and move to objects incrementally.

The drawback of a hybrid language is that it is easy to fall back on the original language, never leveraging the available support for objects. Developers must contend with two disparate development approaches, distinguishing between what is intrinsic to the base language and what is part of the object-oriented extension. Hybrid languages tend to become very complex because they try to cater to two different worlds.

Libraries

A library associated with a programming language is a contribution to your reuse assets. Libraries contain objects that represent basic data structures, applications, framework components, and frameworks. Some libraries are provided in binary form, some include the source code.

Many beginning Smalltalk programmers view the Smalltalk language as both large and complex. In fact, the Smalltalk language has very simple syntax and semantics. The perceived size and complexity is derived from the Smalltalk class libraries, not the language. However, since most of the core functionality (and hence the power of the Smalltalk system) is found in the library, this distinction is not useful for beginners.

In choosing a programming language, you should consider what libraries already exist, especially whether the language vendors or third-party sellers provide domain frameworks appropriate to your development needs, and what kinds of tools are available for managing the library, especially for locating and retrieving code assets. Also consider whether there is support in the language and the tools for combining libraries from multiple vendors, regardless of the languages in which these libraries are written.

Programming Tools

Bob Balzer is a senior researcher at the Information Sciences Institute of the University of Southern California. His research focuses on software engineering, notably automatic programming. He was invited to the ACM OOPSLA '92 conference to be on a panel about supporting the development life cycle. He opened his comments by saying:

> "I do not know why I am here. I am interested in obtaining an order of magnitude improvement in productivity. You are just interested in objects."

He caught the audience's immediate attention. After all, objects are about productivity improvements—faster development, safer maintenance. But to Bob, objects represent a coding model. And Bob wasn't interested in any technology that required him to spend time thinking about coding—ever. His goal is to create tools for specifying the system requirements and then automatically generating the implementation. A change in the requirements causes a change in the specification, and regeneration of the implementation. Much of the early work on CASE tools and 4GL languages had the same vision, although perhaps not with the same ambition that Bob expressed that day. The various visual framework construction tools, whereby the graphical user interface for an application is "painted" and then linked to the underlying business logic, also share this productivity vision. Some of these construction tools generate specifications of the user interface and defer binding these specifications to implementation code until after the system determines the host environment in which the application will run. (A reference to some future thinking about computer-assisted software engineering can be found in [Rich and Waters 1990].)

In selecting implementation tools, you must take into consideration both the process model you use for implementing systems, and the style in which you prefer to interact with the available set of tools. You must take into account the concerns of whomever has to write the system implementation, and others who, in order to maintain or reuse aspects of the system, have to read the implementation.

Implementation Strategy

Generating implementation from specification is one of the future directions for development environments. It is one example of what we refer to as an implementation strategy. Until this approach unfolds as a commercial option, less automated implementation strategies must be considered.

An *implementation strategy* is a collection of activities that the developer has to do, alone and with others, to implement a system. This strategy influences and is influenced by the choice of product process model, the skill levels of the development team members, and whether team and cross-project coordination is required. Implementation tools must help the developers carry out the implementation process, to:

- Describe new kinds of objects in terms of classes or concrete examples

- Describe new objects by combining existing ones (using composition or aggregation)

- Describe new objects by refining existing ones (inheritance or delegation)

- Establish other object relationships

- Restructure objects and their relationships

Any number of different tools can be used to perform these tasks. A standard text editor can be used for editing object descriptions and relationship information. But tools that have knowledge about objects are better able to assist the developer. These tools provide templates for defining classes and their inheritance relationships, for example, rather than leaving it to the developer to remember the proper language syntax.

Incremental development and integration. A typical implementation strategy is one that follows an edit, compile, link, execute, debug cycle. This cycle still exists today, despite major changes in how the steps are carried out. On-line access to creating and testing code is today's version of yesterday's punching holes in decks of cards and submitting them to a computer operator standing behind a glass enclosure. The only way to substantially change the model—to eliminate the explicit compile and link steps—will be use of automatic implementation generation techniques and of simple ways to describe combinations of existing components. In the meantime, on-line access has made one big difference—speeding up the cycle. Speed is further increased by doing work incrementally, only modifying system parts that are directly affected by changes. Similarly, incremental compilers and linkers are important tools, whereby only the code affected by the change is recompiled and reintegrated.

Prototyping. When using a process model based on incremental development and prototyping, it is important to be able to restructure class hierarchies and other class relationships rapidly, even when a large number of instances of the classes already exist. The tools that support incremental development often coincide with tools needed to support prototyping.

Our friend and colleague David Leibs, when asked to describe what is important to him in a development environment, answered that he wants to "grow his code into existence"—to mold it like clay. He likes to discover what he will do. With a little bit of planning, he likes to try a little, watch what happens, and discover more details. He wants to be a "partner with the objects." He doesn't like the idea of describing an object with one set of tools, and then interacting with the object's executable form using some other tools. David likes the Smalltalk Object Inspector. He says it is the best first user interface to an object.

David is a prototyper. But when David's prototyping work is done, he creates a product. He uses the same development environment for both prototyping and production work. Often he throws his prototypes away. Just as often he evolves his prototypes into products.

Many tools that are adequate for developing a prototype are not capable of evolving the prototype into a product. Traditional screen painting/report writing 4GL development tools, for example, may allow for the rapid prototyping of screens and reports, but are typically not capable of modeling sophisticated business aspects of applications. They are often incapable of delivering adequate performance to support resource-intensive applications. On the other hand, some environments are well suited for product development but are inappropriate for prototyping. Typically these tools impose a large overhead—require too much effort—to create the prototype.

Prototyping begs for dynamic binding, unbounded polymorphism, and dynamic type checking. Some part of the development environment must take responsibility for type checking. But this responsibility can be assigned to any number of different tools ranging from compilers (such as the Eiffel compiler) to program verifiers (Lint for the programming language C) to linkers and runtime systems (Smalltalk virtual machine). All of these tools have the same responsibility—to ensure that operations applied to an object are valid for that type of object. They differ as to when they carry out the responsibility and, consequently, in the amount of help they can supply. As a general rule, tools that check types during development have more information available and more options for handling typing errors than do tools that check during execution. When type checking occurs during execution (determining when a message is sent to an object whether it is able to respond), exception handling becomes an important mechanism of the language environment.

During the early stages of development, having to declare all types explicitly can hamper a prototyping process. Prototypers are frequently more interested in trying out their latest ideas than they are in determining and declaring the type relationships among all system elements. As a consequence, full static type checking may not be desired early in the development process. Often a programmer wishes to exercise only a small fraction of the implementation. Static type checking of the entire system may take significant time, and any type error—even one outside of the implementation that will actually execute—is likely to prevent successful compilation.

As development progresses, it becomes more important to incorporate explicit typing information. Although type declarations require effort to write, they are generally beneficial to both the program writer and the program reader. The program writer can better express the relationships between operations and entities, and the program readers (maintainers and reusers) can more easily understand the program. During the later stages of development, there are likely to be more readers than there are writers.

Documentation. In Chapter 6, we discuss expectations for documentation of object-oriented systems. We need to document requirements, designs, scenarios, and how to reuse. Type declarations can also be an important source of documentation, describing implementation intentions.

Software development tools should be fully integrated with documentation tools. For example, when and where developers create classes, they should be able to provide textual descriptions of the classes. Likewise, they should be able to provide on-line documentation for individual methods and attributes. The object model supports a rich set of artifacts and relationships that should be documented. However, the tools should also save the developer from work that computer software can do just as well—implementation-generating tools can and should automatically generate documentation diagrams from analysis and design models or by reverse engineering the code.

Note that the most prevalent strategy for development is to create an implementation that is then documented. Many researchers today are focusing on an alternative strategy, namely, to write documentation to which executable implementations are linked. The purpose of this reversal is to emphasize the importance of maintaining up-to-date documentation and the importance of being able to understand the system through this documentation rather than through code reading.

Testing. Testing tools should capture tests, play back tests for regression analysis, and provide coverage analysis. Tools that profile static and dynamic characteristics of a system need to be specifically designed to work with object-oriented technology. Static testing evaluates characteristics of the implementation itself, such as the degree of coupling between objects. Dynamic testing evaluates characteristics of the running system, such as the amount of memory required, the time to perform particular scenarios, and so on. A popular kind of testing tool for C++ programs is a memory leak analyzer, which is needed because developers can mistakenly allocate but forget to deallocate in-memory object storage.

Traceability. We have two expectations about traceability for development tools. First, we expect to cross-reference objects with their collaborators, and with their analysis and design counterparts. Second, the tools themselves should be well integrated so that creation and maintenance of cross-references is handled automatically by the tools in response to specific development activities. Tools differ in how and when such trace information is made available. Some tools require preprocessing of the entire artifact set to create a special cross-reference index. Other tools construct and maintain this information dynamically, permitting fast and up-to-date navigation of trace relationships.

Team tools. Objects need to be packaged into applications. When multiple developers are creating a software system, the packages are typically created independently, and then combined to form the target systems. At any given time during the process, the packages will most likely be at different stages of development. Tools are needed to assign tasks, manage versions of objects and packages, and configure these packages into the full system. Configuration tools include conflict analyzers and resolution support. Because of the nature of object-oriented technology, the tools have to be useful during prototyping as well as development, and they have to be able to configure partial systems because of the incremental nature of the process model. In some cases, these coordination tools will have to serve developers who are working at different levels of the system.

Tools not specifically designed to support object-oriented development are likely to coordinate through files. Developers store artifacts (typically source code) into files. The files are placed under version and configuration control. This use of files does not map very well to object-oriented systems, where the classes and class relationships are the primary units to be managed. If the unit to be managed is reduced to a single code method or member function (it is not uncommon for a developer to maintain a version history of a single method), there is an explosion in the number of files and they become exceedingly difficult to manage. Good object-oriented team tools are designed to manage the specific artifacts and their configurations in an efficient and unobtrusive manner. A critical challenge in creating team coordination for object-oriented development is to provide management control while retaining the productivity and sense of empowerment typical of object-oriented development.

Interaction Strategy

The implementation strategy defines the activities that the developer must do, alone and with others, to implement the system or prototypes of the system. The *interaction strategy* for a software development environment defines the interaction style with which the developer carries out these activities, the human-factors considerations of the process model and tools.

The research associated with the creation of the Smalltalk-80 system developed a specific interaction strategy, known as the *programmer-as-reader* model [Goldberg 1987]. The basic premise of this model is that most developers spend the majority of their time reading and understanding other people's implementations, as well as their own. We read what has been written, and we should write with full awareness of the expected reader. Development tools for object-oriented languages need to be biased toward the reader because of the importance placed on reuse.

Supporting the programmer-as-reader. Supporting the programmer-as-reader requires an interaction strategy based on system queries and navigation. Reading implementations is inherently a nonlinear task. It is carried out more as a form of query, either by asking explicit questions or by investigating (navigating) links between related parts. In fact, there is a general set of queries that readers issue, identified in [Goldberg 1987] as:

While examining system structure:

What is that? (Where "that" is a token or reference to information)

Where is it? (A fact, implementation, an example use of implementation, an existing algorithm; where is it defined or where is it used?)

Does any part of the system do this? (Presumably the reader can show the system something of interest and be shown a system component that does it.)

What part of the system knows about that?

How did I get here?

How can I get back?

While examining execution:

What is the current state of the system?

Why did that happen?

Why didn't that happen?

These general queries can be restated more specifically in the context of the object model:

Provide a description of an object.

Show me the class hierarchy for an object.

Which objects implement a specific behavior?

Which objects implement a set of behaviors?

Which messages are sent by a code method?

Which objects collaborate with a particular object?

Show me all the uses of (references to) an object in the system.

Show me the state of an object.

What is the most recent message that was sent to an object?

Show me the current list of incomplete message-sends.

And so on. Development environment tools for object-oriented technology should be specifically designed to support this query and navigation style of interaction.

Figure 16.1 shows the original Smalltalk-80 System Browser, a tool used to construct queries about Smalltalk objects. Five different subviews, each with its own special query facilities, are provided. Each of the four top subviews presents a different perspective on the Smalltalk class library: categories, classes, protocols, and methods. Associated with each subview is a menu of query and navigation options. The query options encompass a variety of different forms for searches and cross-references, including pattern matching and selection from menu lists. The subviews of the browser show the response to a query, such as the name of a class shown in the context of its class hierarchy. Cross-referencing allows the reader to explore the various reference relationships that exist among the objects, such as message collaborators and class composition.

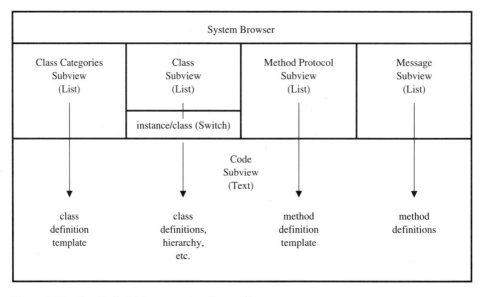

Figure 16.1   Smalltalk-80 Programming System Browser

Depending on the selections and modes of the four top subviews, the bottom sub-view of the System Browser displays either category-class relationships or protocol-method relationships. It also displays the definition of a class (including its variable names), the hierarchy of the class (superclasses and subclasses), or the class comment (a textual description about the class). It can also display the Smalltalk implementation of a particular method. Regardless of the information displayed, the reader can always select a piece of text—corresponding to some Smalltalk token such as a message or class name—and ask the System Browser to "explain" the token. The resulting explanation provides not only a description of the token, but executable queries for exploring the token's relationship to other aspects of the same object or other objects in the system.

In a well-designed environment, the interaction strategy pervades all tools. The same query model available in one tool is available in the others. The Smalltalk-80 Process Inspector, shown in Fig. 16.2, is a good example. This tool is often referred to as the debugger, but this is a misnomer. Debugger connotes a tool that is used to determine what is wrong with implementation (to remove bugs). The Process Inspector is used for this purpose, but it is also used to determine what is right with the implementation. Often the best way to understand the implementation of a system is to run it, and then interrupt the execution when the system exhibits some interesting behavior. In Smalltalk, interrupting the system causes control to transfer to the Process Inspector, where the reader can examine the executing implementation, by viewing variable values, stepping through message-sends, and viewing dynamic interactions. The cross-referencing capabilities of the Browser are also available in the Process Inspector.

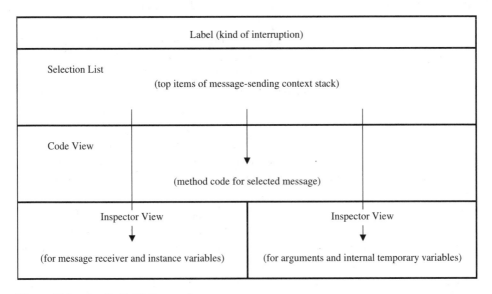

Figure 16.2 Smalltalk-80 Process Inspector

Writing. Developers should be encouraged to write object-oriented implementations with the expectation that they will be read. Tools should facilitate the construction of systems that embody and exhibit the properties of good object-oriented designs and implementations.

Object-oriented systems contain information that can be used to support the reader's interaction strategy for querying and navigating the system. For example, the inheritance relationship is expressed directly in the implementation. The reading tools can use this information to navigate and to query the object model about inheritance relationships. However, to support the complete set of queries desired by the reader, information not inherently a part of the object model must be captured while writing (implementing) systems. For example, to query for the classes that are contained in a particular group (e.g., application or subsystem) category, the Smalltalk developer must specify the category-class relationship, which is not a formal part of the language. Of course, the development tools can facilitate the capturing of this information so the developer/writer provides it as a natural part of the development process.

Writing tools must support the reuse of existing artifacts, and incremental development. The developer should be able to implement some portion of the system, try it out, and then create more of the implementation. Developing incrementally depends on a high degree of interaction between the writing and the reading tools. In a Smalltalk system, this interaction is supported by the Process Inspector, whose middle subview contains the implementation for the method that is selected in the topmost subview. This subview is identical to the bottom subview of the Browser, so not only can readers examine the implementation and use the explain facility, they can also edit and recompile. Within the context of the Process Inspector, the roles of writer and reader are interchangeable. This facilitates incremental development and prototyping.

A tool like the Process Inspector also allows implementation to be deferred. Imagine that an application has been executing for 30 minutes when an error occurs and control transfers to the Process Inspector. In the context of inspecting, the developer determines that the system was interrupted because a particular variable was not properly initialized. The permanent fix is to edit a method to provide an initial value. However, this approach will require that the system be restarted, potentially having to repeat 30 minutes of work. An alternative is to log the error and provide a default value for the uninitialized variable (using one of the two inspector tools contained within the Process Inspector), and then continue the execution from the point of failure. The developer can later fix the method that contains the error.

The query-and-navigation interaction strategy motivated the design of Smalltalk Browsers, Object Inspectors, and Process Inspectors. It was a rewarding model to apply because the structure of objects and object relationships lend themselves well to navigation and query. Our recommendation for object-oriented technology is to look for tools that support the developer as reader, and provide a well-integrated set of tools for coordination of the dual desires for writing and reading.

Object-Oriented Databases

A database is an important part of almost any system—it holds the information that persists between uses of the system. Databases are distinguished by their data models and data management facilities. The structure of a hierarchical data model is a tree, and the structure of a network data model is a lattice. The structure of a relational data model is a table. And, not surprisingly, the structure of an object data model is an object and its relationships. Database management supports transaction control, queries, locking, and versioning. Most database management systems today are associated with some form of query language, such as SQL, which allows an application program to access stored information. The query language for an object-oriented database is based on sending messages to the stored objects.

A number of properties distinguish an object-oriented database (OODB) from other kinds of databases. First, data types defined by the developers are treated the same as any built-in data types. Transactions can be long, involving a number of operations on complex data types. A query is expressed in terms of messages to objects. As with other forms of object development, the schema for an object-oriented database is expected to evolve over time. The object-oriented database management systems are designed to permit incremental definition of the schema without disrupting the ongoing use of the database. The rules for an OODB, as set by the OMG standards effort (ODBMG-93) [Atwood 1993], are:

- There is one type system across the object-oriented programming language and the database.

- The language binding respects the syntax of the base object-oriented programming language.

- The binding is structured as additions to the object-oriented programming language.

- It is acceptable to mix the base language expressions of the object-oriented programming language with the additions of the database's object manipulation language.

- There is no difference in the expression of operations between transient and persistent objects. Generally, any message that can be sent to a transient object can be sent to a persistent one.

There are a number of reasons why you might choose an OODB. Some of the reasons carry more weight if you have chosen an object-oriented programming language, although you can use an OODB with a traditional language. One reason is the ability to manage persistent objects using the same language that is used to manage transient objects. The advantage is that you can create a system that manages transient objects, insert declarations that the objects are to be persistent and therefore enable them to migrate to the database, and continue to use the same expressions. This consistency of language usage means that there is only one language the programmers have to learn, and no need to map between different language constructs.

The consistency of language is not, however, the primary reason for the interest in OODBs. Rather, it is the ability quickly to store and retrieve large data types—representations of complex information structures as might be found in computer-aided design, document management, systems engineering simulations, and CASE tools. Relational databases were designed for data processing applications, where the data could be naturally represented as tables of values. They were especially tuned for short transactions, typical of on-line transaction processing systems. Complex information structures were either ignored by the relational database vendors or simulated using complex table joins. It is difficult to get reasonable performance from such simulations. Skilled SQL programmers expend considerable effort modifying table structures to meet performance expectations.

An advantage of an OODB for applications written in an object-oriented language is the ability to retain the implementation object model in the external storage. One OODB user indicated that the ability to retain the same model in the application as in the database helped the development team complete their task in a few weeks. Relational database programmers, assigned to do the same task, were still trying to revise the table structures to achieve acceptable performance. At the time of our interview, they had already been working on the task for ten weeks.

A passive database contains just data. To process the data, it must first be retrieved from the database and then manipulated by an application program. An active database allows functions to be executed in the database system. In terms of an OODB, this means that the methods are stored along with the object's data in the database. And therefore the database stores the executable business or technical model (see Chapter 14, Fig. 14.5). When you want to ask questions, or manipulate information stored in the database, you send a message to the appropriate database objects. The database objects execute their methods inside the database. The ability to do so means that less time is spent transferring information from the database to the application execution environment, and the database operations are applied only to the appropriate objects in the database. Stored procedures in relational databases propose to solve a similar problem.

How to Choose a Database

Table 16.2 lists the various combinations of programming languages and database systems, identifying the key advantages and disadvantages of each combination. To summarize, a relational database is preferable when:

- Data types are simple and the relationships among the data types are simple

- Transactions are short lived

- Very little navigation over the data (requiring table joins) is required

- A low degree of schema evolution is expected

An object-oriented database is preferable when:

- Data types are complex types defined by the user

- Transactions are long lived

- Multiple versions of data are required to support experimentation

- Navigation by reference is critical to the application

Any database should be evaluated for its ability to provide all the facilities of a conventional database system, such as:

- Data model for representing and manipulating the stored information

- Persistence across sessions

- Concurrent access by multiple users

Table 16.2 Advantages and Disadvantages of Choosing Different Combinations of Programming Languages and Database Systems for Applications

Programming language	Database	Advantages	Disadvantages
object-oriented	relational	keeps legacy data where it already is	conversion from tables to objects required, inconsistent language between persistent and transient information
embedded SQL	object-oriented	SQL is familiar to the developers	different query and programming languages
object-oriented	object-oriented	same language for persistent as well as transient information, support for objects everywhere	may have to move existing data to new database
SQL, or SQL with objects	extended relational	incremental change from prior practices; addition of object-like concepts and stored procedures	hybrid language solution with object SQL, retains complexity of tuning the schema
object-oriented	extended relational	retains prior data and incrementally adds the objects into the applications	conversion from tables to objects required, inconsistent language between persistent and transient information

- Transaction management that ensures consistency and stability of the data

- Recovery from crashes

- High-level query language for accessing stored information

- Performance at the desired speed for accessing and updating the information

- Security to protect information from unauthorized use

- Ability to scale to required dataset size

There are a number of object-oriented database systems on the market. If you decide to use an OODB, find out whether the database provides a binding to your programming language of choice, and supports your preferred object modeling concepts. For example, if you decide that multiple inheritance is important to you, then a criterion for choosing a database system is whether the data-definition and data-manipulation languages support multiple inheritance.

Your choice of a database will also be influenced by which platforms the database runs on, how well it performs for the size and type of data you have to support, and whether the database management system adheres to industry-accepted standards.

Summary

In this chapter, we explored the advantages and disadvantages of different features of object-oriented programming languages, and supplied guidelines for choosing programming languages, libraries, tools, and databases.

You choose a programming language based on support for the object concepts that you decide are critical to your development efforts. Of critical importance are the size and quality of the libraries of frameworks and components available for the language, and the ability of the language system to call on frameworks and components written in other languages. You choose your programming tools to support the product process model you wish to use, and you often choose a programming language based on which tools are available. You should also choose the language based on its suitability to the kinds of applications you are building and the ability of your programmers to learn the language. Many languages today are going through transitions, often motivated by standardization efforts or the need to account for features available in competing languages. Look to see if these development directions meet your organization's language expectations.

An interaction strategy for a development environment defines the style the developer uses to carry out implementation activities. The Smalltalk-80 research lead to a strategy that treats the programmer as a reader who explores other people's implementations through system queries and navigation in order to learn how to create combinations, refinements, or original work. In a well-designed environment, the interaction strategy pervades all tools. Pick a development environment whose interaction strategy is a good match to the way your developers like to work.

Languages, libraries, and tools should support the ability to create applications that access information in non-object-oriented databases. But the arguments in favor of object-oriented databases are compelling. Object-oriented databases can rapidly store and retrieve large and complex data structures, eliminate the need to transform a well-defined object model into an alternative data model (such as relational tables), and enable you to program queries in the same language that is used for the rest of the application.

Additional Reading About Software Development Environment Choices

Barstow, D., Shrobe, H., and Sandewall, E., eds., *Interactive Programming Environments*, McGraw-Hill: New York, 1984.

> This book contains papers written by 42 prominent contributors in the field of interactive programming environments. Many of the papers describe research in 1984 that has made, or is still trying to make, its way into commercial products today. For example, the marketing hyperbole surrounding today's software development products echoes the friendly, cooperative, and forgiving environments of Interlisp-D (papers by Sheil, Teitelman, and Barstow) and Smalltalk (papers by Goldberg and Goldstein). Also of interest are the papers by Stallman (which discusses extensibility of the EMACS editor environment), Sandewall (which describes alternatives to the edit-compile-link-run cycle when using interactive programming environments), and Winograd (which discusses how programming will become a process not of writing new programs but of modifying existing ones).

Cattell, R. G. G., *Object Data Management: Object-Oriented and Extended Relational Database Systems*, Addison-Wesley: Reading, Mass., 1991.

> Cattell has sifted through the noise and provided a well-organized and readable description of data management systems that manipulate objects. The book points out how nonobject data management systems fail to meet the data needs of particular classes of applications. He goes on to introduce object data management systems and to discuss how they do meet the needs of today's data-sophisticated applications. The book is comprehensive in its technical coverage, and also provides a description of several products and prototypes.

Definitive books on object-oriented programming languages:

Actors
Agha, G., *ACTORS: A Model of Concurrent Computation in Distributed Systems*, MIT Press: Cambridge, Mass., 1986.

C++
Stroustrup, B., *The C++ Programming Language*, Addison-Wesley: Reading, Mass., 1985. Second edition appeared 1991.

CLOS
Bobrow, D. G., DiMichiel, L. G., Gabriel, R. P., Keene, S. E., Kiczales, G., and Moon, D. A., Common Lisp Object System Specification, X3J13 Document 88-002R, *ACM SIGPLAN Notices*, 23, September 1988.

Eiffel
Meyer, B., *Eiffel: The Language*, Prentice Hall International: United Kingdom, 1992.

Objective C
Cox, B., *Object-Oriented Programming: An Evolutionary Approach*, Addison-Wesley: Reading, Mass., 1986.

Self
Ungar, D. and Smith, R., Self: the power of simplicity, Proceedings of the 1987 ACM OOPSLA Conference, *ACM SIGPLAN Notices*, 22(12), 227-42, December 1987.

Simula
Dahl, O. J., Myhrhaug, B., and Nygaard, K., *Simula 67, common base language*, Norwegian Computing Center, Technical publication #S-2, 1968.

Smalltalk
Goldberg, A. and Robson, D., *Smalltalk-80: The Language and its Implementation*, Addison-Wesley: Reading, Mass., 1983. Revised as Goldberg A. and Robson, D., *Smalltalk-80: The Language*, Addison-Wesley: Reading, Mass., 1989.

CHAPTER 17

Select a Software Development Environment

To select a software development environment based on object-oriented technology, you need to select a programming language, libraries of reusable frameworks and components, tools for creating and changing objects and their relationships, database(s) for storing class descriptions and instances, and methods and tools for analysis and design.

Framework for Selecting a Software Development Environment

Selecting the software development environment is a special kind of resource-improvement project, as shown in Fig. 17.1. The goals of the project are to select methods, programming languages, libraries, tools, and databases.

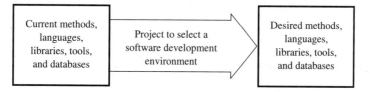

Figure 17. Resource-Improvement Project to Select a Software Development Environment

Managers know that smart developers are more important than the tools, the languages, the methods—any aspect of the development environment. Smart people can do a good job, no matter what. Indeed, there is evidence that some developers are ten times more productive than average developers, using the same development environment [DeMarco and Lister 1987]. But tools do make a difference. Good supporting technology that the developers like to use makes it possible for average individuals to perform well, for more skilled individuals to perform better, and for the efforts of a team of developers to be better than the sum of the parts. Hence the principle for the decision framework emphasizes coordination.

Framework Principle. Team members work together most effectively when there is a strategy for coordinating methods, tools, libraries, languages, databases, and delivery.

By using the word "coordinating" in the principle, we emphasize the importance of looking at your development environment in terms of all of the activities your developers have to do to meet goals and objectives, and of making sure that your choices in support of these activities interrelate and complement one another. You need to support the efforts of all team members, including any development done by end users. Choices about your software development environment are strategic decisions because considerable resources are required to develop and coordinate these choices. You will not have to invest in every decision at once, but make sure that each investment makes progress toward a consistent vision of the future.

Framework Goal. Set up a development environment for all team members that enables the team to create, maintain, and deliver applications.

The steps of the framework for selecting a software development environment are:

Software Development Environment

- Assess the current resource situation
- Understand the software to be developed
- Determine the characteristics of the user environment
- Establish a program for evaluating options

Assess the Current Resource Situation

Past practices influence decisions about the future. Your developers are accustomed to particular working styles, analysis-and-design methods, tools, and programming languages. If you want to establish new development processes and resources that are based on object-oriented technology, you need to know your starting point. This knowledge will help you understand the changes that will be necessary and prepare you for the costs of the transition. You should focus on a transition strategy that is practical for your organization. Developers do not all have the same knowledge and experiences, nor do they need to. In Chapter 14, we point out that developers create different kinds of software and that this software is expressed at different levels of system complexity. All of the developers need to work together, to share analyses, designs, and code. They have to be able to maintain one another's software results. Developers working at different levels of a system have to coordinate requests and expectations. The extent to which you have a variety of developers at different skill levels influences your choice of methods, programming languages, libraries, and tools. For example, if you plan to develop business applications on top of business frameworks, themselves on top of system frameworks, you must select development tools and methods that allow your developers to coordinate and work together at all three levels.

An organization should acknowledge and appreciate its culture before it adopts any new technology. Even the best technology is doomed to fail in an organization that is not prepared to accept it. We begin with the most obvious cultural issue:

> **Bow to forgone conclusions.** If the primary decision maker has a strong prejudice toward one choice over the others, the decision has already been made—right or wrong.

Making Change Decisions

If the decision isn't already a forgone conclusion, then begin by determining your current resource and process situation. Assess your current technology resources, methods, and personnel resources. With these assessments completed, you can evaluate your organization's culture.

Saturation level. Many organizations institute multiple changes at once—changes in hardware, operating system, windowing system, graphical widgetry, database, and network. Change is an opportunity. It can be exciting for your personnel and beneficial to the bottom line. But too much change at one time can be debilitating. Instead of energizing the organization, change can create an atmosphere of frustration—less work gets done while new skills are slowly learned, customer complaints are backlogged, work piles up. Introducing yet another technology change into an already saturated organization is likely to give poor results.

Disposition toward change. What is your organization's disposition toward change? Does it thrive on change or does it avoid it at all cost? What is the best way for you to make changes, in an evolutionary or a revolutionary style? For example, in an evolutionary culture, developers who currently use C may prefer to use C++ if it is viewed as a natural progression. Some incremental change may be required to maintain use of existing applications or databases. The evolutionary culture prefers to balance the old with the new. Where there is a low tolerance for change of any kind, then either there will be no new technology, or the new will be very similar to the old. In such a situation, change has to be introduced slowly and incrementally.

Developers in a revolutionary culture have no desire to let the past dictate the future. Starting over is acceptable if it helps to meet the desired goals and objectives, even when an evolutionary option exists. Organizations with a high tolerance for change treat the decision to acquire new technology as an opportunity to rethink their prior ways of doing business. New technology can be introduced more aggressively.

Making Change Decisions

Work with your people. People don't resist change, they resist being changed.

Whether evolutionary or revolutionary, you need everyone's cooperation to accomplish change.

Tolerance for risk. You must also have a good understanding of your organization's tolerance for different kinds of risk. In particular, technology market momentum is a major source of risk. *Technology market momentum* is an external property of a technology that indicates the degree to which the technology has been accepted or endorsed by the marketplace. We have purposely chosen the word "momentum" to reuse its definition from physics: mass times velocity. Market momentum is measured by the quantity of resources (mass) that the marketplace has dedicated to a technology, and the speed (velocity) at which the technology is being adopted.

Software system vendors add momentum to a particular programming language by developing compilers or programming environments that support it. Software developers add momentum to a language by using it to develop products. Authors add their momentum by devoting their time to writing books about it. Standards organizations add momentum by dedicating the resources to standardize it. Using this definition for momentum, object-oriented technology as a whole has tremendous momentum: There are a large number of books, tools (some of which only claim to be object-oriented), new and evolving languages, standards activities, and efforts to develop businesses selling reusable assets.

We prefer the term "momentum" to a word such as "maturity." Maturity connotes that something is complete and has reached the fullness or perfection of development or growth. This fosters reasoning of the form: Since language X is more mature than language Y, language X must be technically superior to language Y. This may or may not be true. Our definition of momentum purposely tries not to convey a sense of technical superiority. It is simply a means of illustrating that the industry, rightly or wrongly, has chosen to endorse one solution over another. This implies no judgment as to whether one language is "better" than another. It merely observes that, for reasons that may not be clearly understood or reasonable, one language has achieved a stronger momentum than another in the marketplace.

The importance of momentum is that it is inversely related to risk. The less momentum a technology has, the more risk an organization assumes by using it. For example, a language that today has little momentum may never evolve into a major force in the marketplace. By betting on this language today, an organization assumes the risk that it may not be available tomorrow, or at least may not be any better supported tomorrow than it is today. Since there are many sources of momentum, there are many sources of risk. To a given organization, some risks are likely to be more important than others. The level and types of risk that are acceptable depend on the culture of the specific organization.

Understand the Software to Be Developed

Some development environments are specialized for creating GUI-centric, database-centric, or domain-specific applications. For example, suppose you are interested in creating a graphical user interface. You would look for a development environment that includes special editors for laying out windows (screens) and linking visual widgets in each screen to underlying business logic. You would also look for libraries containing the visual widgets you expect to use.

Each kind of software you build might require a different development environment. Creating First-of-Its-Kind software may require a different set of tools than for software that is a Variation-on-a-Theme. Creating prototypes may require tools different from those for creating final products. And creating highly visual presentations may require libraries and methods different from those for creating text-based presentations.

Determine the Characteristics of the User Environment

In Chapter 14, we discuss expectations about the user environment that influence the choice of development environment. For example, not all methods, languages, libraries, tools, or databases can create results that are portable across platforms, provide open interfaces, factor functionality for distribution on a network, or use a client/server architecture. You need to know the general characteristics of the results your users expect, and pick a development environment that targets these expectations.

Establish a Program for Evaluating Options

There are likely to be several possible choices for each component of a software development environment. This step of the decision framework asks you to set up a project to evaluate which choice best meets your requirements. The first activity of this project is to choose which technologies you will evaluate (for example, programming languages or analysis methods or database systems) and the criteria for selection. These criteria should be ordered by importance to you. The most important criteria can then be used to screen which competing products you will examine in more detail.

When ranking criteria, you should be aware of the research findings of Galletta [Galletta, King, and Rateb 1993], who studied the effects of expertise on creating a weighted set of criteria for selecting software products (databases were used in the study). To summarize the findings:

- Experts are more likely to agree on the important criteria and their relative weights than are novices.

- Experts, more than novices, believe they know what is important, and are more willing to give these criteria higher weighting. Novices have a tendency to give all criteria a midpoint weight.

- Experts are about twice as unwavering as novices in applying the weights they assigned when making the actual selections. Novices are less likely to adhere to their weight assignments after they have made them.

- Experts make choices different from those of novices, especially in the first- and last-place rankings.

Evaluation projects can be time consuming and costly. It is important at the outset to understand your overall resource constraints: how much time and money is available, and who is available to carry out the evaluations. Preferably, the initial screening process will eliminate many contenders, saving you time and effort.

The next step is to collect data about each product to determine the extent to which each meets the selection criteria. Sometimes this data is collected by running tests or benchmarks. A *benchmark* is a standard set of tests. Organizations often seek industry-accepted benchmarks to simplify the data-collection task (see [Conte and Hwu 1991] for a characterization of benchmarks).

Benchmarks provide a way to compare one product's performance against that of all others with respect to the execution of the benchmark. You might choose a product that performs the best. Or, you could choose any of the products that simply meet or exceed your requirements. Using a standard benchmark saves you the resources needed to create and validate your own benchmark. Sometimes, you can use published benchmark values for your evaluation, rather than running your own tests—saving you both time and money.

There are problems with benchmarks. Vendors can tune their products to the benchmarks. Benchmark cheating occurs when a product contains code that caters to a specific benchmark while not necessarily adding any general improvement in real-world performance. Clearly this confounds the validity of the results.

Benchmarks may test only a small aspect of a product, an aspect that is not relevant to your planned use. For an overview of common benchmarks measuring hardware speed, see [Weicker 1990]. Weicker points out that "fair benchmarking would be less of an oxymoron if those using benchmark results knew what tasks the benchmarks really perform and what they measure." A variety of benchmarks applicable to object-oriented technology are in common use for comparing the performance of systems written with different object-oriented and non-object-oriented languages. But most test only low-level capabilities. Common choices include the Stanford Suite of integer benchmarks, the Puzzle benchmarks and the Richards operating system simulation [Chambers and Ungar 1991], and the slopstones (Smalltalk Low-Level OPeration Stones) and smopstones (Smalltalk Medium-Level OPeration Stones) [Samuelson 1993]. Unfortunately, these benchmarks are generally not good predictors of real day-to-day performance in a business situation. For example, one of the smopstone tests computes prime numbers, which is not a common business task.

Table 17.1 shows the benchmark results of ParcPlace Smalltalk Version 4.1 executing on 21 of the 29 different platform configurations on which the system ran in 1993. Because the ParcPlace system runs portably across all of these platforms, the benchmarks are useful for comparing the performance of different platforms when executing the exact same system (here, the development environment). Note that for purposes of the example, the absolute values of the numbers are not relevant; only the relative comparison is important.[1] These numbers cannot be used to compare implementations using language systems from multiple Smalltalk vendors or to compare Smalltalk to C++.

There are two commonly used benchmarks for object-oriented data management: OO1 [Cattell 1991] and OO7 [Carey, DeWitt, and Naughton 1993]. OO1, referred to as the Sun Benchmark, was the first widely accepted benchmark that attempted to predict DBMS performance for engineering design applications. OO7 provides a more comprehensive profile of the performance of an OODBMS than OO1. Its workload attempts to mimic the workload of CAD/CAM/CASE applications, although not in detail.

---

[1] It is only of historical interest, but the number 100 is equated to the benchmark result obtained in the early 1980s using the Xerox research machine called a Dorado.

Table 17.1 Platform Performance Numbers for ParcPlace Smalltalk Version 4.1, Computed in 1993

Processor	Machine	Result
SuperSPARC	Sun SPARCstation 10, Model 41 (SunOS 4.1.3)	1300
PA-RISC	HP 9000, model 720	1178
80486	Sequent 486/50 (xterm: NCD RISC mono)	1100
SuperSPARC	Sun SPARCstation 10, Model 30 (SunOS 4.1.3)	1024
80486	Sequent 486/50 (with HP 425 is X server)	908
80486	486/66	831
PA-RISC	HP 9000, model 710	805
SPARC	Sun SPARCstation 2 (SunOS 4.1.3)	687
80486	Sequent 486/50 (xterm: NCD 68xxx mono)	624
IBM	IBM RS/6000 340H	622
SPARC	Sun SPARC LX (Solaris 2.1)	527
80486	486/33 clone (Windows 3.1)	514
SPARC	Sun SPARCstation IPC	486
68040	Macintosh Quadra 950	465
R2000	DECstation 5000/25	452
80486	Toshiba 4400 SXC (Windows 3.1)	430
80486	486/33 clone (OS/2 2.0)	427
SPARC	Sun SPARCstation 1 with CGX	393
68040	Macintosh Quadra 700	352
IBM	IBM RS/6000 220H	296
68040/25	HP 425	294

Case Study Results

Software Development Environment Camps

In the case studies, we observed that the many strategies for choosing methods and languages fell into four camps. Figure 17.2 illustrates these camps. In that figure, and in others, we use the following icons:

Object-oriented—We use this icon both for artifacts created with object-oriented technology and to represent the structure of the real-world domain

 Traditional—The mapping of the problem to a hierarchical structure using a traditional (non–object-oriented) analysis, design. or implementation

Ad hoc—No particular mapping of the problem

Figure 17.2 is divided into three columns. The first column represents the real world—the situation that we are trying to model. The same real-world starting point is assumed for each of the four camps. We use the same icon to represent the real world and the mapping of the problem to an object model indicating our posture that the real world can be viewed as a collection of interacting objects.

The second column represents the outputs of the analysis and design. For simplicity, we combine analysis and design, even though there may be large differences in the methods employed by any one camp. In this figure, we do not distinguish among the different artifacts generated by an analysis method (such as structured-analysis function hierarchies and data flow diagrams) and a design method (such as structured-design structure charts). Our goal is only to show the various ways that case study organizations have mixed traditional and object-oriented methods and programming languages. Also, in this figure we assume that traditional and object-oriented methods are not mixed in carrying out analysis and design.

The third column represents the implementation that follows from the analysis and design.

The curved arrow in the second row indicates that some kind of special transformation is needed to map the traditional analysis and design results into the constructs of an object-oriented programming language. You can label this transformation whatever you like. We label it *magic*. It is magic to take the carefully separated data and functions and somehow combine them to form objects.

The figure also shows an arrow in the third row. This arrow represents a transformation from the object-oriented analysis and design models to the traditional implementation model. We label this transformation *unfortunate*. It is unfortunate in the sense that the developers have retained a consistent problem and solution model through the design phase, formulated in terms of objects. Now the developers have to make arbitrary transformations in the model because the selected programming language does not provide full support for object-oriented modeling concepts.

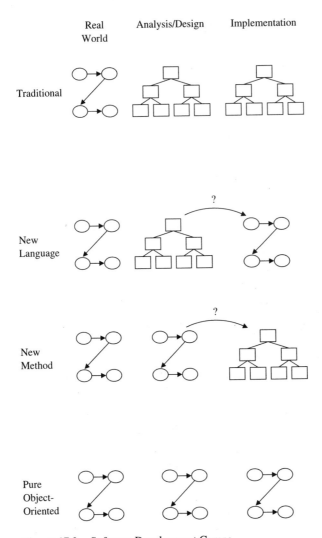

	Real World	Analysis/Design	Implementation	Description

Traditional — The dominant camp of the last 20 years, where object-oriented technology is used for neither methods nor implementation. Methods employ functional decomposition, data-flow or information modeling, structure charts, and ER diagrams. Implementation is done in procedural languages.

New Language — Traditional methods are used for analysis and design, but object-oriented languages are used for implementation. This camp retains its methods' training and tools investment, but is willing to try a new programming language.

New Method — Object-oriented methods are used for analysis and design, but procedural languages are used for implementation. The benefits of object-oriented technology are sought in the form of object models of complex problems, but traditional languages remain an organizational requirement.

Pure Object-Oriented — Object-oriented technology is used throughout development, a graphical portrayal of "objects all the way down."

Figure 17.2   Software Development Camps

Three charts summarize the analysis and design choices made by the case study projects. The first chart, Chart 17.1, indicates the number of projects that used ad hoc, traditional, and object-oriented analysis. Categorizing was done in a subjective manner—it was object-oriented if the project manager said so. The second chart, Chart 17.2, similarly summarizes the numbers of projects that used the three kinds of design approaches. And the third chart, Chart 17.3, cross-correlates the information in the other two charts.

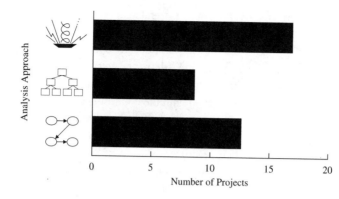

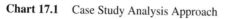

Chart 17.1   Case Study Analysis Approach

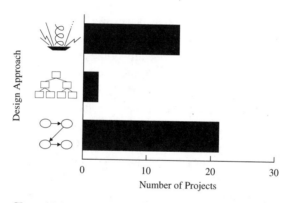

Chart 17.2   Case Study Design Approach

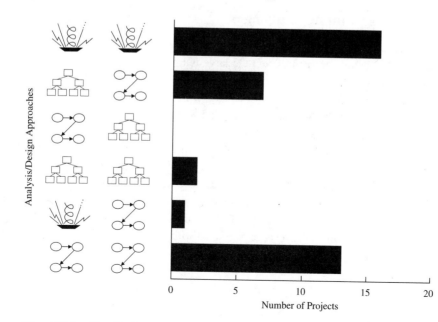

Chart 17.3   Case Study Analysis and Design Approach

All of the developers employed an object-oriented approach to implementation—otherwise they would not have been in the study!

Most of the projects did ad hoc analysis and design. This may be partly because the projects we studied were started in the late 1980s and very early 1990s, predating the flurry of articles and books that have since appeared about analysis-and-design methods for object-oriented technology. Later, even with the contributions of Booch, Rumbaugh *et al.*, Shlaer-Mellor, and others, the organizations we interviewed still thought it important to refine and combine—picking notations and techniques from the different offerings to create a result that best matched their organization's needs.

In our data, seven projects used traditional analysis followed by object-oriented design. No project that conducted an object-oriented analysis followed with a traditional design. We encountered two magical projects, ones that used traditional analysis and design, and then used an object-oriented programming language. One of these case study projects used C++, and the other Smalltalk. Both were successful projects, despite the effort required to create the object-oriented implementations out of traditional design results. We attribute their successes to the quality of the team members.

We had only one project that used ad hoc analysis followed by object-oriented design. This project was implemented in C++. Although ultimately viewed as successful, the project was completed a year late. We had anticipated more projects in this camp for several reasons. In the time frame in which we did this study, there was little discussion about object-oriented methods; the few discussions that did exist focused on object-oriented design. Generally, the early adopters just started designing and coding, without analysis. However, many projects (13) argued they did do object-oriented analysis, given the options available at the time.

Choice of Programming Languages

Within our case studies, there is no direct correlation between language choice and project success. This is not surprising given the large number of project management issues that affect a project. Of the 39 projects studied, most selected either C++ or Smalltalk (Smalltalk-80, Smalltalk/V, and ENFIN), as shown in Chart 17.4. A few of the companies and projects we reviewed used both C++ and Smalltalk. (When different dialects of the same language were reported, we counted the language only once.) We also studied projects that used CLOS, Eiffel, Objective C, and an object modification to PL/1. Although each language and related development environment presents some technical differences, the managerial issues do not appear to be considerably different. The one exception is training and the ability to hire already trained personnel. Most college graduates with a background in C feel more comfortable using C++ than any other object-oriented language. Programmers who are experienced with COBOL or 4GL languages seem to resist C++.

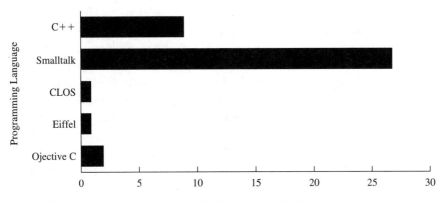

Chart 17.4   Programming Languages Used in the Case Studies

Our sample is clearly small. Much depended upon our ability to convince project leaders to spend time sharing their experiences. It was considerably easier to convince Smalltalk customers to accommodate us, and hence the heavy weighting toward Smalltalk.

Choice of Databases

Chart 17.5 shows the forms of external storage used by the case study projects. Thirteen of the projects used no database at all. One project used an object-oriented database to store the artifacts created during development. The remaining projects developed end-user applications that required database access.

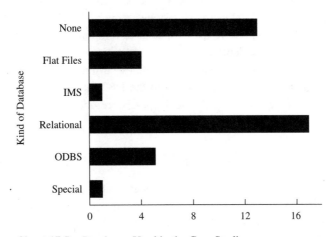

Chart 17.5   Databases Used in the Case Studies

Most of the companies with which we have worked, as well as the case study projects, have used relational database management systems for storing application information. Several of the companies also experimented with using object-oriented databases for storing libraries of class descriptions. The primary reason for choosing a relational database is that the technology has proved to be a robust way to create a scalable corporate database server, and there are a number of vendors with mature data modeling and administration products. Recognizing the market penetration of relational databases, most vendors of object-oriented development and delivery environments provide mechanisms for accessing these databases.

Organizations choose an object-oriented database when the data elements are large and complex, and retrieving them with relational technology is too slow. As the object-oriented database vendors continue to add the features and tools that are available with relational databases, these systems become competitive alternatives. In addition, OODB vendors participate in standards-setting efforts. Of special interest is the effort to create C++ and Smalltalk language bindings for the databases so the database queries and transaction commands will be formulated in the same syntax as the general programming language. The advantage of this is that everything is represented as an object, which can be transient or persistent as a matter of programmatic declaration. No special embedded query language will be required. The software will be written in a consistent manner, which facilitates maintenance.

One of the case studies used multiple databases. The production database, where the majority of the organization's business data resides, was DB2—its choice was dictated by history. All new applications were required to cooperate with this database. The organization also wanted to store a large number of scanned images that could be examined on demand by end-user applications. Because of the sheer volume of images (approximately 27 million), the organization selected ViewStar—a database that is specially designed for managing images. The third database, Gemstone, supported the software development environment. The developers were using special development tools built on top of a Smalltalk environment. These tools were used to create an interconnected set of analysis artifacts. Gemstone was used to store and retrieve these artifacts. The fourth database was Oracle. It stored information that was similar to the DB2 information, and was used for testing application software because the developers were not permitted to conduct tests with the production database.

Illustration 1: Languages Face-off Using Multiple Comparisons

Working for an application development environment vendor, we have seen many different clients carry out evaluations. One customer, whose current software was created with a combination of Natural (a 4GL), PL/1, and APL, assigned a team to recommend the next-generation development environment. After some preliminary investigation, the team narrowed their choices to C, C++, Ada, and Smalltalk. The team concluded that a comparison of technical documentation alone would be inconclusive, and recommended a realistic use test.

To set up the test, the team selected three different applications they considered characteristic of the kinds of applications the company develops. They wrote a short requirements specification for each application, and then they sought out internal developers who were experts in each of the languages. The team located C, C++, and Ada experts, but had to bring in a consultant as the Smalltalk expert.

The experiment required each language expert to develop all three applications in the same order. They could take as much time as necessary, but it was expected that all three applications could be completed within a week as they were not large applications, and resources for the evaluation (the time of the experts and evaluation team members) were limited. Evaluation team members were available to the developers to answer any questions about the requirements. Each language was evaluated one at a time, which could have affected the results as the evaluation team honed its explanations over time.

The evaluation criteria included the time to complete each application, the ease with which the evaluation team understood the development process, and the extent to which they believed the developers in their organization could replicate the expert's behavior. They chose Smalltalk because the Smalltalk expert completed the three applications in a significantly shorter time, and the Smalltalk applications demonstrated easier extensibility for improved maintenance.

Illustration 2: Languages Face-off Using a Single Large Comparison

Rather than base a comparison on several small applications, a single larger example representing a result of significance to the corporation can be written with different languages, and then compared. *Computer World* in 1992 reported a comparison conducted by EDS in which two different teams developed the same inventory control system, one using PL/1 and the other Smalltalk. Care was taken to keep the skill level of the two teams the same.

The PL/1 team developed a fully functional manufacturing inventory subsystem, based on a 300-page functional specification they created using a non-object-oriented analysis method. The PL/1-based system made use of a relational database. The developers on the team were all EDS employees. The Smalltalk team was given both the functional specification and the running PL/1 system, and asked to recreate it using object-oriented technology, including an object-oriented database. Team members consisted of consultants from the database company.

The results are shown in Table 17.2. EDS uses a product process model they call SLC, which supports extensive data collection. As a result, detailed data on staff-hours and system size for both the PL/1 and the Smalltalk teams were collected. The PL/1 version of the system provided a character-oriented user interface. The Smalltalk team chose to use Facets, a GUI application generator, rather than create a character-oriented interface. The Smalltalk team had actually taken less time than shown in the table. To make sure that the comparison was fair, the Smalltalk staff-hour numbers were adjusted to reflect the anticipated effort involved if the Smalltalk version had implemented a character-oriented user interface, for which the Facets facilities were not well suited.

Table 17.2 Data from the EDS Experiment

Measure	PL/1 Team	Smalltalk Team	Difference
Staffing average	8	3	2.5 to 1
Elapsed time	19 months	3.5 months	5 to 1
Person months	152	11	14 to 1
Lines of code	265K	22K	12 to 1
Response time on complex query	10 Sec	30 Sec	0.3 to 1
Response time on simple query	2 Sec	2 Sec	1 to 1

The results favor Smalltalk (and therefore object-oriented technology), but appear suspect. The comparison is not completely fair because the Smalltalk team had the advantage of using the PL/1 team's result as a way to understand the specifications. The ratios just seem too big. But if the Smalltalk results are decreased by a factor of three, there is still a two-to-one time difference, a five-to-one person-month difference, and a four-to-one size difference in the code to be maintained. Still impressive.

The results of this productivity project convinced management that a follow-on project was warranted. The goal of this next study was to understand whether EDS employees can learn object-oriented technology faster than the typical six-to-nine months reported in the trade press.

Illustration 3: Methods Face-off Using a Survey Approach

One of the case study projects used a broad-based survey of existing object-oriented design methods to select one for use in the organization, having already selected the Shlaer-Mellor analysis method. (The process model for this case study was documented as Illustration 2 in Chapter 8.)

A questionnaire was sent out to various vendors to learn the details of their design methods, asking:

1. To what extent does the OOD method address the following OO principles:

   - Abstraction
   - Encapsulation
   - Inheritance
   - Polymorphism/Dynamic binding
   - Delegation

2. Is the method classless or class based?

3. If it is class based, are there guidelines for designing reusable components and generic class hierarchies, and accommodating class evolution?

4. To what extent does the method address the following object design issues:

   - Concurrency
   - Distribution
   - Exception handling
   - Internationalization
   - Persistence
   - Security
   - Synchronization/Scheduling
   - Memory management

5. Are guidelines provided for estimating performance (time and space)?

6. Is the method independent of programming language?

7. Are programming-language guidelines provided? If so, what languages are covered?

8. What models are encompassed by the method?

9. What notation is used for modeling?

10. What case tools are available that support the method/model/notation?

11. What training is available (courses/schedule/cost/customization/consulting)?

12. What case studies are provided with the training?

13. Where, and for what type of applications, has this method been used successfully? Can references be provided?

14. Does the method address postdesign issues (e.g., code development, testing, maintenance, project management)?

15. Is the method compatible with object-oriented analysis? If so, which analysis methods are supported?

16. Are design measures available?

After examining six written questionnaire responses, the project leaders selected three as finalists, primarily based on the completeness of the notation, its documentation, and prior industry experience using the method. Each of the major proponents of these methods was invited to give an oral presentation. The winning method was Booch's.

Illustration 4: Champions Face-off Face to Face

The technique of having proponents of different choices compete shows up in several formats. Three examples follow, in which the formats are: create software for comparison, debate within the organization, and solicit cross-vendor criticism.

Vendors create software demonstrations. Based on their business requirements and a market survey, one of the case study teams narrowed the field of software development environments to two possibilities. One environment was based on non-object-oriented technology: a relational database with a 4GL programming language and GUI builder. The other choice used object-oriented technology with Smalltalk as the programming language, a GUI builder, and access to relational databases. In the evaluation, each vendor was asked to create a software solution based on a problem description designed by the evaluation team leader. The responses were presented in an open meeting, attended by the evaluators and members of both vendor development teams.

At the outset, the team leader assumed that both vendors would succeed in completing the development assignment. Creating software was important to this project, but even more important was the ability to maintain the resultant software. So the real evaluation took place at the open meeting. The plan was to ask each vendor to present its result and explain how the product contributed to the successful completion of the task. And then the team leader would ask each vendor to change the result—in the meeting, while all participants watched.

Unfortunately, the vendor proposing non-object-oriented technology was unable to complete the original assignment. During the demonstration of the partial result, the system crashed and the presenters ended up talking their way through what should have happened. The object-oriented technology team completed the original assignment, demonstrated it, and then quickly made the requested change. Needless to say, objects won the day!

Company advocates debate the environment choice. One organization wanted to select a Smalltalk environment to be used in its development centers worldwide. The organization already had experience in using three different Smalltalk environments, and wanted to standardize on one.

To select the specific Smalltalk environment, the organization set up an evaluation project that resembled a debate. The idea was to debate the specific merits and demerits of each Smalltalk environment in an open forum in front of a moderator and an evaluation panel composed of team members from the organization's tools group. The tools group is chartered to approve all technologies used by development groups throughout the organization. The moderator was an outside consultant, a recognized expert in object-oriented technology, with specific Smalltalk development know-how. The debaters were employees of the company, not vendor representatives. Each was chosen because he or she was recognized as the strongest advocate for a particular Smalltalk environment.

The stage was set for the debate. The evaluation committee asked specific questions of the various debaters, and each responded with a product-specific answer. The moderator controlled the discussion by making sure that the appropriate issues were addressed and that no debater avoided an issue. The moderator was also permitted to ask questions. In addition, the debaters had considerable latitude to cross-examine one another.

The result of the debate was useful. The evaluation committee was able to rule out one of the environments immediately. In addition, all of the participants had a much better understanding of how Smalltalk was and could be used within the organization. However, deciding between the remaining two Smalltalk environments required information—pricing and future enhancement plans of the vendors—that could not be provided by the debaters. And so another evaluation project, involving the vendors, was initiated.

Cross-vendor critique or appraisal. A time-honored evaluation approach is to publish a request-for-proposal (RFP). Interested vendors respond in writing. The twist is to ask the competing vendors to review one another's responses, to find inconsistencies, factual discrepancies, and omissions in the competitive bids. The vendors are both motivated and often more adept at providing such critiques, which then provide the organization with the set of questions to be asked during the follow-on phase of evaluation.

The difficulty with this approach is maintaining the confidentiality of certain responses, such as special prices and product futures. Often a consultant can help moderate the process in those cases where confidentiality is critical. Or responses can be given in two parts, one designated as confidential. We have seen this evaluation approach be quite effective, given vendors who are willing to participate.

Summary

In this chapter, we reviewed the need to assess your current development environment; to determine who will use the environment to create analyses, designs, and code; and to identify the kinds of software you will produce and the characteristics of the delivery setting. We then briefly discussed some ideas for evaluating options, and reviewed various evaluation techniques used in the case study projects.

Not every organization is prepared for the changes brought by new languages, libraries, tools, databases, and methods. Look at your organization's level of saturation with new technologies, disposition toward change, and your tolerance to risk. Take into account the risk we call technology market momentum, which is the extent to which some technology has captured market attention whether or not it is the best choice for you.

Evaluate your options using techniques such as benchmarking. We pointed out some of the benchmarks currently available for comparing object-oriented products. Our case studies showed the different ways people have mixed and matched analysis-and-design methods with programming languages. Using new methods with traditional (non-object-oriented) programming languages is an unfortunate situation, while continuing to use traditional methods with object-oriented languages is magic. Our preference is for a purely object-oriented approach, so that you can obtain the benefits associated with maintaining traceability among your analysis, design, and implementation object models.

The case studies illustrate approaches to evaluation. You can compare languages by building simple or complex examples. You can send surveys to vendors. You can have your vendors face off in a competition in which you challenge their marketing claims, using either internal advocates or vendor experts. We have participated in all of these, finding the face-to-face (vendor-to-vendor) contests the most fun and informative.

Additional Reading About Evaluating Software Development Environments

Moreau, D. and Dominick, W., A Programming Environment Evaluation Methodology for Object-Oriented Systems: Part I—The Methodology, *Journal of Object Oriented Programming*, 3(1), 38–52, May/June 1990(a).

Moreau, D. and Dominick, W., A Programming Environment Evaluation Methodology for Object-Oriented Systems: Part II—Test Case Application, *Journal of Object Oriented Programming*, 3(3), 23–32, September/October 1990(b).

This two-part series of articles offers a method for evaluating object-oriented systems which includes a test case application. It is interesting both for the example method and its start-to-finish recommendations for setting up an experiment to determine which software development environment to select.

Weiderman, N. H., Habermann, A. N., Borger, M. W., and Klein, M. H., A Methodology for Evaluating Environments, *The Second ACM SIGSOFT/SIGPLAN Symposium on Practical Software Development Environments*, 199-207, December 1986.

This paper reports on an effort at the Carnegie Mellon University Software Engineering Institute to provide the requirements for an effective environment evaluation methodology and to apply this methodology to several Ada environments. The approach focuses on the activities of the user rather than the tools of the environment, with the intent to test and report on a broad set of functionality considered necessary by the evaluators. Despite its age, this paper remains one of the only accessible and practical sources on this topic.

CHAPTER 18

What Is in a
Training Plan?

Tell me and I'll forget;
show me and I may remember;
involve me and I'll understand.

Chinese Proverb

The title of this chapter contains the word "Training." We could have substituted the word "Educating." The two words are often used synonymously, although they have substantially different meanings. Training is most often used in the context of vocational education. After a training program, the student should have a skill that is immediately applicable to doing a job, although training is used to imply that the student has learned a limited skill, with little ability to generalize and extend the skill. Gibson, in communicating the training needs of object-oriented technology [Gibson 1991], preferred the term "education." Education implies that the learner has assimilated the context of the skill, including when and where to use different techniques, how to apply them, and why they are useful in particular situations—all of which facilitate extending and generalizing the skill.

Most employers think it is not their job to educate their employees—this should have occurred when they were in school. At the most, employers believe it is their responsibility to train employees in the specific skills they require to do their jobs. The assumption is that employees already have the requisite educational background to assimilate the training at the deep level implied by education. Unfortunately, an education in object-oriented technology has generally not been available in schools over the last decade. As a consequence, if employers provide only developer's training on the syntax of an object-oriented programming language, the developers will be unlikely to understand the best way to apply the language. When schools do not provide the requisite object-oriented education, this task must be assumed by corporations.

We approach our training discussion with the assumption that we have to educate the whole team. The discussion distinguishes subject areas, proficiency levels, and training formats. We conclude with specific recommendations for how to train the different team members.

Subject Areas

Training that covers each aspect of the software development life cycle should be considered for both technical and managerial team members. Let's examine several areas in which training is required.

Concepts About Object-Oriented Technology

The goal of a first course in object-oriented technology is to educate team members in basic concepts. This course should cover the concepts and benefits of object-oriented technology that we present in Chapter 3, notably developing for maintainability and developing with reuse. The course should show how these key points are supported by features such as object encapsulation, polymorphism, inheritance, and dynamic binding.

Several key topics must be addressed by this course. First, object-oriented technology is used to develop systems, not to write lines of code. Students must be taught to focus on architecture, rather than on algorithms. Second, the names of objects and their services reflect the vocabulary of the domain. Students must learn the importance of using the vocabulary of the problem domain when developing object-oriented models. Third, the objects in an object-oriented system are classified and categorized with respect to one another and to objects in existing libraries. Students must learn basic classification skills, since these are often left untaught in schools.

There is no official, standard terminology for object-oriented technology, although there have been several attempts [Object Management Group 1992]. For that matter, there isn't even general agreement about the core set of concepts that constitute object-oriented technology. Without a standard, it is impossible to determine whether a course covers all of the concepts. Worse still, different courses define common terms—such as object state—in very different ways. Fortunately, there is a body of object-oriented terminology and definitions that many practitioners use. We use these terms and definitions in this book. Any concept course that unnecessarily invents new terms and definitions should be avoided. If your team members learn strange terminology, they will have a difficult time communicating with their industry peers. Also, be wary of courses that make a religious issue out of choosing which concepts are fundamental to object-oriented technology and which are not. Since there is no standard set of concepts, this discussion is inappropriate. For the beginner, it is really not productive to discuss whether multiple inheritance is a core concept or not. It is more important to discuss any concept that may have practical use to the students, and leave out the dogma.

Not everything about objects is simple and easy to learn. Many concepts must be explained using practical examples drawn from a domain that is familiar to the students. Comparative examples are especially useful because they show how the same problem is solved both with and without object-oriented concepts.

The course should tell what is hard about object-oriented technology. For example, it is difficult to derive the vocabulary that represents your business. Determining the proper responsibilities of each object is also difficult. Designing for reuse is as much an art as an engineering activity. The course must also describe the technical details and difficulties of using encapsulation, polymorphism, inheritance, and dynamic binding.

Object-Oriented Analysis

Object-oriented analysis (OOA) training teaches students how to conceptualize, model, and represent the requirements of a given problem domain. Training in OOA must introduce the key concepts that underlie one or more specific analysis methods. The training must also describe techniques and guidelines that are used to examine a problem domain and determine a set of object-oriented artifacts that meet the stated goals and objectives. And the training must describe or reference one or more notations for representing the analysis object model. An OOA (as well as an OOD) course should have the students work through at least one complete example to illustrate and reinforce the concepts.

Many OOA training courses only describe one or more notations. Such courses are of limited value because they teach only how to represent the analysis artifacts, not how to conceptualize and model a problem to determine the proper artifacts. A more valuable approach is to teach both the conceptualization and modeling techniques of a particular method, and a supporting notation.

Avoid OOA training courses that are overly simplistic. For example, avoid courses that suggest that you: Take the written requirements specification and underline the nouns—these will be your objects. Then, underline the verbs—these will be the services of the associated objects (nouns). Finally, underline the adjectives—these will be the attributes of the objects. Such an approach makes numerous assumptions, which in practice are simply not true. Unfortunately, many contemporary OOA training courses use precisely this approach, or some equally poor variation. Look for training that provides insight into the problem of finding objects in the problem domain and modeling the problem in terms of objects.

An OOA training course should teach when and where to apply OOA, and how to review the analysis artifacts. This advice is critical because object-oriented development, as we describe in Chapter 6, can differ from past practices.

OOA training should be independent of any implementation language. Analysis focuses on the problem statement, independent of technology constraints. An implementation language injects unnecessary technology constraints into the discussion.

Object-Oriented Design

Object-oriented design (OOD) training teaches architectural and detailed design using object-oriented techniques. As we discuss in Chapter 15, OOA and OOD have much in common—the conceptualization, modeling, and notation aspects are nearly identical. Issues addressed during OOD which are not considered during OOA can be taught in a separate course, or OOA and OOD can be taught in combination. Because of their common techniques, we prefer teaching analysis and design as a single course.

OOD training must tell how to make both strategic and tactical object-oriented design decisions. Strategic decisions define:

- Architecture—how subsystems are discovered and modeled in terms of objects

- User interaction—how end users interact with the system

- Information management—how to deal with persistent forms of information elements

- Communications—how communications take place among system elements, or with elements external to the system

- Control—how the system determines what to do next

Tactical decisions include:

- Choice of algorithms, especially ones designed as templates to be completed by subclasses

- Choice of middleware for adapting the interface of one collection of objects to the message-sending expectations of another

- Choice of data structures, especially those needed for best performance and memory management

Learning just a design notation (or the specific design features added to an analysis notation), will not teach you how to design. An OOD course is likely to use one or more programming languages to illustrate detailed design decisions, even though many OOD decisions are independent of language choice. Unless you specifically want a design course tailored to the nuances of a particular programming language, look for language-independent OOD training.

Especially be wary of a design course that assumes analysis is not necessary!

Framework Design

Framework design training is an advanced course that provides the student with skills for defining abstractions and for creating understandable and reusable frameworks.

Framework design is the crafting of a collection of objects to capture the reusable abstractions of a given problem domain. Learning to design frameworks is a difficult task. In fact, not everyone is capable of becoming a framework designer. As our colleague David Leibs—himself an excellent framework designer and chief architect of ParcPlace's VisualWorks 1.0 product—once said, "Good framework designers have personality disorders." There is something strange and wonderful about the way such people immerse themselves in the process of framework design—our colleague claims that "you do not design the framework, you live the framework." In the end, the framework is truly a reflection of the designer.

Framework design is difficult to do because proper abstractions are not easy to devise, and even when the proper abstractions are already known, it is technically challenging to organize an understandable and reusable framework.

Framework design training teaches students how to design objects that embody the proper balance of generalized and specialized knowledge. If an object description is too general, ways to specialize it might not be obvious. If an artifact is too specific, it will embody assumptions that limit its reusability. Framework design training must teach students this balancing skill.

The framework design course must help students understand what makes a framework effective as a foundation for building applications. A framework is usually not a single object, but a collection of objects that work together to provide a foundation for reuse. Not only must you learn to define objects that balance generality with specificity, you must learn to generalize these objects to arrive at an abstract collection of interacting objects. Learning to devise appropriate generalization is the essence of the course. The course must also teach communication skills. A framework is useless unless it is well documented, describing its purpose and usage.

Good framework design is a skill best learned through an apprenticeship to good framework designers, and through examination, use, or modification of existing frameworks. This approach is like taking a famous painting and exploring the artist's design decisions, such as taking a Van Gogh farm scene and changing the blue thatched roof of a cottage to orange and seeing why the artist might have preferred the blue! Framework design is an art that you learn from the masters.

Although the apprentice model is best, there is still value in a course format. What follows is a sample course plan.

Choose one large framework, several medium frameworks, and many small examples that illustrate different aspects of framework design. Begin with the small examples, each one crafted to illustrate a particular framework design trade-off issue, such as understandability versus performance. We present the background on the example and then begin a debate. Each student assumes the role of a team member—developer, user, or tester—and argues why one trade-off is better than another at meeting the stated goals and objectives. We discuss a series of small examples in this way, taking about an hour for each.

Next, we tackle medium-sized frameworks. An example that we have used in the past is that of a discrete event-simulation framework, such as the one fully described in the Smalltalk-80 language book [Goldberg and Robson 1983]. At this level, examples can be supplemented with published material to provide written reinforcement for what is said in the classroom. We might spend a day dissecting and describing the various aspects of the framework. The primary emphasis is on what decisions were made and why. A software implementation of the framework is made available on-line for hands-on perusal, use, and extension.

Finally, we examine one large example framework. In many cases, real-world issues do not show up until this point. In the small and medium framework examples, we can finesse difficult questions and make isolated decisions, targeted to singular objectives. With large frameworks, we take a systems approach and concern ourselves with meeting all of the project's system objectives simultaneously. Examples of large frameworks are the Smalltalk model-view-controller (MVC) framework or a library for creating graphical user interfaces, such as Interviews [Linton and Calder 1987]. In the past, we have used the real-world redesign of the MVC framework from ParcPlace Smalltalk-80 Version 2.5 to Objectworks\Smalltalk Release 4.0 [Leibs and Rubin 1992] as an example. The discussion of a large example takes at least one day.

Implementation Environment

Implementation environment training teaches topics such as the use of a particular programming language, a set of development tools, and a library of reusable components. This training is directed at technical developers.

Implementation environment training should include some form of programming language training such as C++ or Smalltalk. It is important that the training teach developers how the fundamental object-oriented concepts are mapped onto the mechanisms of a particular programming language. For example, inheritance is a concept that can be realized by different mechanisms. Smalltalk and C++ both have their own ways to support inheritance. Developers must learn the syntax and semantics of the programming language, but the training must address pragmatic issues of how to use the language to solve real problems.

Most implementation environment training will also teach the use of particular development tools, including browsers, compilers, and debuggers. Finally, many development environments come with libraries of reusable components, so training must provide a road map to the library, and specific details on the most frequently reused components.

When evaluating an implementation environment course, be especially careful if the language involved is a hybrid, such as C++ or CLOS. It is dangerous to learn these languages as extensions to their underlying base languages. Seek out training that presents C++ from an object-oriented perspective, and not just as C with class extensions. This topic is a controversial one (what isn't, when objects are involved?), discussed in detail in [Antebi 1990].

The more effective implementation environment training courses allocate at least 50 percent of course time to hands-on practice with the environment, doing exercises that reinforce materials from the lectures. Students are more likely to retain their understanding of a language in which they have done actual work.

After seven years of designing and teaching a Smalltalk environment course, we believe it combines many of the aspects that are necessary in an effective implementation environment course. We present our course outline in Table 18.1 as an example. This particular course assumes no prior knowledge of object-oriented technology and so it includes training on object-oriented concepts with a brief introduction to OOA.

Project Management

Project-management training teaches managers how to structure and manage successfully a software development effort that uses object-oriented technology. It must explain how object-oriented technology affects planning, controlling, directing, organizing, and staffing a project. At the project level, this training should teach how to set up a product process model, create teams, devise a training plan, select analysis-and-design methods, and select an implementation environment. Some project managers in the organization may require special training on how to introduce object-oriented technology into an organization to meet organization software development goals and objectives, or how to create a corporate reuse program or measurement program. This may be taught in the same course with the core project management material or in a separate one.

This book, of course, was designed to function as a training vehicle in the area of project management. The Table of Contents is a check-off list for the contents of a course on project management.

Other Subject Areas

There are a number of other courses that could enhance an organization's object-oriented technology curriculum. We list a few here with a brief synopsis of course content.

Table 18.1 . VisualWorks Course Outline

Course Offerings

1. Object-Oriented Basics

   - Introduce object-oriented concepts and definitions
   - Compare traditional solutions with object-oriented solutions
   - Exercise: Simulate a local area network

2. Introduction to the User Interface

   - Describe the various user interface components necessary for using the Smalltalk development environment
   - Exercise: Exploring the user interface

3. Object-Oriented Techniques

   - Overview of Object Behavior Analysis. This provides a brief introduction to the basic concepts of analysis so developers can see the big picture.
   - Object-oriented classification techniques. Describes many of the fundamental techniques for organizing an object model.
   - Exercise: Designing an object-oriented LAN

4. Basic System Tools

   - Introduction to some of the basic tools of the Smalltalk environment
   - Exercise: Using the basic system tools

5. Smalltalk Language: Objects and Expressions

   - Discuss many of the concepts and elements of the Smalltalk language: classes, instances, messages, methods, literals, variables, block and message expressions
   - Exercise: Evaluating Smalltalk expressions in the Smalltalk environment

6. Smalltalk Language: Messages & Method Lookup

   - Discuss message types, precedence, cascading, and return values
   - Discuss messages for instance creation, coercion, and control structures
   - Discuss method lookup, self, and super
   - Exercise: Additional work on evaluating Smalltalk expressions

7. System Browser

   - Describe the organization of the system browser
   - Exercise: Using the system browser

8. System Classes

   - Shared object protocols
   - Important system classes
   - System class categories
   - Exercise: Exploring system classes and shared behavior

9. VisualWorks\Smalltalk and the External Environment

   - The structure of the VisualWorks environment
   - Platform-independent I/O
   - Crash recovery
   - Exercise: Crash recovery system

continued

Table 18.1   continued

Course Offerings

10. Debugging Tools

    - Notification of definition errors
    - Notification of execution interrupts
    - Using the system debugger
    - Exercise: Find the bugs!

11. Building Applications

    - Application building process
    - Exercise: 1/3-day lab for building applications

12. Building User Interfaces

    - Introduction to the UI builder
    - An implementation of a simple counter interface
    - Exercise: Building a simple user interface

13. Model-View-Controller Framework

    - Overview of the MVC metaphor
    - An implementation of MVC
    - Exercise: Exploring simple MVC programs

14. Building VisualWorks Applications

    - Introduction to the VisualWorks graphical layout components
    - An implementation of a personal financial manager
    - Exercise: Building a complete application
    - Exercise: Completing the personal financial manager

Corporate object model. If an organization does an enterprise-wide or domain analysis, defining an object model that pervades most, if not all, of the applications to be built by in-house developers, then it is important to provide a course specifically to review this object model and how to create applications using it. The object model itself will influence how specialization should take place, thus influencing the choice of product process model. Course content should include examples of how the corporate object model has already been used in the organization. A particular product process model could be recommended in this course.

Framework reuse. Whereas the course on the corporate object model is specific to a particular framework, and the framework design course focuses on producing a framework, a course on the general technique of development by reusing frameworks could be useful. This course would target those developers expected to consume rather than produce frameworks. Special techniques for using frameworks covered in the course could include how to look for framework specialization hooks and how to integrate components into frameworks. Typically, an organization has business application developers (see Chapter 12) who could benefit from taking this course or the one on the corporate object model.

Object-oriented database systems (OODB). This course should be both theoretical and practical, covering the basic concepts of object-oriented database systems and their relationship to programming languages, and how to apply the concepts to defining the OODB schema. Much of this latter topic overlaps the content of a course on OOA and OOD, implying that the methods courses are prerequisites. This course would then focus on the specific OODB selected by the organization, its data definition language, and the data modeling language. The course should also cover traditional database topics, such as transaction management, concurrency, consistency, and recovery, as they apply to a specific OODB.

Managing reuse process model. Members of the Reuse Team (see Chapter 12 and Appendix C) require special training to support the organization's reuse process model. This course would help all team members understand one another's roles, giving a basic understanding of the organization's policies for reuse definition, acquisition, certification, classification, and communication. If the organization has selected specialized reuse tools for managing the reuse repository, these should also be introduced. More advanced courses on certification and classification could target the librarian or administrator roles.

Measurement. At Hewlett-Packard, a course on measurement is documented in [Grady and Caswell 1987]. The objective of the course is "to provide background and hands-on experience to project managers and engineers so they can immediately use software metrics in their own environment to make informed decisions in the software development process." The course covers defect tracking, estimation techniques and tools, use of code analyzers to refine estimates, and establishing a test release plan. The structure of the course is based on a single case study of a project. A measurement course targeted at planning and controlling projects using object-oriented technology would cover similar topics, with specific recommendations for how to measure the size and functionality of an object-oriented system (see Chapter 20). It would also help predict work effort on a project, and provide suggestions on how to use data to improve process, resources, and products. A course targeted to self-improvement for programmers was devised by Watts Humphrey [Humphrey 1995]. It can be modified to take into consideration the different ways in which measurement is done when the development approach uses objects.

Train the trainers. A cost-saving approach for larger organizations is to provide internal training support. Teachers have to be trained too, and kept up to date on the fast-changing world of object-oriented technology. Many vendors of courses are willing to license their course materials and train your internal teachers in techniques for delivering the materials. An additional form of training for teachers consists of attending technology seminars and conferences.

Subject Area Proficiency Levels

We are frequently asked how much and what kind of training is necessary to get someone up to speed in a particular subject area. We answer by first describing four proficiency levels, which define what it means to be "up to speed." Then we define the training needed to reach each of the proficiency levels in the subject areas of object-oriented analysis, object-oriented design, implementation environment, and project management. Not all team members need to be experts in every aspect of object-oriented technology, but each member should understand the roles and responsibilities of all team members.

Proficiency Levels

Our proficiency scale has four values: conceptual, basic, functional, and advanced. Someone who has a basic understanding of a subject area is more knowledgeable than someone with a conceptual understanding. We do not define a natural low point on the scale, a level at which a person is completely ignorant of the subject area.

Conceptual. An individual at the conceptual level has a preliminary grasp of the concepts, but is not yet prepared for project assignments that require a working knowledge of the subject area. Most people require no formal training to reach this level. Reading books or magazine articles often suffices.

Basic. An individual at the basic level has a working knowledge of the subject area, and can recognize what he or she does not know. A person at this level can work on small assignments, but is not ready for critical-path product development. This level of proficiency is typically reached with some initial training and simple assignments.

Functional. An individual at a functional level has good working knowledge of the subject area, possesses a set of usable skills, and is able to ask clarification questions to refine these skills. A person at this level needs minimal guidance to complete assignments. Most productive product development efforts are staffed by people at this level. This level is attained through a mix of training and direct experience on multiple projects.

Advanced. An individual at an advanced level is an expert in the subject area. This person is the authority to whom others turn to for advice and solutions to unusual problems. An individual at an advanced level is often a contributor to the technology. This level is attained over an extended period of time by a person working as a practitioner on multiple projects.

Time to Attain a Proficiency Level

Our discussion of proficiency levels assumes that the students are learning about the use of object-oriented technology to do their jobs. We assume they already possess basic analysis and design skills, or programming skills, or are experienced project managers.

The following charts show how much time we estimate is needed to learn each subject area to reach each of the four proficiency levels, assuming the student is of average intelligence. The X-axis of each chart indicates the four proficiency levels, and the Y-axis indicates time in months. Because we provide time estimates as a range, each chart contains two data series. The higher series plots the upper bound for each estimate, and the lower series plots the lower bound. Our estimates assume regular training efforts that progress at learning paces comfortable for the average student. There are styles of training, such as immersion programs, that aim for the lower bounds. We illustrate experience with such programs in Chapter 19.

The first chart (Chart 18.1) indicates that it will take between six and eight months to reach a functional level of proficiency in OOA/OOD. Functional and advanced levels are reached only after work on actual development projects. Advancing a level depends mainly on the number of projects in which you participate and the amount of effort you contribute.

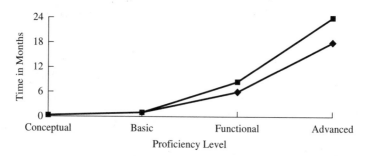

Chart 18.1   Time to Achieve OOA and OOD Proficiency Levels

When we say that not everyone is capable of becoming a designer of reusable frameworks, we mean that not everyone can reach a functional or advanced level of proficiency in this subject area. Moving from a basic to a functional level as a framework designer involves substantial effort, as demonstrated by the estimates shown in Chart 18.2. Developers must evolve their skills for two or more years, especially if they work on their own. If they work as apprentices, they may only need one year to reach the functional level.

The data backing up our estimates on the time needed to learn an implementation environment (Chart 18.3) comes from seven years of direct experience teaching ParcPlace Smalltalk and VisualWorks environments to more than 3000 people. We have had the good fortune to follow up with a number of these people as they developed their products. And we have compared our Smalltalk training estimates with estimates from

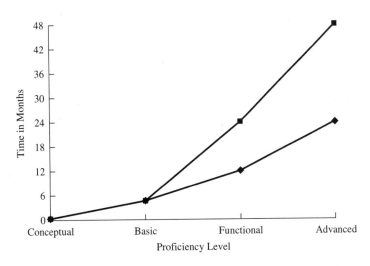

Chart 18.2   Time to Achieve Framework Design Proficiency Levels

experienced C++ trainers, including those in our own company. As a result, we learned that it is not possible to provide a precise correlation between Smalltalk and C++ training estimates. The imprecision reflects the differences in effort required to learn language, tools, and libraries. For example, it takes much less time to teach someone the Smalltalk language because Smalltalk has a simpler syntax and semantics. But most C++ programmers do not have to learn new tools; they rely mostly on their prior C-based tools. And the C++ libraries are generally smaller and less likely to be viewed as an integral part of learning the language than are the Smalltalk libraries. The result is that implementation environments for the two languages take about the same amount of time to learn.

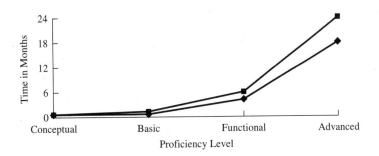

Chart 18.3   Time to Achieve Implementation Environment Proficiency
                 Levels

Our time estimates for learning an implementation environment assume that the student is already a programmer, with a functional level of proficiency in at least one high-level general purpose language such as COBOL or C. The estimates also assume that the person is already familiar with object-oriented concepts. For the average person, it will take five to six months to reach a functional level of proficiency in the Smalltalk environment. The cofounder of one training company, with more than seven years' experience in teaching C++ to C programmers, claims that C programmers with appropriate training become functional C++ programmers in four to six months [Banahan 1992].

Chart 18.4 shows the estimates for learning project management when using object-oriented technology, assuming the learner already has experience as a technical manager. Even the most experienced managers may not appreciate the issues in planning and controlling a project using the incremental and iterative development strategies, prototyping, and consuming reusable assets. The time we allot assumes that learning has to take place in the context of several actual projects.

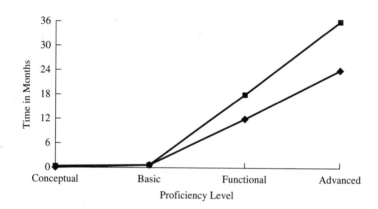

Chart 18.4   Time to Achieve Project Management Proficiency Levels

At the functional level, a manager has real-world experience planning, executing, and tracking development involving objects, and is able to make the decisions we outline in this book. The only way to reach this level is by managing one or more (sub)projects under the tutelage of a mentor or project manager, over the course of six months to one year.

Table 18.2 summarizes the effort required to attain the various levels of proficiency in the subject areas of OOA/OOD, Framework Design, Implementation Environment, and Project Management. Time denotes total elapsed time, so that one month to reach a basic level is the cumulative time for both conceptual and basic. The table contains our recommendations on how training should take place, and on the kind of hands-on experience required to develop skills.

Training Formats

There are a variety of different training formats useful in helping developers and managers reach their target proficiency levels: prepared, mentoring, and self study.

Table 18.2 Effort to Obtain Proficiency Levels in Each Subject Area

Subject Areas	Conceptual	Basic	Functional	Advanced
OOA/ OOD	Reads about analysis and design in references (Chapter 15), or attends conference tutorial (2 wks)	Conceptual plus attends a formal OOA/OOD course (1 mo)	Basic plus completes the analysis and design of one small or medium project (6–8 mos)	Functional plus completes at least two medium to large projects and several smaller projects (1.5–2 yrs)
Framework Design	Reads subset of design references (Chapter 15) (2 wks)	Conceptual plus attends a design for reuse course; examines existing frameworks in depth (4 mos)	Basic plus develops one medium-sized framework (1–2 yrs)	Functional plus develops at least two large-sized frameworks (2–4 yrs)
Implementation Environment	Reads language references (Chapter 16) or attends conference tutorial (2–3 wks)	Conceptual plus attends a formal course (or self-study course) on specific environment (3–4 wks)	Basic plus 3-4 months full-time usage (5–6 mos)	Functional plus additional year of usage covering different areas of library (1.5–2 yrs)
Project Management	Reads project management references (this book or recommended additional readings) or attends conference tutorial (1–2 wks)	Conceptual plus attends a formal course or workshop (3–4 wks)	Basic plus successfully plans and executes one small/medium project (1–1.5 yrs)	Functional plus successfully plans several different types of projects (2–3 yrs)

Prepared, Face-to-Face Presentations

Prepared presentation is a popular training format in which one or more presenters offer prepared materials to participants. This kind of training occurs in many forms, such as executive presentations, conference tutorials, and classroom-style training classes. Students are typically given a copy of the presentation material or an accompanying notebook. Such training relies heavily on the quality of both the speaker and the presentation material.

Executive seminars. These seminars, often delivered at conferences, target high-level executives who wish to have a conceptual understanding of object-oriented technology. In choosing an executive seminar, make sure the presenter can speak authoritatively and concisely to your upper management. You should also review the materials in advance to verify that the presentation is not full of uninteresting technical details, theory, or jargon. Look for material based on real-world examples.

Conference tutorials. Conference tutorials are half-day or full-day presentations on specific topics by presenters with direct and preferably practical experience in the subject areas. Most tutorials present basic- or functional-level information, relegating advanced material to workshops, where experts gather to teach one another.

Tutorials depend upon the quality of the speaker, which varies from one individual to another. Before attending a tutorial, examine the background of the presenter, information that is often available in the conference brochure. You should also solicit the opinions of others who have attended this person's tutorials in the past—most tutorial speakers are repeat offenders! Tutorials can be expensive—it might be more cost-effective to buy and read the book upon which a tutorial is often based. The best tutorials are given by experienced practitioners who have good communication skills.

Classroom training. Classroom training is a good choice when the subject matter is complex, as it allows for a combination of prepared material and *in situ* customization. The prepared material should be well planned and should embody the cumulative experience of both the instructor and colleagues in teaching the complex topic. Having an instructor available to answer questions in the context in which they arise allows students to explore a complex issue from their own point of view. Such training exists for all object-oriented technology subject areas, at all levels of proficiency. It is provided by professional training companies and universities.

Class size tends to be smaller than in conference tutorials, and class composition tends to be homogeneous. Such classes are easier for the instructor and for the students. The instructor can assume a uniform skill level when introducing examples and providing explanations. Students can ask questions with some expectation that other students are interested in the answers as well. Hearing answers to questions raised by other students is an important part of the learning process. Class composition, of course, is controlled in this way only when the class prerequisites are clearly stated and a single person monitors sign-up. Such control is certainly possible when the class is given at your site and you choose the students.

There are some rules of thumb about choosing classroom training which highlight the teacher rather than the materials, and emphasize that effective classroom training requires excellent instructors who have a comprehensive command of the subject material and good presentation skills.

Training

Teach from experience. Good instructors practice what they preach. Hands-on experience gives the instructor the confidence to answer tough questions.

Instructors should be able to think on their feet, which comes from experience in and out of the classroom.

When selecting a course, rather than accepting a verbal description of the course material, you can ask the training organization to send you an outline and sample material for your examination. Don't expect to be able to read it instead of taking the course. Rather, examine it to see whether the material is well presented on paper. Does it make sense on its own, without additional explanation? Is there a good mix of text and graphics? If you were taking the class, would you like to have the student manual in front of you? What kind of collateral material is included in the student book? Does the book include extra reading materials or references?

Mentoring

A mentor is an expert who works directly with a small team of people in a hands-on manner. Mentors typically do not use prepared material in the form of a student manual or overhead transparencies. Rather, the mentor is expected to evaluate the needs of the team members and to customize a set of activities to help them meet their goals and objectives. The form of these activities depends on the subject area. If a team is being mentored in how to use an implementation environment, then most of the activities will involve online use of the implementation environment. If a team is being mentored in the use of a particular analysis or design method, then the consultant can lead the team through the use of the method on a specific project.

Mentors are often found in consulting companies with special apprentice programs. A mentor could also come from within your own company—team members teaching one another or someone from outside the team assigned temporarily to provide the mentoring.

There are three basic kinds of mentoring, defined by the level of the mentor's involvement.

Mentor does it, you watch. The first approach is where the mentor does the work and the team members watch. We know one mentor who teaches people how to use an implementation environment by solving a problem in front of an audience, thinking "out loud" to explain what is going on in his expert head. Team members observe and ask questions—learning by osmosis.

This approach has the benefit that the team gets to observe how an expert strategizes and solves a problem. When the performance is over, the team has an end result available for study.

Unless team members are skilled observers, however, most of what the expert does is missed. The expert is impressive, but perhaps too impressive—leaving the team with reduced confidence in their own ability to do similar work. Examples that can be demonstrated this way are often simple. It is hard to learn how to handle complex, large problem issues by listening to a mentor think out loud. Most of the hard decisions are made in the head of the mentor and not relayed during the performance.

Our assessment is that this approach has limited usefulness compared with formal classroom training.

Mentor and you do it together. An alternative is for both team members and the mentor to work closely on the same problem—a form of apprenticeship.

Team members now become active participants. The responsibility for solving the problem is jointly owned by mentor and team members. The mentor's job is that of technical leader, to structure and divide the problem. The mentor then either solves individual subproblems directly with the assistance of team members, delegates all subproblems to team members, or some mixture. Team members learn from exposure to the mentor's decision-making process, and from direct involvement in solving parts of the problem.

A mentor can work successfully with about five people. Because of the intense demands for the mentor's attention, less aggressive team members often get neglected and therefore do not learn. Moreover, the mentor does the critical part—strategizing and partitioning the effort into tractable parts. When the mentoring is over, no one team member has experienced this leadership role. The team may not be able to stand on its own, unless of course the mentor is one of the permanent team members.

Despite these drawbacks, this approach has proved powerful for small teams, especially when supplemented with some initial classroom instruction.

You do it, mentor watches. A final approach to working with a mentor is where your team members do the work and the mentor oversees the activities. In this approach, the team experiences all aspects of the work effort, learning while doing. A team member provides the central leadership for the project. The mentor is available to answer specific questions and to provide general guidance.

Team members must have at least basic skills because they are doing the work. Ultimately, the team reaps the rewards of knowing that they solved the problem. Management also has a stronger belief that its developers can be successful with the new technology.

Our experiences with this approach have been mixed—it depends on the caliber of the team members. We favor its use in conjunction with an organization's first project, after some initial classroom training.

Self-Study

In some organizations, resources constrain the use of formal training and mentoring. Either there is insufficient money or there is not enough time for people to leave their current assignments to attend a training class. Such organizations prefer a self-study approach, whereby team members learn a subject area on their own time, or on the job during off-peak times. Material comes in the form of tutorial manuals, books, magazines, journals, and videos. Maintaining an up-to-date library accessible to the team emphasizes the importance you place on self-study learning.

Training Plan

People playing different roles on the team require different skills and therefore different training. We provide a summary of training requirements and minimal proficiency levels in the form of a table for each role. Each table consists of three columns. The first shows the order in which subject areas should be learned, the second the desired proficiency level, and the third the recommended format. Proficiency levels are indicated as C for Conceptual, B for Basic, F for Functional, and A for Advanced. Whenever we write "A," we are aware that such people may not be available. Functional proficiency will often suffice.

The sequence should not imply that the first subject is learned up to the desired proficiency level before training in the next subject begins. Rather, where a functional level is required, say for object-oriented concepts, training in the next subject—such as OOA or project management—can begin after the basic level is attained. Starting a second subject area can assist in improving skills in the first area.

Everyone should have a conceptual understanding of project management to understand the roles and interactions of various team members. This information can be acquired through self-study. We do not list project management in the training sequence when only a conceptual level is expected.

Nontechnical management. Executive vice-presidents, CIOs, or even higher-level management come under this heading. They do not practice object-oriented analysis, design, or implementation, but they do make decisions about which products to develop, and decisions concerning the object-reuse, training, and measurement programs. They make better decisions when they understand the benefits and pitfalls of the technology. The consequential training plan for the nontechnical managers is shown in Table 18.3. Which managers should take these seminars? Our rule of thumb is that training should go up to the level of management affected by the use of the technology, including the managers who have to approve resource allocations.

Table 18.3 Training Plan for Nontechnical Managers

Subject and Sequence	Level	Training Format
Object-oriented concepts	C	Executive seminars; Self-study, including this book

First-line project manager. A first-line manager is involved in the day-to-day management of the project, and needs to make decisions requiring some technical knowledge. The plan in Table 18.4 indicates courses in four subject areas.

Table 18.4 Training Plan for First-line Project Managers

Subject and Sequence	Level	Training Format
Object-oriented concepts	F	Executive seminars; Self-study, including this book
Project management	A	Conference tutorial; Classroom; On-the-job experience
OOA/OOD	B	Self-study (optional)
Implementation environment	B	Self-study (optional)

Reuse manager. This person manages the Reuse Team, which is in charge of carrying out the reuse process model, and takes specific responsibility for identifying and acquiring reusable assets. The training plan in Table 18.5 recommends basic level studies in project management, analysis-and-design methods, and framework design.

Table 18.5 Training Plan for Reuse Managers

Subject and Sequence	Level	Training Format
Object-oriented concepts	F	Executive seminars; Self-study, including this book
Project management	F	Conference tutorial; Classroom; On-the-job experience
OOA/OOD	B	Classroom
Framework design	B	Classroom

Technical manager/object coach. A technical manager has a technical background and is a respected technical leader of the organization. So is the object coach. We show the same training plan for both in Table 18.6. The manager, of course, has more hands-on day-to-day management responsibility, whereas the coach is guiding the entire team to make sure that decisions are understood and consistently applied.

Table 18.6 Training Plan for Technical Managers and Object Coaches

Subject and Sequence	Level	Training Format
Object-oriented concepts	A	Classroom; On-the-job experience
Project management	F	Conference tutorial; Classroom; On-the-job experience
Implementation environment	F	Classroom; On-the-job experience
OOA/OOD	F	Classroom; On-the-job experience
Framework design	F	Classroom; On-the-job experience

Analyst/designer. The training plan for analysts and designers are treated together in Table 18.7 because, for the most part, the skill levels for these team members are the same. The personalities and technical know-how may differ, as an analyst spends most of the time interacting with end users, while the designer is closer to the technology issues. Each should be advanced in the respective subject area.

Table 18.7 Training Plan for Analysts and Designers

Subject and Sequence	Level	Training Format
Object-oriented concepts	A	Classroom; On-the-job experience
OOA/OOD	A	Classroom; On-the-job experience
Implementation environment	B	Classroom
Framework design	B	Classroom; Self-study

Framework designer. The framework designer needs advanced capability in all technical areas, with functional knowledge in the use of the implementation environment. Table 18.8 indicates our expectations that framework designers attain advanced skills in most subject areas.

Table 18.8 Training Plan for Framework Designers

Subject and Sequence	Level	Training Format
Object-oriented concepts	A	Classroom; On-the-job experience
OOA/OOD	A	Classroom; On-the-job experience
Implementation environment	F	Classroom
Framework design	A	Classroom; Self-study; On-the-job experience

Product programmer/prototyper. The role of prototyper can be played by the analyst, the designer, or someone else. Prototyping is a form of development, and for this reason we combined the product programmer and prototyper in preparing the plan in Table 18.9.

Table 18.9 Training Plan for Product Programmers and Prototypers

Subject and Sequence	Level	Training Format
Object-oriented concepts	F	Classroom; On-the-job experience
Implementation environment	F	Classroom; On-the-job experience
OOA/OOD	B	Classroom

Reuse evaluator. The reuse evaluator is a special tester who invents new uses for proposed reusable assets. As such, this person is a developer who must have domain knowledge to create new applications to exercise an existing framework or components. Table 18.10 shows a training plan to bring reuse evaluators to functional skill levels in concepts and the use of the organization's implementation environment, and basic understanding of methods and framework design.

Table 18.10 Training Plan for Reuse Evaluators

Subject and Sequence	Level	Training Format
Object-oriented concepts	F	Classroom; On-the-job experience
Implementation environment	F	Classroom; On-the-job experience
OOA/OOD	B	Classroom
Framework design	B	Classroom

Case Study Results

Of the 32 projects in Phase 1 (as defined in Chapter 1), we considered 19 to be successful. Of these 19 projects, 14 had some form of classroom or other formal training. One company used outside mentors who did all of the work while the team watched. The team had some understanding of the framework, enough to do some specialization but not enough to modify the framework itself or create their own. The remaining four projects hired primarily professional software engineers with computer science backgrounds, and depended on their educational background to equip them for self-study on object-oriented technology. They were asked which books the team members read and would recommend to others; the most popular were Meyer's *Object Oriented Software Construction* [Meyer 1988] and (the first half of) Booch's *Object-Oriented Design with*

Applications [Booch 1991]. Brad Cox's early book was often mentioned [Cox 1986], and, more recently, David Taylor's book *Object-Oriented Technology for the Manager* [Taylor 1991].

Of the 11 ongoing projects, four used classes in implementation environments only, and the rest relied on educational background. Of the two failed projects, neither did formal training; one relied on reading the tutorial provided by the implementation environment vendor, and the other relied on the educational background of team members. In most cases, educational background was some form of engineering degree from a university and work experience as a software engineer. All of the projects in Phase 2 used classroom training, with four of the projects using mentors as well.

Chart 18.5 summarizes the different training formats used by the successful or ongoing projects. It indicates that classroom training was the most frequently used format. The numbers do not add up to 39 because many projects used multiple formats. We have not distinguished the various forms of mentoring, but in four cases the team members went to a separate site and were mentored for one to two weeks by outside consultants. In three cases, the company set up a process by which internally trained personnel became mentors for new hires, for as long as three months.

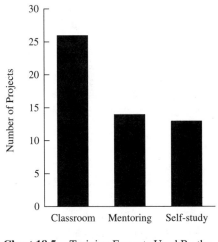

Chart 18.5   Training Formats Used By the
Successful or Ongoing Projects

Chart 18.6 examines which subject areas were taught in the successful and ongoing projects, using the three different formats. Of the 19 projects that used classroom teaching, many taught multiple subject areas (hence the total number of projects is greater than 19). Classroom work concentrated on languages and tools. We separated the cases where object-oriented database training was provided.

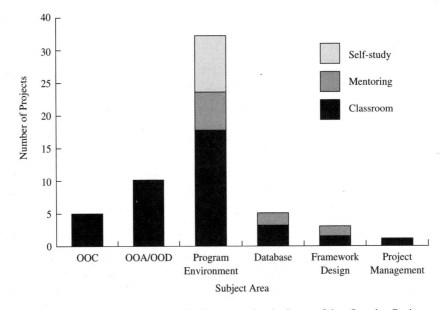

Chart 18.6   Subject Areas Taught in Classrooms by the Successful or Ongoing Projects

Early adopters did not distinguish learning a language from learning basic concepts and analysis and design. This historically has been a problem throughout software engineering, not just with object-oriented technology. The good news, however, is that early adopters have learned that it is important to focus on good project management, and on careful up-front analysis and design. They write papers, give talks, and generally, when asked, bring up the importance of training in specific subject areas.

Summary

We recommend that you educate your entire development team in the effective use of object-oriented technology. Your goal should be to educate each team member to the skill level appropriate for each subject area: object-oriented concepts, object-oriented analysis and design, framework design, implementation environment, and project management. The required skill level depends on the team member's role. Not all team members need to be experts in all areas of object-oriented technology, although each should understand the responsibilities of the other team members. Our proficiency scale has four levels: conceptual, basic, functional, and advanced. There are many different training formats from which you can choose. We described classroom presentations, on-the-job training, mentoring, and self-study. We also provided a training plan for each of the team roles.

Additional Reading About Training

Every year there is a special training section in *Object Magazine or Journal of Object-Oriented Programming—JOOP* March/April 1993 is an example. These special sections describe the latest commercial offerings in training about object-oriented technology, and therefore are worth checking out.

CHAPTER **19**

Set Up a Training Plan

Training and education costs can be large expenditures when adopting object-oriented technology. The purpose of this chapter is to advise you on how to set up a training plan that gives team members the specific object-oriented technology skills to do their jobs, and gives you the best return on your investment.

Framework for Setting Up a Training Plan

By following the steps of the training framework, you can set up a plan for improving the skills and proficiency levels of team members. Training a team is a resource-improvement project, as shown in Fig. 19.1.

Figure 19.1   Resource-Improvement Project to Develop Plan to Train Team Members

To set up a training plan, you must first assess the current skills of your team members. Then you must define the desired skills and proficiency levels. After establishing the resources you currently have and the ones you wish to have, you can define a training plan.

The principle for this decision framework emphasizes the importance of a training plan, and the goal summarizes the nature of the project to set up such a plan.

Framework Principle. Success with a new technology depends on proper education of all team members in the use of the technology.

Framework Goal. Develop a training plan to give your team members the additional skills they need to use new processes and resources to achieve desired results.

There are three primary steps and several substeps for meeting the framework goal:

Team Training Plan

- Determine skills of team members

- Define desired skills of team members

  - Decide who should be trained
  - Decide on the subject areas to teach
  - Define the desired skills and proficiency levels
  - Decide whether product deliverables should result from the training effort, and if so, define them

- Define training resources and activities

  - Determine the appropriate formats for training
  - Determine how much time and money is available for training
  - Decide on the order of training activities

It is important to remember that training is not a static, one-time event. Technology evolves, markets evolve, and businesses must evolve as well. Team members need to keep up. Training needs to be ongoing. Managers who are committed to high-quality personnel reward their people with opportunities for continuing education which directly support them in doing their jobs better. Whether a one-time event or an ongoing activity, training is meaningful only if the skills taught have relevance to the job. The key to learning about object-oriented technology is to have a project to work on soon after the training.

Determine Skills of Team Members

The first step of the framework is to assess the skills of your developers. You measure the proficiency levels of team members in several subject areas: object-oriented concepts, object-oriented analysis, object-oriented design, framework design, programming environment, and project management. Not only should you assess their skills with object-oriented technology (if any), you should also assess their general software development skills. You assess what they know about how to develop software systems. You may also wish to assess their reuse skills, to find out who can take responsibility as reuse engineers or other Reuse Team members.

Define Desired Skills of Team Members

To define the desired skills of team members, first determine the roles needed to support your selected team structure. Knowing the desired team roles, you can use the tables in the previous chapter to determine the necessary skills (subject areas and proficiencies). In some cases, training in non–object-oriented skills may be necessary to learn object-oriented skills. For example, a team in one case study was planning to develop sophisticated object-oriented applications using personal computers with graphical windowing systems. They had never used such a platform. This team first needed to learn how to operate personal computers and their windowing systems.

Once the roles and the skills have been defined, you must identify the specific team members who will fulfill the roles. For a first project using object-oriented technology, you may choose existing team members who have most of the needed skills. In other circumstances, such as training all of the developers in an organization, there may be no specific criteria for selecting team members.

Regardless of how the developers are chosen, you must determine the differences between their current skills and the skills needed for the roles they will play. These differences will indicate the appropriate training. It is important to prioritize subject areas for each team member. It makes little sense to train people in a large number of subject areas all at once, especially if all the new information will not be used immediately.

Finally, decide whether you expect a product deliverable from the training effort. For example, you may wish to develop a first prototype of your product software as part of the training program. Many forms of mentoring can be used to teach developers the necessary skills while working on a real software project.

Define Training Resources and Activities

The third step of the training framework is to define one or more projects to change the current situation into the desired one. Training is frequently resource-limited, in terms both of time and money. A training plan must recognize and conform to resource constraints.

Begin by determining the appropriate training format for your team members. In the previous chapter, we discuss many such options and the situations in which they are most useful. In practice, most organizations prefer either on-the-job training or classroom training. The on-the-job training commonly consists of either self-study (videos, books, tutorial manuals) or mentoring. These two differ greatly in effectiveness and expense. Whereas mentoring can be viewed as a consulting expense, classroom instruction is viewed as a real training expense. It may be possible to mix these approaches to achieve the best overall training in the face of a limited training budget.

The final framework step is to determine the sequence of training activities relative to one another and to other development activities. For example, should you teach analysis and design before programming, or vice versa? As we illustrate in the previous chapter, this will depend on the students—analysts and designers prefer to learn the methods first and the language second, while programmers prefer it the other way around. It is important that students learn basic software engineering skills before embarking on studies of object-oriented technology.

The best way to understand training projects is to examine real examples. We now present several examples from our own work and that of the case studies.

Case Study Results

Illustration 1: The Reading Club

In most projects, developers have ongoing responsibilities that cannot be preempted while they take a training course, especially a course delivered at a remote site. One case study organization had the added difficulty of being located in a city that had no easy access to skilled trainers. This organization formed a Reading Club. Self-study is a solution in both of these situations. Where two or more people have decided to learn on their own, they can help one another.

The company produces financial planning and accounting software, with six products already on the market. The company is small, with only 10–12 developers (plus two development managers) producing and maintaining the software products. The rest of the company provides revenue-producing customer service.

Current skill set. All of the developers were skilled 4GL programmers, accustomed to producing software products using the Clipper database and development tools. Upper management was nontechnical and unwilling to convert everyone at once to a new development environment. The lead technical manager had a strong computer science background and a willingness to learn new languages and tools. He also felt comfortable as a mentor and teacher.

Desired skill set. The lead technical manager had the authority to choose the new language and database. He selected object-oriented technology, but he did not understand which aspects of the technology would be important: Templates? Multiple inheritance? So, he chose a language that he thought had the most features, C++. He also decided to use an SQL-based database server as the repository for financial information, and chose a product from Gupta Systems based on price and availability on PC platforms. This manager also wanted everyone in upper management and the developers to understand the basic concepts of object-oriented technology. Each developer needed to know Borland C++; some needed SQL.

Training approach. The technical manager learned about object-oriented technology by reading books and attending a conference that concentrates on objects. He personally taught the company directors, using one-on-one meetings augmented by background articles that emphasized the maintainability and portability benefits. This personal training continued for two months, until a formal presentation to management resulted in the desired allocation of resources. The presentation focused on three issues: the company's current inability to accommodate customer change requests, the potential speed of other companies to accommodate change and bite away at the company's customer base, and the fact that competitors were already beginning to use objects.

In parallel, the technical manager created a Reading Club for the programmers. They were required to read:

All of Meyer's book *Object Oriented Software Construction* [Meyer 1988].

The first half of Booch's book *Object-Oriented Design with Applications* [Booch 1991].

Meyer's book *Eiffel: The Language* (as an intellectual exercise only) [Meyer 1992].

The programmers read one chapter a week on their own time. Once a week they gathered to discuss the chapter's content with the technical manager. The technical manager told us that this approach—combining self-study and group discussion—proved to be a very effective way to provide a basic education in object-oriented technology. Once this level was reached, upper management approved classroom training for C++.[1] A single five-day course was attended by 12 developers. They were also given access to a 21-lesson Borland video about C++, and the *C++ Primer* by S. Lippman [Lippman 1989]. An additional class on SQL was also given. The technical manager was very pleased with the effectiveness of the video classes.

Training continued concurrent with project development. Five (later six) programmers maintained the prior products one day each week and used the other four days to do the new work. The technical manager handed out assignments—primarily small subsystem prototypes—to be done by each programmer; the results were reviewed as a group. The Reading Club thus transitioned from reading other people's books to reading and discussing one another's designs and code.

---

[1] This strategy is a smart one. Our experience in teaching a Smalltalk language course is that students who have a basic level of proficiency with object-oriented concepts before they attend the class gain the most from the course. These students find that the course review of object-oriented concepts reinforces their understanding and enables them to focus their attention on how Smalltalk mechanisms support object-oriented concepts.

Illustration 2: Continuing Education Programs

One of the Phase 2 companies has a continuing education program for its information technology professionals, and it includes a set of courses on object-oriented technology.

The company is in the financial industry and needs to create new products rapidly in response to changing market conditions. Developers use a wide variety of hardware and software systems, ranging from mainframes (IBM 3090, Tandem) to workstation servers (Sun, Data General) to desktop computers (PCs, NeXT). Inconsistent tracking of their 4 million legal commitments was creating a financial loss for the company. The goal of the project we examined was to remedy this situation, creating a new tracking, processing, and updating system.

In total, the project included four analyzers, four designers, six coders, eight testers, four managers, and three people assigned to converting a legacy system. Development was done on NeXT workstations. The end-user database manager was from Sybase. The system objectives were:

- Process 5 million large-scale transactions overnight, twice a month

- Perform acceptably fast for 100 simultaneous users

- Provide a two-minute response time for any real-time request from a user

At the time of the interviews, the project was still ongoing, but was close enough to completion to forecast a successful outcome.

Current skill set. None of the proposed team members or managers was knowledgeable about object-oriented concepts, none had experience developing on the NeXT workstation, and all were accustomed to a Waterfall product process model. Most of the team members had experience developing mainframe applications using traditional methods.

Desired skill set. Functional knowledge of object-oriented concepts was required of all developers. Each team member was assigned to a specific area of the development life cycle—analysis, design, implementing, and testing—and required functional knowledge of that area. Coders needed basic knowledge of Objective C and the associated development environment (tools and library) for this project. Because the managers planned to use an incremental development approach similar to a Spiral model, developers needed a basic level of understanding of their roles within this process model.

Training approach. As part of the larger effort to transition the company's information systems from a mainframe culture to the use of a client/server architecture, a formal Certification and Continuing Education Program was designed and implemented. This program was designed for information technology professionals, to ensure that they would have a command of fundamental skills, and to provide access to courses for maintaining and extending those skills.

All project team members went through the Education Program, taking the core curriculum and then classroom training appropriate to their specializations (analysis, design, implementation). All new skills were immediately applied in a development project.

Description of a continuing education program. Management's commitment to a high-quality workforce was demonstrated by their guarantee that each professional would have at least seven and up to 12 training days per year. The idea of "certification" is to provide a framework within which courses are selected, courses that directly relate to the employee's job and career objectives. Courses focus on improved job performance but are not directly tied to promotion. Object-oriented technology became a core part of the curriculum.

The company's goal is for at least 80 percent of all eligible employees to participate in the continuing education program. Courses involve either classroom training or self-study. The education program is summarized in Table 19.1 and Table 19.2. Interdisciplinary

Table 19.1 Continuing Education Program Core Curriculum

Course Name	Description
Required Courses	
Intro I	Knowledge about the company's specific business
CIS Overview	Knowledge about the structure, operations, and guidelines by which systems are built in the company
One Course from These Areas	
Problem Solving and Analysis	Analysis and design concepts and techniques
Technological Environment	Fundamental skills to operate a specific platform
Consulting and Communications Skills	Presentation, writing, and consulting skills needed to work on a team and with clients

Table 19.2 Additional Continuing Education Courses

Course Name	Description
Business Knowledge	Specific details about the company's business practices
Analysis and Design	Object-oriented analysis and design
Programming	Techniques and concepts of object-oriented languages and tools
Systems Administration and Operations	Techniques and tools of specific operating systems and networks
Project Leadership	General leadership skills including project management
Interdisciplinary Studies	Topics that span several areas, such as expert systems, image processing, and object-oriented databases

Studies is a catchall for topics not easily categorized. This company chose to treat object-oriented databases as one such topic, since it spans database, programming language, tools, and applications. This program maps well to our recommended subject areas: business know-how, object-oriented basic concepts, analysis and design, programming environment, and project management.

Illustration 3: Mentoring Success Story

The history of this project is unusual. Training was used to help the team make technical decisions. Methods and tools were chosen only if the team could learn how to use them. Several times, the team took courses anticipating a management decision to select a particular technology, only to find out that management had made a different choice. The training story for this case study starts with the decision to use structured analysis and design.

Training Project 1

Current skill set. The company was a high-technology manufacturer, about to carry out a long-term project involving both hardware and software development. The initial assumption was that structured approaches to analysis and design would be used to create a requirements specification. No one on the proposed team was skilled in classical structured analysis.

Desired skill set. Team management selected a CASE tool that supported a notation for Yourdon/DeMarco SA/SD methods. Team members needed to understand the methods and the tool.

Training approach. Twelve people took one week of classroom training to learn how to use the CASE tool. Eight months into the project, management decided to use object-oriented technology rather than structured analysis and design. The training therefore did not apply.

Training Project 2

Current skill set. A technical leader from another division was transferred to serve as chief architect on the project. He had taught himself object-oriented technology and was instrumental in convincing management to turn to objects for better productivity and flexibility. The rest of the team did not understand the technology. They saw the decision as changing their careers, and they were excited. The choice of object-oriented technology dictated that object-oriented analysis-and-design methods be used. However, no one on the team knew anything about these methods. Management was convinced that a choice of object-oriented technology meant that implementation should be done in C++, especially since many of the team members were familiar with C. However, team members convinced management that the language choice should be deferred until after the analysis had been completed.

Desired skill set. All team members needed basic knowledge about the various analysis-and-design methods, and functional knowledge of the method selected for the project.

Training approach. An intense exploration of analysis-and-design methods was carried out. Various speakers were invited to present their methods. Courses were taken during the decision process. In particular, two courses on the Shlaer-Mellor analysis method were given: one week on information modeling for 20 people, and 1.5 days on state and process modeling for 12 people. Class members included nondevelopment personnel. A questionnaire was sent out to various vendors to learn the details of their analysis-and-design methods. The questionnaire is documented in Chapter 17 as Illustration 3 (selecting a method based on a survey approach). After the organizers reviewed responses to the questionnaire, Grady Booch was invited to give a two-day training class with 24 attendees.

Team members were encouraged to read the books on object-oriented technology available at the time. The ones considered good were Cox, Shlaer-Mellor, and Meyer [Cox 1986, Shlaer and Mellor 1988, Meyer 1988]. They also circulated among themselves any applicable magazine articles and papers that they discovered.

While the methods were being reviewed, other team members were ready to start the first prototyping effort. Smalltalk was selected as the prototyping language.

Training Project 3

Current skill set. Team members knew C, not Smalltalk.

Desired skill set. Developers needed a functional proficiency in Smalltalk and its development environment.

Training approach. A one-week introductory classroom course on Smalltalk was taken by ten out of the 23 developers. Eight of these developers, including the chief architect, then participated in a Smalltalk apprentice program, a mentoring activity managed by outside consultants. It consisted of two weeks of working with the outside mentors at the mentors' offices, followed by two weeks of working on their own project, followed by another two weeks with the outside mentors. The result was a basic level of Smalltalk proficiency plus an ability to use components from a library of about 300 class definitions provided by the mentors.

Another six months into the project, management thought it was time to get ready for production work using C++, the language that management assumed would be selected.

Training Project 4

Current skill set. None of the team members knew C++ or its various development tools. They had all taken Smalltalk training.

Desired skill set. Functional knowledge of C++ on the part of all developers.

Training approach. The company hired an outside training group to teach C++. Twenty-four students in two courses were taught Turbo C++.

By this time, one year had passed since the decision had been made to use object-oriented technology. After a heated debate between management and developers, management reversed its C++ decision and accepted Smalltalk as the product implementation language. This decision resulted from the successful demonstration of a prototype, with all functionality complete and exceeding management expectations. Replicating this work in C++ would have been costly because much of the prototype resulted from reusing an outside consultant's and several vendors' Smalltalk libraries.

Training Project 5

Current skill set. Six developers who had a functional knowledge of Smalltalk and its development environment remained with the project.

Desired skill set. Twenty more Smalltalk programmers were needed. A persistent store was also needed, so the team required knowledge of at least one object-oriented database.

Training approach. Smalltalk became part of the company's standard training curriculum, based on a course provided by a local university professor. A course from each of two object-oriented database vendors was also given as a way to help the team make a selection.

The product process model used by the team was devised to support quality objectives. The quality assurance department thought that additional training on testing and code walkthroughs would be appropriate. A course on Fagen inspection principles was given, but the techniques were not pursued.

Illustration 4: A Popular Idea—Quick Start Training Projects

A Quick Start (or immersion) program is an intense, multifaceted approach to training in several subject areas. It is best used when team members need to perform immediately with new technology skills they do not have. Such programs, when administered properly, can decrease the time required for developers to reach basic and functional proficiencies. When administered poorly, students have remarked that this approach is like trying to drink water from a fire hose.

Quick Start programs should be used to teach only a small number of skills because even the best students can absorb only a limited amount of new material in a short period of time. In addition, the desired skills should be closely related, since this type of program needs to have each newly learned skill reinforce and leverage the others.

For example, the ParcPlace Quick Start program we devised targets a basic level for understanding object-oriented concepts and analysis-and-design methods, and a functional proficiency in Smalltalk. It is a multifaceted program of instruction that involves formal classroom instruction, coupled with various forms of mentoring. We suggest a program of eight logical weeks that can be spread out over a longer or shorter actual time period, depending on the target skills and proficiency levels. In all cases, program size is limited to at most 14 students with at least two trainers/mentors. A maximum student-to-teacher ratio of seven to one is desirable to retain the attention of each student. We intentionally avoid language and tool training until after the concepts of object-oriented technology are understood.

Here is a schedule of activities:

Preliminary. Before we begin the actual training, we sit down with the project leader and determine the goals and objectives of the training program. After learning the goals and objectives, we sometimes assist the project leader in selecting good candidate team members to work on the project. Finally, we work together to determine an appropriate prototype project for the team to develop during the program.

Week 1. A four-day object-oriented methodology course develops basic proficiency in object-oriented concepts and a conceptual understanding of the OBA method.

During the fifth day, we work with the team to begin preliminary analysis of the prototype application. During this activity, we use the apprentice model of mentoring, where the mentor acts as the facilitator for the gathering of information during the initial OBA steps. The team members act not only as analysts but as domain experts.

Week 2. This week begins by continuing to apply OBA to the prototype, working in groups of three or four. Each group begins its own analysis, starting with the initial results generated during the previous week. Full responsibility for the analysis is in the hands of the individual team members. The mentor floats from team to team, answering questions as they arise.

At the end of the week, the teams will have developed a good initial analysis and design of the desired prototype.

Week 3. This week is spent taking an introductory course on the Smalltalk language and application development environment (an outline of this course is provided in the previous chapter).

Weeks 4–5. During this period, students return to their teams and implement parts of their designs using Smalltalk and its application development environment. Because this is the first time they are using an object-oriented approach, we expect the team members to make changes to the analysis and design as they proceed through the implementation. The mentor again floats from group to group, providing assistance as needed.

Week 6. This week is spent in the classroom exploring various advanced Smalltalk programming issues based on the desires and needs of the team members. Each topic is augmented with on-line exercises.

Week 7. The team returns to work on the prototype, now nearing completion. Each prototype is tested and documented. As in previous weeks, the mentor floats from group to group, providing assistance.

Week 8. Final work on the prototype is permitted during the first day. Next, each group presents its analysis, design, and prototype to the other teams, and optionally to their management. During the presentation, other teams ask questions. The mentor acts as moderator and examiner.

During each presentation, the mentor records a particular aspect of each prototype that could be changed. After all of the presentations have been completed, each team is asked to turn over their analysis, design, and implementation artifacts to one of the other teams. The mentor then requests that each team make a change to the prototype now in their possession. They are not permitted to consult with the team that originated the prototype and are allotted no more than a day to do this task. If they finish early, they are assigned another change.

The remaining day is used to discuss the maintenance changes and any other issues that are still unresolved.

The exercise of switching prototypes and making maintenance changes is very educational. Team members get an opportunity to examine another application in detail, which reinforces what has already been learned, and provides an opportunity to maintain someone else's object-oriented system. From management's perspective, this maintenance exercise reinforces the idea that changes can be made safely by a team other than the one that originated the application.

Illustration 5: A Bad Situation That Got Better

In this case study, we describe a company that initially chose the Quick Start approach to training but executed it poorly. Team members were overwhelmed by new information they could not assimilate. Unlike Illustration 3 (the mentoring success story), the team members were not enthusiastic about learning a new technology so quickly. After recognizing the failure of this format for this situation, management altered the plan, opting to train a smaller team using a mentoring format. The mentoring approach, coupled with some follow-on classroom training, eventually gave the team members the skills they needed to do their jobs.

Quick Start Training Project 1

Current skill set. All of the team members were mainframe developers. They were accustomed to using 4GLs, COBOL, PL/1, and Telon. Not one of them had ever used a computer they could carry! In fact, many of them had never touched a mouse before. Their educational backgrounds consisted mainly of MIS degrees with a sprinkling of computer science and engineering.

Desired skill set. A team of 20 developers, chosen by management because they were available, was asked to develop PC- and workstation-based applications using Smalltalk and an object-oriented database. Given their current skill set, they needed to learn everything: new operating systems and windowing systems, in addition to object-oriented concepts, Smalltalk, and object-oriented databases. This team was not going to perform the overall system analysis, so management decided they would not need training in object-oriented analysis methods, but they would require training in object-oriented design. Team members were to be trained to a functional proficiency in all of the desired subject areas.

Training approach. Management decided that classroom training would be appropriate for its developers. It also decided that a massive training effort up front would be the best approach. No reason to delay. If we're going to use this object stuff, let's get to it. This decision was taken without a clear understanding of when the first project would begin, since the developers had to wait for the analysis to be finished. As it turned out, the first project did not begin for many months, and most of the skills learned by the developers had begun to fade before they could be put to use.

The initial training project consisted of four different training courses attended by all 20 team members. All courses were completed before any project work started. The first class was a week-long introduction to Smalltalk taught on Macintosh computers. Since none of the developers had ever used a Mac or a GUI, this was the wrong first class for this team. It would have been much better to train the team first on the new (to them) operating and windowing system features before attempting to teach Smalltalk. As a result, many of the students were distracted by platform differences and did not learn object-oriented concepts or Smalltalk. At the end of the class, many students felt lost.

The following week, the students attended an object-oriented database class. This class was unsuccessful due to the poor training materials and the instructor's lack of knowledge. The problem was exacerbated by subtle differences in the object-oriented concepts that were used in this class, compared with the Smalltalk class. By the end of the class, the team had learned nothing about object-oriented databases, and was more confused about basic object-oriented concepts.

After one week of recovery, the team was sent to another class—this one specifically about the use of a Smalltalk user interface forms builder. This class was successful because most students finally saw something that looked familiar—many of them had developed forms-based user interfaces on the mainframe using Telon or other 4GLs. The tool they were learning allowed them to create similar types of forms-based screens. Unfortunately, their lack of basic object-oriented concepts caused them difficulties when they tried to understand how to integrate underlying business logic with the forms.

A fourth week of training—a follow-on Smalltalk course—was scheduled at this time. However, management decided that the team was not ready. An assessment of skills showed that the majority of the team members had at best a conceptual proficiency in object-oriented concepts, Smalltalk, and object-oriented databases. There was, though, a small set who had acquired a basic understanding of Smalltalk. Given that so few had attained even a basic proficiency, the managers agreed to give the team members some breathing room for self-study.

Several weeks later, the team attended a customized intermediate-level Smalltalk class, although, arguably, many of the students would still have benefited from a remedial introductory course. The intermediate course lasted one week. At the end, the students were divided into teams, and each team was assigned one person at the basic level or better. Each team was to use Smalltalk to develop a small calendar application. The purpose of the project was to give team members some practical experience developing applications in Smalltalk.

The teams were allotted three weeks to develop their application. During this time, they were able to solicit help and feedback from the instructor. At the end of the three-week period, the instructor reviewed each project with the teams. The instructor and the other groups provided feedback. For many team members, this project helped them achieve a basic level of proficiency in Smalltalk. Others were still lost.

Mentoring Training Project 2

Current skills set. Some team members with basic skills in Smalltalk, most with a conceptual level of proficiency in object-oriented concepts and Smalltalk programming.

Desired skills set. Functional ability to carry out the actual development project was required of all team members.

Training approach. At the end of the classroom training program, the developers were assigned to their respective positions on the actual development project. At this point, given the discomfort of the team members with their unacquired new skills, management decided that a mentoring style of development would be useful. Two mentors were brought in to support the 20 developers. One was assigned to work with the small team of developers who had reached the higher proficiencies during the prior training program. The second mentor worked with the rest.

The mentor assigned to the advanced team was a Smalltalk expert. He and the team worked together to build parts of the system. Team members told us that the greatest contribution made by this mentor was a sense of development style. In particular, the mentor would critique the team's Smalltalk code by walking through it line by line and pointing out how he would have done it differently. The team really wanted to know where their code "stank" and how it could be improved. In addition, the mentor would walk the team through his own designs and explain why he had made the choices that he did. Team members found this to be an invaluable way of learning the pragmatics of Smalltalk. This mentor worked with the team for more than a year. According to the team leader, it took them about one year before they felt at ease applying the mentor's style.

The second mentor worked with the less advanced team members. The mentoring approach used with the first team was unacceptable. Whereas the first team encouraged criticism of their work, this team was offended by it. They were experts in a 4GL language and did not like the idea that they were now novices. Because of this, the mentor did most of the work himself, while the team members watched. Watching did give them some ideas; the team offered suggestions based on their domain knowledge. Seeing the domain mapped to Smalltalk code helped them understand how familiar concepts are represented as objects.

Mentoring yielded positive results for both teams. The first team became much more proficient in object-oriented concepts and Smalltalk. The second team slowly overcame their resistance to new ideas, having seen some examples that they could understand and having minimally contributed to their development. Most of these team members reached a basic proficiency in object-oriented concepts and Smalltalk.

Several months after the mentors left, all 20 team members attended an object-oriented design course. This occurred almost one and a half years after the first training class. The results were quite good. The class helped to reinforce much of what the team members had learned during mentoring, and provided some new insight on how to develop reusable architectures. It brought everyone up to a basic level of proficiency in framework design.

Summary

We recommended that you assess the skills of current team members, and then decide who will be on the teams assigned to create applications and reusable frameworks and components. The members of these teams must have skills ranging from conceptual to advanced, covering all the subjects that Chapter 18 outlines. You must define training resources and specific training formats, the curricula, and schedules needed to transfer these skills to the selected team members. We suggested various training plans that you might adapt, and illustrated these from the case studies. In particular, we provided a curriculum for a Quick Start program, and a formal set of courses spanning several years and several levels of proficiency. Training is most effective when immediately reinforced by on-the-job experience.

The experiences of the case studies suggest some additional approaches to training. Where training courses are not available or are too expensive, self-study efforts can be effective, such as the Reading Club we described as Illustration 1. Most organizations consider ongoing education to be both an obligation and a responsible way to get the best from the people they employ. Continuing education programs take a number of forms, such as funding for employees to take courses at local colleges and to attend seminars and conferences, as well as providing extensive in-house training such as that shown in the case study in Illustration 2.

Just-in-time training, on-the-job training, and Quick Start programs all provide ways in which mentors—skilled technologists with lots of experience—can participate on projects and make sure that the team both produces the desired project outcomes and develops new skills that will be generally useful to the organization. The mentoring success story of Illustration 3 is just one of many examples of the importance of including in the team the roles of Object Coach and Object Technology Expert. Quick Start programs, mentored by experts, should be carefully planned, and the team members put through such programs should be carefully selected for their tolerance of the accelerated work pace. The Quick Start program we put together as Illustration 4, typical of commercially offered immersion programs, was designed for team members who were prepared for rapid assimilation of several subject areas at once. Illustration 5 describes a failed Quick Start effort, inappropriate given the choice of team members. The company recovered from the initial failure by applying a more appropriate learning format.

CHAPTER 20

What Is Measurement?

When you can measure what you are speaking about, and express it in numbers, you know something about it; but when you cannot measure it, when you cannot express it in numbers, your knowledge is of a meager and unsatisfactory kind; it may be the beginning of knowledge, but you have scarcely in your thoughts advanced to the stage of science.

Lord Kelvin

Measurement serves two purposes: to determine the extent to which stated goals and objectives are being met, and to assess the current situation as input to setting new project goals and objectives. Whenever you plan a project, you should define the measures by which you will determine whether you have achieved the project goals and objectives.

What Is a Measure?

A *measure* associates a number with a specific attribute of an entity. So to measure some entity, we first determine which attribute of the entity is of interest. It doesn't make sense to say that we are going to measure the program code, if we haven't specified which aspect of the code is to be measured. It does make sense to say that we plan to measure the size of the program code. There are two types of attributes: internal and external. *Internal attributes* are measured in terms of the product, process, or resource itself, and *external attributes* are measured in terms of how the product, process, or resource relates to its environment. For example, as illustrated in Fig. 20.1, height is an internal attribute of a tree because it can be measured solely in terms of the tree. However, whether or not a tree has a beautiful appearance is an external attribute, since it must be measured not only in terms of the tree but by the viewer. Table 20.1, adapted from [Fenton 1991], illustrates internal and external attributes for example software products, processes, and resources.

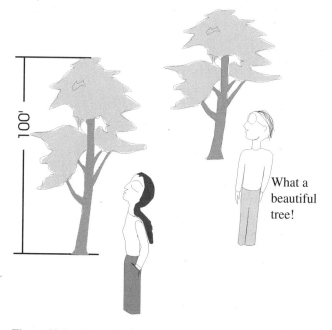

Figure 20.1   Example of an Internal and External Attribute
of a Tree

A measure must be well defined and useful. By well defined, we mean that the measure is based on empirical observation, is consistent with intuition, and represents a mapping onto an appropriate number system.[1]

To be able to measure means that you are able to express how entities relate to one another in terms of a common internal or external attribute. For example, you can dip your fingers into two different cups of water and observe that one cup of water is hotter than the other. This empirical observation forms the basis for a measure of water temperature. Now suppose someone claims that the complexity of a C++ program can be measured by counting the number of tokens with capital letters that occur in the code. Does

---

[1] See [Fenton 1991, Zuse 1990] for a description of the theory of measurement from which we derived our description of well-defined measures.

Table 20.1 Internal and External Attributes of Products, Processes, and Resources

	Internal	*External*
Products		
Specifications	size, reuse, modularity, redundancy, functionality, syntactic correctness	comprehensibility, safety, maintainability, traceability
Designs	size, reuse, modularity, coupling, cohesiveness, functionality	quality, complexity, safety, maintainability, traceability
Code	size, reuse, modularity, coupling, functionality, algorithmic complexity, control-flow structuredness	reliability, usability, safety, maintainability, traceability
Test Data	size, coverage level	quality
Processes		
Constructing specification	time, effort, number of required changes	quality, cost stability
Detailed design	time, effort, number of specification faults found	cost-effectiveness, cost
Testing	time, effort, number of bugs found	cost-effectiveness, stability, cost
Resources		
Personnel	price	productivity
Teams	size, communication level, structuredness	productivity, quality
Software	price, size	usability, reliability
Hardware	price, speed, memory size	reliability
Office	size, temperature, light	comfort, quality

this relation between tokens with capital letters and complexity capture your intuition about C++ code? If not, then the measure is not well defined.

A measure is useful if it can be used meaningfully to assess a current situation, control a process, or predict attributes of an entity. The purpose of the measure should be known in advance. Collecting data associated with the measure should help meet the goals and objectives of the organization. In the GQM approach described in the next section, any measure that answers one or more questions in the GQM tree is considered useful.

There are other characteristics of a good measure. First, the data for the measure has to be easy to collect and validate. Second, the measure should define a normal range of acceptable data values as an aid in interpreting the results. Third, timeliness is important—a well-defined measure that provides information after it is needed is not very helpful.

The Goal-Question-Metric Approach

You can determine useful measures in a number of ways. One that we recommend is Goal-Question-Metric (GQM) [Basili and Rombach 1988, AMI 1992]. GQM is a top-down approach. You decompose a primary goal into simpler subgoals; a subgoal can itself have subgoals. For each subgoal you define a set of questions, and for each question a set of measures that collect data to answer the question. In this sense, subgoals with questions are objectives in that they have to be time-targeted and measurable. An example primary goal is:

Improve the speed of getting new products to market.

Team members state subgoals in terms of the products, processes, and resources for which they are responsible. For example, given the goal of improving time to market, the reuse and product development managers might define the following subgoals:

Improve potential reusability of assets in the library.
Improve the efficiency of reuse engineers when working on projects.

The project development managers may also pose subgoals:

Reduce requirements-capturing time.
Improve early defect removal rate.

Team members then propose a set of questions that must be answered to quantify the subgoal, questions that define the measures. For example, in support of reducing requirements-capturing time, a development manager may ask:

How much time is spent capturing requirements?
How many people are involved in capturing requirements?

The team can answer these questions by measuring the staff-hours that personnel spend capturing requirements. The measures would be collected before and after changing the processes and resources for capturing requirements, to determine whether time and staffing resources have been reduced.

The relationship among goals, subgoals, questions, and measures forms a tree structure, as shown in Fig. 20.2 (Q and M stand for question and measure, respectively).

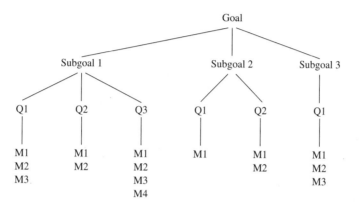

Figure 20.2   Structure of a Goal-Question-Metric Tree

Creating the GQM top-down decomposition requires a model of how processes, resources, and products are related to one another. For example, a maintenance model might indicate that overall C++ code maintainability is inversely correlated with the number of nonmember functions, member functions, and classes defined as friends.[2] Without an appropriate model, it is difficult to formulate the proper questions for a subgoal. Lacking a model also makes it difficult to reuse existing measures. In prior chapters, we discuss appropriate models for object-oriented software development. We also present goals for six decision frameworks that we decompose into steps that you should follow. We can now suggest some of the questions for each step that measure your progress toward the framework goals. These questions are shown in Table 20.2. The measures we propose later in this chapter supply answers to many of these questions.

If you follow the advice of this book, you should consider collecting the data that allows you to answer questions about each of the decision frameworks that you address, such as those listed in Table 20.2. Of course, you may have other questions more appropriate to your organization's interests.

---

[2] Any friend of a class can directly access the nonpublic members of the class without using the class's interface. Such couplings can complicate maintenance.

Table 20.2 Decision Framework Questions

Decision Framework	Questions
Product Process Model	What is the size of the system?
	How many defects are in the system?
	What kinds of defects are in the system?
	How complex is the system?
	What is the average response time to a change request?
	What percentage of existing system parts were changed to accommodate new functionality?
	What percentage of the system functionality and implementation is documented?
	What percentage of the system has test coverage?
	What type and quantity of reuse was achieved during the project?
	How many artifacts passed and how many failed the reuse evaluation tests?
Planning and Controlling	What is the time estimate for carrying out a particular task?
	How much of the estimated work effort has been completed?
	How much of the estimated work effort remains to be done?
	What is the current deviation from plan?
	What is the average deviation from estimated task durations?
	How many changes were made to scheduled task dependencies?
	How much time was spent replanning?
Reuse Process Model	What is the average level of potential reusability of library assets?
	What percentage of the artifacts developed on a particular project are potentially reusable on other projects?
	How often has a reusable asset been successfully reused?
	How much time is spent to certify, classify, store, locate, retrieve, understand, use, and maintain reusable assets?
	What percentage of the reusable assets have documentation sufficient to assist a developer in reusing the asset?
	What percentage of the reusable assets have been tested according to the organization's guidelines for testing products?
	How many reusable assets have been certified?

continued

Table 20.2 *continued*

Decision Framework	Questions
Team Structure	With how many other team members must each team member communicate to carry out his or her responsibilities?
	How many different responsibilities are defined for each team role?
	What percentage of the team members have the right proficiency in the subject areas needed to carry out their roles?
	What percentage of the tasks are assigned to a team member who has responsibility to carry out the task?
	How productive is each developer?
	How productive is the project team?
Software Development Environment	How much effort has been (or will be) expended on the software development environment evaluation project?
	How much did it (or will it) cost to port a result from one platform to another?
	What percentage of the desired concepts are addressed by the analysis-and-design method?
	What is the level of technology marketplace momentum for the selected languages, tools, databases, and methods?
Training	What percentage of the developers found that their training was effective in transferring needed skills?
	How long does it take to train team members to each proficiency level in each subject area?
	What percentage of the course materials and instructors are adequate to support the course objectives?
	What percentage of the team members found the format for delivering training or mentoring appropriate to their needs?

Measuring Size, Productivity, and Effort

Many of the questions in Table 20.2 refer to the size of some product, the productivity of some resource, or the effort of some process. *Size* measures the magnitude of some product (an internal product measure). For example, how large was the last system you developed? There are many measures of product size. The two most common are length and functionality measures. Lines of code (LOC) is the classic software measure of length. Figure 20.3 illustrates the idea of length as a measure of size—where length is in feet for a bicycle or an automobile.

Figure 20.3   Basic Measurement Perspective of Size

Functionality is an alternative sizing measure. Function points [IFPUG 1994a] is a measure of functionality. Figure 20.4 illustrates the idea of a functionality measure of size, where functionality is the seating capacity of a vehicle.

Figure 20.4   Functionality Perspective of Size

Length and functionality size measures quantify different size aspects of a software product—much as height and strength quantify different size aspects of a person. For a software product, we recommend that you report the size in terms of both length and functionality.

In our case studies, we asked, how large was your software development effort? Use whatever measure you think is appropriate. The developers who had any data at all responded using either LOC or number of class definitions—both length measures (see Appendix A, Charts A.3 and A.4). In the following section, we consider whether LOC and number of class definitions are good length measures to use with object-oriented software products.

Length Measure: Lines of Code

Lines of code—a well-defined measure? For more than 45 years, the most common measure of software system (product) size has been LOC. Unfortunately, there is no standard for counting LOC, with the result that much of the LOC data that has been collected over the past decades cannot be compared because of differences in the way people counted. Also, developers using modern software development environments can create applications by laying out graphical screens and filling in property dialog boxes. Using these environments, the majority of the executable code is generated by the application builder. As a result, LOC no longer measures what developers directly create. For all of these reasons, LOC has no stature as a well-defined measure of software product size.

The inheritance and encapsulation concepts provided by object-oriented languages complicate the rules for counting LOC. Any LOC measure would have to determine when code from superclasses is or is not counted again in subclasses. Since each language provides its own mechanisms for inheritance and encapsulation, LOC counts are not comparable across languages. The size data from the case studies presented in Appendix A Chart A.3 must be interpreted with extreme care since the data represents LOC of products written in different languages.[3]

Lines of code—useful for determining effort and productivity? LOC is not useful for computing or predicting productivity and work effort. Economists define *productivity* as the goods or services produced per unit of labor or expense. According to this definition, as real costs decline, the cost per unit of goods or services should also decline. As productivity goes up, the number of goods or services produced per unit of time should go up. It is certainly possible to report productivity numbers in terms of LOC—for example, the productivity of a developer is 100 LOC per month. However, the LOC size measure is negatively correlated with improvements in a programming language. As the level of

---

[3] Actually, the situation is even worse with regard to comparability, since each case study project team used different counting rules.

language expressiveness increases, the developer writes less code to express more functionality. As a result, use of more advanced languages appears to make programmers less productive.

Effort measures the amount of elapsed time needed to perform some task, for example, the number of uninterrupted staff-hours needed to test an object. Measuring effort directly does not require a size measure; we simply note how long it takes to carry out a task. However, as Chapter 7 discusses, effort is something we frequently wish to predict. Most effort-estimation models, such as COCOMO [Boehm 1981], base their effort prediction on LOC. COCOMO is used to produce estimates of effort during early phases of software development, before the exact LOC measure of a product is known. So the expected LOC of the result has to be predicted as well. These predictions are often significantly different from the actual size of the system, which means that the effort estimate is necessarily inaccurate as well. For this reason, should you decide to use COCOMO with object-oriented technology, you would replace LOC by the number of object abstractions. The number of object abstractions have to be the ones you expect to find in the implementation model in order to be comparable to Boehm's LOC approach. But since you can know only the number of object abstractions in the implementation after implementation has been completed, this approach is not very useful. It would be better to calibrate a historical model to the number of object abstractions in the analysis model.

Since the amount of code within an object-oriented system is often small, the LOC measure is particularly ill suited for quantifying the productivity of object-oriented developers. For example, the average length of a ParcPlace Smalltalk (VisualWorks Version 1.0) method is 7 LOC. The median length is 3 LOC. The real productivity of object-oriented developers is not their ability to create many small methods rapidly. Rather, productivity is better measured in terms of the time to create the object abstractions with their associated responsibilities and contracts.

Because LOC is not well defined and not useful for determining effort and productivity, we recommend against its use as a means of reporting object-oriented code size. However, if you are obligated to report LOC, be certain to define how you will measure LOC in your particular programming language. Try to automate the counting if possible to make sure that the measure is consistently applied.

Be aware that, because of problems we have raised with LOC, it is not sensible to make productivity comparisons such as: "The productivity of our developers has increased from 3 LOC per month using traditional languages to 10 LOC per month using object-oriented languages." These comparisons will lead only to misguided conclusions.

Length Measure: Number of Object Abstractions

Number of object abstractions—a well-defined measure? An object abstraction, as the basic unit of organization within an object-oriented system, is a reasonable candidate as a length measure of object-oriented systems. Some of our case study organizations reported their system size in terms of the number of object classes. In object-oriented languages that include classes, the number of classes is one way we can measure the number of object abstractions within a system. The measure is defined as:

Count the number of unique class definitions that occur in the implementation.

A well-defined measure based on object abstractions should count object abstractions produced throughout the development life cycle. In particular, each object-oriented analysis-and-design method should provide a way to count object abstractions in the resulting models. In OBA, for example, the number of object abstractions in the analysis model equals the number of roles that are not explicitly labeled as examples. Since not all object-oriented programming languages are class based (Self is an example), you will have to define alternative measures for determining the number of object abstractions in each implementation language. To the extent that such measures count the unique syntactic object abstractions (class definitions) coded in the programming language, you will be able to obtain comparable cross-language results.

Number of object abstractions—useful for determining effort and productivity?
The number of object abstractions is not useful for computing or predicting productivity and effort. The measure provides only a simple count of the number of abstractions, without any regard to complexity or the difficulty in conceiving the abstraction. In general, any measure that is useful for determining effort and productivity must take into account the complexity of the entities to be produced.

We recommend you use the measure of the number of object abstractions to communicate the basic (length) size of an object system. However, until this measure is supplemented with appropriate complexity measures, it can be used only as a rough approximation for estimating effort and productivity. Also, recall from our example in Chapter 7 that it is error-prone to track overall project progress based on the estimated number of object abstractions in the problem domain. There will almost always be additional object abstractions in the implemented system.

Functionality Measure: Function Points

Two measures of functionality in software systems are Albrecht's Function Point Analysis (FPA) [Albrecht 1986, Dreger 1989, IFPUG 1994a] and DeMarco's Bang [DeMarco 1982]. The primary objective of both of these size measures is to predict effort and cost, and to assess productivity based on a basic unit of product size. Bang is specific to the DeMarco structured analysis-and-design method, and therefore is not applicable unless that method is used.

Function Point Analysis. Function Point Analysis (FPA) sizes an application from an end-user perspective, rather than from the technical details of a particular implementation language. Introduced by Allan Albrecht of IBM in the late 1970s, FPA defines a *function* *point* to be one end-user business function. The analyst counts only those functions approved by and beneficial to the end user. FPA is the method of choice for measuring the size of a product from the customer's point of view, for more than 1000 major corporations around the world [IFPUG 1994a].

Function points is an artificial measure, however, equivalent to cost per square foot in home construction or the Dow Jones Industrial Average stock indicator. Contractors do not build a house one square foot at a time, even though they find it useful to describe the project in terms of square feet [Jones 1991]. Similarly, software professionals do not build software one function point at a time, although they find it useful to describe the product in terms of function points.

In 1986, the International Function Point User Group (IFPUG) was formed to assist in communicating data and information about FPA. The members work together to resolve conceptual issues about the use of function points. The objectives for counting function points, as promoted by IFPUG, are:

- Measure the functionality that the user requests and receives independent of the technology used for implementation

- Provide a size measure to support quality and productivity analyses

- Provide a means to estimate the cost of software development

- Provide a way by which function points can be compared across organizations

To meet these objectives, IFPUG produced the Function Point Counting Practices Manual [IFPUG 1994a]. This manual provides a standard set of definitions, rules, and techniques for counting function points.

Figure 20.5 summarizes the function point counting method. The first step is to determine the type of system involved: a new system installation, an enhancement to a system, or an existing system. The second step is to identify the boundary between the system and the end user, to determine which functions should be included in the count. According to FPA, an application is a collection of five kinds of components: inputs, outputs, inquiries, interfaces to other applications, and logical internal files. The first three are referred to as transaction function types, while the last two are data function types. The third step is to count the different data and transaction function types. Specific counting rules adjust the counts based on the complexity of the components— some logical internal files, for example, are more complicated than others and are assigned more function points. The component counting techniques provide guidelines on how to determine the level of complexity, and IFPUG defines a table that maps component complexities to weighted values. Given the type of component and its complexity, we look in the table to find the appropriate number of function points to assign to the system's functions. The total of all of these function points is called the unadjusted function points.

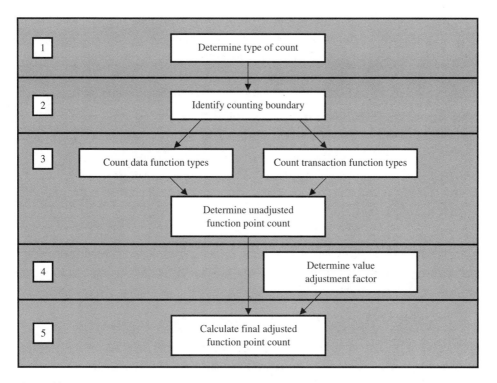

Figure 20.5 Function Point Counting Method

The fourth step is to assess 14 general system characteristics, such as transaction rate and complexity of transaction processing. Each characteristic will have either no influence, strong influence, or some level of intermediate influence on the count of function points. A combination of these characteristics provides an adjustment factor (also known as the technical complexity factor). The final step is to calculate the final adjusted function point count using the unadjusted function points and the adjustment factor. The specific formula depends on the type of system as determined in the first step.

Function Point Analysis—a well-defined measure? The underlying premise of FPA is that customers can more easily understand the size of a delivered system in terms of the number of business functions rather than the number of lines of code. IFPUG has developed counting rules that promote uniformity in counting practices across organizations. A field experiment on the reliability of function point counting showed that the function point counts from pairs of raters using the standard counting method differed, on average, by only plus or minus 10 percent [Kemerer 1990]. Given the uniformity of counting, we can say that 500 function points, as measured by a company in San Francisco, California, provides exactly the same amount of functionality as 500 function points measured by a company in Tokyo, Japan, or Oslo, Norway.

FPA was originally conceived as a means of sizing MIS applications, and was originally biased toward counting large mainframe MIS applications. A variant of function points, referred to as feature points, counts everything in FPA plus characteristics of algorithms. It extends FPA to scientific and engineering applications [Jones 1991]. Additional apparent inconsistencies of FPA advanced by Symons [Symons 1991] include:

- Components are sometimes difficult to identify in modern systems development practice. What, for example, is a "logical file" in a relational database environment?

- For any given component, the most complex component can get at most only twice the function points of the simplest component, which does not support the intuitive complexity range.

- A logical inquiry, when programmed in batch mode, is treated as a separate input and output, receiving more than twice as many points as it would if programmed as an on-line inquiry delivering an immediate answer to the user.

- System organization is sometimes penalized in unjustifiable ways. The IFPUG rules assign more function points to a collection of discrete systems than to a single integrated system. As function points are currently defined, when a collection of discrete systems is replaced by an integrated system, the number of function points will decrease because the number of end-user application interfaces decreases.

There have been a number of adaptations to function points, such as the feature points mentioned earlier, Mark II Function Points [Symons 1991], Asset-R Function Points [Reifer 1990], and 3D Function Points [Whitmire 1992]. IFPUG's continued position is that FPA is well defined without any of these modifications.

Function Point Analysis—useful for determining effort and productivity? Despite its failings, FPA is a well-defined size measure, and function points are a useful economic unit for determining productivity and effort. As real costs decline, the cost per function point also declines. If you spend $100,000 to develop 100 function points, the cost per function point is $1,000. If you reduce your development cost 50 percent to $50,000 for 100 function points, the cost per function point is also reduced 50 percent to $500. If you can improve your productivity from 10 function points per month to 15 function points per month, your overall output is improved. In terms of effort, if you wish to develop a new application that will consist of 525 function points, and you know that your team development productivity is 15 function points per month, you can predict that it will take approximately 35 months to complete the application.

We see function points as a well-defined size measure that is useful for computing the productivity and effort of a completed MIS project. Using function points, it is meaningful to compare productivity results of object-oriented projects with non–object-oriented projects. It makes sense for you to say, "The productivity of our developers has increased from three function points per month using traditional development to ten function points per month using object-oriented development." The important prerequisite is knowing how to count function points in object-oriented development projects.

Function points and object-oriented products. The IFPUG New Environments Committee is responsible for proposing new function point counting techniques. As of 14 September 1993 [IFPUG 1994b], the committee concluded that, since a given product has the same number of function points regardless of which implementation technology is used in its construction, the existing function point measure discussed in the IFPUG Counting Practices Manual can be used for measuring object-oriented systems.

The fact that FPA is independent of implementation technology does not make it independent of analysis-and-design methods, and so IFPUG recommends changes to step 3 in Fig. 20.5. However, the recommended modifications make no mention of how to handle interfaces, and contain a superficial judgment that you can treat class hierarchies as logical internal files, a position that will need better elaboration and justification.

Another approach to applying function points to object-oriented technology is described by Whitmire in [Keyes 1993]. This approach identifies function point components by examining static object models (models of objects and their relationships with one another), and the incoming and outgoing messages that cross the application boundary (which Whitmire refers to as interaction links). The basic function point counting approach illustrated in Fig. 20.5 is used.

The application boundary is determined by identifying which classes are internal to the software part of the system. Once the boundary has been established, the transaction function types—inputs, outputs, and inquiries—are determined from interaction links. The complexity of each input, output, and inquiry is determined by the number of classes accessed by each transaction. Generally speaking, each class represents an internal logical file. However, classes that form an aggregation (a purchase order is an aggregation of order items) are counted as one logical internal file. The number of classes in the aggregation is used to determine the complexity of the logical internal file (one for purchase order and the other for order item). Also, abstract classes in a class hierarchy are counted as internal logical files if they are relevant to the application domain (provide specification). If an abstract class exists only to provide implementation, it is not counted, but its code is assumed to be defined in all derived classes, which are counted separately (i.e., multiple times).

An external interface file represents data that is maintained internally by some other application, and is accessed directly by the application we are counting. In object-oriented development, objects should never access externally maintained data. Rather, a message is sent to request data from the containing object. These message-sends will almost always be counted as external inquiries. As such, Whitmire proposes that we ignore external interfaces.

After the inputs, outputs, inquiries, and internal logical files have been counted, the unadjusted function point count is determined. The value adjustment factor is computed according to IFPUG practices, which is then used to compute the final adjusted function point. The resulting count should be comparable to function point counts of other applications developed using non–object-oriented techniques. To the extent that object-oriented analysis-and-design methods generate artifacts that map to the descriptions of the four component types, they will be able to use Whitmire's approach. Otherwise, a new mapping will have to be created for the specific artifacts that result from a particular method.

In practice, there is no well-known accepted approach to counting function points in projects making use of object-oriented technology. Most organizations with which we deal count object-oriented function points using the same approach they use to count traditional function points, if they count anything at all. Typically, these organizations have data-intensive applications, so the standard counting practices work because the elements counted are easily identified in the object model resulting from an object-oriented analysis method.

The standard counting technique does not work for other kinds of applications. The approach described by Whitmire offers some promise, but it is not well known, must be described in greater detail, and must be tested on a wide-scale basis before we will know its efficacy. We recommend that if you are interested in using function points with object-oriented analysis-and-design methods, you will have to expand on Whitmire's approach (where the traditional approach is not applicable). Get your method vendor to work with you to specify how to count function points based on the elements of the models that the analysis-and-design method produces.

Measuring Quality

Quality, as we define it in Chapter 6, is a catchall term that refers to external product attributes, such as reliability and correctness. You can use the GQM method or a technique known as Quality Templates to define end-user product quality requirements.

Quality Templates. Quality Templates were proposed by Tom Gilb as a way to capture the information necessary for measuring an external product attribute [Gilb 1988]. Table 20.3 provides a generic description and example of the information that is captured in a Quality Template. The first item in the Quality Template is the name and description of the objective to be met. In the example, the objective is Average Response Time. The next item lists any prerequisites that have to be met before you can measure the attribute. In the example, there must be data in the database before you can run the test, and there must be software tools that execute specific tests.

Date indicates the date by which the test must be run. This date can reference the project schedule, as it does in the example. Test describes a precise test or measure to

Table 20.3 Example Quality Template for Average Response Time

Aspect	Definition	Example
Name and Description	Unambiguous and meaningful to the end user	Average Response Time—average time needed for system to perform common queries
Prerequisites	Conditions that must be met before measurements are meaningful	Test data exists in the database, test framework exists
Date	Date by which the test should be run	Alpha Testing (actual date obtained from project schedule)
Test	Precise test or measure used to determine the value on the provided scale	Perform the five most frequent forms of queries 20 times each. Compute the average elapsed time for all queries.
Scale	Scale along which measurements will be made	Number of elapsed seconds
Worst	Worst acceptable limit on the scale; worse than this is defined as failure	30 seconds
Plan	Level on the scale that must be met by Date	20 seconds
Best	Engineering limit, state-of-the-art, best ever	10 seconds
Current	Some existing system for comparison with Plan and Worst cases	40 seconds
Reference	Reference to more detail	See query document for a description of the five test queries and the information content of the database
Source	Authority for the objective	Marketing

determine the value of the attribute. This test can be a common measure, such as counting the number of classes, or something more specific to the product, such as the outcome of performing the five most frequent forms of queries 20 times each. Scale is a number scale used for comparing the values resulting from the test.

The next four entries in the Quality Template refer to numbers on the scale. Worst describes the worst acceptable test result. Anything worse than this is a system failure. If this quality attribute is critical, then failing to be at least as good as Worst is a total system failure. Plan is the value you are trying to achieve by Date. Best represents a value on the scale associated with an engineering limit or state-of-the-art practice. If you were measuring reliability, Best would be 100 percent. Best is informative because it tells clients and managers there is unexploited potential in this attribute. However, the goal of the project is not to achieve Best, but to achieve Plan.

Current is an equivalent test result for the existing system and is useful for comparison purposes. The final two aspects are Reference and Source. Reference points to more information about the test conditions or how to achieve the planned result. Source refers to the person or organization who stated the objective, and therefore can authorize any changes. Any of these aspects can have multiple entries—for example, there can be multiple Prerequisites. In such cases, each entry is qualified so it can be uniquely referenced.

Quality Templates serve two fundamental purposes. First, they encourage analysts and customers to work together to define measurable quality objectives for a product. Second, they provide essential input to the design process. Quality Templates give designers the information they need to make appropriate design trade-offs. Assuming a complete set of templates, a designer who has simultaneously satisfied all of the provided templates can be confident that the design exhibits the user's planned level of quality.

Reporting Quality in Terms of Defects

There are four reasons to track reported defects: to describe the product's quality in terms of the number and kinds of defects, to track whether the quality is improving because the number of defects is decreasing, to identify when and how defects are introduced so the development process can be improved, and to make sure defects get fixed.

Defect measures are an important indicator of quality. In Chapter 6, we recommend that you track incidents, defects, and changes using the templates we provide, and report results using the direct and indirect measure that we describe in this section. You should use prototyping and inspections to uncover defects in analysis-and-design artifacts. We expect the analysis-and-design methods to provide definitions of consistency, and method tools to support consistency checks. Inspections should also be used to uncover defects in documentation artifacts. You should use testing as your primary means of uncovering defects in detailed design and code artifacts. If you work in life-critical domains, you should consider using formal methods and correctness proofs to uncover defects as well.

Reports. You can report both direct and indirect measures of incidents, defects, and changes. Direct measures are simple counts of the various incident, defect, and change reports. It is often more informative to measure the number of reports that have a particular characteristic, such as the number of reused components that had to be changed, or the number of defects where the software could not be used at all. Exactly what is reported depends on the nature of the project.

There are several indirect measures that you should use as well. One such report might list aged defects—defects that have not been removed after two years, after one year, and after six months. Others, mostly based on the recommendations of [DeMarco 1982], include:

Project defect density	Known defects detected prior to delivery, expressed as the number of defects per unit, such as defects per ten class definitions.
Project spoilage	Cost to remove all known defects prior to delivery, normalized to cost per unit, such as $2000 per class.
Defect removal efficiency	Ratio of known defects removed from the product prior to customer release to the total number of known defects found in the application during its useful life, expressed as a percentage.
Product defect density	Known defects delivered in the product expressed as the number of defects per unit, such as defects per class.
Product spoilage	Cost to remove all known defects from the time the system is delivered until it is retired, normalized to cost per unit, such as $500 per class.
Total spoilage	Sum of project and product spoilage.
Six-month product spoilage	Cost to remove all known defects during the first six months after delivery, normalized to cost per unit. It is commonly believed that the product spoilage during the first six months is a good indicator for the rate of spoilage during the life of the system.

Measuring Complexity

Complexity measures the number of parts and their interconnections. Measures of complexity are typically based on internal product attributes, such as cohesion, coupling, and structuredness.

Cohesion	The degree to which tasks performed by a single system component are functionally related.

Coupling
: The interdependence among components in a computer system.

Structuredness
: The extent to which a system is organized into a recognizable pattern, out of a small number of well-defined parts.

Complexity measures are used to predict development and maintenance effort, or to indicate some aspect of product quality, such as understandability, correctability, or extensibility.

Inherent and Added Complexities

There are two forms of complexity: inherent and added. *Inherent complexity* is the number of domain elements and their interdependencies that are intrinsic to a problem. Certain domains are inherently more complex than others. For example, controlling the equipment of the space shuttle is inherently more complex than controlling a microwave oven. Inherent complexity is a property of a problem; it cannot be eliminated or reduced without changing the problem itself. The COCOMO effort-prediction model accounts for inherent application complexity by adjusting its formula's exponent and coefficient based on the application's type. FPA uses the inherent complexities of individual components to adjust the overall function point count.

Added complexity is complexity introduced by the software artifacts you create when developing a solution to a problem. It includes elements of the analysis, design, and implementation models, such as scripts, classes, and class hierarchies. Added complexity exists because of technology constraints imposed by industry standards, by the choice of computing environment, and by goals not required by the problem statement (such as goals for greater extensibility). Most traditional and object-oriented complexity measures have to do with added complexities.

Object-Oriented Design and Code Complexity Measures

The contemporary object-oriented measurement literature addresses object-oriented design complexity [Chidamber and Kemerer 1991, Henderson-Sellers and Edwards 1994, Li and Henry 1993, Lorenz and Kidd 1994, Tegarden, Sheetz, and Monarchi 1993]. The majority of the measures described by these authors are simple counts of particular attributes, for example, the number of direct subclasses and the number of methods that access a variable. All of the measures examine attributes in terms of basic object-oriented concepts—polymorphism, encapsulation, and inheritance. In addition, all of the authors use the concepts of coupling and cohesion in choosing their measures. The majority of the measures provided by Chidamber and Li are well defined. Several of the measures provided by Tegarden are not well defined, either because they are not intuitive or because they are poorly described. Lorenz and Kidd offer a large number of easy-to-collect measures, some of which are not particularly well defined and others whose usefulness the authors are still evaluating.

The major problem with these measures is that the authors provide little insight on how to interpret the resulting data. For example, Chidamber and Kemerer claim that the depth of the inheritance tree is useful for "behavior prediction, design complexity and potential reuse of inherited methods." Let's use their proposed measure and see what we can conclude. Chart 20.1 shows the results of applying the depth-of-inheritance measure to all 395 classes in the ParcPlace Systems ObjectWorks for Smalltalk Version 4.1 product (excluding the metaclasses).

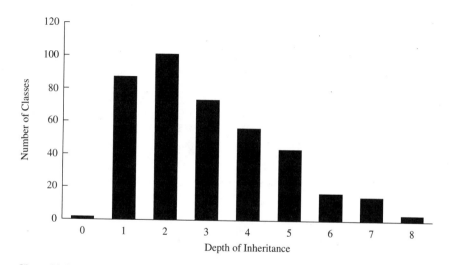

Chart 20.1   Results of Applying the Depth of Inheritance Measure to All Classes in ParcPlace ObjectWorks for Smalltalk, Version 4.1

ParcPlace Smalltalk has a single class hierarchy whose root is the class Object. The depth for class Object is 0. The average depth of a class is 2.95, and the median depth is 3. Now what? It is difficult to draw any useful conclusions—it is not clear what a median depth of 3 means. The depth-of-inheritance count is an example of a simple-to-compute measure that is useless without a framework for interpretation, which the proponents of this measure fail to provide.

Some measurement advocates provide erroneous or ill-defined guidelines for interpreting measurement data. For example, some advocates claim that the design of any system that has a class hierarchy deeper than four is "suspect." It is dangerous to make such general claims. Some problems are sufficiently complex to warrant hierarchies of depth greater than four because they are best understood with such hierarchies. Many object-oriented complexity measures, such as depth of the inheritance tree, assume they are only measuring design complexity, when in fact they are measuring both design and the inherent complexity of the problem. Design measures have to be interpreted in the context of the problem analysis.

Furthermore, object-oriented design and implementation complexity measures proposed to date have not been defined in terms of a realistic model of object-oriented software development and maintenance. Rather, they have been driven by what is easy to measure. The use of the collected data is left as an exercise for further research. This defect of complexity measures is not specific to object-oriented measures. As Kearney [Kearney *et al.* 1986] points out, most traditional software complexity measures—such as Software Sciences [Halstead 1977] and Cyclomatic Complexity [McCabe 1976]—are without theoretical basis. Object-oriented complexity measures that can be interpreted and used to effect real change must be grounded in a development process model appropriate to the use of object-oriented technology. Although there is more than one process model for developing object-oriented software, most include strategies for incremental and iterative development, consuming reusable assets, incremental testing and integration, and prototyping to obtain requirements and design information.

To benefit from today's object-oriented complexity measures, you will have to develop your own framework for interpreting the resulting data. This framework can be developed by selecting a set of complexity measures and applying them to your ongoing and completed software projects. You can analyze the data collected in this way to determine typical ranges for each measure. For example, if you determine that your application domains historically are modeled with hierarchies in the range of five to seven classes deep, you can conclude that a similar application with a hierarchy of depth 12 is worth scrutinizing.

If you also measure quality attributes such as testability, maintainability, and usability, you can attempt to discover correlations between your historical complexity attributes and quality attributes. Such correlations provide you with additional knowledge for interpreting complexity data. Finally, you can examine your product process models and hypothesize correlations between internal and external attributes. You can use these correlations to determine which complexity and quality attributes are important to measure. Or, if you have already been collecting data, the proposed model can be used to confirm or refute your hypothesized correlations.

Measuring Reuse

The extent to which reusable artifacts have been tested and proved reliable will directly and proportionally improve the quality of the system in which they are reused and the productivity of the people who create with them. There are three important aspects of reuse measures: potential reuse, the influence of reuse on size measures, and the influence of reuse on effort measures.

Measuring Potential Reuse

Potential reuse is a measure of the likelihood that an artifact developed on one project will be reusable on other projects. Three factors influence potential reusability: inherent reusability, domain reusability, and organizational reusability (that is, support for the reuse process model). A weighted measure of these three factors provides a measure of potential reuse.

Inherent reusability. Inherent reusability refers to the likelihood that an asset is reusable based on its internal attributes or predicted external attributes. There are many attributes that can be used to measure inherent reuse. Three of these are:

- Completeness of the asset's interface specification, which indicates its potential as a component of multiple applications (an internal product measure)

- Generality of the asset with respect to the opportunities it presents for specialization (an internal product measure)

- Understandability of the asset—one of the quality aspects, which indicates how easy it will be for developers to reuse the asset (an external product measure)

Many of the complexity and quality measures that have been and will be defined for object-oriented artifacts are useful as indicators of inherent reusability.

Domain reusability. Domain reusability refers to the likelihood that an artifact is reusable based on the probability that future application domains will be similar to the domain for which the artifact was created. To measure domain similarity, you can describe the needs of new applications in terms of the same classification scheme used to classify reusable assets. The domain reusability of the artifact can then be determined by computing the degree to which its classification matches that of the applications.

Organizational reusability. Organizational reusability is a compound measure of the organization's ability to identify, certify, classify, store, communicate, locate, and retrieve reusable assets.

Influence of Reuse on Size Measures

Effective reuse is a measure of the type and quantity of reuse that has occurred on a given project. Most people who report effective reuse data do not provide a clear indication of what they measured. For example, the claim "we achieved 80 percent reuse on our project" is vacuous. A software development project uses many different types of artifacts such as analyses, designs, code, test suites, and documentation, and this claim does not indicate which types of artifacts were counted. Also, there are different ways artifacts can be reused. For example, implementation artifacts can be reused as-is, through inheritance, or through generic or parameterized classes. A report on effective reuse should indicate the different forms of reuse that were counted, and even provide a breakdown by type— for example, 20 percent code reuse via inheritance, 40 percent via parameterized classes, and so on. If artifacts can be adapted for reuse, types and levels of adaptation should be reported—for example, 18 percent of the code modules were reused with slight revisions (less than 25 percent modification).

Most managers report on interproject reuse—that is, reusing artifacts that were developed by other projects. It is essential that the manager report which externally developed components are being counted, especially when reporting on applications developed in languages like Smalltalk. In Smalltalk, numbers, strings, and characters are utility objects provided as part of a standard library of reusable objects. In most languages (including hybrid object-oriented languages), numbers, strings, and characters are part of the language definition (that is, they are built into the compiler). Should you treat these objects as reused when you write Smalltalk applications? If you count these as reusable objects, the measure for Smalltalk reuse is likely to be larger than for C++ for the same application (given that all other variables are the same).

You might also wish to report on effective intraproject reuse, that is, the extent to which artifacts developed on a project are reused within the project. This type of measure has more relevance when measured during maintenance. An interesting example is reported for the Customer-Related Information System II developed for Brooklyn Union Gas [Davis and Morgan 1993]. After the initial system had been in operation for more than two years, a new feature was added to the system. This feature consisted of a new dialog with four displays that allowed users to correct mismatches between field conditions and database contents. When the programmer was done, the developers counted the number of raw lines of code added to the system. The analysis showed that 2000 lines had been added, but a total of 40,000 lines of code had been used. The ratio of new code to reused code was 1 to 20. The 40,000 line count included only behaviors that implemented business functions; technical behaviors such as dialog management were not counted.

Influence of Reuse on Effort Measures

Reusing software artifacts affects how you measure and predict effort. If you measure effort in terms of uninterrupted staff-hours, you must account for the time it takes to carry out the reuse process model steps: the time to locate, retrieve, understand, and use the assets. If you are developing reusable assets, you need to measure the additional effort that is expended to ensure that the artifacts are indeed reusable assets.

Table 20.4 FPA Measure of Reusability

Score As	Descriptions to Determine Degree of Influence
0	No reusable code.
1	Reusable code is used within the application.
2	Less than 10 percent of the application considered more than one user's needs.
3	Ten percent or more of the application considered more than one user's needs.
4	The application was specifically packaged and/or documented to ease reuse, and the application is customized by the user at source code level.
5	The application was specifically packaged and/or documented to ease reuse, and the application is customized for use by means of user parameter maintenance.

The effort to carry out a task is a function of the expected level of reuse—of both the type and the quantity of reuse. The greater the expected reuse, the less effort you should need to carry out the task.[4] The predicted level of effort to do a task is determined by two factors: which assets are available, and the predicted amount of adaptation of the assets that will be required.

The basic COCOMO effort estimation model uses the number of newly created source instructions as an independent variable in computing effort. Intermediate COCOMO accounts for reused code by multiplying the number of source instructions adapted from existing software by an adaptation adjustment factor. This factor is based on the effort to adapt the design and code, and to test and integrate the result. A modified COCOMO based on the number of object abstractions would have to make similar adjustments.

FPA is frequently used to account for the effort to create new reusable code. The fourth step of counting function points assesses 14 general system characteristics believed to make the job of developing a system more complex. Characteristic number ten is Reusability, defined to be the degree to which the application and the code in the application have been specifically designed, developed, and supported to be usable in other applications. The person counting function points is asked to measure the degree to which this characteristic influences the application as a whole. Table 20.4 defines this measure.

---

[4] In general this statement is true. But there are some situations where the effort to reuse is the same as or more than the effort to develop without reuse. There still may be a good reason for reusing, such as consistency leading to lower maintenance costs.

Framework for Setting Up a Software Measurement Program

A software measurement program defines which measures to collect, and how and when measures will be collected within an organization. The program specifies the people, organizational structure, tools, and policies needed to meet measurement objectives. Each organization will have its own individual measurement program.

The project to create a measurement program is shown in Fig. 20.6.

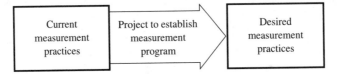

| Current measurement practices | Project to establish measurement program | Desired measurement practices |

Figure 20.6   Process-Improvement Project to Establish a Software Measurement Program

Although it is certainly possible to establish a measurement program in the context of a single project, the real return on investment occurs when common measurement practices are applied across many projects within an organization. The measurement data collected from prior projects can be used to predict the costs of future development efforts, and to control an ongoing development effort.

Collecting data must be an integral part of each developer's and each manager's job.

Measurement

Measurement is everyone's job. Data collection must be an integral part of all software development job roles.

One specific concern you must address when setting up a measurement program is that everyone understands the goals and objectives of the program. You conscientiously have to avoid "goal displacement," whereby the original goal (improving the product, process, or resources) is displaced by a secondary goal (making the measures look good).

Some organizations have a special group assigned to the collection of measurement data. However, all team members should view themselves as responsible for supporting that group. To the extent possible, data collection should be automated. Data that cannot be collected automatically should be collected at the time it becomes available and verified immediately. It is important to archive the raw data and the derived data to enable an independent audit.

According to DeMarco [DeMarco 1982], measurement activities ought to cost from 5–10 percent of the staffing cost of the effort monitored. DeMarco indicates that, in the beginning of carrying out a measurement program, the cost will be at the high end of this range, since proportionately more time will be spent learning, setting up new procedures, reconstructing past history, and working by trial and error. The ongoing maintenance costs for measurement are at a 5–10 percent level as well.

You must know the precision of the data that you collect so you can provide error estimates with your analyses of the data. Each datum should have an associated precision value that is consistent with the process or device used to make the measurement. It is also important to know how data will be used so you can determine the proper level of measurement precision. It is pointless to measure staff effort in seconds if you plan to report in person-months and to accept error in units of days.

The principle for the decision framework for setting up a software measurement program states that measurement is essential. And the goal states the need to decide what data you require.

> *Framework Principle.* Effective software measurement is an essential engineering activity.

> *Framework Goal.* Set up a measurement program to identify the data you require, a means of collecting this data, and a way to use the results to meet goals and objectives.

The steps of the decision framework follow from the goal:

- Define project goals and objectives

- Determine measures based on goals and objectives

- Use measurement data to assess, predict, and control

- Update the measurement plan

Software Measurement Program

Define Project Goals and Objectives

The first step, to establish clear project goals and objectives, is emphasized throughout this book. You must determine measures that help you establish your goals and objectives, assess whether you are making progress toward your goals and objectives, and determine when you successfully reach them. This requirement is true whether these goals and objectives are defined for long-term continuous improvement efforts that affect multiple projects, or whether they are defined for a single product development project.

Determine Measures Based on Goals and Objectives

Goals and objectives are statements of desired outcome. They do not dictate the form of the measure, but rather what you should measure. The problem is to determine which measures to use. GQM and Quality Templates are top-down approaches that assist in defining measures. Both approaches are flexible and can be used for different types of organizations with different types of goals.

Use Measurement Data to Assess, Predict, and Control

Measurement data is used to assess, predict, and control some attribute of a product, process, or resource. Even when the context is known, you must be careful to use the data for the original purpose, and to do so in statistically appropriate ways.

Plan before you collect. Know what you plan to do with the data you collect, before you collect it.

To understand how to interpret the data, refer back to your GQM tree or Quality Templates to find the context in which you defined why the data should be collected. The context is defined by the GQM model as the questions to be answered to determine whether a subgoal has been reached; the measurement data is used to answer one or more of these questions. As you traverse the GQM tree, the measures for subgoals can be combined to derive new measures associated with higher-level goals. As a word of caution, we offer the following two maxims:

Advertise before you collect. Never use data to assess individual developers unless you have informed them, in advance, of this purpose.

Team members are often wary of data collection activities that they think will be used to evaluate them. So if it is your intent to use data to measure your team members, make sure that they know exactly how the data will and will not be used. Team members who believe the data is being used improperly will not collect it or will report it inaccurately. When you communicate the value you expect to gain from analysis of the data, your development team is more likely to support the data collection.

Data Collection

DeMarco's revised Heisenberg's uncertainty principle. Measuring any project parameter, and attaching evident significance to it, will affect the usefulness of that parameter.

If team members know you are measuring a particular attribute, and they know that this attribute is significant (especially to their personal evaluation), they will attempt to optimize the measure. This effort can be good if your goal is to optimize the attribute, as in the case where sales-people know that their bonus is related to commissionable sales and therefore they attempt to optimize their sales. However, it can be bad if your overall goal with respect to the attribute is not to optimize it, but rather to collect data for assessing the true current value of the attribute.

Care must also be taken to ensure that appropriate statistical techniques are applied to the resulting data. The following illustration demonstrates the danger of applying statistical techniques that are inappropriate to the measurement scale.

> In 1987, members of IFPUG discovered and reported that all of the 1984–85 average yield data that had been derived from function point counts were not meaningful [IFPUG 1987]. Specifically, they determined that it is not meaningful to compute department average productivity by dividing the total function points of a set of projects by the total hours spent developing those projects. This determination came about when measurement experts realized that no exact scale for function points had been agreed upon, and that most likely the scale cannot be developed beyond that of an interval scale.[5] During 1984 and 1985, department averages were computed as a ratio of total project function points to total project hours. Averages cannot be computed on an interval scale. Today, under the assumption that function points are measured on an interval scale, IFPUG recommends that department averages be defined as the average of the individual project's productivity—that is, separately compute each individual project's function point delivery rate, then compute the average of the productivities.

Given the immature state of object-oriented measures, users should be cautious. Other than measures based on simple counts, many of the newly proposed measures are not well defined enough to establish the proper measurement scale.

Update the Measurement Plan

Measurement provides a systematic way of learning from past experience and applying that learning to current activities. Over time, a measurement program must evolve to satisfy the needs of the organization. Just as we advocate in Chapter 7 that you must plan to replan when setting project schedules, you must plan to replan your measurement program. Such planning is the heart of a continuous improvement attitude.

---

[5] An interval scale of measurement is one in which differences between pairs of points anywhere on the scale are represented by equal intervals, but the zero point is arbitrary.

Summary

A measure associates a number with a specific attribute of an entity. In the case of software engineering, the attributes of interest are those belonging to products, processes, and resources. A measure should be well defined and useful. We discussed whether various size measures such as length (lines of code, number of object abstractions) and functionality (function point analysis) are well defined and useful for purposes of answering questions about systems built with object-oriented technology.

In this chapter, we introduced the Goal-Question-Metric (GQM) approach to deriving measures from goals. GQM suggests that team members decompose the project's primary goal into subgoals that describe the desired attributes of the products, processes, and resources. The team members then specify the measures needed to answer questions about each subgoal. We applied GQM to the goals of each decision framework for succeeding with objects and suggested questions you should consider answering when carrying out your projects.

You should measure the quality of a product. We described how to use Gilb's Quality Templates to measure fitness for use. Ways to predict quality are the number of defects in the product and the product's complexity. We examined how to measure the complexity of the problem domain and of the software artifacts, and then looked at why the current recommendations for measuring complexity of object-oriented systems are inadequate.

We explored three aspects of reuse measures—potential reuse, the influence of reuse on size measures, and the influence of reuse on effort measures. Potential reuse is a measure of the likelihood that an artifact developed on one project will be reusable on other projects, whereas effective reuse measures the type and quantity of reuse that occurred in a given project. You will likely want to report on effective reuse—either within a project or across multiple projects.

We made a number of recommendations you should consider:

Use GQM as the primary approach to determine which measures are appropriate.

Do not use LOC for measuring length size, rather use the number of object abstractions.

Do not use object abstractions to predict effort or productivity until such time as complexity measures can be associated with these abstractions.

Use function points to report function length size. Use the standard counting approach on data-oriented applications. On other applications, work with the vendor of the analysis-and-design method to adapt the Whitmire approach, modified to count the specific elements in the method's object model.

Use Gilb Quality Templates to define measurable project-specific quality objectives.

In Chapter 6, we provide templates for logging defects, incidents, and changes to deliverables. Use these templates, or your own—making sure they are well defined and used consistently.

Report both direct and indirect defect measures.

Complexity measures are not yet mature. To use any, you will have to develop your own framework for interpreting the data.

If reusing is part of your development, you should report size as a collection of numbers depending on the reuse details desired. Report total size. Report the contribution of reuse, and specifically what is reused, the type of reuse, and what you did to change any by-adaptation reuse. Account for the time it takes to carry out the reuse process model steps: the time to locate, retrieve, understand, and use the assets.

Finally, we defined the decision framework for setting up a software measurement program, based on the definitions of various measures and how they are used in the context of object-oriented technology.

Start collecting data now. The key to measurement is to use your own data so that interpretation is calibrated against historical evidence.

Additional Reading About Measurement

Fenton, N. E., *Software Metrics: A Rigorous Approach*, Chapman & Hall: London, 1991.
  This book is the most approachable of all of the measurement books available today. The book is part of the educational material generated by the EEC ESPRIT METKIT (metrics education tool kit) project. Fenton provides a rigorous framework for describing software measurement, and systematically categorizing various types of measurement within this framework. Along the way, he points out the inadequacies of many measures in common use today.

Grady, R. B. and Caswell, D. L., *Software Metrics: Establishing a Company-Wide Program*, Prentice Hall: Englewood Cliffs, N.J., 1987.
  This book describes the successful Hewlett-Packard (HP) measurement program. Grady and Caswell were members of the HP Metrics Council, which established and oversaw the measurement program. They share their experiences in selling HP upper management and development team members on a technically sound program. In doing so, Grady and Caswell provide a clear description of the technical issues surrounding specific software measures, and address many of the human elements that are necessary to establish a successful corporate measurement group, including training.

Humphrey, W. S., *A Discipline for Software Engineering*, Addison-Wesley: Reading, Mass., 1995.
  Watts Humphrey is best known for introducing the SEI capability maturity models, a yardstick by which many software organizations measure themselves. Mature organizations have stable, well-defined, and repeatable processes by which software is created and maintained—processes that are continually monitored for improvement. These processes depend on mature individual team members. The purpose of this book is to define the activities individuals should follow to be able to plan, carry out, and evaluate their assigned programming tasks. The author recommends basic coding standards, size measures, planning and reporting templates, and testing formats and reports. This textbook is for students who know how to write computer programs, but who have not yet acquired the disciplined approach to programming that is needed in large team efforts.

CHAPTER 21

Failing with Objects

In a time of drastic change, it is the learners who inherit the future. The learned find themselves equipped to live in a world that no longer exists.

Eric Hoffer

G-d gave everyone one mouth and two feet. When you want to know a person's true intent, watch the feet.

Richard Reich

You fail because you choose to fail.

Adele and Kenny

Organizations worldwide are looking to object-oriented technology as some sort of magic with which to fix their software systems development practices. Good project management will allow you to benefit from the use of the technology; its absence will lead to failure. You need to understand the different aspects of object-oriented technology, preparing yourself and your teams to benefit from the technology. You cannot just talk about what you need to do, you have to act on what you say.

Good Project Management Leads to Success

We wrote 20 chapters to tell you one important message:

Objects are only as beneficial as your ability to benefit from them.

Your ability to benefit from a decision to bring object-oriented technology into your organization depends on understanding your expectations for the kinds of products you want to build, the nature of the processes you will use to build the products, and the resources you have available. You have to be willing to change your processes and resources if you are to change the kinds of software systems you build. This involves changes in product process models, including how you plan and control projects; embracing a systematic reuse process model that creates a repository of reusable assets that your developers trust; creating team structures that mirror the structure of the system to be built and the process model for building it; adopting appropriate methods and tools; providing ongoing training and mentoring; and instituting a software measurement program that will give you the information you need to link cause and effect.

This is a lot to do. It is a costly investment. You cannot do it all at once. You have to set your vision for the use of object-oriented technology and incrementally move toward that vision. The cost of the investment will quickly be recouped as you benefit from a more mature and productive development situation.

Some of you might not make the investment.

Poor Project Management Leads to Failure

We ask you in this book to make decisions, positioned as decisions for succeeding. It is our experience that the decisions in Table 21.1 lead to failure. Check off the ones you are making. Count your check marks. If you score high, your chances for failure are good.

There are additional failures related to organizational issues. You can make promises you cannot keep. You can ignore the culture of your organization, pushing new technology too fast or on the wrong people. You can try to make big changes without convincing your developers that the benefits are worth the effort. You can fail to promote your successes, and let others promote your failures. You can discourage the object champions. You can expect the process to be painless. And you can expect objects to be the solution to all your development problems.

Table 21.1 Decisions that Lead to Failure in the Use of Object-Oriented Technology

Kinds of Failures	*Failure-related Decisions*
Failure related to goals and objectives	Never make a real management commitment to the use of object-oriented technology.
	Misalign expectations for the use of object-oriented technology with the organization's values for its products, processes, and resources.
	Expect outcomes from a project that are not the explicit goals or objectives of the project.
	Expect a change in product quality without a change in processes or resources.
	Position object-oriented technology as the goal, rather than as the means to the goal.
	Oversell objects—do not control management expectations.
	Attempt to adopt all aspects of object-oriented technology at once.
	Do not make a fair assessment of your current software development situation.
Failure related to product process models	Fail to select a product process model.
	Expect one process model to work for all projects.
	Resist the shift to doing more analysis and less coding.
	Ignore the opportunity to learn from prototypes.
	Treat a prototype as a product.
	Confuse the role of reuse consumer with that of reuse producer.
	Ignore the opportunity for incremental integration.
	Make quality assurance the other developer's job.
Failure related to planning	Continue to plan projects without acknowledging the uncertainty associated with an incremental and iterative development process that includes prototyping.
	Insist on detailed schedules that do not acknowledge missing information or decisions that cannot be made without further investigation.
	Insist on detailed schedules that do not have the developers' concurrence.
	Report progress based on amount of consumed resources.
	Report progress based on lines of code or numbers of classes completed.

continued

Table 21.1 *continued*

Kinds of Failures	Failure-related Decisions
Failure related to reuse process model	Ignore the need to manage reuse systematically.
	Demand that all projects provide reusable assets, regardless of their goals.
	Expect the first project to provide reusable assets.
	Expect to get substantial reuse immediately upon moving to object-oriented technology.
	Expect immediately to install a mature reuse process model.
	Expect that all developers are able to create reusable assets.
	Bribe developers to reuse.
	Bribe developers to submit reusable artifacts to a common repository.
	Believe that objects magically make producing and consuming reuse easy.
Failure related to team structures	Choose a team structure that does not mimic the project's process model and the target system's structure.
	Choose team members with skills that are inappropriate to the required roles.
	Choose people for team roles because they happen to be available.
	Leave the role of object technology expert vacant on your development projects.
	Mix up Application Team roles with roles needed on the Reuse Team.
	Put the project manager on the critical development path.
	Assign responsibility without authority.
	Force developers to use object-oriented technology.

continued

Table 21.1 *continued*

Kinds of Failures	Failure-related Decisions
Failure related to software development environments	Treat C++ as a better C.
	View the language as THE technology.
	Treat a notation as a method.
	Rely on smart people alone, without supportive resources.
	Fail to coordinate your choices for analysis-and-design methods, and implementation and change-management tools, so as to lose traceability between artifacts of the life cycle.
	Select a software development environment that does not allow you to test the software in the targeted delivery configuration.
	Select an environment that is a mismatch for creating software in the targeted delivery configuration.
	Select an environment that is too hard for team members to learn.
	Select an environment that is object-oriented in name alone.
Failure related to training	Provide no training. Just assume that your developers will pick it up as they go along.
	Teach everything about objects at once.
	Forget to teach related subject areas.
	Ask people to learn too much at once, without sufficient time to assimilate.
	Confuse conceptual knowledge with functional proficiency.
	Fail to train management, at least up to the level where their jobs are affected.
Failure related to measurement	Don't collect any measurement data.
	Collect data about everything.
	Collect data without knowing what you will do with it.
	Forget to inform the team why they are being asked to collect specific data.
	Create a situation in which data collection interferes with the team members' primary tasks.
	Report effective reuse as a single number.
	Insist on 80 percent expected reuse on every project.

The Last Word

We have worked with many consultants and organizations—large and small—who have chosen to succeed. These are the people who took the time to learn, and to make careful decisions about how to manage their projects. They are succeeding in changing their ability to build understandable and maintainable software systems, leveraged by the availability of reusable object assets.

How does an organization succeed with objects?
One decision at a time.

Adele and Kenny, with due respect to Frederick Brooks

McClure: "Confession is good for the soul—"
d'Agapeyeff: "—but bad for your career."

from [Nauer and Randell 1969]

We carried out our case studies in two phases. In the first phase, we conducted face-to-face interviews. We had formulated an outline of what we expected we would write in a future book, and we gave the outline to each project that we studied, mostly in advance of our visit. In many cases, the interviewees completed a written response based on the outline. The written responses gave us the initial project descriptions in an efficient manner, including project team structures and the backgrounds of all team members.

The interviews we conducted were free-form and tape recorded. We did not necessarily adhere to the sequence of questions from the outline when the interviewees wanted to talk about particular issues or experiences. Before the end of the interview, however, we made sure that each question had been answered. We refer to the responses to these first interviews as Phase 1.

Subsequently, we worked with a client to formulate a questionnaire that could be used to survey system and project characteristics. We used this questionnaire to study additional projects. The purpose of these new studies was to confirm the conclusions we had drawn from the first phase. The questionnaire was completed by project leaders or information systems managers, usually without our being present. It is reproduced in Appendix B. We refer to these studies as Phase 2.

In conducting the case studies, we were interested in six general aspects of each project.

Motivation	Why was the project started? How visible was the project in the company in terms of expected influence on the business? What were the expectations of management beyond completing the project itself? Why was object-oriented technology chosen to carry out the project?
Organization	How did the project and its team fit into the organization, and how did this positioning affect the manager's ability to obtain training and appropriate tools? Who were the project team members? What background experience did they bring to the project? How was the team structured, and why was that structure chosen?

Processes	What project process model was employed, and how did that process affect the cost of development, meeting goals and objectives, and return on the investment? Were conclusions drawn as to which results or technology could be transferred to other projects in the organization? What process differences could be attributed to the use of object-oriented technology?
Methods	Which analysis-and-design methods were used, if any? Were there significant obstacles—managerial, skills of existing personnel, past practices—to the use of object-oriented methods for analysis or design?
Tools	Which languages, development tools, analysis-and-design tools, project management tools, and so on, were available to the project? Which ones were used? What were the issues in learning to use the new tools? Were any tools developed in-house? If any were, why? What additional tools would have helped?
Multiple projects	How did the project structure and process model differ when multiple projects were carried out simultaneously? What were the models for obtaining reuse of prior experiences?

Case Study Demographics

In Phase 1, we studied 32 projects carried out in 19 companies. Thirteen companies contributed one project each to the study. Of the other six companies, two companies provided two projects each, two provided three projects, another company provided four projects to the study, and yet another contributed five projects. When these projects were multiple projects within a single company, the teams were located in different geographic locations. We were often able to interview the project's customers as well. Doing so helped us to assess the project's level of success.

In Phase 2, we studied an additional seven projects in seven companies. Of the total of 39 projects, most were based in the United States, with three in Canada, three in Australia, and three in Europe. Therefore, it is reasonable to assume that our studies reflect an American point of view. We also had access to the data collected by Technology Transfer International from six Japanese companies. None of the Japanese companies reported projects that employed object-oriented technology; rather, the studies provided information on issues of corporate reuse.

Charts A.1 and A.2 indicate the industries in which Phase 1 and Phase 2 companies participate, and the types of projects we investigated. Since the earliest adopters of object-oriented technology were found in telecommunications, manufacturing, government, and financial industries, most of the companies we studied are in these categories. The main emphasis of the projects—such as network configuration management, factory automation and control, and scheduling and planning software—was to create simulations of engineering or business processes, with interactive graphical user interfaces.

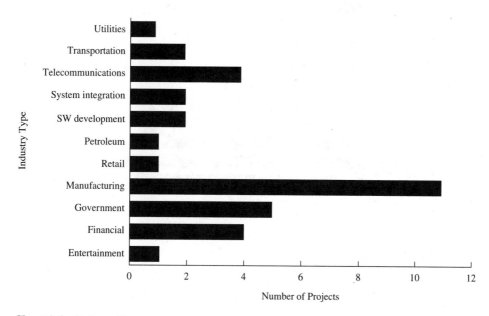

Chart A.1   Industry Types

The various information management systems included: tracking and processing financial portfolios, expediting freight handling, managing policy claims, and tracking customer service calls. Most of the projects resulted in new approaches to giving end users access to, and flexible manipulation of, retrieved information. A number of the project teams treated object-oriented technology as a new opportunity to model business domains, and to provide information services based on these domain models.

The goal of 31 of the projects was to create a product. By product, we mean either a program or system intended for sale in a public market (to users outside the company that created the result), or a program or system intended for deployment to the private market (to users inside the company of origin). Five projects did not pursue product development. And three team leaders answered that a product was a possible outcome, but not the measure of whether the project was a success.

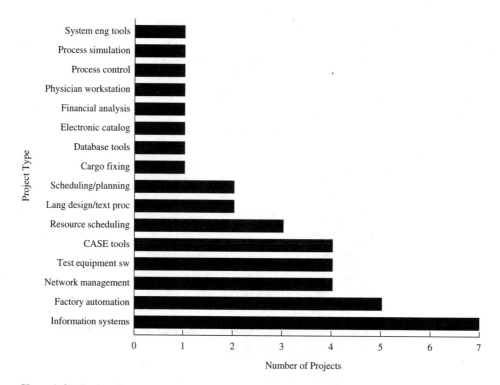

Chart A.2   Project Types

We asked the teams whether their projects completed successfully and why. In the case studies, we counted 20 projects as successful. This count includes all Phase 2 projects. All Phase 2 projects claimed that they were successful from three points of view: the interviewee, the customer, and the manager.

Two projects from Phase 1 were not successful, and 14 were still ongoing at the time of the interviews. We consider three completed projects to be unknowns in the sense that they did not have goals and objectives against which success could be measured. In the various charts reporting case study data, these three projects are treated as successful because, despite the absence of clear goals at the outset of the projects, the teams believed that they were successful. We have learned that three additional projects completed successfully after the interviews were conducted, and another project was canceled.

Questions our clients often ask are: Can object-oriented technology be used for large projects, where there are more than ten developers, and where more than a few thousand lines of code will be created? Can the technology be used in conjunction with already existing applications or databases? The projects we studied varied greatly in size, as measured in terms of the number of people (Table A.1), length of project (Table A.2), and amount of code produced (Charts A.3 and A.4).

Sizing the projects was difficult in that the number of participants varied over the project's duration, and data on actual staff hours was typically not available. In the charts,

Table A.1 Number of People on the Projects

	Successful	*Ongoing*	*Unsuccessful*
1–5	4	4	0
6–10	6	4	0
11–25	9	4	0
26–50	3	1	1
> 100	2	0	1

Table A.2 Length of Time to First Release

	Successful	*Ongoing*	*Unsuccessful*
<1 year	4	3	0
1–2 years	13	7	1
>2–4 years	4	3	0
4+ years	3	0	1

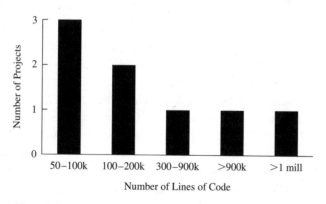

Chart A.3 Lines of Code

we identify the maximum number of persons, stating the count as full-time equivalents. Most of the projects consisted of 10–15 persons, most of whom were developers. The number of years to first full release of the product, or to the date of our interviews, averaged two years.

We asked the project managers we interviewed to size their systems using whatever measure they thought was appropriate. Many people used lines of code, others used the number of class definitions. We show these numbers in the charts. We say more about the interpretation of these numbers in Chapter 20.

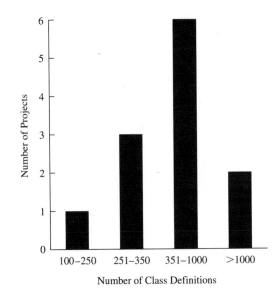

Chart A.4   Number of Class Definitions

We have often been told that no very large project has been carried out with an object-oriented language, as compared with the many large projects completed in COBOL. A typical business information system written in COBOL might have 2–3 million lines of code, or more. We have witnessed comparable-sized C++ systems. However, we saw no evidence that this large size was necessary. Our look at projects completed using object-oriented technology suggests little about size. Our own experience, moreover, indicates that one payoff of more effort is less code.

There are two clear distinctions between the case studies in Phases 1 and 2: time and training. Phase 1 projects started as early as 1987, while in Phase 2 most projects were carried out after 1990. In Phase 1 projects, training consisted mainly of self-study. The team members seem to be saying: We are smart and we can learn on our own. Consultants had to convince companies that planned training programs are the most effective way to introduce the new technology. By the 1990s, training became an expected part of the decision to use object-oriented technology. The focus on training is emphasized by the across-the-board use of training programs in Phase 2 projects, matched by the increased educational opportunities in college courses. Many of the Phase 2 companies have in-house training organizations, or at least regularly budget time and expenses for employees to attend training sessions.

We reference specific additional details about the case studies in the book chapters, including detailed illustrations of case study projects.

Appendix B
Suggested Survey Questions
for Project Managers

We used this survey in Phase 2 of the case studies. You might use it to gather information about your organization and its projects to help you make the decisions we describe in this book.

About the Interviewee

The following questions describe who is answering the questions.

1. What is your job title?

2. What do you do—that is, how do you describe your job?

3. In what fields do you have formal training?

Business Characterization

The following questions collect information about the business context in which the project was carried out.

4. What is the business mission of your organization?

5. In which industry or industries do you participate? (For example, Financial, Manufacturing, Retail, Petroleum, Government, Service, or . . . ?)

6. What is important to your organization in terms of computer or software system product characteristics, in order to feel or be successful?

7. What is important to your organization in terms of development processes or resources, in order to feel or be successful?

Organization Overview

The following questions collect information about the organization context in which the project was carried out.

8. What types of hardware and software systems are used in the organization?

9. Which systems must remain in use regardless of transitions to new technology?

10. What are your long-term objectives for technology support in your organization?

Project Description

The following questions (11–49) collect information about a specific project. You should complete these questions for each project that used object-oriented technology.

11. What type of software result are you trying to create? (For example, factory automation and control system, network management, information management, method case tools, resource scheduling, or . . . ?)

12. What motivated doing this project?

13. Who decided that this project should be carried out?

14. We are interested in the level of visibility of the result of the project. What is the highest level in the organization where there is awareness of the project?

15. Later we will ask you for a timeline of your project that includes the buildup of team members. For now, please indicate:

    How many people worked on the project at its peak? _____

    How many people were:

analyzers? _____	documentors? _____
designers? _____	testers? _____
coders? _____	managers? _____
others? _____	

    _____

    _____

16. What was the length of the project to first release? _____

    Is the project ongoing? _____

17. How much *new* software was developed? _____

    (Use whatever measures are available, such as lines of code, number of function points, or number of different kinds of objects.)

18. What programming languages were used? If multiple languages were used, indicate relative percentage of the resulting software written in each language.

    for prototyping, if any: _____

    for production development: _____

19. What computer systems did you use?

    during development: _____

    during testing: _____

    during deployment: _____

20. What database systems did you use?

    during development: _____

    during testing: _____

    during deployment: _____

21. State the goal of the project:

    _____

    _____

22. State any of the measurable objectives of your project—for example, performance or reliability requirements:

_____

_____

23. Is it a goal of your project to create a deployable product?

for internal use _____ for external sale _____

24. Did you set the goal of your project based on the result of a business reengineering process? _____

25. Did your project complete successfully?

from your point of view _____

from your customer's point of view _____

from your manager's point of view _____

26. Describe the members of your project team, including responsibility and reporting hierarchy:

_____

_____

Use additional space to draw the organization chart, if appropriate.

27. What training was provided to team members? List each team member and the training in analysis, design, programming language, database technology, project management, reuse concepts and tools, or other skills.

type of training	form (internal class, mentoring, consulting)	length of training	who was trained

Project or Situation Characterization

The following questions attempt to characterize your project in terms of the kind of system that you built. In questions with multiple-choice answers, please check the option that best applies.

28. Think of the overall purpose of your system. To carry out this purpose, consider the number of independent parts, and their descriptions in terms of services they provide and interactions with other parts.

What is the number of independent parts of the problem? _____

List the kinds of parts you considered: _____

What is the average number of services provided by each part? _____

What is the approximate number of interactions among the parts? _____

In your view, what is your system's inherent complexity? (By *complexity* we mean the measure of the combinations of parts, services, and interactions that describe the problem.)

_____ high

_____ medium

_____ low

29. Capacity is a measure of volume or the potential quantity of information to be handled. What is the unit of time for measuring capacity in your system?

_____

What is the typical measure of capacity during this time period (that is, the number of parts handled during a given unit of time)?

_____

_____

Please define what you consider to be high, medium, or low capacity:

high: _____

medium: _____

low: _____

30. With respect to the average number of transactions in your system, are there peak transaction periods? _____

If so, what is their frequency?

_____ daily

_____ weekly

_____ monthly

_____ quarterly

_____ seasonally

_____ annually

Is it critical to handle peaks specially? _____

31. Consider the manner in which information is to be accessed in the system. Where does the information come from? Is there a fairly standard set of access queries, or is the pattern of queries more ad hoc and unpredictable? (Check each that applies.)

    _____   one source of information

    _____   two or more sources of information

    _____   ad hoc or unpredictable pattern of access

    _____   predictable pattern of access

32. If a customer requests a change to the completed system, how quickly must the change be completed?

    _____   complete the changes within hours or less

    _____   complete the changes in days

    _____   complete the changes after weeks or longer

33. All processing in the system is:

    _____   done locally

    _____   distributed between local and remote

    _____   distributed where local activity makes use of remote shared services

34. Answer this question if the system involves a human interacting with the system. Consider the responsiveness requirements. When the user makes a request, then:

    _____   responsiveness should be immediate, < second

    _____   responsiveness should be observable, < minute

    _____   responsiveness not relevant

35. Answer this question if the system involves an interface to a human user. What is the nature of this user interface?

    _____   graphical interface

    _____   character-based interface

    _____   database-oriented transaction screen

36. To what extent are parts of the system to be designed for reuse?

    _____ none

    _____ all

    _____ some of the parts—which? _____

37. Is it a project goal to eliminate redundancies in the project (i.e., focus on intraproject reuse)? _____

38. What percentage of the system is concerned with:

    user interface   _____%

    business logic   _____%

    communications   _____%

    database management   _____%

    other _____   _____%

39. In what other ways would you characterize your software system project which you thought made it

    more suitable for object-oriented technology:

    _____

    less suitable for object-oriented technology:

    _____

Project Technology Description

40. We are discussing your project because you are using object-oriented technology, at least in the form of the programming language that you chose. Why did you choose object-oriented technology? Please indicate, for each reason, whether the reason proved valid—that is, if you had an expectation for object-oriented technology, was it fulfilled?

    Reason: Achieved or not?

    _____   _____

    _____   _____

    _____   _____

    For the reasons not achieved, please state why not:

    _____

    _____

41. Is this the first project using object-oriented technology for your organization?

    _____

    If not, what other kinds of projects have been done?

    by your group: _____

    by your company: _____

    by yourself: _____

42. Did you use or adapt a process model (software development life cycle phases and reasons for transitioning between phases) that has been described in the literature? If so, which one? If not, can you briefly describe the process you used on your project?

    _____

    _____

    _____

    On a separate sheet of paper, draw a diagram of the process model, if possible.

43. Define *prototyping* as you and your organization use the term (if at all):

    _____

    _____

44. Did your process include prototyping? _____

    If so, how many prototypes did you create? _____

    List the type of prototype (analysis, design, or user interface—A, D, or U) and the reasons for the prototypes you created. Did your prototypes evolve (E) into the next stage, or were they thrown away (T)? Mark each prototype for type, A, D, or U, and use as E or T.

    Type and use of prototype: *Reason for doing the prototype:*

    _____ / _____   _____

    _____ / _____   _____

    _____ / _____   _____

45. On another sheet of paper, show the timeline for the project, indicating

    - start and stop dates
    - number of team members

    for the following stages:

    - getting approval for the project
    - each phase of your process model, being clear as to the purpose of the phase and any prototyping done in support of the phase
    - training

46. What methodologies, if any, did you use in the project?

    For analysis: _____

    For design: _____

47. What tools were used for each methodology? Indicate whether they were purchased (P) or built by the organization (B).

    _____

    _____

48. What development tools were used? Indicate whether they were purchased (P) or built by the organization (B).

    _____

    _____

49. What were your guidelines for tools selection?

    for analysis: _____

    for design: _____

    for development: _____

Organizational Issues About Reuse

50. What does your organization value as reusable assets?

    _____

    _____

51. At what level is reuse managed/supported in the organization?

    _____

52. Who takes responsibility for reuse in your organization—managers, developers, or someone else?

    _____

53. Who pays for creating reusable assets?

    _____

54. Who pays for maintaining the reusable assets?

    _____

55. Are reuse measures collected, evaluated, and reported? If so, what are they?

    _____

    _____

56. Are there economic or other incentives for reuse? If so, what are they?

    for reusing: _____

    for creating reusable components: _____

57. Do you have a special library of reusable artifacts? _____

58. Where do you store your reusable assets?

    _____

59. Is there a corporate librarian for your reusable components? _____

    If so, who does this person report to? _____

    What are this person's responsibilities? _____

60. How do you identify the reusable assets you want to have?

    _____

    _____

61. Where do your reusable assets come from? Check all that apply:

    _____ purchase commercial product from outside the organization

    _____ purchase from outside as part of a development contract

    _____ obtain from another project within the organization

    _____ create within the development project

62. Do you certify reusable assets? _____

    If so, what is the purpose of certification, levels of component types and certification, and properties you expect for each certification level?

    _____

    _____

63. What collateral information must be stored with your reusable assets?

    _____

    _____

64. How are assets classified? That is, what is the representation form of assets to be stored?

    _____

    How was the classification structure developed?

    _____

    How are assets cataloged based on the classification schema?

    _____

65. How do people know what is available as a reusable asset of the organization?

66. How do people locate desired assets?

67. How do people retrieve desired assets?

68. Do you have any special tools for understanding assets?

69. Are there guidelines for how projects reuse the assets—that is, what are the permitted modifications?

70. How will delivered applications be affected by a new version of a reused asset?

71. Who is responsible for collecting incident reports regarding library assets?

72. What level of backward compatibility of assets makes sense?

73. How are reusers known?

74. Do you view cloning as a form of reusing?

75. What are the managerial concerns about reuse in your organization?

76. How does an emphasis on reuse change the performance review and reward structures for individual engineers?

_____

_____

77. What was reused in your project?

_____

_____

78. What are your plans for maintenance of your project results?

_____

Appendix C
Team Member Job Descriptions

From the case study projects, we derived job descriptions for new roles that are needed when using object-oriented technology. The roles for the different kinds of teams overlap, as shown in Fig. C.1. For example, the role of reuse engineer is found on Application, Cross-Project, and Reuse Teams. A Framework Team creating a reusable framework and components will require a reuse evaluator, a role that is also needed on the Reuse Team. Each of the teams requires someone to provide technical, administrative, and people management.

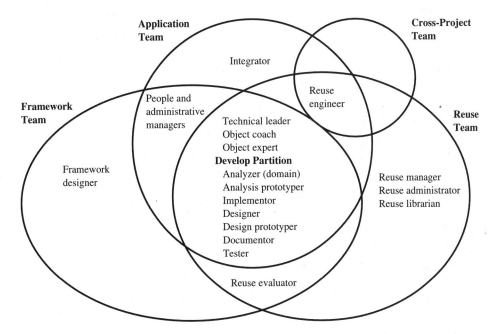

Framework Team

Application Team

Integrator

People and administrative managers

Technical leader
Object coach
Object expert
Develop Partition
Analyzer (domain)
Analysis prototyper
Implementor
Designer
Design prototyper
Documentor
Tester

Framework designer

Cross-Project Team

Reuse engineer

Reuse Team

Reuse manager
Reuse administrator
Reuse librarian

Reuse evaluator

Figure C.1   Teams and Overlapping Roles

Nineteen different roles are identified in Fig. C.1, ten of which we view as special to object-oriented technology. In this chapter, we provide job descriptions for these ten significant roles. We describe job functions, the typical hiring manager, required skills, and evaluation criteria. We present the job descriptions starting with the roles for developing product partitions, then the special members of the Framework Team, and ending with the roles for managing the reuse process model.

Title: Analysis Prototyper

Functional job description. The analysis prototyper develops executable prototypes during the analysis phase. The prototyper works with the analyst to create an executable version of the proposed set of objects and behaviors. Together, the analyst and prototyper are responsible for deriving an analysis model for the system. This responsibility involves interviewing end users, examining existing requirements documents, and studying reference documents that describe the domain. The analysis prototyper also works with end users to solicit feedback, which influences subsequent prototypes.

The analysis prototyper is primarily concerned with rapidly constructing a prototype, which is used to evaluate the proposed requirements. The design quality of the prototype is not important. To meet these goals, the analysis prototyper should reuse appropriate software components and frameworks.

The analysis prototyper and analyst can be the same person, if the analyst is a competent prototyper who finds it easier to think through the details of analysis by developing a prototype implementation.

Hiring manager. Product development manager or other person responsible for overall management of a particular software project.

Individual skills. The analysis prototyper need not be a sophisticated programmer if 4GL-like tools for object-oriented prototyping are available. The analysis prototyper must be able to ignore details such as performance, architectural quality, and size, as these are not essential during this phase of development.

The prototyper should be skilled in the company's selected prototyping environment. This person should be able to interact well with nontechnical people, especially when end-user interaction is expected.

Educational requirements differ from company to company. We look for a B.S., preferably in computer science, or someone with at least two years of experience as a developer in a corporate information systems group or database development group.

Basis for evaluation. The analysis prototyper is evaluated not only on how fast prototypes are built, but also on the robustness and usability of the prototypes in support of user experimentation. Because speed of development and robustness are critical, the prototyper is also evaluated on effective reuse of components in the organization's library. A prototyper is not evaluated on whether the resulting prototype can be evolved into a product. Doing so introduces a conflict—building the prototype quickly is frequently at odds with creating a deliverable implementation.

Title: Design Prototyper

Functional job description. The design prototyper develops executable prototypes during the design phase. The prototyper works with the designer to create an initial executable version of the proposed product. This person should have some level of presentation or documentation skills to participate in the design review discussions.

The design prototyper is the designer's pragmatic conscience, and is expected to verify that the design ideas can be implemented. The design prototyper can be the same person as the designer.

Hiring manager. The product technical strategist or leader for the project. Often, the design prototyper formally reports to the product development manager, and informally reports to the designer.

Individual skills. The design prototyper should be an excellent developer, who can create the design prototype, and an excellent explainer, who can work with the designer to prepare design documents. The design prototyper is a conceptual thinker, one who understands the structure and dynamics of an architecture. This person can organize requirements into conceptual categories, rather than being distracted by the details of the implementation. Often it is the design prototyper who interacts with reuse engineers to propose new reusable components for the organization's library.

The design prototyper is an excellent developer in the company's selected prototyping or delivery environment, or has the ability to learn the environment quickly. The design prototyper should have previous system development experience.

Educational requirements vary with the company's expectations for its development staff. We look for a B.S. or M.S., preferably in computer science, with four years of experience as a product developer. The company's product plans determine special emphases, such as a background in graphics, user interface, communication, or database development.

Basis for evaluation. The designer and the design prototyper are evaluated on the extent to which the resulting design meets the stated functional requirements and quality objectives of the project. They must create a design that can be built. A design prototyper is specifically evaluated on the ability to create timely prototypes that reveal whether the design is workable. It is more likely that a design prototype will be evolved into a product than it is that analysis prototypes will. So it is fair to evaluate design prototypers on their ability to develop evolvable prototypes.

Title: Object Coach

Functional job description. The object coach is a general resource, available to answer all team members' questions about the use of object-oriented technology, and to make sure that everyone is aware of and understands any decisions involving object-oriented technology. This person may also have the expertise to be the team's reuse engineer. The coach reviews results to make sure that object-oriented technology is properly applied. This person is also the object champion. On the first few object-oriented projects, developers may lose sight of how object-oriented technology is helping them meet project goals. The coach is responsible for keeping other team members focused and motivated with respect to object-oriented technology.

Hiring manager. Product development manager or person responsible for overall management of an individual software project, or a subproject manager.

Individual skills. Demonstrable expertise in most areas of object-oriented technology, with advanced levels of proficiency in object-oriented concepts and development. The object coach is proficient in using the organization's selected analysis-and-design methods, and development environment. This person has good interpersonal skills, and is a patient, able explainer.

Basis for evaluation. The basis for evaluation is the ability to help the team members understand project goals and objectives, and effectively apply object-oriented technology. The best way to evaluate the coach is to ask the team members whether the coach helped them understand and use objects.

Title: Object Technology Expert

Functional job description. The object technology expert provides expertise at several levels. The expert points out how objects influence the organization's work, and makes strategic recommendations on how best to use objects. This person might consult on analysis, design, and programming environment issues, or comment on the many different types of artifacts developed during a project. The particular responsibilities of the job depend on the specific situation.

Hiring manager. Product development manager or person responsible for overall management of an individual software project, or a subproject manager. The object technology expert can be hired by upper management as a mentor or consultant for the other managers.

Individual skills. An object technology expert should have an advanced level of proficiency in object-oriented concepts and at least one analysis/design method. In addition, this person should have demonstrable expertise in all other areas of object-oriented technology—development environments, databases, operating environments, user interfaces—or at least the ones appropriate to the tasks at hand. Besides technology skills, an expert must be a good explainer and have the proper interpersonal skills to fit in with a variety of team structures. The object technology expert can be an outside consultant, in contrast to the object coach, who should be a staff member who really knows what is going on in the company and builds a good rapport with team members.

Basis for evaluation. The key evaluation criterion is the quality of the expert's advice. This person should also be evaluated on effectiveness at communicating expert knowledge.

Title: Framework Designer

Functional job description. The framework designer determines the architecture for a general set of parts that can be used to form applications within a specific domain, and designs an initial set of components for specializing the framework.

Hiring manager. Product development manager or project technical manager, or the manager of the Reuse Team.

Individual skills. The framework designer should be an excellent developer, with the special skill of being able to think abstractly about a domain. The framework designer must know how to design objects that embody the proper balance of generalized and specialized knowledge, be capable of understanding the big picture of the domain, understand how to translate this understanding to software, and be able to communicate the framework concepts. Qualifications are the same as for any software designer, but typically with several more years of work experience.

Basis for evaluation. The framework designer is evaluated on the ease with which the framework can be understood and reused by knowledgeable application developers within the specific domain. Excellent framework designers can usually create a good result after two or three attempts. So another evaluation criterion can be the speed with which the result is obtained.

Title: Reuse Administrator

Functional job description. The reuse administrator is responsible for identifying and acquiring new reusable assets for the corporate or project library. The administrator consults with analysis and design prototypers to identify strategic requirements and to help plan the acquisition of reusable assets. If the development is contracted to an outside organization, the reuse administrator monitors the contract.

As part of the development life cycle, design reviews are conducted and project reports provided. The administrator can participate in reviews to identify places where reuse can be leveraged, and work with reuse engineers to identify opportunities for adding reusable assets to the library. Additionally, this person must be an active industry watcher who procures reusable artifacts from commercial sources when appropriate.

Hiring manager. Reuse manager.

Individual skills. The reuse administrator should have excellent interpersonal, verbal, and written communication skills. The reuse administrator understands abstractions, is able to describe requirements, and can manage strategically important development relationships. This person needs negotiation skills to deal with outside contractors or multiple internal interests. The reuse administrator is not a developer, but monitors development activities, and has to be able to understand technical needs. The reuse administrator knows the organization—who is doing what and how the parts of the organization interrelate. If the reuse team is small or just getting started, this role is usually played by the reuse manager.

Basis for evaluation. The reuse administrator is evaluated on how well the contents of the library support the organization's development needs, and on whether the library is the right size to meet the development needs of the company—neither lacking assets nor containing superfluous entries. The quality of the library is measured by whether developers are willing and able to incorporate software found in the library into prototypes and products. This should lead to reduced development costs over time.

Title: Reuse Evaluator

Functional job description. The reuse evaluator determines whether software components have been designed for broad applicability—that is, whether the components have the potential for reuse. Reuse evaluation does not eliminate the need for traditional testing, the purpose of which is to verify whether the assets work according to specification. Since there are many potentially reusable components, and testing all of them may not be feasible, this person (perhaps in conjunction with the reuse administrator) is responsible for choosing those components with the greatest reusability potential within the organization. Reuse evaluation determines the potential reuse of the proposed asset. The result of  the evaluation is information that can contribute to deciding whether to certify the artifact as a reusable asset.

Hiring manager. Reuse manager or quality assurance manager.

Individual skills. The reuse evaluator should be an excellent developer, with the special skill of being able to devise alternative ways to test for potential reuse. The reuse evaluator is able to scout around the organization to learn about prior, current, and expected future software development needs. This person is highly creative and inquisitive, able to imagine projects that do not exist, and able to test the usability of components in new situations. Such testing requires developing parts of projects to see how the proposed reusable asset might fit.

Basis for evaluation. The reuse evaluator is evaluated on the completeness, accuracy, and ingenuity of the test suites used to test individual components, and on how well components are selected for reuse evaluation. In addition, if the organization has a certification process for its reuse library, this person is evaluated on providing the proper certification materials with any asset that is to be included in the library.

Title: Reuse Engineer

Functional job description. The reuse engineer creates and maintains reusable assets, and updates reusers of these assets. The reuse engineer must be able to locate, retrieve, understand, and use the reusable assets as required. If the Expert Services Reuse Model is adopted, the reuse engineer participates directly in product development projects, bringing technical competence and knowledge of the assets available for reuse. While working on the projects, the engineer may identify new opportunities for creating reusable assets.

The reuse engineer:

- Stays informed of what is in the library of reusable assets

- May create the assets, or assist in obtaining them from external commercial sources, including making any modifications necessary to certify the assets according to the organization's documentation and format guidelines

- Provides consulting to the analysis-and-design prototypers on the available reusable assets

- Participates in design reviews to make sure that reuse is properly planned

- Can offer ideas for generalizing applications into reusable frameworks

- Contributes to maintenance enhancements

Hiring manager. Reuse manager.

Individual skills. The reuse engineer should be a skilled developer, with technical competence in the organization's selected software development environment. This person has an ability to recognize good reuse opportunities, both creation and utilization, and is able to work with a variety of project teams.

Basis for evaluation. The reuse engineer is evaluated on the quality of the reusable assets, and ability to support individual development projects with the reusable assets. The reuse engineer is evaluated on how well the contents of the library support the needs of the organization. Since the reuse engineer may participate in application projects, the evaluation should also consider the contributions the reuse engineer makes to these projects. The reuse engineer is evaluated on whether such projects make appropriate reuse of the assets in the library.

Title: Reuse Librarian

Functional job description. The reuse librarian is responsible for certifying, classifying, and storing new reusable assets in the corporate or project library. The librarian is responsible for making sure that the assets placed in the library meet the organization's agreed-upon certification guidelines. This responsibility could include acquiring further documentation, examples, or test suites. In addition, the reuse librarian catalogs the assets by using the selected classification scheme. It is likely that the librarian participated in setting the certification rules and designing the classification scheme.

Hiring manager. Reuse manager.

Individual skills. The reuse librarian should be skilled at applying certification guidelines, which at times will require subjective evaluation. The reuse librarian must have a keen ability to take a new asset and understand its relationship to a large body of existing assets. This person must have a conceptual understanding of the technology used to construct the library of components, experience in organizing and using large volumes of data with many potential connection complexities, and technical competence in using the library's storage and retrieval system. Background in the domain of the assets contained in the library is preferred. Educational background should include training in library science, a natural science, or computer science.

Basis for evaluation. The reuse librarian is evaluated on the quality of the library as measured by whether all library assets meet certification guidelines. Evaluation also depends on whether developers are able to find assets and incorporate the assets into actual products, and on the support provided to the other Reuse Team members.

Title: **Reuse Manager**

Functional job description. The reuse manager plans and controls the reuse process. Responsibilities include setting the guidelines and policies for certification and classification, working with other managers to decide how to identify and acquire reusable assets, selecting the various reuse library tools, and determining policies for communicating, updating reusable assets and reusers. Additionally, the reuse manager is one of the chief evangelists for reuse within the organization. In this capacity, the manager meets regularly with different members of the organization to keep them abreast of the reuse process and its successes within the company.

Note that we expect the reuse manager to be the reuse champion. If this single responsibility were positioned as its own role, the reuse manager and reuse administrator roles would become much more alike.

Hiring manager. Within an organization, there might be several levels of shared libraries, each with its own reuse manager. The manager of the corporate reuse team is hired by the chief information officer or information systems manager. An individual project or a group of projects within a department might each manage reuse libraries, and the hiring manager would be the project development manager or department manager.

Individual skills. The reuse manager should be well versed in the pragmatics of reuse technology, and have sufficient knowledge of the organization to make workable decisions surrounding the reuse process. This person is a capable people manager, and has effective evangelical skills. The reuse manager also has effective interpersonal skills, and good negotiation skills for acquiring third-party reusable assets.

Basis for evaluation. The reuse manager is evaluated on how well the reuse library meets the goals and objectives of the organization by providing potentially reusable assets. In addition, the reuse manager is evaluated on how well the services of the team provide for appropriate and effective levels of reuse on application projects. This person should also be evaluated on whether the reuse team influences the developers in the organization to make use of the reusable assets. If the team is unknown to a majority of the managers and developers, then the reuse manager has done a poor job of evangelizing. The reuse manager is also evaluated, like any other people manager, on hiring skills, effectiveness at setting personnel objectives, and proficiency in handling day-to-day people issues.

Glossary of Terms

Overview

Entries in this glossary are arranged alphabetically. An entry may be a single word, such as *analysis*, a phrase, such as *analysis prototype*, or an acronym, such as *GQM*. If a term has more than one definition, the definitions are listed with numerical prefixes.

The following cross-references are used to show a term's relationship to other terms in the glossary:

- *See* refers to a preferred term or to a term whose definition serves to define the term that has been looked up.

- *See also* refers to a related term.

- *Synonymous with* refers to a synonym.

- *Contrast with* refers to a term with a substantially different meaning.

Definitions

abstract class. A class that provides common specification and partial implementation for a collection of other classes. No instances can be created from an abstract class. *Contrast with concrete class.*

abstraction. 1. Logical description of the commonality among a collection of objects. 2. The process of identifying the common characteristics of a collection of objects.

activity. A step or major unit of work carried out to meet project goals and objectives. Activities represent the high-level steps (such as analysis, design, and coding) of a process model. *See also task.*

adaptation reuse. *See by-adaptation reuse.*

added complexity. The additional complexity (beyond the inherent complexity) introduced by the software artifacts created when developing a solution to a problem. *See also complexity. Contrast with inherent complexity.*

analysis. The software development activity for studying and formulating a model of a problem domain. Analysis focuses on what is to be done, design focuses on how to do it. *Contrast with design.*

analysis method. The specific concepts, techniques, and steps for carrying out analysis. *See also analysis, method.*

analysis prototype. A prototype created to clarify and solicit the requirements specification. *See also design prototype.*

application. 1. Related capabilities that satisfy a customer need. 2. A set of interacting objects that provide a well-defined set of services that implement capabilities required by a customer.

application framework. *See software framework.*

application team. A team that develops external system capabilities to meet end-user needs. Also the team that plays the consumer role in the producer/consumer process model.

appropriate reuse. To reuse components when reusing helps better meet a project's goals and objectives. *See also reuse.*

architecture. 1. A collection of subsystems that represent strategic decisions of how to solve a problem. 2. The primary result of high-level design.

artifact. A result of a software development process. *Synonymous with product.*

as-is reuse. Reusing an artifact without modifying it. *Contrast with by-adaptation reuse.*

assess. *See assessment.*

assessment. To measure attributes of and draw conclusions about products, processes, or resources.

asset. An artifact that has been certified as having value to the organization, such as something reusable across projects.

attribute. 1. A data element of a class. 2. A measurable characteristic of a product, process, or resource. *See also internal attribute, external attribute.*

available prototype. A prototype that is made available to users beyond the immediate development team. Unlike a product, an available prototype is not officially documented, sold, or supported. *See also prototype.*

base class. C++ class from which other classes can inherit data and member functions. *Synonymous with superclass. See also derived class.*

behavior. 1. The manner in which something conducts itself. In the real world, people and things exhibit behavior. For example, a car can accelerate, decelerate, and break down, as well as many other behaviors. In the software world, systems and their constituent parts (subsystems, objects, and so on) exhibit behavior. 2. A set of related behaviors constitutes a system capability. 3. A behavior that appears in the interface of an object is a service. *See also system capability, service.*

binary portability. Ability to port an application from one platform to another by moving the binary representation of the system to the target platform, and starting up a runtime execution environment that can then execute the application.

binding. The association of a message name with a specific implementation. *See also dynamic binding, static binding.*

black box reuse. Reuse of a component through strict examination and use of its external interface. *Contrast with white box reuse, glass box reuse.*

bounded polymorphism. Polymorphism that limits reuse to classes defined within the same class hierarchy. For example, two subclasses of the same class can define the same service name. *See also polymorphism, unbounded polymorphism.*

business process reengineering (BPR). The fundamental rethinking and radical redesign of business processes to achieve dramatic improvements in critical, contemporary measures of performance, such as cost, quality, service, and speed [Hammer and Champy 1993].

by-adaptation reuse. Reusing an artifact by first making modifications to it. *Contrast with as-is reuse.*

capability. *See system capability.*

certification. Reuse process model activity for ensuring that an asset can be trusted for inclusion within the reuse repository.

class. Description of a set of objects that provide the same services and information. A class is a template for the creation of instances. A class itself may be an object. *See also instance.*

class hierarchy. A collection of classes organized in a hierarchical fashion where classes at adjoining levels are related by inheritance.

classification. 1. Organizing objects into related sets (often classes). 2. Reuse process model activity for assigning information (such as name, author, keywords, and so on) to reusable assets so they can be located.

client/server architecture. A system structure in which some applications play the role of client or master, and others play the role of server or slave. Clients request information or action from servers. Servers provide services to clients.

cloning. Copying of an artifact for purposes of reuse. A cloned artifact does not enjoy enhancements made to the artifact from which it was copied.

COCOMO. *See constructive cost model.*

coding. Software development activity of expressing a design in a programming language. *Synonymous with implementation. See also activity.*

complexity measure. An internal product measure of the number of parts and the nature of their interconnectedness. *See also added complexity, inherent complexity.*

component. 1. A part of a larger whole. 2. Software artifact used to develop prototype and product frameworks and applications.

composition (object). 1. The logical combining of several objects to form a new conceptually distinct object. 2. An object that is composed out of and delegates responsibility to other objects. *See also delegation.*

concurrency policy. A coordination policy that allocates permissions to developers (such as read or write) based on already allocated permissions and the rules for multiple developer interaction. *See also coordination policy, security policy.*

configuration management. Method for identifying, defining, releasing, and changing system artifacts in any arrangement that constitutes a configuration—a system baseline or release.

constructive cost model. A software cost and schedule estimating method, developed by Barry Boehm, that uses lines of code to predict effort. Based on historical data accumulated by an organization.

consumer. A software development role with a primary responsibility for using reusable assets. *Contrast with producer.*

contract. An agreement between two objects where one object agrees to use the service of the second object, and the second object agrees to provide the service. *See also service.*

controlling. The set of management activities needed to ensure that the actual project work goes according to plan. It measures performance against plan, reveals when and where deviation exists, and institutes corrective action when necessary. *See also planning.*

coordination. Minimal-interference combination of software development activities and methods, with resources such as people, tools, libraries, and databases, to produce software products.

coordination policy. Rules for administering permissions (such as read and write) among a group of developers. *See also security policy, concurrency policy.*

cost accounting. Collecting and assigning project cost data to appropriate accounting categories. *See uninterrupted staff-hours.*

cross-platform portability. Ability to implement and execute application software on one kind of machine and have it execute on a different kind of machine. *See also binary portability.*

cross-project (reuse) team. A team that facilitates reuse across several concurrent projects. Team members pick up reusable artifacts from one project and deposit them in another.

current situation. How an organization currently practices software development. Defined in terms of products, processes, and resources. *See also situation, desired situation.*

decision framework. An organized sequence of decisions that you must address to be successful with object-oriented technology. A decision framework must be refined with organization-specific details in order to be used. *Contrast with software framework.*

defect. 1. An imperfection in a software development artifact that would not exist if the development process were perfect—if no developer errors were committed. 2. A difference between desired and observed results.

delegate responsibility. *See delegation.*

delegation. When one object sends a message to a second object to fulfill one of its responsibilities. Delegation is an alternative to inheritance for sharing the behavior of objects.

derived class. C++ class that inherits data and member functions from a base class. *Synonymous with subclass.*

design. The software development activity during which strategic and tactical solution decisions necessary for meeting client functionality and quality requirements are made. Analysis focuses on what is to be done, design focuses on how to do it. *Contrast with analysis.*

design pattern. A recurring structure or approach to a solution.

design prototype. A prototype developed to explore and understand some aspect of a system's architecture. *See also analysis prototype.*

desired situation. How an organization would like to develop software. Defined in terms of products, processes, and resources. *See also situation, current situation.*

distributed system. A system whose components are distributed among processes within the same computer, or among different computers on a shared network.

documentation. 1. Collection of documents on a given subject. 2. The software development activity of creating documents. *See also activity.*

domain. A sphere of thought, action, or knowledge in a subject matter area or discipline. A software system solves a problem in one or more domains.

domain analysis. 1. An activity used to understand and model the basic abstractions found in a discipline. The resulting domain model can be used for developing multiple applications within the domain. 2. Used in a project to develop domain-specific reusable frameworks and components before beginning projects to develop specific applications in the domain. *Contrast with harvesting-after-the-fact and on-the-fly-identification.*

domain reusability. Likelihood that an artifact is reusable based on whether the organization's future application domains are similar to the domain for which the artifact was first created. *See also potential reusability.*

dynamic binding. Association of a message name with a specific implementation at code execution time. *See also binding. Contrast with static binding.*

dynamic type checking. 1. Determining at code execution time that an object can respond to a particular message. 2. Determining the type of a variable, argument, or return value at runtime, when each is bound to a specific object. *See also type checking, static type checking.*

effective reuse. A measure of both the type and quantity of reuse that occurs on a project. *See also expected reuse.*

effort measure. An internal process measure that quantifies the resources (such as elapsed time) needed to perform some task. *See also uninterrupted staff-hours.*

encapsulation. The act of enclosing elements within a container, as an object encapsulates information and behavior. Encapsulation supports information hiding, which restricts access to the internal information and implementation descriptions of an object.

enumerative classification scheme. An approach to asset classification based on a predetermined decomposition of the classification domains. An asset is classified by determining the location in the decomposition that best identifies it. The basis for the Dewey decimal system. *See also faceted classification scheme, keyword/attribute classification scheme.*

evolutionary prototyping. Development of a system by creating a series of prototypes, where each subsequent prototype evolves from some or all of the artifacts in the previous prototype. *See also prototyping.*

expected reuse. A prediction of the type and quantity of reusing a project will achieve. *See also effective reuse.*

exploratory programming. The incremental development of a program or set of programs, based on incomplete specifications.

external attribute. A property of a product, process, or resource that is measured in terms of how the product, process, or resource relates to its environment. *Contrast with internal attribute.*

external system capability. User-visible behaviors or features of a system. *See system capability. See also internal system capability.*

faceted classification scheme. An approach to asset classification based on a set of domains (facets) and tags. An asset is classified by choosing a proper tag from each facet. The basis for the library classification system used in India. *See also enumerative classification scheme, keyword/attribute classification scheme.*

feasibility prototype. A prototype used to determine the efficacy of some approach. Analysis-and-design prototypes can also be feasibility prototypes. *See also prototyping.*

figure-of-merit. A number between 0 and 1, associated with a task in a project plan, which is used to convey the importance of the task in meeting a project milestone. The sum of all tasks' figures-of-merit leading to a single milestone should be 1.

FPA. *See function point analysis.*

framework. *See decision framework, software framework.*

framework team. A team whose purpose is to create a reusable software framework and components. This team plays the producer role in the producer/consumer process model.

function point. One end-user business function. *See function point analysis.*

function point analysis. Measures an application's size in terms of function points from an end-user perspective, rather than from the details of a particular implementation language. *See also function point.*

functionality measure. An internal product size measure that determines the amount of functionality delivered to the customer. *See also function point analysis.*

glass box reuse. Reuse of a component by examination of both its internal structure and external interface, but using only the external interface. *Contrast with black box reuse, white box reuse.*

goal. A statement of desired outcome described in terms of products, processes, or resources. *See also objective.*

goal-oriented measurement. The derivation of measures from goals and objectives that are relevant to the specific needs of the organization.

goal-question-metric (GQM). A top-down approach for determining useful measures. A primary goal is divided into subgoals, which are further decomposed into a set of questions. A set of measures is associated with each question.

GQM. *See goal-question-metric.*

harvest-after-the-fact. Examination of a completed project to identify potentially reusable assets. *Contrast with on-the-fly-identification, domain analysis 2.*

hybrid programming language. A programming language that grafts together two or more programming styles. For example, C++ combines procedural C programming with object-oriented programming. *Contrast with pure programming language.*

implementation. 1. The description of a behavior in computer executable code. 2. The software development activity of developing code. *Synonymous with code or coding.*

implementation strategy. Collection of activities that the developer has to do, alone and with others, to implement a system. *See also interaction strategy.*

incident. An undesirable or unexpected result that is detected during product development or in the field.

incremental development. A strategy for developing systems based on making progress in small steps. For software, a system is constructed in parts rather than attempting to build the entire system at one time. *See also iterative development, opportunistic development.*

incremental integration. The software development activity of integrating partitions as they become available, rather than waiting to integrate any partition until all partitions are available. *See also partition, integration.*

inherent complexity. A measure of the quantity and strength of interobject and intraobject linkages that are intrinsic to a problem. *Also see complexity. Contrast with added complexity.*

inherent reusability. Likelihood that an artifact is reusable based on its internal properties. Well-designed, high-quality artifacts exhibit greater inherent reusability than do poorly designed, low-quality artifacts. *See also potential reusability.*

inheritance. A relationship among classes, where one class shares the specification and perhaps the implementation of one or more other classes. *See also single inheritance, multiple inheritance.*

inspection. A technique that is useful for uncovering defects contained in documents. Also applies statistical process control techniques to help identify software process improvements to prevent the occurrence of defects in future documents.

instance. A particular occurrence of a class of objects. A member of a class's set of objects. The term "instance" is often used synonymously with "object" when classes are not considered objects—as in the expression "classes and instances." *See also class.*

integration. The software development activity of combining independently created partitions or components so as to form a coherent whole. *See also activity, incremental integration.*

interaction strategy. The style or manner by which the developer interacts with tools to carry out the activities to create the implementation model. *See also implementation strategy.*

internal attribute. A property of a product, process, or resource that is measured strictly in terms of the product, process, or resource itself. *Contrast with external attribute.*

internal system capability. Behaviors that are required within the design to support external system capabilities. *See system capability. See also external system capability.*

interproject reuse. Reuse that occurs between different projects. *Contrast with intraproject reuse.*

intraproject reuse. Creation and reuse of components within the same project. *Contrast with interproject reuse.*

iteration. Repeating a previously executed process.

iterative development. A strategy for developing systems that allows for the controlled reworking of part of a system to remove mistakes or to make improvements based on user feedback. *See also incremental development, opportunistic development.*

keyword/attribute classification scheme. An approach to asset classification based on assigning keywords and attribute values (such as name and date) to an asset. Most file systems use this approach. *See also enumerative classification scheme, faceted classification scheme.*

legacy system. A production system that was designed for technology assumptions that are no longer true.

life cycle. *See process model.*

linking pin (role). A team role that links together and facilitates the communication among multiple teams.

maintenance. The software development activity during which corrective, adaptive, and perfective changes are made to a software product. *See also activity.*

maxim. A guideline helpful in making decisions. A rule of thumb or "battle scar" derived from personal experience. A maxim may or may not apply in a particular organizational situation. *See also principle.*

measure. Association of a number or symbol to an entity to characterize a specific attribute.

message-passing. The means by which objects communicate with one another—to provide information, send information, and invoke actions. Sending messages is how work gets done in an object-oriented system.

method. 1. A specific way of carrying out an activity. A step-by-step procedure that takes you from a set of inputs to an end result. Defined in terms of concepts, techniques, and steps. *Used synonymously with methodology.* 2. The Smalltalk language name for an implementation code body.

methodology. *See method.*

milestone. Project schedule element that marks progress. Milestones identify major project accomplishments, such as delivering a first version of the system or passing a design review. *See also task.*

modularity. A property of a system that has been decomposed into a set of components that can be individually developed and tested, and easily integrated, reused, and maintained.

multiple inheritance. When a class has an inheritance relationship with two or more other classes. *See also inheritance, single inheritance.*

notation. Language used to communicate the artifacts that result from applying a method.

object. Description of a set of behaviors and the information needed to support the behaviors.

object broker. Special system component that allows objects to call upon one another's services, independent of the location of the objects, of which programming language was used to describe the objects, or of which network protocols are used for object-to-object communication.

object-oriented. 1. An adjective used to describe many different software development products, processes, and resources, such as programming languages, user interfaces, applications, databases, and analysis-and-design methods. 2. A product, process, or resource that can be extended by composition of existing parts or by refinement of behaviors. Changes in original parts propagate, so that compositions and refinements that reuse these parts change appropriately.

object-oriented database. A database that stores, retrieves, and updates objects using transaction control, queries, locking, and versioning.

object-oriented technology. Technology used to develop software systems in terms of objects. *See technology.*

objective. A time-targeted and measurable statement of desired outcome, described in terms of products, processes, or resources. *See also goal.*

on-the-fly identification. Identification of interproject reuse opportunities while projects are ongoing. *Contrast with harvesting-after-the-fact, domain analysis.*

open systems. A software system whose architecture permits components developed by independent organizations to be combined.

opportunistic development. A tactic for carrying out the steps of a method in a nonsequential fashion. Analogous to how people solve jigsaw puzzles. Rather than attempting to solve the puzzle by combining the pieces left to right and then top to bottom, most people combine pieces based on perceived opportunities.

organizational reusability. Influence of the organization's reuse process model on artifact reusability. *See also potential reusability.*

package. 1. Collection of classes and initialized instances of classes. Particularly useful for configuration management. 2. In the programming language Ada, the principal structuring unit that encapsulates data and function. *Often used synonymously with class.*

partition. A set of capabilities that identifies the boundaries of a subproblem. An analysis partition is a set of related analysis capabilities—for example, a set of related business transactions. A design partition is a subsystem within the overall architecture—for example, the database subsystem, the user interface subsystem, and so on. *See also subsystem.*

pilot project. An initial or introductory project whose purpose is to explore the use of one or more new processes or resources within the organization.

plan. *See project plan.*

planning. The set of management activities used to describe how project goals and objectives will be met. *See also project plan, controlling.*

planning under uncertainty. The development of a project plan that specifically addresses the presence of unknown or uncertain information.

polymorphism. Literally, "many shapes." In object-oriented technology, using the same service name in the interface of multiple objects. For example, a dog can speak by barking, and a cat can speak by meowing, and so on. *See also bounded polymorphism, unbounded polymorphism.*

portability. *See binary portability, cross-platform portability.*

potential reusability. Likelihood that an artifact developed on one project is reusable on other projects. Defined as a weighted measure of an artifact's inherent, domain, and organizational reusability. *See also inherent reusability, domain reusability, organizational reusability.*

principle. A rule or a fundamental truth that guides you in making decisions, independent of organizational situation. *See also maxim.*

pristine life cycle. The natural, time-sequenced order of steps for manufacturing or processing a single product of a business. To be pristine means that the details of scaling up a process for multiple instances of a product are not considered.

problem domain. *See domain.*

process. 1. The activities and methods used to build products. 2. An entity whose attributes are measured. *See also product and resource.*

process model. Collection of maxims, strategies, activities, methods, and tasks that are organized to achieve a set of goals and objectives. *Synonymous with life cycle. See also product process model, reuse process model.*

producer. A software development role with a primary responsibility for creating reusable assets. *Contrast with consumer.*

producer/consumer process model. A process model that intermingles projects that produce reusable assets with those that consume reusable assets.

product. 1. Application intended for sale outside the company that created it, or a program or system intended for deployment to users inside the company that created it. 2. Any result of a software development process whose attributes are measured. *See also process, resource.*

product process model. A process model that is used to develop software products. *Synonymous with software development life cycle.*

productivity. *See productivity measure.*

productivity measure. A measure of goods or services produced per unit of labor or expense (an external resource measure).

programmer-as-reader model. A specific developer interaction model based on the premise that most programmers spend the majority of their time reading and understanding other people's code.

programming by refinement. The ability to create desired software by specifying differences (refining) from existing software.

project. A set of activities that uses the processes and resources of the current situation to create or maintain a product, or that modifies these processes or resources to be more like those defined by the desired situation.

project plan. Description of the work to be done (tasks) and the resources (such as time, people, materials) needed to accomplish goals and objectives. The plan's tasks correspond to the selected process model.

project schedule. 1. Primary element of the project plan that indicates the tasks to be carried out, including their interdependencies. The project schedule assigns a start time, duration, and resources to each task. 2. Time-ordered sequence of deliverables, and how these deliverables are to be obtained.

prototype. A preliminary, or intentionally incomplete or scaled-down version of a system. The result of a prototyping activity. *See also available prototype, analysis prototype, design prototype, feasibility prototype.*

prototyping. A software development activity used to buy information to reduce risk involving a problem or solution. *See also prototype.*

pure programming language. A programming language that supports a single uniform style of development. Examples among object-oriented languages are Smalltalk and Eiffel. *Contrast with hybrid programming language.*

quality. 1. Product's fitness for use. 2. Something that is free of defects.

quality assurance. A strategy for ensuring that an organization's processes and resources create quality products within required constraints.

quality measure. A catchall term used to refer to external product attributes such as reliability, maintainability, understandability, and usability. *See also measure.*

quality template. A software development artifact that provides a structured way to capture and represent the relevant information for measuring an external product (quality) attribute.

rapid prototyping. A prototyping activity that is intended to be carried out quickly. Does not refer to the execution speed of the resulting prototype.

resource. 1. Input to a process that yields a product. For example, developers, software tools, hardware environment, or other assets. 2. An entity whose attributes are measured. *See also process, product.*

responsibility. 1. Purpose or obligation of a system or subsystem *(synonymous with capability)* or an object *(synonymous with behavior)*. 2. Defines an important duty of a team member role.

reuse. The act of using what already exists to achieve what is desired. *Synonymous with reusing.*

reuse process model. Thirteen-step process dealing with the definition, acquisition, distribution, and maintenance of reusable assets. *See also process model.*

reuse team. The team whose charter is to manage the reuse process model.

reusing. *See reuse.*

role. A job type defined in terms of a set of responsibilities.

scenario. A sequence of actions that can take place in the problem space. Specific types of scenarios are scripts and use cases.

script. *See scenario.*

security policy. A coordination policy that allocates permissions to developers (such as read or write permissions) based on user authentication and security clearance levels. *See also coordination policy, concurrency policy.*

service. A public behavior of an object that is accessible through the object's interface. A service is invoked by another object via a message send. *See also behavior.*

single inheritance. When a class has an inheritance relationship with exactly one other class. *See also inheritance, multiple inheritance.*

situation. The products, processes, and resources that exist within an organization at a point in time. *See also current situation, desired situation.*

size measure. An internal product measure of a product's magnitude. *See also measure.*

software development environment. Collection of methods, languages, libraries, tools, and database services needed to create software systems.

software development life cycle. *See product process model.*

software engineering. Development of software based on theoretical foundations and practical disciplines traditional to engineering.

software framework. A set of objects that define the basic abstractions of a particular set of applications or of a domain. A software framework must be refined with application-specific details in order to be used. *Contrast with decision framework. See also component.*

software scaffolding. The code that is used temporarily to bridge a gap between parts of a system. Scaffolding is often used to support the interoperation of legacy systems and new systems.

specification. 1. A formal description of the interface to a system or one of its components. One component forms a contract with another component based on its specification. 2. A set of requirements provided by a customer that describes a desired system. These requirements are part of the input to an analysis method. *See also contract.*

static binding. Association of a message name with a specific implementation at code execution time. *See also binding. Contrast with dynamic binding.*

static type checking. 1. Ensuring that before the system executes, every message sent to an object will be handled by at least one service. 2. Determining the type of a variable, argument, or return value at compile time. *See also type checking, dynamic type checking.*

strategy. A collection of ideas that describes and directs the larger vision of how activities in a process model will be carried out, without consideration for the details of the techniques or tasks involved.

subclass. A class that is a refinement or an extension to one or more other classes (its superclasses). A subclass inherits the specification and possibly the implementation from its superclasses. *See also derived class, superclass.*

subsystem. 1. A collection of parts that work together to provide a well-defined set of services. 2. A collection of internal capabilities. *Used synonymously with component.*

superclass. A class that is refined or extended by one or more other classes (its subclasses). *See also subclass, base class.*

supertask. A task on a project plan defined at a level of abstraction more convenient for management reporting. It is defined in more detail in terms of other tasks. *See also task.*

system. An organized collection of components that interact. A collection of external capabilities. *Used synonymously with application.*

system capability. 1. A statement of what a system is supposed to do. 2. A set of system behaviors that provide measurable value either to the user or to the developer. *See also external system capability, internal system capability.*

systematic reuse. Reuse based on a planned formal process model.

task. 1. The smallest unit of work on a project schedule. 2. Specific use of a method within a process model. *See also milestone, supertask.*

team. Group of people fulfilling particular roles and working together in a coordinated fashion to meet a clear set of goals and objectives.

team structure. Arrangement of team roles that affects how team members communicate, how assignments are allocated, and how reporting is handled.

technique. The specific details, algorithms, or heuristics employed by a method. For example, many analysis methods recommend the use of a factorization technique (breaking large classes into a collection of smaller, more modular classes).

technology. Technical means of achieving a practical purpose. In the context of software development, all aspects of software engineering needed to yield practical results, such as: programming languages, analysis-and-design methods, and software measures. *See also object-oriented technology.*

technology market momentum. An external technology property that indicates the degree to which a technology has been accepted or endorsed by the marketplace.

testing. 1. Examining a software artifact to detect differences between existing and required conditions. *See also quality assurance.* 2. The evaluation of data resulting from a measurement. *See also measurement.*

traceability. 1. The ability to ascertain the derivation of an artifact. 2. A property of a set of artifacts where it is possible to determine from which requirement an artifact is derived, and which artifacts are derived from a particular requirement.

transformational reuse. Reuse of a tool or generator that takes specifications as input and generates more detailed programs as output.

type checking. Ensuring that a message sent to an object will be understood by the object. A message is understood by an object if the object specifies a corresponding service in its interface. *See also dynamic type checking, static type checking.*

unbounded polymorphism. Polymorphism that allows classes that do not share a common superclass to reuse the same service name. *See also polymorphism, bounded polymorphism.*

uninterrupted staff-hours. Number of uninterrupted hours that a person spends working on a task. A recommended measure of effort. *See also effort measure.*

use case. *See scenario.*

vertical prototype. A prototype used to understand a complete slice (narrow analysis, design, and coding) of a system.

well-founded measure. A measure that is based on empirical observation, coupled with intuition, and that represents a mapping onto an appropriate number system.

white box reuse. Reuse of a component through examination and use of the component's internal structure as well as external interface. *Contrast with black box reuse, glass box reuse.*

wrapper. A technology used to encapsulate a component (or an entire system, such as a legacy system) so it behaves like an object. The wrapper provides a formal specification of the interface to the wrapped component. Other components can use the wrapped component by sending it messages.

References

ACM Turing Award Lectures, The First Twenty-Five Years 1966–1985, ACM Press: Reading, Mass., 1987.

Agha, G., *ACTORS: A Model of Concurrent Computation in Distributed Systems*, MIT Press: Cambridge, Mass., 1986.

Albrecht, A. J., Measuring Application Development Productivity, *Proceedings of the Joint SHARE, GUIDE and IBM Application Development Symposium,* October 1979. Reprinted in Jones, T. Capers, *Programming Productivity—Issues for the Eighties,* IEEE Press, Catalog Number EH0239-4, 35–44, 1986.

Alexander, C., Ishikawa, S., and Silverstein, M., *A Pattern Language: towns, buildings, construction*, Oxford University Press: New York, 1977.

AMI Consortium, *AMI: Application of Metrics in Industry Handbook,* AMI Consortium: London, 1992.

Antebi, M., Issues in teaching C++, *Journal of Object-Oriented Programming*, 3(4), 11–21, November/December 1990.

Arango, G., Domain analysis methods, Chapter 2 in Schäfer, W., Prieto-díaz, R., and Matsumoto, M., *Software Reusability*, Ellis Horwood: United Kingdom, 1994.

Arnold, P., Bodoff, S., Coleman, D., Gilchrist, H., and Hayes, F., *An Evaluation of Five Object-Oriented Development Methods*, Hewlett Packard Laboratories, Bristol, United Kingdom, Report No. HPL-91-52, June 1991.

Atwood, T., ODMG-93: The object-DBMS standard—at last!, *Object Magazine*, 3(3), 37–44, September/October 1993.

Banahan, M., Cross-over training: Making the transition from C to C++, *C++ Report*, 4(8), 44–48, October 1992.

Barnes, B. H. and Bollinger, T. B., Making Reuse Cost-Effective, *IEEE Software*, 8(1), 13–24, January 1991.

Barstow, D., Shrobe, H., and Sandewall, E., eds., *Interactive Programming Environments*, McGraw-Hill: New York, 1984.

Basili, V. R. and Rombach, D., The TAME Project: Towards Improvement-Oriented Software Environments, *IEEE Transactions on Software Engineering*, 14(6), 758–73, 1988.

Beck, K., CRC: Finding objects the easy way, *Object Magazine*, 3(4), 42–44, November/December 1993.

Beck, K. and Cunningham, W., A laboratory for teaching object-oriented thinking, Proceedings of the 1989 ACM OOPSLA Conference, *ACM SIGPLAN Notices*, 24(10), 1–6, October 1989.

Berard, E., *Essays on Object-Oriented Software Engineering, Vol. 1,* Prentice Hall: Englewood Cliffs, New Jersey, 1993.

Biggerstaff, T. and Perlis, A., eds., *Software Reusability: Volume I, Concepts and Models*, ACM Press: Reading, Mass., 1989(a).

Biggerstaff, T. and Perlis, A., eds., *Software Reusability: Volume II, Applications and Experience*, ACM Press: Reading, Mass., 1989(b).

Biggerstaff, T. and Richter, C., Reusability Framework, Assessment, and Directions, Chapter 1 in Biggerstaff, T. and Perlis, A., eds., *Software Reusability: Volume I Concepts and Models*, ACM Press: Reading, Mass., 1989.

Bobrow, D. G., DiMichiel, L. G., Gabriel, R. P., Keene, S. E., Kiczales, G., and Moon, D. A., Common Lisp Object System Specification, X3J13 Document 88-002R, *ACM SIGPLAN Notices*, 23, September 1988.

Boehm, B., *Software Engineering Economics*, Prentice Hall: Englewood Cliffs, New Jersey, 1981.

Boehm, B., A Spiral Model of Software Development and Enhancement, in Thayer, Richard, ed., *Software Engineering Project Management*, IEEE Computer Society Tutorial, Catalog Number EH0263-4, 1988.

Booch, G., *Object-Oriented Design with Applications*, Benjamin Cummings: Redwood City, Calif., 1991.

Booch, G., *Object-Oriented Analysis and Design With Applications*, 2d ed., Benjamin Cummings: Redwood City, Calif., 1994.

Bourgeois, K., Technology Transfer of Mature Reuse Practices, *Proceedings of the Fifth Annual Workshop on Software Reuse,* Palo Alto, Calif., October 26–29, 1992.

Brooks, F. P., *The Mythical Man Month*, Addison-Wesley: Reading, Mass., 1975.

Burnett, M., Goldberg, A., and Lewis, T., eds., *Visual Object-Oriented Programming*, Manning Publications: Greenwich, Conn., 1995.

Carey, M. J., DeWitt, D. J., and Naughton, J. F., The OO7 Benchmark, *SIGMOD Record,* 22(2), 12–21, June 1993.

Cattell, R. G. G., *Object Data Management: Object-Oriented and Extended Relational Database Systems*, Addison-Wesley: Reading, Mass., 1991.

Chambers, C. and Ungar, D., Making Pure Object-Oriented Languages Practical, Proceedings of the 1991 ACM OOPSLA Conference, *ACM SIGPLAN Notices,* 26(11), 1–15, November 1991.

Chidamber, S. R. and Kemerer, C. F., Towards a Metrics Suite for Object-Oriented Design, Proceedings of the 1991 ACM OOPSLA Conference, *ACM SIGPLAN Notices,* 26(11), 192–211, November 1991.

Cockburn, A., The impact of object-orientation on application development, *IBM Systems Journal*, 32(3), 420–44, March 1993.

Coleman, D., Arnold, P., Bodoff, S., Dollin, C., Gilchrist, H., Hayes, F., and Jeremaes, P., *Object-Oriented Development: The Fusion Method*, Prentice Hall: Englewood Cliffs, New Jersey, 1994.

Connell, J. L. and Shafer, L., *Structured Rapid Prototyping*, Yourdon Press: Englewood Cliffs, New Jersey, 1989.

Connell, J. L. and Shafer, L., *Object-Oriented Rapid Prototyping*, Yourdon Press: Englewood Cliffs, New Jersey, 1995.

Constantine, L. L., Work Organization: Paradigms for Project Management and Organization, *Communications of the ACM*, 36(10), 35–43, October 1993.

Conte, T. M. and Hwu, W. W., Benchmark Characterization, *IEEE Computer*, January 1991.

Cox, B., *Object-Oriented Programming: An Evolutionary Approach*, Addison-Wesley: Reading, Mass., 1986.

Cox, B., Superdistribution and electronic objects, *Dr. Dobb's Journal,* 17(10), 44–48, October 1992.

Cusumano, M., *Japan's Software Factories: A Challenge to U.S. Management*, Oxford University Press: New York, 1991.

Dahl, O. J., Myhrhaug, B., and Nygaard, K., *Simula 67, common base language,* Norwegian Computing Center, Technical Publication #S-2, 1968.

Davis, J. and Morgan, T., Object-Oriented Development at Brooklyn Union Gas, *IEEE Software,* 10(1), 67–75, January 1993.

Davis, M. J., STARS Framework for Reuse Processes, *Proceedings of the Fourth Annual Workshop on Institutionalizing Software Reuse,* Center for Innovative Technology, Reston, Virginia, 1991.

DeGrace, P. and Stahl, L. H., *Wicked Problems, Righteous Solutions: A Catalogue of Modern Software Engineering Paradigms*, Yourdon Press: Englewood Cliffs, New Jersey, 1990.

DeMarco, T., *Controlling Software Projects: Management, Measurement and Estimation,* Yourdon Press: Englewood Cliffs, New Jersey, 1982.

DeMarco, T. and Lister, T., *PeopleWare: Productive Projects and Teams,* Dorset House: New York, 1987.

Deutsch, L. P. and Schiffman, A. M., Efficient Implementation of the Smalltalk-80 System, *Proceedings of the 11th Annual ACM Symposium on the Principles of Programming Languages,* Salt Lake City, Utah, January 1984.

Dreger, J. B., *Function Point Analysis,* Prentice Hall: Englewood Cliffs, New Jersey, 1989.

Fafchamps, D., Organizational Factors and Reuse, *IEEE Software,* 11(5), 31–41, September 1994.

Favaro, J., Procurement Issues in Software Reuse at the European Space Agency: A Case Study, *The Second International Workshop on Software Reusability,* Position Paper Collection, Lucca, Italy, March 24–26, 1993.

Fenton, N. E., *Software Metrics: A Rigorous Approach,* Chapman & Hall: London, 1991.

Fraser, S., Pragmatic Approaches to Software Reuse at BNR, Ltd., *Proceedings of the Fourth Annual Workshop on Institutionalizing Software Reuse,* Center for Innovative Technology, Reston, Virginia, 1991.

Freeman, P., ed., *Tutorial: Software Reusability*, IEEE Computer Society Press: Washington D.C., 1986.

Galletta, D., King, R. C., and Rateb, D., The Effects of Expertise on Software Selection, *Data Base,* 24(2), 7–20, May 1993.

Gamma, E., Helm, R., Johnson, R., and Vlissides, J., *Design Patterns: Elements of Object-Oriented Software Architecture,* Addison-Wesley: Reading, Mass., 1995.

Gibson, E., Flattening the Learning Curve: Educating Object-Oriented Developers, *Journal of Object-Oriented Programming,* 3(6), 24–26, February 1991.

Gilb, T., *Principles of Software Engineering Management*, Addison-Wesley: Reading, Mass., 1988.

Gilb, T. and Graham, D., *Software Inspection: Effective Method for Software Project Management*, Addison-Wesley: Reading, Mass., 1993.

Goldberg, A., Programmer as Reader, *IEEE Software*, 4(5), 62–70, September 1987.

Goldberg, A., ed., *History of Personal Workstations*, ACM Press: Reading, Mass., 1988.

Goldberg, A. and Robson, D., *Smalltalk-80: The Language and its Implementation*, Addison-Wesley: Reading, Mass., 1983. Revised as Goldberg, A. and Robson, D., *Smalltalk-80: The Language*, Addison-Wesley: Reading, Mass., 1989.

Goldberg, A. and Rubin, K. S., Talking to Project Managers . . . Case Studies in Prototyping—Parts 1, 2, *HOTLINE on Object-Oriented Technology*, 1(6), April 1990, 1(7), May 1990.

Grady, R. B. and Caswell, D. L., *Software Metrics: Establishing a Company-Wide Program*, Prentice Hall: Englewood Cliffs, New Jersey, 1987.

Graham, I., *Object-Oriented Methods*, Addison-Wesley: Wokingham, England, 1994.

Halstead, M. H., *Elements of Software Science,* Elsevier North Holland: New York, 1977.

Hammer, M. and Champy, J., *Reengineering the Corporation: A Manifesto for Business Revolution*, Harper Business: New York, 1993.

Harmon, P. and Taylor, D., *Objects in Action: Commercial Applications of Object-Oriented Technologies*, Addison-Wesley: Reading, Mass., 1993.

Harry, M. J. and Lawson, J. R., *Six Sigma Producibility Analysis and Process Characterization,* Motorola University Press: Reading, Mass., 1992.

Henderson-Sellers, B. and Edwards, J., The object-oriented systems lifecycle, *Communications of the ACM,* 33(9), 142–59, 1990.

Henderson-Sellers, B. and Edwards, J., *BookTwo of Object-oriented Knowledge: The Working Object*, Prentice Hall Australia: Sydney, Australia, 1994.

Hetzel, B., *The Complete Guide to Software Testing*, QED Information Sciences: Wellesley, Mass., 1988.

Humphrey, W. S., *Managing the Software Process*, SEI Series in Software Engineering, Addison-Wesley: Reading, Mass., 1989.

Humphrey, W. S., *A Discipline for Software Engineering*, Addison-Wesley: Reading, Mass., 1995.

Hutt, A., ed., *Object Analysis and Design: Description of Methods*, Wiley and Sons: New York, 1994(a).

Hutt, A., ed., *Object Analysis and Design: Comparison of Methods*, Wiley and Sons: New York, 1994(b).

Hyman, M. S., Literate C++, *Computer Language,* 7(7), 67–68, 70, 72, 74–77, 79, July 1990.

International Function Point Users Group (IFPUG), *1987 Spring Conference Proceedings*, Scottsdale, Ariz., April 15–17, 1987.

International Function Point Users Group (IFPUG), *Counting Practices Manual*, Westerville, Ohio, January 1994(a).

International Function Point Users Group (IFPUG), *Metric Views, Newsletter,* Westerville, Ohio, January 1994(b).

Jacobson, I., Christerson, M., Jonsson, P., and Övergaard, G., *Object-Oriented Software Engineering: A Use Case-Driven Approach*, ACM Press: Reading, Mass., 1992.

Jenson, R. L. and Bartley, J. W., Parametric Estimation of Programming Effort: An Object-Oriented Model, *Journal of Systems and Software,* 15(2), 107–14, May 1991.

Johnson, R., Documenting Frameworks Using Patterns, *ACM SIGPLAN Notices*, 27(10), 63–76, October 1992.

Jones, C., *Applied Software Measurement: Assuring Productivity and Quality,* McGraw-Hill: New York, 1991.

Jorgensen, P. C. and Erickson, C., Object-Oriented Integration Testing, *Communications of the ACM*, 32(9), 31–38, September 1994.

Karlsson, E. A., Sørumgård, S., and Tryggeseth, E., Classification of Object-Oriented Components for Reuse, *Proceedings of TOOLS Europe '91*, Dortmund, Germany, Prentice Hall: United Kingdom, 1991.

Kearney, J. K., Sedlmeyer, R. L., Thompson, W. B., Gray, M. A., and Adler, M. A., Software Complexity Measurement, *Communications of the ACM,* 29(11), 1044–50, 1986.

Kemerer, C. F., *Reliability of Function Point Measurement: A Field Experiment*, MIT Sloan School of Management WP #3193-90-MSA, Cambridge, Mass., 1990.

Keyes, J., ed., *Software Engineering Productivity Handbook,* Windcrest/McGraw-Hill: New York, 1993.

Knuth, D., *Literate Programming*, University of Chicago Press: Chicago, 1992.

Koltun, P. and Hudson, A., A Reuse Maturity Model, *Proceedings of the Fifth Annual Workshop on Software Reuse,* Palo Alto, Calif., October 26–29, 1992.

Krasner, G. and Pope, S. T., A Cookbook for Using the Model-View Controller User Interface in Smalltalk-80, *Journal of Object-Oriented Programming*, 1(3), 26–49, August/September 1988.

Lavoie, D., Baetjer, H., Tulloh, W., and Langlois, R., *Components Software: A Market Perspective on the Coming Revolution in Software Development*, Special Research Report, Patricia Seybold: Cambridge, Mass., 1993.

Leibs, D. J. and Rubin, K. S., Reimplementing Model-View-Controller, *Smalltalk Report*, 1(6), 1–7, March/April 1992.

Li, W. and Henry, S., Maintenance Metrics for the Object-Oriented Paradigm, *Proceedings of the First International Software Metrics Symposium*, Baltimore, Maryland, 52–59, May 21–22, 1993.

Linton, M. and Calder, P. R., The Design and Implementation of Interviews, *USENIX Association C++ Workshop Proceedings*, 256–67, USENIX Association: Berkeley, Calif., November 1987.

Lippman, S., *C++ Primer*, Addison-Wesley: Reading, Mass., 1989.

Lorenz, M. and Kidd, J., *Object-Oriented Software Metrics,* Prentice Hall: Englewood Cliffs, New Jersey, 1994.

Love, T., *Object Lessons: Lessons Learned in Object-Oriented Development Projects,* SIGS Books: New York, 1993.

Martin, J. and Odell, J. J., *Object-Oriented Analysis and Design*, Prentice Hall: Englewood Cliffs, New Jersey, 1992.

McCabe, T. J., A Complexity Measure, *IEEE Transactions on Software Engineering,* 2(4), 308–20, December 1976.

McGregor, J. D., Functional Testing of Classes, *Proceedings of the Pacific Northwest Software Quality Conference*, Software Research Institute: San Francisco, May 17–20, 1994.

Meyer, B., *Object-oriented Software Construction*, Prentice Hall International: United Kingdom, 1988.

Meyer, B., The new culture of software development, *Journal of Object-Oriented Programming,* 3(4), 76–81, November/December 1990.

Meyer, B., *Eiffel: The Language*, Prentice Hall International: United Kingdom, 1992.

Meyer, B. and Nerson, J. M., eds., *Object-Oriented Applications*, Prentice Hall: Englewood Cliffs, New Jersey, 1993.

Mills, H., *Chief programmer teams: Principles and procedures,* IBM FSC Report 71-5108, IBM Federal Systems Division: Gaithersburg, Maryland, 1971.

Monarchi, D. E. and Puhr, G. I., A Research Typology for Object-Oriented Analysis and Design, *Communications of the ACM*, 35(9), 35–47, September 1992.

Moore, J. W., A National Infrastructure for Defense Reuse, *Proceedings of the Fourth Annual Workshop on Institutionalizing Software Reuse*, Center for Innovative Technology, Reston, Virginia, 1991.

Moreau, D. and Dominick, W., A Programming Environment Evaluation Methodology for Object-Oriented Systems: Part I—The Methodology, *Journal of Object Oriented Programming*, 3(1), 38–52, May/June 1990(a).

Moreau, D. and Dominick, W., A Programming Environment Evaluation Methodology for Object-Oriented Systems: Part II—Test Case Application, *Journal of Object Oriented Programming*, 3(3), 23–32, September/October 1990(b).

Murphy, G., Townsend, P., Laberge, P., and Juzenas, M., Engineering Software With Objects, Chapter 3 in Meyer, B. and Nerson, J. M., eds., *Object-Oriented Applications,* Prentice Hall: Englewood Cliffs, New Jersey, 1993.

Nauer, P. and Randell, B., eds., *Conference on Software Engineering*, NATO Scientific Affairs Division: Garmisch, Germany, 1969.

Object Management Group, *The Common Object Request Broker: Architecture and Specification*, OMG Document Number 91-12-1, OMG Publications: Boulder, Colo., 1991.

Object Management Group, *OMA Guide, Chapter 4: The OMG Object Model*, OMG Document Number 92-9-2, OMG Publications: Boulder, Colo., 1992.

Object Management Group, *Common Object Services Specification, Vol. 1*, OMG Document Number 94-1-1, Wiley and Sons: New York, March 1994.

Paulk, M. C., Curtis, B., and Chrissis, M. B., *Capability Maturity Model for Software,* Software Engineering Institute, Carnegie Mellon University, CMU/SEI-91-TR-24, 1991.

Paulk, M. C., Weber, C. V., Curtis, B., and Chrissis, M. B., *The Capability Maturity Model: Guidelines for Improving the Software Process*, Addison-Wesley: Reading, Mass., 1995.

Peters, T., *Thriving on Chaos: Handbook for a Management Revolution,* Harper Perennial: New York, 1987.

Plauger, P. J., *Programming on Purpose, Volume III About People*, Prentice Hall: Englewood Cliffs, New Jersey, 1993.

Poulin, J. S., Caruso, J. M., and Hancock, D. R., The business case for software reuse, *IBM Systems Journal,* 32(4), 567–94, 1993.

Ramamoorthy, C. V., Prakash, A., Tsai, W. T., and Usuda, Y., Software Engineering: Problems and Perspectives, *Computer*, 17(10), 191–209, October 1984.

Reenskaug, T., Andersen, E., Berre, A. J., Hurlen, A., Landmark, A., Lehne, O. A., Nordhagen, E., Ness-Ulseth, E., Oftedal, G., Skaar, A. L., and Stenslet, P., OORASS: seamless support for the creation and maintenance of object oriented systems, *Journal of Object-Oriented Programming*, 5(6), 27–41, October 1992.

Reenskaug, T. and Skaar, A. L., An Environment for Literate Smalltalk Programming, Proceedings of the 1989 ACM OOPSLA Conference, *ACM SIGPLAN Notices,* 24(10), 337–45, October 1989.

Reifer, D. J., Asset-R: A Function Point Sizing Tool for Scientific and Real-time Systems, *Journal of Systems and Software,* 11(3), 159–72, March 1990.

Rich, C. and Waters, R. C., *The Programmer's Apprentice*, ACM Press: Reading, Mass., 1990.

Robinson, P., *Hierarchical Object-Oriented Design*, Prentice Hall International: United Kingdom, 1992.

Rosson, M. B. and Alpert, S. R., The Cognitive Consequences of Object-Oriented Design, *Human-Computer Interactions,* 5(4), 345–79, 1990.

Royce, W. W., Managing the Development of Large Software Systems, in Thayer, Richard, ed., *Software Engineering Project Management*, IEEE Computer Society Tutorial, Catalog Number EH0263-4, 118–27, 1988. Reprinted from *Proceedings of IEEE WESCON*, 1–9, 1970.

Rubin, K. S. and Goldberg, A., Object Behavior Analysis, *Communications of the ACM*, 35(9), 48–62, September 1992.

Rubin, K. S. and Goldberg, A., Getting to Why, Supplement in *Journal of Object-Oriented Programming*, 6(4), 5, 8–10, July/August 1993.

Rumbaugh, J., Blaha, M., Premerlani, W., Eddy, F., and Lorensen, W., *Object-Oriented Modeling and Design*, Prentice Hall: Englewood Cliffs, New Jersey, 1991.

Samuelson, B., Smalltalk Benchmarking Revisited, *The Smalltalk Report,* 2(8), 1, 16–21, June 1993.

Schäfer, W., Prieto-díaz, R., and Matsumoto, M., *Software Reusability,* Ellis Horwood: United Kingdom, 1994.

Selic, B., Gullekson, G., and Ward, P. T., *Real-Time Object-Oriented Modeling*, Wiley and Sons: New York, 1994.

Shlaer, S. and Mellor, S. J., *Object-Oriented Systems Analysis: Modeling the World in Data*, Yourdon Press: Englewood Cliffs, New Jersey, 1988.

Shriver, B. and Wegner, P., eds., *Research Directions in Object-Oriented Programming*, MIT Press: Cambridge, Mass., 1987.

Smith, M. F., *Software Prototyping: Adoption, Practice and Management*, McGraw-Hill: London, 1991.

Stamelos, I., *Software Project Cost Estimation: An Object-Oriented Approach*, CSELT Technical Reports, Torino, Italy, 21(1), 53–67, March 1993.

Stroustrup, B., *The C++ Programming Language*, Addison-Wesley: Reading, Mass., 1985. Second edition appeared 1991.

Symons, C. R., *Software Sizing and Estimating: Mk II FPA (Function Point Analysis),* Wiley and Sons: Chichester, United Kingdom, 1991.

Taylor, D., *Object-Oriented Technology for the Manager*, Addison-Wesley: Reading, Mass., 1991.

Tegarden, D., Sheetz, S., and Monarchi, D., A Software Complexity Model of Object-Oriented Systems, *Decision Support Systems: The International Journal*, January 1993.

Thayer, R., ed., *Software Engineering Project Management*, IEEE Computer Society Tutorial Series, Order Number 751, IEEE Catalog Number EH0263-4, 1988.

Thomsett, R., *Third wave project management: a handbook for managing the complex information systems of the 1990s,* Prentice Hall: Englewood Cliffs, New Jersey, 1993.

Ungar, D. and Jackson, F., Tenuring Policies for Generation-Based Storage Reclamation, Proceedings of the 1988 ACM OOPSLA Conference, *ACM SIGPLAN Notices,* 23(11), 1–17, November 1988.

Ungar, D. and Smith, R., Self: the power of simplicity, Proceedings of the 1987 ACM OOPSLA Conference, *ACM SIGPLAN Notices,* 22(12), 227–42, December 1987.

Weicker, R. P., An Overview of Common Benchmarks, *IEEE Computer*, December 1990.

Weiderman, N. H., Habermann, A. N., Borger, M. W., and Klein, M. H., A Methodology for Evaluating Environments, *The Second ACM SIGSOFT/SIGPLAN Symposium on Practical Software Development Environments*, 199–207, December 1986.

Weinberg, G., *The Psychology of Computer Programming*, Von Nostrand Reinhold: New York, 1971.

Wexelblat, R., ed., *History of Programming Languages I*, Academic Press: New York, 1981.

Wexelblat, R. and Bergin, T., eds., *History of Programming Languages II*, forthcoming. Preprints appear in *ACM SIGPLAN Notices*, March, 1993.

Whitmire, S. A., 3D Function Points: Scientific and Real-Time Extensions to Function Points, *Proceedings of the 1992 Pacific Northwest Software Quality Conference*, June 1, 1992.

Wirfs-Brock, R., Wilkerson, B., and Wiener, L., *Designing Object-Oriented Software,* Prentice Hall: Englewood Cliffs, New Jersey, 1990.

Yourdon, E., *Decline and Fall of the American Programmer*, Yourdon Press: Englewood Cliffs: New Jersey, 1992.

Yourdon, E., ed., *Classics in Software Engineering*, Yourdon Press: New York, 1979.

Zuse, H., *Software Complexity: Measures and Methods,* Walter de Gruyter: Berlin, 1990.

Index

A

abstract class, 130–131, 503
abstraction, 43, 354, 503
activity, 86–87, 144, 154, 335, 364, 503
adaptor, 212
Agha, G., 373
Albrecht, A. J., 447
Alexander, C., 2, 123
AMI Consortium, 440
AMS, 330–332
Antebi, M., 401
analysis, 48, 51–52, 86, 136–137, 336–339, 503
  choosing methods, 344–350
  defects, 126
  domain, 119, 227, 508
  method, 87, 337–339, 504
  model space, 337–339
  partition, 118
  prototype, 98, 148, 504
  prototyper, 278, 283, 494–495
  steps, 337–339
  techniques, 337, 340–344
  training, 397–398
  variant, 105
application, 43, 47, 245, 504
  framework, (*see* software framework)
  productization team, 282–285, 318, 504
  prototyping team, 285
  testing, 131
application programming interface (API), 323
Arango, G., 227
architecture, 43, 317–318, 398, 504
  client/server, 139, 229, 316, 324–326, 505
  portability, 322
  system, 10, 49, 96, 118
Arnold, P., 350
articulation space, 337–339
artifact, 102, 125, 203, 504
assessment, 21, 504
  current situation, 29
  midcourse, 76–78
  pilot project, 76
  report, 78
  scorecard, 78–80
asset, 92, 102, 203, 222, 234, 254–260, 504
Asset-R Function Points, 450
attribute, 20, 28–29, 504
  external, 214–215, 437–439, 509
  internal, 214–215, 437–439, 511
Atwood, T., 369

B

Baetjer, H., 255
Balzer, B., 359–360
Banahan, M., 408
Bang (measure), 447
Barnes, B. H., 105, 212–213, 230
Barstow, D., 7, 372

Basili, V. R., 440
Beck, K., 172, 342
behavior, 39, 49, 129, 342, 504
Belarmino, L., 311
Bemer, B., 4
benchmark, 380–382
Berard, E., 90
Betts, M., 204
Big Bang Theory, 95
Biggerstaff, T., 220, 249
binary portability, 321, 505
binding, 129, 505
   dynamic, 355, 362, 508
   static, 355, 517
Blackwell, G., 337
Bobrow, D. G., 373
Boehm, B., 87, 89, 145, 158, 168, 446
Bohm, C., 2
Booch, G., 61, 90, 123, 188, 416–417,
   425, 429
Booch Notation, 123, 336
Boole, G., 335
Bouldin, B. M., 83
Bourgeois, K., 237
Brooks, F., 2, 201
Burnett, M., 47
business mission, 23
business processes, 23
business process reengineering (BPR),
   23–24, 505
Byte Magazine, 17

C

capability, 118
   external system, 118, 144, 153, 509
   internal system, 118, 144, 153, 511
   maturity model (CMM), 30

CARDS project, 235
Carey, M. J., 381
Cattell, R. G. G., 373, 381
certification, 235, 505
   potential reuse, 237
   quality measure, 236–237
Chambers, C., 381
change (in product, process, resource),
   133–134
   recording, 134
Chidamber, S. R., 456–457
chief programmer, 181
class, 7, 42–43, 354, 505
   abstract, 130–131, 503
   base, 356, 504
   derived, 356, 507
   hierarchy, 46, 129, 455, 457, 505
   implementation, 42, 130, 210, 357
   specification, 42, 130, 210, 357
   subclass, 43, 53, 130, 210, 357–358
   superclass, 43, 130, 131, 210, 357–358
classification schemes, 238–239, 264,
   505
   enumerative, 238, 508
   faceted, 238, 509
   keyword/attribute, 239, 511
client/server architecture, 139, 229, 316,
   324–326, 505
cloning, 209–210, 506
Cockburn, A., 94
coding, (*see* implementation), 506
cohesion, 455
Coleman, D., 142, 343, 351
complexity, 455
   added, 456, 503
   cyclomatic, 458
   inherent, 52, 456, 510
   measure, 455–458, 506

component, 42, 44, 506
  evaluator, 286
  strategic, 222
  testing, 131
composition, 50–51, 360–361, 506
  object, 41–42, 50–51
Computer World, 203–204
concept space, 337–339
concurrency policy, 320, 506
configuration management, 319, 506
Connell, J. L., 97, 115
Constructive Costing Model
    (COCOMO), 158–159, 446, 456,
    461, 506
Constantine, L. L., 280
consultants, 74–75, 290, 298, 393, 411,
    497
consumer (reuse), 102, 104, 217, 233,
    282, 506
consuming reusable assets, 102–104, 282
Conte, T. M., 380
contract, 53, 54, 119, 122, 141, 343, 506
controlling (a project), 143, 160–166, 506
Conway, M., 3
coordination, 315, 319–320, 506
  policy, 320, 506
CORBA, 323
corporate reuse program, 82, 266–268
correctness proofs, 126
cost accounting, 160–161, 507
  uninterrupted staff hours, 160, 446,
    460–461, 518
cost estimating, (*see* estimation),
    157–160
coupling, 456
Cox, B., 61, 233, 373, 417, 429
Cox, J., 204
CRC Cards, 172, 342

cross-platform portability, 321, 507
Cunningham, W., 150, 172, 342
Cusumano, M., 271
cyclomatic complexity, 458

D

Dahl, O. J., 3, 7, 373
databases, 48, 387–388
Davis, J., 201, 460
Davis, M. J., 235
decision framework, 1, 13–14, 507
  benefits of object-oriented technology,
    13, 56
  make an initial commitment to objects,
    13, 64
  measurement questions, 442–443
  product process model, 14, 134–135
  project goals and objectives, 13,
    20–23
  project plan and control, 14, 151–152
  reuse process model, 14, 221–223
  software development environment, 14,
    375–376
  software measurement program, 14,
    462–463
  team structure, 14, 292–293
  team training plan, 14, 421–422
defect, 125, 133, 507
  detection, 125–126
  recording, 132–134
  reporting, 454–455
  template for recording, 133
Defense Software Repository System
    (DSRS), 243
DeGrace, P., 115
delegate responsibility, 42, 47, 59
delegation, 47, 357, 507

DeMarco, T., 32, 160, 168, 295, 299, 376, 428, 447, 455, 462, 464

Department of Defense, U. S., (DoD), 169, 227, 239, 243

design, 48, 51–52, 86, 123, 136–137, 339. 507
  choosing methods, 344–350
  complexity measures, 455–458
  defects, 126
  for reuse, 104–105, 212–214
  method, 90, 123
  model space, 337, 339–340
  partition, 119
  pattern, 123, 211, 507
  prototype, 98–101, 125, 148, 495, 507
  prototyper, 283, 495, 498
  training, 398–399

Deutsch, P., 322

developers
  coordination of, 319–320
  kinds of, 317

development
  incremental, 54, 95–96, 124, 143, 148, 150, 154, 283, 344, 349, 361, 510
  iterative, 94–95, 124, 143, 147, 150, 155, 349, 511
  levels of, 317–319
  opportunistic, 95, 155, 340, 513

DeWitt, D. J., 381

Dijkstra, E. W., 3, 4

distributed open system, 322–323, 507

distributed system object model (DSOM), 323

Dr. Dobb's Journal, 332

documentation, 87, 122–124, 362–363, 508

domain, 43, 508
  analysis, 119, 227, 508
  reusability, 215, 459, 508

Dreger, J. B., 447

E

EDS, 389

Edwards, J., 90, 137, 456

encapsulation, 40, 46, 55, 67, 240, 353–354, 445, 508
  circumvention, 354
  multiple levels, 209, 354, 356

end user, 95, 97, 104, 294

Engelbart, D., 3

enumerative classification scheme, 238, 508

estimation
  by analogy, 159–160
  by decomposition, 159
  by expert opinion, 159
  by historical models, 157–159

expert services model, 256–259, 257, 269, 274, 279

exploratory programming, 7, 509

F

faceted classification scheme, 238, 509

Fafchamps, D., 275

Favaro, J., 233

Fenton, N. E., 438, 467

figure-of-merit, 144, 162–163, 509

Forbes, 203

framework
  decision, 1, 13–14, 507
  design training, 399–400
  designer, 286, 415, 497–498
  documenting, 123
  evaluator, 286
  reuse training, 403–404
  software, 1, 43–45, 53, 55, 91–93, 206, 211, 285, 316, 516
  team, 285–287, 318
  testing, 105, 131

Fraser, S., 81, 243
Freeman, P., 220
function point, 444, 447–452, 509
  3D function points, 450
  Mark-II function points, 450
Function Point Analysis (FPA), 447–452, 461, 509

G

Galletta, D., 380
Gamma, E., 212
Gary, R. J., 63
Gibson, E., 395
Gilb, T., 10, 37, 126
goal, 20, 56, 509
  decision framework, 20–23
  failure-related decisions, 471
goal-question-metric (GQM), 162, 440–443, 510
Goldberg, A., 7, 17, 87, 100, 190, 337, 339, 364, 373, 400
Grady, R. B., 132, 467
Graham, I., 126, 351

H

Halstead, M. H., 458
Hammer, M., 23
Harmon, P., 201
Harry, M. J., 30
Heinlein, R., 90
Henderson-Sellers, B., 90, 137, 456
Hetzel, B., 125
hierarchy, 43, 50, 129, 455, 457
Hoffer, E., 469
Hopper, Admiral G. M., 277
Humphrey, W. S., 30, 37, 132, 277, 404, 467

Hutt, A., 344, 350
Hyman, M. S., 124

I

IFPUG, 444, 447, 448, 451, 465
implementation, 39, 50, 86, 109, 162, 320, 327, 345, 354–355, 358, 510
  reuse, 208, 210, 213, 234
  strategy, 360–364, 510
  testing, 127–130
implementation environment, 359–368
  training, 400–401
incident, 132, 510
  template for recording, 132
incremental development, 54, 95–96, 124, 143, 148, 150, 154, 283, 344, 349, 361, 510
information engineering, 341, 343
inherent reusability, 214, 459, 510
inheritance, 46, 55, 239–240, 353, 445, 510
  depth of (measure), 456–457
  of implementation, 208, 210, 354
  of specification, 210, 354
  multiple, 129, 354, 357, 512
  single, 129, 357, 516
  testing, 130–131
inspection, 126, 510
instance, 42, 210, 511
integration, 87, 121–122
  incremental, 122, 361, 511
interaction strategy, 364–368, 511
iteration, 94, 511
iterative development, 94–96, 124, 143, 147, 150, 155, 349, 511

J

Jacobson, I., 142, 342, 351
Jenson, R. L., 158

job descriptions, (*see* roles)
Johnson, R., 123
Jones, C., 448, 450
Jorgensen, P. C., 131

K

KandA Widget Company, 31–36,
    135–136, 226, 244
Karlsson, E. A., 238
Kearney, J. K., 458
Kelvin, Lord, 437
Kemerer, C. F., 449, 456–457
Keyes, J., 451
keyword/attribute classification scheme,
    239, 511
Knuth, D., 123
Koltun, P., 30, 268
Krasner, G., 171

L

Lavoie. D., 255
legacy system, 327–330, 511
Leibs, D. J., 361, 400
Li, W., 456
libraries, 81, 101, 103, 206, 214, 222,
    235, 238, 242, 253–260, 262,
    289–290, 318, 353, 359, 401
Licklider, J., 2
life-cycle (*see* process model)
life styles inventory, 297
likelihood factors, 145–146, 148
lines of code (LOC), 443, 445–446
linking pin, 279, 511
Linton, M., 400
Lippman, S., 425
literate programming, 123–124

Lorenz, M., 456–457
Love, T., 127

M

maintenance, 4, 45–46, 51–52, 54–55,
    87, 321, 327, 460, 511
    reuse, 208–209, 213, 233, 245–246, 253
    team, 291–292
Martin, J., 343, 351
Matsushita Electric, 23
maxim, 9, 86, 135–136, 512
maxims for frameworks
    acquire reusable assets, 230
    data collection, 464
    effective reuse, 215
    KandA battle scars, 135–136
    making change decisions, 377, 378
    measurement, 462
    notations, 346
    plan and control, 148, 149, 150
    potential reuse, 214
    process model, 121
    reuse organization, 251–252
    reuse process, 222
    reuse rewards, 265
    shared vision, 11
    training, 410
    team management, 295
    team members, 298
    team roles, 294
    team size, 296
McCabe, T. J., 458
McGregor, J. D., 125, 129
McIlroy, D., 4
measure, 437–440, 512
    assessment report, 78–80
    decision framework, 462–463

effort, 443–452, 460–461, 508
failure-related decisions, 473
functionality, 444, 509
goal-oriented, 439–440, 509
depth of inheritance, 456–457
object abstractions, 446–447
productivity, 443–452, 514
quality, 236–237, 452–455
reuse, 458–461
size, 443–452, 459–460, 516
training, 404
useful, 439
well-defined, 438, 518
mentoring, 70, 74–75, 160, 298,
    411–412
message-passing (sending), 7, 40–41, 50,
    52, 512
method, 48, 87, 335–336, 512
analysis, 87, 337–339, 504
binding, 357
design, 87, 339–340, 507
selection criteria, 348
tool, 346–347
Meyer, B., 51, 61, 90, 373, 416, 425,
    429
milestone, 144, 146–147, 162–163, 512
progress tracking, 162
required, 152
Mills, H., 181, 280
mission statement, 25
model-view-controller (MVC), 51, 171,
    212, 400
modeling concepts, 337–339
Modular Continuity, 51
modularity, 4, 45, 512
Monarchi, D., 351, 456
Moore, J. W., 235
Moreau, D., 394

motivation to adopt object-oriented
    technology, 66
by fear, 67
by greed, 67
by logic, 67–68
motto, 25
multiple inheritance, 129, 354, 357, 512
Murphy, G., 201
Myers-Briggs type indicator, 297

N
NATO, 3, 10
Nauer, P., 3, 475
notation, 336, 337, 346, 397–398, 512

O
object, 7, 39, 512
as customizable components, 205
as pluggable components, 204
attacking complexity, 52
build partial systems, 53–54
build systems resilient to change, 53
come in different sizes, 51
helps build systems, 49–55
lifetime, 355, 358
live all the way down, 51–52, 384
map real world, 50
natural units for reuse, 55
Object Behavior Analysis (OBA), 87, 91,
    190–196, 239, 339, 342, 447
object broker, 323, 512
object coach, 278, 284, 414–415, 496
object composition, 41–42, 50–51
object linking and embedding (OLE), 323
Object Management Group (OMG), 333

Object Modeling Technique (OMT), 123, 341

object-oriented, 45–49, 512
  analysis-and-design method, 48–49, 336–340
  application, 47–48
  concepts training, 396
  database, 48, 368–371, 388, 404, 513
  language, 46–47, 354–359
  technology, 1, 513
  user-interface, 47–48

Object-Oriented Role Analysis (ORASS), 123

object technology center, 80

object technology expert, 284, 496–497

objective, 20, 56, 513

objectologist, 94, 150

Objectory, 342

open systems, 322, 513

opportunistic development, 95, 155, 340, 513

opportunistic marketing, 242

organizational reusability, 215, 459, 513

organizational reuse models, 253, 260–261
  ad hoc, 253–254, 274
  commercial-off-the-shelf (COTS), 253, 261–262
  expert services model, 256–259, 269, 274, 279, 290
  product center model, 259–261, 269, 274
  supply and demand model, 255–256, 274

P

package, 320, 513

Pan, A., 297

partition, 117–121, 513
  analysis, 118
  breadth-first, 119–120
  definition of, 118
  depth-first, 119–120
  design, 119
  domain-analysis, 119
  enterprise-wide, 119
  examples, 138–141
  system, 181, 282

patterns, 211–212
  design, 123, 211, 507

Paulk, M. C., 30, 37

Pawson, R., 204

Perlis, A., 4, 296

Peters, T., 26

Pitta, J., 204

pilot project, 71, 513
  guidelines for choosing, 71–73
  setting up, 73
  staffing, 74

plan, 143

planning, 96, 118, 143, 513
  decision framework, 151–152
  failure-related decisions, 471
  under uncertainty, 147–151, 513

Plato, 143

Plauger, P. J., 123

polymorphism, 41, 46, 55, 129, 353–354, 513
  bounded, 354, 356–357, 505
  unbounded, 354, 356–357, 362, 518

portability, 321, 514
  binary, 321, 505
  cross-platform, 321–322, 507

potential reusability, 214–215, 228, 235, 237, 258, 459, 514

Poulin, J. S., 276

principle, 9, 514
  of decision frameworks, 20, 56, 64, 135, 152, 222, 293, 376, 422, 463
  of decision making, 10
  of system architecture, 10

pristine life cycle, 120, 514

process, 20, 437, 514

process improvement projects, 21

  change product development process
      model, 135

  change planning and controlling, 151

  establish reuse process, 221

  establish software measurement
      program, 462

process model, 85, 514

  definition of, 85–87

  decision framework, 134–135

  failure-related decisions, 471

  fountain model, 90, 137, 138, 170, 173

  producer/consumer, 102–105, 212, 514

  product, 345

  recursive/parallel, 90

  select, 70

  spiral, 89–90, 99, 114, 138, 176

  time driven, 295

  transform, 89

  waterfall, 87–88, 94, 97, 105, 110, 114,
      138, 150, 170

process model illustrations

  concept development, 190–200

  concepts driven, 218

  contract driven, 169–179

  creating a reusable asset, 185–190

  just-do-it, 182–185

  milestone driven, 169–179, 197

  security driven, 180–182, 281

  series of prototypes, 111–112, 190

  time driven, 110–111

producer (reuse), 102, 104–105, 212, 285,
    514

producer/consumer process model,
    102–105, 212, 514

producing reusable asset, 104–105

product, 20, 222, 437, 514

product process model, 345, 514

productivity, 445

proficiency levels, 405, 422

  for team roles, 413–416

programmer-as-reader model, 364, 514

programming by refinement, 7, 514

programming language

  choosing, 353–359, 386–387

  hybrid, 358–359, 510

  pure, 358–359, 515

programming tools, 359–368

  browser, 365–366

  debugger, 369–368

  inspector, 366–367

project, 20, 515

  control, 143, 164

  management training, 401

  milestone, 144, 146–147, 162–163, 512

  plan, 143, 515

  process improvement, 21, 135, 151,
    221, 462

  resource improvement, 21, 293, 375,
    421

  schedule, 144–147, 515

  task, 144–146, 517

  tracking progress, 161

  work model, 164

project types

  Creating Reusable Assets, 92–93, 114

  First-of-Its-Kind, 91, 114, 216, 379

  Legacy Rewrite, 92, 114, 154, 216

  System Enhancement and
    Maintenance, 93, 114, 154

  Variation-on-a-Theme, 91–92, 114,
    154, 186, 216, 379

prototype, 96–97, 125–126, 164, 261,
    379, 515

  analysis, 98–101, 148, 494–495, 504

  available, 190–192, 504

  definition of, 96

  design, 98, 101, 125, 485, 507

feasibility, 99, 152, 509
vertical, 98, 518
prototyping, 55, 96–102, 108–110, 121,
137, 148, 361–362, 368, 515
as quality assurance strategy, 125–126
controlling, 164–166
definition of, 96–102
language mechanisms, 354–355
evolutionary, 99, 199–200, 508
planning, 148
rapid, 96, 515
success and failures, 100–102
Ptech, 343

Q

quality, 515
assurance, 124–134, 515
measures, 236–237, 452–455, 515
template, 452–455, 515
tracking progress, 163

R

Ramamoorthy, C. V., 97
RAPID project, 227
REBOOT project, 238
Reenskaug, T., 123, 124
Reich, R., 469
Reifer, D. J., 450
resource(s), 20, 437, 515
dynamically allocated, 151
fixed, 151
resource improvement project, 21
create appropriate teams, 293
select software development
environment, 375
train team members, 421
responsibility, 42, 342, 515
Responsibility-Driven Design, 172, 341

reusability
domain, 215, 459, 508
inherent, 214, 459, 510
organizational, 215, 459, 513
potential, 214–215, 228, 235, 237, 258,
459, 514
reuse, 102–103, 210–211, 516
adaptation by a central team, 247–248
administrator, 267, 404, 498
algorithm, 211
appropriate, 102
as form of technology transfer,
252–253
as-is, 207, 246–247, 504
black box, 208, 213, 505
by-adaptation, 207, 247–248, 505
cafeteria analogy, 205–207
consumer, 102, 104, 217, 233, 282, 506
corporate issues, 262–269
corporate program, 266–268
engineer, 256–257, 267, 290, 499–500
evaluator, 286–287, 416, 499
glass-box, 208, 509
in Japan, 271
interproject, 103, 511
intraproject, 103, 263, 511
Lego analogy, 204–205
library (*see* library)
librarian, 267, 299, 404, 500–501
manager, 267, 290, 414, 501–502
maturity, 268
motivating, 264–266
organizational models, 253–262
producer, 102, 104–105, 212, 285, 514
producer/consumer equation, 212–214
rewarding, 265
superdistribution, 233
systematic, 114, 516
team, 256, 267, 289–290, 291, 404, 516
transformational, 209, 518

value of, 212–216

white box, 208–209, 518

reuse identification and acquisition
   strategies

  domain analysis, 119, 227, 508

  harvest-after-the-fact, 228, 510

  on-the-fly identification, 228, 513

reuse measure

  appropriate reuse, 102, 104, 257,
    265–266, 504

  effective reuse, 215, 223, 508

  expected reuse, 215, 508

  potential, 14–215, 228, 235, 237, 258,
    459, 514

reuse process model, 221, 516

  acquire, 223, 230–234, 260

  certify, 223, 234–237, 260

  classify, 223, 237–240, 260

  communicate, 223, 241–242, 260

  define, 223–224

  failure-related decisions, 472

  identify, 223, 225–230, 260

  locate, 224, 242–244, 260

  maintenance, 245–246, 253, 261

  retrieve, 242–224, 260

  store, 223, 240–241, 260

  training, 404

  understand, 224, 244, 261

  update assets, 224, 245–246

  update reusers, 224, 245–246, 261

  use, 224, 244, 261

Rich, C., 360

role, 277–278, 516

  administrative manager, 278

  analysis prototyper, 283, 494–495

  analyzer, 99, 278, 283, 415

  chief programmer, 181

  component evaluator, 286

  definition of, 277

  design prototyper, 283, 495, 498

  designer, 99, 283–284, 415

  documentor, 284

  end user, 95, 97, 104, 294

  framework designer, 286, 415,
    497–498

  framework evaluator, 286

  linking pin, 279

  object coach, 278, 284, 414–415, 496

  object technology expert, 284, 496–497

  people manager, 278

  pollinator, 288

  prototyper, 283, 285, 416

  reuse administrator, 267, 404, 498

  reuse engineer, 256–257, 267, 290,
    499–500

  reuse evaluator, 286–287, 416, 499

  reuse librarian, 267, 290, 404, 500–501

  reuse manager, 267, 290, 414,
    501–502

  technical leader, 278, 414–415

  tester, 284

Robinson, P., 351

Rosen, M., 311

Ross, D., 3

Rosson, M. B., 339

Royce, W. W., 87

Rubin, K. S., 87, 100, 190, 337, 339, 351

Rumbaugh, J., 123, 341, 351

S

Samuelson, B., 381

San Joaquin Delta College, 311–313

scenario, 341, 342, 516

Schäfer, W., 249

schedule, 144–147, 515

scorecard, 78–80

scripting, 342

security policy, 320, 516

Selic, B., 345

service, 40–41, 47, 49–50, 55, 118, 208–209, 210–211, 341, 516
Shecker, S. C., 63
Shlaer, S., 178, 339, 343, 351, 429
Shriver, B., 333
situation, 20, 507
  current, 20, 507
  desired, 20, 507
Six Sigma, 30
Sketchpad, 2
Smith, M. F., 115
software development environment, 48, 51, 53–54, 64, 70, 315, 318, 321, 327, 360, 364, 375, 516
  camps, 382–386
  definition of, 315
  decision framework, 375–376
  failure-related decisions, 473
  training, 400–401
software engineering, 3, 516
  history, 2–6
Software Engineering Institute (SEI), 30, 31
software factory, 271
software framework, 1, 43–45, 53, 55, 91–93, 206, 211, 285, 316, 516
software scaffolding, 330, 516
specification, 52–54, 119, 129–130, 208–209, 211–212, 339, 342, 516
  inheritance, 210, 354
Stamelos, I., 158
STARS project, 235
strategy, 86, 517
  consuming reusable assets, 102–104, 282
  documenting, 122–124
  incremental development, 54, 95–96, 124, 143, 148, 150, 154, 283, 344, 349, 361, 510
  integrating changes, 87, 121–122, 361
  iterative development, 94–96, 124, 143, 147, 150, 155, 349, 511
  partitioning, 117–121
  producing reusable assets, 104–105
  prototyping, 55, 96–102, 108–110, 121, 137, 148, 361–362, 368, 515
  quality assurance, 124–134, 515
Stroustrup, B., 373
structuredness, 456
subclass, 43, 53, 130, 210, 517
subsystem, 51, 118, 517
  testing, 131
superclass, 43, 130, 210, 517
supertask, 144, 517
Symons, C. R., 450
system
  architecture, 10, 49, 96, 118
  based on objects, 49–55
  capability, 144, 153–154, 163, 517
  legacy, 327–330, 511
  open, 513
  partial, 54
  tracking progress, 163

T

task, 87, 144–146, 154–157, 163, 517
  costs, 157–160
  cost models (*see* estimation)
  duration, 157
  figure-of-merit, 144
  for incremental development, 154
  for iterative development, 155
  likelihood factor, 145–146, 148
  size, 156
  tracking progress, 163
Taylor, D., 61, 417

team, 277, 517
  application productization team,
    282–285, 504
  application prototyping team, 285
  cross-project team, 287–289, 507
  definition of, 277
  decision framework, 292–293
  failure-related decisions, 472
  finding members, 296–298
  framework team, 285–287
  job descriptions, 493–502
  maintenance team, 291–292
  Maven Model, 186
  retaining team members, 292
  reuse team, 256–258, 286, 289–291
  selecting, 292–298
  structure, 277–300, 517
  tools, 363–364
team structure illustrations
  battlefield commander, 281
  egoless, 281
  enterprise-wide components, 309–310
  geographically distributed, 305–308
  hierarchical, 280–281
  military, 281
  multiple framework, 308–309
  pollinators, 310–311
  Star Trek model, 311–313
technique, 48–49, 86–87, 336, 517
technology, 1, 518
  market momentum, 348, 378, 518
  transfer, 251
technology transfer, 252–253
Technology Transfer International, Inc.,
  15, 271
Tegarden, D., 456–457
testing, 87, 126, 363, 518
  applications or subsystems, 131
  class, 128–129

class hierarchies, 129–131
frameworks and components, 131
implementations, 127–132
member functions, 128
polymorphism, 129
reuse certification, 236, 247–248
state-based, 129
structure-based, 129
Thayer, R., 168
Thomsett, R., 279
traceability, 20, 86, 136, 345, 348, 363, 518
training
  decision framework, 421–422
  failure-related decisions, 473
  formats, 408–413
  plan, 75, 413–416, 421
  proficiency levels, 405–408
  Quick Start, 430–435
  subject areas, 396–405
Tuckman's Model, 297
type checking, 357–358, 518
  declarations, 355
  dynamic, 355, 357–358, 362, 508
  static, 355, 357–358, 517

U

Ungar, D., 358, 373, 381
uninterrupted staff-hours, 160, 446,
  460–461, 518
use cases, 343
user interface
  object-oriented, 47–48,
  prototyping, 99–100, 164
  testing, 127–128

V

values, business and team, 26–29
value proposition, 56–58, 66

variant analysis, 105
virtual hallway, 252, 288

W

Weicker, R. P., 381
Weiderman, N. H., 394
Weinberg, G., 197, 281
Wexelblat, R., 17
Whitmore, S. A., 450, 451–452
Wirfs-Brock, R., 172, 341, 351
work model, 164–165
wrapper, 327–328, 518

X

Xerox Palo Alto Research Center
   (PARC), 6, 53, 241

Y

Yourdon, E., 17, 428

Z

Zuse, H., 438